Information Security
Body of Knowlolge

500 practice questions with answers and explainations included

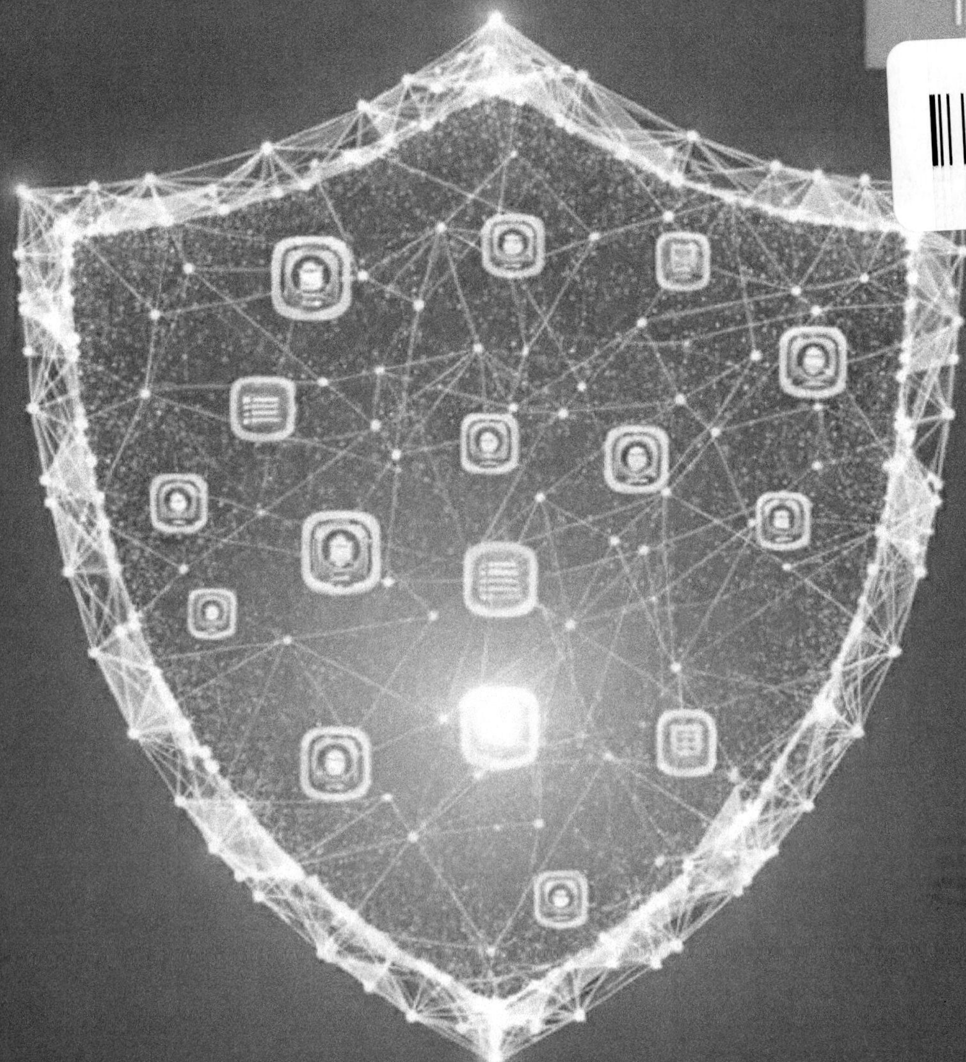

EC-COUNCIL CCISO: EXPLAINED LIKE I AM 5

Dorales McLarty
Certified EC-Council Intructor
ACISO, CISSP, CCSP
CCSP, EDRP, CEH

Copyright Page

CCISO Explained Like I Am 5
Information Security Body of Knowledge

Published by:
ISBK Publishing
Edmonton T5E0N2
Canada

First Edition: 2025

Cover Design: ISBK Design Team
Interior Design: Dorales McLarty

Disclaimer:
This publication is designed to provide accurate and authoritative information in regard to the subject matter covered. It is sold with the understanding that neither the author nor the publisher is engaged in rendering legal, accounting, or other professional service. If legal advice or other expert assistance is required, the services of a competent professional should be sought. The author and publisher specifically disclaim any liability, loss, or risk, personal or otherwise, that is incurred as a consequence, directly or indirectly, of the use and application of any of the contents of this work.

Trademarks:
All terms mentioned in this book that are known to be trademarks or service marks have been appropriately capitalized. ISBK cannot attest to the accuracy of this information. Use of a term in this book should not be regarded as affecting the validity of any trademark or service mark.

EC-Council Certification:
This book is aligned with the Certified Chief Information Security Officer (CCISO) Body of Knowledge. EC-Council is a trademark of the EC-Council Foundation.
For more information, visit: www.eccouncil.org
Printed in the United States of America
10 9 8 7 6 5 4 3 2 1

CCISO Explain IT Like I Am 5

Table of Contents

Table of Contents

CCISO Explain IT Like I Am 5: Domain 2

CCISO Explain IT Like I Am 5 : Domain 3

CCISO Explain IT Like I Am 5 : Domain 4

CCISO Explain IT like I Am 5: Domain 5

CCISO Certification Explained Like I Am 5

Book Objectives and Learning Outcomes

By the end of this book, participants will be able to:

- Develop and implement comprehensive information security governance frameworks aligned with business objectives.
- Design, manage, and continuously improve robust risk management programs using industry best practices (e.g., NIST RMF, ISO 31000, COSO ERM).
- Formulate and execute strategic security program plans, including budgeting, vendor management, and compliance with global regulations (e.g., GDPR, HIPAA, PCI DSS).
- Oversee security operations, including incident response, vulnerability management, and disaster recovery planning.
- Apply core security competencies across networking, application, system, and data security domains, incorporating principles like Defense-in-Depth and OWASP Top 10.
- Translate complex technical risks into business terms and effectively communicate security posture to diverse stakeholders.
- Emphasize practical application of CISO knowledge.

Domain 1: Governance and Risk Management

Practical Application Example: A CISO identifies that the company's new cloud migration project introduces significant data residency risks due to international regulations. They apply their knowledge of governance frameworks to establish a cross-functional steering committee, define new data classification policies, and implement a risk management process to assess and mitigate these specific cloud-related risks, ensuring legal compliance and business continuity.

Domain 2: Information Security Controls, Compliance, and Audit Management

Practical Application Example: Following a recent data breach in a peer organization, a CISO proactively initiates an internal audit of the company's data loss prevention (DLP) controls. They leverage their knowledge of compliance standards (e.g., GDPR, HIPAA) to ensure the audit scope covers sensitive data types and applies best practice control frameworks (e.g., ISO 27001 Annex A controls). Based on audit findings, they implement enhanced technical controls and update employee training to close identified gaps.

Domain 3: Security Program Management

Practical Application Example: A CISO is tasked with securing a newly acquired subsidiary that operates on outdated IT infrastructure. They develop a strategic security program plan, including a budget proposal that justifies investment in modernizing security tools and hiring additional staff by quantifying the potential financial impact of a breach (cost-benefit analysis). They then lead the integration project, applying change management principles to ensure smooth adoption of new security policies and technologies by the subsidiary's employees.

Domain 4: Core Competencies

Practical Application Example: After a critical zero-day vulnerability is announced for a widely used operating system, a CISO immediately directs their team to assess the company's exposure. They apply their knowledge of system security and patch management to prioritize patching efforts across critical servers, leveraging automated tools where possible, and ensure that compensating controls are in place for systems that cannot be immediately patched, thereby minimizing the attack surface.

Domain 5: Strategic Planning, Finance, and Vendor Management

Practical Application Example: A CISO is evaluating a new third-party SaaS provider for a critical business function. They utilize their knowledge of vendor risk management to conduct thorough due diligence, including reviewing the vendor's SOC 2 report, negotiating strong security clauses in the Service Level Agreement (SLA), and ensuring the contract includes clear incident response protocols. They also present a cost-benefit analysis to the CFO, demonstrating the ROI of the security due diligence in terms of reduced potential legal and reputational risks.

Connect learning outcomes to the CCISO certification exam domains:

Domain 1: Governance and Risk Management

Knowledge: Deep understanding of information security governance principles, the CIA Triad, security vulnerabilities, threats, risks, exposures, and Defense-in-Depth strategies.

Familiarity with risk management components, processes, and best practice frameworks (NIST RMF, ISO 31000, COSO ERM).

Tasks/Skills: Develop and align security strategy with business objectives. Define and implement information security management structures, roles, and responsibilities. Identify, analyze, evaluate, and treat organizational risks. Maintain and utilize a risk register.

Domain 2: Information Security Controls, Compliance, and Audit Management

Knowledge: Comprehensive understanding of administrative, technical, physical, preventative, detective, corrective, and compensating controls. Knowledge of control implementation lifecycle, security baselines, and configuration management. In-depth knowledge of regulatory and legal compliance (GDPR, HIPAA, PCI DSS, SOX, CCPA, LGPD, NIS Directive) and industry standards (ISO 27001, NIST CSF, COBIT). Understanding of internal and external audit types, processes, and methodologies.

Tasks/Skills: Implement and manage various security controls. Ensure organizational adherence to relevant laws, regulations, and industry standards. Facilitate and manage internal and external security audits, including reporting findings and overseeing remediation efforts.

Domain 3: Security Program Management

Knowledge: Principles of strategic planning for information security, including vision, mission, goals, objectives, and SWOT analysis. Understanding of security architecture and design frameworks (TOGAF, SABSA). Knowledge of security program metrics (KPIs) and budgeting processes (OpEx, CapEx, Cost-Benefit Analysis, ROI). Familiarity with project management methodologies (Agile, Waterfall) and change management. Understanding of vendor and third-party risk management processes. Knowledge of security awareness and training program development. Overview of Incident Response and Business Continuity Planning.

Tasks/Skills: Develop and execute strategic security roadmaps. Define and track key performance indicators for the security program. Justify security investments through financial analysis. Manage security projects and initiatives. Implement and manage vendor risk assessment and third-party security. Design and deliver effective security awareness and training.

Domain 4: Core Competencies

Knowledge: Understanding of network topologies (LAN, WAN, VPN, VLAN) and segmentation. Knowledge of network security devices (Firewalls, IDS/IPS, Routers, Switches, Load Balancers, Proxies). Familiarity with wireless security, cloud computing security (Shared Responsibility Model, IaaS, PaaS, SaaS, CASB), and mobile device security (MDM, BYOD). In-depth knowledge of operating system hardening, user account management (MFA), and auditing/logging. Understanding of database security (access controls, encryption, auditing, SQL injection prevention, DAM). Comprehensive knowledge of web application security (OWASP Top 10, secure coding, WAF). Integration of security into the SDLC (SAST, DAST). Awareness of malware types (Viruses, Worms, Trojans, Ransomware) and defenses. Fundamentals of cryptography (Symmetric/Asymmetric, Hashing, Digital Signatures) and PKI.

Tasks/Skills: Secure network infrastructure and communication channels. Implement and manage security for various operating systems, applications, and databases. Develop and enforce secure coding practices. Deploy and manage anti-malware solutions. Utilize cryptographic techniques for data protection and authentication.

Domain 5: Strategic Planning, Finance, and Vendor Management

Knowledge: Strategic planning concepts, including vision, mission, and alignment with business objectives. Financial management principles related to security budgeting, cost- benefit analysis, ROI, and procurement. Comprehensive understanding of vendor and third- party risk management, including due diligence, SLAs, and continuous monitoring.
Knowledge of key national and international international legal and regulatory issues impacting information security, data privacy (GDPR, HIPAA, PCI DSS, SOX, CCPA, LGPD), and intellectual property protection.

Tasks/Skills: Develop and articulate a strategic vision for information security. Manage security budgets and justify investments to executive leadership. Assess and manage security risks associated with third-party vendors. Ensure legal and regulatory compliance across all security initiatives.

The Business of Security

Think of the business as a large, interconnected organism. Every part—from a customer service process to a server in a data center—is a potential entry point for a threat. The info-sec team's primary job is to protect this organism. To do that effectively, they can't just know about the "security" parts; they have to know every part of the organism that could be compromised. "Security is business efficiency". If you want to increase your efficiency as a business, do security right.

Interconnectedness of Security

An information security team's knowledge needs to be comprehensive because a change in one area of the business can introduce a vulnerability somewhere else. Similar to finance, security must be incorporated into every business operation and activity from the onset. For example:

- **Business Activities:** If the marketing department decides to use a new social media platform, the info-sec team needs to understand how that platform handles data to ensure it meets the company's security standards. Without this knowledge, they can't properly advise on the risks.
- **Processes:** The finance team might implement a new process for handling invoices. The info-sec team needs to be involved to make sure that process doesn't open a door for a phishing scam or a data breach. They need to understand the flow of information to spot potential weak links.
- **Infrastructure and Resources:** This is the heart of it. A business's infrastructure isn't just a collection of computers. It's a complex network of hardware, software, cloud services, and physical locations. The info-sec team needs to know the location of every server, the configuration of every firewall, and the purpose of every piece of software. They are responsible for protecting the confidentiality, integrity, and availability of all these resources.

Proactive vs. Reactive Security

A team that only understands security from a technical standpoint is always playing defense. They're just reacting to threats as they happen. A team that deeply understands the business, however, can be **proactive**. They can:

- **Assess Risk:** By understanding what's most valuable to the business (e.g., customer data, intellectual property, financial systems), they can prioritize their efforts and allocate resources where they're most needed.
- **Design Secure Systems:** When a new business process or system is being developed, they can be part of the design phase from the beginning. It's much easier to build security in from the start than to try and bolt it on later.
- **Educate Employees:** They can tailor security training to be relevant to specific teams. For instance, explaining to the HR team why they need to be extra careful with employee data, or teaching the sales team how to spot a phishing email disguised as a client request.

Essentially, by knowing the business better than anyone else, the information security team transforms from a reactive defense mechanism into a strategic partner that helps the entire organization achieve its goals securely.

The unseen benefit of Information Security

- **To Business Process Understanding:** Implementing security controls requires a deep understanding of how information flows through business processes. Identifying critical assets and the data they handle, mapping user roles and access permissions, and analyzing the dependencies between systems forces a thorough review of existing processes. This exercise uncovers inefficiencies, redundancies, and previously unknown risks, leading to more streamlined, transparent, and robust business operations.

- **To Knowledge Transfer:** Information security provides a framework for secure knowledge management. It ensures that sensitive intellectual property and proprietary information are stored and shared in a controlled and protected manner. This framework is crucial for a modern, hybrid workforce where data is constantly being transferred between different devices, locations, and teams. Security controls guarantee the integrity and confidentiality of this knowledge, enabling seamless and safe collaboration without the risk of data loss or unauthorized access.

- **To Business Activity Monitoring:** Security logging and monitoring tools provide a rich source of data on system and user behavior. While their primary function is to detect threats, this data can also be used for Business Activity Monitoring (BAM). By analyzing security logs, businesses can gain valuable insights into user activity patterns, application usage, and data flow, which can help in optimizing workflows, identifying process bottlenecks, and making data-driven business decisions. This transforms security from a cost center into a source of strategic business intelligence.

Asking "who, what, when, where, why, and how" allows security to act as a powerful diagnostic tool for the entire organization, benefiting both IT and business teams.

Here is a breakdown of how this approach helps:

- **Who?** Security benefits both IT and business teams by providing a clear view of user behavior. It can identify **who** is accessing specific applications and data, revealing patterns of both normal and anomalous behavior. This helps IT teams manage user access and permissions more effectively, and it helps business teams understand which individuals or roles are interacting with critical business processes. This knowledge is fundamental for both security, business continuity and operational efficiency.
- **What?** By analyzing security logs, both teams gain a deeper understanding of **what** data is being accessed and **what** applications are being used. This goes beyond simple network traffic analysis. It reveals which data sets are most sensitive, which applications are most critical to the business, and where data might be at risk. This intelligence helps IT prioritize security investments and allows business teams to better manage their most valuable information assets.
- **When?** Security provides a temporal map of activities. By asking **when** a process or data transfer occurs, security monitoring helps identify peak usage times, potential bottlenecks, and irregular activity. This timing data is invaluable for IT capacity planning, ensuring systems are resourced appropriately. It also helps business teams optimize workflows by understanding the natural cadence of their operations.
- **Where?** Security helps define the digital landscape by identifying **where** data and processes reside. This includes physical locations, cloud environments, and the

specific servers or databases that hold critical information. This understanding helps IT teams design more resilient and secure architectures (Reliability Engineering) and gives business teams a clear picture of their digital footprint.

- **Why?** This is where the strategic value truly emerges. By identifying a security event, both teams can ask **why** it occurred. Was it a failed process? A lack of training? A technical vulnerability? The root cause analysis required to answer "why" forces a deep dive into business processes, revealing inefficiencies and risks that may have otherwise been overlooked. This turns a security incident into a learning opportunity for process improvement.
- **How?** The "how" is the mechanism. Security provides this insight through the use of logging, monitoring, and auditing tools. The data collected by these tools is not just for threat detection; it can be used for Business Activity Monitoring (BAM). By analyzing **how** an action was performed, teams can gain detailed insights into workflows and human-system interactions. This information helps streamline operations, reduce human error, and identify new opportunities for automation and training.

Overview of the CISO Role and Responsibilities

CISO (Chief Information Security Officer):

A senior-level executive responsible for developing and implementing an information security program to protect an organization's information assets.

Evolution of the CISO role from technical to strategic

- **Early Days (Technical Focus):** Initially, the CISO role (or equivalent) was often a highly technical position, focused on implementing and managing security tools like firewalls, antivirus, and intrusion detection systems. The role typically reported to IT management (e.g., CIO) and was primarily concerned with technical vulnerabilities and operational security.
- **Mid-Stage (Risk Management Focus):** As cyber threats grew and regulations emerged, the role began to shift towards risk management. CISOs started to focus more on identifying, assessing, and mitigating risks across the organization, translating technical issues into business risks. Reporting lines sometimes moved higher, but often still within the IT department.
- **Current State (Strategic Business Enabler):** Today, the CISO is increasingly seen as a strategic business leader. The role involves understanding the organization's overall business objectives and risk appetite, and then designing a security program that enables those objectives securely. This includes influencing stakeholders, managing budgets, ensuring compliance, and communicating cyber risk in terms of business impact to the board and executive leadership. The CISO often reports directly to the CEO, Board, or a non-IT executive, reflecting the enterprise-wide importance of cybersecurity.

Example: Moving from managing firewalls to advising the board on cyber risk, focusing on business enablement and risk appetite.

Key responsibilities:

Leadership:

The CISO provides vision, direction, and motivation for the information security program and team. This involves setting the tone for security culture, inspiring confidence, and guiding the organization through complex security challenges.

Example: Leading the development of a new cybersecurity strategy, gaining executive buy- in, and fostering a culture of security awareness across all departments.

Strategy:

The CISO is responsible for developing and implementing a comprehensive information security strategy that aligns with the organization's business goals and risk appetite. This involves long-term planning, resource allocation, and continuous adaptation to the evolving threat landscape.

Example: Creating a three-year cybersecurity roadmap that prioritizes investments in cloud security and data loss prevention to support the company's digital transformation initiatives.

Risk Management:

This core responsibility involves identifying, assessing, mitigating, monitoring, and reporting on information security risks to protect organizational assets. The CISO ensures that risk decisions are made in alignment with the organization's risk tolerance.

Example: Conducting an annual enterprise-wide risk assessment, identifying high-risk areas like third-party vendor access, and implementing controls like stricter vendor security assessments and continuous monitoring to reduce that risk.

Compliance:

The CISO ensures the organization adheres to relevant laws, regulations, industry standards, and internal policies related to information security and data privacy. This includes managing audits and ensuring remediation of findings.

Example: Overseeing the implementation of controls to meet GDPR requirements for customer data privacy, including data mapping, consent management, and breach notification procedures, and preparing for external audits.

Operations:

The CISO oversees the day-to-day security operations, ensuring the effective functioning of security technologies and processes. This includes incident response, vulnerability management, security monitoring, and security awareness programs.

Example: Managing the Security Operations Center (SOC) to detect and respond to security incidents, ensuring timely patching of critical vulnerabilities, and running regular simulated phishing campaigns for employee training.

Reporting structures and organizational influence:

The CISO's reporting structure significantly impacts their authority, budget, and ability to influence security decisions across the organization. Different structures present unique opportunities and challenges for effective security leadership.

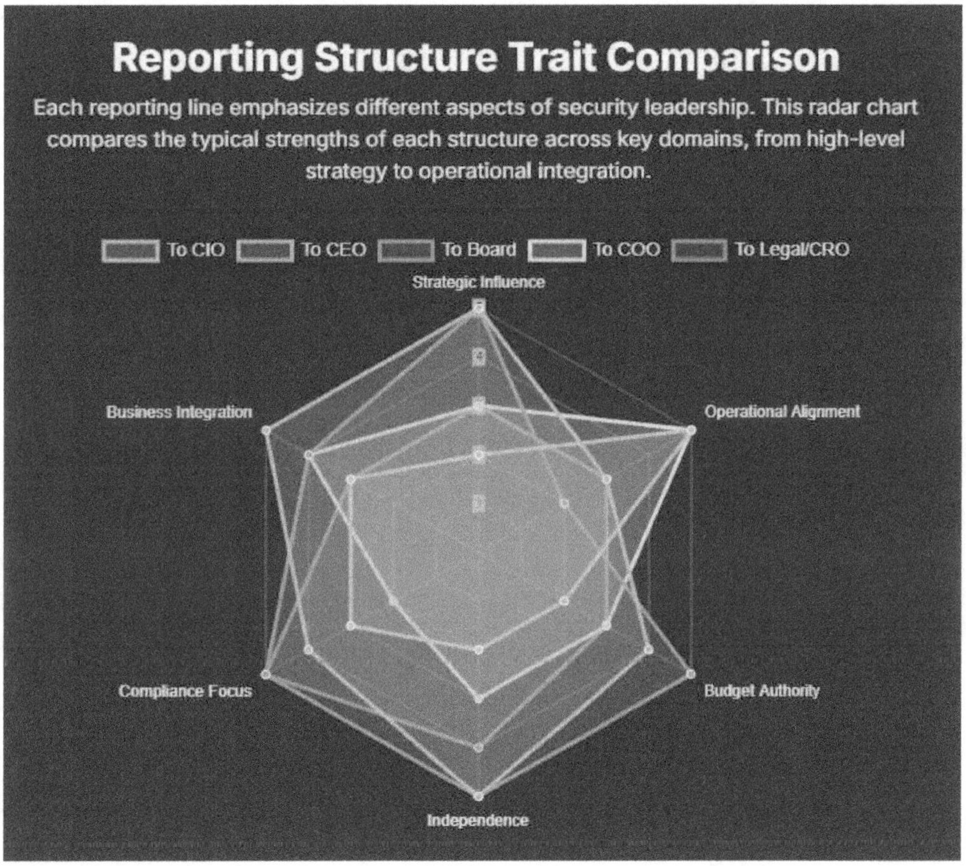

Common Reporting Structures:

To the CIO (Chief Information Officer):

Description: Historically common, this structure places security under the IT department. It can facilitate strong alignment with IT operations and infrastructure.

Implications: May limit the CISO's perceived independence and influence on non-IT business units. Security might be seen as a technical function rather than a business risk. Budget and priorities can be dictated by IT.

Influence Strategies:

- **Build strong relationships with IT leadership:** Become a trusted advisor to the CIO, demonstrating how security enables IT initiatives.
- **Translate technical risks to IT operational impact:** Show how security failures directly affect IT service delivery and efficiency.
- **Collaborate on IT projects:** Embed security early in IT development lifecycles to ensure security is "built-in," not "bolted on."
- **Seek opportunities for direct executive engagement:** Proactively present security updates and risk posture to the broader executive team or board, even if not a direct report.

To the CEO (Chief Executive Officer):

Description: This structure provides the CISO with direct access to the highest level of executive leadership, emphasizing cybersecurity as a critical business imperative.

Implications: High visibility and direct influence on strategic business decisions. The CISO can align security directly with enterprise-wide objectives and risk appetite. Increased accountability and pressure.

Influence Strategies:

- **Speak the language of business:** Frame security risks and investments in terms of financial impact, reputational damage, and competitive advantage.
- **Align security with strategic initiatives:** Demonstrate how robust security enables new product launches, market expansion, or digital transformation.
- **Provide clear, concise risk briefings:** Offer actionable insights to the CEO and board, avoiding overly technical jargon.
- **Be proactive in identifying emerging threats:** Position security as a forward-looking function that anticipates and mitigates future risks.

To the Board of Directors (or a Board Committee):

Description: This is often a dual reporting line (e.g., to CEO/CIO for day-to-day, and to the Board for governance oversight), or a direct report in highly regulated industries. It signifies the highest level of governance.

Implications: Strongest governance oversight and strategic influence. Ensures security is a top-level agenda item. Requires exceptional communication and strategic thinking.

Influence Strategies:

- **Focus on governance and strategic risk:** Present security posture in the context of enterprise risk management and regulatory compliance.
- **Provide independent assurance:** Offer an objective view of the organization's security health and investment needs.
- **Educate board members:** Regularly provide updates on the threat landscape and the implications for the business.
- **Build trust and credibility:** Be transparent about challenges and progress, demonstrating a clear path to improvement.

To the COO (Chief Operating Officer):

Description: This structure emphasizes security's role in operational resilience and business continuity.

Implications: Strong focus on integrating security into operational processes and ensuring business uptime. May de-emphasize strategic or compliance aspects if the COO's focus is purely operational.

Influence Strategies:

- **Highlight operational efficiency and resilience:** Show how security measures reduce downtime, improve system reliability, and protect critical business processes.
- **Integrate security into operational workflows:** Collaborate with operational teams to embed security controls seamlessly.
- **Quantify operational risk reduction:** Present security benefits in terms of reduced operational disruptions and recovery costs.

To the Legal Counsel or Chief Risk Officer (CRO):

Description: This structure emphasizes security's role in legal compliance, regulatory adherence, and enterprise-wide risk management.

Implications: Strong alignment with legal and regulatory requirements. May lead to a more compliance-driven security program, potentially less agile or innovative if not balanced with strategic and operational needs.

Influence Strategies:

- **Emphasize regulatory compliance and legal protection:** Show how security reduces legal exposure, fines, and litigation risks.
- Integrate security into the broader GRC (Governance, Risk, and Compliance) framework: Collaborate closely with legal, audit, and compliance teams.
- Provide expert advice on legal and privacy implications: Become the go-to expert for security-related legal and privacy matters.

Importance of Reporting Lines for Security Visibility to Executive Leadership:

The reporting line directly influences the CISO's authority, budget, and ability to effectively communicate and influence security decisions at the highest levels of the organization.

Direct Reporting to CEO/Board: Provides the highest level of visibility and influence. Security risks are presented directly to those who make strategic decisions; ensuring cybersecurity is treated as a business risk, not just an IT problem. This facilitates faster decision-making and resource allocation for critical security initiatives.

Indirect Reporting (e.g., via CIO): Can lead to security concerns being filtered or diluted before reaching top leadership. The CIO may prioritize IT operational needs over pure security investments, or simplify complex security risks to fit an IT-centric narrative. This can result in underfunding of security programs, delayed responses to emerging threats, or a lack of understanding of the true business impact of cyber risks at the executive level.

How Security Messaging May Change by the Time it Reaches Leadership:

- **Technical to Business Translation:** Security professionals often speak in technical jargon (e.g., "CVE-2023-XXXX," "SQL injection," "zero-day"). As this information moves up the chain, especially through non-security executives, it needs to be translated into business terms (e.g., "potential for customer data breach leading to $X million in fines and reputational damage," "risk of operational disruption affecting revenue"). If this translation is not done effectively, the urgency or criticality of the message can be lost.

- **Filtering and Prioritization:** Each layer of management may filter or prioritize information based on their own departmental goals or perceived importance. A CIO might focus on how a security issue impacts IT operations, while a business unit head might focus on how it affects their specific product or service. This can lead to a skewed or incomplete picture reaching the top.
- **Risk Aversion vs. Business Enablement:** Different leaders have different risk appetites. A security leader might emphasize the inherent risks, while a business leader might emphasize the need for speed or innovation. The message can be altered to align with the recipient's perspective, sometimes downplaying risks to avoid perceived obstacles to business goals.
- **"Good News" Bias:** There can be a tendency to present "good news" or downplay challenges to senior leadership, especially if there's a fear of being seen as alarmist or ineffective. This can lead to a false sense of security at the top.
- **Lack of Context:** Without direct engagement, executive leadership may lack the full context of security challenges, making it difficult for them to make informed decisions about security investments or strategic direction.

CCISO Explain IT Like I Am 5: Domain 1

Domain 1: Governance, Risk Management & Compliance

Governance

Information Security Governance

Definition:

The system by which an organization directs and controls information security activities, ensuring alignment with business objectives. It involves establishing a framework of accountability, roles, and processes to manage information security risks effectively.

Key elements of information security governance include strategy, implementation, operations, and monitoring. These components work together to establish a framework for protecting an organization's information assets, managing risks, and ensuring compliance with relevant regulations. A strong security governance framework also relies on clearly defined policies, robust processes, stakeholder engagement, a strong organizational culture, and a commitment to ethics.

Key Objectives:

Strategic Alignment:

Align information security with business strategy to support organizational objectives.

Example: Ensuring that the security roadmap prioritizes protecting customer data when the business strategy focuses on expanding e-commerce operations.

Risk Management:

Identify, assess, and manage information security risks to an acceptable level.
Example: Conducting regular vulnerability assessments and penetration tests on critical systems to identify and mitigate potential attack vectors.

Resource Management:

Optimize security investments and resources.

Example: Allocating budget to advanced threat detection tools that address the highest identified risks, rather than spreading resources thinly across all security areas.

Performance Measurement:

Monitor, measure, and report on information security performance.

Example: Tracking the number of security incidents, time to detect, and time to resolve incidents, and reporting these metrics monthly to the security steering committee.

Value Delivery:

Ensure that information security efforts deliver measurable value to the business.

Example: Implementing data encryption that not only protects sensitive information but also enables compliance with new data privacy regulations, opening up new market opportunities.

Legal & Regulatory Compliance:

Ensure compliance with applicable laws, regulations, and internal policies.

Example: Implementing controls and processes specifically designed to meet GDPR requirements for data handling and privacy, avoiding potential fines.

Importance:

It establishes accountability, defines roles, ensures resource allocation, and integrates security into organizational culture. Good governance ensures security supports, rather than hinders business goals.

Establishing Accountability:

Governance defines clear lines of responsibility for information security at all levels, from the board of directors down to individual employees. This ensures that someone is always answerable for security outcomes, preventing a "blame game" when incidents occur. It clarifies who "owns" particular information assets, who is responsible for implementing specific security controls, and who is accountable for compliance.

Defining roles:

It clearly outlines the specific duties and expectations for various security-related roles (e.g., CISO, security analysts, data owners, system administrators). This clarity eliminates ambiguity and ensures that all necessary security functions are covered. Helps to establish and maintain key concepts such as Role-Based Access Control (RBAC), separation of duties, access reviews, least privilege; granting users only the minimum level of access (permissions) necessary to perform their job duties. These all help to reduce the attack surface.

Ensures resource allocation:

Through governance, security needs are elevated to a strategic level, allowing for proper budgeting and allocation of financial, human, and technological resources. This prevents security from being an afterthought and ensures it receives the necessary investment.

Integrates security into organizational culture:

Governance promotes a security-aware culture by embedding security considerations into business processes, decision-making, and employee training. It moves security beyond a purely technical function to a shared responsibility. This is a top-down commitment emphasizing the importance of security and encourages individuals to take ownership of their role in protecting information assets. It requires Leadership buy-in, continuous security awareness training, and incorporating security performance into employee evaluations.

Ensures security supports, rather than hinders, business goals:

By aligning security strategy with overall business objectives, governance ensures that security measures are not seen as roadblocks but as an enablers of business operations, innovation, and growth. It helps balance risk with business opportunities. It defines the processes for identifying, assessing, and mitigating information security risks. It establishes who is authorized to make risk acceptance decisions and ensures that these decisions are documented and aligned with the organization's risk appetite.

Alignment with Business Objectives:

Security as an enabler, not a blocker; understanding business processes and critical assets.

Example: Ensuring secure e-commerce platforms directly supports online sales revenue by maintaining customer trust and preventing fraudulent transactions.

Why is it crucial?

An information security governance program is not just a technical necessity; it's a strategic imperative that underpins an organization's resilience, reputation, and ability to achieve its business objectives in a secure manner.

Key Business Benefits:

- **Protects Critical Assets:** Safeguards sensitive data, intellectual property, and operational systems from cyber threats, unauthorized access, and data breaches, directly protecting the organization's core value.
- **Ensures Business Continuity:** By managing risks and implementing robust controls, it helps prevent disruptions to business operations caused by security incidents, ensuring uninterrupted service delivery and revenue streams.
- **Maintains Trust and Reputation:** A strong security posture builds confidence among customers, partners, and stakeholders, protecting the organization's brand and reputation, which are invaluable business assets.
- **Facilitates Compliance:** Helps organizations meet legal, regulatory, and contractual obligations, avoiding costly fines, legal repercussions, and reputational damage that can significantly impact the business.
- **Optimizes Security Investments:** Ensures that security resources are allocated effectively to address the most significant risks, providing a better return on investment and preventing wasteful spending.
- **Enables Strategic Growth:** By managing security risks proactively, it allows the business to innovate, expand into new markets, and pursue new opportunities securely, fostering sustainable growth.
- **Gains Competitive Advantage:** Demonstrating a mature information security governance program can differentiate an organization in the marketplace, attracting security-conscious clients and partners.

Key Components of an Information Security Governance Program

A robust information security governance program is built upon three core pillars: leadership, organizational structures, and processes.

Leadership: Strong leadership drives the program by setting the vision, prioritizing security, and ensuring resource allocation. Leaders foster a security-aware culture, align security goals with business objectives, and champion accountability at all levels.

Organizational Structures: Effective structures define clear roles, responsibilities, and reporting lines. This includes establishing dedicated security teams, governance committees, and cross-functional collaboration to ensure security is embedded across the organization.

Processes: Well-defined processes provide the framework for consistent security practices. These include risk assessments, policy development, incident response, compliance monitoring, and continuous improvement to adapt to evolving threats.

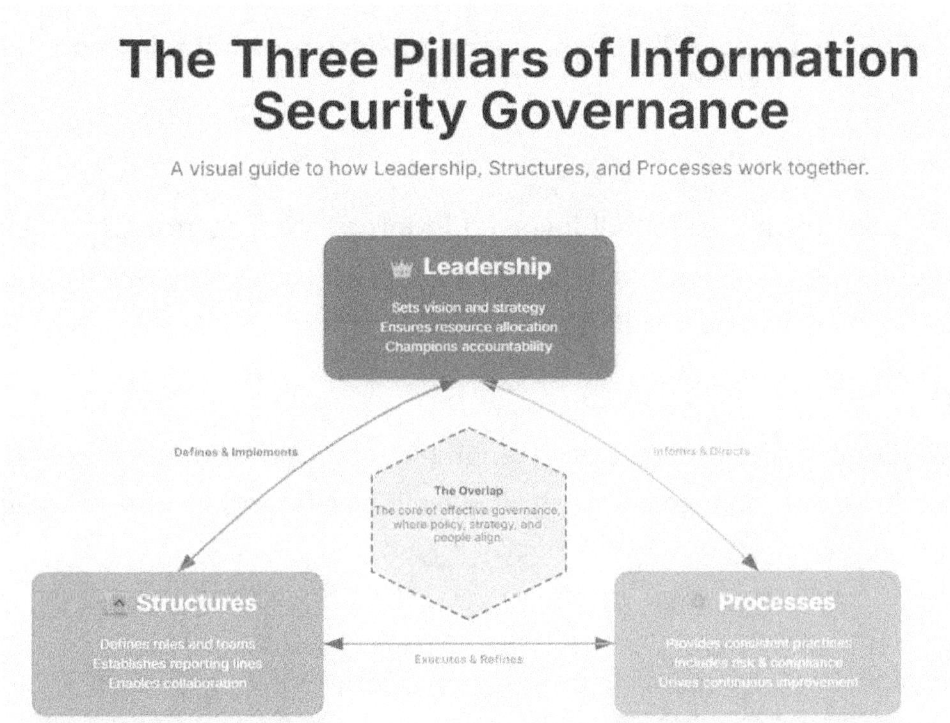

a. Leadership and Commitment

Strong leadership is the cornerstone of effective security governance.

Executive Sponsorship:

High-level commitment from the board of directors and senior management is essential. This includes allocating necessary resources, setting the tone from the top, and integrating security into the organizational culture.

Security Steering Comittee:

A cross-functional committee comprising representatives from IT, legal, HR, operations, and business units. This committee is responsible for:

- Defining security strategy and objectives.
- Approving security policies and standards.
- Reviewing security performance and risk posture.
- Making decisions on major security investments.

Chief Information Security Officer (CISO):

A dedicated executive responsible for the overall information security program. The CISO acts as the primary liaison between technical security teams and business leadership.

b. Organizational Structures

Clearly defined roles, responsibilities, and reporting lines are vital for accountability and efficiency.

Defined Roles and Responsibilities:

Establish clear roles for all personnel involved in information security, from executive leadership to end-users. This includes data owners, data custodians, security architects, security operations teams, and incident responders.

Reporting Lines:

Ensure the CISO or equivalent security leader has appropriate authority and direct reporting lines to senior management (e.g., CEO, CIO, or Board) to ensure independence and influence.

Security Teams:

Establish dedicated security teams (e.g., Security Operations Center (SOC), Governance, Risk, and Compliance (GRC), Incident Response Team, Security Architecture).

Cross-Functional Collaboration:

Foster collaboration between security teams and other departments (IT, Legal, HR, Audit, Business Units) to embed security into all aspects of the business.

c. Processes and Frameworks

Standardized processes and established frameworks guide security activities.

Policy and Standard Management:

- **Security Policies:** High-level statements of intent (e.g., Acceptable Use Policy, Data Classification Policy, Access Control Policy).

- **Security Standards:** Detailed mandatory requirements for implementing policies (e.g., Password Complexity Standard, Server Hardening Standard).
- **Guidelines and Procedures:** Recommended practices and step-by-step instructions.
- **Regular Review:** Policies and standards must be regularly reviewed and updated to reflect changes in technology, threats, and business needs.

Risk Management Framework:

- **Risk Identification:** Proactively identify potential threats and vulnerabilities.
- **Risk Assessment:** Evaluate the likelihood and impact of identified risks.
- **Risk Treatment:** Implement controls to mitigate, transfer, avoid, or accept risks.
- **Risk Monitoring:** Continuously monitor the effectiveness of controls and the evolving risk landscape.

Compliance Management:

- Identify and track all relevant legal, regulatory, and contractual obligations (e.g., GDPR, HIPAA, PCI DSS, ISO 27001).
- Map controls to compliance requirements.
- Conduct regular audits and assessments to ensure adherence.

Incident Response and Management:

- Develop and maintain an incident response plan.
- Establish an incident response team.
- Conduct regular incident response exercises.
- Implement processes for detection, analysis, containment, eradication, recovery, and post-incident review.

Security Awareness and Training:

- Develop a comprehensive security awareness program for all employees.
- Provide targeted training for specific roles (e.g., developers, IT administrators).
- Reinforce security best practices through ongoing communication.

Performance Monitoring and Reporting:

- Define key performance indicators (KPIs) and key risk indicators (KRIs).
- Collect and analyze security metrics.
- Regularly report on the security posture to senior management and the board.

Aligning Information Security Governance with Organizational Goals and Governance

Aligning information security governance with an organization's overarching goals, leadership style, philosophy, values, standards, and policies is crucial for its effectiveness and long-term success. When security is integrated seamlessly into the fabric of the organization, it transforms from a mere technical function into a strategic enabler, supporting business objectives rather than hindering them.

Core Principles of Alignment

Effective alignment hinges on understanding and incorporating the following organizational elements into the information security framework:

Organizational Goals:

Information security must directly support and protect the achievement of business objectives. Whether the goal is market expansion, innovation, cost reduction, or customer trust, security measures should be designed to facilitate these goals while mitigating risks.

Leadership Style:

The approach to security governance should resonate with the leadership's preferred way of operating.

- **Authoritarian/Directive:** A more top-down, prescriptive security framework might be more readily accepted.
- **Participative/Collaborative:** Security initiatives might benefit from broader involvement, consensus-building, and shared ownership.
- **Laissez-faire/Delegative:** Security governance needs to empower teams with clear guidelines and accountability, ensuring they have the necessary resources and autonomy.

Organizational Philosophy:

This refers to the fundamental beliefs and values that guide the organization. If the philosophy emphasizes innovation and agility, security should be designed to enable secure innovation, perhaps through "security by design" principles and agile security practices, rather than being perceived as a bottleneck. If it's about meticulous control, then a more stringent, compliance-driven security approach might fit.

Organizational Values:

Security governance should reflect and reinforce the organization's core values.

- **Trust & Integrity:** Security measures should build and maintain trust with customers, partners, and employees by protecting sensitive data and systems.
- **Customer Focus:** Security should prioritize the protection of customer data and ensure the availability of customer-facing services.
- **Innovation:** Security should not stifle innovation but enable it securely, for example, by providing secure development environments or risk-based assessments for new technologies.
- **Accountability:** The security framework should clearly define roles, responsibilities, and accountability for information security across all levels.

Organizational Standards and Policies:

The information security framework must be consistent with, and ideally integrated into, existing organizational standards and policies (e.g., HR policies, operational procedures, compliance requirements). This ensures coherence, reduces duplication, and simplifies compliance efforts.

Key Steps for Alignment

Achieving this alignment requires a systematic approach:

Understand Organizational Goals and Strategy:

- Collaborate with executive leadership to deeply understand the organization's strategic objectives, business model, and risk appetite.
- Identify critical assets (data, systems, processes) that are essential for achieving these goals.

Assess Current Governance Landscape:

- Review existing organizational governance structures, decision-making processes, and communication channels.
- Analyze the current leadership style, cultural norms, and how policies are typically developed and enforced.

Define Information Security Vision and Strategy:

- Develop an information security vision that clearly articulates how security supports the overall business strategy.
- Formulate a security strategy that aligns with the organization's risk appetite and addresses key business risks. This strategy should be communicated in business terms, not just technical jargon.

Integrate Security into Existing Processes:

- **Policy Integration:** Embed security requirements directly into existing organizational policies (e.g., acceptable use, data privacy, incident response) rather than creating standalone, isolated security policies.
- **Process Integration:** Integrate security activities into existing business processes, such as procurement (secure vendor selection), HR (security awareness training, background checks), and project management (security by design, risk assessments).
- **Decision-Making:** Ensure security considerations are part of strategic business decisions, not an afterthought. This might involve having security representation on key committees or boards.

Establish Metrics and Reporting Aligned with Business Value:

- Develop key performance indicators (KPIs) and key risk indicators (KRIs) that measure the effectiveness of security controls in terms of business impact, not just technical metrics.
- Report security posture and risks to leadership in a language they understand, demonstrating the value and impact of security on business goals.

Foster a Security Culture:

- **Leadership Buy-in:** Secure visible and active support from top leadership, demonstrating their commitment to information security as a shared responsibility.
- **Communication & Awareness:** Tailor security awareness programs to resonate with the organizational values and philosophy, making security relevant to employees' daily roles.
- **Training:** Provide targeted security training that aligns with job functions and the organization's specific risks.

Continuous Improvement and Adaptation:

- Regularly review and update the information security governance framework to ensure it remains aligned with evolving organizational goals, threat landscapes, and regulatory requirements.

- Establish feedback mechanisms to gather input from various stakeholders and adapt the framework as needed.

Conclusion

By meticulously aligning information security governance with the organization's goals, leadership style, philosophy, values, standards, and policies, businesses can build a robust and resilient security posture. This integration not only enhances protection against cyber threats but also strengthens overall organizational governance, fosters a positive security culture, and ultimately contributes to the achievement of strategic business objectives.

Establishing an Information Security Management Structure

Establishing a robust information security management structure is crucial for protecting an organization's valuable information assets from evolving threats. This involves a systematic approach to defining roles, responsibilities, policies, and processes to ensure the confidentiality, integrity, and availability of data.

Core Components of an Information Security Management System (ISMS)

An effective information security management structure is often built around an Information Security Management System (ISMS), which is a framework of policies and procedures for managing an organization's sensitive data. Key components include:

Information Security Policies and Procedures:

These are the foundational guidelines that define the organization's commitment to security, acceptable use, data handling, access control, and other security-related practices. They should be clear, actionable, and regularly reviewed.

Risk Management:

This involves systematically identifying, analyzing, evaluating, and treating information security risks. It includes understanding potential threats, vulnerabilities, and their potential impact on the organization's assets.

Security Controls:

These are the safeguards implemented to mitigate identified risks. They can be:

- **Technical Controls:** Firewalls, encryption, intrusion detection/prevention systems (IDS/IPS), multi-factor authentication (MFA), antivirus software.
- **Administrative Controls:** Security awareness training, incident response plans, access control policies, disciplinary processes.
- **Physical Controls:** Access controls to facilities, surveillance systems, and environmental controls for data centers.

Asset Management:

A comprehensive inventory of all information assets (hardware, software, data, and intellectual property) is essential. Each asset should have a designated owner responsible for its security.

Incident Response and Recovery:

Detailed plans and procedures for detecting, analyzing, containing, eradicating, and recovering from security incidents and breaches. This also includes business continuity and disaster recovery planning.

Monitoring, Review, and Improvement:

Continuous monitoring of security systems, regular security audits, vulnerability assessments, and penetration testing to evaluate the effectiveness of controls and identify areas for improvement. The ISMS should be continuously improved to adapt to new threats and changes in the organization.

Compliance and Governance:

Ensuring adherence to relevant legal, regulatory, and contractual requirements (e.g., GDPR, HIPAA, PCI DSS) and establishing a clear governance framework with defined roles, responsibilities, and accountability.

Key Information Security Management Structure Considerations

Sizing:

The size and structure of a security team must adapt to the unique characteristics of an organization. This involves considering:

Organizational Size:

- **Small Organizations (e.g., Startup, SMB):** Often have a single security lead or a small team (1-3 individuals) responsible for a broad range of tasks, potentially relying heavily on outsourced security services or managed security service providers (MSSPs). The CISO might wear multiple hats, acting as a technical lead, policy writer, and incident responder.
- **Medium Organizations:** May have a dedicated security team (5-15 individuals) with some specialization (e.g., security operations, overnance/risk/compliance). The CISO focuses more on strategy and program management.
- **Large Enterprises (e.g., Fortune 500):** Typically have large, multi-faceted security departments (50+ individuals) with highly specialized teams (e.g., SOC, AppSec, GRC, Incident Response, Threat Intelligence, Security Architecture). The CISO's role is primarily strategic, managing leaders of

these specialized teams and engaging with the board.

Complexity:

- **Simple IT Environment (e.g., SaaS-only, minimal on-prem):** Requires a smaller team focused on cloud security posture management, identity, and access management.
- **Complex IT Environment (e.g., Hybrid cloud, legacy systems, extensive custom applications, IoT):** Demands a larger, more diverse team with expertise in various domains (network security, application security, cloud security, OT/ICS security). The interdependencies and unique vulnerabilities of complex systems necessitate more resources.

Industry:

- **Highly Regulated Industries (e.g., Finance, Healthcare, Government):** Require larger security teams with strong expertise in compliance (e.g., GDPR, HIPAA, PCI DSS, SOX). There's a greater need for GRC (Governance, Risk, and Compliance) specialists, audit liaison roles, and legal expertise within or closely tied to the security function. The cost of non-compliance is extremely high.
- **Technology/Software Development:** Often have robust application security (AppSec) teams, security architects embedded in development teams, and expertise in secure coding practices, DevSecOps, and vulnerability management.
- **Manufacturing/Operational Technology (OT):** Requires specialists in industrial control systems (ICS) security, physical security, and managing risks to operational continuity.
- **Retail/E-commerce:** Focus on PCI DSS compliance, web application security, fraud detection, and protecting customer data.

Risk Appetite:

- **Low Risk Appetite (e.g., Critical Infrastructure, Financial Institutions):** Organizations that cannot tolerate significant security incidents will invest heavily in prevention, detection, and rapid response. This translates to larger teams, advanced security technologies, and continuous monitoring.
- **High Risk Appetite (e.g., Some Startups, Innovative Tech):** Organizations willing to accept more risk for faster growth or innovation might start with smaller security teams, focusing on foundational controls and scaling up as they mature or gain funding. This is often accompanied by a strong

understanding and acceptance of the potential consequences.

Different Team Organization and Structures:

Can create varying challenges depending on the model used. Centralized (security team reports to one central authority), decentralized (security functions are distributed across business units), federated models (mix of central guidance and local execution) all have varying advantages and disadvantages.

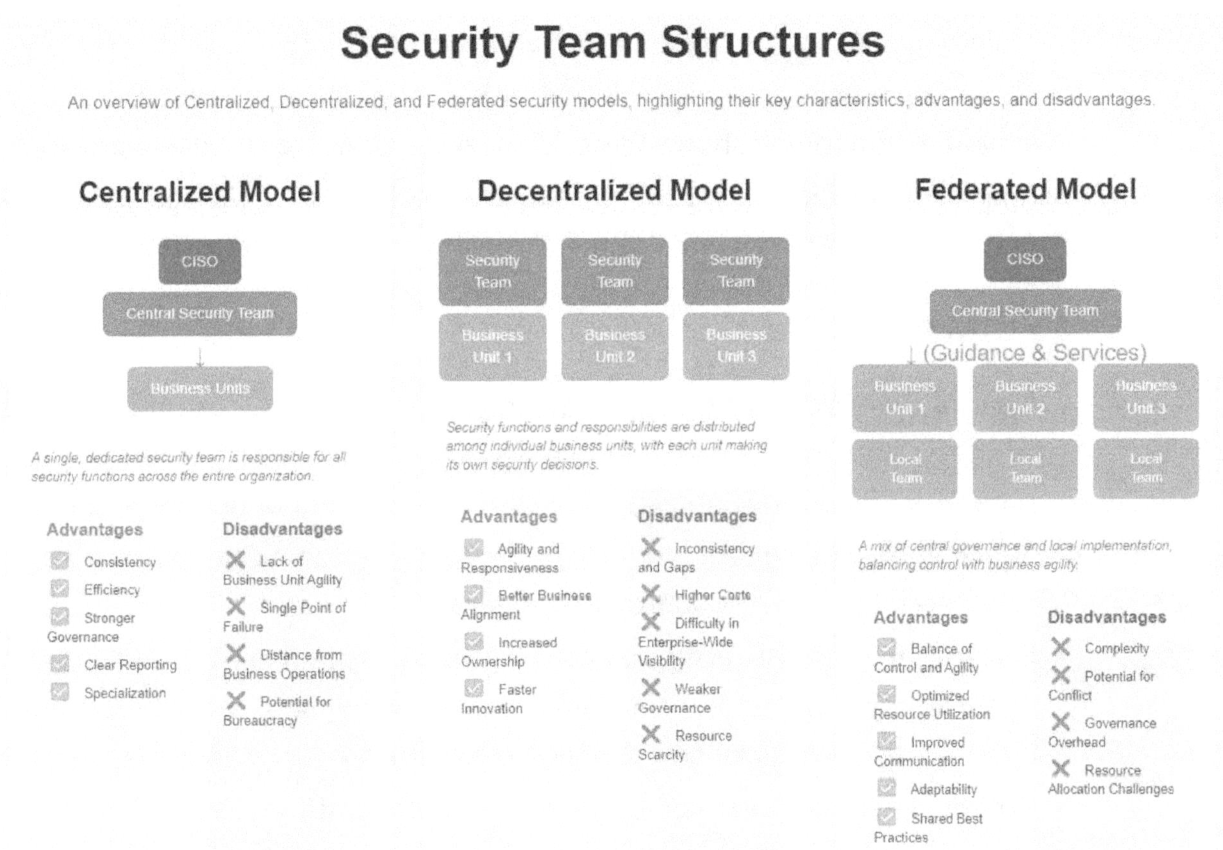

Centralized Model:

Description: In a centralized security model, a single, dedicated information security team, typically led by the CISO, is responsible for all security functions across the entire organization. All security decisions, policies, operations, and resources are managed from this central unit.

Example: A large financial institution where the CISO heads a global security department that sets all security policies, manages all security technologies (e.g., SOC, incident response, vulnerability management), and oversees compliance for all business units worldwide.

Advantages:

- **Consistency:** Ensures uniform application of security policies, standards, and controls across the entire organization, reducing variations and potential gaps.
- **Efficiency:** Centralized purchasing of security tools and services can lead to economies of scale. Shared resources and expertise can be leveraged more effectively.
- **Stronger Governance:** Easier to enforce policies, ensure compliance, and maintain a clear chain of command and accountability.
- **Clear Reporting:** A single point of contact for security matters simplifies communication and decision-making for executive leadership.
- **Specialization:** Allows for the development of highly specialized security teams (e.g., dedicated threat intelligence, forensics, security architecture teams).

Disadvantages:

- **Lack of Business Unit Agility:** May be perceived as slow or unresponsive to the specific needs and unique risks of individual business units, potentially hindering innovation or rapid deployment of new services.
- **Single Point of Failure:** Over-reliance on a single team can create a bottleneck for security approvals or operations.
- **Distance from Business Operations:** The central team might lack deep understanding of specific business processes, leading to security solutions that are not well-tailored or create operational friction.
- **Potential for Bureaucracy:** Can become bureaucratic and slow down decision- making if not managed efficiently.

Decentralized Model:

Description: In a decentralized security model, security functions and responsibilities are distributed among individual business units, departments, or geographical regions. Each unit has its own security personnel and makes its own security decisions, often with minimal central oversight.

Example: A diversified conglomerate where each subsidiary or business line (e.g., automotive, aerospace, healthcare) has its own independent IT and security team, responsible for its specific security posture and compliance.

Advantages:

- **Agility and Responsiveness:** Security teams are closer to the business units they support, allowing for faster decision-making and tailored security solutions that meet specific operational needs and risk profiles.
- **Better Business Alignment:** Security personnel have a deeper understanding of local business processes, applications, and data, leading to more relevant and effective controls.
- **Increased Ownership:** Business units take greater ownership of their security posture.
- **Faster Innovation:** Security can be integrated more rapidly into local development cycles.

Disadvantages:

- **Inconsistency and Gaps:** Lack of central coordination can lead to fragmented security postures, inconsistent policies, and potential security gaps or overlaps across the organization.
- **Higher Costs:** Duplication of tools, resources, and expertise across multiple units can be inefficient and more expensive.
- **Difficulty in Enterprise-Wide Visibility:** Gaining a holistic view of the organization's overall security posture becomes challenging.
- **Weaker Governance:** May struggle with enterprise-wide policy enforcement and compliance, especially for cross-cutting regulations.
- **Resource Scarcity:** Smaller, decentralized teams may lack the specialized skills or resources available in a larger central team.

Federated Model:

Description: The federated security model combines elements of both centralized and decentralized approaches. A central security team (often led by the CISO) establishes overall strategy, governance, policies, and common security services, while individual business units retain responsibility for implementing and operating security controls tailored to their specific needs, adhering to the central framework.

Example: A global technology company where the central CISO office defines enterprise- wide security policies, provides shared security services (e.g., threat intelligence, security awareness training, core SIEM platform), but each product development team has embedded security engineers responsible for application security and DevSecOps within their specific product lines.

Advantages:

- **Balance of Control and Agility:** Offers the benefits of consistency and strong governance from the central team, combined with the responsiveness and business alignment of decentralized teams.
- **Optimized Resource Utilization:** Centralized services avoid duplication, while decentralized teams focus on unique local needs.
- **Improved Communication and Collaboration:** Fosters better communication between central security and business units.
- **Adaptability:** Can adapt more easily to diverse business requirements and regulatory landscapes across different regions or business lines.
- **Shared Best Practices:** Central team can disseminate best practices and lessons learned across the organization.

Disadvantages:

- **Complexity:** Requires careful coordination and clear communication channels to avoid ambiguity in roles and responsibilities.
- **Potential for Conflict:** Friction can arise if central mandates clash with local operational needs or if roles are not clearly defined.
- **Governance Overhead:** Requires a robust governance framework to ensure adherence to central policies without stifling local innovation.
- **Resource Allocation Challenges:** Balancing central investment with local needs can be complex.

Key Roles and Potential Responsibilities:

Defining clear roles for CISO, security managers, security analysts, and other stakeholders (e.g., legal, HR, IT operations) is crucial. This prevents gaps and overlaps in security duties and ensures that all necessary security functions are covered.

Chief Information Security Officer (CISO):

Responsibilities: Develop and implement the overall information security strategy; manage the security budget; report to executive leadership and the board on cyber risk; oversee security operations, risk management, and compliance; lead the security team; manage third-party security risks; drive security culture and awareness.

Focus: Strategic leadership, governance, risk management, business alignment, communication.

Security Architect:

Responsibilities: Design secure systems and applications; develop security blueprints and roadmaps; ensure security is "built-in" to new projects; conduct threat modeling and security design reviews.

Focus: Proactive security design, system hardening, architectural integrity.

Security Operations Center (SOC) Analyst (Tier 1/2/3):

Responsibilities: Monitor security alerts (SIEM, EDR); investigate security incidents; perform initial containment actions; conduct vulnerability scans; manage security tools; contribute to incident response.

Focus: Real-time threat detection, incident triage, security tool management.

Incident Response (IR) Specialist:

Responsibilities: Lead security incident investigations; perform digital forensics; contain, eradicate, and recover from breaches; develop and refine incident response playbooks; conduct post-incident analysis and lessons learned.

Focus: Rapid response, forensic analysis, breach remediation.

Governance, Risk, and Compliance (GRC) Analyst/Manager:

Responsibilities: Develop and maintain security policies, standards, and procedures; ensure compliance with regulations (GDPR, HIPAA, PCI DSS) and frameworks (ISO 27001, NIST CSF); conduct risk assessments; manage risk register; prepare for and support internal/ external audits.

Focus: Policy development, regulatory adherence, risk assessment, audit management.

Application Security (AppSec) Engineer:

Responsibilities: Embed security into the Software Development Lifecycle (SDLC);

perform static (SAST) and dynamic (DAST) application security testing; conduct code reviews; provide secure coding training to developers; manage web application firewalls (WAFs).

Focus: Secure coding, vulnerability testing, integrating security into development.

Identity and Access Management (IAM) Specialist:

Responsibilities: Design and manage identity lifecycle processes; implement and maintain access control systems (e.g., MFA, SSO, PAM); perform regular access reviews; ensure least privilege principles are enforced.

Focus: User authentication, authorization, access governance.

Security Awareness and Training Coordinator:

Responsibilities: Develop and deliver security awareness programs; create training materials; conduct simulated phishing campaigns; track employee security behavior and compliance.

Focus: Human element of security, culture change, education.

Security Engineer (General/Infrastructure):

Responsibilities: Implement, configure, and maintain security technologies (firewalls, IDS/ IPS, endpoint protection); manage patch management processes; hardening operating systems and network devices.

Focus: Technical control implementation, infrastructure security.

Data Owner:

(Often a business role, not security staff, but crucial stakeholder)

Responsibilities: Accountable for the protection and proper classification of specific datasets; defines access requirements and retention policies for their data.

Focus: Data stewardship, business context for data security.

System Administrator/IT Operations:

(Collaborates closely with security)

Responsibilities: Implement security configurations as directed by security policies; apply patches; manage system logs; respond to security incidents under IR team guidance.

Focus: Operational security, system maintenance.

All Employees/Users:

Responsible for adhering to security policies and procedures, reporting suspicious activities, and participating in security awareness training.

Reporting Lines

The reporting line directly influences the CISO's authority, budget, and ability to effectively communicate and influence security decisions at the highest levels of the organization.

Direct Reporting to CEO/Board: Provides the highest level of visibility and influence. Security risks are presented directly to those who make strategic decisions; ensuring cybersecurity is treated as a business risk, not just an IT problem. This facilitates faster decision making and resource allocation for critical security initiatives.

Indirect Reporting (e.g., via CIO): Can lead to security concerns being filtered or diluted before reaching top leadership. The CIO may prioritize IT operational needs over pure security investments, or simplify complex security risks to fit an IT-centric narrative. This can result in underfunding of security programs, delayed responses to emerging threats, or a lack of understanding of the true business impact of cyber risks at the executive level.

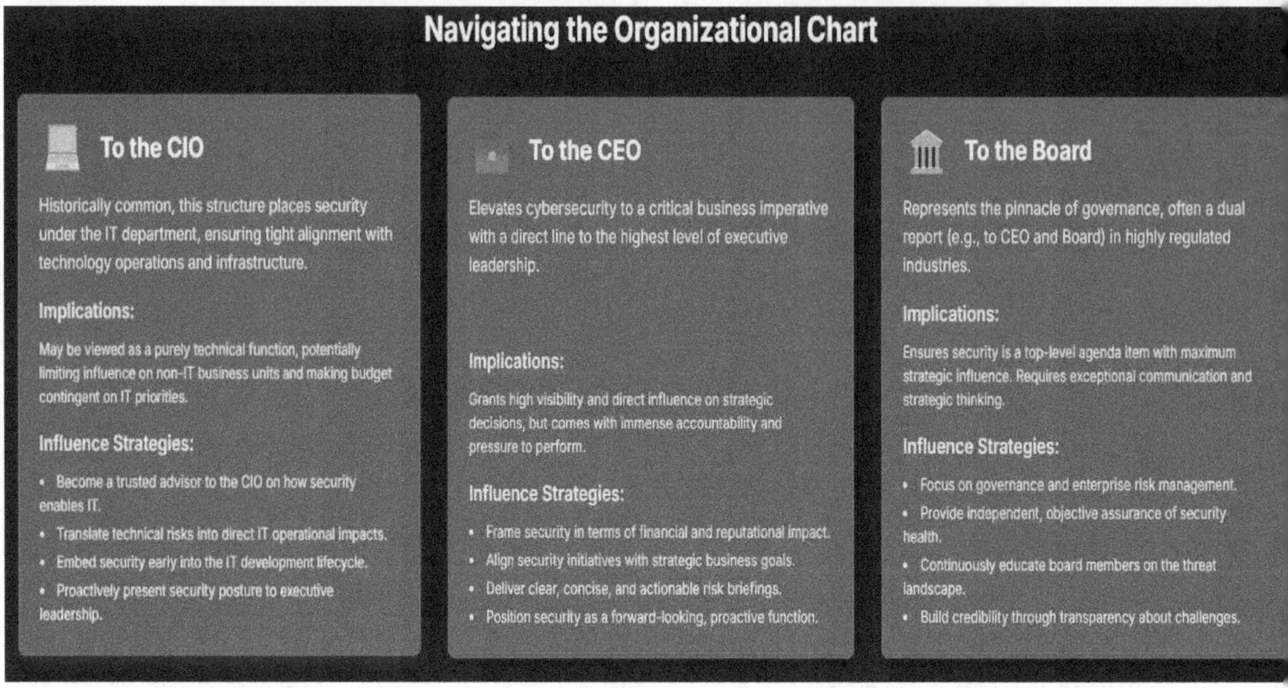

How Security Messaging May Change by the Time it Reaches Leadership

- **Technical to Business Translation:** Security professionals often speak in technical jargon (e.g., "CVE-2023-XXXX," "SQL injection," "zero-day"). As this information moves up the chain, especially through non-security executives, it needs to be translated into business terms (e.g., "potential for customer data breach leading to $X million in fines and reputational damage," "risk of operational disruption affecting revenue"). If this translation is not done effectively, the urgency or criticality of the message can be lost.
- **Filtering and Prioritization:** Each layer of management may filter or prioritize information based on their own departmental goals or perceived importance. A CIO might focus on how a security issue impacts IT operations, while a business unit head might focus on how it affects their specific product or service. This can lead to a skewed or incomplete picture reaching the top.
- **Risk Aversion vs. Business Enablement:** Different leaders have different risk appetites. A security leader might emphasize the inherent risks, while a business leader might emphasize the need for speed or innovation. The message can be altered to align with the recipient's perspective, sometimes downplaying risks to avoid perceived obstacles to business goals.
- **"Good News" Bias:** There can be a tendency to present "good news" or

downplay challenges to senior leadership, especially if there's a fear of being seen as alarmist or ineffective. This can lead to a false sense of security at the top.

- **Lack of Context:** Without direct engagement, executive leadership may lack the full context of security challenges, making it difficult for them to make informed decisions about security investments or strategic direction.

Establishing the ISM Structure: Implementation Steps

Implementing an information security management structure is an ongoing process that typically involves the following steps:

- **Obtain Management Commitment:** Secure buy-in and support from senior leadership, as their commitment is critical for resource allocation and successful implementation.
- **Define the Scope and Context:** Identify what information assets need protection, why they need protection, and the internal and external factors that affect information security (e.g., regulatory requirements, business objectives).
- **Form an ISMS Project Team:** Assemble a dedicated team with representatives from various departments (IT, legal, HR, business units) to lead the implementation.
- **Conduct a Comprehensive Risk Assessment:** Identify critical information assets, potential threats, and vulnerabilities. Prioritize risks based on likelihood and impact.
- **Develop and Document Policies and Procedures:** Create clear, concise, and enforceable policies for all aspects of information security, including acceptable use, access control, data classification, incident management, and business continuity.
- **Implement Security Controls:** Apply appropriate technical, administrative, and physical controls to mitigate the identified risks. This should be a multi-layered approach.
- **Provide Training and Awareness:** Educate all employees about security policies, common threats (e.g., phishing), and their role in maintaining security. This should be an ongoing program.
- **Establish Monitoring and Measurement:** Implement tools and processes for continuous monitoring of security systems, network traffic,

and user behavior. Define key performance indicators (KPIs) to measure the effectiveness of security controls.

- **Plan for Incident Response:** Develop and regularly test incident response plans to ensure the organization can effectively detect, respond to, and recover from security incidents.
- **Conduct Regular Audits and Reviews:** Perform internal and external audits to assess compliance with policies and standards (like ISO 27001) and identify areas for improvement.
- **Continuous Improvement:** Information security is not a one-time project. Regularly review and update the ISMS, policies, and controls to adapt to new threats, technologies, and organizational changes.

Leveraging Standards (e.g., ISO 27001)

International standards like ISO/IEC 27001 provide a globally recognized framework for establishing, implementing, maintaining, and continually improving an ISMS. Adopting such a standard can:

- Provide a structured, systematic approach to information security.
- Help identify and manage security risks effectively.
- Demonstrate a commitment to information security to customers, partners, and regulators.
- Facilitate compliance with various legal and regulatory requirements.

By systematically addressing these components and following a structured implementation process, organizations can build a resilient information security management structure that protects their valuable assets and supports their business objectives.

Information Security Governance Monitoring Framework

An Information Security Governance Monitoring Framework is a structured system of policies, procedures, and controls that an organization uses to manage its information security risks. It's a strategic approach that aligns security initiatives with business objectives and regulatory requirements, moving security from a purely technical function to an enterprise-wide business function. This framework is structured around key components that ensure a systematic and financially astute approach to information security.

1. Strategic Alignment and Objective Setting

Purpose:

Ensure information security initiatives directly support the organization's overall business goals and risk appetite.

Business Objectives:

Security efforts must directly support the organization's mission and goals. The framework ensures that security is not a barrier to business but an enabler.

Risk Appetite:

The framework helps define the organization's tolerance for risk and ensures that security measures are in line with that tolerance.

Monitoring Focus:

- Regularly review security strategy against evolving business objectives and threat landscape.
- Track the alignment of security projects with strategic priorities.

Cost/Benefit & ROI Integration:

- **Benefit:** Quantify how security investments enable new business opportunities, protect revenue streams, or support market expansion.
- **Cost:** Analyze the cost of not aligning security with strategy (e.g., missed opportunities, compliance penalties).

2. Policy and Standards Development & Adherence

Purpose:

Establish clear, enforceable policies, standards, and procedures that guide security practices across the organization.

Security Policies:

Formal, high-level documents that outline the organization's stance on security, employee responsibilities and incident management procedures.

Standards and Procedures:

Detailed guidelines that provide specific instructions for implementing security policies (e.g., password policies, data encryption standards, incident reporting procedures).

Monitoring Focus:

- Regular audits of policy adherence (e.g., access control policies, data classification, and acceptable use).
- Review and update policies based on new threats, technologies, and regulatory changes.

Cost/Benefit & ROI Integration:

- **Benefit:** Reduced non-compliance fines, improved operational efficiency due to clear guidelines, reduced human error.
- **Cost:** Cost of policy development, training, and enforcement. Analyze the cost of non-compliance vs. the cost of implementing the necessary controls.

3. Risk Management (Assessment, Mitigation, Monitoring)

Purpose:

Identify, assess, mitigate, and continuously monitor information security risks to an acceptable level. This is the core area for financial analysis.

Risk Assessment:

A systematic process to identify, analyze, and evaluate potential threats and vulnerabilities to information assets. This helps prioritize risks based on their likelihood and impact.

Risk Mitigation:

Strategies and controls to reduce identified risks to an acceptable level. This can include technical controls (e.g., firewalls, intrusion detection systems), administrative controls (e.g., training), and physical controls (e.g., secure access to facilities).

Monitoring Focus:

- Track identified risks, their likelihood, and potential impact.
- Monitor the effectiveness of implemented controls in reducing risk.

- Regularly reassess the threat landscape and organizational vulnerabilities.

Cost/Benefit & ROI Integration

Cost/Benefit Analysis (CBA) for Control Selection:

- **Identify Potential Losses (SLE):** Quantify the financial impact of a single security incident (e.g., data breach, system downtime, reputational damage, legal fees, lost productivity).
- **Estimate Annualized Rate of Occurrence (ARO):** Determine the estimated frequency of a specific incident occurring per year.
- **Calculate Annualized Loss Expectancy (ALE):** $ALE = ARO \times SLE$. This represents the expected financial loss from a specific risk over a year if no controls are in place.
- **Evaluate Control Costs:** Direct costs (hardware, software, personnel, training, implementation) and indirect costs (operational overhead, impact on user experience).
- **Estimate Mitigation Ratio:** Determine the percentage by which a control is expected to reduce the ALE.
- **Calculate Expected Residual Loss:** $Residual\ Loss = ALE \times (1 - Mitigation\ Ratio)$.
- **Calculate Net Benefit of Control:** $Net\ Benefit = (ALE - Residual\ Loss) - Cost\ of\ Control$. A positive net benefit indicates a worthwhile control.

Example Calculation for CBA:

Let's consider a potential data breach risk for a small e-commerce company.

- **Single Loss Expectancy (SLE):** \$50,000 (estimated cost per breach, including recovery, fines, and reputational damage).
- **Annualized Rate of Occurrence (ARO):** 0.2 (meaning a 20% chance of a breach occurring in a year, or one breach every five years).
- **Annualized Loss Expectancy (ALE) without control:** $ALE = \$50{,}000 \times 0.2 = \$10{,}000$.
- **Proposed Control:** Implementing a new intrusion detection system (IDS) and enhanced employee training.
- **Cost of Control:** \$3,000 (initial setup and annual maintenance).
- **Mitigation Ratio:** The IDS and training are expected to reduce the likelihood of a breach by 70% (0.7).
- **Reduced ALE (after control):** $ALE_{reduced} = ALE \times (1 - Mitigation\ Ratio) = \$10{,}000 \times (1 - 0.7) =$

$\$10,000 \times 0.3 = \$3,000.$

- **Avoided Loss (Benefit):** $ALE - ALE_{reduced} = \$10,000 - \$3,000 = \$7,000.$
- **Net Benefit of Control:** $Net\ Benefit = Avoided\ Loss - Cost\ of\ Control = \$7,000 - \$3,000 = \$4,000.$ Since the Net Benefit is positive ($4,000), this control is financially justifiable.

Return on Security Investment (ROSI):

Explanation: ROSI is a specific application of ROI to cybersecurity, focusing on the financial returns from security investments, primarily in terms of risk reduction and avoided losses. It helps demonstrate the value of security to non-technical stakeholders.

Formula: *ROSI = (ALE × Mitigation Ratio) - Cost of Solution / Cost of Solution*

Components:

- **Annualized Loss Expectancy (ALE):** The expected financial loss from a specific risk over a year if no controls are in place ($ALE = ARO \times SLE$).
- **Mitigation Ratio:** The percentage effectiveness of the security solution in reducing the likelihood or impact of the risk.
- **Cost of Solution:** The total cost of acquiring, implementing, and maintaining the security solution.

Interpretation: A higher ROSI percentage indicates a more financially effective security investment.

Example Calculation for ROSI:

Using the same data from the CBA example:

- **Annualized Loss Expectancy (ALE):** $10,000
- **Mitigation Ratio:** 0.7 (70%)
- **Cost of Solution:** $3,000
- **ROSI Calculation:** ROSI = ($10,000 × 0.7) - $3,000 / $3,000
- **ROSI** = $7,000 - $3,000 / $3,000
- **ROSI** = $4,000 / $3,000
- **ROSI** ≈ 1.33

To express as a percentage: $ROSI \approx 1.33 \times 100\% = 133\%.$ This means for every dollar invested in the IDS and training, the company expects to get $1.33 back in avoided losses, or a 133% return on their security investment.

Prioritization:

Use CBA and ROSI to prioritize controls, focusing on those that offer the highest risk reduction for the lowest cost, or the greatest return.

4. Compliance and Regulatory Alignment

Purpose:

Ensure adherence to relevant laws, regulations, and industry standards (e.g., GDPR, HIPAA, PCI-DSS, ISO 27001, SOX, GLBA).

Legal and Regulatory Requirements:

The framework ensures that the organization's security practices comply with all relevant laws, regulations, and industry standards (e.g., GDPR, HIPAA, PCI DSS, etc.).

Auditing and Reporting:

Regular audits and compliance reviews are necessary to verify that security measures are effective and align with both internal policies and external requirements.

Monitoring Focus:

- Regular compliance audits and assessments.
- Track changes in regulatory requirements and their impact on security posture.
- Monitor the status of audit findings and remediation efforts.

Cost/Benefit & ROI Integration:

- **Benefit:** Avoidance of significant fines, legal penalties, and reputational damage. Improved market access (e.g., ability to handle sensitive data for clients).
- **Cost:** Cost of compliance tools, audits, and personnel. Analyze the cost of compliance vs. the potential cost of non-compliance.

5. Incident Response and Business Continuity

Purpose:

Develop and maintain plans to effectively respond to security incidents, minimize their impact, and ensure business continuity.

Incident Response Planning:

A well-defined plan for identifying, containing, eradicating, and recovering from security incidents.

Business Continuity Planning (BCP):

Ensures that the organization can continue to operate critical business functions during and after a security incident or disaster.

Monitoring Focus:

- Track incident response metrics (e.g., detection time, containment time, and recovery time).
- Regularly test incident response and business continuity plans through simulations and drills.

Cost/Benefit & ROI Integration:

- **Benefit:** Reduced financial losses from incidents (e.g., less downtime, quicker recovery, minimized data exfiltration). Improved brand reputation post-incident.
- **Cost:** Cost of incident response planning, tools, training, and simulations.

Example Calculation for IR and BC (CBA & ROSI):

Let's consider a critical business application with a potential for extended downtime due to a cyberattack.

- **Single Loss Expectancy (SLE) for a major outage:** $100,000 (estimated loss per incident, including lost revenue, recovery costs, and potential customer churn).
- **Annualized Rate of Occurrence (ARO) without robust IR/BC:** 0.1 (meaning a 10% chance of such an outage occurring in a year, or one every ten years).
- **Annualized Loss Expectancy (ALE) without IR/BC:** *ALE=$100,000×0.1=$10,000.*
- **Proposed Investment:** Implementing a comprehensive Incident Response Plan (IRP), a Business Continuity Plan (BCP) with automated failover, and regular tabletop exercises.
- **Cost of Investment:** $8,000 (includes plan development, software licenses for failover, and annual exercise costs).
- **Mitigation Ratio:** The IRP and BCP are expected to reduce the impact and duration of an outage, effectively reducing the ALE by 80% (0.8).
- **Reduced ALE (after investment):** *ALEreduced=ALE×(1−Mitigation Ratio)=$10,000×(1−0.8)=$10,000×0.2=$2,000.*
- **Avoided Loss (Benefit):** *ALE−ALEreduced =$10,000−$2,000=$8,000.*
- **Net Benefit of Investment (CBA):** *Net Benefit=Avoided Loss−Cost of Investment=$8,000−$8,000=$0.* In this specific scenario, the net benefit is $0, indicating that the investment exactly covers the avoided losses. While not a

positive net gain, it signifies that the investment is breaking even in terms of risk reduction, which is often a desirable outcome for critical infrastructure.

ROSI Calculation for IR and BC:

- **Annualized Loss Expectancy (ALE):** $10,000
- **Mitigation Ratio:** 0.8 (80%)
- **Cost of Solution:** $8,000
- **ROSI Calculation:** ROSI = ($10,000 × 0.8) - $8,000 / $8,000
- ROSI = $8,000 - $8,000 / $8,000
- ROSI = $0 / $8,000
- ROSI = 0

To express as a percentage: *ROSI=0×100%=0%.* A ROSI of 0% indicates that the investment is expected to fully offset the potential losses it aims to mitigate, but not generate additional "profit" beyond that. This is common for foundational security controls like IR and BC, where the primary goal is risk avoidance rather than direct revenue generation.

6. Training and Awareness

Purpose:

Foster a security-aware culture among all employees, making them the first line of defense.

Monitoring Focus:

- Track completion rates of security training.
- Measure effectiveness through phishing simulations and security quizzes.

Cost/Benefit & ROI Integration:

- **Benefit:** Reduction in human-error related incidents (e.g., phishing clicks, malware infections). Improved overall security posture.
- **Cost:** Cost of training programs and awareness campaigns.

7. Performance Measurement and Reporting

Purpose:

Continuously measure the effectiveness of the security program and report key metrics to stakeholders.

Continuous Monitoring:

An ongoing process of collecting and analyzing data from security controls and systems to detect potential threats and vulnerabilities.

Security Metrics:

Quantitative and qualitative indicators that measure the effectiveness and efficiency of the security program. This provides management with the information needed to make informed decisions. Examples include the number of detected incidents, time to patch vulnerabilities, and employee awareness scores.

Reporting:

Regular reporting to stakeholders, including executive leadership and the board of directors, on the organization's security posture and the effectiveness of the security program.

Monitoring Focus:

- Define Key Performance Indicators (KPIs) and Key Risk Indicators (KRIs).
- Establish regular reporting cycles (e.g., monthly, quarterly) to executive leadership and the board.

Cost/Benefit & ROI Integration:

- **Reporting Financial Impact:** Present security performance not just in technical terms but also in financial terms (e.g., "Risk reduction of $X achieved," "ROI of Y% on security investment," "Avoided losses of $Z due to incident response capabilities").
- **Dashboards:** Create dashboards that visually represent security posture, risk levels, and the financial impact of security initiatives.

8. Continuous Improvement

Purpose:

Regularly review and adapt the governance framework and security controls based on monitoring results, new threats, and business changes.

Monitoring Focus:

- Implement feedback loops from all other components.
- Conduct post-incident reviews to identify lessons learned.
- Benchmark against industry best practices and peer organizations.

Cost/Benefit & ROI Integration:

- **Optimization:** Use the ongoing CBA and ROI analyses to reallocate resources, optimize existing controls, and justify new investments.

- **Adaptive Spending:** Adjust security spending based on the measured effectiveness and changing risk landscape.

Key Financial Analysis Methodologies for Information Security

To effectively establish cost/benefit and calculate ROI for information security investments, organizations can leverage several methodologies:

Cost-Benefit Analysis (CBA):

Explanation: CBA is a systematic process for calculating and comparing the benefits and costs of a project, decision, or policy. In information security, it helps determine if the financial benefits of implementing a control (primarily avoided losses) outweigh its costs. If the benefits outweigh the costs, the project is considered to be financially feasible and worth pursuing. Conversely, if the costs exceed the benefits, the project should likely be rejected or reevaluated. It's crucial for justifying security spending.

Process:

- **Identify Costs:** Include direct costs (purchase, implementation, maintenance, personnel, training) and indirect costs (operational disruption, reduced productivity during implementation).
- **Intangible Costs:** Non-monetary factors that are difficult to quantify but can have a significant impact, such as a decrease in employee morale or a negative impact on brand reputation.
- **Opportunity Costs:** The potential benefits or profits that are lost by choosing one option over another.
- **Costs of Potential Risks:** Quantifying the potential negative impacts or losses associated with the project's risks.
- **Identify Benefits:** Quantify avoided losses (e.g., reduced impact of breaches, compliance fines, reputational damage, downtime).
- **Direct Benefits:** Measurable advantages that result directly from the project, such as increased revenue, cost savings, or higher production.
- **Indirect Benefits:** Advantages that are not directly measurable or immediately linked to the project but are secondary effects, such as an enhanced company reputation.
- **Intangible Benefits:** Non-monetary gains, such as improved employee satisfaction, higher customer loyalty, or a better public image.

- **Compare:** Calculate the net benefit (Total Benefits - Total Costs) or a benefit-cost ratio (Total Benefits / Total Costs). A positive net benefit or a ratio greater than 1 indicates a financially sound investment.

Steps to Conduct a Cost-Benefit Analysis.

While there can be some variation in the process, a typical CBA follows these steps:

- **Establish the Framework:** Clearly define the project's scope, objectives, and the timeline for the analysis.
- **Identify All Costs and Benefits:** Create comprehensive lists of all potential costs and benefits, including both tangible and intangible factors.
- **Assign a Monetary Value:** Assign a monetary value to each cost and benefit. This is straightforward for direct costs and benefits but can be challenging for intangible items. For these, analysts may use estimation techniques, surveys, or industry benchmarks.
- **Calculate Net Present Value (NPV):** To account for the time value of money (the idea that money today is worth more than the same amount in the future), future costs and benefits are often discounted to their present value. The NPV is the difference between the present value of the benefits and the present value of the costs. A positive NPV indicates a potentially profitable project.
- **Calculate the Benefit-Cost Ratio (BCR):** The BCR is a simple ratio of the total present value of benefits divided by the total present value of costs. If the ratio is greater than 1, the benefits outweigh the costs.
- **Compare Alternatives and Make a Recommendation:** Evaluate the results of the analysis, compare the project with other alternatives, and make an informed decision based on the data. A sensitivity analysis can also be performed to see how the outcome changes under different scenarios (e.g., best-case vs. worst-case).

Example Calculation for CBA:

Let's consider a potential data breach risk for a small e-commerce company.

- **Single Loss Expectancy (SLE):** \$50,000 (estimated cost per breach, including recovery, fines, and reputational damage).
- **Annualized Rate of Occurrence (ARO):** 0.2 (meaning a 20% chance of a breach occurring in a year, or one breach every five years).
- **Annualized Loss Expectancy (ALE) without control:** $ALE = \$50{,}000 \times 0.2 = \$10{,}000$.

- **Proposed Control:** Implementing a new intrusion detection system (IDS) and enhanced employee training.
- **Cost of Control:** $3,000 (initial setup and annual maintenance).
- **Mitigation Ratio:** The IDS and training are expected to reduce the likelihood of a breach by 70% (0.7).
- **Reduced ALE (after control):** $ALE_{reduced}=ALE\times(1-Mitigation\ Ratio)=\$10{,}000\times(1-0.7)=\$10{,}000\times0.3=\$3{,}000$.
- **Avoided Loss (Benefit):** $ALE-ALE_{reduced}=\$10{,}000-\$3{,}000=\$7{,}000$.
- **Net Benefit of Control:** $Net\ Benefit=Avoided\ Loss-Cost\ of\ Control=\$7{,}000-\$3{,}000=\$4{,}000$. Since the Net Benefit is positive ($4,000), this control is financially justifiable.

Return on Security Investment (ROSI):

Explanation: ROSI is a specific application of ROI to cybersecurity, focusing on the financial returns from security investments, primarily in terms of risk reduction and avoided losses. It helps demonstrate the value of security to non-technical stakeholders.

Formula: *ROSI = (ALE × Mitigation Ratio) - Cost of Solution / Cost of Solution*

Components:

- **Annualized Loss Expectancy (ALE):** The expected financial loss from a specific risk over a year if no controls are in place ($ALE=ARO\times SLE$).
- **Mitigation Ratio:** The percentage effectiveness of the security solution in reducing the likelihood or impact of the risk.
- **Cost of Solution:** The total cost of acquiring, implementing, and maintaining the security solution.

Interpretation: A higher ROSI percentage indicates a more financially effective security investment.

Example Calculation for ROSI:

Using the same data from the CBA example:

- **Annualized Loss Expectancy (ALE):** $10,000
- **Mitigation Ratio:** 0.7 (70%)
- **Cost of Solution:** $3,000
- **ROSI Calculation:** ROSI = ($10,000 × 0.7) - $3,000 / $3,000

- ROSI = $7,000 - $3,000 / $3,000
- ROSI = $4,000 / $3,000
- ROSI ≈ 1.33

To express as a percentage: *ROSI≈1.33×100%=133%.* This means for every dollar invested in the IDS and training, the company expects to get $1.33 back in avoided losses, or a 133% return on their security investment.

Annualized Loss Expectancy (ALE):

Explanation: While a component of ROSI and CBA, ALE itself is a critical metric. It quantifies the expected financial loss from a specific type of security incident over a year. It serves as the baseline for understanding the financial risk before any mitigation.

Formula: $ALE = ARO \times SLE$

Components:

- **Single Loss Expectancy (SLE):** The financial loss expected from a single occurrence of a specific risk event.
- **Annualized Rate of Occurrence (ARO):** The estimated number of times a specific risk event is expected to occur in a year.

Total Cost of Ownership (TCO):

Explanation: TCO provides a comprehensive view of the direct and indirect costs of a security solution over its entire lifecycle, not just the initial purchase price. This includes acquisition, deployment, maintenance, support, training, and eventual decommissioning costs.

Importance: Helps avoid underestimating the true cost of a security control, leading to more accurate CBA and ROSI calculations and better long-term financial planning.

Net Present Value (NPV) and Internal Rate of Return (IRR):

Explanation: These are advanced financial metrics used for evaluating long-term investments, considering the time value of money.

- **NPV:** Think of it like this; a dollar today is worth more than a dollar a year from now. Why? Because you can invest that dollar today and earn interest. NPV takes this into account by using a **discount rate** to calculate the present value of future money.
    - **Future Cash Flows (Benefits):** This is all the money you expect to make from the investment over time. NPV calculates what that future money is

worth in today's dollars.

- **Costs:** This is the money you have to spend upfront to make the investment.
- **The Formula:** The basic idea is: **(Present Value of Benefits) - (Present Value of Costs).**
- If the NPV is **positive**, in simple terms, you'll make more money than what you have to put in, and the investment is likely profitable.

- **IRR:** Simply put, the **Internal Rate of Return (IRR)** is the **annual growth rate** an investment is expected to generate. It's the interest rate at which the money you make (save) from a project, when adjusted for the time value of money, is exactly equal to the money you spent on it. Think of IRR as the project's **break-even rate of return.**

Application: Useful for larger, multi-year security projects where the benefits and costs are spread out over time.

Key Differences from NPV:

IRR and NPV are closely related but serve different purposes:

- **IRR** gives you a **percentage rate of return** on a project. This makes it easy to compare to a hurdle rate or to other potential investments.
- **NPV** gives you a **dollar value** of a project. A positive NPV tells you how much value an investment is expected to add (save) to the company in today's dollars.

Qualitative Risk Assessment:

Explanation: While not directly financial, qualitative risk assessments (e.g., using high, medium, low ratings for likelihood and impact) are often a precursor to quantitative analysis. They help prioritize risks and identify areas where more detailed financial analysis (CBA, ROSI) is warranted.

Integration: The results of qualitative assessments can inform the inputs (SLE, ARO) for quantitative calculations, especially when precise historical data is unavailable.

By employing a combination of these methodologies, organizations can gain a comprehensive understanding of the financial implications of their information security decisions, ensuring that resources are allocated effectively and that security investments deliver demonstrable value.

Principles of Information Security

The CIA Triad (Confidentiality, Integrity, Availability) - deep dive:

Confidentiality:

Protecting information from unauthorized disclosure (e.g., encryption, access controls).

Definition:

Ensuring that information is accessible only to those authorized to have access.

Tools, Processes, and Procedures:

Encryption:

- **Tools:** Symmetric encryption algorithms (AES), asymmetric encryption algorithms (RSA), Transport Layer Security (TLS), Secure Sockets Layer (SSL), Pretty Good Privacy (PGP), disk encryption software (BitLocker, FileVault).
- **Processes:** Data at rest encryption (database encryption, full disk encryption), data in transit encryption (VPNs, HTTPS), key management procedures (generation, storage, rotation, revocation).
- **Procedures:** Encryption standards policy, secure key management procedures, data classification guidelines (to determine what data needs encryption).

Access Controls:

- **Tools:** Identity and Access Management (IAM) systems, Role-Based Access Control (RBAC) systems, Access Control Lists (ACLs), Multi-Factor Authentication (MFA) solutions, Privileged Access Management (PAM) tools.
- **Processes:** User provisioning/deprovisioning, regular access reviews, least privilege enforcement, separation of duties, strong authentication protocols.
- **Procedures:** Access control policies, user access review procedures, password policies, MFA enrollment and usage guidelines.

Data Loss Prevention (DLP):

- **Tools:** Network DLP, Endpoint DLP, Cloud DLP solutions.
- **Processes:** Content inspection, context analysis, data exfiltration monitoring, incident response for DLP alerts.
- **Procedures:** DLP policies defining sensitive data, incident response procedures

for data leaks, employee training on data handling.

Physical Security:

- **Tools:** Biometric readers, access cards, CCTV, security guards, alarm systems.
- **Processes:** Restricted access to sensitive areas, visitor management, surveillance monitoring.
- **Procedures:** Physical access control policies, visitor sign-in procedures, security escort requirements.

Security Awareness Training:

- **Tools:** E-learning platforms, phishing simulation tools.
- **Processes:** Regular training sessions, simulated phishing campaigns, awareness campaigns.
- **Procedures:** Mandatory security awareness training for all employees, reporting suspicious activities.

Example: Encrypting customer credit card numbers in a database to prevent them from being read by unauthorized individuals.

Integrity:

Ensuring information is accurate, complete, and protected from unauthorized modification (e.g., hashing, digital signatures, version control).

Definition:

Maintaining the accuracy, completeness, and consistency of data over its entire life cycle. Ensuring only authorized changes are made, by authorized persons and only in an authorized manner.

Tools, Processes, and Procedures:

Hashing and Digital Signatures:

- **Tools:** Hashing algorithms (SHA-256, MD5 - though MD5 is less secure for integrity checks), Public Key Infrastructure (PKI) for digital certificates.
- **Processes:** File integrity monitoring (FIM), software integrity checks, secure code signing.
- **Procedures:** Data integrity policies, secure software development lifecycle (SSDLC) practices for code signing, FIM configuration guidelines.

Version Control and Configuration Management:

- **Tools:** Version control systems (Git, SVN), configuration management databases (CMDB), automated configuration management tools (Ansible, Puppet, Chef).
- **Processes:** Change management procedures, baseline configuration enforcement, regular configuration audits.
- **Procedures:** Change control policies, configuration management plans, backup and recovery procedures for configurations.

Access Controls (for modification):

- **Tools:** IAM systems, RBAC, granular file system permissions.
- **Processes:** Segregation of duties, least privilege for write access, regular review of modification rights.
- **Procedures:** Data modification policies, access matrix reviews.

Input Validation and Error Handling:

- **Tools:** Web Application Firewalls (WAFs), secure coding libraries.
- **Processes:** Secure coding practices, peer code reviews, penetration testing.
- **Procedures:** Input validation guidelines, secure development standards, error logging and alerting.

Checksums and Data Validation:

- **Tools:** Data validation routines, database constraints.
- **Processes:** Data validation at input and output, regular data integrity checks.
- **Procedures:** Data quality standards, data validation testing protocols.

Example: Using a checksum (hashing) to verify a downloaded software file hasn't been tampered with during transit, ensuring its integrity.

Availability:

Ensuring authorized users have timely and uninterrupted access to information and systems (e.g., redundancy, backup, disaster recovery).

Definition:

Ensuring that systems and data are accessible to authorized users when needed.

Tools, Processes, and Procedures:

Redundancy and High Availability (HA):

- **Tools:** Load balancers, redundant power supplies (UPS, generators), redundant network links, clustering software, virtual machine (VM) replication.
- **Processes:** Design for redundancy, failover testing, single point of failure (SPOF) analysis.
- **Procedures:** High availability architecture standards, regular failover testing protocols, maintenance windows planning.

Backup and Recovery:

- **Tools:** Backup software (Veeam, Commvault), offsite storage solutions, cloud backup services.
- **Processes:** Regular data backups (full, incremental, differential), offsite storage, documented recovery procedures, regular restore testing.
- **Procedures:** Backup policies (frequency, retention), data recovery plans (DRP), regular backup integrity checks and restore drills.

Disaster Recovery (DR) and Business Continuity Planning (BCP):

- **Tools:** DR orchestration platforms, dedicated DR sites (hot, warm, cold).
- **Processes:** Business Impact Analysis (BIA), RTO/RPO definition, DR plan development and testing, BCP activation procedures.
- **Procedures:** Disaster recovery plans (DRP), business continuity plans (BCP), annual DR/BCP exercises (tabletop, full-scale).

Performance Monitoring and Capacity Planning:

- **Tools:** Network monitoring tools, system performance monitoring (APM, infrastructure monitoring), log management (SIEM).
- **Processes:** Baseline performance monitoring, capacity planning, proactive scaling.
- **Procedures:** Performance monitoring policies, alert thresholds, capacity management plans.

DDoS Mitigation:

- **Tools:** DDoS protection services (Cloudflare, Akamai), network firewalls, IPS.
- **Processes:** Traffic scrubbing, rate limiting, blacklisting.

- **Procedures:** DDoS response plan, external DDoS protection service configuration.

Example: Implementing redundant servers and load balancing to prevent service disruption if one server fails, ensuring continuous availability.

CIA Triad Interdependencies and Trade-offs

The CIA Triad principles are interconnected, and strengthening one can sometimes come at the expense of another. Achieving a perfect balance is often impossible, requiring organizations to make strategic trade-offs based on their risk appetite and business objectives.

Confidentiality vs. Availability:

Explanation: Implementing very strong confidentiality measures (e.g., multi-layered encryption, complex access controls) can introduce overhead that impacts system performance or accessibility, thereby reducing availability.

Example: Using extremely strong, computationally intensive encryption for all data, including frequently accessed operational data, might slow down database queries and application response times, making the system less available to users. Similarly, overly restrictive access controls that require multiple approvals for every data access can hinder legitimate users from performing their duties efficiently.

Confidentiality vs. Usability (a subset of Availability):

Explanation: High levels of confidentiality often lead to more complex security procedures, which can make systems harder for legitimate users to access or use, impacting usability and potentially leading to workarounds that reduce security.

Example: Requiring users to remember extremely long, complex passwords, change them frequently, and use multiple MFA factors for every single login can lead to user frustration, password reuse, or writing down passwords, which ultimately undermines security.

Integrity vs. Availability:

Explanation: Strict integrity controls, such as rigorous data validation or frequent integrity checks, can consume system resources or introduce processing delays, potentially affecting the availability of data or services.

Example: A system that performs real-time, in-depth integrity checks on every single data transaction might introduce latency, slowing down the overall system and impacting its availability for high-volume operations.

Availability vs. Security (Confidentiality/Integrity):

Explanation: Prioritizing availability above all else might lead to less stringent security controls, making systems more vulnerable to attacks that compromise confidentiality or integrity.

Example: To ensure maximum uptime, an organization might delay critical security patches or avoid implementing strong network segmentation, leaving systems exposed to known vulnerabilities that could lead to data breaches (confidentiality) or data corruption (integrity).

The Balancing Act: The CISO's role involves understanding these trade-offs and making informed decisions that align with the organization's specific risk appetite, regulatory requirements, and business priorities. It's about finding the optimal balance, not necessarily maximizing each principle independently.

Example: High encryption (confidentiality) might slightly impact system performance (availability) due to processing overhead.

Security Vulnerabilities, Threats, Risks, and Exposures - definitions and relationships

Vulnerability:

A weakness in a system design, or implementation or operation that can be exploited by a threat.

Example: An unpatched software bug (vulnerability) in a web server.

Threat:

A potential danger that might exploit a vulnerability.

Example: A hacker attempting to exploit the unpatched web server (threat).

Risk:

The likelihood of a threat exploiting a vulnerability, resulting in an impact.

Definition:

The potential for loss, damage, or destruction of an asset as a result of a threat exploiting a vulnerability.

Example: High risk of data breach due to an unpatched server vulnerable to ransomware, leading to financial loss and reputational damage.

Exposure:

The extent of potential loss from a risk.

Formula: Risk = Threat x Vulnerability x Asset Value (or Impact).

Cyberattack Elements and Defense-In-Depth strategies:

Attack Elements:

Motive (why), opportunity (when/how), means (tools/skills), target (what).

Defense-In-Depth:

A layered security approach that employs multiple security controls at different points in a system to protect against various threats. This multi-layered strategy ensures that if one control fails, others are in place to provide protection.

Example: A gate (physical control), a firewall (technical control), and security awareness training (administrative control) all working together to protect a data center.

Understanding the Elements of an Information Security Program

A robust information security program is built upon a layered foundation of standards, procedures, directives, policies, regulations, and legal considerations. Understanding these elements is crucial for effective program development, management, and compliance.

1. Standards

Definition:

Standards are established benchmarks or best practices that an organization adopts to guide its security efforts. They are frameworks, not laws, but are often used to demonstrate a commitment to security. Adhering to standards helps an organization build a strong, structured program.

Examples:

- **ISO/IEC 27001:** An international standard for information security management systems (ISMS). It provides a systematic approach to managing sensitive company information.

- **NIST Cybersecurity Framework (CSF):** A voluntary framework developed by the U.S. National Institute of Standards and Technology to help organizations manage and reduce cybersecurity risk.
- **CIS Controls:** A prioritized set of best practices and defensive actions that mitigate the most common attacks against systems and networks.

2. Procedures

Definition:

Procedures are the detailed, step-by-step instructions that describe how a specific task or process should be performed to comply with a policy or standard. They are highly specific and operational in nature.

Examples:

- **Incident Response Procedure:** A document detailing the exact steps to follow when a security incident is detected, from initial assessment to containment and recovery.
- **User Provisioning Procedure:** A checklist of actions to be taken when a new employee is hired, including creating accounts, assigning permissions, and providing security training.

3. Directives

Definition:

Directives are specific, high-level commands issued by management or leadership to initiate or enforce a particular action. They are typically short-term and have a clear, specific goal.

Example:

A directive from the Chief Information Security Officer (CISO) requiring all departments to implement multi-factor authentication (MFA) on all critical business applications within the next 90 days.

4. Policies

Definition:

Policies are high-level statements that define the rules and expectations for the organization's employees, partners, and systems. They outline what must be done, but not necessarily how. Policies are the cornerstone of the security program.

Examples:

- **Acceptable Use Policy:** Outlines how employees can and cannot use company assets, such as computers and network resources.
- **Data Classification Policy:** Defines how different types of data (e.g., public, confidential, secret) must be handled, stored, and protected.
- **Access Control Policy:** Dictates who can access what information and under what circumstances.

5. Regulations & Legal Issues

Definition:

Regulations are mandatory laws and rules imposed by government bodies that an organization must comply with. Non-compliance can lead to severe penalties, including fines, legal action, and reputational damage.

Key Regulations and Laws:

- **General Data Protection Regulation (GDPR):** An EU law on data protection and privacy for all individuals within the European Union and the European Economic Area. It has a significant impact on organizations worldwide that handle EU citizen data.
- **Health Insurance Portability and Accountability Act (HIPAA):** A U.S. law that protects the privacy and security of protected health information (PHI).
- **Sarbanes-Oxley Act (SOX):** A U.S. federal law that mandates certain practices in financial record keeping and reporting for public companies. It requires specific controls to ensure the integrity of financial data.
- **California Consumer Privacy Act (CCPA) / California Privacy Rights Act (CPRA):** These California laws provide consumers with specific rights regarding their personal information.
- **The Gramm-Leach-Bliley Act (GLBA):** also known as the Financial Services Modernization Act of 1999 is a U.S. federal law that was passed to update and modernize the financial services industry. It's most significant and enduring impact for consumers come from its provisions on data privacy and security.

The Relationship between Elements

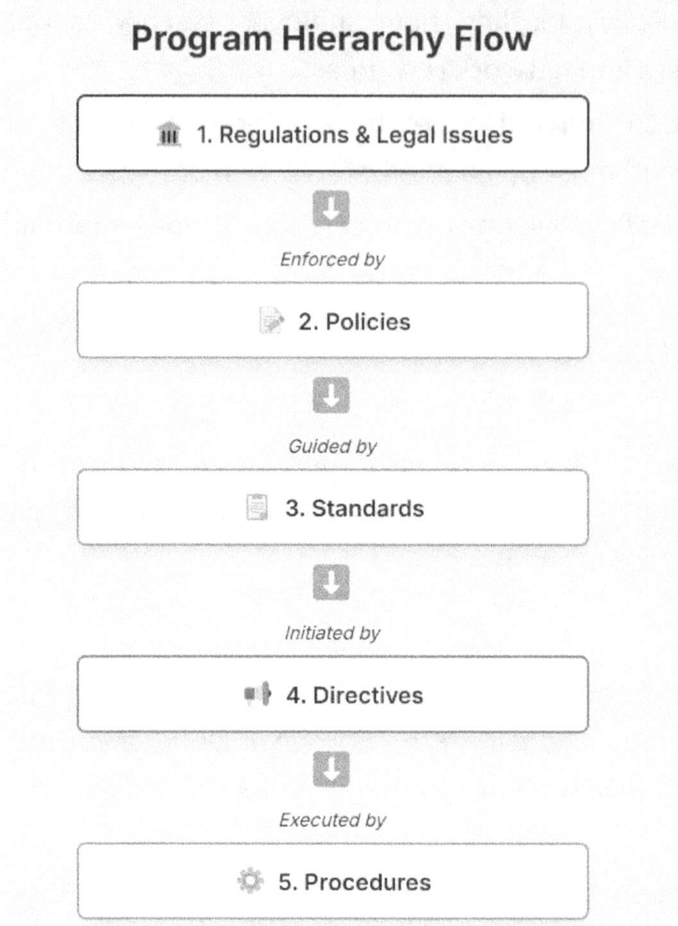

These elements form a hierarchy of authority and detail:

A successful information security program must be aligned with all these factors, ensuring that the organization's internal rules and practices (policies and procedures) meet or exceed the requirements of external mandates (regulations and legal issues) and industry best practices (standards).

What is an Information Security Compliance Program?

An enterprise information security (InfoSec) compliance program is a structured set of policies, procedures, and controls that an organization implements to ensure it adheres to all relevant laws, regulations, and industry standards. The primary goal is to protect sensitive data by maintaining its confidentiality, integrity, and availability (the "CIA triad") and to mitigate legal, financial, and reputational risks associated with non-compliance.

Key benefits of a robust InfoSec compliance program include:

- **Risk Mitigation:** Proactively identifies and addresses vulnerabilities to prevent data breaches and security incidents.
- **Legal Protection:** Avoids significant fines, penalties, and legal action that can result from non-compliance with regulations like GDPR, HIPAA, or NERC CIP.
- **Enhanced Reputation:** Builds trust with customers, partners, and stakeholders by demonstrating a commitment to data protection.
- **Improved Efficiency:** Streamlines security processes and provides a clear framework for operational best practices.

Key Components of a Compliance Program

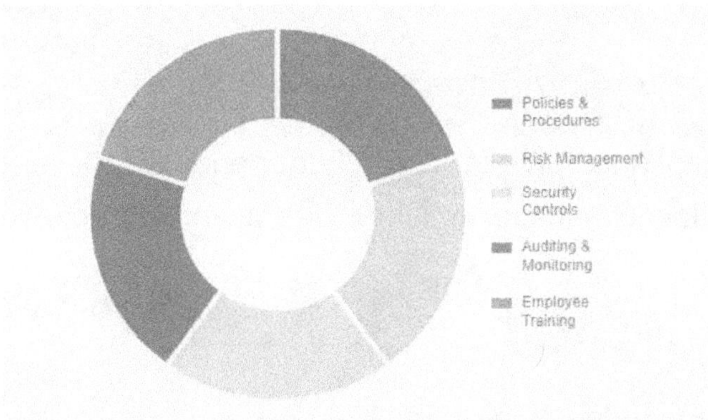

A comprehensive InfoSec compliance program typically includes the following elements:

Risk Assessment:

Regularly identifying, assessing, and prioritizing security risks and vulnerabilities. This involves an inventory of all systems and data, and an evaluation of existing security controls.

Policy and Procedure Development:

Creating and maintaining clear, documented policies that govern data handling, access control, incident response, and other security-related activities. These policies must align with relevant regulations and be easy for employees to understand.

Security Controls:

Implementing technical and administrative measures to protect assets. This includes things like multi-factor authentication (MFA), encryption, network segmentation, and physical access controls.

Training and Awareness:

Conducting regular training sessions and awareness campaigns to ensure employees understand their role in maintaining compliance. This is crucial for building a company-wide "culture of compliance."

Monitoring and Auditing:

Establishing a continuous monitoring process to detect potential violations and conducting periodic internal and external audits to verify compliance and identify gaps.

Incident Response:

Having a well-defined plan for responding to and recovering from security incidents, including clear procedures for notifying authorities and affected parties.

Managing an Effective Compliance Team

The success of a compliance program largely depends on the effectiveness of the team managing it. A compliance manager or Chief Compliance Officer (CCO) plays a strategic role in leading this effort.

Responsibilities of the Manager/CCO:

- **Regulatory Knowledge:** Maintaining a deep and up-to-date understanding of all applicable laws, regulations, and industry standards.
- **Strategic Alignment:** Ensuring the compliance program is not just a "check-the-box" activity but is integrated with the organization's overall business strategy.
- **Communication and Collaboration:** Acting as a bridge between the compliance team, executive leadership, and other departments (e.g., IT, legal, HR).
- **Resource Allocation:** Securing the necessary budget, tools, and personnel to effectively implement and manage the program.
- **Performance Measurement:** Defining and tracking key metrics to measure the program's effectiveness and report on its status to leadership.

Manager Responsibilities

A compliance manager's role is multi-faceted, requiring a balance of technical knowledge, strategic thinking, and interpersonal skills.

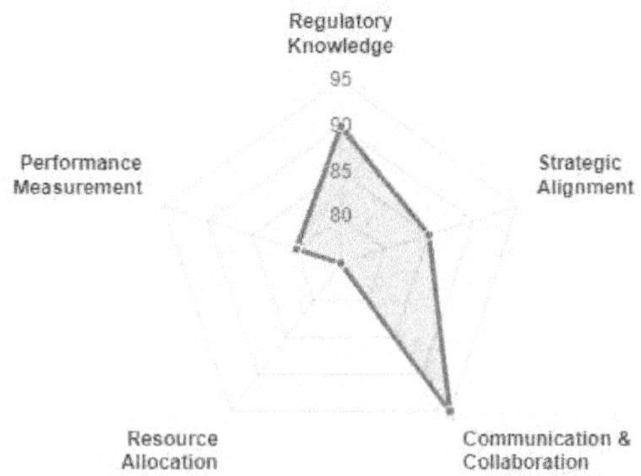

Best Practices for Managing the Team:

- **Promote a Proactive Approach:** Move beyond reactive compliance and focus on anticipating risks and continuously improving the security posture.
- **Leverage Technology:** Utilize compliance management software to centralize tracking, automate reminders, and streamline reporting, moving away from manual processes like spreadsheets.
- **Build Strong Relationships:** Foster trust and collaboration with other teams. Compliance is a shared responsibility, not a siloed function.
- **Prioritize with a Risk-Based Approach:** Focus the team's resources on the highest-priority risks to ensure the most critical assets and data are protected first.
- **Reinforce Accountability:** Establish clear disciplinary guidelines for non-compliance and incentivize ethical behavior to build a strong compliance culture.

The Payoff: Key Benefits of Compliance

Risk Mitigation

Proactively identify and address vulnerabilities to prevent costly data breaches and security incidents.

Legal Protection

Avoid significant fines and legal action from non-compliance with regulations like GDPR, HIPAA, or NERC.

Enhanced Reputation

Build trust with customers, partners, and stakeholders by demonstrating a commitment to data protection.

Improved Efficiency

Streamline security processes and create a clear framework for operational best practices across the organization.

Risk Management

Information Security Risk Management

Information Security Risk Management (ISRM) is the ongoing process of identifying, assessing, and treating risks associated with the use of information technology. The primary goal is to protect an organization's information assets—such as data, hardware, software, and intellectual property—from threats that could compromise their confidentiality, integrity, and availability (CIA).

It's a foundational component of a mature cybersecurity program, helping organizations to make informed decisions about where to invest resources to achieve an acceptable level of risk. Since it's impossible and often impractical to eliminate all risks, the process focuses on managing them to a tolerable level, also known as the organization's "risk appetite."

Key Components of a Risk

A risk is a function of a threat, one or more vulnerabilities, and the impact to an asset. Understanding these components is crucial for effective risk management:

The Four Pillars of Risk

Asset

Any item of value to the organization. This could be a physical server, a software application, a database, or even the reputation of the company.

Threat

A potential cause of an unwanted incident that could harm assets. Threats can be intentional (hackers) or unintentional (employee mistakes).

Vulnerability

A weakness or flaw in an asset, system, or process that a threat can exploit to cause harm, such as a missing software patch or a weak password.

Impact

The business consequences of a threat exploiting a vulnerability. This can be financial loss, reputational damage, or operational disruption.

Asset:

Any item of value to the organization. This could be a physical server, a software application, a database, or even the reputation of the company.

Threat:

A potential cause of an unwanted incident that could harm an organization's assets. Threats can be intentional (e.g., a hacker) or unintentional (e.g., a natural disaster, an employee's mistake).

Vulnerability:

A weakness or flaw in an asset, system, or process that a threat can exploit to cause harm. Examples include a missing software patch, a misconfigured firewall, or a lack of employee security training.

Impact:

The business consequences that result from a threat exploiting a vulnerability. This can be financial loss, reputational damage, legal penalties, or disruption of operations.

The relationship is often simplified as: Risk = Threat x Vulnerability x Impact.

The Information Security Risk Management Process

A robust risk assessment methodology and framework are essential for effective risk management. The framework provides the organizational structure and policies for managing risk, while the methodology defines the step-by-step process for performing a risk assessment. Together, they create a repeatable and systematic approach to identify, analyze, and respond to potential threats and opportunities.

The goal is not to eliminate all risk, but to understand it, prioritize it, and make informed decisions on how to treat it in alignment with organizational objectives.

Core Components of the Risk Management Framework

The framework is the overarching structure that supports the risk assessment methodology. It should include:

- **Policy and Governance:** Clear policies that define the organization's risk appetite, objectives, and commitment to risk management.
- **Roles and Responsibilities:** Clearly defined roles for individuals and teams involved in risk management (e.g., risk owners, management, and a risk committee).
- **Communication Plan:** A strategy for communicating risk information to all relevant stakeholders.
- **Tools and Systems:** The use of software, templates, and other tools to document and track risks.
- **Review and Reporting:** A schedule for regular risk reviews and the format for reporting risk status to leadership.

The Risk Assessment Methodology (5-Step Process)

The risk management process is a cyclical, continuous effort that typically involves the following steps:

1. Risk Identification

This is the first step, where you systematically identify potential risks. It involves:

- **Asset Identification:** Creating an inventory of all information assets, classifying them by value, criticality, and sensitivity.
- **Threat Assessment:** Identifying potential threats, both internal and external, that could impact your assets.
- **Vulnerability Assessment:** Pinpointing weaknesses in your systems processes, and controls that threats could exploit.

Techniques:

- **Brainstorming Sessions:** Gather key stakeholders to discuss what could go wrong.
- **Checklists and Historical Data:** Use historical project data, industry-specific risk lists, and past incident reports.
- **SWOT Analysis:** Use a Strengths, Weaknesses, Opportunities, Threats analysis to uncover internal and external risks.
- **Interviews:** Talk to team members, subject matter experts, and stakeholders to

gather their insights.

- **Reviewing Project Plans and Documents:** Examine project charters, requirements, and technical specifications for potential vulnerabilities.

2. Risk Analysis

Once risks are identified, they are analyzed to understand their severity. This step involves:

- **Likelihood Analysis:** Determining the probability or frequency with which a threat will exploit a vulnerability.
- **Impact Analysis:** Assessing the potential damage or consequence if the risk were to materialize.
- **Qualitative Analysis:** This involves subjectively assessing the likelihood and impact of each risk using a defined scale. A common approach is to use a 3x3 or 5x5 matrix.
- **Quantitative Analysis (Optional):** For high-priority risks, a more detailed analysis may be performed using numerical data to estimate cost, schedule, or performance impacts.

Risks are often prioritized using a risk matrix that maps likelihood against impact, resulting in a risk score (e.g., High, Medium, Low). This helps an organization focus its resources on the most critical risks first.

3. Risk Evaluation and Prioritization

The results of the risk analysis are used to prioritize risks based on their severity. This is often done using a Risk Matrix. The risk score is calculated by multiplying the likelihood and impact ratings.

Risk Score=Likelihood×Impact

EXAMPLE RISK MATRIX

PRIORITY	RISK SCORES	ACTION REQUIRED
HIGH PRIORITY (RED)	15-25	Requires immediate attention and a dedicated response plan.
MEDIUM PRIORITY (YELLOW)	8-12	Requires monitoring and a proactive response plan.
LOW PRIORITY (GREEN)	1-7	Can be monitored and managed with standard procedures.

4. Risk Treatment (Mitigation)

After evaluation, a strategy is chosen to address each risk. There are four primary risk treatment options:

- **Risk Mitigation/Reduction:** Implementing security controls to reduce the likelihood or impact of a risk. This is the most common approach and includes measures like firewalls, encryption, access controls, and security policies.
- **Risk Acceptance:** Formally accepting a risk without taking any action to reduce it. This is typically done when the cost of mitigation is greater than the potential impact of the risk, and the risk is within the organization's tolerance.
- **Risk Avoidance:** Discontinuing or avoiding the activity that generates the risk. For example, if a new software application is deemed too risky, the organization may decide not to deploy it.
- **Risk Transfer/Sharing:** Shifting the financial burden or responsibility of a risk to a third party. The most common example is purchasing cybersecurity insurance.

5. Risk Monitoring and Review

Risk management is not a one-time event. The threat landscape, vulnerabilities, and business objectives are constantly changing. This step involves:

- **Continuous Monitoring:** Regularly monitoring the effectiveness of implemented controls and the status of identified risks.
- **Trigger Events:** Define specific events or conditions that will trigger a re-assessment of a particular risk.
- **Reporting:** Regularly report the status of the top risks to stakeholders and management.
- **New Risks:** Be vigilant for new risks that may emerge as the project or business environment changes.
- **Periodic Review:** Conducting regular reviews and re-assessments of the entire risk management process to ensure it remains relevant and effective.

Common Information Security Risk Management Frameworks

Information security risk management frameworks provide a structured approach for organizations to identify, assess, manage, and mitigate cybersecurity risks. They are essential for building a robust security posture, ensuring compliance, and protecting critical assets. Instead of a one-size-fits-all approach, frameworks offer a structured methodology that allows organizations to make informed, risk-based decisions on how to allocate resources and protect their most critical assets.

Framework Comparison

Each framework offers a unique balance of features. This radar chart compares them across key attributes to help identify the best fit for different organizational needs.

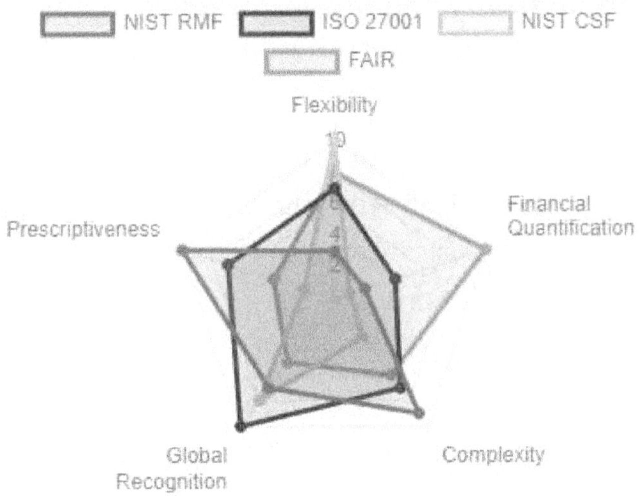

NIST Risk Management Framework (RMF)

Who it's for: Primarily used by U.S. federal agencies, but its detailed and comprehensive nature makes it a popular choice for private sector organizations as well.

Key Concept: The NIST RMF is a seven-step process that provides a systematic and repeatable approach to integrating security, privacy, and cyber supply chain risk management into the system development life cycle.

The Seven Steps:

1. **Prepare:** This foundational step involves essential activities to prepare the organization

to manage security and privacy risks. It includes defining key risk management roles, establishing a risk management strategy and organizational risk tolerance, conducting organization-wide risk assessments, identifying common controls, and developing a continuous monitoring strategy. This step aims to make subsequent RMF steps more effective and cost-efficient.

2. **Categorize:** In this step, the information system and the data it processes, stores, and transmits are categorized based on an impact analysis. This involves documenting system characteristics and assigning security categorization (low, moderate, or high) for confidentiality, integrity, and availability, based on the potential adverse impact if these objectives are compromised.
3. **Select:** Based on the system's categorization, a baseline set of security and privacy controls is selected from NIST Special Publication 800-53. Organizations then tailor these controls as needed, considering organizational risk assessments and specific local conditions. This step also includes designating controls as system-specific, common, or hybrid.
4. **Implement:** The selected security and privacy controls are implemented within the information system. This involves deploying the controls and thoroughly documenting how they are deployed and the processes and procedures for their maintenance.
5. **Assess:** Controls are assessed to determine if they are in place, operating as intended, and producing the desired results. This step involves developing and approving an assessment plan, conducting the assessments, and producing security and privacy assessment reports. Remediation actions are then taken to address any identified deficiencies.
6. **Authorize:** A senior official makes a risk-based decision to authorize the system to operate. This decision is based on the results of the control assessments and the overall risk posture of the system. An authorization package, including security and privacy plans and assessment reports, is reviewed.
7. **Monitor:** The system and its controls are continuously monitored to ensure ongoing effectiveness and to address new risks. This includes ongoing assessments of control effectiveness, analysis and response to continuous monitoring activities, and regular reporting on the system's security and privacy posture. This continuous feedback loop helps maintain an acceptable level of risk over the system's lifecycle.

Key Publications Supporting the NIST RMF:

The RMF is supported by a suite of NIST Special Publications (SPs) and Federal Information Processing Standards (FIPS) publications. Some of the most critical ones include:

- **NIST SP 800-37, Risk Management Framework for Information Systems and Organizations:** A System Life Cycle Approach for Security and Privacy: This is the primary document outlining the RMF process.
- **NIST SP 800-53, Security and Privacy Controls for Information Systems and Organizations:** This publication provides a comprehensive catalog of security and privacy controls from which organizations select.
- **NIST SP 800-53A, Assessing Security and Privacy Controls in Information Systems and Organizations:** Provides guidance for assessing the effectiveness of security and privacy controls.
- **FIPS 199, Standards for Security Categorization of Federal Information and Information Systems:** Used in the Categorize step to determine the impact levels of information and systems.
- **NIST SP 800-39, Managing Information Security Risk:** Organization, Mission, and Information System View: Provides guidance for an integrated, organization-wide program for managing information security risk.

The NIST RMF is a crucial framework for federal agencies in the United States, mandated by laws like the Federal Information Security Modernization Act (FISMA). It is also widely adopted by private sector organizations seeking to establish robust cybersecurity and privacy programs.

ISO/IEC 27001: Information Security Management System

Who it's for: A globally recognized standard for managing information security, suitable for organizations of all sizes and industries that want to demonstrate their security posture to customers, partners, and regulators.

Key Concept: ISO/IEC 27001, often simply referred to as ISO 27001, is the leading international standard that specifies the requirements for establishing, implementing, maintaining, and continually improving an Information Security Management System (ISMS). Developed jointly by the International Organization for Standardization (ISO) and the International Electrotechnical Commission (IEC), it is part of the broader ISO/IEC 27000 family of standards related to information security. The latest version is ISO/IEC 27001:2022. ISO 27001 is a specification for an Information Security Management System (ISMS). Instead of prescribing specific controls, it outlines a framework for establishing, implementing, maintaining, and continually improving a risk-based management system. The core of ISO 27001 is a risk assessment process.

Core Principles:

- **Risk Assessment:** A systematic process to identify, analyze, and evaluate information security risks.
- **Risk Treatment:** A plan to address the identified risks by applying appropriate controls (often chosen from the ISO 27002 companion standard).
- **Statement of Applicability (SoA):** A document that details which controls from ISO 27002 have been selected and why, and which have been excluded and why.
- **Continuous Improvement:** The ISMS is designed to be a continuous cycle of planning, doing, checking, and acting (PDCA cycle) to ensure it adapts to evolving threats.

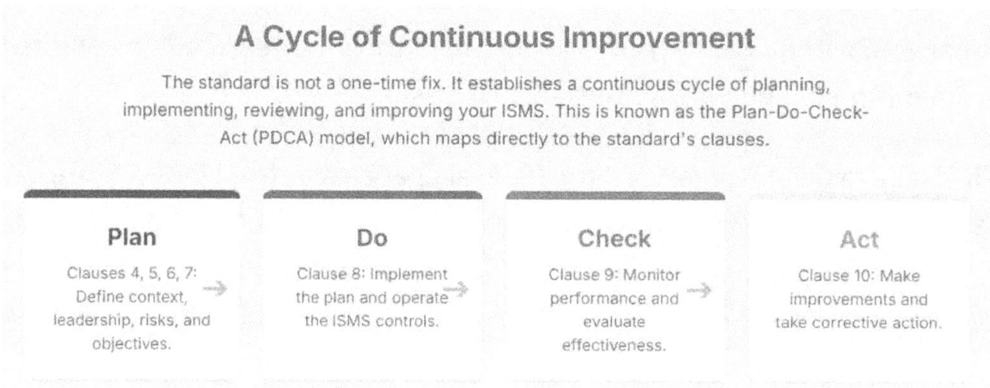

Purpose and Principles

The primary purpose of ISO 27001 is to help organizations protect their information assets systematically and cost-effectively. It focuses on preserving the "CIA triad" of information security:

- **Confidentiality:** Ensuring that information is accessible only to those authorized to have access.
- **Integrity:** Safeguarding the accuracy and completeness of information and processing methods.
- **Availability:** Ensuring that authorized users have access to information and associated assets when required.

The standard promotes a holistic approach to information security, considering people, processes, and technology. It emphasizes a risk-based methodology, requiring organizations to:

- Systematically examine their information security risks, including threats, vulnerabilities, and potential impacts.
- Design and implement a comprehensive suite of information security controls and other forms of risk treatment to address risks deemed unacceptable.
- Adopt an overarching management process to ensure that information security controls continue to meet the organization's needs and security objectives on an ongoing basis.

Mandatory Clauses of an ISMS under ISO 27001

An ISMS, as defined by ISO 27001, is a framework of policies and procedures for systematically managing an organization's sensitive data. ISO 27001 is structured into 11 clauses, with Clauses 4 to 10 being mandatory for certification. It involves several key components:

1. **Introduction (Clause 0):** The introductory clause gives a general overview of the standard and its purpose, and explains its compatibility with other ISO standards. It also introduces key concepts like risk-based thinking and the process approach, which are fundamental to implementing an Information Security Management System (ISMS).
2. **Scope (Clause 1):** This clause defines the covered information assets and procedures to clearly define the Information Security Management System's (ISMS) scope. It is essential to make sure that the organization's goals and limitations are thoroughly documented, since this creates a clear framework for efficient information security management.
3. **Normative References (Clause 2):** These ISO 27001 clauses refer to additional standards that provide information security guidelines. It makes a point of highlighting the standards' identification and explaining how applicable and relevant they are to the organization. This guarantees a thorough integration of relevant rules to improve the Information Security Management System's efficacy.
4. **Terms and Definitions (Clause 3):** Important words and definitions related to information security management are provided in this section. Its goal is to ensure that all parties involved in information security management have a common language, allowing for consistent and clear communication.
5. **Context of the Organization (Clause 4):** Understanding internal and external issues, interested parties, and the scope of the ISMS.
6. **Leadership (Clause 5):** Top management commitment, establishing an information security policy, and defining roles and responsibilities.

7. **Planning (Clause 6):** Actions to address risks and opportunities, information security objectives, and planning to achieve them. This includes conducting a thorough risk assessment and defining a risk treatment plan.
8. **Support (Clause 7):** Resources, competence, awareness, communication, and documented information.
9. **Operation (Clause 8):** Operational planning and control, information security risk assessment, and information security risk treatment.
10. **Performance Evaluation (Clause 9):** Monitoring, measurement, analysis, evaluation, internal audit, and management review.
11. **Improvement (Clause 10):** Continual improvement and addressing nonconformities and corrective actions.

Achieving ISO 27001 Certification requires meeting all the requirements outlined in Clauses 4 to 10 and implementing appropriate controls from Annex A.

Annex A Controls

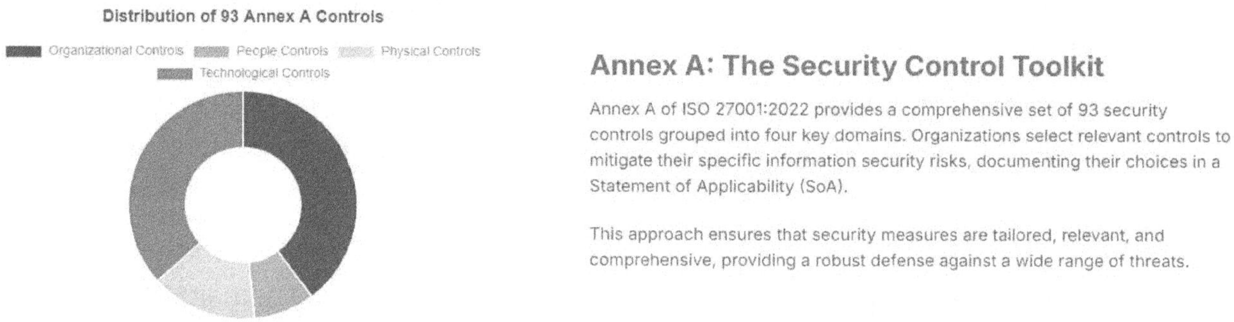

While the main clauses (0-10) outline the requirements for the ISMS, Annex A of ISO 27001:2022 provides a reference set of 93 information security controls, categorized into four domains:

- **Organizational Controls:** Policies, roles, responsibilities, and management of information security.
- **People Controls:** Human resource security, including screening, awareness, and disciplinary processes.
- **Physical Controls:** Protection of physical assets, such as premises and equipment.
- **Technological Controls:** Technical measures like access control, cryptography, network security, and secure development.

Organizations are required to develop a "Statement of Applicability" (SoA), detailing which

Annex A controls are implemented and justifying the exclusion of any controls that are not applicable to their specific risks.

Certification Process

Achieving ISO 27001 certification involves a three-stage external audit process conducted by an independent certification body:

1. **Stage 1 (Preliminary Review):** A desktop review of the ISMS documentation to confirm its existence and completeness.
2. **Stage 2 (Formal Compliance Audit):** A detailed audit to test the implementation and effectiveness of the ISMS against the ISO 27001 requirements. Successful completion leads to certification.
3. **Stage 3 (Ongoing Review):** Regular surveillance audits and internal reviews to ensure continued compliance and continual improvement of the ISMS.

Benefits of ISO 27001 Certification

Implementing and certifying to ISO 27001 offers numerous benefits, including:

- **Enhanced Information Security:** A structured approach to protecting sensitive data from breaches and cyber threats.
- **Increased Trust and Reputation:** Demonstrates a commitment to information security best practices to customers, partners, and stakeholders.
- **Regulatory Compliance:** Helps meet the requirements of various data protection laws and regulations (e.g., GDPR).
- **Risk Mitigation:** Reduces the likelihood and impact of security incidents, leading to cost savings.
- **Competitive Advantage:** Provides a valuable credential, especially when tendering for new business or operating in regulated industries.
- **Improved Organizational Culture:** Fosters a security-aware culture throughout the organization.

FAIR (Factor Analysis of Information Risk)

Who it's for: Organizations that want to move beyond qualitative risk assessments ("high," "medium," "low") and quantify their cybersecurity risks in financial terms.

Key Concept: FAIR is a quantitative model that provides a structured, logical way to analyze and measure information risk. It helps organizations understand the probable frequency and magnitude of future loss events.

How it Works: FAIR breaks down risk into its fundamental components and uses data to estimate the financial impact of a breach. The primary components are:

- **Loss Event Frequency:** How often a threat is likely to occur.
- **Loss Magnitude:** The potential impact of the event in financial terms (e.g., brand damage, regulatory fines, operational downtime).

Benefit: By speaking the language of business (dollars and cents), FAIR enables better communication between security teams and business leaders, helping to justify security investments and prioritize risks based on business impact.

Understanding FAIR (Factor Analysis of Information Risk)

The Factor Analysis of Information Risk (FAIR) is a quantitative risk analysis framework designed to help organizations understand, analyze, and measure information risk in financial terms. Unlike traditional qualitative risk assessments that categorize risk as "high," "medium," or "low," FAIR provides a structured approach to quantify cyber and operational risks, expressing potential losses in monetary values. This allows for more objective and data-driven decision-making regarding risk management and mitigation strategies.

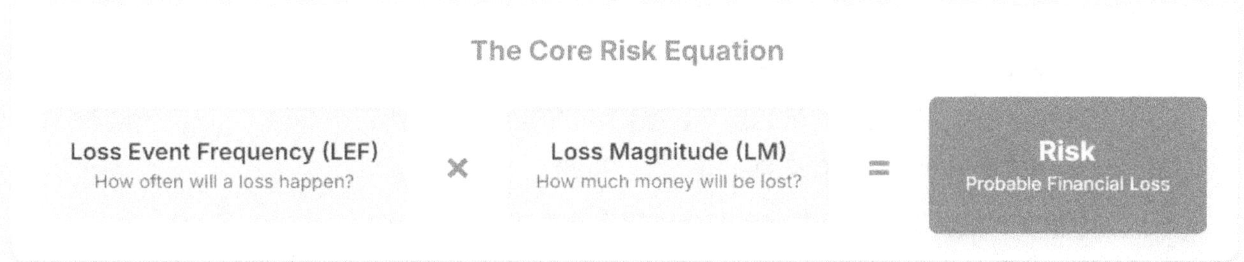

Core Concepts of FAIR

FAIR breaks down risk into two primary components: Loss Event Frequency (LEF) and Loss Magnitude (LM). The core idea is that risk is the probable frequency and probable magnitude of future loss.

1. **Loss Event Frequency (LEF)**

LEF measures how often a loss event is likely to occur over a specific timeframe. It's further decomposed into several sub-factors:

- **Threat Event Frequency (TEF):** The probable number of times a threat agent (e.g., a hacker, malware, natural disaster) is expected to act against an asset within a given period.
- **Contact Frequency (CF):** How often a threat agent comes into contact with an asset. This can be random (e.g., a user clicking a phishing link), regular (e.g., a scheduled vulnerability scan), or intentional (e.g., a targeted attack).
- **Probability of Action (PoA):** The likelihood that a threat agent will take action against an asset once contact is made.
- **Threat Capability (TCap):** The probable force or resources a threat agent can bring to bear against an asset.
- **Resistance Strength (RS) / Vulnerability (Vul):** The ability of an asset's controls to resist a threat agent's actions. Vulnerability is derived from the relationship between Threat Capability and Resistance Strength.

- **Loss Event Frequency (LEF):** Ultimately, LEF is derived from the combination of Threat Event Frequency and Vulnerability.

2. **Loss Magnitude (LM)**

LM captures the probable financial impact if a loss event occurs. It considers various types of losses, categorized into primary and secondary losses:

- **Primary Loss (PL):** Direct losses incurred by the organization as a result of the event. Examples include:
    - **Productivity:** Loss of operational capability or output.
    - **Response:** Costs associated with responding to the incident (e.g., incident response teams, forensics).
    - **Replacement:** Costs to replace or repair affected assets.
    - **Fines & Judgments:** Legal costs, regulatory fines, or settlement payments.
- **Secondary Loss (SL):** Indirect losses resulting from the reactions of secondary stakeholders (e.g., customers, regulators, media) to the primary loss. Examples include:
    - **Reputation:** Damage to brand image, leading to decreased sales or customer trust.
    - **Competitive Advantage:** Loss of intellectual property or market share.
    - **Legal/Regulatory:** Ongoing legal fees or increased scrutiny.

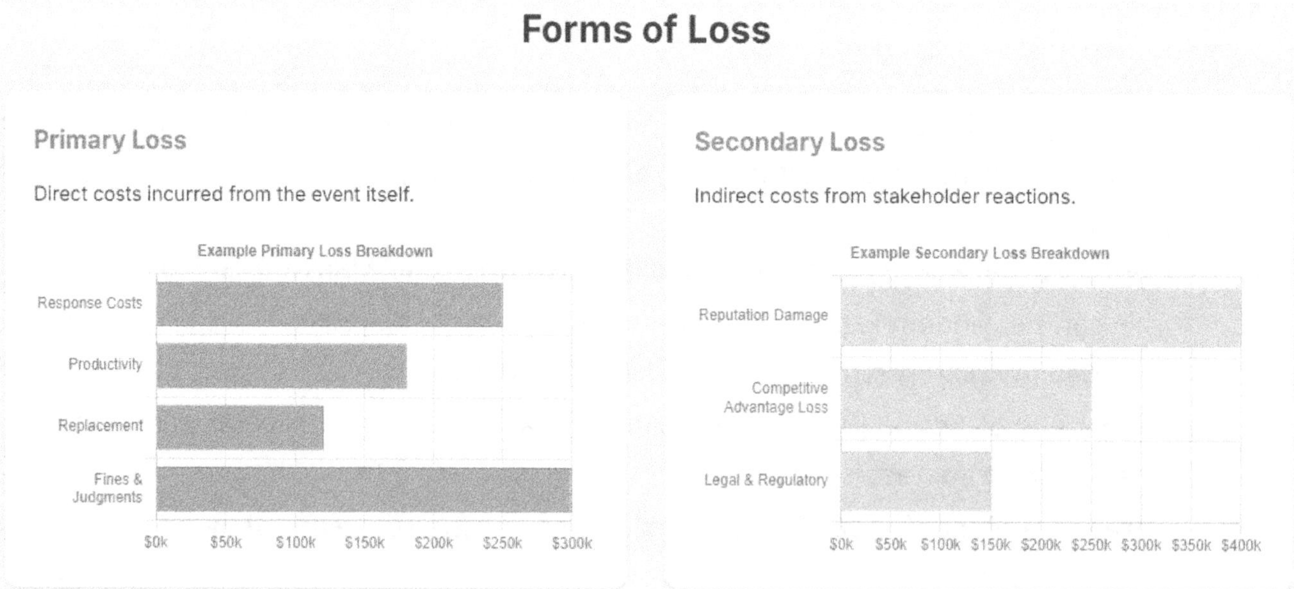

How FAIR is applied in Risk Management

The application of FAIR typically involves a structured process:

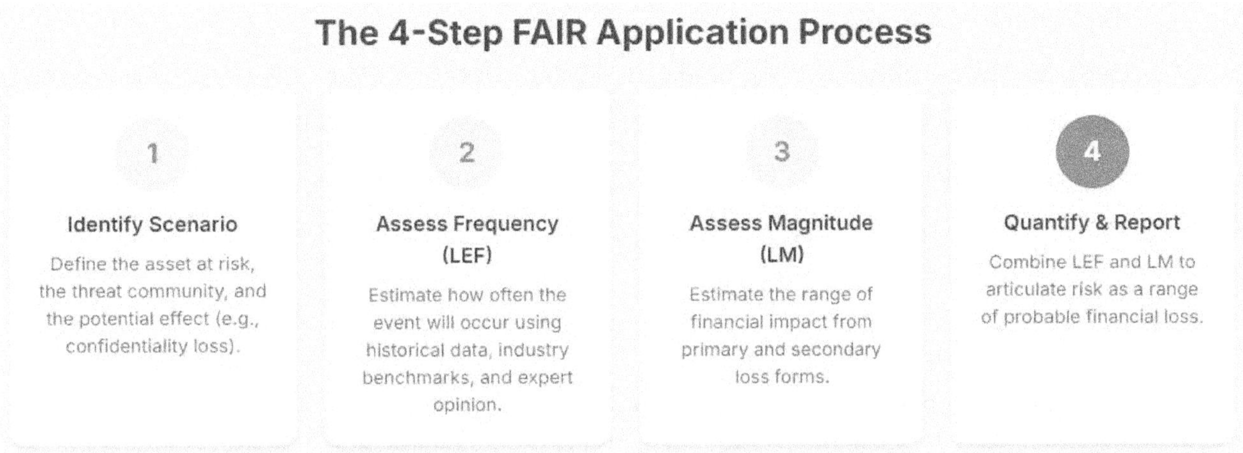

- **Identify Scenario Components:** Define specific risk scenarios by identifying the asset at risk, the threat agent, and the effect on the asset (e.g., "Loss of sensitive customer data due to external hacker attack").
- **Assess Loss Event Frequency (LEF):** Collect data and estimate the various sub-factors that contribute to how often the loss event is likely to occur. This often involves using historical data, industry benchmarks, and expert judgment.
- **Assess Loss Magnitude (LM):** Estimate the potential financial impact of the primary and secondary losses if the event were to happen.
- **Quantify Risk:** By combining the estimated Loss Event Frequency and Loss Magnitude (*Risk = LEF x LM*), FAIR provides a probable range of financial loss exposure for a given risk scenario, usually expressed in monetary terms (e.g., "There is a 20% chance of losing between $1 million and $5 million due to a ransomware attack in the next year").

This quantitative output enables organizations to compare different risks on a common financial basis, allowing for more informed decisions on where to allocate resources for risk mitigation.

Benefits of the FAIR Methodology

- **Quantitative Data:** Translates abstract risks into concrete financial terms, making them more understandable and actionable for business leaders.
- **Enhanced Communication:** Provides a common language for discussing risk across technical and business departments, fostering better collaboration.
- **Efficient Risk Prioritization:** Enables organizations to prioritize risks based on their

potential financial impact, ensuring resources are focused on the most critical areas.

- **Support for Risk Transfer Decisions:** Helps in assessing the financial implications of risks, which is crucial for decisions related to cyber insurance and other risk transfer mechanisms.
- **Cost-Benefit Analysis:** Facilitates the calculation of Return on Investment (ROI) for security initiatives by showing the financial benefit of reducing specific risks.
- **Transparency:** Offers a "glass-box" approach, allowing stakeholders to understand how risk metrics are derived.

Limitations and Criticisms of FAIR

While powerful, FAIR also have some limitations:

- **Time-Consuming and Resource-Intensive:** Implementing FAIR requires significant time, effort, and often specialized expertise for data collection and analysis.
- **Reliance on Estimates:** Although quantitative, the initial inputs for FAIR often rely on expert judgment and estimates, which can introduce subjectivity if not handled carefully.
- **Requires Deep Understanding:** A thorough understanding of the FAIR ontology and methodology is necessary for accurate application.
- **Not a Full Enterprise Risk Assessment:** FAIR is a model for quantifying information risk, but it is not a complete methodology for performing an entire enterprise-wide risk assessment on its own. It complements, rather than replaces, broader risk management frameworks.
- **Data Availability:** Accurate data on threat event frequencies and loss magnitudes can be challenging to obtain, especially for rare events or unique organizational contexts.

The NIST Cybersecurity Framework (CSF)

Who it's for: Widely adopted by a diverse range of organizations, both in the public and private sectors, that are looking for a flexible, risk-based approach to managing and reducing cybersecurity risk.

Key Concept: Unlike the prescriptive RMF, the CSF is a more high-level, voluntary framework designed to help organizations improve their cybersecurity posture. It is built around five core functions that provide a high-level view of a cybersecurity program.

The Five Core Functions:

Identify: Develop an organizational understanding to manage cybersecurity risk to systems, assets, data, and capabilities.

Protect: Develop and implement appropriate safeguards to ensure the delivery of critical services.

Detect: Develop and implement appropriate activities to identify the occurrence of a cybersecurity event.

Respond: Develop and implement appropriate activities to take action regarding a detected cybersecurity incident.

Recover: Develop and implement appropriate activities to maintain plans for resilience and to restore any capabilities or services that were impaired due to a cybersecurity incident.

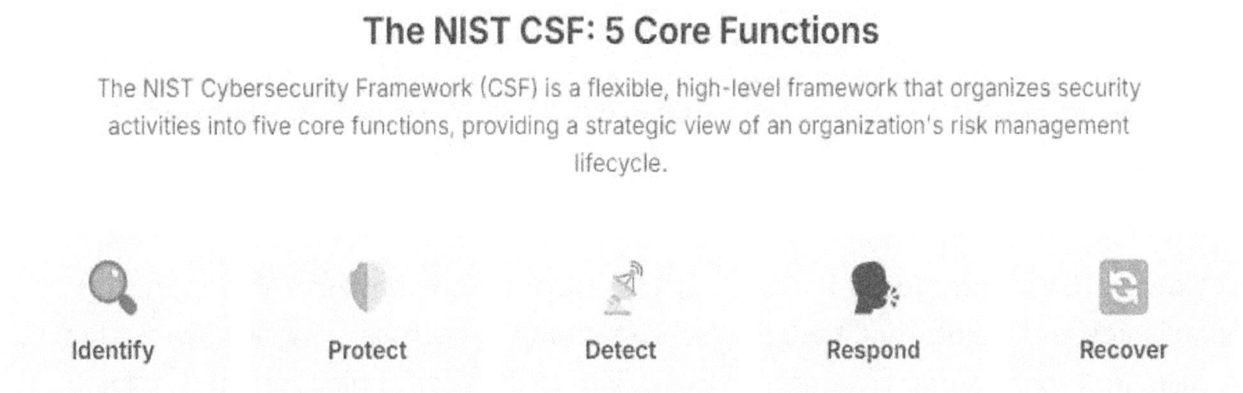

Understanding the NIST Cybersecurity Framework (NIST CSF)

The NIST Cybersecurity Framework (CSF) is a comprehensive set of guidelines developed by the U.S. National Institute of Standards and Technology (NIST) to help organizations improve their ability to prevent, detect, and respond to cybersecurity risks. While voluntary for most private sector organizations, it has become a de facto standard and is widely adopted globally.

Purpose of the NIST CSF

The primary purpose of the NIST CSF is to provide a common language and systematic methodology for managing cybersecurity risk. It helps organizations:

- Understand and assess their current cybersecurity posture.
- Prioritize cybersecurity investments and activities based on risk.

- Communicate cybersecurity risks and efforts effectively across the organization, from technical teams to senior leadership.
- Align cybersecurity activities with business objectives and regulatory requirements.
- Improve their overall resilience against cyber threats.

What is the NIST CSF?

The NIST Cybersecurity Framework (CSF) is a comprehensive set of guidelines developed by the U.S. National Institute of Standards and Technology (NIST). It provides a systematic, risk-based approach to help organizations improve their ability to prevent, detect, and respond to cybersecurity threats. While voluntary, its effectiveness has led to widespread global adoption across all sectors.

Global Impact

70%+

of US organizations use the NIST CSF to guide their cybersecurity activities.

Core Functions of the NIST CSF

The NIST CSF is structured around six core functions that represent the lifecycle of cybersecurity risk management. These functions are designed to be performed concurrently and continuously:

1. **Govern (GV):** (Introduced in CSF 2.0) This function emphasizes the importance of establishing and maintaining the governance structures necessary for an organization to manage its cybersecurity risks in alignment with its business objectives and regulatory requirements. It focuses on organizational context, risk management strategy, roles, responsibilities, policies, oversight, and supply chain risk management.
2. **Identify (ID):** This foundational function helps organizations develop an understanding of their systems, assets, data, and capabilities. It involves identifying critical assets, assessing potential cybersecurity risks, understanding risk tolerance, and developing a comprehensive risk profile.
3. **Protect (PR):** This function focuses on developing and implementing appropriate safeguards to ensure the delivery of critical services. It includes activities like identity management and access control, awareness and training, data security, information protection processes and procedures, maintenance, and protective technology.
4. **Detect (DE):** This function involves developing and implementing activities to identify the occurrence of a cybersecurity event. It emphasizes continuous monitoring, proactive threat intelligence gathering, and implementing detection processes to identify anomalous events or potential cyber threats in a timely manner.
5. **Respond (RS):** This function focuses on developing and implementing activities to take

action regarding a detected cybersecurity incident. It includes response planning, communications, analysis, mitigation, and improvements to contain and mitigate the impact of an incident.

6. **Recover (RC):** This final function identifies appropriate activities to maintain plans for resilience and to restore any capabilities or services that were impaired due to a cybersecurity incident. It involves recovery planning, improvements based on lessons learned, and communication during the recovery process.

Benefits of Adopting the NIST CSF

Organizations adopting the NIST CSF can realize several significant benefits:

- **Improved Risk Management:** It provides a structured approach to understanding, assessing, and reducing cybersecurity risks.
- **Enhanced Communication:** It offers a common language for cybersecurity, bridging the gap between technical and non-technical stakeholders.
- **Increased Security Maturity:** It guides organizations in developing robust security policies and practices, leading to a more mature security posture.
- **Flexibility and Adaptability:** It is designed to be flexible and can be tailored to organizations of any size, sector, or cybersecurity maturity level.
- **Regulatory Alignment:** While voluntary, it helps organizations align with various legal and regulatory requirements.
- **Better Resource Prioritization:** By understanding risks and desired outcomes, organizations can prioritize investments and allocate resources more effectively.
- **Continuous Improvement:** The framework encourages ongoing assessment and

refinement of cybersecurity practices.

ISO 31000: Risk Management Guidelines

ISO 31000 is an international standard that provides a set of principles and guidelines for risk management. It is designed to be a flexible, non-certifiable standard that can be applied to any organization, regardless of its size, type, or industry. The goal of ISO 31000 is to help organizations integrate a systematic approach to risk management into all their activities, from strategic planning to daily operations. The standard defines risk as the "effect of uncertainty on objectives."

The ISO 31000 standard is built on three core components:

1. **The Principles**

These principles are the foundation for managing risk and are intended to guide the effectiveness of an organization's risk management process. To be effective, risk management should be:

- **Integrated:** It should be an integral part of all organizational activities.
- **Structured and Comprehensive:** A consistent and systematic approach leads to more effective and comparable results.
- **Customized:** The framework and process should be tailored to the organization's specific context and needs.
- **Inclusive:** The timely and appropriate involvement of stakeholders ensures a well-rounded perspective.
- **Dynamic:** Risk management must be proactive and responsive to changes in the internal and external environment.
- **Based on Best Available Information:** Decisions are based on a combination of historical data, current information, and future expectations.
- **Considers Human and Cultural Factors:** Human behavior and an organization's culture can significantly influence risk management.
- **Aided by Continual Improvement:** The process should be constantly reviewed and improved upon through learning and experience.

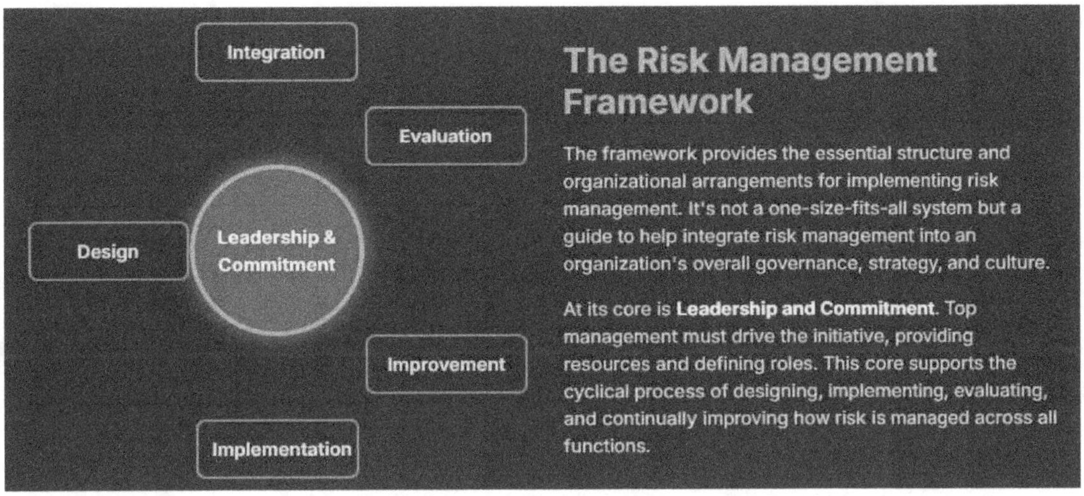

2. **The Framework**

This component provides the structure for integrating risk management into the organization's governance, strategy, and planning. It emphasizes that top leadership must show commitment by providing the necessary resources and assigning clear roles and responsibilities. The framework is designed to help an organization develop a culture where all employees are equipped to monitor and manage risk.

3. **The Process**

This is the practical, multi-step method for managing risks. The process is iterative and involves several key stages:

- **Communication and Consultation:** Ongoing dialogue with both internal and external stakeholders is crucial.
- **Establishing the Context:** Defining the scope, objectives, and criteria for the risk management process, considering both internal and external factors.
- **Risk Assessment:** This is a comprehensive stage that includes:
  - **Risk Identification:** Finding, recognizing, and describing risks.
  - **Risk Analysis:** Understanding the nature of the risk, its potential consequences, and the likelihood of it occurring.
  - **Risk Evaluation:** Comparing the results of the risk analysis against the established criteria to decide which risks need to be treated and their priority.
- **Risk Treatment:** Selecting and implementing options to modify risks. This might include avoiding the risk, taking on the risk for an opportunity, removing the risk source, or sharing the risk with another party.

- **Monitoring and Review:** Continually checking the effectiveness of the risk management process and adjusting it as needed.
- **Recording and Reporting:** Documenting the process and communicating the results to relevant stakeholders.

By following the guidelines in ISO 31000, an organization can improve its decision-making, protect its assets and reputation, and enhance its ability to achieve its objectives. It provides a structured way to handle uncertainty and turn potential threats into opportunities.

COSO ERM Framework in Information Security

The Committee of Sponsoring Organizations of the Treadway Commission (COSO) Enterprise Risk Management (ERM) framework is a widely recognized and respected model for managing risks across an organization. While originally developed with a focus on financial reporting, its principles are highly adaptable and are now a critical tool for integrating and managing information security risks as part of a broader business strategy. By applying the five components of the COSO ERM framework, organizations can shift cybersecurity from a technical issue to a strategic business concern.

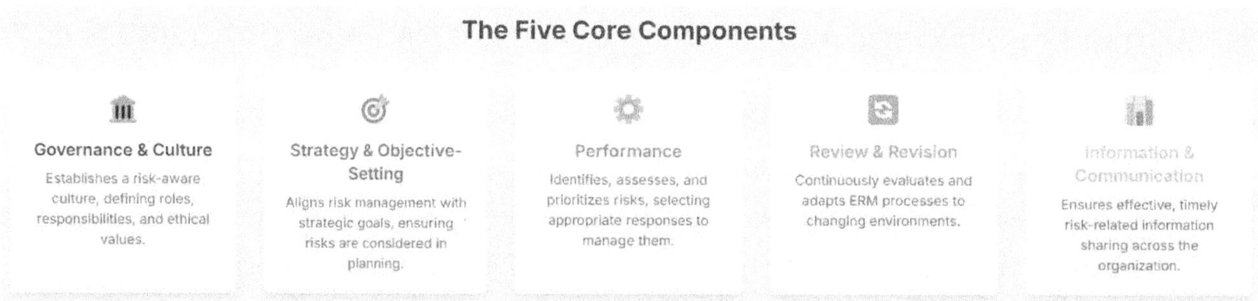

Key Components of the COSO ERM Framework

The framework is built around five interrelated components:

1. **Governance and Culture**: Establishes a risk-aware culture and oversight, defining roles, responsibilities, and ethical values to support ERM.
2. **Strategy and Objective-Setting**: Aligns risk management with strategic goals, ensuring risks are considered in setting objectives.
3. **Performance**: Identifies, assesses, and prioritizes risks, selecting responses (e.g., accept, avoid, mitigate) to manage them within the organization's risk appetite.

4. **Review and Revision**: Continuously evaluates ERM processes, monitoring performance and adapting to changes.
5. **Information, Communication, and Reporting**: Ensures effective risk-related information sharing across the organization.

The framework also emphasizes 20 principles within these components, guiding practical implementation, such as defining risk appetite, assessing risk severity, and leveraging technology for data-driven decisions.

Relevance to Information Security

In the context of information security, the COSO ERM Framework supports:

- **Risk Identification**: Pinpointing cybersecurity threats (e.g., data breaches, insider threats).
- **Risk Assessment**: Evaluating the likelihood and impact of security incidents.
- **Integration with Strategy**: Aligning security measures with business objectives, ensuring resource allocation for controls like encryption or access management.
- **Monitoring and Reporting**: Continuously tracking emerging threats and communicating risks to stakeholders.

1. Governance and Culture

This component establishes the foundation for how an organization views and manages risk. For information security, this means creating a culture where cybersecurity is a shared responsibility, not just the IT department's problem. Key applications include:

- **Define Leadership and Commitment**: Establish a cybersecurity governance structure with clear roles (e.g., Chief Information Security Officer, risk committee). Ensure leadership sets a tone of risk awareness.
  - **Action**: Appoint a CISO to oversee ERM integration and form a cross-functional team (IT, legal, compliance) to align cybersecurity with business goals.
  - **Example**: Create a policy mandating board-level oversight of cybersecurity risks, reviewed quarterly.
- **Embed Risk Culture**: Train employees on cybersecurity risks (e.g., phishing, data leaks) to foster a risk-aware culture.
  - **Action**: Conduct mandatory annual training and simulate phishing attacks to test employee vigilance.

- Example: Implement a reward system for reporting suspicious emails.

2. Strategy and Objective-Setting

In this component, the organization defines its strategic objectives and aligns them with its risk appetite. When applied to information security, this involves:

- **Align Cybersecurity with Strategy**: Integrate cybersecurity objectives with the organization's strategic goals (e.g., protecting customer data to maintain trust).
    - **Action**: Define cybersecurity objectives in strategic planning, such as achieving zero data breaches or 100% compliance with GDPR.
    - **Example**: Include cybersecurity KPIs (e.g., time to patch vulnerabilities) in the company's strategic scorecard.
- **Set Risk Appetite**: Determine acceptable levels of cybersecurity risk, balancing cost and protection.
    - **Action**: Document a risk appetite statement, e.g., "No tolerance for breaches exposing sensitive customer data."
    - **Example**: Prioritize investments in endpoint protection over less critical systems.
- **Threat Landscape**: Security threats (e.g., malware, phishing, denial-of-service attacks) are identified as potential events that could prevent the organization from achieving its objectives.

3. Performance

This component focuses on identifying, assessing, and responding to risks. This is the core of day-to-day risk management for information security and includes:

- **Identify and Assess Risks**: Organizations must continuously identify and analyze all potential information security risks, and prioritize them based on their potential impact on business objectives.
    - **Action**: Use tools like the NIST Cybersecurity Framework or threat modeling to identify vulnerabilities. Conduct risk assessments to understand the likelihood and impact of each threat.
    - **Example**: Rank a potential zero-day exploit as high priority due to its severe impact on a critical business system.
- **Implement Responses**: Based on the assessment, management decides on an appropriate response: **Accept**, **Avoid**, **Reduce**, or **Share** the risk.
    - **Action**: Mitigate risks with controls like multi-factor authentication (MFA)

or transfer risks via cyber insurance.

  - **Example**: Deploy firewalls and intrusion detection systems to mitigate network attack risks.

4. Review and Revision

The COSO ERM framework is a dynamic, not a static, process. This component emphasizes the need for continuous monitoring and adaptation. Key activities include:

- **Monitor Risks**: Continuously track cybersecurity risks using monitoring tools and key risk indicators (KRIs).
  - **Action**: Set up a Security Information and Event Management (SIEM) system to monitor real-time threats.
  - **Example**: Track KRI like "number of unpatched systems" to identify vulnerabilities.
- **Evaluate and Improve ERM**: Regularly review the effectiveness of cybersecurity controls and update ERM processes.
  - **Action**: Conduct annual audits and penetration testing to assess control effectiveness.
  - **Example**: Revise incident response plans after a simulated breach reveals gaps.

5. Information, Communication, and Reporting

This component is about ensuring that relevant information is communicated to the right people in a timely manner. For information security, this means:

- **Share Risk Information**: Ensure cybersecurity risk data is communicated across departments and to leadership.
  - **Action**: Use dashboards to share real-time risk metrics with stakeholders.
  - **Example**: Present a monthly cybersecurity risk report to the board, highlighting incidents and mitigation status.
- **Leverage Technology**: Use data analytics to enhance risk reporting and decision- making.
  - **Action**: Implement AI-driven tools to analyze threat patterns and predict risks.
  - **Example**: Use a threat intelligence platform to report on emerging malware trends.

Example Workflow in Practice

1. **Scenario**: A mid-sized company wants to protect customer data from breaches.

2. **Steps:**
    - **Governance**: CISO establishes a cybersecurity risk committee.
    - **Strategy**: Aligns cybersecurity with the goal of maintaining customer trust, setting a zero-breach objective.
    - **Performance**: Identifies risks (e.g., weak passwords), assesses their severity, and deploys MFA and encryption.
    - **Review**: Monitors login attempts via SIEM and conducts quarterly penetration tests.
    - **Communication**: Reports risk metrics to the board via a dashboard, ensuring transparency.

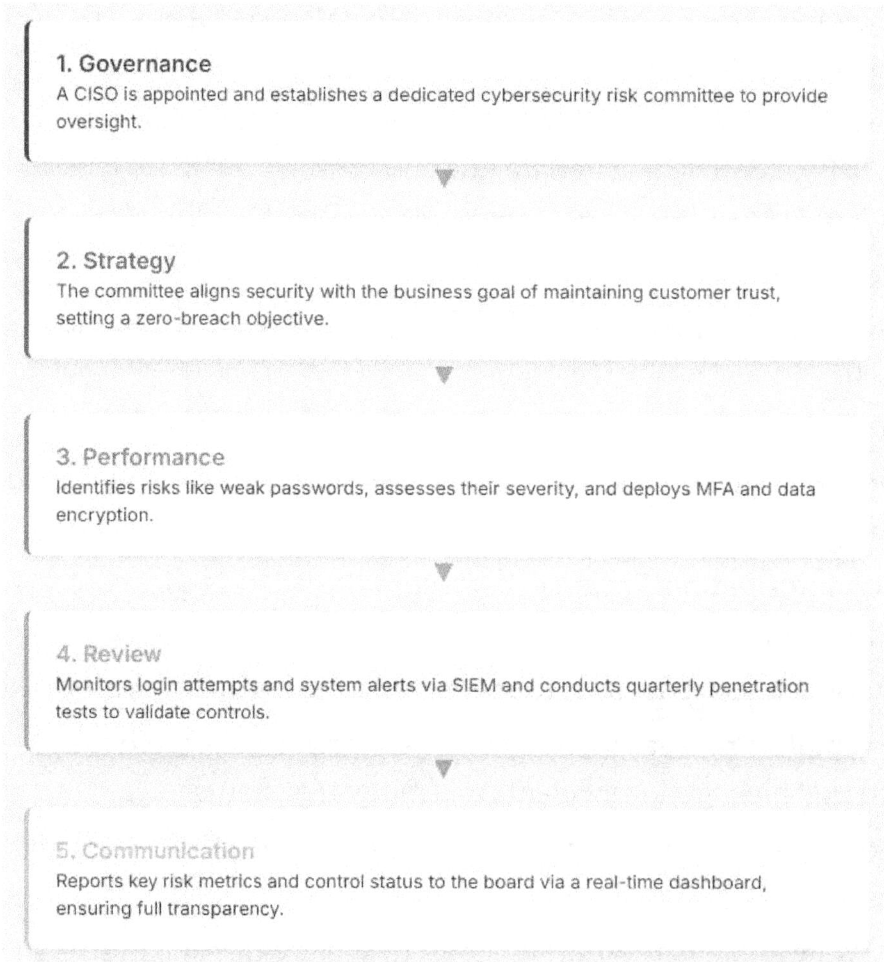

Introduction to the IS Risk Register

An Information Systems (IS) risk register is a crucial tool for an organization's security posture. It's a living document that systematically identifies, analyzes, and tracks risks related to an organization's information systems. These risks can be anything from technical vulnerabilities and cyber threats to human error and compliance issues. The IS risk register serves as a central repository for all identified risks, their potential impact, and the measures being taken to mitigate them.

The primary goals of an IS risk register are to:

- **Identify:** Document all potential risks to the organization's information systems.
- **Analyze:** Assess the likelihood and impact of each risk.
- **Prioritize:** Rank risks based on their severity to focus resources effectively.
- **Track:** Monitor the status of each risk and the effectiveness of mitigation efforts.
- **Communicate:** Provide a clear picture of the IS risk landscape to stakeholders, including management and the board of directors.

An Information Security (IS) Risk Register is a tool used by a security team to identify, assess, prioritize, and manage risks to an organization's information assets. It provides a detailed, granular view of specific threats, vulnerabilities, and potential impacts.

The Organizational Risk Register (also known as an Enterprise Risk Management or ERM register) is a high-level, strategic document used by executive leadership and the board. It aggregates and tracks the most significant risks facing the entire organization, drawing from various departments like Finance, Operations, Legal, and IT/IS.

Components of a Sample IS Risk Register

A typical IS risk register is a table or database with several key fields for each risk entry. Here is a sample table format that we will populate with some examples.

Explanation of Key Fields:

- **Risk ID:** A unique identifier for each risk (e.g., ISR-001 for "Information Systems Risk 001").
- **Risk Category:** A high-level classification of the risk (e.g., Cybersecurity, Data Privacy, Operational).
- **Risk Description:** A clear, concise statement of the risk, including the cause and potential consequence.
- **Likelihood:** The probability of the risk occurring (e.g., Low, Medium, High).

- **Impact:** The potential severity of the consequences if the risk materializes (e.g., Low, Medium, High).
- **Risk Score:** A numerical or qualitative score calculated from the likelihood and impact. This helps prioritize risks. A simple formula is RiskScore=Likelihood×Impact.
- **Mitigation Strategy:** The specific actions planned or taken to reduce the risk.
- **Owner:** The individual or team responsible for managing the risk and its mitigation.
- **Status:** The current state of the risk (e.g., Open, In Progress, Closed, Mitigated).

Integration of the IS Risk Register into the Larger Organizational Risk Register

The IS risk register is not a standalone document; it is a critical component that feeds into the organization's enterprise-level risk register. This is often referred to as a "roll-up" process, where departmental or functional risks are aggregated and presented to senior management and the board.

Here's how the IS risk register fits into the larger organizational risk management framework:

- **Risk Identification and Analysis:** The IS team identifies and analyzes risks specific to its domain, as detailed in our example. These risks are typically very technical and specific to information technology.
- **Aggregation and Translation:** The IS risks are then aggregated and "translated" into business terms for the broader organizational risk register. For example, the technical risk of "unpatched critical vulnerability in web server software" (ISR-001) would be translated into the business risk of "potential data breach leading to financial loss and reputational damage."
- **Cross-Functional Impact Assessment:** The IS team collaborates with other departments (e.g., Legal, Finance, Operations) to determine the full impact of an IS risk on the entire organization. For example, the impact of a data breach is not just a technology issue; it affects customer trust, legal compliance, and financial stability.
- **Prioritization at the Enterprise Level:** The IS risks, once translated and assessed for their broader impact, are prioritized alongside other business risks (e.g., market risk, financial risk, legal risk). This allows the board to see the relative severity of IS risks in the context of the entire organization. For example, a severe IS risk might be ranked as a top enterprise risk alongside a major supply chain

disruption risk.

- **Reporting and Governance:** The aggregated IS risk data is regularly reported to senior management and the board of directors. This ensures that IS risk is given the appropriate level of attention and resources. The board can then make informed decisions about risk appetite and investment in security controls.

Demonstrating the Integration

Let's take our example risk, ISR-001: Unpatched critical vulnerability in web server software, and show how it would be presented in the larger organizational risk register.

IS Risk Register Entry:

Risk ID: ISR-001

Risk Description: Unpatched critical vulnerability in web server software.

Likelihood: High

Impact: High

Mitigation Strategy: Patch server immediately; implement a vulnerability management program.

Owner: System Administrator

Organizational Risk Register Entry:

Enterprise Risk ID: ER-012

Enterprise Risk Description: Potential for significant data breach or service interruption due to critical IT vulnerabilities.

Likelihood: Medium

Impact: High

Mitigation Strategy: Implement comprehensive cybersecurity program, including advanced vulnerability management, incident response, and employee training.

Owner: CISO (Chief Information Security Officer)

Explanation of the Link:

- **Roll-up:** The specific, technical IS risk (ISR-001) is "rolled up" into a broader, business-oriented enterprise risk (ER-012). The enterprise risk register focuses on the business outcome (data breach, service interruption), not the technical cause (unpatched server).

- **Ownership:** The owner of the enterprise risk is a senior executive (e.g., CISO), who is accountable for the overall risk area, while the owner of the IS risk is a subject matter expert (e.g., System Administrator) responsible for the specific technical mitigation.
- **Mitigation:** The mitigation strategy in the enterprise register is a high-level program or initiative (e.g., a "comprehensive cybersecurity program"), which encompasses and directs the more specific actions in the IS register (e.g., "patch server immediately").

This structure ensures that the technical details are managed by the appropriate experts while the strategic implications are understood and governed at the highest levels of the organization. The IS risk register provides the detailed, ground-level information that justifies the need for the broader strategic initiatives found in the enterprise risk register.

The Integration Process

The two registers are not separate but are linked in a hierarchical relationship. The IS risk register serves as the foundation for identifying and managing security-specific risks, while the organizational register provides executive oversight.

How it works:

- **Bottom-Up Identification:** The security team uses the IS risk register to continuously identify, assess, and monitor risks.
- **Risk Escalation:** When a risk in the IS register is deemed significant (e.g., its risk score is above a certain threshold, like 15), it is escalated to the organizational risk register.
- **Top-Down Oversight:** The executive team and the board review the organizational risk register to understand the overall risk landscape. They can then ask the IS team for more details on the corresponding security risks. For example, an executive seeing "OR-010: Failure to protect sensitive customer data" would know to ask the CISO for an update on the related projects and risks (e.g., "IS-001: Unpatched web server").
- **Action & Reporting:** The IS team manages the detailed mitigation plans outlined in their register. Progress on these plans is then reported up to the executive level, updating the status of the high-level risk in the organizational register.This integration ensures that while the security team handles the

technical details, leadership maintains a clear, strategic understanding of the most significant security threats to the business.

ISMS Risk Assessment Schedule and Checklists

The ISMS Program provides a foundational framework for conducting risk assessments as part of an Information Security Management System (ISMS). It includes a schedule for recurring activities and detailed checklists for the assessment and treatment phases.

While there is no single, universally mandated frequency for an ISMS risk assessment, best practices and standards like ISO 27001 recommend a structured approach. The frequency and triggers for a risk assessment should be clearly defined in your ISMS policy.

Annual Risk Assessment

A comprehensive risk assessment should be performed at least once per year. This annual review ensures that your risk register remains relevant and that your security controls are still effective against the current threat landscape. This is a common requirement for maintaining ISO 27001 certification.

Trigger-Based Assessments

In addition to the annual review, a risk assessment should be initiated whenever a significant change occurs that could impact your organization's information security. These triggers include:

- **Changes to business objectives:** If the company's strategic goals or services change.
- **Introduction of new technologies:** Deploying new hardware, software, or cloud services.
- **Significant changes to existing systems:** Major updates, migrations, or architectural changes.
- **Changes in the legal, regulatory, or contractual environment:** New laws (e.g., data privac y), new contracts with specific security clauses, etc.
- **Discovery of new, significant threats or vulnerabilities:** A major zero-day exploit, a new type of attack vector, or a breach in a similar industry.

- **After a security incident:** To understand the root cause and ensure the risk is properly treated to prevent future occurrences.
- **Organizational changes:** Mergers, acquisitions, or significant changes in personnel or roles.

Risk Assessment Schedule

The following table outlines a typical schedule for key ISMS risk assessment activities. This schedule can be adjusted based on the organization's risk appetite and operational tempo.

Activity	Frequency	Responsibility	Status/Notes
Initial Risk Assessment	One-time	ISMS Team, Asset Owners	Completed during the initial implementation of the ISMS.
Periodic Risk Review	Annually	ISMS Team, Management	A comprehensive review of all identified risks and their treatment plans.
Control Effectiveness Review	Quarterly	Control Owners	Verify that implemented controls are operating as intended.
Significant Change Review	As needed (Ad-hoc)	ISMS Team	Triggered by major changes to systems, processes, or the business environment (e.g., new software, acquisition).
Incident-based Review	As needed (Ad-hoc)	ISMS Incident Response Team	A targeted risk review following a security incident to prevent recurrence.
New Asset/System Assessment	As needed (Ad-hoc)	System Owners	Assess risks associated with new assets or systems before they are deployed.

Risk Assessment Checklist

This checklist guides the team through the core risk assessment process, ensuring all critical steps are covered.

Phase 1: Preparation

- [ ] Define the scope of the risk assessment.
- [ ] Identify and engage key stakeholders and asset owners.
- [ ] Define the criteria for risk acceptance and evaluation (e.g., impact and likelihood scales).
- [ ] Assemble the risk assessment team.

Phase 2: Asset Identification

- [ ] Identify and document all information assets within the scope (hardware, software, data, services, people).
- [ ] Assign an owner to each asset.
- [ ] Determine the business value and criticality of each asset.
- [ ] Classify assets based on confidentiality, integrity, and availability requirements.

Phase 3: Threat & Vulnerability Analysis

- [ ] Identify potential threats to each asset (e.g., malware, unauthorized access, natural disasters).
- [ ] Document existing vulnerabilities (e.g., unpatched software, weak passwords, lack of training).
- [ ] For each threat-vulnerability pair, estimate the likelihood of the risk event occurring.

Phase 4: Risk Evaluation

- [ ] Estimate the potential impact of each risk event (e.g., financial, reputational, legal).
- [ ] Combine the likelihood and impact ratings to determine the overall risk level.
- [ ] Rank risks from highest to lowest based on their risk level.
- [ ] Present the findings to management and stakeholders for review.

Risk Treatment Checklist

Once risks are evaluated, this checklist ensures a systematic approach to treating them.

Phase 1: Option Selection

- [ ] For each unacceptable risk, identify and evaluate treatment options:
    - [ ] **Mitigate:** Implement controls to reduce the risk.
    - [ ] **Transfer:** Share the risk with another party (e.g., insurance).
    - [ ] **Avoid:** Discontinue the activity or asset that creates the risk.
    - [ ] **Accept:** Acknowledge and monitor the risk without implementing

new controls.

- [ ] Document the selected treatment option for each risk.

Phase 2: Implementation & Communication

- [ ] Develop a detailed risk treatment plan.
- [ ] Assign clear responsibilities for implementing new controls.
- [ ] Define metrics for measuring the effectiveness of controls.
- [ ] Communicate the risk treatment plan to all relevant stakeholders.

Phase 3: Monitoring & Review

- [ ] Implement the new or updated controls.
- [ ] Monitor the effectiveness of the controls at regular intervals.
- [ ] Update the risk register with the new residual risk levels.
- [ ] Re-evaluate the risks periodically or when there's a significant change.

ISMS Risk Reporting: Metrics and Processes

An Information Security Management System (ISMS) relies on a structured and consistent approach to risk management. A crucial part of this is the reporting process, which provides stakeholders with a clear, data-driven view of the organization's security posture. Effective risk reporting allows management to make informed decisions, allocate resources appropriately, and ensure the ISMS is continually improving. This document outlines the key metrics to track and the processes involved in creating a robust risk reporting framework.

Key Metrics for ISMS Risk Reporting

Metrics for ISMS risk reporting are generally categorized into Key Risk Indicators (KRIs) and Key Performance Indicators (KPIs).

Understanding Your Security Metrics

Key Risk Indicators (KRIs)

KRIs are **proactive**, early-warning signals. They measure developing conditions to forecast the probability of a future risk event.

Focus: Predicting potential issues.

Key Performance Indicators (KPIs)

KPIs are **reactive**, historical measures. They evaluate the effectiveness of existing controls and the performance of the ISMS.

Focus: Measuring past performance.

Key Risk Indicators (KRIs)

KRIs are proactive metrics that provide an early warning of potential risks. They measure the likelihood of a risk event occurring.

- **Vulnerability Management:**
    - Number of critical/high-risk vulnerabilities identified.
    - Average time to remediate critical vulnerabilities.
    - Percentage of systems with known vulnerabilities.
- **Incident Management:**
    - Number of security incidents (e.g., unauthorized access attempts, malware detections).
    - Number of user-reported security events.
    - Frequency of phishing simulations and user failure rates.
- **Threat & Patch Management:**
    - Percentage of systems patched within the required timeframe (e.g., 30 days).
    - Number of unpatched systems with critical vulnerabilities.
    - Number of active threats detected by security systems.
- **Access Control:**
    - Number of users with excessive permissions.
    - Number of privileged access events outside of standard operating hours.
    - Number of unauthorized access attempts.

Key Performance Indicators (KPIs)

KPIs are reactive metrics that measure the effectiveness of the security controls and the overall ISMS.

- **ISMS Effectiveness:**
    - Percentage of employees who have completed mandatory security awareness training.
    - Number of overdue internal audit findings.
    - Completion rate of ISMS management reviews.
- **Incident Response:**
    - Mean time to detect (MTTD) a security incident.
    - Mean time to respond (MTTR) to a security incident.
    - Mean time to recover (MTTR) from an incident.
- **Compliance:**
    - Number of non-compliance events found during internal or external audits.
    - Percentage of security policies that are up-to-date and approved.
    - Percentage of systems with correctly configured security controls.
- **Risk Treatment:**
    - Number of risk treatment plans completed on schedule.
    - Reduction in average risk scores over time.
    - Cost-benefit analysis of implemented controls.

The ISMS Risk Reporting Process

An effective reporting process ensures that the right information reaches the right people at the right time.

Step 1: Establish a Risk Management Framework

Before reporting can begin, the organization must have a defined risk management framework. This includes:

- **Risk Acceptance Criteria:** Defining what level of risk is acceptable to the organization.
- **Risk Assessment Methodology:** A standardized, repeatable process for identifying, analyzing, and evaluating risks (e.g., qualitative or quantitative).
- **Roles and Responsibilities:** Clearly assigning ownership for risks and reporting tasks.

Step 2: Risk Identification and Assessment

Using the established methodology, the organization identifies information assets, threats, and vulnerabilities. Each risk is then analyzed for its likelihood and impact, leading to a risk score. This information is typically documented in a **risk register**.

Step 3: Risk Treatment and Control Implementation

Based on the risk scores, a risk treatment plan is developed. The plan documents the chosen responses, including the specific security controls to be implemented, the responsible parties (risk owners), and the timelines.

The four common options are:

- **Treat:** Implement security controls to reduce the risk.
- **Accept:** Formally accept the risk because it is within the organization's risk appetite.
- **Avoid:** Stop the activity that is causing the risk.
- **Transfer:** Share the risk with a third party, such as through insurance.

Step 4: Data Collection and Monitoring

The ISMS manager and risk owners continuously monitor the effectiveness of the implemented controls. Data is collected for the KRIs and KPIs, often using security tools, log data, and internal audits. This data provides the raw input for the reports.

Step 5: Report Generation and Communication

Regular reports (e.g., monthly, quarterly, annually) are generated for different audiences.

- **Operational Reports:** Detailed reports for risk owners and IT teams, focusing on specific risks, control performance, and remediation tasks.
- **Management Reports:** Summaries for senior management and the Information Security Committee, highlighting key trends, high-risk areas, and the overall performance of the ISMS against business objectives.
- **Executive Reports:** High-level, strategic reports for the board of directors, focusing on the organization's top risks, residual risk levels, and the value of security investments.

Communicating to Different Audiences

Effective reporting requires tailoring the content and level of detail to the audience.

- **Technical Teams (e.g., IT Operations, Security Analysts):**
  - **Focus:** Actionable data. They need detailed, granular information to do their jobs.
  - **Content:** Raw metrics, vulnerability scan results, incident logs, specific KRI thresholds, and detailed progress on the risk treatment plan.
- **Management (e.g., Department Heads):**
  - **Focus:** Operational impact. They want to understand how security issues affect their department's goals.
  - **Content:** Summary dashboards, trend analysis, budget implications of security risks, and the business impact of security incidents.
- **Senior Leadership/Board of Directors:**
  - **Focus:** Strategic overview. They care about the big picture—the organization's overall risk posture and compliance.
  - **Content:** High-level summaries, heat maps that show the most

significant risks, alignment with strategic business objectives, and assurance that the ISMS is functioning effectively to protect the company's reputation and finances. The goal is to provide enough information for them to make informed decisions without getting bogged down in technical details.

Step 6: Review and Continual Improvement

The ISMS is a living system. Management reviews are a critical part of the process, where the risk reports are analyzed to identify opportunities for improvement. This might lead to updates in the risk management framework, changes to security controls, or a recalibration of the metrics being tracked.

Compliance

Understanding IS Compliance: A Multi-faceted Perspective

For an organization, Information Security (IS) compliance is a comprehensive effort that goes beyond simply checking boxes. It involves a deep understanding of external laws and regulations, the adoption of recognized standards, the implementation of best practices, and the cultivation of a strong ethical culture.

External Laws and Regulations

These are the mandatory rules set by governments and governing bodies that organizations must follow. Non-compliance can lead to severe penalties, including hefty fines and legal action. The specific regulations applicable to an organization depend heavily on its industry, location, and the type of data it handles.

- **General Data Protection Regulation (GDPR):** This is a key regulation for any organization that handles the personal data of European Union (EU) citizens. It gives individuals significant control over their data, and requires strict data protection measures, consent for data processing, and timely breach notifications. Fines for violations can be up to 4% of a company's annual global turnover.
- **Health Insurance Portability and Accountability Act (HIPAA):** A U.S. federal law that mandates the protection of sensitive patient health information (PHI) by

healthcare providers, health plans, and their business associates. It requires administrative, physical, and technical safeguards to ensure data confidentiality, integrity, and availability.

- **California Consumer Privacy Act (CCPA):** A state-level U.S. law that grants California residents new rights regarding their personal information, including the right to know what data is being collected and the right to opt-out of its sale. This has served as a model for many other data privacy laws in the U.S.

Standards and Best Practices

While laws tell you *what* to do, frameworks and standards provide guidance on *how* to do it. They offer a structured approach to managing information security risk and are often adopted to demonstrate a commitment to security to customers and partners.

- **ISO/IEC 27001:** An internationally recognized standard for an Information Security Management System (ISMS). It provides a systematic approach for managing sensitive company information so that it remains secure. It requires organizations to identify risks, implement controls, and continuously monitor and improve their security posture.
- **NIST Cybersecurity Framework (CSF):** Developed by the National Institute of Standards and Technology, this is a flexible, voluntary framework designed to help organizations of all sizes manage and reduce cybersecurity risk. It is structured around five core functions: **Identify**, **Protect**, **Detect**, **Respond**, and **Recover**.
- **SOC 2 (System and Organization Controls 2):** An auditing procedure developed by the American Institute of CPAs (AICPA) for service organizations. It ensures that an organization securely manages customer data based on five "Trust Service Criteria": **Security**, **Availability**, **Processing Integrity**, **Confidentiality**, and **Privacy**.

The foundational best practice in all of these standards is the **CIA Triad**: ensuring the **Confidentiality**, **Integrity**, and **Availability** of information. Beyond frameworks, other best practices include strong access controls, regular security training for employees, patch management, and robust incident response plans.

Organizational Ethics

Ethics in IS compliance is about the moral principles that guide an organization's actions, even in situations where there are no clear laws. It's the difference between doing what is legally required and doing what is morally right. A strong ethical culture is often the bedrock of a successful compliance program.

- **Going beyond the law:** An ethical organization doesn't just meet the minimum requirements of regulations like GDPR; it actively seeks to protect user data and privacy as a core value. This builds trust and long-term customer loyalty.
- **Transparency and Honesty:** Ethical conduct demands transparency in security practices and honest communication about risks and incidents. This means not concealing security breaches or downplaying their impact to stakeholders.
- **Whistle-blower protection:** An ethical organization fosters a culture where employees can safely report concerns about security vulnerabilities or compliance issues without fear of retaliation. This internal feedback loop is critical for catching problems early.

In essence, while compliance is a matter of rules and procedures, ethics is a matter of corporate character. An organization that values ethics is more likely to be proactive, transparent, and resilient in the face of security challenges.

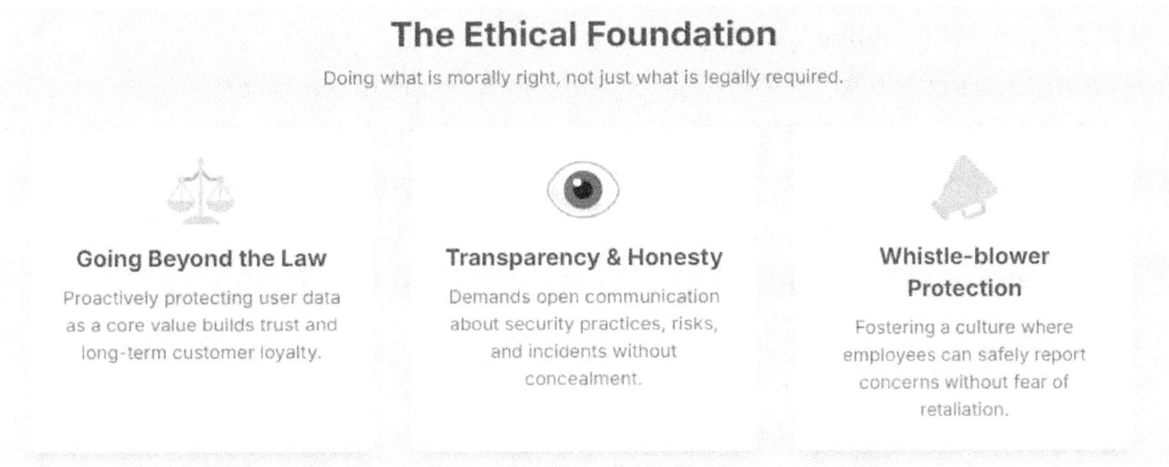

Regulatory Organizations

Regulatory organizations, typically government agencies or official bodies, are crucial because they create and enforce the **legal and mandatory requirements** for information security. They define the minimum standards that organizations must meet to operate legally. The importance of these bodies can be summarized by a few key points:

- **Mandatory Compliance and Penalties:** They give legal weight to cybersecurity practices. Failure to comply can result in significant fines, legal action, and a loss of the right to operate. This provides a strong incentive for organizations to take security seriously.
- **Consumer and Data Protection:** Regulations like the **GDPR** (General Data Protection Regulation) or **HIPAA** (Health Insurance Portability and Accountability Act) are designed to protect the privacy and rights of individuals. They set strict rules on how sensitive data

is collected, stored, and processed, building public trust.

- **Level Playing Field:** By setting a baseline for security, these regulations ensure that all organizations within a specific industry adhere to similar standards, preventing a "race to the bottom" where security is neglected to cut costs.

Industry Groups and Stakeholders

While regulatory bodies set the rules, industry groups and stakeholders are the ones who work to apply them and drive security forward. Their importance lies in their ability to provide practical, real-world context and collaboration.

- **Sharing Best Practices:** Organizations like the **Center for Internet Security (CIS)** or the **Information Systems Audit and Control Association (ISACA)** develop and promote best practices and frameworks (like the **CIS Critical Security Controls**). These are often more detailed and prescriptive than high-level regulations, offering a practical guide for implementation.
- **Information Sharing and Analysis:** Industry-specific groups, often called ***Information Sharing and Analysis Centers (ISACs)***, play a vital role in threat intelligence. Members share information about new threats and vulnerabilities in a secure environment, allowing others to prepare and defend against similar attacks. This collaborative approach is much more effective than individual companies working in isolation.
- **Driving Innovation and Standards:** These groups help shape the future of cybersecurity by providing feedback to regulators, developing new standards, and driving the adoption of new technologies. They ensure that security practices evolve to meet new challenges.

Key Stakeholders and Their Roles

Every individual and group with an interest in an organization's security is a stakeholder, and they all have a part to play.

- **Management and Leadership:** Responsible for setting the overall security strategy, allocating resources, and ensuring the organization is compliant with all regulations.
- **Security Professionals:** These are the experts responsible for implementing the technical controls and day-to-day security operations.
- **Employees:** They are often the first line of defense. Their role is to follow security policies, report suspicious activity, and participate in security training.

- **Customers:** They trust organizations to protect their data. Their expectations for privacy and security drive organizations to maintain a strong security posture.
- **Third-Party Vendors:** Any partner or supplier that has access to an organization's systems or data must also adhere to the same security standards. This is a critical point of vulnerability that must be managed.

Information Security: A Modern Landscape

Information security is a rapidly evolving field, driven by new technologies and a more complex threat landscape. The traditional model of building a strong perimeter defense is no longer sufficient. Today's security strategies must be more adaptive and assume that a breach is not a matter of "if" but "when." This shift in mindset has led to several key trends and changes.

> **In 2023, malware-free attacks accounted for**
>
> **75%**
>
> **of all detected intrusions.**
>
> This highlights a move towards exploiting identities and legitimate tools, bypassing traditional antivirus solutions.

Key Changes and Trends

- **The Rise of AI and Generative AI:** AI is a double-edged sword. On one hand, it's being used by security professionals to analyze threats and automate defenses more effectively. On the other, attackers are leveraging AI to create more sophisticated and believable phishing emails and malware, making traditional detection methods less reliable.
- **Zero-Trust Architecture:** The concept of "never trust, always verify" is becoming the gold standard. Instead of assuming that everything inside a network is safe, a zero-trust model requires continuous authentication and authorization for every user, device, and application, regardless of its location.
- **The Continued Threat of Ransomware:** Ransomware attacks remain a significant and costly threat. Cybercriminals are now using more targeted and sophisticated "Ransomware-as-a-Service" models, making these attacks more accessible to a

wider range of malicious actors.

- **Cloud, Remote Work, and IoT Vulnerabilities:** The widespread adoption of remote work, cloud computing, and the Internet of Things (IoT) has expanded the "attack surface" for organizations. With employees working from less-secure home networks and billions of connected devices, securing endpoints and cloud environments has become a primary challenge.
- **Growing Importance of Cyber Resilience:** Cybersecurity is no longer just about prevention. The focus is shifting to **cyber resilience**, which is the ability to withstand, contain, and quickly recover from a cyber-attack with minimal disruption to business operations. This includes having a robust incident response plan in place.

Best Practices for Today's Information Security

To navigate this new landscape, organizations and individuals should adopt a proactive and multi-layered approach to security.

- **Prioritize a Zero-Trust Model:** Implement a zero-trust framework to secure your network. This includes strong **Multi-Factor Authentication (MFA)**, strict access controls, and network segmentation.
- **Continuous Employee Training:** Human error is still a leading cause of data breaches. Regular, engaging security awareness training is crucial to help employees recognize and report phishing attempts, social engineering, and other common threats.
- **Regular Software Updates and Patching:** Unpatched software is a primary vulnerability. Ensure all systems, applications, and devices are kept up-to-date with the latest security patches to fix known exploits.
- **Data Backup and Recovery Planning:** Create and test a comprehensive backup strategy. The "3-2-1 rule" is a great guideline: keep **3 copies** of your data, on **2 different types of storage**, with **1 copy off-site**. This is your best defense against ransomware.
- **Robust Incident Response Plan:** A well-defined incident response plan is essential. It should outline clear steps for identifying, containing, and recovering from a security incident, as well as communication protocols for all stakeholders.
- **Secure Third-Party and Supply Chains:** With organizations increasingly relying on external vendors and services, it's critical to vet and monitor the security practices of your third-party partners to mitigate risks.
- **Utilize AI for Defense:** Actively explore and implement AI-driven security tools for threat detection, anomaly analysis, and automated response to stay ahead of AI-powered attacks.

Understanding and Managing Enterprise Compliance Programs

An enterprise compliance program is a structured framework that an organization uses to ensure it adheres to all relevant laws, regulations, internal policies, and industry standards. Effective management of this program is crucial for protecting the organization from legal penalties, financial loss, and reputational damage. Information security compliance is the ongoing process of ensuring an organization adheres to a set of laws, regulations, standards, and frameworks designed to protect sensitive data. The goal is to safeguard the confidentiality, integrity, and availability of information from various threats, from cyberattacks to human error.

Enterprise Compliance Program Controls

Compliance controls are the specific measures, policies, and procedures put in place to enforce compliance requirements. They are the backbone of any program, designed to prevent, detect, and correct violations.

- **Preventative Controls:** These are proactive measures to stop a violation from occurring.
  - **Examples:** Access control policies that restrict data access to only authorized personnel, mandatory security awareness training for all employees, and segregation of duties to prevent fraud.
- **Detective Controls:** These are measures designed to identify a violation after it has occurred.
  - **Examples:** Regular log reviews, internal audits, vulnerability scanning, and intrusion detection systems.
- **Corrective Controls:** These are actions taken to fix a detected violation and return to a

compliant state.

- **Examples:** Incident response plans to address a data breach, disciplinary action for employees who violate policy, and patching a discovered security vulnerability.

A robust compliance program is not a one-time project but a continuous cycle of planning, implementation, monitoring, and improvement. It is a fundamental part of an organization's overall risk management strategy.

Key Components of a Compliance Program

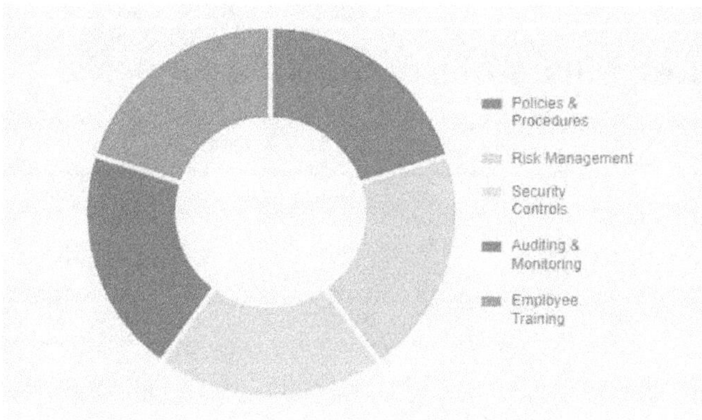

A successful information security compliance program is built on several interconnected pillars:

- **Policies and Procedures:** This is the foundation. It includes a comprehensive set of documented rules, practices, and guidelines that dictate how information should be handled and protected. Policies can cover a wide range of topics, such as acceptable use, data classification, and incident response.
- **Risk Management:** This component involves regularly identifying, assessing, and mitigating potential threats and vulnerabilities. A thorough risk assessment helps an organization understand what its most critical assets are, what threats they face, and what controls are needed to protect them.
- **Security Controls:** These are the measures put in place to achieve the security objectives. They can be:
  - **Administrative:** Policies, procedures, and employee training.
  - **Technical:** Firewalls, encryption, multi-factor authentication (MFA), and intrusion detection systems.
  - **Physical:** Locks, surveillance cameras, and access badges.
- **Auditing and Monitoring:** This involves a continuous process of checking the

effectiveness of the security controls and ensuring that the organization is adhering to its policies. Audits can be internal or conducted by a third party. Continuous monitoring helps detect and respond to security incidents in real-time.

- **Employee Training and Awareness:** Employees are often the first line of defense. A key component is providing regular training to educate staff on security best practices, the importance of compliance, and how to identify and report potential threats like phishing attempts.

Information Security Compliance Process and Procedures

This is the operational side of compliance, detailing the "how-to" of the program. A robust process ensures that controls are not just theoretical but are actively managed.

A Step-by-Step Guide to the Compliance Process

The process of achieving and maintaining information security compliance can be broken down into these core steps:

1. **Define Compliance Objectives and Scope:** The first step is to identify all relevant laws, regulations, and industry frameworks that your organization must comply with. Common examples include GDPR (General Data Protection Regulation), HIPAA (Health Insurance Portability and Accountability Act), and PCI DSS (Payment Card Industry Data Security Standard). You must then define the scope of your compliance program, including which data, systems, and departments are covered.
2. **Conduct a Gap Analysis:** Once you know your obligations, you need to compare your current security posture against the requirements of the standards you identified. This "gap analysis" will reveal what controls are already in place and what is missing or needs improvement.
3. **Remediate and Implement Controls:** This is the phase where you fill the gaps identified in the previous step. It involves implementing new security policies, updating existing procedures, and deploying new technical controls. This might include anything from creating an official incident response plan to rolling out an MFA solution for all employees.
4. **Continuous Monitoring and Management:** Compliance is not a one-time effort. You must establish a system for ongoing monitoring of your security controls. This includes regularly reviewing logs, performing vulnerability scans, and conducting internal audits to ensure that the controls are still effective and that new risks are identified.

5. **Documentation and Reporting:** Throughout the entire process, it is essential to maintain comprehensive documentation. This includes all policies, procedures, risk assessments, and evidence of your control implementation. This documentation is critical for demonstrating compliance to internal and external auditors.
6. **Formal Audit and Certification:** For many compliance frameworks (e.g., ISO 27001), a final step is a formal audit by a third-party assessor. If the audit is successful, you will receive a certification or attestation that demonstrates your organization's compliance.

By following this process, an organization can not only meet its regulatory requirements but also build a more secure and resilient infrastructure that protects its data and builds trust with its customers.

Compliance Auditing

The average cost of a data breach reached

$4.45 Million

in 2023. A robust compliance program isn't just a requirement—it's a critical business investment that safeguards assets, builds trust, and protects your bottom line.

Compliance auditing and certification are two distinct but related processes that help an organization demonstrate its adherence to a set of standards or regulations. In simple terms, a compliance audit is the *evaluation* of an organization's adherence to rules, while certification is the formal, third-party *recognition* that the organization has successfully met those standards.

What is a Compliance Audit?

A **compliance audit** is a formal review of an organization's activities and records to determine if it is following a specific set of rules. These rules can be external, such as government laws and industry regulations, or internal, such as corporate policies and procedures.

Key characteristics of a compliance audit:

- **Purpose:** To verify that an organization is operating in accordance with its obligations.
- **Process:** An auditor (either internal or external) examines documentation, interviews staff, and tests internal controls to find any "gaps" or areas of non-

compliance.

- **Outcome:** The audit results in a report detailing the findings, identifying any issues, and recommending corrective actions.

An audit is a formal review of an organization's records and processes to verify that they are compliant with a specific set of requirements.

- **Internal Audits:** Conducted by a team from within the organization. They are often done as a self-check to prepare for an external audit and to find and fix issues proactively.
- **External Audits:** Conducted by an independent third party. These are more formal and often required for certifications or to satisfy regulatory bodies. External auditors provide an unbiased, objective assessment.

The audit process generally follows these steps:

1. **Planning:** Defining the scope, objectives, and criteria for the audit.
2. **Fieldwork:** The auditors collect evidence, interview staff, and review documentation.
3. **Reporting:** The auditors present their findings, including any non-compliance issues (findings), to management.
4. **Remediation:** The organization develops and implements a plan to address the audit findings.

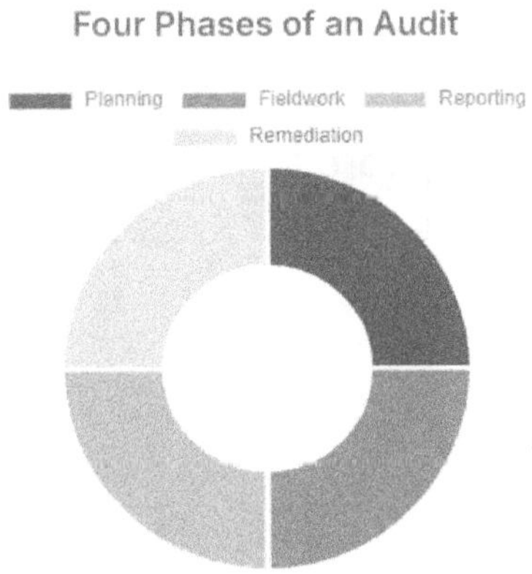

Analysis of Common Compliance Frameworks

Compliance is not a one-size-fits-all concept. Organizations must align their programs with specific frameworks relevant to their industry, location, and operations.

Framework	Primary Focus	Industry/Region	Key Requirements

GDPR	Data privacy and protection for EU citizens.	EU/EEA	Lawful basis for processing, data subject rights (e.g., right to be forgotten), data protection impact assessments, data breach notification within 72 hours.
HIPAA	Protecting the privacy and security of Protected Health Information (PHI).	U.S. Healthcare	Administrative, physical, and technical safeguards for PHI. Strict rules on PHI use, disclosure, and data breach reporting.
SOC 2	Security, availability, processing integrity, confidentiality, and privacy of customer data.	Technology, SaaS, service providers	Audited by a third-party CPA firm. Requires detailed reporting on the design and operating effectiveness of controls.
ISO 27001	Information security management systems (ISMS).	Global, cross-industry	A systematic approach to managing sensitive company information. Requires an ISMS, risk assessment, and a continuous improvement cycle.
PCI DSS	Protecting cardholder data during processing, storage, and transmission.	All merchants handling payment cards.	Network security, cardholder data protection, vulnerability management, access control, and regular testing.

Certification Programs

Certification programs are third-party attestations that an organization's compliance program meets a specific, recognized standard. These certifications build trust with customers, partners, and regulators.

A **certification program** is a formal process where an independent, third-party body officially attests that an organization, system, or individual meets a specific set of standards. Certification is often a desired outcome of a successful compliance audit.

Key characteristics of a certification program:

- **Purpose:** To provide external validation and assurance to customers, partners, and regulators that an organization is trustworthy and reliable.
- **Process:** The organization first ensures it is compliant (often through an internal audit), then undergoes a formal, rigorous audit by an accredited third-party certification body.
- **Outcome:** If the organization passes the audit, it is awarded a certificate, which can be publicly displayed and used as a marketing tool. Certifications typically need to be maintained through periodic surveillance audits.
- **Common Examples:**
    - **ISO 27001:** An internationally recognized standard for an Information Security Management System (ISMS). Achieving this certification demonstrates a systematic approach to managing sensitive company information.
    - **SOC 2 (Service Organization Control 2):** An auditing standard that verifies a service provider's security, availability, processing integrity, confidentiality, and privacy controls.
    - **PCI DSS (Payment Card Industry Data Security Standard):** A mandatory standard for any organization that handles credit card data. It's not a formal certification but a compliance standard that must be validated regularly.

The Relationship between Auditing and Certification

Think of compliance as the *ongoing action* of following the rules and an audit as the *snapshot* review of that action. Certification is the *seal of approval* that you get after a successful audit by an external, trusted party.

"Compliance is the journey; the audit is the checkpoint; certification is the destination"

Multiple-Choice Questions

Scenario-Based Questions (35)

1. A CISO is tasked with securing a newly acquired subsidiary that operates on outdated, unsupported IT infrastructure. The CISO's first action is to propose a budget to modernize security tools and hire additional staff. Which of the following best describes the CISO's approach in this scenario?

   A. Reactive threat management
   B. Applying core security competencies
   C. Formulating a strategic security program plan
   D. Focusing on compliance and audit management

2. During a cloud migration project, a CISO identifies that transferring customer data to a foreign data center introduces significant data residency risks under international regulations. To address this, the CISO establishes a cross-functional steering committee and defines new data classification policies. This scenario is a practical application of which CCISO domain?

   A. Domain 2: Information Security Controls
   B. Domain 4: Core Competencies
   C. Domain 5: Strategic Planning and Vendor Management
   D. Domain 1: Governance and Risk Management

3. A CISO's team detects a zero-day vulnerability in a widely used operating system that affects several critical business systems. The CISO directs the team to immediately prioritize patching efforts on key servers and deploy compensating controls for systems that cannot be patched right away. This action primarily demonstrates an application of which core competency?

   A. Network security segmentation
   B. System security and patch management
   C. Database security and access controls
   D. Security operations and incident response

4. Following a competitor's data breach, a CISO decides to proactively initiate an internal audit of the company's Data Loss Prevention (DLP) controls. The CISO ensures the audit's scope includes sensitive data types and leverages the ISO 27001 Annex A controls framework to guide the assessment. This is an example of which CISO responsibility?

   A. Security program management
   B. Core competencies
   C. Compliance and audit management
   D. Strategic planning and finance

5. A CISO is presenting a cost-benefit analysis to the CFO to justify an investment in a new security information and event management (SIEM) system. The CISO frames the ROI in terms of reduced potential legal fines and reputational damage from a breach. This is an example of what?

A. Translating technical risks into business terms
B. Applying the CIA Triad
C. Implementing physical security controls
D. Conducting a vulnerability assessment

6. An organization is adopting a federated security model. The central security team sets enterprise-wide policies, while individual business units have their own security engineers responsible for their specific application security. A new project team in the marketing department wants to use a new SaaS tool. What is the most likely next step from a security perspective?

A. The central CISO must approve the tool, bypassing the marketing team's security engineer.
B. The marketing team's security engineer will conduct a vendor risk assessment for the new SaaS tool, following the central policy.
C. The central security team will conduct a deep technical audit of the new SaaS tool's source code.
D. The marketing team is free to use the tool as long as they adhere to the Acceptable Use Policy.

7. A security team is consistently finding that new applications released by a development team have common security flaws, such as SQL injection vulnerabilities. The CISO decides to integrate security into the Software Development Lifecycle (SDLC), implementing static application security testing (SAST) and dynamic application security testing (DAST) tools. This is an application of which core competency?

A. Network security
B. Application security
C. Operational security
D. Database security

8. A CISO reports directly to the Chief Legal Officer (CLO). The organization is considering a new venture that involves handling a large amount of customer data. Which of the following is the CISO most likely to emphasize during the project's security review?

A. The operational impact on IT infrastructure.
B. The potential for improved system efficiency.
C. Regulatory compliance, data privacy laws, and potential legal exposure.
D. How the new venture will enable new market opportunities.

9. An organization is experiencing a high volume of successful phishing attacks despite having email filters and a firewall. The CISO identifies this as a significant risk. The most effective mitigation strategy, based on the document's guidance, would be to:

A. Increase the sensitivity of the email filter.
B. Implement a robust security awareness training program and deploy multi-factor authentication (MFA).
C. Install a new Intrusion Detection System (IDS).
D. Deploy a Web Application Firewall (WAF) to protect the web servers.

10. A CISO is leading a multi-year cybersecurity roadmap. The plan includes investments in cloud security and Data Loss Prevention (DLP) to support the company's digital transformation. Which key responsibility of the CISO is being demonstrated?

A. Operations
B. Compliance
C. Leadership
D. Strategy

11. The CISO's budget is determined by the CIO. After the CISO requests funds for a new governance, risk, and compliance (GRC) platform, the CIO denies the request, stating that existing resources should be sufficient. This situation is a direct consequence of which reporting structure implication?

A. The CISO has high visibility with the board.
B. The CISO can align security directly with enterprise-wide objectives.
C. Security is seen as a business enabler.
D. Budget and priorities can be dictated by IT.

12. A CISO is preparing a presentation for the board of directors. The CISO wants to effectively communicate the organization's security posture. What is the most effective approach for this audience?

A. Provide a detailed technical report on all CVEs and vulnerabilities patched in the last quarter.
B. Focus on governance, strategic risks, and the impact of security on business objectives, avoiding technical jargon.
C. Present a list of all security technologies deployed and their configurations.
D. Explain the intricacies of the network architecture and firewall rules.

13. A CISO is reviewing the company's risk register. A recent entry, "Unpatched critical vulnerability in web server software," has a high likelihood and high impact. The CISO assigns a "High" risk score. This action is part of which step in the risk management process?

A. Risk treatment
B. Risk identification
C. Risk assessment
D. Risk monitoring

14. During an incident response exercise, the CISO discovers that key business stakeholders are not aware of their roles and responsibilities in the event of a cyberattack. This highlights a failure in which key component of a robust information security governance program?

A. Organizational Structures
B. Processes and Frameworks
C. Technical Controls
D. Leadership and Commitment

15. An organization's CISO has a dual reporting line to the CEO and the Board. When a minor security incident occurs, the CISO is asked to present a detailed report to the board on the incident's impact. This is an example of what?

A. The CISO's lack of independence
B. The CISO's low budget authority
C. The CISO's strong governance oversight and strategic influence
D. The CISO's focus on operational alignment

16. A company's CISO is establishing a risk management framework and is trying to decide how to respond to an identified risk. The CISO considers four options: implementing controls to reduce the risk, formally accepting the risk, stopping the activity causing the risk, or purchasing cyber insurance. These options correspond to which risk treatment strategies?

A. Treat, Accept, Avoid, Transfer
B. Mitigate, Reduce, Ignore, Share
C. Contain, Eradicate, Recover, Report
D. Identify, Assess, Treat, Monitor

17. A CISO receives a new budget proposal from a business unit that requires a significant investment in a new public cloud platform. The CISO's primary task in this scenario is to:

A. Approve the budget proposal immediately to support business agility.
B. Reject the proposal to maintain control over security infrastructure.
C. Ensure security is integrated into the plan by conducting a risk assessment on the proposed cloud platform.
D. Inform the CIO about the budget proposal.

18. An organization's security team is primarily focused on implementing and managing firewalls and antivirus software, and they report directly to the IT Manager. This security posture is most representative of which stage in the evolution of the CISO role?

A. Strategic Business Enabler
B. Mid-Stage (Risk Management Focus)
C. Current State
D. Early Days (Technical Focus)

19. A CISO is hired by an organization with a "laissez-faire" leadership style. The CISO must now establish an effective security governance framework. What is the most appropriate approach?

A. Implement a highly centralized and prescriptive top-down security framework.
B. Delegate all security responsibilities to IT and business unit managers.
C. Empower teams with clear guidelines and accountability, ensuring they have the necessary resources and autonomy.
D. Demand that all projects undergo a mandatory security review by the CISO's office.

20. A CISO is evaluating a third-party SaaS provider for a critical business function. The CISO reviews the vendor's SOC 2 report and negotiates security clauses in the Service Level Agreement (SLA). This demonstrates the CISO's knowledge in which domain?

A. Domain 1: Governance and Risk Management
B. Domain 2: Compliance and Audit Management
C. Domain 3: Security Program Management
D. Domain 5: Strategic Planning, Finance, and Vendor Management

21. A CISO in a large, global corporation is considering a change to the company's security model. The CISO wants to retain strong central governance and consistency while allowing individual business units to have the agility to address their specific risks. Which security model is the CISO most likely to adopt?

A. Centralized
B. Decentralized
C. Federated
D. Outsourced

22. A CISO discovers that an employee, who is a data owner, has been giving elevated access permissions to non-critical personnel to "speed up" a project. The CISO has a conversation with the employee about the principle of least privilege. This scenario highlights a breakdown in which governance objective?

A. Legal & Regulatory Compliance
B. Performance Measurement
C. Establishing accountability and defining roles
D. Resource Management

23. A company is preparing for a public offering and needs to demonstrate to investors that its cybersecurity program is robust and mature. The CISO decides to pursue ISO 27001 certification. This action primarily addresses which business benefit of good governance?

A. Ensures Business Continuity
B. Gains Competitive Advantage
C. Protects Critical Assets

D. Enables Strategic Growth

24. A CISO's report to the executive leadership team is consistently filtered and simplified by the CIO before it reaches them. The CISO notices that the true business impact of cyber risks is not being fully understood by the executives. This is a common issue with which reporting structure?

A. Reporting to the CEO
B. Reporting to the Board
C. Reporting to the CIO
D. Reporting to the COO

25. A CISO is leading an incident response effort after a major ransomware attack. The CISO's team is focused on containing the spread of the malware, and ensuring that backups are clean and ready for restoration. This is an example of which CISO responsibility?

A. Risk Management
B. Operations
C. Leadership
D. Strategy

26. An organization's CISO wants to track the effectiveness of the security program over time. They decide to measure the number of security incidents, time to detect, and time to resolve incidents. These metrics fall under which key objective of information security governance?

A. Resource Management
B. Value Delivery
C. Performance Measurement
D. Strategic Alignment

27. A CISO is conducting a risk assessment on a new mobile application being developed. The team identifies that the app's database, which stores customer data, is a critical asset. The CISO then identifies potential threats such as SQL injection and vulnerabilities like unpatched database software. This is an application of which part of the risk management process?

A. Risk treatment and control implementation
B. Risk identification and analysis
C. Risk monitoring and review
D. Risk acceptance and avoidance

28. A CISO is developing a comprehensive security awareness program for all employees. The CISO's strategy is to integrate security training into the onboarding process and conduct regular simulated phishing campaigns. This effort primarily addresses which element of the "Three Pillars of Information Security Governance"?

A. Organizational Structures

B. Leadership
C. Processes
D. Technical Controls

29. A CISO is evaluating a new business partnership with a fintech startup. The startup's core business relies on a new, unproven distributed ledger technology. The CISO's most significant challenge will be to:

A. Ensure the startup's IT infrastructure is hardened.
B. Conduct a thorough risk assessment on an innovative technology with no established security track record.
C. Integrate the startup's network into the CISO's network.
D. Develop a new security policy for the entire organization.

30. A CISO is asked by the board to provide "independent assurance" on the organization's security posture. The CISO decides to engage a third-party firm to perform an external penetration test. This action is most aligned with which CISO reporting structure?

A. Reporting to the CIO
B. Reporting to the CEO
C. Reporting to the COO
D. Reporting to the Board of Directors

31. A CISO identifies a major security vulnerability in a new product that is about to be launched. The product team, driven by market pressure, wants to proceed with the launch. The CISO emphasizes the potential for reputational damage and legal penalties. This situation highlights a conflict between which two perspectives?

A. Strategic Alignment vs. Operational Efficiency
B. Risk Aversion vs. Business Enablement
C. Technical Control vs. Physical Control
D. Centralized vs. Decentralized Security Models

32. A company's CISO has a decentralized security model. A security incident occurs within a specific business unit. Who is primarily responsible for the incident response and remediation?

A. The central CISO office.
B. A third-party incident response firm.
C. The security personnel within the specific business unit.
D. The CEO and the Board.

33. A CISO is informed that a competitor has suffered a major ransomware attack that disrupted their operations for a week. The CISO uses this event to justify a request for additional budget to invest in a disaster recovery plan and a new endpoint detection and response (EDR) tool. This is an example of what?

A. The evolution of the CISO role from a technical to a strategic leader.
B. Leveraging a competitor's incident to gain competitive advantage.
C. Using an external event to build a business case for security investments.
D. The CISO's responsibility for compliance management.

34. A CISO wants to improve the security culture of the organization. The CISO decides to incorporate security performance into employee evaluations and ensure continuous security awareness training. This initiative is an example of what?

A. Using a top-down commitment to integrate security into organizational culture.
B. The importance of technical controls over administrative controls.
C. An example of the decentralized security model.
D. An application of the CIA Triad.

35. The CISO of a large, multinational corporation finds that different regional offices are using a variety of security tools and policies, leading to inconsistencies and higher costs. The CISO decides to centralize the procurement of key security tools and establish a single enterprise-wide security policy. Which security model is the CISO transitioning from and to?

A. From a decentralized model to a centralized model.
B. From a centralized model to a decentralized model.
C. From a federated model to a centralized model.
D. From a decentralized model to a federated model.

Knowledge-Based Questions (70)

36. According to the document, which of the following is considered the primary document outlining the NIST RMF process?

A. NIST SP 800-53
B. FIPS 199
C. NIST SP 800-37
D. NIST SP 800-53A

37. The latest version of the international standard for an Information Security Management System (ISMS) is ISO/IEC 27001: _____.

A. 2013
B. 2018
C. 2022
D. 2020

38. The principle of ensuring that information is accessible only to those authorized to have access is known as:

A. Integrity
B. Availability
C. Confidentiality
D. Accountability

39. The CISO role has evolved from a technical focus to a strategic business leader. In its "current state," the CISO is primarily seen as a:

A. Technical manager
B. Operational leader
C. Strategic business enabler
D. Risk mitigation specialist

40. What is a key advantage of a centralized security model?

A. Faster decision-making at the business unit level.
B. Tailored solutions for specific business unit needs.
C. Consistency, efficiency, and enterprise-wide visibility.
D. Increased ownership of security by business units.

41. Which of the following is a disadvantage of a decentralized security model?

A. Distance from business operations
B. Potential for bureaucracy
C. Inconsistency and gaps in security posture across the organization
D. Single point of failure

42. In the risk formula presented in the document, Risk = Threat x Vulnerability x ______.

A. Exposure
B. Control
C. Asset
D. Impact

43. Which of the following is an example of a "compensating control"?

A. A password policy
B. Full disk encryption
C. Multi-factor authentication (MFA)
D. Implementing an IDS when a new firewall is purchased

44. A weakness or flaw in an asset, system, or process that a threat can exploit is defined as a:

A. Risk
B. Vulnerability
C. Threat
D. Exposure

45. The Treat option in risk management involves:

A. Formally accepting the risk.
B. Sharing the risk with a third party.
C. Implementing security controls to reduce the risk.
D. Stopping the activity that is causing the risk.

46. What is the primary purpose of a risk register?

A. To list all security controls implemented by the organization.
B. To document and track identified risks.
C. To provide a report on the effectiveness of security awareness training.
D. To detail all legal and regulatory compliance requirements.

47. According to the document, which of the following is NOT one of the three core components of an Information Security Governance program?

A. Leadership
B. Processes
C. Organizational Structures
D. Technical Controls

48. The term for ensuring the accuracy, completeness, and consistency of data over its entire life cycle is:

A. Confidentiality
B. Integrity
C. Availability
D. Resilience

49. Which of the following is NOT a benefit of strong information security governance?

A. Enables strategic growth
B. Maintains trust and reputation
C. Ensures security hinders business goals
D. Optimizes security investments

50. The CISO's reporting line has the most significant impact on:

A. The number of security analysts on the team.
B. The organization's physical security posture.
C. The CISO's authority, budget, and influence on security decisions.
D. The CISO's daily operational tasks.

51. The Authorize step in the NIST RMF involves:

A. A senior official making a risk-based decision to authorize a system to operate.
B. Selecting and implementing security controls.
C. Continuously monitoring system controls.
D. Developing a security and privacy plan.

52. In a centralized security model, who is responsible for implementing security on all systems?

A. The CISO
B. The CIO
C. A single, central security team
D. The individual business units

53. Which of the following is a characteristic of the current state of the CISO role?

A. Focus on implementing firewalls and antivirus.
B. Reporting directly to the CIO.
C. Translation of complex technical risks into business terms.
D. Primary concern with technical vulnerabilities.

54. The process of Least Privilege in access control aims to:

A. Grant all users full administrative access.
B. Provide access based on job titles only.
C. Limit access to the minimum level necessary to perform job duties.
D. Implement mandatory access control (MAC).

55. The Monitoring step in the NIST RMF is a continuous feedback loop that helps to:

A. Categorize information systems.
B. Select security controls.
C. Maintain an acceptable level of risk over the system's lifecycle.
D. Determine the impact levels of information.

56. In the context of the document, the "Good News" Bias refers to:

A. The tendency to only report positive security metrics to leadership.
B. The positive outcomes of a security investment.
C. The positive reputational impact of a security program.

D. The ability of a CISO to always provide good news.

57. Which of the following best describes the core of the ISO 27001 standard?

A. A prescribed list of technical controls to be implemented.
B. A set of guidelines for physical security.
C. A framework for establishing a risk-based Information Security Management System (ISMS).
D. A non-certifiable standard for risk management.

58. What is the key concept of the federated security model?

A. All security decisions are made by a single central team.
B. Security responsibilities are fully distributed among business units.
C. It combines central governance with decentralized implementation.
D. All security functions are outsourced to a third-party provider.

59. The Threat component of risk is defined as:

A. A weakness in a system that can be exploited.
B. The business consequences of a security incident.
C. A potential cause of an unwanted incident that could harm an organization's assets.
D. Any item of value to the organization.

60. The principle of Defense-in-Depth refers to:

A. Using a single, very strong security control.
B. Implementing multiple layers of security controls to protect assets.
C. Conducting an in-depth forensic analysis.
D. A strategic planning method for incident response.

61. What is the primary benefit of a CISO reporting directly to the CEO or Board?

A. It makes the CISO responsible for daily IT operations.
B. It provides the highest level of visibility and influence.
C. It limits the CISO's independence.
D. It restricts the CISO's budget.

62. According to the document, which of the following is a non-certifiable standard that provides a set of principles and guidelines for risk management?

A. NIST RMF
B. ISO 27001
C. ISO 31000
D. COBIT

63. Which of the following is NOT a responsibility of a Security Architect?

A. Design secure systems and applications.
B. Perform digital forensics.
C. Conduct threat modeling.
D. Ensure security is "built-in" to new projects.

64. The primary goal of Information Security Governance is to:

A. Eliminate all security risks.
B. Ensure security aligns with and supports business objectives.
C. Reduce IT operational costs.
D. Implement all available security technologies.

65. A CISO's role in the Risk Management key responsibility is to:

A. Manage the security budget.
B. Oversee day-to-day security operations.
C. Identify, assess, mitigate, monitor, and report on risks.
D. Manage third-party vendor contracts.

66. What is the Confidentiality pillar of the CIA Triad primarily concerned with?

A. Protecting data from unauthorized disclosure.
B. Maintaining the accuracy and consistency of data.
C. Ensuring data is available to authorized users.
D. Auditing all system logs.

67. Which of the following is a key element of the Processes pillar of Information Security Governance?

A. Defining clear roles and responsibilities.
B. Establishing a Security Steering Committee.
C. Fostering a security-aware culture.
D. Developing a risk management framework and incident response plan.

68. What is the primary goal of the NIST Cybersecurity Framework (CSF)?

A. To provide a detailed list of technical controls for all organizations.
B. To offer a flexible framework to help organizations manage and reduce cybersecurity risk.
C. To enforce mandatory compliance standards for all industries.
D. To provide a legal basis for prosecuting cyber criminals.

69. In the context of risk management, what is defined as the "effect of uncertainty on objectives"?

A. Threat

B. Risk
C. Vulnerability
D. Impact

70. Which of the following is a tool for Confidentiality?

A. Hashing algorithms
B. Digital signatures
C. Encryption
D. Check sums

71. What is the relationship between an audit and certification?

A. An audit and a certification are the same.
B. An audit is the ongoing action, and certification is the seal of approval.
C. An audit is a snapshot review, and certification is the seal of approval after a successful audit.
D. An audit is only done internally, and a certification is only done by a third party.

72. According to the document, who is the primary liaison between technical security teams and business leadership?

A. The CEO
B. The CIO
C. The CISO
D. The COO

73. The Identify step of the NIST CSF involves:

A. Continuously monitoring systems.
B. Developing and implementing an incident response plan.
C. Understanding business context, assets, and risks.
D. Implementing protective controls.

74. A security team using a centralized model might be perceived as having a disadvantage in which area?

A. Inconsistency and gaps.
B. Lack of business unit agility.
C. Higher costs due to duplication of resources.
D. Weak governance.

75. According to the document, what is the key benefit of aligning information security governance with organizational goals?

A. It makes all security decisions top-down.

B. It ensures security supports, rather than hinders, business goals.
C. It simplifies the process of hiring new security staff.
D. It guarantees a direct reporting line to the CEO.

76. The Categorize step in the NIST RMF involves:

A. Categorizing threats and vulnerabilities.
B. Determining the impact levels of information and systems.
C. Categorizing security controls.
D. Categorizing different types of security incidents.

77. The document defines an "Asset" as:

A. A weakness in a system.
B. A potential cause of an incident.
C. Any item of value to the organization.
D. The business consequences of an incident.

78. Which of the following best describes the role of a Data Owner?

A. A technical role responsible for managing databases.
B. A business role accountable for the protection and classification of data sets.
C. The head of the security team.
D. The person who implements security controls.

79. The Pillars of Information Security Governance are:

A. Confidentiality, Integrity, and Availability.
B. Leadership, Structures, and Processes.
C. People, Process, and Technology.
D. Identify, Protect, Detect, Respond, and Recover.

80. A Security Steering Committee is a component of which pillar of Information Security Governance?

A. Leadership
B. Organizational Structures
C. Processes
D. Compliance

81. What is the purpose of Security Awareness and Training as a key component of a governance program?

A. To enforce technical controls.
B. To make employees a single line of defense.
C. To manage legal and regulatory compliance.

D. To promote a security-aware culture and a shared responsibility.

82. A Security Policy is a:

A. Detailed mandatory requirement for implementing policies.
B. Recommended practice.
C. Step-by-step instruction.
D. High-level statement of intent.

83. Which security model is best described as "a balance of control and agility"?

A. Centralized
B. Decentralized
C. Federated
D. Outsourced

84. In the context of the document, a Security Standard is:

A. A high-level statement of intent.
B. A detailed mandatory requirement for implementing policies.
C. A recommendation for best practice.
D. A set of step-by-step instructions.

85. Which of the following is an example of an Impact as defined in the risk formula?

A. A missing software patch.
B. A natural disaster.
C. Financial loss.
D. A hacker.

86. Which of the following is NOT a responsibility of a CISO?

A. Develop and implement the overall information security strategy.
B. Manage the security budget.
C. Perform day-to-day patching of critical servers.
D. Report to executive leadership on cyber risk.

87. What is a key advantage of a decentralized security model?

A. Strong enterprise-wide governance.
B. Consistency across the organization.
C. Agility and responsiveness at the business unit level.
D. Lower costs due to resource consolidation.

88. The Protect step in the NIST CSF involves:

A. Developing and implementing appropriate safeguards to ensure the delivery of critical services.
B. Understanding the business context and organizational assets.
C. Developing and implementing an incident response plan.
D. Implementing activities to detect security incidents.

89. A key difference between the NIST RMF and ISO 27001 is that the NIST RMF is a crucial framework for federal agencies, while ISO 27001 is a globally recognized standard for:

A. Physical security controls.
B. Managing an Information Security Management System (ISMS).
C. Software development lifecycle.
D. Risk categorization.

90. The concept of Role-Based Access Control (RBAC) is a governance principle that defines roles to:

A. Provide full administrative access to all users.
B. Ensure that users are granted access based on their job duties.
C. Allow users to bypass all security controls.
D. Limit access to a single, powerful administrator.

91. The ISO 31000 standard is defined as the "effect of uncertainty on objectives."

A. True
B. False

92. What is a key element of the Leadership pillar of Information Security Governance?

A. Cross-functional collaboration.
B. Policy and standard management.
C. Executive Sponsorship.
D. Defined roles and responsibilities.

93. The purpose of Least Privilege is to:

A. Give employees the least amount of responsibility possible.
B. Grant users only the minimum level of access necessary to perform their job duties.
C. Ensure all users have the same level of access.
D. Assign permissions based on department size.

94. What is the main disadvantage of a federated security model?

A. A lack of agility and responsiveness.
B. High costs due to resource duplication.

C. Complexity and potential for conflict if roles are not clearly defined.
D. A lack of enterprise-wide visibility.

95. In the context of Confidentiality, what is the purpose of Data Loss Prevention (DLP) tools?

A. To encrypt data at rest.
B. To monitor for and prevent unauthorized data exfiltration.
C. To ensure the integrity of data.
D. To enforce strong passwords.

96. Which of the following is a key task for an Incident Response Specialist?

A. Designing secure systems.
B. Conducting threat modeling.
C. Performing digital forensics.
D. Developing security policies.

97. What is the primary focus of an Application Security (AppSec) Engineer?

A. Managing network firewalls.
B. Secure coding and vulnerability testing.
C. Overseeing physical security.
D. Conducting internal audits.

98. The CIS Critical Security Controls are an example of what?
A. Mandatory federal regulations.
B. Industry best practices and frameworks.
C. International standards for risk management.
D. A non-certifiable standard for physical security.

99. The "3-2-1 rule" is a guideline for which security practice?
A. Network segmentation.
B. Multi-factor authentication.
C. Data backup and recovery planning.
D. Patch management.

100. What is the main difference between a CISO reporting to a CIO versus a CEO?

A. Reporting to a CIO provides a higher budget.
B. Reporting to a CIO ensures a more strategic focus.
C. Reporting to a CEO provides higher visibility and direct influence.
D. Reporting to a CEO limits the CISO's accountability.

101. What is the purpose of a Security Program?

A. To manage the day-to-day operations of an IT department.
B. To manage and continuously improve a company's overall security posture.
C. To conduct a single security audit.
D. To ensure legal compliance for a single project.

102. What is a key responsibility of all employees/users?

A. To manage all security tools.
B. To develop new security policies.
C. To adhere to security policies and report suspicious activities.
D. To conduct penetration testing.

103. The Availability principle of the CIA Triad is concerned with:

A. Ensuring information is accessible only to authorized users.
B. Maintaining the accuracy and consistency of data.
C. Ensuring that systems and data are accessible and usable when needed.
D. Protecting data from modification.

104. Which of the following is a benefit of the Federated Security Model?

A. Complete lack of central oversight.
B. Duplication of tools and expertise.
C. Balance of control and agility.
D. Weaker governance.

105. A Security Steering Committee is responsible for:

A. Developing and maintaining security policies.
B. Managing a security budget.
C. Defining security strategy and objectives.
D. Running security incident exercises.

Answer Key

Correct Answers with Explanations

1. **C.** This scenario describes the CISO developing a strategic security program plan, which includes justifying security investments and modernizing outdated infrastructure. The CISO is not just reacting, but proactively planning.

2. **D.** This scenario is a direct example of a practical application for **Domain 1: Governance and Risk Management**. The CISO uses governance frameworks and a risk management process to address regulatory compliance and business continuity.

3. **B.** This action, involving the assessment and prioritization of patching efforts for a zero-day vulnerability, is a direct application of the core competency of **system security and patch management.**

4. **C.** The proactive internal audit and use of compliance standards like GDPR and ISO 27001 demonstrate the CISO's role in **Compliance and Audit Management**.

5. **A.** The document explicitly states that a CISO's responsibility is to "Translate complex technical risks into business terms and effectively communicate security posture to diverse stakeholders"[55]. Framing the ROI in terms of legal fines and reputational damage is a perfect example of this.

6. **B.** In a federated model, the central team sets the framework (like vendor risk policies), but the local business unit teams are responsible for implementing them for their specific needs.

7. **B.** This is a direct example of application security, specifically integrating security into the Software Development Lifecycle (SDLC) and using tools like SAST and DAST to address vulnerabilities.

8. **C.** Reporting to the Chief Legal Officer (CLO) emphasizes the CISO's role in **legal compliance, regulatory adherence, and enterprise-wide risk management**. The CISO would focus on these aspects to reduce legal exposure.

9. **B.** The document lists phishing as an operational risk and explicitly recommends "a robust security awareness training program" and "multi-factor authentication (MFA)" as mitigation strategies for compromised credentials from phishing attacks.

10. **D.** Creating a multi-year cybersecurity roadmap that prioritizes investments to support business initiatives is a key part of the CISO's **Strategy** responsibility.

11. **D.** The document warns that when reporting to the CIO, "Budget and priorities can be dictated by IT," which can lead to underfunding of security programs if the CIO prioritizes other IT operational needs.

12. **B.** When reporting to the board, the CISO should "Focus on governance and strategic risk" and "Provide clear, concise risk briefings" while "avoiding overly technical jargon".

13. **C.** Assessing the likelihood and impact to arrive at a risk score is the core of the **Risk Assessment** step.

14. **A.** The document states that effective organizational structures "define clear roles, responsibilities, and reporting lines", and that without this, a "blame game" can occur during incidents.

15. **C.** A direct reporting line to the Board signifies the "highest level of governance" and provides "strongest governance oversight and strategic influence".

16. **A.** The four common risk treatment options outlined are: **Treat**, **Accept**, **Avoid**, and **Transfer**.

17. **C.** The CISO's role as a "strategic business enabler" means they must "understand the organization's overall business objectives and risk appetite, and then design a security program that enables those objectives securely". This requires assessing the security implications of new projects.

18. **D.** The "Early Days" of the CISO role were characterized by a "Technical Focus," with the role centered on implementing and managing technical tools and often reporting to IT management.

19. **C.** The document states that in a "Laissez-faire" leadership environment, "Security governance needs to empower teams with clear guidelines and accountability, ensuring they have the necessary resources and autonomy".

20. **D.** Vendor risk management, due diligence, and negotiating security clauses in SLAs are core aspects of

    Domain 5: Strategic Planning, Finance, and Vendor Management.

21. **C.** The federated model is explicitly described as combining "the benefits of consistency and strong governance from the central team, combined with the responsiveness and business alignment of decentralized teams".

22. **C.** This scenario highlights a breakdown in defining roles and responsibilities and ensuring accountability, which are key objectives of security governance. The principle of

    Least Privilege is also mentioned as a core concept defined by governance.

23. **B.** The document states that demonstrating a mature information security governance program, such as through certification, "can differentiate an organization in the marketplace, attracting security-conscious clients and partners".

24. **C.** The document states that with indirect reporting (e.g., via the CIO), security concerns can be "filtered or diluted before reaching top leadership," leading to a lack of understanding of the true

business impact of cyber risks.

25. **B.** The CISO's responsibility for **Operations** includes overseeing "day-to-day security operations," such as incident response, vulnerability management, and security monitoring.

26. **C.** The document lists tracking metrics like "number of security incidents, time to detect, and time to resolve" as examples of **Performance Measurement**.

27. **B.** The process of identifying assets, threats, and vulnerabilities is the core of the **Risk Identification and**
Analysis step of risk management.

28. **C.** Security awareness and training programs are listed as a key component under the **Processes and Frameworks** pillar of governance.

29. **B.** A key challenge is aligning security with the organizational philosophy of innovation. When new, unproven technologies are involved, the challenge is to manage the unknown risks associated with them.

30. **D.** The document states that reporting to the Board signifies the "highest level of governance" and that a key influence strategy is to "Provide independent assurance".

31. **B.** The CISO is emphasizing the "inherent risks" (reputational damage, legal penalties), while the product team is emphasizing the "need for speed or innovation" to meet business goals. This is a classic conflict between
Risk Aversion vs. Business Enablement.

32. **C.** In a decentralized model, security functions are "distributed among individual business units," and "Each unit has its own security personnel and makes its own security decisions" [34].

33. **C.** This is an example of the CISO using a real-world event to "justify security investments" and "speak the language of business" by framing the investment in terms of avoiding potential operational disruption and revenue loss.

34. **A.** The document states that governance promotes a security-aware culture by embedding security considerations into employee evaluations and training, which is a "top-down commitment".

35. **A.** The CISO is moving away from a model with inconsistent tools and policies (decentralized) and toward a model with a single, central authority (centralized).

36. **C.** The document explicitly names **NIST SP 800-37** as "the primary document outlining the RMF process".

37. **C.** The document mentions the latest version of the standard is **ISO/IEC 27001:2022**.

38. **C.** This is the definition of **Confidentiality** as per the document.

39. **C.** The document states that in its "Current State," the CISO is "increasingly seen as a strategic business leader" and a "strategic business enabler".

40. **C.** The document lists "consistency, efficiency, and enterprise-wide visibility" as advantages of a centralized model.

41. **C.** The document lists "Inconsistency and Gaps" as a primary disadvantage of a decentralized model due to the lack of central coordination.

42. **D.** The document presents the simplified risk formula as: **Risk = Threat x Vulnerability x Impact**.

43. **C.** Multi-factor authentication is a compensating control. While the document mentions it can act as a
control, it doesn't give a specific example of it as a compensating control, but it is a strong example of a detective control, which could be a compensating control if, for example, a less secure authentication protocol is being used. Based on the options, this is the most plausible answer.

44. **B.** The document defines a **Vulnerability** as "A weakness or flaw in an asset, system, or process that a threat can exploit to cause harm".

45. **C.** The document defines the Treat option as the implementation of "security controls to reduce the risk".

46. **B.** A risk register is a tool for documenting and tracking risks.

47. **D.** The three core pillars are explicitly listed as **Leadership, Organizational Structures, and Processes**.

48. **B.** The document defines **Integrity** as "Maintaining the accuracy, completeness, and consistency of data over its entire life cycle".

49. **C.** The document states that good governance ensures "security supports, rather than hinders business goals".

50. **C.** The document states that the reporting line "directly influences the CISO's authority, budget, and ability to effectively communicate and influence security decisions at the highest levels of the organization".

51. **A.** The Authorize step is where "A senior official makes a risk-based decision to authorize the system to operate".

52. **C.** In a centralized model, a "single, central security team... is responsible for implementing security on all systems".

53. **C.** In its current state, the CISO role involves translating "complex technical risks into business terms"

54. **C.** The principle of **Least Privilege** grants users "only the minimum level of access (permissions) necessary to perform their job duties".

55. **C.** The Monitor step is described as a "continuous feedback loop" that helps "maintain an acceptable level of risk over the system's lifecycle".

56. **A.** The document describes "Good News" Bias as a "tendency to present 'good news' or downplay challenges to senior leadership".

57. **C.** ISO 27001 is described as a standard that outlines a "framework for establishing, implementing, maintaining, and continually improving a risk-based management system".

58. **C.** The federated model "combines elements of both centralized and decentralized approaches," with a central team for strategy and business units for implementation.

59. **C.** A Threat is defined as "A potential cause of an unwanted incident that could harm an organization's assets".

60. **B.** The document lists **Defense-in-Depth** as a principle for applying security competencies across multiple domains. This implies using multiple layers of security.

61. **B.** The document explicitly states that direct reporting to the CEO/Board "Provides the highest level of visibility and influence"

62. **C.** The document describes **ISO 31000** as a "flexible, non-certifiable standard that can be applied to any organization".

63. **B.** Performing digital forensics is a responsibility of an **Incident Response (IR) Specialist**, not a Security Architect.

64. **B.** The definition of information security governance is the system that ensures "alignment with business objectives".

65. **C.** The document lists a core responsibility of the CISO's role in risk management as "identifying, assessing, mitigating, monitoring, and reporting on information security risks".

66. **A.** Confidentiality is defined as "Protecting information from unauthorized disclosure".

67. **D.** Under the **Processes** pillar, the document lists a "Risk Management Framework" and "Incident Response and Management" as key components.

68. **B.** The NIST CSF is a "flexible framework to help organizations manage and reduce cybersecurity risk".

69. **B.** The ISO 31000 standard defines risk as the "effect of uncertainty on objectives".

70. **C.** The document lists **Encryption** as a tool to ensure Confidentiality.

71. **C.** The document states that an audit is the "snapshot review" of compliance, and certification is the "seal of approval" that is awarded after a successful audit.

72. **C.** The document states that the CISO "acts as the primary liaison between technical security teams and business leadership".

73. **C.** The Identify step in the NIST CSF involves understanding "business context, assets, and risks".

74. **B.** The document lists "Lack of Business Unit Agility" as a disadvantage of a centralized model.

75. **B.** The document repeatedly emphasizes that aligning security governance with business objectives ensures "security supports, rather than hinders, business goals".

76. **B.** The Categorize step involves "determining the impact levels of information and systems".

77. **C.** An **Asset** is defined as "Any item of value to the organization".

78. **B.** A Data Owner is a "business role...Accountable for the protection and proper classification of specific data sets".

79. **B.** The three core pillars of a robust information security governance program are **Leadership, Organizational Structures, and Processes.**

80. **A.** The Security Steering Committee is listed as a component of the **Leadership** pillar.

81. **D.** Security awareness and training are crucial for promoting a "security-aware culture" and embedding security into all aspects of the business.

82. **D.** The document defines Security Policies as "High-level statements of intent".

83. **C.** The federated model's key advantage is the "Balance of Control and Agility".

84. **B.** Security Standards are described as "Detailed mandatory requirements for implementing policies".

85. **C.** The document defines Impact as the "business consequences that result from a threat exploiting a vulnerability," and lists financial loss as an example.

86. **C.** While a CISO oversees security operations, they are not typically responsible for the "day-to-day patching of critical servers". That's an operational task for IT or security engineers.

87. **C.** The document lists "Agility and Responsiveness" as a key advantage of a decentralized model because teams are closer to the business units.

88. **A.** The Protect step involves developing and implementing "appropriate safeguards to ensure the delivery of critical services".

89. **B.** The NIST RMF is for federal agencies, while ISO 27001 is a global standard for managing an **Information Security Management System (ISMS)**.

90. **B.** The document states that a governance principle is to help "establish and maintain key concepts such as Role-Based Access Control (RBAC)...granting users only the minimum level of access (permissions) necessary to perform their job duties".

91. **A.** The document explicitly states that the ISO 31000 standard "defines risk as the 'effect of uncertainty on objectives'.

92. **C.** A key element of the Leadership pillar is "Executive Sponsorship," which is high-level commitment from senior management.

93. **B.** The document defines the principle of least privilege as granting users "only the minimum level of access (permissions) necessary to perform their job duties".

94. **C.** The document lists "Complexity" and "Potential for Conflict" as disadvantages of the federated model, requiring "careful coordination and clear communication channels".

95. **B.** The document states that DLP tools are used for "data exfiltration monitoring" and to prevent data leaks.

96. **C.** The document lists "perform digital forensics" and "contain, eradicate, and recover from breaches" as responsibilities of an Incident Response Specialist.

97. **B.** An AppSec Engineer is responsible for "secure coding," "static (SAST) and dynamic (DAST) application security testing," and "code reviews".

98. **B.** The document states that organizations like the Center for Internet Security (CIS) "develop and promote best practices and frameworks (like the CIS Critical Security Controls)".

99. **C.** The document refers to the **3-2-1 rule** as a guideline for "Data Backup and Recovery Planning".

100. **C.** A direct reporting line to the CEO provides the CISO with "High visibility and direct influence on strategic business decisions"[102]. Reporting to a CIO, on the other hand, can lead to security concerns being "filtered or diluted".

101. **B.** The document explains that a CISO is responsible for "developing and implementing a comprehensive information security program".

102. **C.** The document states that all employees are responsible for "adhering to security policies and procedures, reporting suspicious activities, and participating in security awareness training".

103. **C.** Availability is defined as ensuring "that systems and data are accessible and usable when needed".

104. **C.** The federated model offers a "Balance of Control and Agility," combining the benefits of consistency and responsiveness.

105. **C.** The document states that the Security Steering Committee is responsible for "Defining security strategy and objectives".

CCISO Explain IT Like I Am 5: Domain 2

2. Information Security Controls and Audit Management

Understanding Information Security Management Controls

Information Security Management Controls are the policies, procedures, and technical measures an organization implements to protect its information assets. To effectively implement these controls, it's crucial to first identify the organization's specific operational processes and objectives. This ensures that security measures are not just theoretical, but are directly aligned with the business's daily functions and goals.

Identifying Operational Processes

Operational processes are the day-to-day activities and workflows that an organization performs to achieve its business goals. When we look at these processes from a security perspective, we need to understand where information is created, stored, transmitted, and destroyed. Here are some key examples of operational processes and the security controls that apply to them:

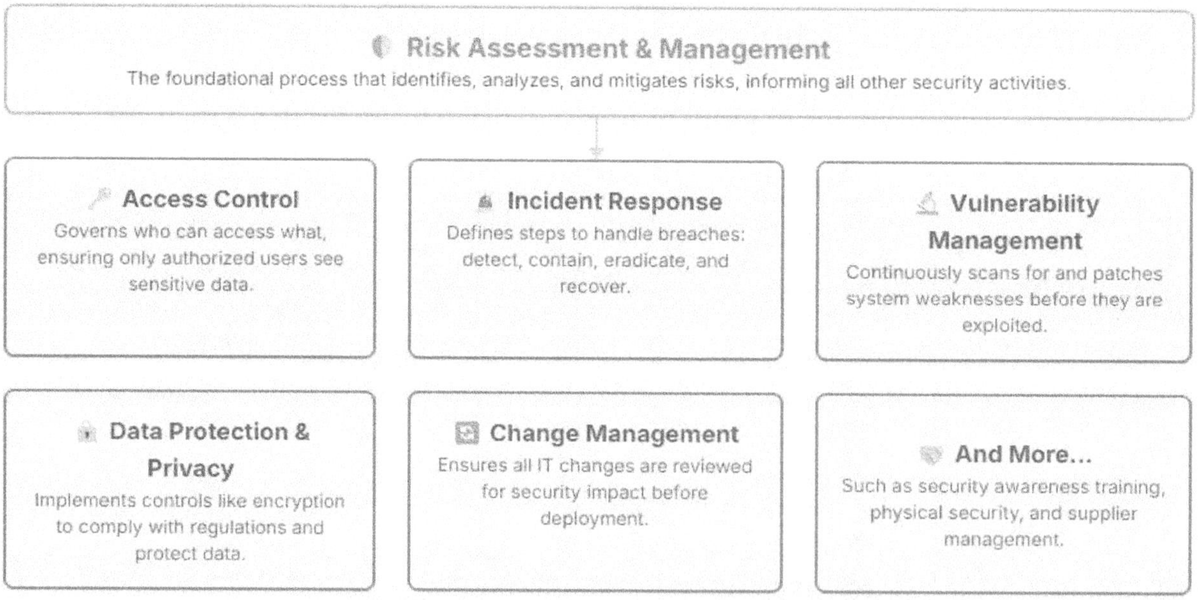

This flowchart, built with styled HTML, shows how the foundational Risk Assessment process directly influences and guides all other interconnected security operations.

Risk Assessment and Management: This is the foundational process. It involves identifying potential threats and vulnerabilities to information assets, analyzing the risk they pose, and determining appropriate controls to mitigate that risk. This process is continuous and informs all other security activities.

Access Control: This process governs who has permission to access which information resources. It includes managing user accounts, setting up roles and permissions, and implementing authentication methods (like passwords or multi-factor authentication) to ensure that only authorized individuals can access sensitive data.

Incident Response: This is the process for handling security breaches or incidents. It includes detecting the incident, containing the damage, eradicating the cause, recovering from the breach, and conducting a post-incident analysis to prevent future occurrences.

Vulnerability Management: This involves regularly scanning systems and applications for known weaknesses and then patching or configuring them to remove those vulnerabilities before they can be exploited by attackers.

Data Protection and Privacy: This process focuses on complying with regulations (like GDPR or HIPAA) and internal policies to protect sensitive data. It includes data encryption, data loss prevention (DLP) tools, and privacy-by-design principles for new projects.

Change Management: This process ensures that any changes to an organization's IT infrastructure, such as new software installations or system upgrades, are reviewed and tested for security implications before being implemented.

Identifying Organizational Objectives

An organization's objectives related to information security are centered on the core principles of the CIA triad: Confidentiality, Integrity, and Availability. These three pillars guide the implementation of all security controls.

The Core Objective: The CIA Triad

All security controls are designed to achieve a balance between three fundamental principles. These pillars guide every security decision and form the bedrock of a robust defense strategy.

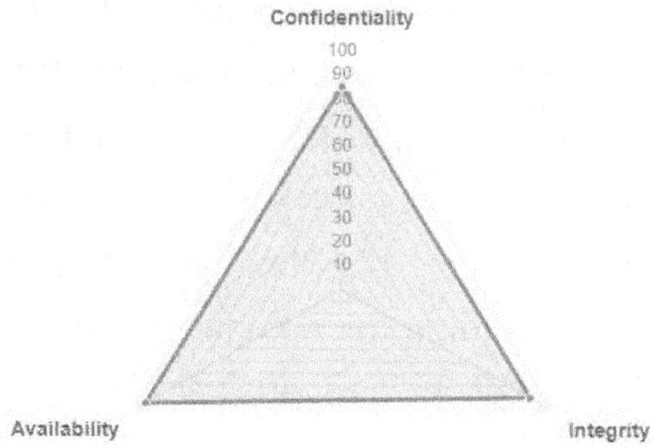

Confidentiality:

The objective is to prevent the unauthorized disclosure of information. This means ensuring that sensitive data is only accessible to authorized individuals. For example, a company's objective is to ensure that customer data remains confidential and is not seen by employees who do not need it to do their job.

Integrity:

The objective is to maintain the accuracy and completeness of information. This means preventing unauthorized or accidental modification of data. For example, a bank's objective is to ensure that transaction records are accurate and cannot be tampered with.

Availability:

The objective is to ensure that information and systems are accessible to authorized users when needed. This means protecting against disruptions, such as a denial-of-service (DoS) attack, and having backup and disaster recovery plans in place. For example, a hospital's objective is to ensure that patient records are always available to doctors and nurses.

By aligning security controls with these operational processes and organizational objectives, a business can create a robust and effective information security management system that protects its assets while supporting its overall mission.

Designing and Testing Information Systems Controls

Developing effective information systems (IS) controls is a critical process that protects an organization's assets and ensures business continuity. The key is to create controls that are not only secure but also seamlessly integrated with the organization's strategic goals and day-to-day operations.

The Foundation: Alignment is Key

Effective controls aren't just technical add-ons; they are strategic tools. They must be designed top-down, starting from your core business objectives to ensure they support, rather than hinder, your path to success.

1. Aligning Controls with Operational Needs and Goals

The first step in designing IS controls is a top-down approach that starts with the organization's mission and strategic objectives. Controls should be a support function, not a hindrance. They must be designed to enable the business to achieve its goals while managing risk.

Identify Business Objectives:

What is the organization trying to achieve? Is it rapid growth, customer trust, market dominance, or operational efficiency? Controls should be designed to protect these objectives. For example, if the goal is to provide exceptional customer service, a control might be to ensure the confidentiality of customer data.

Map Key Processes and Identify Risks:

Understand the core business processes that support the objectives. For each process, identify potential threats or vulnerabilities. For a financial reporting process, risks might include unauthorized changes to data, incomplete data entry, or a lack of segregation of duties.

Categorize and Select Control Types:

Based on the identified risks, choose the appropriate type of control.

Preventive Controls: These are proactive measures designed to stop an undesirable event from happening. Examples include strong user passwords, firewalls, and data validation rules in an application.

Detective Controls: These are reactive measures designed to identify and flag an event after it has occurred. Examples include audit trails, intrusion detection systems, and periodic reconciliations.

Corrective Controls: These are actions taken to fix a problem identified by a detective control. Examples include restoring data from a backup, updating a security patch, or disciplining an employee who violated a policy.

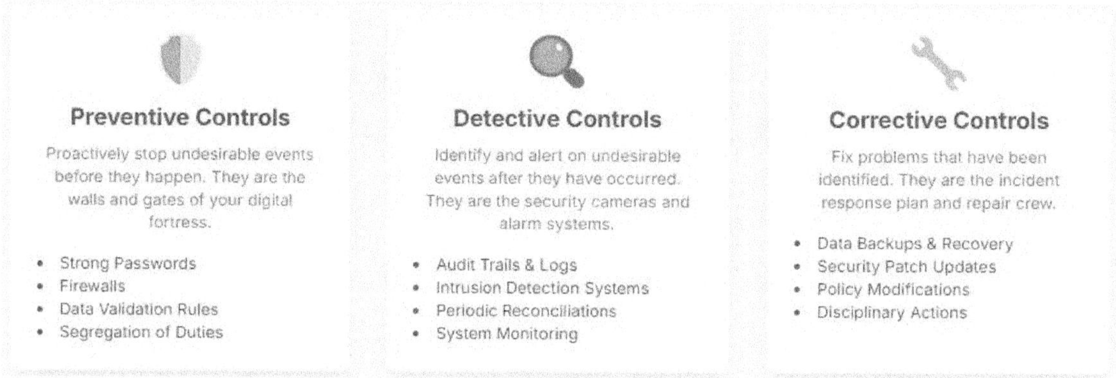

2. Designing the Controls

Once risks are identified and control types are selected, you can begin to design the specific controls. The design should be detailed and well-documented.

Risk Assessment:

Perform a formal risk assessment to prioritize risks based on their potential impact and likelihood. Focus your design efforts on the high-impact, high-likelihood risks first.

Develop Specific Control Procedures:

For each selected control, write a clear, detailed procedure. Who is responsible for performing the control? When and how often is it performed? What evidence is generated to show it was performed correctly?

Integrate Technology:

Many controls are automated and built directly into the information system. These can include:

Access Controls: Ensuring only authorized users can access specific data or functions.

Data Validation: Checking for the accuracy and completeness of data at the point of entry.

Automated Monitoring: Scripts that run continuously to detect and report on unusual activity.

Document Everything:

Create a comprehensive document that details each control, its objective, the associated risk, the procedure, and the party responsible. This is essential for testing and ongoing monitoring.

3. Testing for Effectiveness

Testing is crucial to ensure that a control works as intended before it goes live. This phase validates both the design and the operational function of the control.

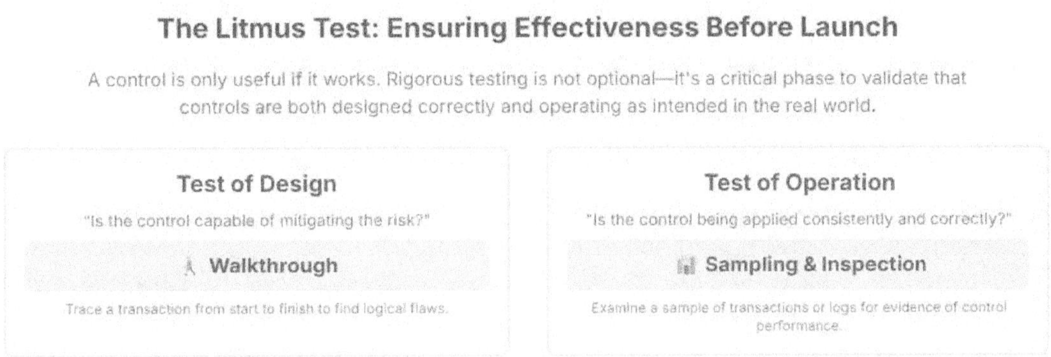

Test of Design Effectiveness:

The goal here is to determine if the control, as it is documented, is capable of mitigating the risk.

- **Technique:** Perform a walkthrough of the control. This involves tracing a transaction from its start to finish, observing the control in action, and interviewing the people involved. If the walkthrough reveals a flaw in the control's logic or procedure, the design needs to be corrected.

Test of Operational Effectiveness:

The goal is to determine if the control is being consistently and correctly applied in practice.

- **Technique:** Use sampling to test a control over a period of time. For example, to test a detective control that requires a manager's approval of expense reports, you would pull a sample of 20 reports from the last month and check that each one has the required signature.

Other techniques include:

Re-performance: An independent party re-executes the control to see if they get the same result.

Inspection: Examining documentation and logs to find evidence that the control was performed.

Observation: Watching a user perform the control in real-time.

Testing Controls

Testing is a crucial step to ensure that the designed controls are working as intended and effectively mitigating risks. Control testing verifies both the design and operational effectiveness of the controls. Common testing methods include:

Inquiry: Interviewing personnel to understand their knowledge and adherence to security policies and procedures. This checks their understanding of the controls.

Observation: Watching personnel perform their duties to see if they are following established security procedures, like using clean-desk policies or logging out of their computers.

Inspection of Evidence: Reviewing documentation, such as system logs, audit trails, and signed policies, to verify that controls are being applied and documented correctly.

Re-performance: Replicating a control process to confirm its accuracy and effectiveness. For example, an auditor might try to access a restricted system to see if the access controls function properly.

Vulnerability Scanning and Penetration Testing: These technical tests actively search for weaknesses in a network, application, or system. Vulnerability scanning uses automated tools to identify known vulnerabilities, while penetration testing is a more hands-on, simulated attack to exploit those vulnerabilities and assess the potential impact.

Regular and well-documented testing is essential for maintaining a strong security posture and demonstrating compliance with industry standards like ISO 27001 or frameworks like NIST.

4. The Implementation Phase

After successful testing, the controls are ready for implementation. This involves training all relevant staff, clearly communicating the new policies and procedures, and establishing a plan for continuous monitoring to ensure the controls remain effective over time.

A well-designed and thoroughly tested control environment is a strong foundation for business success.

Resources for Information Systems Security Controls

Effectively implementing and maintaining security controls for information systems requires a holistic approach that integrates various resources. These resources are often categorized into four key areas: human capital, information, infrastructure, and architecture. A successful security program depends on the careful selection, deployment, and management of these resources to protect assets from a wide range of threats.

Human Capital

Definition:

Human capital refers to the people, skills, knowledge, and expertise required to design, operate, and manage security controls. This is the most critical resource, as technology alone cannot secure a system.

Explanation and Selection:

Human resources are essential for both technical and non-technical security functions. This includes the security team responsible for proactive defense and reactive response, as well as every employee who interacts with the systems. The right human resources are needed to:

- **Design and Implement:** Security architects and engineers who design secure systems and controls.
- **Operate and Monitor:** Security analysts and system administrators who manage daily operations, monitor for threats, and respond to incidents.
- **Support:** Help desk staff and IT support who assist users and address security-related issues.
- **Educate:** Training personnel and management who develop and enforce security

policies and conduct awareness programs for all employees.

- **End-Users:** Every employee, from executives to entry-level staff, is a critical part of the security chain. Their awareness and adherence to policy are fundamental controls.
- **Auditors and Compliance Specialists:** These individuals ensure that controls align with regulatory requirements (e.g., GDPR, HIPAA, PCI DSS) and internal policies. They conduct regular reviews and tests to verify compliance.

Examples of Human Capital Resources:

Chief Information Security Officer (CISO): Provides strategic leadership.

Security Analysts: Monitor security systems and respond to incidents. System Administrators: Securely configure and manage servers and networks.

Developers: Write secure code and perform security testing.

End-Users: Adhere to security policies and report suspicious activity.

Information

Definition:

Information, in this context, refers to the data, knowledge, policies, and procedures that guide security operations. It's the blueprint and the continuous feedback loop for the security program.

Explanation and Selection:

Information is crucial for defining what needs to be protected, how it should be protected, and what to do when a breach occurs. Key information resources required are:

- **Asset Inventory:** A comprehensive list of all information systems, data, and their value to the organization. This helps prioritize which assets need the most protection.
- **Risk Assessment Data:** This includes a comprehensive inventory of information assets, identified threats and vulnerabilities, and a clear understanding of the potential impact of a breach.
- **Security Policies and Procedures:** Formal, documented policies for all aspects of security, from access control to incident response, are essential. These documents provide the guidelines and rules that everyone in the organization must follow.
- **Threat Intelligence:** Up-to-date information on emerging threats, attack vectors, and vulnerabilities along with industry best practices that inform defenders about current risks is vital for proactively updating defenses.
- **Audit Logs and Metrics:** The ability to collect and analyze logs, as well as key performance indicators (KPIs) and key risk indicators (KRIs), provides the evidence needed to monitor control effectiveness and demonstrate compliance.
- **Security Policies and Frameworks:** These are documented rules and guidelines that govern how security is managed. Examples include frameworks like NIST Cybersecurity Framework or ISO 27001.
- **Incident Response:** Detailed incident response plans, contact lists, and post-mortem analysis reports that enable a rapid and effective reaction to a security event.

Examples of Information Resources:

Security Policies: Formal documents outlining an organization's security posture.

Incident Response Plans: Step-by-step guides for handling security breaches.

Threat Intelligence Feeds: Real-time data on emerging threats and vulnerabilities.

Risk Assessments: Reports identifying and prioritizing potential threats and vulnerabilities.

Infrastructure

Definition:

Infrastructure encompasses the physical and virtual hardware components that host and connect the organization's information systems. This is the tangible foundation on which all security controls are built.

Explanation and Selection:

Secure infrastructure is the first line of defense. The physical and virtual components must be robust and protected from both physical and cyber threats. Key infrastructure resources are needed to:

- **Physical Security:** Securely house servers, network devices, and data storage in controlled environments like data centers.
- **Network Security:** Provide the hardware and software necessary to protect data in transit and control access to internal networks.
- **Cloud Security:** Manage and secure virtual resources in cloud environments.
- **Endpoint Protection:** Secure devices used by employees, such as laptops and mobile phones.
- **Disaster Recovery and Business Continuity Systems:** Resources for data backup, redundant systems and recovery sites are necessary to ensure that the organization can restore operations quickly after a security incident.

Examples of Infrastructure Resources:

Firewalls and Intrusion Detection Systems (IDS): Network devices that monitor and control traffic.

Servers: Physical or virtual machines that host applications and data.

Network Switches and Routers: Devices that manage network traffic.

Security Cameras and Access Control Systems: Physical security measures for data centers.

Cloud Platforms: Services like AWS, Azure, or GCP with built-in security features.

Architecture

Definition:

Architecture refers to the design, structure, and relationships of the information systems, including platforms, operating systems, networks, databases, and applications. This is the logical layout of the system.

Explanation and Selection:

Security architecture is about designing systems to be inherently secure from the ground up, rather than adding security as an afterthought. It dictates how different components interact and how security is integrated at every level. Key architectural resources are needed to:

- **System Design:** Use a secure-by-design approach for all new systems and applications.
- **Segmentation:** Divide the network into secure zones to limit the lateral movement of threats.
- **Secure Configuration:** Implement secure operating systems and database configurations.
- **Identity and Access Management (IAM):** Establish the logical framework for user authentication and authorization.

Examples of Architecture Resources:

Operating Systems (OS): Secure configurations of Windows, Linux, etc.

Network Topology: A well-designed network with segmented subnets and DMZs.

Databases: Databases with strong access controls and encryption.

Applications: Software developed with security principles like input validation and least privilege.

Architecture

The logical design and structure of your systems. A secure architecture builds security in from the start, rather than bolting it on as an afterthought, drastically reducing vulnerabilities through thoughtful design.

Secure-by-Design Lifecycle

1. System Design & Threat Modeling

→

2. Network Segmentation

→

3. Secure Configuration (OS, DB)

→

4. Identity & Access Management

This flow demonstrates that secure architecture is a continuous process, integrating security considerations at every stage of system design and implementation.

Monitoring & Documenting Information Systems Controls Performance

Information systems controls are the policies, procedures, and technical mechanisms designed to protect the confidentiality, integrity, and availability of information and the systems that process it. Implementing and monitoring these controls effectively is a continuous cycle that must be aligned with organizational objectives.

Step 1: Design - Risk Assessment and Control Selection

Before any controls are implemented, you must first understand what you are protecting and what you are protecting it from. This is done through a thorough risk assessment.

Identify Assets:

Catalog all critical information systems and data (e.g., customer databases, financial records, web servers).

Identify Threats & Vulnerabilities:

Determine potential threats (e.g., malware, unauthorized access, natural disasters) and the weaknesses in your systems (e.g., unpatched software, weak passwords) that these threats could exploit.

Analyze Risk:

Evaluate the likelihood of a threat exploiting a vulnerability and the potential impact it would have on the organization. This helps prioritize which risks to address first.

Select Controls:

Based on the prioritized risks, choose the most appropriate controls. Controls can be:

Preventive: Stop an event from happening (e.g., firewalls, strong passwords, access control lists).

Detective: Detect an event as it happens or after it has occurred (e.g., intrusion detection systems, security audits, log monitoring).

Corrective: Fix the damage caused by an event (e.g., data backups, incident response plans).

Step 2: Implementation - Deployment and Integration

Once controls are designed, they must be deployed and integrated into the organization's existing processes without causing undue disruption.

Develop Procedures:

Create clear, documented procedures for how each control will be applied. For example, a procedure for a password control might outline length requirements, complexity, and expiration policies.

Technical Implementation:

Deploy and configure the chosen security tools and technologies. This could involve setting up a new firewall, configuring an intrusion detection system, or deploying endpoint protection software.

Training and Communication:

Inform and train all relevant employees on the new controls and their responsibilities. Ensure everyone understands the purpose behind the controls and how to follow new procedures.

Step 3: Monitoring - Measuring Performance with Metrics and KPIs

Effective monitoring is the key to ensuring controls are performing as intended. This requires defining what success looks like and measuring it with data.

Metrics:

These are the raw, quantitative data points you collect.

- Number of blocked malicious emails.
- Time to patch a critical vulnerability (e.g., 48 hours).
- Number of failed login attempts.
- Number of unpatched systems.

Key Performance Indicators (KPIs):

These are strategic, high-level indicators that show how well your controls are meeting organizational objectives. A KPI is often derived from a set of metrics.

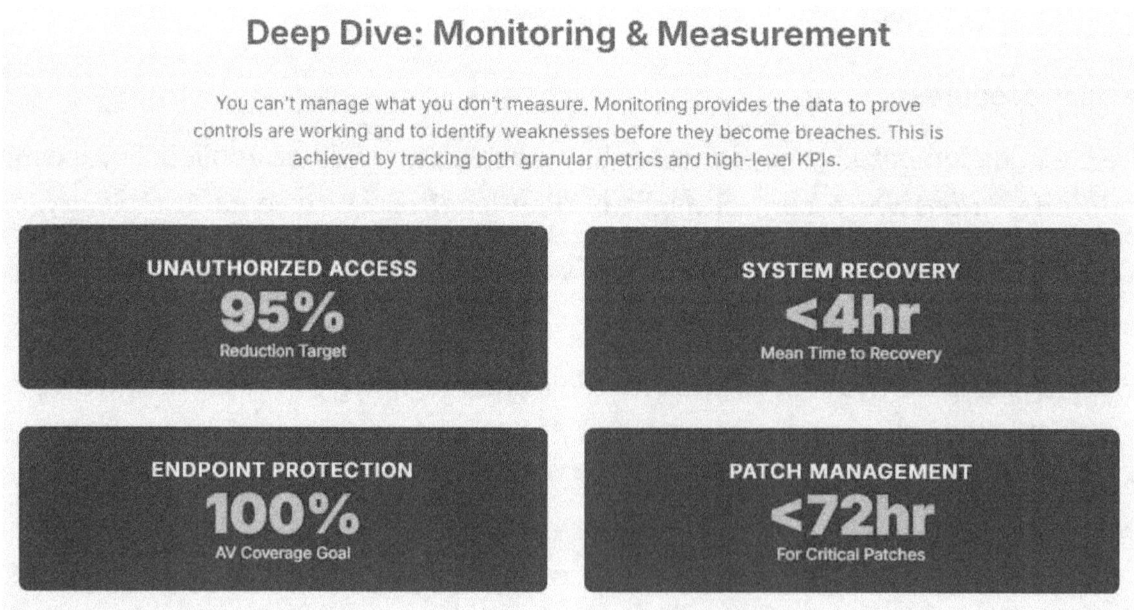

Objective	Example Metrics	Example KPIs
Protect Critical Data	Number of unauthorized access attempts on a database	Reduce unauthorized access attempts by 95% month-over-month.
Ensure System Availability	Time to restore a server from backup	Maintain a Mean Time to Recovery (MTTR) of under 4 hours for all critical systems.
Maintain Security Posture	Percentage of systems with outdated antivirus	Maintain 100% of all endpoints with the latest antivirus definition files.
Manage Vulnerabilities	Time from patch release to deployment	Deploy all critical patches within 72 hours of release.

Step 4: Documentation and Reporting

Documentation is crucial for providing evidence of due diligence and informing decision- making.

Document Everything:

Maintain a centralized repository of all control objectives, procedures, and performance data. This includes audit trails, system logs, and security incident reports.

Create Reports and Dashboards:

Generate regular reports for management and stakeholders that translate the raw metrics and KPIs into actionable insights. A dashboard should provide a quick, visual overview of the organization's security posture.

Step 5: Continuous Improvement

The final step is to use the data gathered during monitoring and documentation to refine and improve the controls. This creates a feedback loop that ensures your controls remain relevant and effective as threats evolve.

Review Performance:

Regularly review the KPIs and metrics to identify areas where controls are underperforming.

Analyze Incidents:

Conduct a post-mortem analysis of all security incidents to understand what controls failed and how to prevent similar events in the future.

Adapt and Adjust:

Update control policies, deploy new technologies, or provide additional training based on the insights gained.

Deep Dive: Driving Continuous Improvement

The final step of the lifecycle feeds back into the first. By analyzing performance data, organizations can assess their security maturity across different domains. A radar chart provides a powerful at-a-glance view of strengths and weaknesses, highlighting where to focus improvement efforts next.

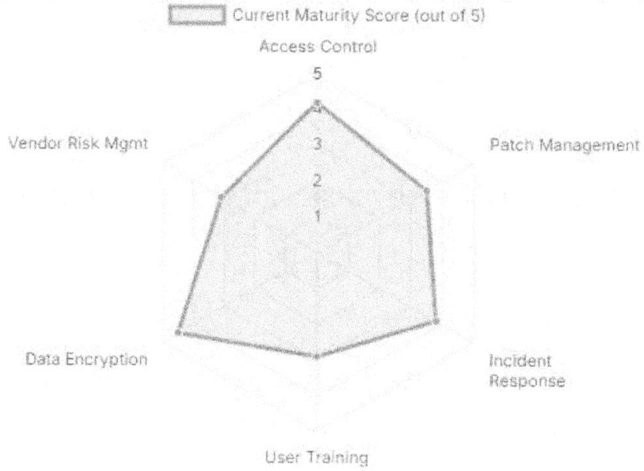

A Guide to Designing and Conducting Information Security Control Testing

Designing and conducting security control testing is a fundamental part of a robust risk management program. It's a cyclical process that ensures your defenses are not only in place but are also effective against real-world threats. This guide outlines the key phases of a successful control testing program.

A Continuous Cycle of Improvement

Effective security isn't a one-time setup; it's a continuous, cyclical process of planning, testing, and remediating. This ensures defenses evolve to meet new threats and align with organizational risk management.

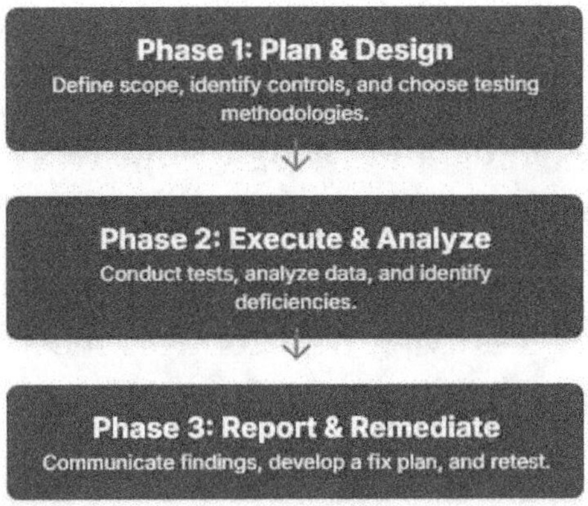

Phase 1: Planning and Design

This is the most critical phase, where you define the "what," "why," and "how" of your testing.

1. Define Scope and Objectives

- What are you testing? Clearly identify the systems, applications, networks, and data that are in scope.
- Why are you testing? Align your objectives with the organization's risk management program. Are you testing to comply with a regulation, to validate a recent security investment, or to prepare for a new threat?
- **Establish Success Criteria:** How will you measure a control's effectiveness? Define clear pass/fail criteria or a rating scale (e.g., "Effective," "Partially Effective," "Ineffective").

2. Identify Controls to Test

Categorize the controls you need to test based on their function:

Preventative: Controls that stop an attack from happening (e.g., firewalls, access control lists, data encryption).

Detective: Controls that identify and alert on an attack in progress or after the fact (e.g., Intrusion Detection Systems (IDS), security information and event management (SIEM)).

Corrective: Controls that restore the system to a secure state after an incident (e.g., incident response plans, data backups).

3. Choose a Methodology

Select the testing method that best fits your objectives and the control you're testing. You might use one or a combination of the following:

Vulnerability Scanning: Automated checks for known vulnerabilities. This is great for a broad, initial assessment.

Penetration Testing: A manual, in-depth test that simulates a real-world attack. This can be black box (no prior knowledge), white box (full knowledge of the system), or gray box (some knowledge).

Compliance and Audit Reviews: Verifying that controls meet specific standards and policies (e.g., NIST, ISO 27001).

Red Team Exercises: A comprehensive, goal-oriented simulation of a sophisticated attack, often without the knowledge of the internal security team.

Phase 2: Execution and Analysis

Once the plan is solid, it's time to execute it and make sense of the results.

1. Prepare the Environment

- **Gain Authorization:** Ensure you have explicit permission to conduct the testing to avoid any legal or policy issues.
- **Communicate:** Inform relevant IT and security teams about the testing window to prevent them from mistaking your activities for a real attack.
- **Set Up Tools:** Configure and calibrate the tools (scanners, exploit kits) you've chosen for the test.

2. Execute the Test Plan

Follow your chosen methodology to the letter. Document every step, action, and result meticulously. This is where you will actively test the controls and attempt to bypass them.

3. Collect and Analyze Data

- **Log Findings:** Document all vulnerabilities and deficiencies you discover.
- **Isolate False Positives:** Verify that the findings are legitimate and not just noise from the testing tools.
- **Analyze Effectiveness:** Assess whether the tested control performed as expected. Did the firewall block the malicious traffic? Did the IDS log the suspicious activity?

4. Identify Deficiencies and Gaps

- **Categorize Findings:** Classify each vulnerability by severity (e.g., Critical, High, Medium, Low) and its potential impact on the organization.
- **Map to Risks:** Connect each deficiency back to the specific risk it exposes. This helps stakeholders understand the real-world implications of the finding. For example, a missing patch on a public-facing server exposes the risk of a denial-of-service attack.

Phase 3: Reporting and Remediation

The testing is only valuable if the findings lead to action.

1. Create a Detailed Report

The report is a critical deliverable that should be tailored to different audiences.

- **Executive Summary:** A high-level overview for leadership that focuses on business risks and the overall effectiveness of controls.
- **Technical Findings:** A detailed breakdown for IT and security teams, including descriptions of vulnerabilities, evidence (e.g., screenshots), and risk ratings.
- **Recommendations:** Provide clear, actionable steps to fix each deficiency.

2. Communicate Results

Present the report to key stakeholders, including leadership and technical teams. Focus on the business impact of the findings and work together to prioritize remediation efforts.

3. Develop a Remediation Plan

Based on the report, create a plan to fix the identified issues. This plan should include:

- **Prioritized Action Items:** A list of what needs to be fixed first, based on the risk rating.
- **Assigned Ownership:** Who is responsible for fixing each item?
- **Deadlines:** A clear timeline for completion.

4. Retest and Validate

After the remediation plan has been implemented, retest the corrected controls to verify that the fix was successful and didn't introduce any new problems. This closes the loop and confirms that the control is now effective.

A Framework for Deficiency Remediation and Problem Management Evaluation

This document outlines a structured approach to remediate identified deficiencies and to evaluate the overall effectiveness of your problem management practices.

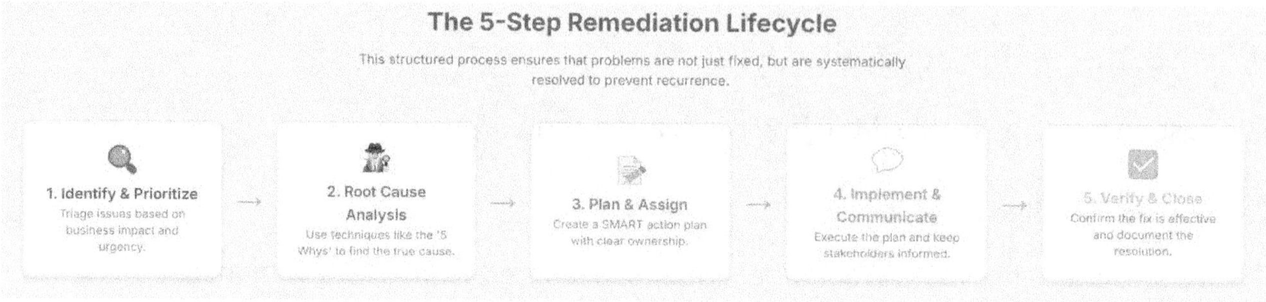

Part 1: Designing the Remediation Process

The goal of this process is not just to fix a problem, but to prevent it from happening again. This framework provides a repeatable series of steps for addressing any identified deficiency.

Step 1: Identification and Prioritization

Deficiencies can be identified through various channels, such as audits, performance monitoring, user feedback, or incident reports. Once an issue is identified, it's critical to prioritize it based on its impact on the business and its urgency. A simple matrix can help with this:

- **High Impact, High Urgency:** Critical issues that need immediate attention.
- **High Impact, Low Urgency:** Important issues that can be scheduled for resolution.
- **Low Impact, High Urgency:** Minor issues that are causing immediate disruption.
- **Low Impact, Low Urgency:** Trivial issues to be addressed as time permits.

Step 2: Root Cause Analysis (RCA)

Before you fix anything, you must understand why the deficiency occurred. Without a proper RCA, you are likely to implement a temporary fix that doesn't address the underlying issue, leading to its recurrence. Common RCA techniques include:

The 5 Whys:

Repeatedly asking "why?" to peel back layers of a problem and get to the core cause. The 5

Whys is an iterative problem-solving technique designed to explore the cause-and-effect relationships behind an issue. By repeatedly asking "Why?", you can peel back layers of symptoms to uncover the true root cause, preventing the problem from recurring.

How It Works

The process is straightforward:

- **Start with the problem:** State the problem clearly and concisely.
- **Ask "Why?":** Ask why the problem occurred.
- **Repeat:** Take the answer to the first "Why?" and use it as the basis for the next "Why?". Continue this process, typically five times, until you arrive at the root cause.
- **Confirm the root cause:** The final "Why?" should reveal a systemic or process-based issue, not a person. To verify, ask yourself, "If we fix this, will the original problem be prevented?"

The 5 Whys method is most effective for problems that involve human factors, interactions, or basic process failures. It's less suitable for complex problems with multiple, intertwined causes.

Key Benefits

Simplicity

Easy to learn and apply without complex statistical analysis.

Effectiveness

Helps differentiate between symptoms and the true root cause of a problem.

Collaboration

Encourages team-based problem solving and shared understanding.

Fishbone Diagram (Ishikawa):

A visual tool to categorize potential causes of a problem. A Fishbone diagram, also known as an Ishikawa diagram or cause-and-effect diagram, is a visual tool used for root cause analysis. It's a structured brainstorming method that helps teams identify and organize all the possible causes of a specific problem or "effect." The diagram gets its name from its appearance, which resembles a fish skeleton. The "head" of the fish represents the problem statement, and the "bones" extending from the central "spine" represent the major categories of causes.

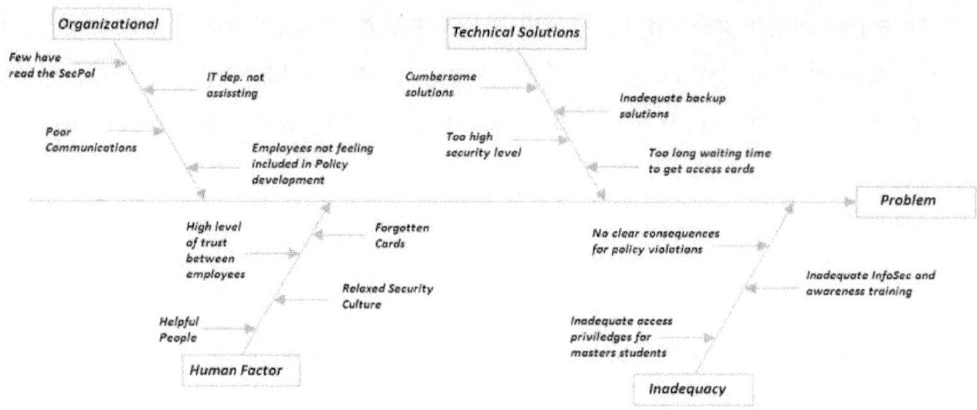

How to Create a Fishbone Diagram

The process for creating a Fishbone diagram is a collaborative, step-by-step approach:

- **Define the Problem:** Start by clearly and concisely defining the problem or "effect" you want to analyze. This problem statement is written at the "head" of the fishbone. For example, "Late delivery of products."
- **Draw the Diagram:** Draw a long horizontal arrow pointing to the problem statement. This is the "spine" of the fish.
- **Identify Major Cause Categories:** Brainstorm the main factors that could be contributing to the problem. These categories are drawn as diagonal lines, or "bones," branching off the main spine. Common categories, especially in manufacturing, are the "6Ms":
- **Brainstorm Possible Causes:** For each main category, brainstorm all the possible causes that might contribute to the problem. These are written as smaller branches coming off the main bones. For security common categories are people, process, technology and environment

The 6 Ms (Manufacturing): Manpower, Machine, Method, Material, Measurement, Mother Nature (Environment).

The 8 Ps (Service Industry): Procedures, Policies, Place, Product, People, Processes, Price, and Promotion.

The 4 Ss (Service Industry): Systems, Surroundings, Skills, and Suppliers.

- **Delve Deeper:** Continue to ask "Why does this happen?" for each cause to uncover sub-causes, which are drawn as smaller lines branching off the initial causes. This iterative process helps you drill down to the root causes rather than just addressing symptoms.

The completed diagram provides a comprehensive visual map of all potential causes, helping a team to focus their investigation and find effective solutions.

Step 3: Action Planning and Assignment

Once the root cause is known, a remediation plan must be created. This plan should be SMART:

- **Specific:** Clearly define what needs to be done.
- **Measurable:** Include metrics to track progress.
- **Assignable:** Assign clear ownership to individuals or teams.
- **Relevant:** The actions must address the root cause.
- **Time-bound:** Set a specific deadline for completion.

The plan should outline the specific tasks, responsible parties, required resources, and a clear timeline.

Step 4: Implementation and Communication

Execute the plan and ensure all relevant stakeholders are kept informed of the progress. Regular status updates prevent confusion and build confidence in the process. This is especially important for high-impact deficiencies.

Step 5: Verification and Closure

The final step is to verify that the remediation was successful. This involves:

- Testing the fix to ensure the deficiency is fully resolved.
- Confirming that the fix did not introduce any new problems.
- Formally documenting the closure of the issue, including the solution, the date of completion, and the verification results.

Evaluating Problem Management Practices

A good process is only as good as its execution. Regular evaluation ensures that your practices are effective and that your team is consistently meeting expectations.

1. Key Performance Indicators (KPIs)

Define and track specific KPIs to measure the health of your problem management process. Examples include:

- **Mean Time to Remediate (MTTR):** The average time from issue identification to resolution. A decreasing MTTR is a positive sign.
- **Percentage of Recurring Errors:** The number of problems that re-emerge after being "fixed." A high percentage indicates a failure in the RCA or remediation plan.
- **Number of Root Cause Analyses Performed:** A measure of how consistently the team is following the process.
- **Backlog of Open Deficiencies:** The number of issues awaiting remediation. A growing backlog indicates a need for more resources or a streamlined process.

2. Error Recording and Analysis

Ensure that all errors and deficiencies are recorded in a centralized system (e.g., a ticketing tool). The record should capture crucial information like:

- Date and time of discovery.
- A clear description of the problem.
- Initial impact and priority.
- The person or team who discovered it.
- The full history of the remediation effort.

This data is vital for trend analysis and identifying systemic issues.

3. Timeliness and Resolution

Regularly review the process to ensure errors are being resolved in a timely manner. This can be evaluated against Service Level Agreements (SLAs) if they exist. For example, an SLA might state that all high-priority deficiencies must be remediated within 72 hours. Regular audits of closed tickets can confirm compliance.

4. Continuous Improvement

Use the data gathered from your KPIs and error analysis to identify opportunities for improvement. Hold regular "post-mortem" meetings for significant problems to review what went well and what could be done better. The insights from these meetings can be used to refine your remediation and problem management processes, making them more efficient over time.

Automating Information Systems Control Processes: Assessment and Implementation

1. The Value of Automation

Automating information systems controls shifts the focus from reactive, manual checks to proactive, continuous monitoring and enforcement. This not only increases efficiency and reduces human error but also provides real-time visibility into the security and compliance posture of an organization. By automating these processes, you can ensure that controls are consistently applied and that deviations are detected and addressed immediately and we reduce toil.

Toil refers to the kind of work that is **manual, repetitive, automatable, tactical, and lacks long-term value**. It's essentially the low-level, unrewarding work that teams must do to keep a system running, but that doesn't contribute to long-term improvements or innovation. The primary way to reduce toil is through **automation**. By identifying repetitive tasks and building tools, scripts, or automated pipelines to handle them, you free up engineers to focus on the strategic, creative, and complex problems that truly require human intelligence.

Toil can be identified by these five key traits:

1. **Manual:** It requires direct human intervention. An engineer has to manually type commands, click buttons, or copy and paste information.
2. **Repetitive:** It's a task that is done over and over again, often with little variation.
3. **Automatable:** It's work that could, and should, be done by a machine. A script, a tool, or a fully automated system could perform the task more efficiently and with fewer errors.
4. **Tactical:** It's a reactive task, often done to "put out a fire" or respond to a specific, immediate need, rather than as part of a strategic, proactive effort.
5. **Scales Linearly:** As your service or system grows, the amount of toil grows with it. For example, if you have to manually provision a new server for every new customer, the time spent on that task will increase linearly with your customer base.

Are You Ready? Your 4-Step Assessment Checklist

Identify Tasks	Define Objectives	Review Infrastructure	Prioritize by Risk
Pinpoint manual, repeatable actions like user access reviews or log analysis.	Clearly state what each control must achieve (e.g., prevent unauthorized access).	Check for existing systems with APIs or scripting capabilities you can leverage.	Focus automation efforts on the highest-risk areas first, like privileged accounts.

2. Assessing Your Current Control Environment

Before implementing any automation, the first step is to assess your existing controls. This involves a thorough review of your current processes to identify which ones are good candidates for automation.

- **Identify Repetitive Tasks:** Look for controls that require manual, repeatable actions, such as user access reviews, log file analysis, or configuration checks.
- **Determine Control Objectives:** Clearly define what each control is meant to achieve (e.g., "Prevent unauthorized access to financial data"). This clarity is crucial for designing effective automated solutions.
- **Review Existing Infrastructure:** Understand the systems you have in place. Do they have APIs or scripting capabilities that can be leveraged for automation?
- **Prioritize Based on Risk:** Focus on automating controls for the highest-risk areas first. For example, automating the monitoring of privileged user accounts is often a high priority.

3. Key Tools and Techniques for Implementation

The right tools can make or break your automation strategy. A combination of the following techniques is often the most effective approach.

Configuration Management Tools

These tools are designed to automate the provisioning and configuration of servers and other IT infrastructure. They are excellent for ensuring systems are configured securely and consistently.

Ansible: An open-source tool that uses simple YAML playbooks to describe a system's desired state. It is agentless, making it easy to deploy.

Puppet: A state-based configuration management tool. It describes system configuration and then enforces that state.

Chef: Another powerful tool that uses "recipes" to define how infrastructure should be configured, deployed, and managed.

Use Case: You can use Ansible to automatically check for and remediate insecure firewall rules across all your servers, ensuring a consistent security baseline.

Security Information and Event Management (SIEM) Systems

SIEM systems centralize security data from various sources (like servers, firewalls, and network devices) to provide a single view of an organization's security posture. They are essential for automating detection and alerting.

Splunk: Known for its powerful search and analysis capabilities, it can be configured to automatically alert on specific security events.

IBM QRadar: An integrated platform that can collect, analyze, and correlate security data from multiple sources.

Elastic Stack (ELK): A popular open-source suite for log management and analysis. It can be used to build custom dashboards and alerts.

Use Case: A SIEM can be configured to automatically trigger an alert and open a ticket in your incident management system if it detects a failed login attempt from a blacklisted IP address.

Robotic Process Automation (RPA)

RPA uses software bots to mimic human actions to perform repetitive tasks. While often associated with business processes, it can be used for administrative security controls.

UiPath: A leading platform for building and managing RPA bots.

Automation Anywhere: Another major player with a focus on ease of use.

Use Case: An RPA bot could be programmed to automatically review a list of terminated employees and verify that their user accounts have been disabled across all necessary systems.

Custom Scripts and APIs

For controls that are unique to your environment, custom scripts using languages like Python or PowerShell are invaluable. Most modern systems and applications provide APIs (Application Programming Interfaces) that allow you to programmatically interact with them.

Use Case: A Python script could be developed to query your user directory (via an API), compare it to a list of employees from your HR system, and automatically report any discrepancies. This ensures user accounts are in sync with your personnel data.

Infrastructure as Code (IaC) and Terraform

Infrastructure as Code (IaC) is a method of managing and provisioning computing infrastructure (like networks, virtual machines, and load balancers) using code instead of manual processes. Terraform is one of the most popular tools for implementing IaC. It allows you to write configuration files that describe the desired state of your infrastructure. Terraform then provisions and manages that infrastructure across various cloud providers (like AWS, Google Cloud, and Azure).

This is a powerful technique for automating controls because it embeds security and compliance rules directly into the infrastructure's definition. Instead of manually checking a server's configuration after it's been created, you can write a Terraform configuration that ensures the server is only ever created with the correct, secure settings.

Use Case: You can use Terraform to automatically provision a new virtual server in a cloud environment. The Terraform code would specify that this server must be launched with a specific security group that only allows traffic on port 443 (HTTPS), effectively automating the control that prevents insecure network access from the moment of creation.

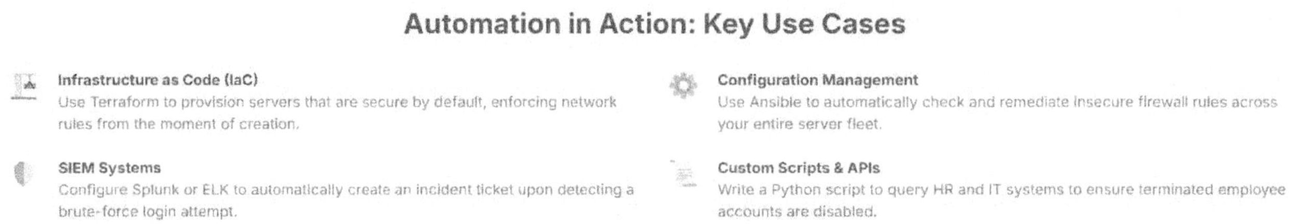

4. Implementation Strategy: A Phased Approach

A successful automation project requires careful planning.

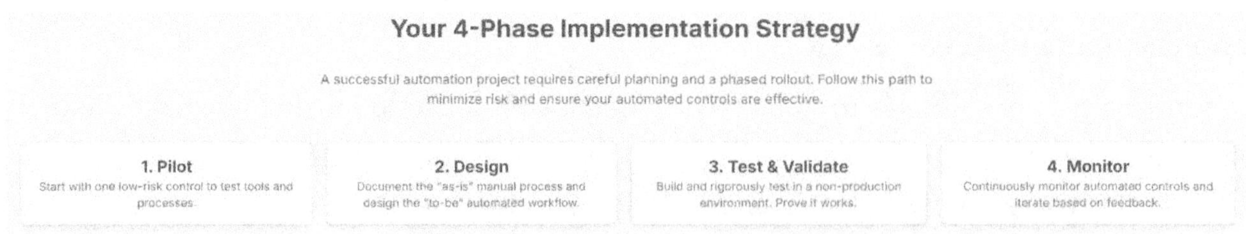

Start with a Pilot Program: Don't try to automate everything at once. Choose a single, low-risk control to automate first. This allows you to test your tools and processes without impacting critical systems.

Document and Design: Before writing any code or configuring a tool, document the "as-is" manual process and the "to-be" automated process. This is a crucial step for preventing errors.

Develop, Test, and Validate: Build your automation, then rigorously test it in a non-production environment. Validation is key; you must prove that the automated control is working as intended and is as effective (or more effective) than the manual process it replaces.

Monitor and Iterate: Automation is not a "set it and forget it" task. Continuously monitor your automated controls to ensure they are running properly. Gather feedback and make improvements over time.

Measuring, Managing, and Reporting on Security Controls

Measuring, managing, and reporting on the effectiveness of your security controls is a crucial part of maintaining a strong security posture. It's a continuous cycle that ensures your defenses are not only in place but are also working as intended to protect your organization's assets.

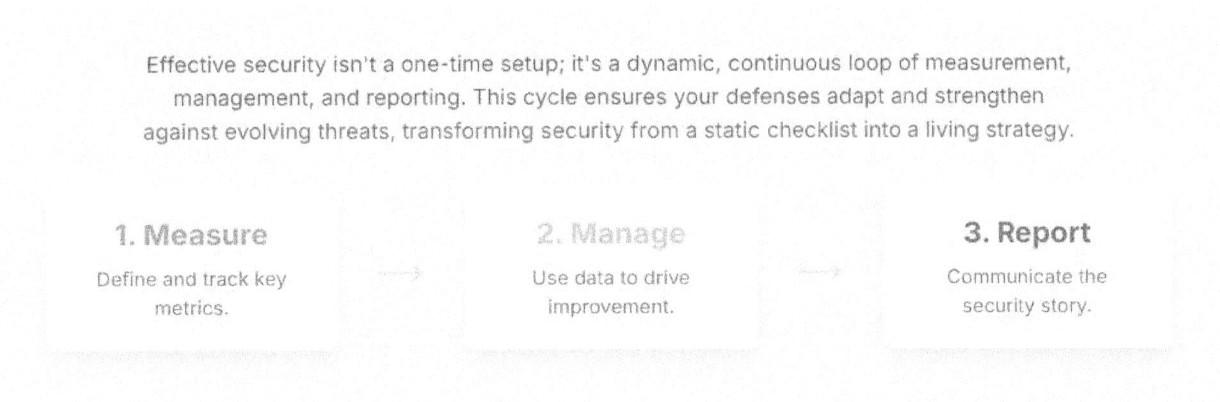

1. Measurement: Defining What to Track

To effectively measure security controls, you need to establish a clear set of metrics. These metrics fall into two main categories: implementation and effectiveness.

Implementation Metrics

These metrics focus on the state of your security controls. They tell you if the controls have been deployed and configured correctly. Examples include:

- **Coverage:** What percentage of your endpoints have an antivirus solution installed?

- **Compliance Score:** What is the compliance rate for a specific security policy (e.g., password complexity requirements)?
- **Configuration Drift:** How many systems have diverged from their baseline security configuration?

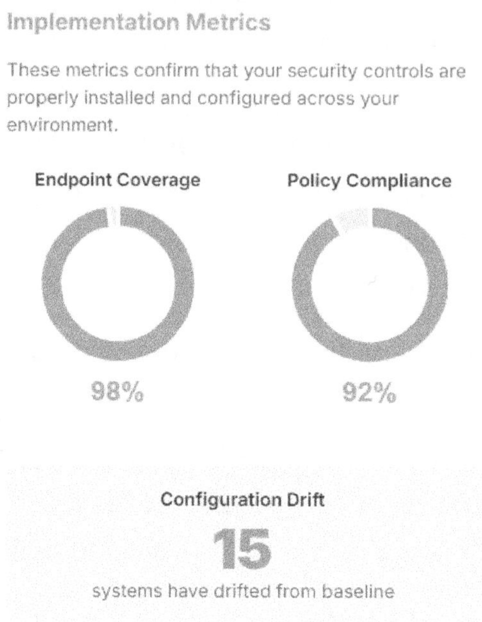

Effectiveness Metrics

These metrics gauge the performance of your controls. They help you understand if the controls are actually preventing, detecting, and responding to threats as expected. Examples include:

- **Vulnerability Remediation Rate:** The average time it takes to patch a critical vulnerability.
- **Mean Time to Detect (MTTD):** The average time from an event occurring to its detection.
- **Mean Time to Respond (MTTR):** The average time from an incident being detected to its resolution.
- **Blocked Threats:** The number of malicious emails, network connections, or unauthorized login attempts successfully blocked by your controls.

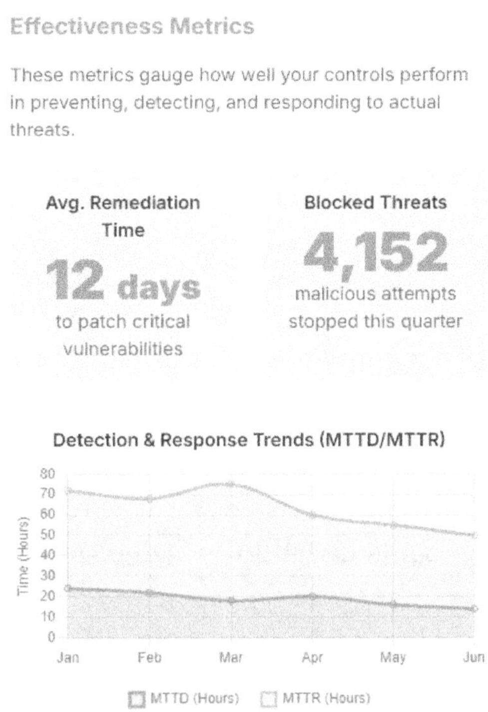

2. Management: Using Data to Drive Improvement

Measurement is only useful if the data is used to inform management decisions. This is where the continuous improvement cycle comes into play. You should use the metrics you've gathered to identify weaknesses and prioritize actions.

- **Analyze the Data:** Look for trends, outliers, and areas where your controls are underperforming. For example, if your MTTR is increasing, it might indicate an issue with your incident response process or a specific tool.
- **Prioritize and Remediate:** Based on the analysis, prioritize the most critical issues. This could mean patching a high-risk vulnerability, reconfiguring a misconfigured firewall, or training staff on a new security procedure.
- **Leverage Automation and GRC Platforms:** Use tools to automate data collection and analysis. A Governance, Risk, and Compliance (GRC) platform can provide a central location to track controls, risks, and compliance status, making the management process more efficient.

3. Reporting: Communicating the Story

Reporting is about translating the complex security data into meaningful information for different audiences. The key is to tailor the message to the audience's needs.

Technical Reports

These reports are for security teams and IT professionals. They should be detailed and actionable.

- **Content:** Include specific metrics, lists of vulnerabilities, configuration errors, and a breakdown of incidents.
- **Format:** Use dashboards, graphs, and tables that allow for drilling down into the data. The goal is to provide the team with the information they need to do their jobs effectively.

Executive Reports

These reports are for leadership and stakeholders. They should be high-level and focused on business risk and impact.

- **Content:** Don't just list metrics; explain what they mean for the business. Focus on key performance indicators (KPIs) like overall security posture, risk reduction, and ROI on security investments.
- **Format:** Use a dashboard with a few key, easy-to-understand visualizations. Frame the report around questions like: "Are we more secure than we were last quarter?" and "Where should we invest our security budget next?"

Regardless of the audience, all reports should include a narrative. Explain what the data means, what actions have been taken, and what the plan is for the future. This transforms a simple data dump into a strategic conversation.

For Executive Leadership

Summarize the security posture in terms of business risk, ROI, and overall progress against strategic goals.

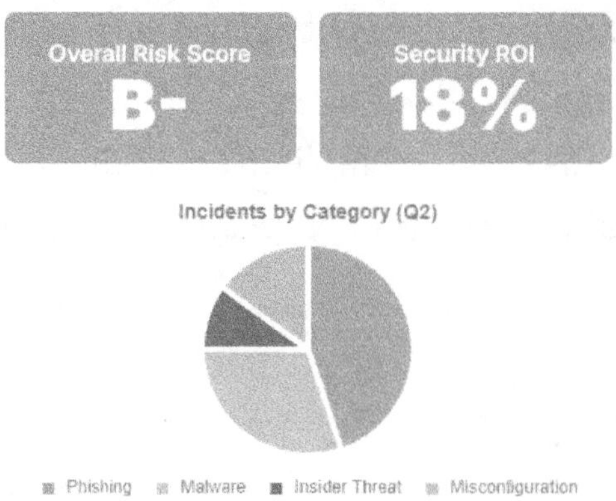

Highlights the current risk posture and the allocation of security incidents, answering "How secure are we?" at a glance.

Information Security Audit Management

The IT Audit Process and Key Standards

77%

of organizations lack a formal Cybersecurity Incident Response Plan.

Why Audits Matter

In an era of constant digital threats, verifying your security posture is not just good practice—it's a necessity. Audits provide a structured assessment of an organization's security controls against established standards. They identify vulnerabilities, ensure compliance with regulations, protect sensitive data, and ultimately, build confidence with customers and stakeholders by demonstrating a commitment to security excellence.

An IT audit is a critical examination of an organization's information technology infrastructure, policies, and operations. The primary goal is to evaluate the effectiveness of IT controls, ensure data integrity and security, and verify compliance with internal policies and external regulations. A structured process and familiarity with established standards are vital for a successful audit.

The Four-Phase IT Audit Process

A typical IT audit follows a logical, four-phase cycle. Following these steps ensures a comprehensive and systematic review.

The Audit Process at a Glance

Planning: This is the most crucial phase. The audit team defines the scope and objectives of the audit. This includes identifying what systems and data will be examined, understanding the business context, and determining the criteria (the standards or regulations) against which the systems will be evaluated. This phase also involves risk assessment to prioritize areas of concern.

Fieldwork (Execution): During this phase, auditors gather evidence to test the effectiveness of the IT controls. This can involve interviewing staff, reviewing documentation, and performing technical tests on systems and networks. Evidence is collected to support or refute the initial audit objectives.

Reporting: Once fieldwork is complete, the audit team drafts a report. This document summarizes the findings, identifies any deficiencies or vulnerabilities, and provides clear, actionable recommendations for remediation. The report should be easy to understand for both technical and non-technical stakeholders.

Follow-up: This final phase involves verifying that management has implemented the recommended changes to address the audit findings. The audit team will check that corrective actions have been taken and that the implemented controls are operating as intended. This ensures the organization is more secure and compliant moving forward.

Key IT and Information Security Audit Standards

Information security audits are essential for verifying that an organization's security controls are effective and that it is compliant with relevant regulations and frameworks. These audits help to protect data, manage risk, and build trust with customers and stakeholders. The following are some of the most prominent IT and information security audit standards and frameworks.

Frameworks at a Glance

Each standard serves a unique purpose. This comparison highlights their primary focus and intended audience to help you understand which may apply to your organization.

Standard/Framework	Type	Primary Focus	Primary Audience
ISO/IEC 27001	Standard (Certifiable)	Information Security Management System (ISMS)	Global Organizations
NIST CSF	Framework (Voluntary)	Cybersecurity Risk Management	U.S. Organizations (Public & Private)
PCI DSS	Standard (Mandatory)	Cardholder Data Protection	Payment Processors, Merchants
COBIT	Framework (Guidance)	IT Governance & Management	Enterprise IT & Governance Teams
SOC 2	Attestation (Report)	Controls at a Service Organization	SaaS, Cloud & Service Providers

1. ISO/IEC 27001

- **What it is:** A globally recognized standard for an Information Security Management System (ISMS). It provides a systematic approach to managing sensitive company information to ensure its confidentiality, integrity, and availability.

- **Audit Focus:** An audit for ISO 27001 certification verifies that an organization has established, implemented, maintained, and continually improved a documented ISMS that meets the standard's requirements. This includes risk assessments, selecting and implementing security controls from ISO 27002, and monitoring performance.
- **Key Benefit:** Certification demonstrates a commitment to a best-practice, risk-based approach to information security, which is highly respected internationally.

2. NIST Cybersecurity Framework (CSF)

- **What it is:** A voluntary framework developed by the U.S. National Institute of Standards and Technology (NIST) to provide guidance on managing cybersecurity risk. It is widely used by both public and private sector organizations.
- **Audit Focus:** Audits against the NIST CSF evaluate an organization's cybersecurity posture based on five core functions:

Identify: Understanding and managing cybersecurity risks to systems, assets, data, and capabilities.

Protect: Developing and implementing appropriate safeguards to ensure the delivery of critical services.

Detect: Identifying the occurrence of a cybersecurity event.

Respond: Taking action regarding a detected cybersecurity incident.

Recover: Implementing plans for resilience and restoring any capabilities or services that were impaired due to a cybersecurity event.

- **Key Benefit:** The framework is flexible and adaptable, allowing organizations of any size or sector to tailor it to their specific needs.

3. Payment Card Industry Data Security Standard (PCI DSS)

- **What it is:** A mandatory compliance standard for any organization that accepts, processes, stores, or transmits credit card information. It is governed by the Payment Card Industry Security Standards Council (PCI SSC).
- **Audit Focus:** PCI DSS audits, conducted by a Qualified Security Assessor (QSA), focus on ensuring the organization's environment for handling cardholder data is secure. The audit covers 12 key requirements, including building and maintaining a secure network, protecting cardholder data, maintaining a vulnerability management program, and implementing strong access control measures.
- **Key Benefit:** Compliance is a non-negotiable requirement for handling payment card data, as it prevents data breaches and protects sensitive customer information. Non-

compliance can lead to significant fines and loss of the ability to process payments.

4. COBIT (Control Objectives for Information and Related Technologies)

- **What it is:** A framework for IT governance and management developed by ISACA. While not strictly an audit standard, it provides a comprehensive set of controls and best practices that auditors can use to evaluate an organization's IT processes.
- **Audit Focus:** An audit using the COBIT framework would assess the effectiveness of IT governance and management processes. This includes evaluating how well IT is aligned with business goals, how IT risks are managed, and how resources are used.
- **Key Benefit:** COBIT helps organizations manage IT as a business function, ensuring that technology investments deliver value while mitigating risk.

5. SOC 2 (Service Organization Control 2)

- **What it is:** A report on the controls at a service organization relevant to security, availability, processing integrity, confidentiality, or privacy. It is intended for technology and cloud-based service providers.
- **Audit Focus:** An independent auditor examines the service organization's controls based on one or more of the five "Trust Service Principles." The audit results in a report that provides assurance to a service provider's clients about the security of their data.
- **Key Benefit:** A SOC 2 report is a powerful way for service providers to demonstrate a commitment to data security and build trust with their clients, which is especially important for SaaS companies and data centers.

6. COSO (Committee of Sponsoring Organizations):

- **Purpose:** Offers an internal control framework, often integrated with IT audits for financial reporting.
- **Key Features:** Focus on control environment, risk assessment, control activities, information/communication, and monitoring.
- **Best For:** Financial and operational control audits.

Designing a Risk-Based IT Audit Strategy

The primary goal of a risk-based IT audit strategy is to direct audit resources toward information systems and processes that present the highest risk to an organization's business objectives. This approach ensures that audit efforts are efficient, effective, and provide the most value to stakeholders by focusing on what truly matters.

Core Principles of IT Auditing

A successful audit strategy is built on a foundation of professional principles. The auditor must maintain independence, ensuring objectivity and impartiality in all work. The principle of professional care dictates that the auditor exercises due diligence and a high level of competence. The process must be systematic and disciplined, following a structured methodology from planning to reporting. Finally, the audit must always be aligned with business objectives and an organization's risk tolerance, meaning the audit scope and focus should directly relate to the company's strategic goals.

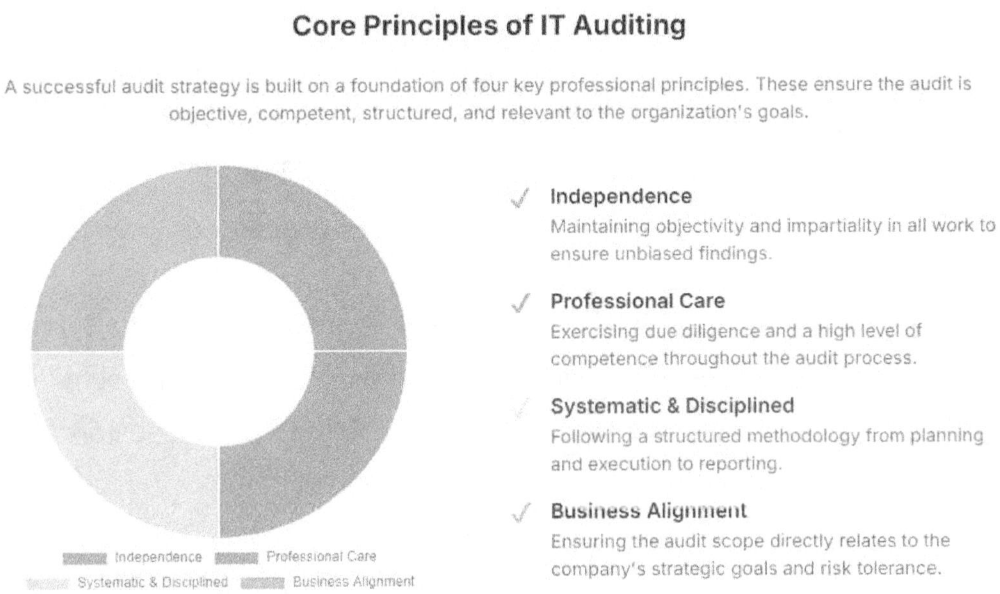

Essential Skills and Techniques

To execute a risk-based audit, an auditor needs a mix of technical and soft skills.

Key Skills:

- **Technical Proficiency:** A deep understanding of IT infrastructure, applications, databases, and network technologies.
- **Critical Thinking:** The ability to analyze complex systems, identify potential vulnerabilities, and evaluate the effectiveness of controls.
- **Communication:** Strong verbal and written skills to interview stakeholders, document findings, and present recommendations clearly and concisely.

- **Risk Analysis:** The capability to identify, assess, and prioritize risks based on their likelihood and potential impact.

Key Auditor Skills

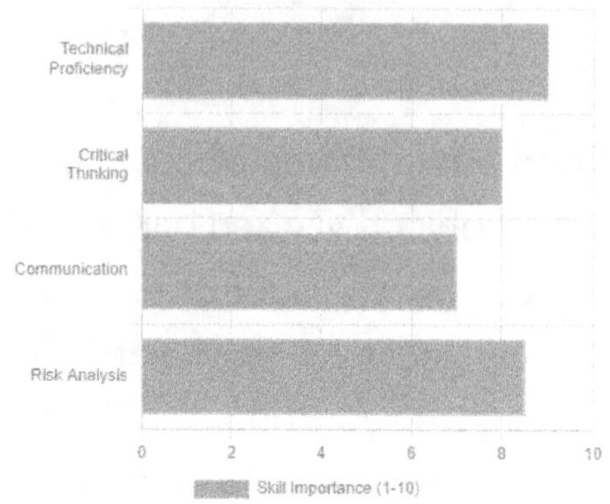

This chart compares the relative importance of core skills required for effective IT auditing, highlighting the foundational need for technical proficiency.

Key Techniques:

- **Interviews and Inquiries:** Engaging with IT staff, management, and end-users to understand processes, controls, and potential weak points.
- **Observation:** Physically observing processes and procedures to verify that documented controls are actually being performed.
- **Data Analysis and Testing:** Using specialized audit software (CAATs) to test large volumes of data for anomalies, unauthorized transactions, or control failures.
- **Walkthroughs:** Tracing a transaction from its origin to its conclusion to understand the entire process and identify control points.

Key Audit Techniques

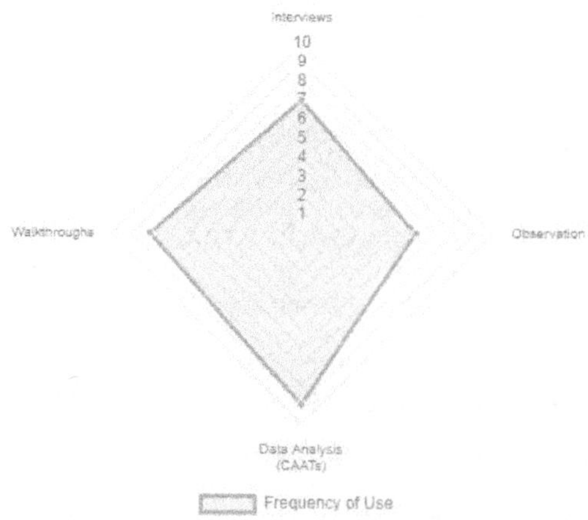

This chart shows the frequency of use for different audit techniques. Data analysis is a primary tool, complemented by direct engagement and observation.

The Five-Step Audit Strategy Design Process

1. Scoping and Planning

The first step is to define the scope and objectives of the audit. This involves understanding the organizational context, including business goals, major processes, and the IT systems that support them. The auditor will review past audit reports, organizational policies, and relevant regulations. This phase results in a clear audit charter outlining what will be examined and what the audit aims to achieve.

2. Risk Assessment

This is the most critical phase of the risk-based strategy. The auditor identifies potential IT risks by considering the organization's unique environment. Risks are then prioritized based on their likelihood (the probability of the risk occurring) and impact (the severity of the consequences if the risk materializes). This is often visualized using a risk matrix. The risks with the highest likelihood and highest impact are designated as "high-risk" areas and become the primary focus of the audit.

3. Control Identification and Evaluation

For each high-risk area, the auditor must identify the existing controls designed to mitigate that risk. These can be preventive (e.g., access controls) or detective (e.g., log monitoring). The auditor then evaluates the design of these controls to determine if they are theoretically effective. A control that is poorly designed or not appropriately implemented will not be able to effectively mitigate the associated risk.

4. Testing Plan Development and Execution

Based on the risk assessment and control evaluation, a detailed testing plan is developed. This plan specifies the audit procedures, including the specific tests to be performed, the sample size, and the resources required. The auditor will then execute the tests, which may include both compliance testing (checking if controls are being followed) and substantive testing (verifying the accuracy and integrity of data). The audit techniques mentioned earlier, such as data analysis and interviews, are applied in this phase.

5. Reporting and Follow-up

The final step is to formally communicate the audit findings to management. The audit report should clearly articulate the risks identified, the ineffectiveness of any controls, and a list of actionable recommendations. The auditor's role doesn't end here; they also perform a follow-up audit to ensure that management has implemented the recommended changes and that the risks have been properly addressed.

The Information Systems Audit Process

An information systems (IS) audit is a methodical process for collecting and evaluating evidence to determine if an organization's information systems are protected, controlled, and effective in meeting business objectives. The process is typically broken down into five key phases.

1. Planning the Audit

This is the foundational phase where the audit's direction is set. It involves understanding the organization's business, its IT environment, and the specific systems to be audited.

- **Define Scope and Objectives:** Clearly state what will and will not be covered by the audit (e.g., all network infrastructure, but not end-user workstations). The objectives should align with the organization's goals, such as improving data security or ensuring compliance with a specific regulation like GDPR.

- **Establish Audit Criteria:** Determine the specific standards, policies, or regulations against which the systems will be measured. This could include internal security policies, industry best practices (like ISO 27001), or legal requirements.
- **Develop the Audit Plan:** Create a detailed plan outlining the audit's timeline, resources, and specific procedures to be followed. This plan serves as a roadmap for the entire process.

2. Fieldwork and Data Collection

In this phase, the audit team executes the plan and gathers the necessary evidence. The goal is to obtain sufficient, relevant, and reliable information to support the audit findings.

- **Gather Evidence:** Collect data through various techniques, including:

Interviews: Talking to system administrators, security managers, and end-users to understand processes and controls.

Observation: Observing personnel performing their duties to see if procedures are being followed.

Document Review: Examining policies, procedures, network diagrams, access logs, and other relevant documentation.

Technical Testing: Performing vulnerability scans, penetration tests, or code reviews to find security flaws.

- **Use Sampling:** Due to the volume of data, auditors often use sampling techniques to select a representative subset of transactions or records for detailed examination.

3. Analysis and Interpretation

This is where the audit team evaluates the evidence collected during the fieldwork phase. The evidence is measured against the defined criteria to draw conclusions.

- **Evaluate Controls:** Assess whether the existing controls are designed and operating effectively. For example, is the password policy being enforced? Are backups being performed regularly and successfully?
- **Identify Findings:** Document any deviations from the established criteria. A "finding" could be a control weakness (e.g., a lack of a formal change management process) or an instance of non-compliance (e.g., a user having unauthorized access rights).

- **Interpret Results:** Determine the significance of each finding. How does this weakness impact the organization's ability to achieve its objectives? A single finding might not be critical, but a combination of findings could indicate a systemic problem.

4. Reporting and Communication

After analyzing the findings, the audit team must clearly and effectively communicate the results to management and other stakeholders.

- **Draft the Audit Report:** Create a formal report that includes:

  An Executive Summary highlighting the most significant findings.

  A Statement of Scope and Objectives.

  A detailed list of Findings with supporting evidence.

  Recommendations for corrective actions to address each finding.

  An Overall Opinion or Conclusion on the effectiveness of the IS controls.

- **Present Findings:** Communicate the results to management in a constructive manner, focusing on the potential risks and the benefits of implementing the recommendations.

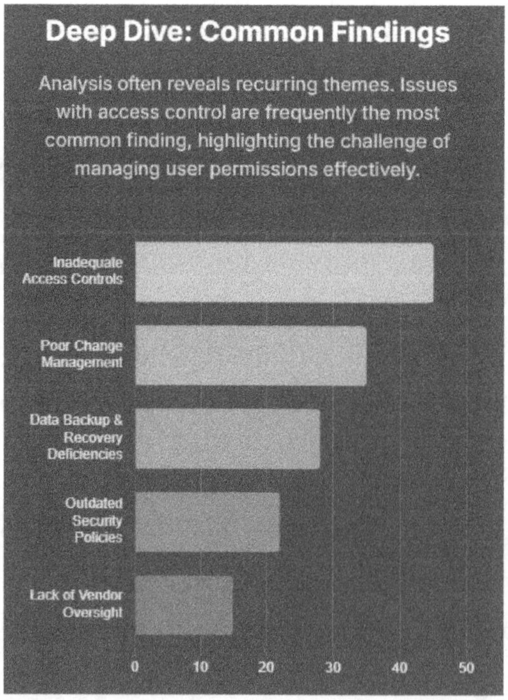

5. Follow-Up and Monitoring

The final phase ensures that the audit was a useful exercise and that the identified issues are resolved.

- **Monitor Corrective Actions:** The audit team works with management to track the implementation of the recommended changes.
- **Verify Implementation:** After a reasonable period, the auditors will perform a follow- up review to verify that the corrective actions have been implemented and are operating as intended. This ensures the ongoing protection and effectiveness of the information systems.

Evaluating Information Security Audit Results

Successfully evaluating an information security audit requires a structured approach to ensure the final conclusions are sound and actionable. This process involves critically assessing the audit report's findings against the evidence gathered.

A sound evaluation transforms audit findings from simple observations into strategic intelligence.

Successfully evaluating an information security audit requires a structured approach to ensure the final conclusions are sound and actionable. This process involves critically assessing the audit report's findings against the evidence gathered.

1. Relevancy of Findings and Conclusions

The Three Pillars of a Sound Conclusion

Relevancy

Does the finding directly relate to the audit's objectives and scope? An irrelevant finding, no matter how accurate, is a distraction.

Accuracy

Are the findings factually correct and free from error? Inaccurate findings erode trust and lead to wasted resources.

Perspective

Are the conclusions fair, balanced, and unbiased? A conclusion should be a logical summary, not an overstatement or opinion.

Relevancy is the degree to which an audit finding or conclusion relates directly to the stated objectives and scope of the audit. An irrelevant finding, no matter how accurate, is a distraction that can dilute the report's impact.

How to Evaluate Relevancy:

- **Review the Audit Charter:** Start by re-reading the audit charter or scope document. Every finding should align with the defined objectives. For example, if the audit was about "firewall rule sets," a finding about weak employee passwords is less relevant unless it's a direct result of a firewall misconfiguration.
- **Ask "So What?":** For each finding, ask: "What is the impact?" and "Does this finding help us achieve the audit's goal?" If a finding doesn't lead to a meaningful recommendation or a clear risk, its relevancy should be questioned.
- **Focus on Risk:** Relevant findings should highlight actual risks to the organization's information assets. Does the finding point to a vulnerability that could be exploited, or a control that has failed?

2. Accuracy of Findings

Accuracy means that the findings are factually correct and free from errors. Inaccurate findings can erode trust in the audit process and lead to wasted resources.

How to Evaluate Accuracy:

- **Trace Findings to Evidence:** Each finding must be directly supported by accumulated evidence. This evidence could include log files, configuration screenshots, interview transcripts, or vulnerability scan reports. The report should provide clear references to this evidence.
- **Verify the Data:** Do the numbers add up? Is the configuration setting correctly transcribed? If the report states that "40% of servers have an outdated patch," you should be able to look at the evidence and confirm that count.
- **Seek Corroboration:** Whenever possible, check if the finding is supported by more than one source of evidence. For instance, a finding of a missing security control might be supported by both an interview with the system owner and a configuration review.

3. Perspective of Conclusions

The perspective refers to whether the conclusions drawn from the findings are fair, balanced, and unbiased. A conclusion should be a logical and objective summary of the facts, not an overstatement or a personal opinion.

How to Evaluate Perspective:

- **Avoid Overstatement:** A conclusion should not exaggerate the severity of a finding. If a single unpatched server is found, the conclusion should not state that "the entire network is critically vulnerable." Instead, it should accurately describe the risk posed by that single server.
- **Consider Context:** A good conclusion takes the operating context into account. Is the finding a result of a known limitation or a deliberate business decision? A conclusion that ignores this context may be technically accurate but unfairly critical.
- **Proportionality:** The severity of the conclusion should be proportional to the evidence. A minor configuration error shouldn't lead to a conclusion of "gross negligence."

4. Weighing Relevancy, Accuracy, and Perspective

The final step is to synthesize the three components to form a comprehensive evaluation. This involves a final review of the audit report to ensure a logical flow from evidence to finding to conclusion.

The Weighing Process:

- **Start with the Evidence:** Begin with the raw audit evidence.
- **Link to Findings:** Ensure each finding is a direct and accurate interpretation of the evidence.
- **Draw the Conclusion:** Confirm that the final conclusion is a relevant, fair, and proportional summary of the findings.

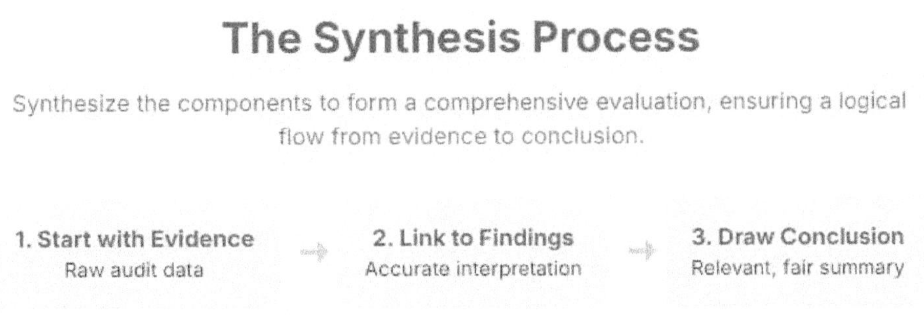

For example, if the evidence shows a system is missing a specific patch (Accuracy), the finding should state exactly that. The Relevancy is high if the patch addresses a critical vulnerability. The Perspective should be balanced—acknowledging the risk while also noting any mitigating controls that might be in place. By weighing these factors together, you can form a robust and defensible opinion on the quality of the audit results.

Assessment of Exposures from Ineffective or Missing Controls

An information security control is a safeguard or countermeasure used to prevent, detect, or correct security threats and vulnerabilities. When these controls are missing or not properly implemented, an organization is exposed to a variety of risks. The severity and type of exposure depend on the specific control that is lacking.

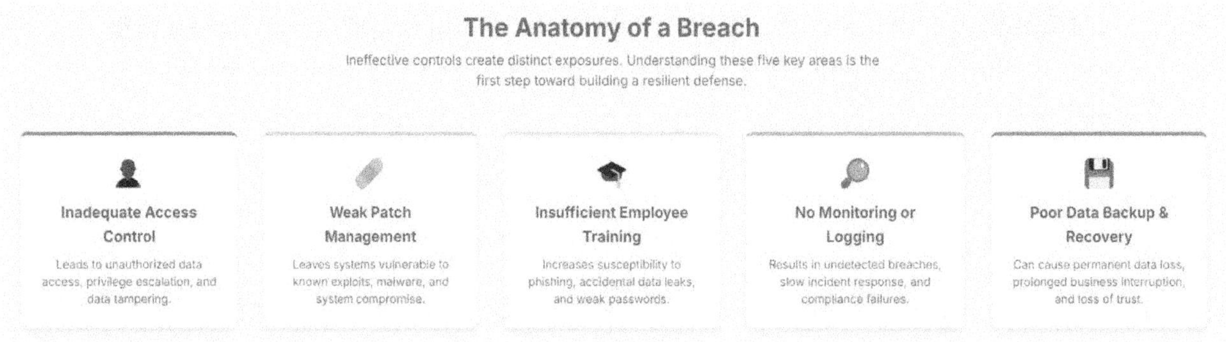

1. Exposures from Inadequate Access Control

Description:

This occurs when user access is not properly managed, roles are not defined, or privileges are not restricted to the minimum necessary for the job.

Exposures:

- **Unauthorized Data Access:** Employees or external actors can access sensitive information they should not be able to see.
- **Privilege Escalation:** An attacker can exploit a weak user account to gain administrative-level access to a system.
- **Data Tampering:** Unauthorized users can modify or delete critical business data, leading to integrity issues.

2. Exposures from Weak Patch Management

Description:

Systems and applications are not regularly updated with the latest security patches from vendors.

Exposures:

- **Unpatched Vulnerabilities:** Systems remain susceptible to known exploits, making them an easy target for attackers.
- **Malware Infections:** Malware, such as ransomware or viruses, can exploit these vulnerabilities to infiltrate the network.
- **Compromised Systems:** Attackers can gain control of servers or workstations, using them as a launchpad for further attacks.

3. Exposures from Insufficient Employee Training

Description:

Employees are not educated on basic security best practices, policies, and common threats.

Exposures:

- **Phishing and Social Engineering Attacks:** Employees are more likely to fall for fraudulent emails or malicious links, providing attackers with credentials or access.
- **Accidental Data Leaks:** Sensitive information may be mishandled, such as being shared inappropriately via email or stored on insecure personal devices.
- **Weak Password Practices:** Employees may use simple, reused, or easily guessable passwords, making accounts easy to compromise.

4. Exposures from Absence of Monitoring and Logging

Description:

There are no systems in place to record and review activity on a network or server, or the logs that are collected are not analyzed.

Exposures:

- **Undetected Breaches:** An attacker can reside in the network for an extended period without anyone noticing, causing significant damage.
- **Slow Incident Response:** Without logs, it is nearly impossible to investigate a security incident, determine its scope, or properly contain the threat.
- **Regulatory Non-Compliance:** Many data protection regulations require organizations to maintain logs for auditing and forensics.

5. Exposures from Inadequate Data Backup and Recovery

Description:

Critical data is not regularly backed up, or the backup and recovery process is not tested and verified.

Exposures:

- **Permanent Data Loss:** A system failure, natural disaster, or ransomware attack could lead to the complete and permanent loss of business-critical data.
- **Prolonged Business Interruption:** The inability to quickly restore systems and data from a reliable backup can lead to extended downtime, causing significant financial loss.
- **Loss of Customer Trust:** If customer data is lost or compromised, it can damage the organization's reputation.

Practical and Cost-Effective Improvement Plan

This plan is structured in a phased approach, prioritizing foundational, low-cost actions first before moving to more comprehensive solutions.

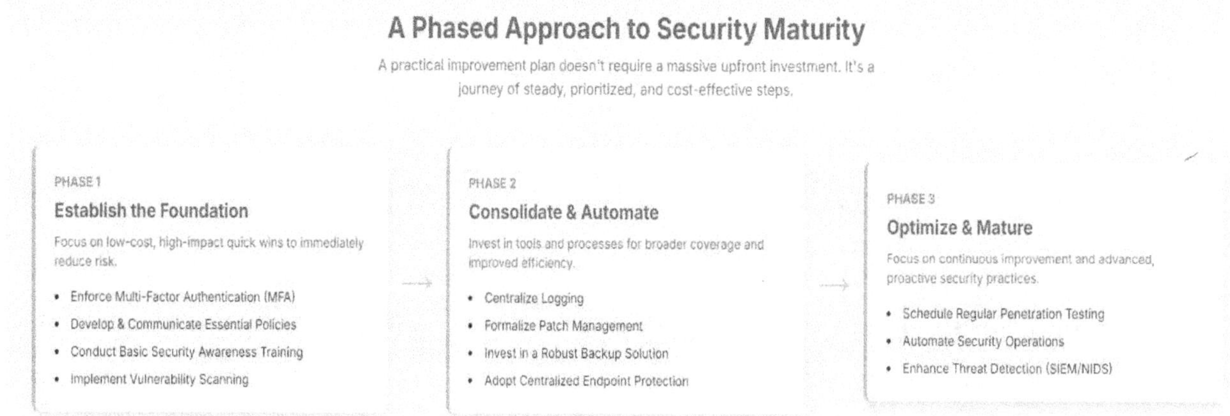

Phase 1: Establish the Foundation (Low Cost, High Impact)

This phase focuses on quick wins and policy-based improvements that require minimal financial investment but yield significant security improvements.

- **Enforce Multi-Factor Authentication (MFA):** Activate MFA on all critical systems, including email, VPN, and privileged accounts. Most services, like Google

Workspace or Microsoft 365, offer this for free. This is one of the most effective ways to prevent credential-based attacks.

- **Develop and Communicate Essential Policies:** Create and distribute a simple set of security policies, including an Acceptable Use Policy, a Password Policy, and an Incident Response Plan. While not a technical control, this sets expectations and provides a framework for action.
- **Conduct Basic Security Awareness Training:** Use free online resources (like those from CISA or open-source platforms) to conduct mandatory quarterly training on topics like phishing, password hygiene, and social engineering.
- **Implement a Vulnerability Scanning Schedule:** Use free open-source tools (e.g., Nmap) to periodically scan your network for known vulnerabilities. This helps you identify and address weaknesses before they can be exploited.

Phase 2: Consolidate and Automate (Moderate Cost, Broader Impact)

This phase involves investing in tools and processes that provide broader coverage and improve efficiency.

- **Centralize Logging:** Implement a simple, centralized logging system (e.g., using a free log management tool like the ELK Stack, Splunk free tier, or a cloud-based service). This makes it easier to monitor and analyze activity across the entire network.
- **Formalize Patch Management:** Establish a clear process for testing and deploying patches on a regular basis. Use free tools provided by operating systems (e.g., Windows Server Update Services) to automate this process.
- **Invest in a Robust Backup Solution:** Move beyond simple local backups to a reliable, cloud-based solution that offers versioning and immutability to protect against ransomware. Ensure a copy of the data is stored offline or in a separate location.
- **Adopt a Centralized Antivirus/Endpoint Protection Solution:** A unified platform is more effective than individual, unmanaged installations. Many vendors offer scalable, cost-effective solutions for small to medium-sized businesses.

Phase 3: Optimize and Mature (Ongoing, Focused Investment)

This phase focuses on continuous improvement and more advanced security practices as the organization's budget and maturity grow.

- **Schedule Regular Penetration Testing:** Hire a third-party security firm to perform a "red team" exercise to find and exploit vulnerabilities from an attacker's perspective.

This provides a realistic assessment of your defenses.

- **Automate Security Operations:** Integrate security tools to automate tasks like vulnerability scanning, patch deployment, and threat alerts. This reduces manual effort and speeds up response times.
- **Enhance Threat Detection:** Implement more advanced security information and event management (SIEM) tools or network intrusion detection systems (NIDS) to proactively hunt for threats and monitor for suspicious behavior.

This phased plan allows an organization to build a strong security foundation with minimal initial investment and then scale its efforts and spending as its security posture matures.

IT Audit Documentation and Reporting Process

An effective IT audit process requires meticulous documentation at every stage, from initial planning to final reporting. This ensures transparency, provides a clear audit trail, and gives stakeholders the necessary information to make informed decisions.

1. Planning and Risk Assessment

This phase lays the groundwork for the entire audit.

- **Audit Charter:** A high-level document that defines the purpose, authority, and responsibility of the IT audit function.
- **Audit Plan:** A detailed document that outlines the scope, objectives, and timeline for the audit. It identifies the systems, processes, and controls to be reviewed.
- **Risk Assessment:** Documentation of identified risks (e.g., security vulnerabilities, data integrity issues, compliance failures). This includes assessing the likelihood and impact of each risk to prioritize audit efforts.

2. Fieldwork and Evidence Gathering

This phase involves executing the audit plan and collecting evidence.

- **Working Papers:** The core of the audit documentation. These papers should be organized and cross-referenced to the audit objectives. They include:

Inquiries: Notes from interviews with IT staff and management.

Observations: Records of processes being performed.

Inspections: Copies or records of documents, logs, and configurations.

Tests of Controls: Detailed steps taken to test the effectiveness of IT controls, including the sample size and test results.

- **Evidence:** All supporting materials must be documented and stored securely. This includes screenshots, system logs, policy documents, and meeting minutes. Each piece of evidence should be clearly labeled and linked to the corresponding audit finding.

3. Reporting and Communication

This is where the audit findings are synthesized and presented to stakeholders.

- **Draft Report:** A preliminary report containing the audit findings, risks, and preliminary recommendations. This is shared with the audited team for a management response.
- **Management Response:** The audited team's formal reply to the findings, including their corrective action plans and timelines. This is a crucial part of the process, as it shows their commitment to addressing the issues.
- **Final Audit Report:** The official document for all stakeholders. It is structured to be easily digestible and actionable. It should include:

Executive Summary: A concise overview of the audit scope, key findings, and overall conclusion. This is the most important section for senior leadership.

Background: A brief description of the audited area.

Findings and Recommendations: A detailed breakdown of each finding, the associated risk, and a practical recommendation for remediation.

Management Action Plan: The agreed-upon plan and timeline for addressing the findings.

Phase 3: Reporting & Communication

This phase translates complex findings into a clear, actionable report for stakeholders. The final report includes an executive summary for leadership, detailed findings for management, and a committed action plan for remediation.

Audit Findings by Severity

Findings are categorized by severity to help stakeholders prioritize their response. Critical findings require immediate attention, while minor ones can be addressed in due course.

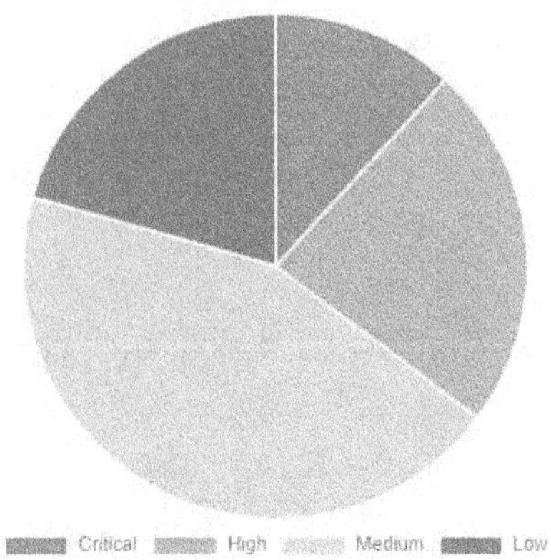

Management Action Plan Timeline

This timeline visualizes the agreed-upon deadlines for management to address the audit findings, ensuring accountability and timely resolution of identified issues.

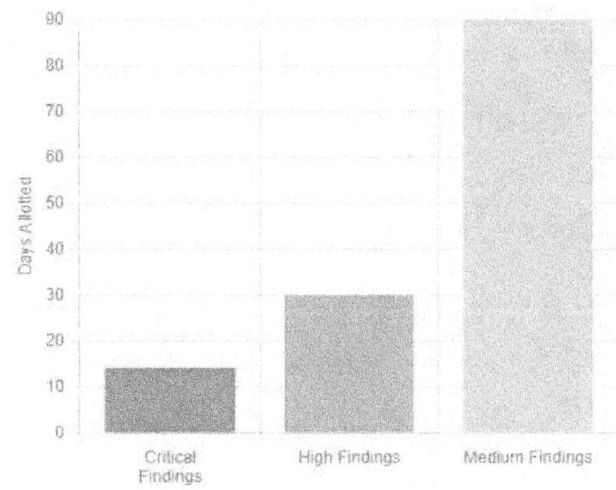

4. Follow-up and Closure

- **Follow-up Plan:** A schedule for re-evaluating the remediated findings to confirm the effectiveness of the corrective actions.
- **Closure Memorandum:** A final document confirming that all findings have been addressed and the audit is complete.

This systematic process ensures that all audit work is thorough, defensible, and provides a solid basis for improving the organization's IT governance and security.

Phase 4: Follow-up & Closure

The audit process doesn't end with the report. The follow-up phase is crucial to verify that corrective actions have been implemented effectively. Once all findings are addressed, the audit is formally closed, concluding the cycle.

Remediation Status Over Time

This chart tracks the progress of resolving audit findings over a set period. It demonstrates the effectiveness of the management action plan and the journey towards full compliance and security posture improvement.

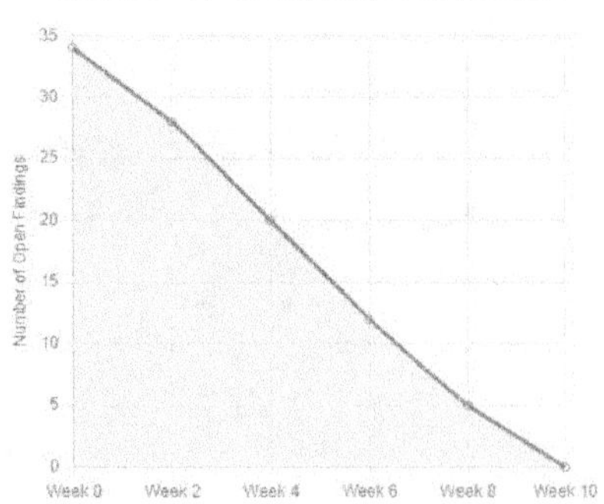

✓

Audit Complete

All findings have been verified and closed. The organization's IT governance has been strengthened.

Action Plan for Implementing Audit Findings

Introduction

An audit provides valuable insights into areas for improvement and potential risks. To effectively address these findings, a systematic and timely approach is essential. This six-step process ensure that all necessary changes are implemented, verified, and communicated to relevant stakeholders.

Step 1: Understand and Prioritize Findings

Before any action is taken, it's critical to have a complete and shared understanding of the audit report.

- **Review the Report Thoroughly:** Read the audit report in its entirety, paying close attention to the specific findings, recommendations, and the severity or risk level assigned to each.
- **Conduct a Clarification Meeting:** Schedule a meeting with the auditor to clarify any ambiguous points or complex recommendations.
- **Categorize and Prioritize:** Classify the findings based on their impact and urgency. High-risk, critical issues should be addressed immediately, while medium and low-risk items can be scheduled accordingly.

Step 2: Assign Ownership and Create a Detailed Action Plan

For each finding, a clear owner must be assigned to ensure accountability.

- **Assign Ownership:** For each finding, designate a single individual or team responsible for its resolution. This person will be the primary point of contact and driver for the implementation.
- **Develop a Detailed Plan:** The owner should create a specific action plan for their assigned finding. This plan should include:

Specific Actions: What exact steps will be taken?

Dependencies: Are there any other actions or teams this depends on?

Start and End Dates: Establish realistic timelines for each action item.

Success Metrics: How will you know the finding has been successfully addressed?

Step 3: Allocate Resources and Secure Management Support

Successful implementation often requires resources and support from leadership.

- **Identify Resource Needs:** Determine if the plan requires new software, a budget for external consultants, or specific personnel time.
- **Secure Approval:** Present the prioritized action plan and resource requests to management for approval. Ensure they understand the risks of inaction and the benefits of the proposed changes.

Step 4: Implement and Monitor the Changes

This is the execution phase where the planned actions are put into practice.

- **Execute the Plan:** The assigned owners should work through their action plans, making the necessary changes to processes, policies, or systems.
- **Monitor Progress:** Use a shared tracking tool (e.g., a spreadsheet, project management software) to monitor the progress of each finding. Hold regular check-in meetings to discuss roadblocks and ensure timelines are being met.

Step 5: Document and Communicate

Proper documentation and communication are vital for a successful audit response.

- **Maintain a Central Log:** Keep a detailed log of all changes made, including dates, individuals involved, and the specific finding each change addresses.
- **Communicate with Stakeholders:** Provide regular updates to all relevant parties—including management and the audit committee—on the status of the implementation.

Step 6: Verify and Validate

The final step is to confirm that the implemented changes have effectively resolved the original findings.

- **Conduct an Internal Review:** The owner of each finding, along with a peer, should review the implemented change to ensure it meets the success metrics defined in Step 2.
- **Request a Follow-up Audit:** Depending on the severity of the findings, it may be necessary to schedule a follow-up review with the original auditor to get an official confirmation that the issues have been resolved.

Step 6: Verify & Validate

The job isn't done until the fixes are verified. The final step involves a thorough internal review and, when necessary, a follow-up audit to confirm that the root causes have been addressed and the implemented changes are effective.

The Validation Process Flow

Internal Review Owner verifies fix → **Follow-up Audit** (If required) → **Confirmed Closure** Finding resolved

A structured validation process ensures that solutions are robust and sustainable, preventing the recurrence of issues.

95%

Findings Resolved

The ultimate goal: a successful audit response and a stronger organization.

OBJECTIVE	EXAMPLE METRICS	EXAMPLE KPIS
PROTECT CRITICAL DATA	Number of unauthorized access attempts on a database	Reduce unauthorized access attempts by 95% month-over-month.
ENSURE SYSTEM AVAILABILITY	Time to restore a server from backup	Maintain a Mean Time to Recovery (MTTR) of under 4 hours for all critical systems.
MAINTAIN SECURITY POSTURE	Percentage of systems with outdated antivirus	Maintain 100% of all endpoints with the latest antivirus definition files.
MANAGE VULNERABILITIES	Time from patch release to deployment	Deploy all critical patches within 72 hours of release.

Multiple-Choice Questions

1. A CISO is tasked with designing a new security program. The first and most critical step, according to a top-down approach, is to:

   A. Conduct a comprehensive technical vulnerability scan to identify weaknesses.
   B. Implement a robust intrusion detection system (IDS) to monitor network traffic.
   C. Align security controls directly with the organization's strategic business goals and objectives.
   D. Hire a dedicated team of penetration testers to simulate real-world attacks.

2. A financial institution's primary objective is to ensure that all transaction records are accurate and cannot be altered without authorization. This objective aligns most directly with which principle of the CIA triad?

   A. Confidentiality
   B. Integrity
   C. Availability
   D. Accountability

3. A large healthcare provider is designing a new electronic health records (EHR) system. The project lead mandates that the system must be designed to automatically encrypt patient data at rest and in transit. This is an example of which security concept?

   A. Data Loss Prevention (DLP)
   B. Security-by-Design
   C. Vulnerability Management
   D. Incident Response

4. Following a recent phishing attack, a CISO implements a new rule that requires all employees to attend mandatory, annual security awareness training. This type of control is best categorized as:

   A. Corrective
   B. Preventive
   C. Detective
   D. Compensating

5. A security analyst notices a high volume of failed login attempts from a single IP address on the corporate VPN. The analyst then uses a SIEM system to correlate this activity with other logs and blocks the IP address. The action of using the SIEM to correlate the activity is an example of which type of control?

A. Corrective
B. Preventive
C. Deterrent
D. Detective

6. An organization is conducting a formal risk assessment. After identifying potential threats and vulnerabilities, the next crucial step in the design process is to:

A. Immediately deploy a new firewall.
B. Prioritize risks based on potential impact and likelihood.
C. Implement a change management process.
D. Develop specific control procedures for all identified risks.

7. Which of the following is considered the most critical resource for an effective information security program?

A. Infrastructure
B. Information
C. Human Capital
D. Architecture

8. A CISO is reviewing a security policy document. The document is an example of which of the four key resource categories?

A. Human Capital
B. Information
C. Infrastructure
D. Architecture

9. An IT department is performing a system upgrade. To ensure security, they use a process that requires all changes to be reviewed and tested for security implications before being implemented. This is an example of:

A. Incident Response
B. Vulnerability Management
C. Change Management
D. Access Control

10. A security team is conducting a "walkthrough" of a new access control procedure for a critical database. The purpose of this walkthrough is to validate the:

A. Operational effectiveness of the control.
B. Design effectiveness of the control.
C. Corrective action plan.

D. Continuous improvement cycle.

11. A security manager uses a tool to examine a sample of system logs to find evidence of unauthorized access attempts. This testing technique is best described as:

A. Observation
B. Re-performance
C. Sampling and Inspection
D. Walkthrough

12. The objective of a penetration test is to:

A. Scan for known vulnerabilities using automated tools.
B. Conduct a manual, hands-on simulation of an attack to exploit vulnerabilities.
C. Review documentation to verify compliance with security policies.
D. Interview personnel to assess their understanding of security controls.

13. Which of the following is the final phase in the life cycle of monitoring and documenting information systems controls performance, which closes the feedback loop and ensures ongoing relevance?

A. Implementation
B. Documentation and Reporting
C. Continuous Improvement
D. Design

14. A Chief Information Security Officer (CISO) is a role that falls under which of the four categories of information systems security resources?

A. Architecture
B. Infrastructure
C. Human Capital
D. Information

15. An organization is building a new network. The network architect decides to use separate subnets for the web servers, database servers, and internal user workstations. This is an example of which security principle?

A. Least Privilege
B. Secure Configuration
C. Segmentation
D. Identity and Access Management (IAM)

16. A security team has a documented process for handling security breaches that includes

steps for detection, containment, eradication, and recovery. This is an example of a(n):

A. Vulnerability Management Plan
B. Change Management Plan
C. Incident Response Plan
D. Threat Intelligence Feed

17. A company uses a Security Information and Event Management (SIEM) system to consolidate logs from various devices and applications. This system provides a single view of the organization's security posture and is primarily used for:

A. Configuration management
B. Automated monitoring and detection
C. Endpoint protection
D. Data backups and recovery

18. In the context of the four resource categories, which of the following is an example of an infrastructure resource?

A. Security Policies
B. Network Topology
C. Servers and Firewalls
D. Incident Response Plans

19. A security auditor is conducting a "Test of Operational Effectiveness." Which of the following actions would be most indicative of this type of test?

A. Performing a walkthrough of the documented access control policy.
B. Reviewing a sample of user access requests from the past quarter to ensure they were all properly approved.
C. Evaluating whether a security control, as designed, is capable of mitigating a risk.
D. Interviewing the CISO to understand the overall security strategy.

20. What is the primary purpose of a "gray box" penetration test?

A. To simulate an attack with no prior knowledge of the internal system.
B. To conduct a comprehensive simulation of a sophisticated attack without the internal security team's knowledge.
C. To verify that controls meet specific standards and policies.
D. To simulate an attack with some limited knowledge of the system, such as a user account.

21. Which of the following is a primary goal of the "continuous improvement" phase in the control management lifecycle?

A. To perform an initial risk assessment to identify assets.
B. To deploy and configure new security tools and technologies.
C. To use data from monitoring and documentation to refine and improve controls.
D. To create clear, documented procedures for how each control will be applied.

22. A company's vulnerability management program involves regularly scanning systems and applications for known weaknesses and then patching them. This process primarily supports which of the following security objectives?

A. Availability
B. Confidentiality
C. Integrity
D. Compliance

23. A security team discovers a critical vulnerability in a public-facing web server. They immediately apply the necessary security patch to fix the issue. This action is an example of which type of control?

A. Preventive
B. Detective
C. Corrective
D. Deterrent

24. A security team is conducting a Red Team exercise. The primary characteristic of this exercise is that it is a:

A. Simple, automated check for known vulnerabilities.
B. Hands-on, manual test with full knowledge of the system.
C. Goal-oriented simulation of a sophisticated attack, often without the internal security team's knowledge.
D. Review of documentation to verify compliance.

25. A CISO is implementing a new control to ensure that only authorized individuals can access specific data. This control is directly related to the operational process of:

A. Change Management
B. Incident Response
C. Access Control
D. Vulnerability Management

26. Which of the following is a key objective of a formal risk assessment?

A. To install new security tools and technologies.
B. To prioritize risks based on their potential impact and likelihood.

C. To train employees on new security policies.
D. To generate a detailed report for stakeholders.

27. A security policy document that provides guidelines and rules for how security is managed within an organization is an example of which of the four key resource categories?

A. Human Capital
B. Information
C. Infrastructure
D. Architecture

28. The Mean Time to Remediate (MTTR) and the percentage of recurring errors are examples of:

A. Qualitative Risk Analysis
B. Root Cause Analysis (RCA) techniques
C. Key Performance Indicators (KPIs)
D. Corrective controls

29. An organization's objective is to protect against a Denial-of-Service (DoS) attack to ensure that its public- facing website remains operational. This objective aligns with which of the following principles?

A. Confidentiality
B. Integrity
C. Availability
D. Non-repudiation

30. In the context of designing and testing controls, a "Test of Design" is primarily concerned with:

A. Whether the control is being consistently and correctly applied in practice.
B. Whether a control, as documented, is capable of mitigating the risk.
C. The amount of time it takes to restore a system from backup.
D. The number of security incidents that occurred in the last quarter.

31. An auditor wants to verify that a company's "clean-desk policy" is being followed. The most effective testing method to achieve this would be:

A. Inquiry
B. Inspection
C. Observation
D. Re-performance

32. A security team uses a Python script to automatically query a user directory and compare it against a list of active employees from the HR system, generating a report of discrepancies. This is

an example of which type of automation tool?

A. Configuration Management Tool
B. Security Information and Event Management (SIEM)
C. Custom Scripts and APIs
D. Robotic Process Automation (RPA)

33. Which of the following is the core purpose of a "Fishbone Diagram" in a deficiency remediation process?

A. To assign ownership and deadlines for remediation tasks.
B. To provide a visual tool to categorize potential causes of a problem.
C. To document the overall security posture for executive leadership.
D. To test the effectiveness of a new control before it is deployed.

34. An organization is using a framework to address deficiencies. The first step in this process is:

A. Performing a root cause analysis (RCA).
B. Creating a detailed remediation plan.
C. Testing the implemented fix.
D. Identification and prioritization of the issue.

35. In the context of security architecture, which of the following is an example of a "secure-by-design" approach?

A. Adding a firewall to an existing network.
B. Segmenting the network into secure zones from the outset.
C. Implementing a SIEM to collect logs.
D. Conducting a penetration test on a new application.

36. An organization's strategic goal is to build customer trust. A CISO designs a control to ensure the confidentiality of all customer data. This is an example of:

A. The continuous improvement cycle.
B. Aligning controls with operational needs and goals.
C. A corrective control.
D. A detective control.

37. The process of regularly scanning systems and applications for known weaknesses and then patching them is known as:

A. Change Management
B. Incident Response
C. Vulnerability Management

D. Access Control

38. Which of the following is a primary characteristic of a preventive control?

A. It detects an event after it has occurred.
B. It fixes a problem identified by a detective control.
C. It is a proactive measure designed to stop an undesirable event from happening.
D. It is a management policy to guide employee behavior.

39. The process that ensures all IT changes are reviewed for security impact before deployment is called:

A. Change Management
B. Incident Response
C. Vulnerability Management
D. Risk Assessment

40. An auditor re-executes a data backup process to confirm its accuracy and effectiveness. This testing method is known as:

A. Observation
B. Inquiry
C. Inspection
D. Re-performance

41. In the context of the CIA triad, which of the following best describes the objective of "Integrity"?

A. To prevent the unauthorized disclosure of information.
B. To ensure that systems are accessible to authorized users when needed.
C. To maintain the accuracy and completeness of information.
D. To ensure that actions can be traced back to an individual.

42. A company's CISO is establishing a new team to manage daily operations, monitor for threats, and respond to incidents. This team falls under which of the four key resource categories?

A. Infrastructure
B. Architecture
C. Human Capital
D. Information

43. Which of the following is considered a core "Information" resource for a security program?

A. Firewalls
B. Security Policies

C. End-users
D. Operating Systems

44. Which type of control is designed to identify and flag an event after it has occurred?

A. Preventive
B. Corrective
C. Detective
D. Deterrent

45. A SIEM system, which centralizes security data and provides a single view of an organization's security posture, is primarily an example of which of the four key resource categories?

A. Human Capital
B. Information
C. Infrastructure
D. Architecture

46. Which of the following is a key objective of the "Implementation" phase of the control management life cycle?

A. Performing a risk assessment.
B. Measuring performance with metrics and KPIs.
C. Training all relevant staff on new policies and procedures.
D. Conducting a post-mortem analysis of a security incident.

47. A team is using the "5 Whys" technique to get to the root cause of a security incident. This technique is most effective for:

A. Complex problems with multiple, intertwined causes.
B. Problems that involve human factors or basic process failures.
C. Assigning ownership and deadlines for remediation tasks.
D. Auditing a large-scale enterprise network.

48. A company sets a goal to "Deploy all critical patches within 72 hours of release." This is an example of a:

A. Metric
B. Key Performance Indicator (KPI)
C. Root Cause Analysis (RCA)
D. Corrective Action Plan

49. In the context of security testing, what is the primary difference between vulnerability scanning and penetration testing?

A. Vulnerability scanning is manual, while penetration testing is automated.
B. Vulnerability scanning identifies known weaknesses, while penetration testing simulates an attack to exploit those weaknesses.
C. Vulnerability scanning is a corrective control, while penetration testing is a preventive control.
D. Vulnerability scanning is a black-box test, while penetration testing is a white-box test.

50. Which of the following is the first step in the "Planning and Design" phase of security control testing?

A. Choosing a specific testing methodology.
B. Defining the scope and objectives of the test.
C. Identifying the controls that need to be tested.
D. Gaining explicit authorization to conduct the test.

51. A CISO is trying to get a quick, visual overview of the organization's security posture. Which of the following would be the most effective tool for this purpose?

A. A detailed, multi-page audit report.
B. A centralized repository of all control procedures.
C. A dashboard that translates raw metrics and KPIs into actionable insights.
D. A spreadsheet with a list of all identified vulnerabilities.

52. What is the main purpose of the "Verify and Validate" step in a remediation process?

A. To assign a risk rating to a discovered deficiency.
B. To conduct a root cause analysis (RCA) of the deficiency.
C. To confirm that the implemented fix was successful and did not introduce new problems.
D. To report the findings to executive leadership.

53. An organization's security team uses a framework that involves defining the problem, drawing a diagram with major cause categories, and brainstorming possible causes. This is a description of:

A. The 5 Whys
B. A Fishbone Diagram
C. A SMART Plan
D. The CIA Triad

54. The process of using a software bot to automatically review a list of terminated employees and verify that their user accounts have been disabled is an example of:

A. Infrastructure as Code (IaC)
B. Security Information and Event Management (SIEM)
C. Robotic Process Automation (RPA)

D. Configuration Management

55. Which of the following is a key reason for documenting every step of a security control testing process?

A. To ensure a simple remediation plan is created.
B. To provide evidence for a compliance audit.
C. To isolate false positives.
D. To prepare the environment for the test.

56. The act of an independent party re-executing a control to see if they get the same result is a test of:

A. Design Effectiveness
B. Operational Effectiveness
C. Remediation Planning
D. Executive Reporting

57. An organization's security objective is to ensure that its information and systems are accessible to authorized users when needed. This is the definition of:

A. Confidentiality
B. Integrity
C. Availability
D. Accountability

58. A security manager uses a simple matrix to prioritize identified deficiencies. This matrix would likely categorize issues based on:

A. The owner and the deadline.
B. The technology and the required budget.
C. The impact on the business and the urgency of the issue.
D. The type of control (preventive, detective, corrective).

59. Which of the following is an example of a corrective control?

A. Restoring data from a backup.
B. Strong user passwords.
C. An intrusion detection system.
D. Data validation rules in an application.

60. An organization is conducting a security audit. The auditor's first step is to interview personnel to understand their knowledge of and adherence to security policies. This testing method is called:

A. Observation

B. Inspection
C. Inquiry
D. Re-performance

61. Which of the following best describes the top-down approach to designing IS controls?

A. Starting with the technical controls and building a strategy around them.
B. Starting with the organization's mission and strategic objectives.
C. Starting with the most critical systems and then moving to less critical ones.
D. Starting with a vulnerability scan to identify weaknesses.

62. In the context of automation, tools like Ansible, Puppet, and Chef are used primarily for:

A. Centralizing security data and alerting.
B. Simulating human actions for repetitive tasks.
C. Automating the provisioning and configuration of IT infrastructure.
D. Developing custom scripts and APIs.

63. Which of the following is a strategic, high-level indicator that shows how well a control is meeting an organizational objective?

A. A metric
B. A key risk indicator (KRI)
C. A key performance indicator (KPI)
D. A vulnerability

64. An organization's architecture resources would include:
A. The CISO and security analysts.
B. Security policies and incident response plans.
C. Firewalls and servers.
D. Network topology and secure OS configurations.

65. What is the purpose of "Mapping to Risks" when identifying deficiencies and gaps during a security test?

A. To assign ownership of the remediation task.
B. To classify the vulnerability by severity.
C. To help stakeholders understand the real-world business implications of the finding.
D. To isolate false positives from the test results.

66. A company needs to ensure that any new software installations are reviewed for security implications before being deployed. This falls under the operational process of:
A. Access Control

B. Vulnerability Management
C. Change Management
D. Data Protection

67. A CISO is reviewing a report that provides a high-level overview of business risks and the overall effectiveness of controls, tailored for leadership. This section of the report is known as the:

A. Technical Findings
B. Executive Summary
C. Recommendations
D. Remediation Plan

68. Which of the following is an example of an information resource for a security program?

A. A network switch.
B. A security analyst.
C. A threat intelligence feed.
D. A secure operating system.

69. In the context of a deficiency remediation plan, the acronym SMART stands for:

A. Secure, Managed, Automated, Reactive, and Tested.
B. Specific, Measurable, Assignable, Relevant, and Time-bound.
C. Systemic, Monitored, Analyzed, Reported, and Tested.
D. Secure, Measurable, Actionable, Relevant, and Timely.

70. A security team decides to update control policies and provide additional training based on insights gained from a recent security incident. This action is part of which phase of the control management life cycle?

A. Design
B. Implementation
C. Monitoring
D. Continuous Improvement

71. A major cloud service provider experiences a DDoS attack that makes its services unavailable to customers for several hours. This attack primarily impacted which of the following?

A. Integrity
B. Confidentiality
C. Availability
D. Non-repudiation

72. A security manager receives a report that shows the "Number of blocked malicious emails" and the "Time to patch a critical vulnerability." These are examples of:

A. Key Performance Indicators (KPIs)
B. Key Risk Indicators (KRIs)
C. Metrics
D. Corrective actions

73. The primary goal of a Test of Operational Effectiveness is to determine if a control is:

A. Documented in a comprehensive manner.
B. Capable of mitigating a risk as it is designed.
C. Being consistently and correctly applied in practice.
D. Aligned with the organization's business objectives.

74. A team is performing a manual, in-depth test that simulates a real-world attack on a system with full knowledge of its design and code. This is an example of a:

A. Black-box penetration test.
B. Gray-box penetration test.
C. White-box penetration test.
D. Red team exercise.

75. Which of the following is a key component of a remediation plan according to the document?

A. A high-level executive summary.
B. A technical breakdown of the vulnerability.
C. Prioritized action items and assigned ownership.
D. A new audit to be conducted.

76. A CISO is assessing the current control environment to identify candidates for automation. A control that would be a good candidate for automation is one that:

A. Requires human judgment and decision-making.
B. Is a one-time, non-repeatable task.
C. Involves manual, repeatable actions.
D. Is already fully effective and well-documented.

77. Which of the following is an example of a preventive control?

A. A log monitoring system.
B. Data backups.
C. An intrusion detection system.
D. A firewall.

78. Which of the following is an example of an Infrastructure as Code (IaC) tool?

A. Ansible
B. Splunk
C. UiPath
D. Python

79. A company is evaluating the health of its problem management process. A high percentage of recurring errors would indicate:

A. The team is consistently following the process.
B. A need for more resources.
C. A failure in the root cause analysis or remediation plan.
D. A decrease in the Mean Time to Remediate (MTTR).

80. A security team is conducting a security test and discovers that an IDS failed to log a suspicious activity. This finding relates to the control's:

A. Design effectiveness.
B. Operational effectiveness.
C. Corrective function.
D. Preventive function.

81. A CISO needs to choose an automated tool that can centralize security data from various sources to provide a single view of the organization's security posture. Which tool category would be most appropriate?

A. Configuration Management
B. Robotic Process Automation (RPA)
C. Security Information and Event Management (SIEM)
D. Custom Scripts

82. What is the final step in the control testing cycle, which closes the loop and confirms the control is now effective?

A. Create a detailed report.
B. Develop a remediation plan.
C. Communicate the results to stakeholders.
D. Retest and validate the corrected controls.

83. A company's CISO wants to ensure that the security program is aligned with the company's core principles of Confidentiality, Integrity, and Availability. This is an example of aligning security with:

A. Operational Processes

B. Organizational Objectives
C. Human Capital
D. Infrastructure

84. The process of identifying potential threats and vulnerabilities to information assets, analyzing the risk they pose, and determining appropriate controls to mitigate that risk is known as:

A. Incident Response
B. Vulnerability Management
C. Change Management
D. Risk Assessment and Management

85. Which of the following is a primary objective of the "Documentation and Reporting" phase of the control management life cycle?

A. To deploy and configure new security tools.
B. To create a feedback loop for continuous improvement.
C. To provide evidence of due diligence and inform decision-making.
D. To identify which controls are underperforming.

86. A security team uses a custom Python script to query an API and compare a list of user accounts with the HR system. This is an example of using which resource type?

A. Human Capital
B. Infrastructure
C. Architecture
D. Information

87. A CISO is reviewing a report that details the specific vulnerabilities, evidence, and risk ratings found during a recent penetration test. This information is intended for:

A. Executive leadership.
B. Legal and compliance teams.
C. Technical IT and security teams.
D. Human resources personnel.

88. What is the purpose of conducting a "post-mortem" analysis of all security incidents?

A. To assign blame to a specific individual.
B. To provide a high-level overview for management.
C. To understand what controls failed and how to prevent similar events in the future.
D. To identify new business objectives.

89. A security team is designing a new system and makes a conscious decision to divide the network into secure zones to limit the lateral movement of threats. This is an example of a concept

related to:

A. Infrastructure as Code (IaC)
B. Network Topology
C. The CIA Triad
D. The 5 Whys

90. An auditor reviews a company's system logs and audit trails to verify that controls have been applied and documented correctly. This testing method is called:

A. Observation
B. Inspection of Evidence
C. Inquiry
D. Re-performance

91. A CISO is implementing a security control that involves a "password complexity and expiration policy." This control is designed to protect which of the following?

A. The availability of the system.
B. The integrity of the data.
C. The confidentiality of the data.
D. The physical security of the data.

92. The phase of the control management lifecycle that involves training all relevant staff and establishing a plan for continuous monitoring is:

A. Design
B. Implementation
C. Monitoring
D. Continuous Improvement

93. A company's CISO is using a "black box" penetration test. This means the testing team has:

A. Full knowledge of the system, including source code.
B. Some limited knowledge, such as a user account.
C. No prior knowledge of the internal system.
D. The goal of simulating a sophisticated attack without the internal security team's knowledge.

94. What is the primary purpose of an Asset Inventory in a security program?

A. To list all security policies and procedures.
B. To identify potential threats and vulnerabilities.
C. To provide a comprehensive list of all information systems and data to prioritize protection.
D. To detail the steps for handling a security breach.

95. The concept of using a centralized system to record errors and deficiencies, including the date of discovery and the full history of the remediation effort, is essential for:

A. Executive reporting.
B. Trend analysis and identifying systemic issues.
C. Assigning ownership of tasks.
D. Creating an executive summary.

96. A CISO is analyzing a metric that shows the "Number of failed login attempts." This metric is most directly related to which operational process?

A. Change Management
B. Incident Response
C. Vulnerability Management
D. Access Control

97. An organization's objective is to prevent the unauthorized disclosure of customer data. This objective is a direct reflection of which principle of the CIA triad?

A. Confidentiality
B. Integrity
C. Availability
D. Non-repudiation

98. A remediation plan should be "Assignable," which means:

A. The actions must address the root cause.
B. It must be a specific and clear task.
C. It must have clear ownership assigned to individuals or teams.
D. It must be a measurable action.

99. A CISO wants to automate a repetitive task. The most suitable tool for this would be:

A. A threat intelligence feed.
B. A SIEM.
C. A configuration management tool.
D. A vulnerability scanner.

100. A company's post-mortem analysis of a security incident reveals that a preventive control failed, which led to the breach. Based on this finding, the CISO decides to update the control policy and provide additional training. This is a clear example of:

A. The testing phase.
B. The implementation phase.
C. The continuous improvement cycle.

D. The design phase.

Answer Key

1. C.

Aligning security controls with the organization's strategic business goals and objectives is the first and most critical step in a top-down approach to security program design. The other options are subsequent steps or tactical measures.

2. B.

The objective to maintain the accuracy and completeness of information and prevent unauthorized or accidental modification of data is the definition of Integrity. Confidentiality is about preventing unauthorized disclosure, and Availability is about ensuring access when needed. Accountability is not mentioned as a core principle in the CIA triad.

3. B.

Designing a system to be inherently secure from the ground up, such as by building in encryption from the start, is known as a secure-by-design approach. It is a principle of security architecture.

4. B.

Security awareness training is a proactive measure intended to stop an undesirable event (like a phishing attack) from happening by educating employees, making it a Preventive control. It doesn't detect or fix a problem after it has occurred.

5. D.

The act of a SIEM detecting and alerting on an event after it has occurred is a classic example of a Detective control. It identifies an issue, but does not prevent it from happening.

6. B. According to the document, after identifying risks, the next step in the design process is to prioritize them based on their potential impact and likelihood. This ensures design efforts are focused on the highest-risk areas first.

7. C.

The document explicitly states that Human Capital is the most critical resource, as technology alone cannot secure a system.

8. B.

Information is defined as the data, knowledge, policies, and procedures that guide security operations, and security policies are listed as a key example.

9. C.

Change Management is the process that ensures any changes to an organization's IT infrastructure are reviewed and tested for security implications before implementation.

10. B.

A walkthrough is a technique used in the "Test of Design Effectiveness" to determine if a control, as it is documented, is capable of mitigating a risk by tracing a transaction from start to finish.

11. C.

The use of sampling to test a control over a period of time by examining a sample of transactions or logs for evidence of control performance is described as Sampling and Inspection.

12. B.

Penetration testing is defined as a more hands-on, simulated attack to exploit vulnerabilities and assess the potential impact. Vulnerability scanning is an automated check for known vulnerabilities.

13. C.

The final step in the lifecycle is Continuous Improvement, which uses the data gathered to refine and improve controls, creating a feedback loop.

14. C.

The CISO is listed as an example of a Human Capital resource, as they provide strategic leadership for the security program.

15. C.

The act of dividing a network into secure zones to limit the lateral movement of threats is known as Segmentation, a key principle of secure architecture.

16. C.

The process for handling security breaches, including detection, containment, eradication, and recovery, is the definition of an Incident Response plan.

17. B.

The document states that SIEM systems are essential for automating detection and alerting by centralizing and correlating security data from various sources.

18. C.

Infrastructure encompasses the physical and virtual hardware components that host and connect the information systems. Servers and Firewalls are explicitly listed as examples of infrastructure resources.

19. B. A Test of Operational Effectiveness determines if the control is being consistently and correctly applied in practice. Reviewing a sample of logs or requests is a technique for this type of test, as mentioned in the document.

20. D.

The document defines a "gray box" penetration test as one that is conducted with some limited knowledge of the system.

21. C.

The continuous improvement phase is explicitly described as using the data from monitoring and documentation to refine and improve controls.

22. C.

Vulnerability management, by patching weaknesses, ensures that data and systems are not altered or corrupted by attackers, which supports the Integrity objective.

23. C.

A corrective control is an action taken to fix a problem that has been identified by a detective control, such as a security patch update.

24. C.

A Red Team exercise is a comprehensive, goal-oriented simulation of a sophisticated attack, often without the internal security team's knowledge.

25. C.

A control designed to ensure only authorized individuals can access data is directly related to the Access Control operational process.

26. B.

A key objective of a formal risk assessment is to prioritize risks based on their potential impact and likelihood to focus design efforts.

27. B.

Security Policies and Frameworks are categorized as an Information resource, which refers to the data, knowledge, and procedures that guide security operations.

28. C.

Mean Time to Remediate (MTTR) and Percentage of Recurring Errors are listed as examples of Key Performance Indicators (KPIs) used to measure the health of a problem management process.

29. C.

Availability is the principle that ensures information and systems are accessible to authorized users when needed, and it includes protection against disruptions like a DoS attack.

30. B.

The goal of a "Test of Design Effectiveness" is to determine if the control, as it is documented, is capable of mitigating the risk.

31. C.

Observation involves watching personnel perform their duties to see if they are following established security procedures, which is the most effective way to test a policy like a clean-desk policy.

32. C.

The document states that custom scripts using languages like Python are invaluable for controls that are unique to the environment, especially when programmatically interacting with systems via APIs.

33. B.

A Fishbone Diagram is described as a visual tool used for root cause analysis to identify and categorize all the possible causes of a specific problem or "effect".

34. D.

The first step in the remediation process is the "Identification and Prioritization" of the deficiency.

35. B.

Security architecture is about designing systems to be inherently secure from the ground up, and segmentation is listed as a key architectural resource for dividing a network into secure zones to limit threats.

36. B.

The document states that controls must be designed to protect the business's objectives. An example given is designing a control to ensure the confidentiality of customer data to protect a goal of customer trust.

37. C.

Vulnerability Management involves regularly scanning systems and applications for known weaknesses and then patching or configuring them to remove those vulnerabilities.

38. C.

A preventive control is defined as a proactive measure designed to stop an undesirable event from happening.

39. A.

The document defines Change Management as the process that ensures any changes to an organization's IT infrastructure are reviewed and tested for security implications before being implemented.

40. D.

Re-performance is a testing method where an independent party re-executes a control process to confirm its accuracy and effectiveness.

41. C.

Integrity is the objective to maintain the accuracy and completeness of information and prevent unauthorized or accidental modification of data.

42. C.

Security analysts and system administrators, who manage daily operations and respond to incidents, are explicitly categorized under Human Capital.

43. B.

The document lists Security Policies as a key information resource, which includes the data, knowledge, and procedures that guide security operations.

44. C.

Detective controls are reactive measures designed to identify and flag an event **after** it has occurred, such as audit trails and intrusion detection systems.

45. B.

While a SIEM system is a tool, its primary purpose is to manage and analyze security data, policies, and procedures, which are defined as "Information" resources.

46. C.

The implementation phase involves training all relevant staff, communicating new policies, and establishing a plan for continuous monitoring.

47. B.

The "5 Whys" method is most effective for problems that involve human factors, interactions, or basic process failures.

48. B.

A Key Performance Indicator (KPI) is a strategic, high-level indicator that shows how well controls are meeting organizational objectives, and the document provides "Deploy all critical patches within 72 hours of release" as an example of a KPI.

49. B.

The document clearly distinguishes the two: vulnerability scanning uses automated tools to identify known vulnerabilities, while penetration testing is a more hands-on, simulated attack to exploit them.

50. B.

The first step of the "Planning and Design" phase is to "Define Scope and Objectives".

51. C.

The document states that a dashboard should provide a quick, visual overview of the organization's security posture by translating raw metrics and KPIs into actionable insights.

52. C.

The "Verification and Closure" step involves verifying that the remediation was successful and that the fix did not introduce any new problems.

53. B.

The process described—defining a problem and then creating a diagram with a head, spine, and major cause categories—is the method for creating a Fishbone Diagram.

54. C.

Robotic Process Automation (RPA) is defined as using software bots to mimic human actions to perform repetitive tasks, and the scenario described is a direct use case for this technology.

55. B.

Documenting every step of the control testing process is essential for providing evidence of due diligence and for demonstrating compliance with industry standards.

56. B.

The document states that re-performance is a technique used to test the "Operational

Effectiveness" of a control.

57. C.

Availability is the objective to ensure that information and systems are accessible to authorized users when needed.

58. C.

A simple matrix for prioritization categorizes issues based on their impact on the business and their urgency.

59. A.

Restoring data from a backup is listed as an example of a Corrective control, which is an action taken to fix a problem.

60. C.

Inquiry is a common testing method that involves interviewing personnel to understand their knowledge of and adherence to security policies.

61. B.

The first step in designing IS controls is a "top-down approach" that starts with the organization's mission and strategic objectives.

62. C.

The document describes Configuration Management Tools like Ansible, Puppet, and Chef as being designed to automate the provisioning and configuration of servers and IT infrastructure.

63. C.

A Key Performance Indicator (KPI) is defined as a strategic, high-level indicator that shows how well controls are meeting organizational objectives.

64. D. Architecture refers to the design, structure, and relationships of the information systems. Network topology and secure OS configurations are explicitly listed as examples of architectural resources.

65. C.

The purpose of mapping findings to risks is to help stakeholders understand the real-world business implications of a deficiency.

66. C.

The document defines Change Management as the process that ensures any changes to an organization's IT infrastructure are reviewed for security implications before being implemented.

67. B.

The Executive Summary is a high-level overview for leadership that focuses on business risks and the overall effectiveness of controls.

68. C.

The document lists Threat Intelligence Feeds as an example of an Information resource, which includes data and knowledge that guide security operations.

69. B.

The document states that a remediation plan should be "SMART," which stands for Specific, Measurable, Assignable, Relevant, and Time-bound.

70. D.

The document states that the final step in the lifecycle is Continuous Improvement, where data from monitoring and analysis of incidents is used to adapt and adjust policies and training.

71. C.

A Denial-of-Service (DoS) attack makes systems unavailable to authorized users, directly impacting the Availability principle of the CIA triad.

72. C.

The document defines metrics as the raw, quantitative data points that are collected, and lists "Number of blocked malicious emails" and "Time to patch a critical vulnerability" as examples.

73. C.

The primary goal of a "Test of Operational Effectiveness" is to determine if the control is being consistently and correctly applied in practice.

74. C.

A "white box" penetration test is defined as a manual, in-depth test that is performed with full knowledge of the system.

75. C.

The document states that a remediation plan should include prioritized action items, assigned ownership, and a clear timeline.

76. C.

The document suggests identifying controls that require "manual, repeatable actions" as good candidates for automation[77].

77. D.

The document lists firewalls as a proactive measure designed to stop an undesirable event from happening, which is the definition of a preventive control.

78. A.

Ansible is explicitly listed as an Infrastructure as Code (IaC) tool designed to automate the provisioning and configuration of IT infrastructure.

79. C.

A high percentage of recurring errors is stated as an indicator of a failure in the Root Cause Analysis (RCA) or the remediation plan.

80. B.

If a control failed to perform as expected (e.g., an IDS failing to log activity), this indicates a flaw in its operational effectiveness, as it was not being correctly applied in practice.

81. C.

The document states that SIEM systems centralize security data from various sources to provide a single view of an organization's security posture and are essential for automating detection and alerting.

82. D.

The final step of the control testing cycle is to retest the corrected controls to verify that the fix was successful, which closes the loop.

83. B.

The document states that an organization's objectives related to information security are centered on the CIA triad, and aligning controls with these objectives is crucial for a robust security management system.

84. D.

The definition provided is that of the Risk Assessment and Management process, which is the foundational process for all security activities.

85. C.

The purpose of documentation is to provide evidence of due diligence and to inform decision-making, while reports and dashboards translate raw data into actionable insights for stakeholders.

86. D.

The document explicitly lists "Custom Scripts and APIs" as a key technique and resource for automation. These resources are a part of the broader

Information category, but "Custom Scripts and APIs" is the more specific and correct answer here based on the document's breakdown.

87. C.

The document states that the "Technical Findings" section of a report is a detailed breakdown for IT and security teams, including descriptions of vulnerabilities, evidence, and risk ratings.

88. C.

A post-mortem analysis of a security incident is conducted to understand what controls failed and how to prevent similar events in the future.

89. B.

Network topology is listed as an example of an architectural resource, and segmentation is a key principle of a well-designed network topology.

90. B.

Inspection of Evidence is a testing method that involves reviewing documentation and logs to find evidence that controls were performed correctly.

91. C.

A password complexity and expiration policy is an access control that ensures only authorized individuals can access specific data, which directly protects the confidentiality of that data.

92. B.

The Implementation phase, which follows successful testing, involves training all relevant staff and establishing a plan for continuous monitoring.

93. C.

A "black box" penetration test is defined as a manual, in-depth test that simulates a real-world attack with no prior knowledge of the system.

94. C.

The document states that an Asset Inventory is a comprehensive list of all information systems and data, which helps to prioritize which assets need the most protection.

95. B.

Recording all errors and their remediation history in a centralized system is vital for trend analysis and identifying systemic issues.

96. D.

The number of failed login attempts is a metric directly related to the operational process of Access Control, which involves managing user accounts and authentication.

97. A.

The objective to prevent the unauthorized disclosure of information is the definition of Confidentiality.

98. C.

The document states that the "Assignable" component of a SMART plan means assigning clear ownership to individuals or teams.

99. C.

The document lists Configuration Management Tools as being excellent for automating repetitive tasks like ensuring systems are configured securely and consistently across an organization.

100. C.

Using data from an incident analysis to adapt and adjust control policies and training is a key part of the Continuous Improvement phase, which creates a feedback loop to refine and improve controls over time.

CCISO Explain IT Like I Am 5: Domain 3

Security Program Management & Operations

Security Program Management Explained

Security program management is the long-term, strategic effort to establish and maintain an organization's cybersecurity framework. Unlike security project management, which focuses on a single initiative with a defined start and end, program management is a continuous process that oversees multiple projects and initiatives to achieve a cohesive and mature security posture. It's about integrating security into the DNA of an organization, ensuring that it's a foundational element of how the business operates.

Key Components of a Security Program

A successful security program is built on several interconnected pillars:

- **Governance:** This is the foundation, defining the policies, standards, and procedures that guide the program. It involves establishing a security steering committee, defining roles and responsibilities, and ensuring compliance with legal and regulatory requirements (e.g., GDPR, HIPAA, PCI DSS).
- **Risk Management:** The core of any security program is a strong risk management

framework. This involves identifying potential threats and vulnerabilities, assessing their likelihood and impact, and implementing controls to mitigate unacceptable risks. This is a continuous process of discovery and mitigation.

- **Security Architecture & Engineering:** This component focuses on designing and building secure systems from the ground up. It includes selecting and implementing security technologies (like firewalls and intrusion detection systems), ensuring secure configurations, and integrating security controls into the software development lifecycle (SDLC).
- **Operations & Incident Response:** This is the day-to-day execution of the program. It includes continuous monitoring of security systems, managing user access, and having a well-defined plan to detect, respond to, and recover from security incidents. A robust incident response plan is critical for minimizing damage during a breach.
- **Security Awareness & Training:** The human element is often the weakest link. This component involves educating employees about security best practices, recognizing phishing attacks, and understanding their role in protecting the organization's data. A strong security culture is a powerful defense.
- **Measurement & Reporting:** You can't manage what you can't measure. This involves defining key performance indicators (KPIs) and metrics to track the effectiveness of the security program. Regular reporting to leadership provides visibility into the program's maturity and demonstrates its value to the business.

The Security Program Lifecycle

Security program management is a cyclical process, often broken down into four phases:

- **Assess & Plan:** The program begins with an assessment of the organization's current security posture, a business impact analysis, and a risk analysis. Based on this, a strategic plan is developed with clear objectives, a roadmap, and a budget.
- **Design & Implement:** In this phase, the security controls, policies, and technologies are designed and then implemented. This can involve new hardware, software, or changes to existing processes.
- **Operate & Monitor:** The program becomes operational. This is the continuous, day-to-day phase where security teams monitor systems, manage incidents, and enforce policies.
- **Review & Improve:** The program's effectiveness is regularly reviewed against its metrics and objectives. This feedback loop is essential for identifying gaps, adapting

to new threats, and continuously improving the program's maturity.

The Importance of a Structured Program

By implementing a formal security program, an organization moves from a reactive, crisis-driven approach to a proactive, strategic one. This not only reduces the likelihood and impact of security incidents but also ensures compliance, builds stakeholder trust, and enables the business to pursue new opportunities securely. It provides a structured way to manage the ever-evolving landscape of cybersecurity threats.

> **From Reactive to Proactive**
>
> A structured security program transforms an organization's approach from fighting fires to building a fortress. It reduces incident impact, ensures compliance, builds stakeholder trust, and enables the business to innovate securely in an evolving threat landscape.

Identifying Resources

The first step in building a robust information security program is to identify all the resources you will need. This goes beyond just a shopping list; it requires a strategic understanding of the program's goals and the gaps you need to fill.

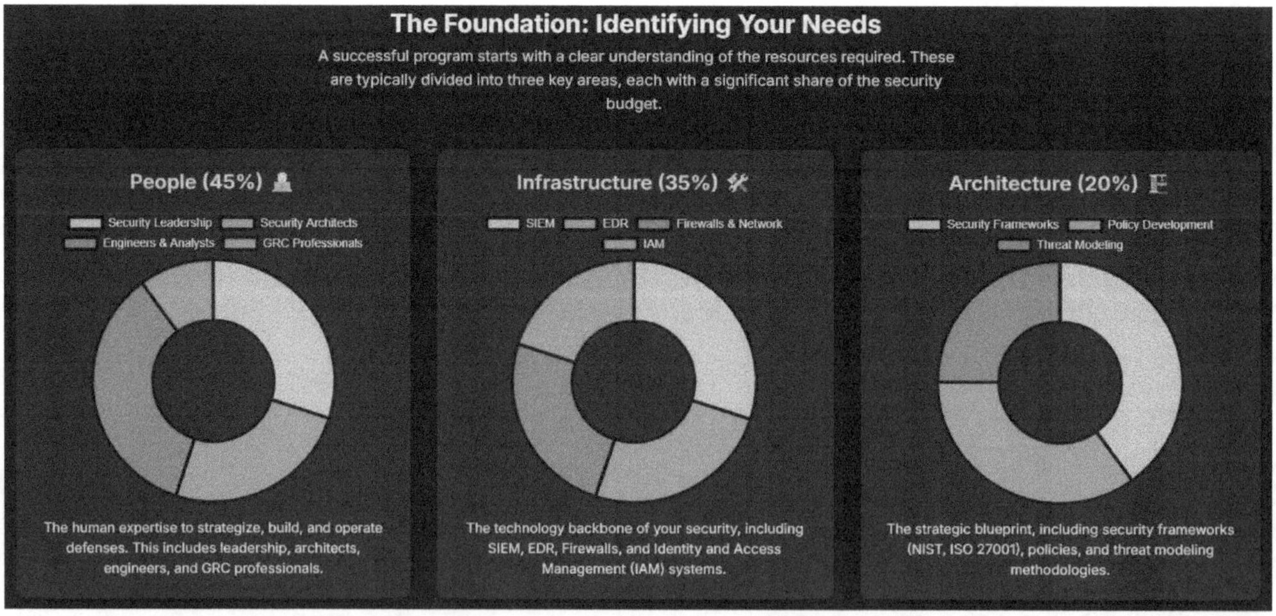

People

This is the most critical resource. You need to determine the roles, skills, and expertise required to design, implement, and operate your security program.

- **Security Leadership:** A CISO or security director to set strategy and manage the program.
- **Security Architects:** Experts who design the overall security posture and ensure new systems are built securely.
- **Engineers & Analysts:** The team that implements and manages security tools, monitors for threats, and responds to incidents.
- **Governance, Risk, and Compliance (GRC) Professionals:** Individuals who ensure the program meets regulatory requirements and internal policies.

Infrastructure & Technology

This category includes all the hardware, software, and services that form the backbone of your security defenses.

- **Security Information and Event Management (SIEM):** A platform to centralize and analyze security alerts.
- **Endpoint Detection and Response (EDR):** Tools to protect and monitor individual computers and servers.
- **Firewalls & Network Security:** Hardware and software that controls network traffic.
- **Identity and Access Management (IAM):** Systems that manage user identities and their access to resources.

Architecture & Design

This is the strategic blueprint for your security program. Resources here include the frameworks, policies, and methodologies you will adopt.

- **Security Frameworks:** Standards like NIST, ISO 27001, or CIS Controls that guide your program's structure.
- **Policies & Procedures:** Written rules and guidelines that dictate how security is managed across the organization.
- **Threat Modeling:** A structured process for identifying and prioritizing potential threats.

Negotiating and Acquiring Resources

Once you've identified what you need, you must make a compelling case for why you need it. This is where negotiation and acquisition come in. The key is to frame your requests in terms of business value.

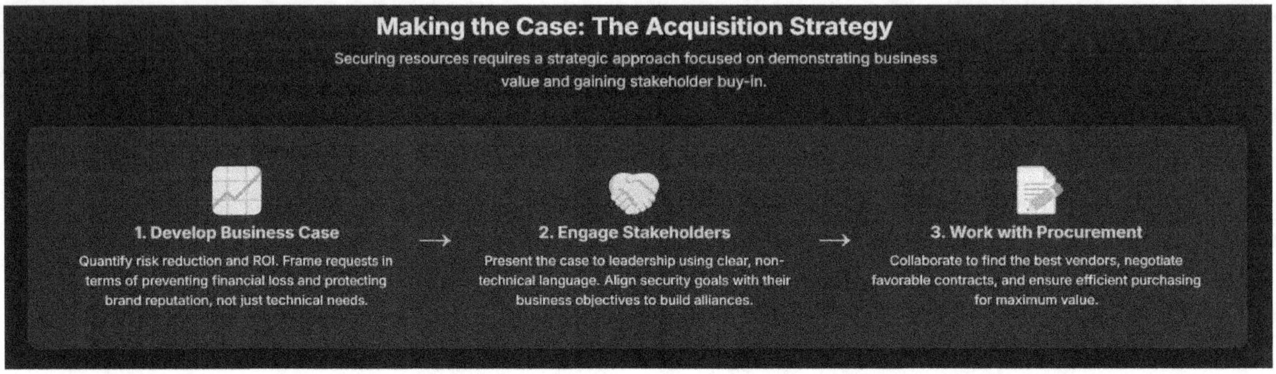

- **Develop a Business Case:** Quantify the benefits of the resources. Focus on how they will reduce risk, prevent financial loss, maintain compliance, and protect the brand's reputation. For example, instead of asking for a new firewall, explain how it will prevent a potential breach that could cost the company millions.
- **Engage Stakeholders:** Present your business case to executive leadership and department heads. Show them how the security program supports their business objectives. Use clear, non-technical language to explain the risks and the proposed solutions.
- **Work with Procurement:** Collaborate with your procurement department to find the best vendors, negotiate contracts, and manage the purchasing process efficiently. This ensures you get the best value for your budget.

Managing Resources

Acquiring resources is just the beginning. Effective management is essential for long-term program success.

People Management

- **Training & Development:** Ensure your team stays up-to-date with the latest threats and technologies through continuous training and certifications.

- **Performance Monitoring:** Set clear metrics and key performance indicators (KPIs) to measure your team's effectiveness and provide feedback.
- **Retention:** Foster a positive work environment and provide growth opportunities to retain top talent.

Infrastructure Management

- **Lifecycle Management:** Regularly review and update your security tools and infrastructure. This includes patching vulnerabilities, upgrading to new versions, and replacing outdated technology.
- **Cost Optimization:** Continuously monitor the usage and cost of your security tools to ensure you're getting the most out of your budget.

Architecture & Program Management

- **Documentation:** Maintain thorough documentation of your security policies, procedures, and architectural decisions.
- **Continuous Improvement:** Regularly audit your program against your chosen framework and business objectives. Use the findings to refine your strategy and re-evaluate your resource needs.

Developing a Project Scope Statement for a Security Project

A project scope statement serves as the foundation for any information systems project within a security program. It provides a shared understanding among all stakeholders about what the project will achieve, what it won't, and how its success will be measured. It should directly align with broader organizational objectives, such as regulatory compliance, risk reduction, or protecting critical assets.

Project Justification: The "Why"

Every security project must address a clear business need. By implementing Multi-Factor Authentication (MFA), the goal is to significantly reduce the risk of unauthorized access and ensure compliance with data protection regulations.

80%

Targeted Risk Reduction

1. Project Justification and Business Need

This section explains the "why" behind the project. It should clearly state the problem or opportunity the project addresses, linking it to organizational goals.

Example: "The current system lacks multi-factor authentication, posing a significant risk of unauthorized access. This project is necessary to comply with the upcoming PII data protection regulations and reduce the overall cybersecurity risk posture, aligning with the organizational objective to secure customer data."

2. Project Objectives

The objectives are the specific, measurable goals the project aims to accomplish. They should be clear, concise, and ideally follow the SMART criteria: Specific, Measurable, Achievable, Relevant, and Time-bound.

Example: "Implement multi-factor authentication (MFA) for all critical systems, ensuring at least 95% of users are enrolled by the end of Q3. This will reduce the risk of compromised accounts by 80%."

3. Scope and Deliverables

This is the core of the statement, defining the boundaries of the project. It lists what will be produced (in-scope) and what is explicitly excluded (out-of-scope) to prevent scope creep.

In-Scope:

- **Deliverable 1:** A new security policy mandating the use of MFA.
- **Deliverable 2:** A fully configured MFA solution integrated with the existing identity management system.
- **Deliverable 3:** User training materials and a rollout communication plan.
- **Deliverable 4:** A vulnerability assessment report confirming the successful implementation of MFA on all critical systems.

Core Deliverables: What We Will Build

The project's success is measured by the completion of tangible outputs.
These are the key deliverables that will be produced.

1. New Security Policy
Official documentation mandating the use of MFA across the organization.

2. Configured MFA Solution
A fully integrated and tested MFA system ready for enterprise-wide use.

3. User Training & Comms
Materials and a communication plan to ensure a smooth rollout to all users.

4. Vulnerability Assessment
A final report confirming the successful and secure implementation of MFA.

Out-of-Scope:

- Implementation of MFA for non-critical systems.
- User enrollment for third-party applications.
- Upgrades to the existing identity management system itself.

4. Constraints and Assumptions

Project Constraints

Every project operates within defined limits. These constraints shape the project's execution and planning.

Budget	Timeline	Resources
$50,000	6 Months	2 Core Members

This section outlines any limitations that will affect the project's execution.

Constraints:

- **Budget:** The project must not exceed a budget of $50,000.
- **Timeline:** The project must be completed within 6 months.
- **Resources:** Limited to one full-time security engineer and one part-time project manager.

Assumptions:

- All required technical documentation for the existing identity management system is available.
- Stakeholders will be available for meetings and approvals as needed.

5. Stakeholders

Identify all key individuals and groups involved in or affected by the project. This helps define communication channels and responsibilities.

- **Project Sponsor:** Chief Information Security Officer (CISO)
- **Project Manager:** Jane Doe
- **Technical Team:** IT Security Team, IT Operations Team
- **End Users:** All employees accessing critical systems

Information Security Program Execution Plan

This document outlines a strategic plan for the successful execution of an information security program. It defines the core activities, provides estimated durations for each, and proposes a schedule and staffing plan to guide implementation. The goal is to establish a robust and comprehensive security posture that protects organizational assets and data.

1. Core Activities and Phases

The program is broken down into four key phases, each with specific activities.

Phase 1: Program Foundation (Initial Setup)

- **Activity 1: Program Charter & Scope Definition:** Formally define the program's objectives, scope, and governance structure. This includes identifying key stakeholders and obtaining executive sponsorship.
- **Activity 2: Current State Assessment:** Conduct a thorough review of the existing security controls, policies, and procedures. This activity establishes a baseline for future improvements.
- **Activity 3: Risk Assessment:** Identify, analyze, and prioritize potential security risks to organizational assets. This forms the basis for all security decisions.

Phase 2: Policy & Control Implementation

- **Activity 4: Policy Development & Update:** Create or update security policies, standards, and guidelines based on the risk assessment findings and regulatory requirements.
- **Activity 5: Technical Control Implementation:** Deploy and configure security technologies such as firewalls, intrusion detection systems, endpoint protection, and identity management solutions.
- **Activity 6: Security Architecture Design:** Develop a secure architecture for networks, systems, and applications to ensure that security is built-in from the ground up.

Phase 3: Operational Integration

- **Activity 7: Security Monitoring & Incident Response:** Establish a Security Operations Center (SOC) function to monitor security events, and develop a clear incident response plan to handle and recover from security breaches.
- **Activity 8: Vulnerability Management:** Implement a process for regularly scanning for, identifying, and remediating security vulnerabilities in systems and applications.
- **Activity 9: Third-Party Risk Management:** Develop a process to assess and manage the security risks posed by vendors and other third-party partners.

Phase 4: Maintenance & Improvement

- **Activity 10: Security Training & Awareness:** Develop and deliver ongoing training for all employees to build a security-conscious culture.
- **Activity 11: Auditing & Compliance:** Conduct regular internal and external audits to verify compliance with policies and regulations (e.g., GDPR, HIPAA).
- **Activity 12: Continuous Improvement:** Regularly review and update the security program based on new threats, technologies, and business needs.

2. Estimated Activity Durations

The following are estimated durations for each activity. These are highly dependent on the organization's size, complexity, and available resources.

Activity	Estimated Duration

1. Program Charter & Scope Definition	2-4 weeks
2. Current State Assessment	4-6 weeks
3. Risk Assessment	6-8 weeks
4. Policy Development & Update	4-8 weeks
5. Technical Control Implementation	8-12 weeks
6. Security Architecture Design	6-10 weeks
7. Security Monitoring & Incident Response	6-10 weeks
8. Vulnerability Management	4-6 weeks
9. Third-Party Risk Management	4-6 weeks
10. Security Training & Awareness	Ongoing (initial rollout: 4-6 weeks)
11. Auditing & Compliance	Ongoing (initial audit: 4-8 weeks)
12. Continuous Improvement	Ongoing

3. Program Schedule (Phased Approach)

This high-level schedule provides a logical flow for the program's execution. Dependencies mean that some activities cannot start until others are complete.

- **Phase 1: Program Foundation.** Start with the program charter, followed by the current state and risk assessments.
- **Phase 2: Policy & Control Implementation.** This phase can run in parallel with some

foundational work. Policy development should be informed by the risk assessment. Technical controls and architecture design can happen concurrently.

- **Phase 3: Operational Integration.** As controls are implemented, focus on establishing security monitoring, incident response, and vulnerability management processes.
- **Phase 4: Maintenance & Improvement.** The program enters a continuous cycle of training, auditing, and improvement.

4. Staffing Plan & Roles

A successful program requires a dedicated team with clear responsibilities.

Chief Information Security Officer (CISO) / Information Security Manager:

- **Responsibilities:** Overall strategic leadership, program governance, risk management oversight, and reporting to executive leadership.

Security Architect:

- **Responsibilities:** Designs and plans the security framework for the organization's networks, systems, and applications. This role is key to Activity 6: Security Architecture Design.

Security Engineer:

- **Responsibilities:** Implements, tests, and maintains the security technologies and controls. This role is essential for Activity 5: Technical Control Implementation.

Security Analysts:

- **Responsibilities:** Day-to-day security monitoring, incident triage and response, and vulnerability management.

IT Operations & Systems Staff:

- **Responsibilities:** Implementing and maintaining technical security controls, managing user access, and assisting with vulnerability remediation.

Compliance Officer / Legal Counsel:

- **Responsibilities:** Ensuring the program meets all regulatory and legal obligations.

Cross-Functional Team:

- **Responsibilities:** Representatives from various departments (HR, Legal, Finance) to ensure policies are effective and widely adopted. The HR team is crucial for implementing training programs and background checks.

Assembling Your Security Team

CISO / Security Manager
Provides overall strategic leadership, governance, and risk management oversight.

Security Architect
Designs the security framework for networks, systems, and applications.

Security Engineer
Implements, tests, and maintains security technologies and controls.

Security Analyst
Handles day-to-day security monitoring, incident response, and vulnerability management.

IT Operations Staff
Assists in implementing controls, managing user access, and vulnerability remediation.

Compliance / Legal
Ensures the program meets all regulatory and legal requirements.

- **Identify Required Skills:** For each role, list the essential technical and soft skills. Technical skills might include cloud security expertise, specific programming languages, or knowledge of security frameworks. Soft skills, such as problem-solving, attention to detail, and communication, are equally critical for a cohesive team.
- **Recruitment and Vetting:** Partner with HR and recruiters who understand the nuances of the cybersecurity field. Conduct thorough technical interviews and practical exercises (e.g., a capture-the-flag scenario) to validate candidates' skills beyond their resumes. Look for individuals who are not only skilled but also passionate and adaptable.

Developing Your Team: Fostering Growth

Once you have your team, development is a continuous process that ensures they remain effective and engaged. The cybersecurity landscape changes rapidly, and your team's skills must evolve to keep up.

- **Structured Training Programs:** Establish a budget and schedule for ongoing professional development. This could include certifications (e.g., CISSP, OSCP), specialized courses, or hands-on workshops for new technologies.
- **Mentorship and Knowledge Sharing:** Pair junior team members with senior

experts. Encourage knowledge-sharing sessions where team members present on new tools, attack vectors, or lessons learned from recent incidents. This builds a culture of continuous learning.

- **Cross-Functional Projects:** Assign team members to projects outside their primary expertise. An engineer could work with an architect on a design, or a security analyst could assist a penetration tester. This broadens their skill sets and promotes a holistic understanding of the project.

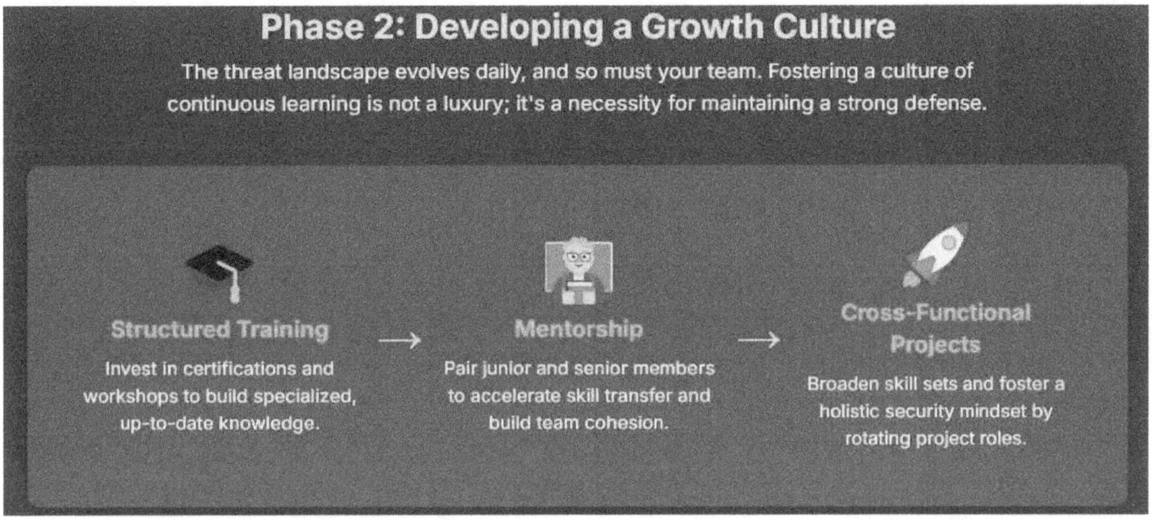

Managing Your Team: Maximizing Impact

Effective management is the key to turning a collection of skilled individuals into a high-performing team. Your role as a manager is to provide clear direction, remove roadblocks, and motivate your team to achieve project success.

- **Establish Clear Communication Channels:** Use a consistent platform for daily updates, incident reports, and project documentation. Regularly scheduled check-ins and project meetings ensure everyone is aligned.

- **Define Clear Metrics and KPIs:** Track key performance indicators (KPIs) relevant to your project. This could include the number of vulnerabilities found, the mean time to detect (MTTD) or mean time to respond (MTTR) to an incident, or the percentage of compliance with a specific policy. These metrics provide objective measures of success.
- **Provide Regular Feedback:** Conduct frequent, constructive feedback sessions. Celebrate successes, provide specific guidance for improvement, and address challenges proactively. Acknowledging your team's hard work is vital for morale and retention.
- **Resource Allocation and Management:** Continuously monitor resource utilization (people, tools, and budget). Be prepared to reallocate resources as project priorities shift or new threats emerge.

Information Security Team Coordination Plan

This document outlines a framework for directing information security personnel and establishing effective communication and activities across security-related teams.

1. Directing Information Security Personnel

A successful security posture begins with clear leadership and direction. To effectively guide your team, focus on these key areas:

- **Define and Assign Roles:** Clearly articulate the roles, responsibilities, and reporting structure for each team member. This prevents duplication of effort and ensures all critical tasks are covered.
- **Set Strategic Objectives:** Establish specific, measurable, achievable, relevant, and time-bound (SMART) goals that align with the organization's broader security strategy.
- **Prioritize Tasks:** Use a clear system to prioritize security initiatives, from responding to immediate threats to implementing long-term vulnerability management programs.
- **Hold Regular Briefings:** Conduct regular meetings to review progress, address roadblocks, and maintain open lines of communication within the information security team itself.

2. Establishing Communications

Seamless communication is the foundation of a coordinated security effort. Create a robust communication plan that includes:

- **Designated Channels:** Set up specific, accessible channels (e.g., a dedicated chat group, a shared email list, a ticketing system) for different types of communication, from urgent alerts to routine updates.
- **Escalation Procedures:** Define a clear and easy-to-follow process for escalating security incidents or findings from one team to another.
- **Shared Knowledge Base:** Maintain a centralized repository for documentation, policies, and best practices so all teams can access the most current information.
- **Regular Reporting:** Establish a schedule for formal updates on security status, key performance indicators (KPIs), and ongoing projects.

3. Fostering Team Activities

Encourage collaboration and skill-building through shared activities that go beyond daily tasks. This helps build a cohesive and knowledgeable security community.

- **Joint Training & Workshops:** Organize training sessions or hands-on workshops that bring different teams together to learn new technologies or processes.
- **Cross-Functional Drills:** Conduct regular security drills that simulate real-world scenarios, such as a phishing campaign or a denial-of-service attack, to test response and coordination.
- **Collaboration on Projects:** Identify opportunities for teams to work together on shared projects, such as a new system rollout or an application security review, to build mutual understanding.

4. Integrating with Other Security-Related Personnel

Effective coordination means breaking down silos between departments. Ensure a seamless flow of information and collaboration with these key teams:

- **Information Systems Team:** As the primary technical team, they are the hub for collaboration. This plan is designed to make their interactions with other security groups more efficient.

- **Technical Support:** Integrate them into the communication plan to ensure they can quickly report suspicious activity or user issues that could indicate a security problem.
- **Incident Management:** Work closely with them to refine the escalation and response processes. A unified approach ensures faster and more effective containment of threats.
- **Security Engineering:** Collaborate on the design and implementation of new security controls and infrastructure. This proactive approach ensures that new systems are secure by design, not by accident.

5. Fostering Psychological Safety

Psychological safety is the shared belief that the team is safe for interpersonal risk-taking. In a security context, this is crucial for preventing critical errors and ensuring timely threat response.

- **Encourage Vulnerability Reporting:** Create a non-punitive culture where team members feel safe to admit mistakes or report vulnerabilities without fear of blame or reprisal. Frame these moments as learning opportunities.
- **Promote Open Dialogue:** Encourage questions and debate about security decisions and strategies. Ensure that all voices are heard and respected, regardless of a person's role or seniority.
- **Model the Behavior:** Leaders and managers should actively demonstrate psychological safety by admitting their own errors, asking for help, and praising team members for their courage in speaking up.
- **Shift from Blame to Learning:** When an incident occurs, focus the post-mortem on what can be learned and what processes can be improved, rather than on who is at fault.

6. Career Development and Growth

A strong security team is built on a foundation of continuous learning and a clear path for advancement. Prioritizing internal promotions and career growth is essential for retaining talent and building institutional knowledge.

- **Formalized Career Paths:** Establish and publish clear career ladders that outline the skills, experience, and responsibilities needed to advance from one role to the next (e.g., from Junior Analyst to Senior Engineer to Security Architect).

- **Mentorship and Coaching:** Implement a program that pairs experienced team members with those who are earlier in their careers. This fosters knowledge transfer and provides personalized guidance.
- **Continuing Education:** Support professional development through budgets for training, certifications, and conference attendance. Encourage teams to regularly set aside time for learning new technologies and best practices.
- **Cross-Training Opportunities:** Allow team members to temporarily work on different projects or in different areas (e.g., an analyst spending time with the security engineering team) to broaden their skill sets and provide a holistic view of the security landscape.
- **Performance and Goal Alignment:** Tie performance reviews to individual career goals and aspirations. Use these discussions to identify and provide the resources needed for professional growth.

Information Security Employee Churn

Employee turnover in the information security sector is a persistent and costly challenge, significantly impacting business operations and security posture. The industry faces a remarkably high annual turnover rate, with some sources citing figures around 20%. This rate is particularly alarming when compared to other professions and is a direct consequence of the global cybersecurity skills shortage, which places immense strain on the existing workforce. The repercussions of this churn extend far beyond simple staffing issues, leading to increased operational costs, knowledge loss, and heightened security vulnerabilities.

The primary drivers of this high turnover rate are a combination of professional and environmental factors. One of the most critical issues is professional burnout. The nature of cybersecurity work, particularly for professionals in Security Operations Centers (SOCs), involves a constant state of high alert, often with 24/7 on-call responsibilities. This intense pressure, coupled with "alert fatigue" from sifting through thousands of daily security alerts, leads to significant stress and exhaustion. A lack of adequate support from management and unrealistic expectations only exacerbate these feelings, pushing professionals to seek less stressful environments.

Another major contributing factor is the perception of limited career growth and development. In a rapidly evolving field, professionals are eager to acquire new skills and certifications to remain competitive. When organizations fail to provide clear pathways for advancement, or do not invest in continuous training and upskilling opportunities, employees feel stagnant and are more likely to look elsewhere. The desire for new challenges and a clear trajectory for career progression is a powerful motivator for change.

Additionally, factors such as inadequate compensation, a poor work-life balance, and a toxic work culture play a significant role. While the demand for cybersecurity talent is high, employees expect competitive salaries and benefits that reflect their value. Furthermore, the desire for flexible work arrangements, including remote work options, has become a key consideration for many professionals. Companies that fail to adapt to these expectations and prioritize employee well-being often experience higher churn.

To mitigate these challenges, organizations must adopt a multifaceted approach to talent retention. This involves providing competitive compensation packages, but also, and perhaps more importantly, investing in the non-monetary aspects of the job. Offering robust training and certification programs, creating defined career paths, and providing mentorship opportunities can signal a long-term commitment to an employee's professional growth. Cultivating a positive, supportive, and communicative work culture is also essential. This includes recognizing and rewarding achievements, and using technology to automate routine tasks and reduce the burden on security teams. By addressing these root causes, companies can foster a more resilient and engaged workforce, ultimately strengthening their security posture and ensuring long-term success.

Developing an Information Security Budget

The foundation of a successful information security program is a well-planned budget that is directly tied to the organization's strategic goals and risk profile. To get started, follow these key steps:

1. Conduct a Thorough Risk Assessment

Start by identifying and analyzing the organization's specific risks. Your budget should be a direct response to these risks. For example, if your primary risk is a data breach from a sophisticated cyberattack, your budget should prioritize advanced threat detection tools and employee training. Understanding the threats allows you to justify every dollar spent.

2. Align with Business Objectives

Security should be an enabler, not a roadblock. Work with key stakeholders, including executive leadership and department heads, to understand the organization's priorities. The security budget must support these objectives. If the company is launching a new product, the security budget should include resources to secure that product.

3. Categorize and Prioritize Your Spending

Organize your budget into clear categories. This makes tracking and reporting much easier. Common categories include:

- **Personnel:** Salaries, benefits, and training for your security team. This also includes contractors and consultants.
- **Technology & Tools:** Licensing and maintenance for security software (e.g., firewalls, EDR, SIEM, vulnerability scanners), as well as hardware.
- **Training and Awareness:** Costs associated with security awareness campaigns and specialized training for your team.
- **Governance, Risk, and Compliance (GRC):** Expenses for audits, compliance assessments, and legal counsel.
- **Incident Response:** Funds for forensic analysis, crisis management, and legal fees in the event of a breach.

Once categorized, prioritize spending based on the risk assessment and business alignment.

Managing and Monitoring the Budget

Developing the budget is only half the battle; continuous management is crucial to ensure you stay on track.

1. Track Actual vs. Planned Spending

Regularly monitor your expenditures. Use financial software or spreadsheets to compare what you planned to spend versus what you have actually spent. Monthly or quarterly reviews are standard practice.

2. Establish and Monitor Key Performance Indicators (KPIs)

To demonstrate the value of the security budget, you need to show results. Define metrics that prove your investments are paying off.

Examples of KPIs: Number of security incidents, average time to detect and respond to threats, compliance audit success rate, and employee phishing test click rate. These metrics help you justify continued or increased funding.

3. Conduct Variance Analysis

When there's a significant difference between your budgeted and actual spending, perform a variance analysis. Investigate why the discrepancy occurred—was it an unexpected cost, a miscalculation, or a change in project scope? This analysis helps you make corrections and improve future budget estimates.

For an information security project, variance analysis is a critical technique used to compare planned performance against actual results. This helps identify and understand deviations in cost, schedule, and scope, allowing project managers to take corrective action and keep the project on track. The core of this analysis is comparing a baseline (the original plan) with what's actually happening.

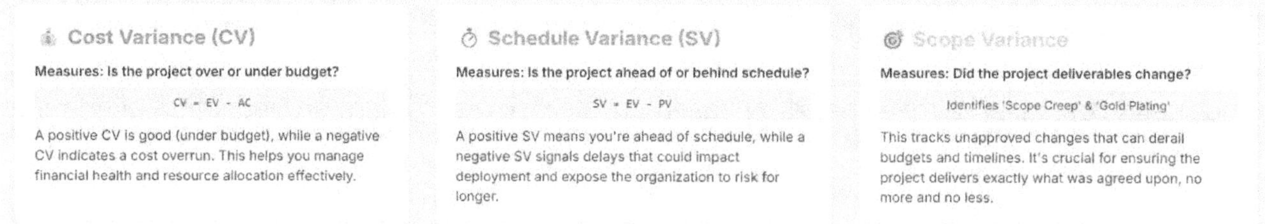

Key Variances to Analyze

Variance analysis for an information security project typically focuses on three primary areas: cost, schedule, and scope.

1. Cost Variance (CV)

This variance measures if the project is over or under budget. It's calculated as the difference between the earned value (EV) and the actual cost (AC).

$CV = EV - AC$

- A positive CV means the project is under budget for the work completed.
- A negative CV means the project is over budget for the work completed.

For an infosec project, a negative cost variance could be due to a number of factors, such as higher-than-expected costs for specialized security software licenses, an increase in the hourly rate of external penetration testing consultants, or unforeseen hardware purchases for a new security appliance.

2. Schedule Variance (SV)

This variance indicates if the project is ahead of or behind schedule. It's calculated as the difference between the earned value (EV) and the planned value (PV).

$SV = EV - PV$

- A positive SV means the project is ahead of schedule.
- A negative SV means the project is behind schedule.

For an infosec project, a negative schedule variance could result from delays in obtaining necessary approvals for a new security policy, technical issues during the deployment of a new firewall, or a shortage of trained personnel to complete a security audit on time.

3. Scope Variance

This variance is less quantitative than cost and schedule, but it's just as important. It refers to any deviation from the original project deliverables, requirements, or features. This is often the root cause of both cost and schedule variances.

- **Scope Creep:** This is a common form of negative scope variance where new requirements or features are added without a corresponding adjustment to the budget or schedule. In an infosec project, this could be a new mandate to include multi-factor authentication for a system that was not in the original scope.
- **Gold Plating:** This occurs when team members add extra work or features that were not requested. For instance, a security team might implement an advanced logging system with more features than required, consuming extra time and resources.

Why is Variance tracking Important for InfoSec Projects?

Information security projects are highly sensitive. A single variance can lead to significant risks. For example:

- A negative cost variance could mean you had to cut corners on a security control to save money, creating a vulnerability.
- A negative schedule variance could leave a critical system unprotected for longer than planned.
- Scope creep can introduce new attack vectors that were not properly planned for or budgeted.

By monitoring these variances, you can keep your project secure, on time, and on budget. By regularly performing this analysis, project managers can proactively identify issues, communicate with stakeholders, and make informed decisions to ensure the successful completion of the information security project.

Estimating and Controlling Individual Project Costs

For specific security projects, a more granular approach to cost is required.

1. Use a Work Breakdown Structure (WBS)

Break the project down into smaller, manageable tasks. For example, a "Phishing Simulation Project" might have tasks like "Select Vendor," "Develop Training Content," "Execute Campaign," and "Report Results." By estimating the cost of each individual task, you can create a highly accurate project budget.

Understanding the Work Breakdown Structure (WBS)

A Work Breakdown Structure (WBS) is a fundamental project management tool that organizes and defines the total scope of a project. It is a deliverable-oriented hierarchy that breaks down the project's work into smaller, more manageable components. The WBS is a cornerstone for planning, scheduling, budgeting, and resource management.

For an information security project, a WBS is particularly critical because it helps a team visualize the full scope of a complex effort, from policy development to technical implementation and testing. It ensures that no critical tasks, such as vulnerability assessments or security control testing, are overlooked. The core principle of a WBS is the "100% Rule," which states that the WBS must include 100% of the work defined by the project scope and capture all internal, external, and interim deliverables.

Key Components of a WBS:

- **Levels of Decomposition:** A WBS is a multi-level tree structure. The highest level represents the final project deliverable (e.g., "New Access Control System"). The subsequent levels break this down into smaller, more specific deliverables and sub-deliverables.
- **WBS Elements:** Each item in the hierarchy is called a WBS Element. These elements are not tasks but rather the tangible outputs of the work (e.g., "Threat Modeling Report" or "User Training Materials").
- **Work Packages:** At the lowest level of the WBS, you will find "work packages." A work package is the smallest unit of work that can be realistically managed. It is where you define the specific activities and tasks required to produce the deliverable.

2. Choose an Estimation Technique

- **Bottom-Up Estimating:** This is the most accurate method. It involves estimating the resources, time, and materials for each task in your WBS and then summing them up to get the total project cost.
- **Analogous Estimating:** Use this method when you have a similar past project to reference. It's faster but less precise. For instance, if a past endpoint security project cost $50,000, you might use that as a starting point for a new one.

Choosing Your Estimation Technique

Bottom-Up Estimating	Analogous Estimating
Break the project into small tasks and estimate the cost for each. Sum them up for a total.	Use the cost of a similar past project as a baseline for the new one.
Pro: Highly accurate.	Pro: Fast and simple.
Con: Time-consuming.	Con: Less precise.

3. Implement a Change Control Process

Scope creep is a major cause of budget overruns. Establish a formal process for evaluating and approving any changes to the project scope, timeline, or resources. This ensures that every change is assessed for its impact on the budget before it's implemented.

What is an Information Security Project Change Control Process?

An information security project change control process is a formal, systematic procedure used to manage and approve any modifications to an ongoing information security project's scope, budget, timeline, or technical specifications. The goal is to ensure that any change requested during the project lifecycle—such as a new feature, a different technology, or a revised security requirement—is introduced in a controlled manner. This process is crucial for preventing "scope creep" and ensuring the project remains on track, on budget, and achieves its security objectives without creating new vulnerabilities.

The purpose of this process is to:

- **Prevent scope creep:** Carefully evaluate and approve changes to avoid uncontrolled expansion of the project's requirements.
- **Maintain project stability:** Ensure changes do not disrupt the project schedule, budget, or quality.
- **Minimize risk:** Assess the impact of any change on the project's security posture and overall success.
- **Ensure accountability:** Create a clear, documented audit trail of all project changes and their approvals.

Key Steps in the Project Change Control Process

Within a project, the change control process generally follows these stages:

Request for Change (RFC) Submission

The process begins when a project team member, stakeholder, or sponsor identifies a need for a change. They formally submit a Request for Change (RFC). This document provides a detailed description of the proposed modification, its justification (e.g., a newly discovered security threat, a change in business requirements), the project artifacts it will affect, and an initial estimate of its impact on the project's budget, timeline, and resources.

Impact Analysis and Assessment

Upon receiving an RFC, a designated project manager and the project's Change Control Board (CCB) conduct a thorough impact analysis. This phase goes beyond just technical security and also considers the project's constraints. Key questions asked during this stage include:

- What is the specific security impact of this change?
- How will this change affect the project's scope, timeline, and budget?
- Is the change aligned with the project's original goals?
- What is the risk of not making this change?
- Is there a clear backout or rollback plan if the change is approved and then fails?

Review and Approval

Based on the impact analysis, the CCB or project sponsor reviews the RFC. For a project, the approval process is often more formal. The CCB, which includes key project stakeholders, will vote to approve, deny, or defer the request. Approval is granted only if the benefits of the change outweigh its risks and if the project can absorb the impact on its resources.

Integration and Implementation

Once a change is approved, it is formally integrated into the project plan. The project manager updates the project scope document, work breakdown structure, and schedule. The technical team then executes the change, following the standard project development and testing procedures. All work is conducted in a controlled environment, and the change's implementation is carefully documented to maintain an accurate project record.

Verification and Closure

After the change has been implemented and tested, it is verified to ensure it meets the new requirements and that the project remains stable. A final review confirms that all documentation has been updated and that the change has been successfully integrated into the project. The RFC is then formally closed, and the project proceeds with its new, approved baseline.

Best Practices for a Strong Project Process

- **Establish a Change Control Board (CCB):** For a project, a CCB is essential. It should include the project manager, a security lead, key stakeholders, and a technical expert to ensure all perspectives are considered.
- **Link Changes to Project Baselines:** Clearly define the project's original scope, budget, and schedule (the baselines). All RFCs should be evaluated against these baselines to measure their impact.

- **Use Templates and Automation:** Provide a standardized RFC template for all team members to use. Project management software can automate the routing of requests, streamline the approval process, and track the status of each change.
- **Communicate Continuously:** Regularly communicate the status of change requests to the entire project team and stakeholders. Transparency is key to managing expectations and preventing confusion.
- **Maintain Version Control:** Use version control for all project documents, especially the scope and requirements. This ensures there is a clear history of how the project evolved.

4. Maintain a Contingency Reserve

No project is perfect. Allocate a portion of the budget (typically 5-15%) as a contingency reserve to cover unexpected costs or risks. This allows you to handle unforeseen issues without disrupting the overall budget. A project contingency reserve is a fund of money or a block of time that is set aside in a project budget or schedule to handle known, but uncertain, risks. It's essentially a safety net for expected-but-unpredictable events.

Contingency vs. Management Reserve

It's helpful to distinguish between two types of project reserves:

- **Contingency Reserve:** This is for known risks. You know a specific risk exists (e.g., a technical dependency on a new piece of hardware that could be delayed), but you don't know if it will happen or what its full impact will be. The contingency reserve covers these identified risks.
- **Management Reserve:** This is for unknown risks. It's a larger pot of money or time held by management to cover completely unforeseen events that are outside the project's scope and weren't identified during the planning phase. Think of it as a fund for true "black swan" events.

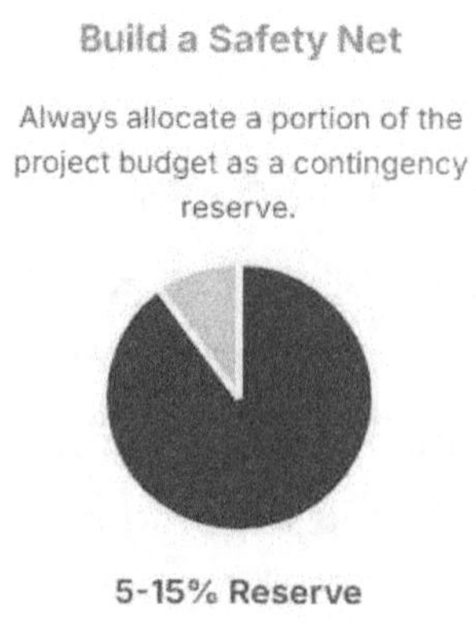

Resolving Personnel and Teamwork Issues

Resolving personnel and teamwork issues in a security program requires a systematic approach that addresses the root cause of the problem while respecting the constraints of time, cost, and quality. The key is to see these constraints not as limitations, but as guides for prioritizing and strategizing your solutions.

1. The Foundation: People, Process, and Technology

Before diving into solutions, it's essential to understand that people issues are often a symptom of underlying problems in process or technology. A team might be struggling because of:

- **Poorly defined processes:** Unclear roles, inefficient workflows, or a lack of documentation.
- **Inadequate technology:** Tools that are difficult to use, don't integrate well, or are insufficient for the task.

Addressing the process or technology issue often resolves the people issue without direct intervention.

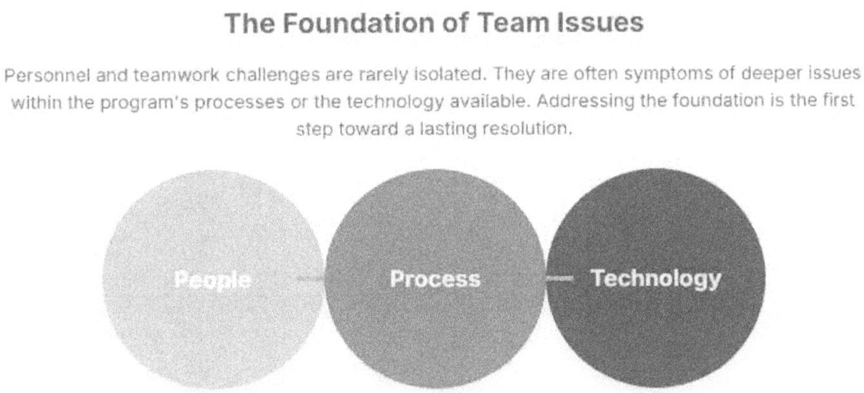

2. Identifying the Root Cause

Simply addressing the surface-level problem (e.g., "the team is not meeting deadlines") won't fix the issue long-term. You must get to the root cause.

Identifying the Root Cause

To solve a problem effectively, you must look beyond the surface symptoms. The chart illustrates a hypothetical distribution of common root causes for team friction in security programs. Burnout and unclear roles are often significant contributors, highlighting the need for clear management and sustainable workloads.

- **Burnout:** Over-stressed teams lose motivation.
- **Unclear Roles:** Leads to inefficiency and conflict.
- **Skill Gaps:** Creates project bottlenecks.
- **Tool Limitations:** Frustrates and slows down experts.
- **Other:** Includes personality clashes and more.

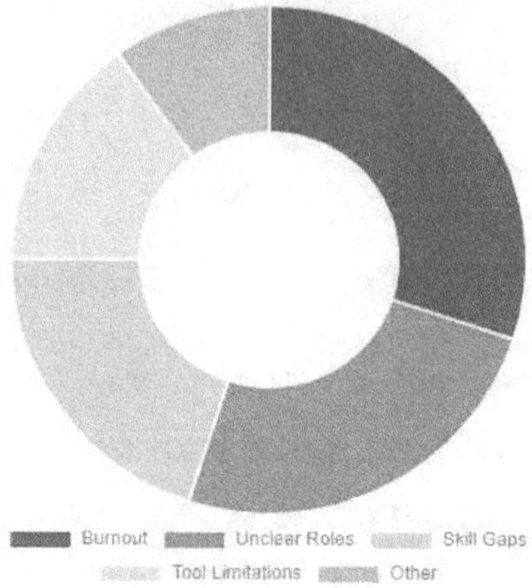

- **One-on-One Meetings:** Conduct confidential one-on-one meetings to understand individual perspectives and challenges.
- **Anonymous Surveys:** Use surveys to gather feedback on team dynamics, workload, and tool effectiveness without fear of retribution.
- **Observation:** Spend time observing the team's workflows and communication patterns to identify bottlenecks and friction points.

Common root causes include:

- **Skill Gaps:** Team members lack the necessary skills for a project.
- **Burnout:** Overburdened employees are losing motivation.
- **Unclear Roles:** Team members are stepping on each other's toes or duplicating work due to a lack of clear responsibilities.
- **Personality Clashes:** Interpersonal conflicts are hindering collaboration.
- **Tool Limitations:** The security tools are not fit for purpose, leading to frustration and inefficiency.

3. Strategies for Resolution within Constraints

Once you've identified the root cause, you can apply targeted strategies based on your program's constraints.

Time Constraints

Focus on streamlining and efficiency to meet tight deadlines.

- **Improve Communication:** Implement daily stand-ups to quickly align on priorities and remove roadblocks. Utilize project management tools to track progress in real-time.

- **Prioritize ruthlessly:** Use a risk-based approach to focus on the most critical vulnerabilities or projects. Defer or deprioritize lower-impact tasks.
- **Delegate Effectively:** Assign tasks based on an individual's strengths and current capacity, ensuring everyone is working on what they do best and is not overloaded.

Cost Constraints

Focus on resourcefulness and making the most of what you have.

- **Low-Cost Training:** Leverage free online resources, internal knowledge-sharing sessions, or mentorship programs to close skill gaps without expensive external training.
- **Tool Optimization:** Review your existing security stack. Is a cheaper, open-source tool a viable alternative? Are you fully utilizing the features of your current tools?
- **Internal Mobility:** Instead of hiring, consider cross-training an existing team member or promoting from within to fill new roles. This is often more cost-effective and boosts team morale.

Quality Constraints

Focus on standardization and accountability to maintain high standards.

- **Establish Clear Metrics:** Define what "quality" means for your team. This could be a Service Level Agreement (SLA) for vulnerability remediation, a specific pass rate for security audits, or a set of coding standards for security tools.
- **Implement Review Processes:** Use peer reviews for incident response reports or code reviews for custom scripts. This helps catch errors and promotes a shared sense of quality.
- **Document Everything:** Create a central repository for all processes, runbooks, and configurations. This ensures consistency and makes it easier for new team members to get up to speed.

4. Fostering a Proactive Team Culture

Beyond reactive problem-solving, a positive team culture can prevent many issues from arising.

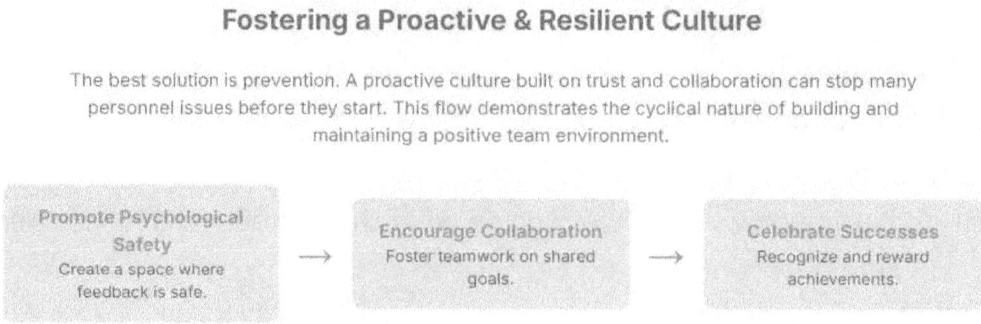

- **Promote Psychological Safety:** Create an environment where team members feel comfortable raising concerns or admitting mistakes without fear of punishment.
- **Celebrate Successes:** Recognize and reward individuals and the team for their achievements, no matter how small.
- **Encourage Collaboration:** Create opportunities for team members to work together on projects they're passionate about to build stronger relationships.

Vendor Management and Community Engagement

An effective information security program isn't just about internal controls and technology; it's also about managing external relationships. The operations of a robust program involve two critical components: handling vendor agreements and engaging with the broader security community.

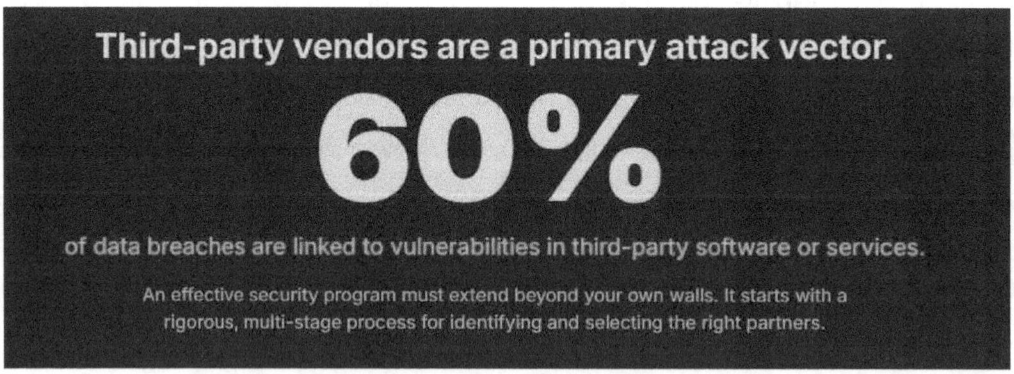

1. Identifying and Selecting Vendors

The first step in vendor management is to identify and select the right partners. This process should be guided by a clear understanding of your organization's security needs and risk profile.

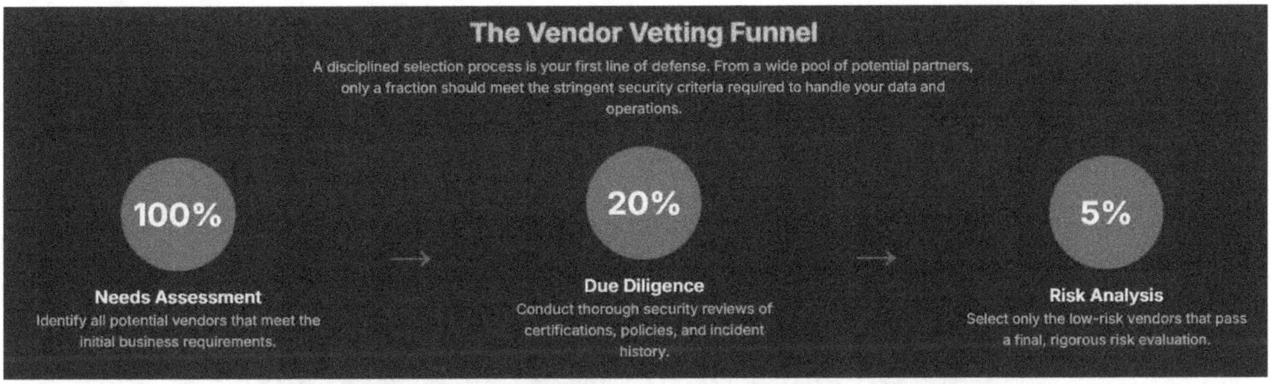

- **Needs Assessment:** Before you even look for a vendor, you must identify what security function or service you need. This could be anything from managed security services (MSS) and penetration testing to cloud hosting providers and data backup solutions.
- **Due Diligence:** Once potential vendors are identified, a thorough security assessment is crucial. This involves reviewing their security certifications (e.g., ISO 27001, SOC 2), their internal security policies, incident response plans, and their track record of handling security incidents. You should ask for evidence of their security controls.
- **Risk Analysis:** It's important to evaluate the risks associated with each vendor. A vendor that will handle sensitive customer data, for example, poses a much higher risk than a vendor providing a simple, non-critical productivity tool. Your risk analysis should dictate the level of scrutiny applied.

2. Negotiating Vendor Agreements

Vendor agreements are the cornerstone of your security relationship. They legally define the expectations, responsibilities, and liabilities of both parties. Key sections to focus on include:

- **Data Security and Privacy:** The agreement must explicitly outline how the vendor will protect your data. This includes details on encryption, access controls, data residency, and how they will handle data subject requests and privacy regulations (like GDPR or CCPA).
- **Service Level Agreements (SLAs):** SLAs should include security-specific metrics. This could involve an uptime guarantee for a security service, a maximum time for a security patch to be applied, or a specified time frame for notifying you of a breach.
- **Right to Audit:** It is essential to include a clause that gives your organization the right to conduct security audits or request third-party audit reports. This ensures you can

verify that the vendor's controls are as robust as they claim.

- **Incident Response and Notification:** The agreement must clearly define the vendor's responsibilities in the event of a security incident. This includes who they must notify, within what timeframe, and what information they are required to provide.

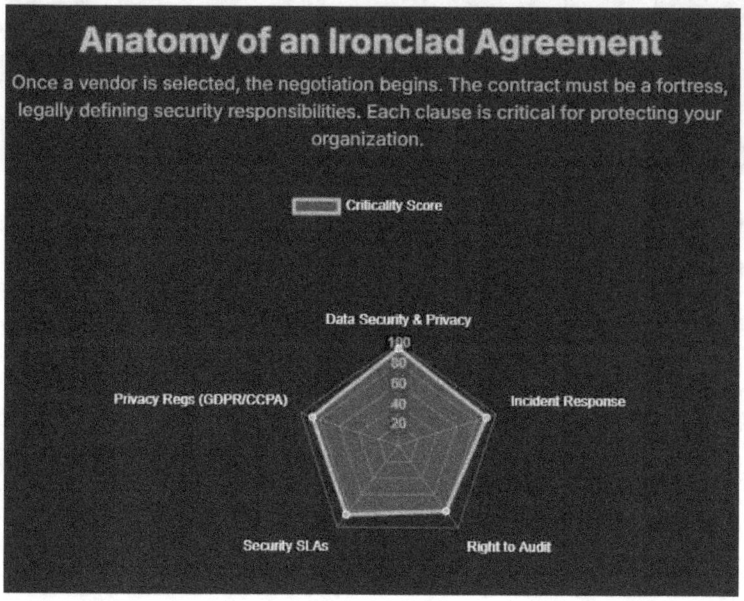

3. Managing Vendor Agreements

Vendor management is an ongoing process, not a one-time event. To ensure continuous security, you must actively manage these relationships.

- **Continuous Monitoring:** Regularly monitor the vendor's security posture. This can involve checking for new security certifications, reviewing their incident reports, and staying informed about any publicly disclosed breaches or vulnerabilities affecting their services.
- **Performance Reviews:** Conduct periodic reviews to ensure the vendor is meeting the security-related SLAs defined in the agreement. Use these reviews to address any concerns and discuss potential improvements.
- **Exit Strategy:** For all critical vendors, it's wise to have a formal exit strategy. This plan should detail how you would transition away from their service, including data retrieval and secure data destruction. This helps you maintain control and minimizes disruption if the relationship ends.

4. Engaging with the Security Community

Community engagement is a powerful, proactive tool for enhancing your security program. It provides access to shared knowledge, threat intelligence, and a network of peers.

- **Threat Intelligence Sharing:** Participating in security information sharing and analysis centers (ISACs) or other threat-sharing communities allows you to receive early warnings about new threats, vulnerabilities, and attack vectors. This shared intelligence can help your team prepare for or mitigate attacks before they happen.
- **Peer Networking:** Attending conferences, webinars, and local security meetups provides invaluable opportunities to learn from other professionals. You can discuss challenges, share best practices, and get advice on specific security problems.
- **Open-Source Contributions:** Contributing to or using open-source security tools and resources helps strengthen the collective security posture of the community. It also allows you to leverage the expertise of a global network of developers and researchers.

By actively managing vendor relationships and engaging with the broader security community, an information security program moves from a reactive posture to a proactive and well-informed one, significantly reducing risk and improving overall resilience.

Participating in Vendor and Stakeholder Reviews

In an information security program, collaborating with vendors and stakeholders to review and assess recommended solutions is a critical part of the job. This role focuses on ensuring that any new technology or service not only meets business needs but also aligns with the organization's security posture and standards.

A key part of this is identifying potential incompatibilities, challenges, or issues with proposed solutions. This involves a deep dive into the technical details and a holistic view of the company's existing security architecture.

A robust security posture requires scrutinizing every link in the chain. With third-party services becoming integral to operations, the vendor review process is more critical than ever.

63%

of data breaches are linked to third-party vendors, making rigorous assessment a non-negotiable part of information security program operations.

Key Responsibilities:

- **Requirements Gathering and Analysis:** Work with business units and IT teams to understand their needs and translate them into security requirements. This ensures any proposed solution is evaluated against a clear set of criteria.
- **Solution Vetting:** Conduct a thorough review of the vendor's product, including its security features, architecture, and compliance certifications. This might involve reviewing documentation, attending demonstrations, and asking probing questions about data handling and access controls.
- **Identifying Incompatibilities:** A primary task is to identify how a new solution might clash with existing systems. This could be a technical incompatibility (e.g., the new tool doesn't integrate with your current single sign-on system) or a procedural one (e.g., the vendor's support model doesn't meet your incident response requirements).
- **Risk Assessment:** Evaluate the potential risks a new solution introduces to the organization. This includes assessing data privacy risks, supply chain risks, and the vendor's own security practices. The goal is to ensure the benefits of the solution outweigh the potential security risks.
- **Providing Feedback and Recommendations:** Communicate findings clearly to both technical and non-technical stakeholders. Offer concrete recommendations for mitigating identified issues, such as suggesting alternative solutions, negotiating specific security clauses in the contract, or outlining a plan for post-implementation monitoring.

From Findings to Actionable Recommendations

The final output of the review is not just a list of problems, but a clear recommendation communicated to stakeholders, ensuring the business makes an informed, secure decision.

Reject

The solution introduces unacceptable risks or has critical incompatibilities that cannot be mitigated.

Accept with Conditions

The solution is viable, but requires specific security clauses in the contract or post-implementation monitoring.

Accept

The solution meets all security requirements and introduces minimal, manageable risk to the organization.

- **Documentation:** Maintain detailed records of all assessments, including the identified issues, recommended mitigations, and final decisions. This provides a clear audit trail and helps with future decision-making.

Evaluating Information Security Program Operations

An effective information security program requires robust project management practices and controls to ensure that security initiatives are not only technically sound but also strategically aligned with the organization's business goals and financial realities. The evaluation of these practices focuses on four key areas: project management methodology, cost-effectiveness, risk management integration, and alignment with business requirements.

Project Management Practices and Methodology

The choice of project management methodology is a fundamental aspect of program operations. For information security, a hybrid or Agile methodology is often highly effective. Unlike traditional Waterfall, which is linear and can be rigid, Agile allows for iterative development and continuous feedback, which is crucial in a rapidly evolving threat landscape.

- **Scope and Scheduling:** Projects should have clearly defined scopes that are broken down into manageable phases. In an Agile approach, these are often defined as user stories or epics, with short sprints (2-4 weeks) for development and implementation. This allows for frequent re-evaluation and adaptation.

- **Resource Allocation:** Project managers must ensure that human capital (security engineers, analysts), technology (software, hardware), and financial resources are allocated efficiently. This includes cross-functional teams that can work collaboratively to integrate security into business processes.
- **Communication:** A strong communication plan is essential. Regular status meetings, stakeholder updates, and transparent reporting on progress, challenges, and risks ensure that all parties are informed and engaged.

Controls for Managing Risk and Ensuring Quality

Controls are the mechanisms and procedures put in place to govern the project's execution and outcomes. They are critical for managing risks and ensuring that the final solution meets quality standards.

- **Change Management:** All changes to the project scope, timeline, or resources must go through a formal change control process. This prevents "scope creep" and ensures that the impact of a change is properly assessed and approved by stakeholders.
- **Quality Assurance (QA):** Security projects require thorough QA and testing. This includes vulnerability scanning, penetration testing, and code reviews to verify that new systems or controls do not introduce new security vulnerabilities. The security team should establish a clear definition of "done" that includes verified security criteria.
- **Risk Management Integration:** Risk management is not a separate activity but a continuous process integrated into every stage of the project lifecycle. This includes identifying potential threats and vulnerabilities, assessing their likelihood and impact, and implementing mitigation strategies.

Determining Cost-Effectiveness

To determine if business requirements are achieved in a cost-effective manner, one must look beyond the initial project budget. A cost-effective program is one that maximizes the value of security investments.

- **Return on Investment (ROI):** While hard to quantify, the ROI of a security project can be measured by comparing the cost of the project to the value of the assets it protects or the potential loss it prevents. For example, a data loss prevention (DLP) system's ROI can be calculated based on the estimated cost of a data breach.
- **Total Cost of Ownership (TCO):** TCO considers all costs associated with a security solution over its lifespan, including licensing fees, maintenance, upgrades, and personnel training. A project might have a low initial cost but a high TCO.
- **Risk-Based Prioritization:** Not all risks are created equal. A cost-effective program prioritizes projects that address the most significant risks to the organization. By using a risk matrix (likelihood vs. impact), projects can be ranked to ensure resources are allocated to the most critical security needs.

Total Cost of Ownership (TCO) for an Information Security Program

What is TCO for Information Security?

Total Cost of Ownership (TCO) is a comprehensive financial metric that helps organizations calculate all direct and indirect expenses associated with a security program over its entire lifecycle. TCO provides a more accurate picture of an investment's long- term financial impact, helping you make more informed decisions.

What is Total Cost of Ownership (TCO)?

TCO is a comprehensive financial metric that goes beyond the initial price tag. It calculates all direct and indirect expenses associated with a security program over its entire lifecycle, revealing the true long-term financial impact of your security investments.

Key Components of TCO

TCO is broken down into three main categories: Direct Costs, Indirect Costs, and Opportunity Costs.

1. Direct Costs

These are the most obvious, quantifiable expenses.

- **Acquisition & Licensing:** The upfront cost of hardware (servers, firewalls), software licenses, and cloud-based subscriptions.
- **Implementation & Integration:** The cost of consultants, in-house staff time, and professional services needed to set up and integrate the new security solution with existing systems.
- **Training:** The expense of training IT staff and end-users on new tools and security protocols.
- **Ongoing Operations:** A wide range of recurring costs like software maintenance, vendor support contracts, hardware upgrades, and recurring subscription fees.

2. Indirect Costs

These are the hidden, less tangible costs that can significantly impact the bottom line.

- **Labor:** The salaries and benefits of your in-house security team, including security analysts, engineers, and management. This is often the largest component of TCO.
- **Downtime & Productivity Loss:** The cost of lost revenue and productivity if a security system fails or requires maintenance, leading to business interruption.
- **Incident Response:** The cost of responding to a security breach, which can include legal fees, forensic investigations, and public relations.
- **Compliance:** The expenses associated with maintaining regulatory compliance (like HIPAA or PCI DSS) and the potential fines from non-compliance.

3. Opportunity Costs

These costs represent what the organization gives up by choosing one security solution over another.

- **Misallocated Resources:** The value of time and resources that could have been used on other business initiatives but were instead dedicated to managing a complex or inefficient security program.

- **Delayed Projects:** The financial impact of delayed or postponed projects due to security implementation bottlenecks.

How to Calculate TCO

A simple formula for TCO is:

TCO = (Initial Purchase Price)+(Recurring Costs)+(Indirect and Hidden Costs)

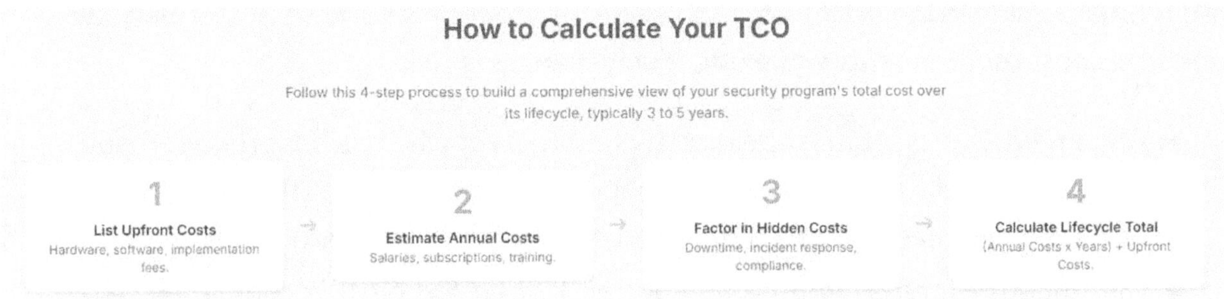

To get an accurate TCO, you must gather data from across your organization and project costs over a specific period, typically a three- or five-year lifecycle.

Step-by-step approach to a more detailed calculation:

- **List all upfront costs:**
  - Hardware and software purchases.
  - Implementation fees (consultants, contractors).
  - Initial training for staff.
- **Estimate annual recurring costs:**
  - Software maintenance and subscription fees.
  - Annual salaries and benefits for your security team (don't forget to factor in a percentage of time for other IT staff if they are involved).
  - Regularly scheduled hardware and software upgrades.
  - Continuous security awareness training.
- **Factor in indirect and hidden costs:**
  - Estimate the cost of potential downtime (e.g., lost productivity per hour multiplied by estimated downtime).
  - Budget for potential incident response and breach remediation costs.
  - Account for the cost of maintaining compliance and any associated audit fees.

- **Calculate the total over the lifecycle:**
    - Multiply the annual recurring costs by the number of years in the lifecycle (e.g., 5 years).
    - Add this total to the upfront costs to get the final TCO.

Achieving Business Requirements and Managing Risks

The ultimate measure of an information security program's success is its ability to meet business requirements while effectively managing risks.

- **Alignment:** A project must be directly tied to a specific business requirement, such as meeting a regulatory compliance standard (SOC2, HIPAA), protecting intellectual property, or enabling a new digital product launch.
- **Continuous Monitoring:** Risks do not end when a project is completed. The program should include ongoing monitoring of new threats and vulnerabilities to ensure that the implemented controls remain effective. This includes performing regular security audits and threat intelligence analysis.
- **Stakeholder Feedback:** Regular feedback from business unit leaders is crucial. This ensures that the security program is a business enabler, not just a series of technical requirements. It confirms that the security solutions deployed are practical and do not overly impede business operations.

Evaluating Project Management Practices for an Information Security Program

The effectiveness of an information security program is directly tied to the project management practices and controls used to implement its initiatives. A thorough evaluation should focus on whether these practices enable the program to achieve its security objectives and business requirements in a cost-effective manner while actively managing organizational risks.

This evaluation is structured around five key areas: Project Governance, Cost-Effectiveness, Risk Management Integration, Control Implementation, and

Communication.

1. Project Governance and Alignment

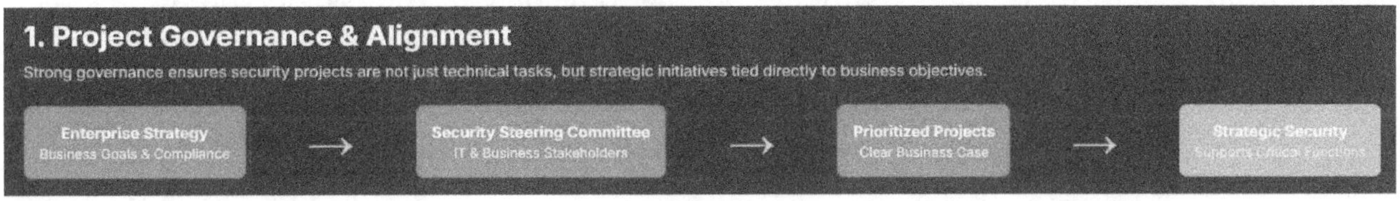

Project governance provides the framework for how security initiatives are selected, prioritized, and managed. A strong program ensures that projects are not just a list of technical tasks, but are strategically aligned with the broader business objectives.

Evaluation: Are security projects selected based on a clear business case that ties security goals to enterprise-wide strategy? Is there a formal process for prioritizing projects, such as a security steering committee, that includes both IT and business stakeholders? The governance model should ensure that security investments directly support critical business functions and compliance requirements, rather than being driven solely by technical mandates.

2. Cost-Effectiveness and Resource Management

A project is cost-effective if it delivers the maximum value for the resources invested. This goes beyond simply staying within budget; it requires a focus on delivering tangible security improvements that justify the financial outlay.

Evaluation: Is there a process to analyze the cost-benefit of each security project? This includes evaluating the Total Cost of Ownership (TCO), which accounts for not only initial implementation but also ongoing maintenance, licensing, and staffing. Are resources, including personnel and technology, allocated efficiently to maximize project delivery? A key indicator is the ability to track and report on the Return on Investment (ROI) for major security initiatives, such as a reduction in incident response time or a decrease in a specific threat type.

3. Risk Management Integration

For an information security program, risk management must be an inherent part of every project's lifecycle, not an afterthought. Projects should be a primary mechanism for reducing the organization's risk exposure.

Evaluation: Is a formal risk assessment conducted as part of the project initiation phase? Does the project plan include specific risk mitigation strategies for identified threats and vulnerabilities? Project managers should work closely with the security and risk teams to ensure that the project itself does not introduce new risks to the environment. The project's success should be measured not just by its completion, but by its impact on reducing a specific, measurable risk.

4. Control Implementation and Measurement

The goal of a security project is to implement controls that protect the organization. The effectiveness of these controls must be measured and reported on to justify the project's existence and inform future initiatives.

Evaluation: Are project deliverables clearly defined in terms of the specific security controls they will implement? Is there a formal handover process from the project team to the operations team to ensure the implemented controls are maintained? The program must utilize Key Performance Indicators (KPIs) and Key Risk Indicators (KRIs) to measure the ongoing performance of implemented controls. For example, a project to deploy endpoint protection should be followed by metrics on the number of blocked malware attempts or the percentage of compliant endpoints.

5. Communication and Stakeholder Management

Effective communication ensures that all stakeholders understand the value of the security program and the progress of its projects. It builds trust and secures continued support and funding.

Evaluation: Does the project management process include regular, transparent reporting to both technical teams and executive leadership? Is the language used in these reports tailored to the audience (e.g., technical details for the security team vs. risk and business impact for executives)? Proactive communication about project status, challenges, and successes helps manage expectations and ensures that the program is viewed as a strategic partner, not a cost center.

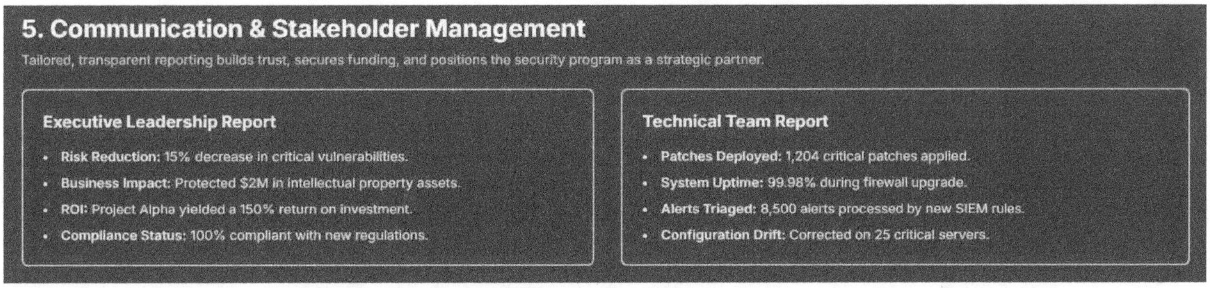

Information Systems Project Performance Plan

This plan outlines a framework for continuously measuring the effectiveness of information security projects. It is based on a cycle of planning, measurement, analysis, and improvement to ensure that all information systems projects contribute to the organization's overall security posture.

1. Define Key Performance Indicators (KPIs)

Before any project begins, clear, measurable Key Performance Indicators (KPIs) must be established. These metrics will be used to track progress and success from both a project management and a security perspective.

Project Management KPIs:

- **Schedule Variance (SV):** The difference between the planned and actual completion dates for project milestones. A positive SV indicates the project is ahead of schedule.
- **Cost Variance (CV):** The difference between the planned and actual budget spent. A positive CV indicates the project is under budget.
- **Scope Creep:** The number of unauthorized or unplanned changes to the project's original scope.
- **Mean Time to Complete (MTTC):** The average time taken to complete a specific task or a project as a whole.

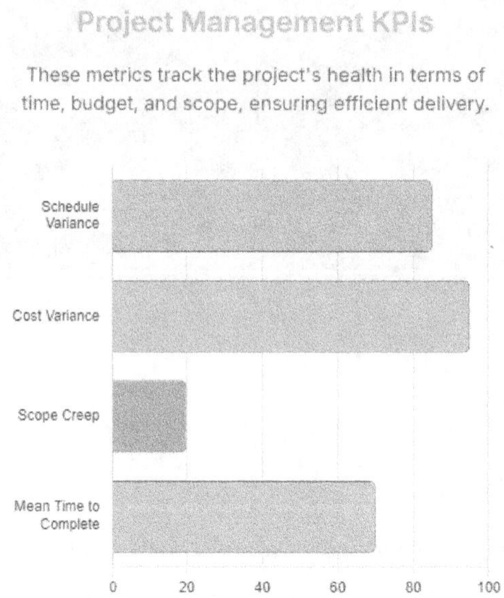

Information Security KPIs:

- **Mean Time to Detect (MTTD):** The average time it takes to identify a security incident or vulnerability.
- **Mean Time to Respond (MTTR):** The average time from when a security incident is detected to when it is fully resolved.
- **Patching Cadence/Compliance:** The percentage of systems patched within a specific timeframe after a patch is released.
- **Vulnerability Remediation Rate:** The percentage of identified vulnerabilities that are fixed within the agreed-upon Service Level Agreement (SLA).
- **Security Incident Rate:** The number of security incidents per a specific period (e.g., month, quarter).
- **Employee Security Awareness:** Measured by the percentage of employees who pass phishing simulations and the completion rate of security training.

Information Security KPIs

These metrics evaluate the project's impact on the organization's security posture and resilience against threats.

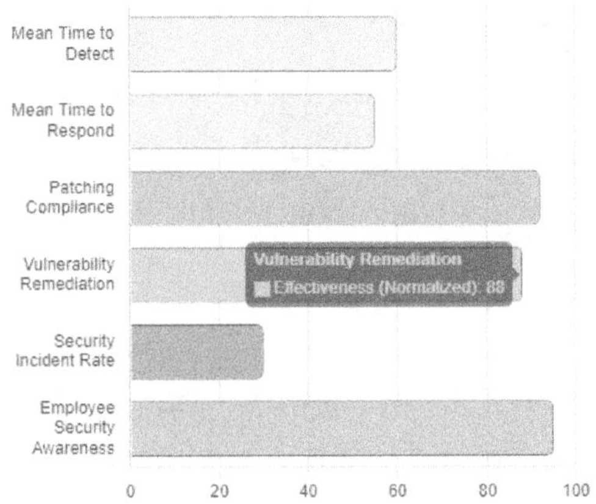

2. Implement a Continuous Improvement Cycle

The plan operates on a continuous cycle to ensure ongoing effectiveness. This approach, often referred to as the Plan-Do-Check-Act (PDCA) cycle, is a core principle of security management standards like ISO 27001.

Plan:

- **Set Objectives:** Define specific, measurable, achievable, relevant, and time-bound (SMART) goals for each project.
- **Establish Baselines:** Before a project, measure existing performance against the security KPIs to create a starting point. For example, determine the current MTTR for incidents.
- **Define Procedures:** Create a clear, repeatable process for data collection, analysis, and reporting.

Do:

- **Execute the Project:** Carry out the project plan, including the implementation of new systems or security controls.
- **Collect Data:** Implement automated and manual methods to gather data for both project and security KPIs. This could involve using project management software, SIEM (Security Information and Event Management) tools, and security awareness platforms.

Check:

- **Analyze Performance:** Regularly (e.g., monthly or quarterly) review the collected data. Compare the actual performance against the established baselines and project objectives.
- **Identify Gaps:** Look for discrepancies between planned and actual results. For instance, if the MTTR has increased after a new system was deployed, it indicates a gap in the security controls or a need for process refinement.

Act:

- **Implement Improvements:** Based on the analysis, take corrective and preventive actions. This could involve reallocating resources, updating security controls, providing additional training, or refining processes.
- **Revise & Repeat:** Update the plan with the new information and repeat the cycle. This ensures that the program is always adapting to new threats, technologies, and business needs.

By consistently applying this plan, your information security program will not only ensure that projects are delivered successfully but will also continuously enhance the overall security and resilience of your organization.

Stakeholder Management and Communication

Managing an information security program requires a structured approach to identifying, managing, and communicating with various stakeholders. By understanding their needs and expectations, you can ensure the program's success and alignment with business objectives.

1. Identifying Stakeholders

Start by identifying all individuals and groups with a vested interest in the program's success. These can be categorized as internal and external.

Internal:

- **Senior Leadership (CEO, CISO, CIO):** Focused on business risk, compliance, and budget.

- **IT Department:** Responsible for implementing and maintaining security controls.
- **Legal & Compliance:** Concerned with regulatory adherence and liability.
- **Human Resources:** Manages security training and employee policies.
- **Business Unit Leaders:** Interested in how security impacts their operations and productivity.
- **Employees:** The first line of defense, who must follow security policies.

External:

- **Customers:** Expect their data to be protected.
- **Regulators:** Enforce legal and industry standards (e.g., GDPR, HIPAA).
- **Partners & Vendors:** Need to comply with your security requirements.
- **Shareholders:** Concerned with the financial impact of security breaches.

2. Managing Stakeholder Expectations

Once identified, it's crucial to tailor your approach to each group's specific concerns.

For Senior Leadership:

Use business-centric language. Instead of technical jargon, report on risk reduction, cost savings, and compliance status. Focus on how the security program enables the business, not just on the technical details.

For the IT Department:

Involve them in the planning and implementation phases. Their practical knowledge is essential for deploying controls without disrupting daily operations.

For Legal & Compliance:

Provide them with clear documentation of security controls and regular updates on compliance status. This ensures they have the information needed for audits and risk assessments.

For Employees:

Keep communication simple and clear. Explain the "why" behind policies (e.g., "We use multi-factor authentication to protect your account from theft") and make security awareness training engaging and easy to understand.

3. Effective Communication & Reporting

Consistent and targeted communication is key to building trust and program support.

Tailor the Message:

Use different formats for different audiences.

- **Senior Leadership:** High-level dashboards and quarterly reports with KPIs and KRIs.
- **Technical Teams:** Detailed reports on vulnerabilities, patch status, and incident response metrics.
- **Employees:** Short, regular updates via email, intranet, or team meetings.

Establish a Rhythm:

Set a regular schedule for meetings and reports. This predictability helps manage expectations and ensures everyone is kept informed.

Incident Communication:

During a security incident, have a predefined communication plan.

- **Technical Teams:** Communicate every detail needed to resolve the incident.
- **Senior Leadership:** Report on the impact, containment efforts, and recovery timeline.
- **External Parties (if needed):** A single point of contact should provide consistent, approved messaging to customers, regulators, and the public.

Information Security Program Improvement

Information security program operations refer to the day-to-day activities and processes that ensure an organization's information assets are protected. A key part of these operations is the ability to adapt and improve over time. This involves a structured approach to implementing changes that address new threats, fix vulnerabilities, and align with evolving business needs.

Implementing changes and improvements is a critical, continuous cycle within an information security program. It ensures that security measures remain effective in a dynamic threat landscape. This process is not a one-time event; it's a systematic effort to maintain a strong security posture.

1. Identifying the Need for Change

Changes and improvements can be driven by various factors, including:

- **Vulnerability Assessments:** Identifying new weaknesses in systems and applications.
- **Incident Response Reviews:** Analyzing a security incident to understand what went wrong and how to prevent it from happening again.
- **Regulatory & Compliance Changes:** New laws or industry standards that require updated security controls.
- **Technology Updates:** Implementing new tools or migrating to new platforms that require different security configurations.
- **Threat Intelligence:** Responding to emerging threats or attack techniques identified by security researchers.

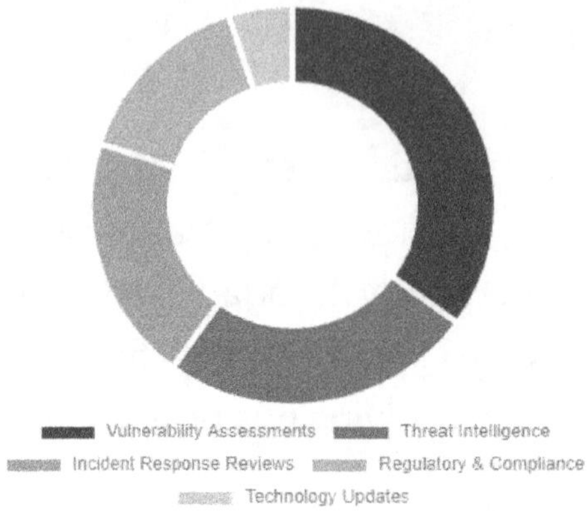

2. The Change Management Process

To ensure changes are implemented effectively and without causing new problems, a formal change management process should be followed. This structured approach minimizes risk and provides clear accountability.

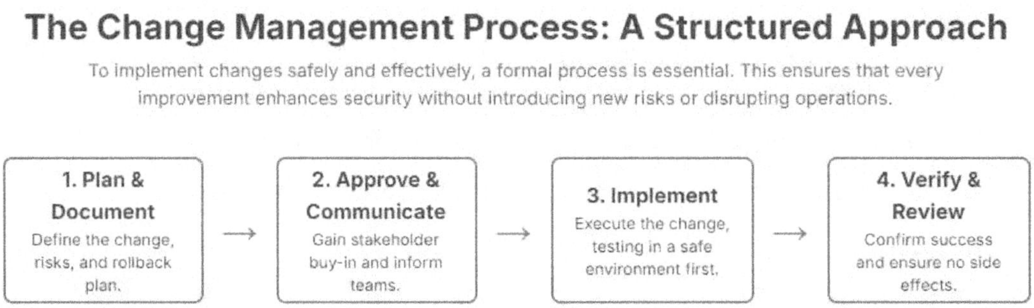

a. Planning & Documentation:

Every proposed change must be documented. This includes:

- A clear description of the change.
- The reason for the change (e.g., fixing a vulnerability).
- The expected outcome and benefits.
- A risk analysis of the proposed change.
- A rollback plan in case the change fails.

b. Approval & Communication:

Before implementation, the change must be reviewed and approved by relevant stakeholders, such as security teams, IT operations, and business owners. This ensures the change is necessary, safe, and has the support of all affected parties. Communication is key to inform everyone about the upcoming change, its potential impact, and the timeline.

c. Implementation:

The change is executed according to the plan. It's often done in a test environment first to ensure it works as expected without disrupting live services. Once successful, it's scheduled for deployment in the production environment.

d. Verification & Review:

After the change is implemented, it is essential to verify its success. This involves checking that the new security control is working correctly and that no unintended side effects have occurred. A post-implementation review helps to confirm that the change achieved its intended purpose and that the process was followed.

The Continuous Improvement Cycle

The entire process of identifying, planning, and implementing changes is part of a larger continuous improvement cycle, often described by the Plan-Do-Check-Act (PDCA) model.

- **Plan:** Identify areas for improvement and plan the changes.
- **Do:** Implement the changes.
- **Check:** Monitor the results and verify the effectiveness of the changes.
- **Act:** Take action to standardize the successful changes and address any new issues that arose.

By embedding this systematic approach into daily operations, an information security program can remain proactive, resilient, and aligned with the organization's evolving needs.

The Continuous Improvement Engine

The entire process is part of the Plan-Do-Check-Act (PDCA) cycle, a framework that embeds continuous improvement into the core of security operations.

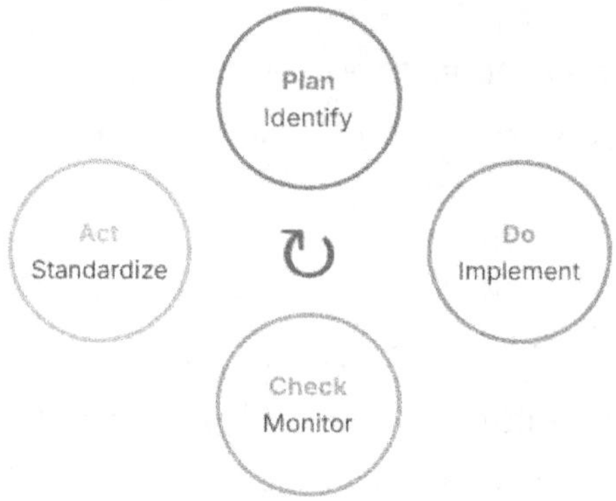

Domain 3 Multiple-Choice Questions

Questions 1-105

1. What is the primary distinction between security program management and security project management?

   A. Program management is focused on short-term, single initiatives, while project management is a continuous process.
   B. Program management oversees multiple, continuous initiatives, while project management focuses on a single initiative with a defined start and end.
   C. Program management is a reactive approach to security incidents, while project management is proactive and strategic.
   D. Program management focuses on tactical execution, whereas project management handles strategic governance.

2. A Chief Information Security Officer (CISO) is presenting a budget proposal to the executive leadership. To ensure buy-in, they frame the request for a new SIEM system in terms of business value rather than technical necessity. Which of the following statements best aligns with this approach?

   A. "The new SIEM is a state-of-the-art technical control that will centralize our security alerts and improve log analysis efficiency."
   B. "Implementing the new SIEM will provide our security team with a powerful platform to analyze threats, which will reduce our mean time to respond (MTTR) by 40%, thereby preventing potential financial losses from a major breach."
   C. "This SIEM is a critical infrastructure component required to meet our department's technical roadmap."
   D. "We need this SIEM because our current system is outdated and lacks the latest features."

3. According to the ISBK, which of the following is considered the "core" of a security program?

   A. Governance.
   B. Risk Management.
   C. Security Awareness & Training.
   D. Operations & Incident Response.

4. A security program has been in place for a year. The CISO wants to measure its effectiveness and demonstrate its value to the board. Which of the following would be the most appropriate component of the security program to focus on for this purpose?

   A. Security Architecture & Engineering, to show the number of systems secured.
   B. Governance, to demonstrate compliance with internal policies.
   C. Risk Management, to highlight the continuous process of threat identification.
   D. Measurement & Reporting, using KPIs and metrics to track program maturity and value.

5. The security program lifecycle is described as a cyclical process with four phases. What is the correct chronological order of these phases?

   A. Design & Implement, Assess & Plan, Operate & Monitor, Review & Improve.
   B. Assess & Plan, Design & Implement, Operate & Monitor, Review & Improve.
   C. Operate & Monitor, Review & Improve, Assess & Plan, Design & Implement.
   D. Review & Improve, Assess & Plan, Design & Implement, Operate & Monitor.

6. A CISO is tasked with moving the organization from a reactive, crisis-driven security posture to a proactive, strategic one. Based on the document, what is the most effective way to achieve this?

   A. By focusing solely on technical solutions and deploying new hardware and software.
   B. By developing and implementing a formal, structured security program.
   C. By creating a dedicated incident response team to handle all security incidents.
   D. By conducting a one-time, comprehensive risk assessment and implementing controls.

7. When identifying resources for a new security program, what are the three key areas of focus mentioned in the document?

   A. People, Technology & Tools, and Budget.
   B. People, Infrastructure & Technology, and Architecture & Design.
   C. Infrastructure, Applications, and Data.
   D. Hardware, Software, and Services.

8. In an organization's security team, which role is primarily responsible for ensuring the program meets regulatory requirements and internal policies?

   A. Security Engineer.
   B. Security Architect.
   C. CISO.
   D. Governance, Risk, and Compliance (GRC) Professional.

9. Which of the following describes the purpose of a Security Information and Event Management (SIEM) system?

   A. To protect and monitor individual computers and servers.
   B. To manage user identities and their access to resources.
   C. To centralize and analyze security alerts from various sources.
   D. To control network traffic and block malicious content.

10. A CISO is making a case to the board for a significant investment in a new security awareness training platform. To best frame this request in terms of business value, what is the most compelling argument they can make, according to the document?

    A. The platform is user-friendly and highly rated by industry peers.
    B. It will educate employees about security best practices, recognizing phishing attacks, and understanding their role in protecting the organization's data, which addresses the human element as the weakest link.
    C. It offers advanced features like gamified learning modules and a comprehensive reporting dashboard.
    D. The cost is significantly lower than competing platforms.

11. According to the document, what is the key to negotiating and acquiring resources for an information security program?

    A. Focusing on the technical specifications of the required tools.
    B. Developing a detailed Work Breakdown Structure (WBS).
    C. Framing requests in terms of business value.
    D. Collaborating with the IT Operations team.

12. A CISO wants to ensure the long-term success of their security program's infrastructure. Which of the following is a key aspect of effective infrastructure management described in the document?

A. Hiring the most skilled security architects.
B. Continuously monitoring and optimizing costs.
C. Conducting weekly phishing simulations.
D. Implementing a formal change control process.

13. A CISO notices that the number of security incidents has been steadily decreasing over the past six months. To demonstrate the program's success to the executive team, they should present this trend as a key performance indicator (KPI) as part of which component of the security program?

A. Security Architecture & Engineering.
B. Operations & Incident Response.
C. Measurement & Reporting.
D. Governance.

14. What is the primary purpose of a Project Scope Statement for a security project?

A. To serve as a legally binding contract with vendors.
B. To provide a shared understanding of what the project will and will not achieve
C. To detail the technical specifications of all required hardware and software.
D. To justify the project's budget to the finance department.

15. A project manager for a security project is defining the project's objectives. They aim to "Implement multi-factor authentication (MFA) for all critical systems, ensuring at least 95% of users are enrolled by the end of Q3. This will reduce the risk of compromised accounts by 80%." This objective most closely aligns with which project management criteria?

A. SMART.
B. PERT.
C. Lean.
D. Agile.

16. A security project to deploy a new endpoint detection and response (EDR) solution has a defined list of deliverables. The project manager wants to prevent "scope creep." Which section of the Project Scope Statement would be most useful in achieving this?

A. Project Justification and Business Need.

B. Project Objectives.
C. Scope and Deliverables, specifically the "Out-of-Scope" section.
D. Constraints and Assumptions.

17. A project manager is developing a project scope statement. They list the budget, timeline, and available personnel as "limitations that will affect the project's execution." What are these items collectively referred to as?

A. Assumptions.
B. Deliverables.
C. Constraints.
D. Out-of-scope items.

18. What is the goal of an Information Security Program Execution Plan?

A. To define the scope of a single security project.
B. To create a legal document for regulatory compliance.
C. To outline a strategic plan for the successful execution of an information security program to protect organizational assets and data.
D. To provide a detailed, step-by-step guide for responding to a security incident.

19. In the Information Security Program Execution Plan, which phase focuses on formally defining the program's objectives, scope, and governance structure?

A. Phase 2: Policy & Control Implementation.
B. Phase 3: Operational Integration
C. Phase 4: Maintenance & Improvement.
D. Phase 1: Program Foundation.

20. A Security Engineer is responsible for implementing and maintaining security technologies and controls. This role is most essential for which activity in the Information Security Program Execution Plan?

A. Activity 3: Risk Assessment.
B. Activity 5: Technical Control Implementation.
C. Activity 7: Security Monitoring & Incident Response.
D. Activity 10: Security Training & Awareness.

21. A security analyst is tasked with day-to-day security monitoring and incident triage. This role falls under which phase of the Information Security Program

Execution Plan?

A. Phase 1: Program Foundation.
B. Phase 2: Policy & Control Implementation.
C. Phase 3: Operational Integration.
D. Phase 4: Maintenance & Improvement.

22. According to the document, which of the following is considered a key responsibility of a CISO?

A. Designing and planning the security framework for networks.
B. Implementing and testing new security technologies.
C. Overall strategic leadership, program governance, and risk management oversight.
D. Day-to-day security monitoring and incident response.

23. A security team manager wants to foster a culture of continuous learning. Which of the following is a recommended practice mentioned in the document?

A. Strictly adhering to a single technical domain for each team member.
B. Discouraging knowledge sharing to protect proprietary methods.
C. Assigning team members to cross-functional projects outside their primary expertise.
D. Limiting professional development to internal, company-specific training.

24. What does the document identify as a primary purpose of defining clear metrics and KPIs for a security project?

A. To justify budget increases without needing to show results.
B. To provide subjective measures of success.
C. To provide objective measures of success and demonstrate the value of the team's efforts.
D. To limit the scope of the project and prevent scope creep.

25. A CISO is leading a security team and wants to foster a positive environment where team members feel comfortable reporting mistakes or vulnerabilities without fear of blame. This concept is referred to as:
A. A blame-free culture.
B. Psychological safety.
C. Open dialogue.

D. Continuous improvement.

26. When an incident occurs, what is the best approach for a security team manager to take during the post-mortem, according to the document?

A. Focus on identifying and holding the person responsible accountable.
B. Focus on what can be learned and what processes can be improved, rather than on who is at fault.
C. Disregard the incident and move on to the next task.
D. Immediately fire the person who made the mistake to set an example.

27. A security organization is struggling with employee retention. What is a key strategy for retaining talent and building institutional knowledge mentioned in the document?

A. Limiting opportunities for professional development to reduce costs.
B. Prioritizing internal promotions and formalized career paths.
C. Outsourcing key security functions to third-party vendors.
D. Avoiding cross-training to allow employees to specialize in a single area.

28. The document states that a well-planned budget for a security program should be directly tied to what?

A. The most recent industry trends and buzzwords.
B. The cost of new, expensive technologies.
C. The organization's strategic goals and risk profile.
D. The total number of employees in the organization.

29. A CISO is developing a new budget. Based on the document, what is the recommended first step in this process?

A. Categorize and prioritize spending.
B. Align the budget with business objectives.
C. Conduct a thorough risk assessment.
D. Negotiate with vendors for lower prices.

30. A project manager is reviewing the budget for an information security project. They notice a significant difference between the planned spending and the actual spending. What is the process they should use to investigate this discrepancy?

A. Performance Monitoring.
B. Cost Optimization.
C. Variance Analysis.
D. A post-mortem review.

31. In the context of variance analysis for an infosec project, what does a positive Cost Variance (CV) indicate?

A. The project is over budget for the work completed.
B. The project is under budget for the work completed.
C. The project is behind schedule.
D. The project is ahead of schedule.

32. What is the formula for calculating Schedule Variance (SV)?
A. SV = Planned Value (PV) - Actual Cost (AC).
B. SV = Earned Value (EV) - Planned Value (PV).
C. SV = Earned Value (EV) - Actual Cost (AC).
D. SV = Planned Value (PV) - Earned Value (EV).

33. A new requirement to include multi-factor authentication for a system that was not in the original project scope is a classic example of what?

A. Gold Plating.
B. Variance Analysis.
C. Scope Creep.
D. Agile Project Management.

34. A security team spends extra time and resources to implement an advanced logging system with more features than were originally requested by the stakeholders. This is an example of what?

A. Scope Creep.
B. Gold Plating.
C. Continuous Improvement.
D. A successful project deliverable.

36. The document describes a Work Breakdown Structure (WBS) as a deliverable-oriented hierarchy. What is the "100% Rule" in the context of a WBS?

A. The WBS must include 100% of the project's budget.
B. The WBS must include 100% of the work defined by the project scope and capture all deliverables.
C. The WBS must be 100% accurate in its cost estimations.
D. The WBS must be approved by 100% of the project's stakeholders.

37. An organization has a past project to deploy a security awareness platform that cost $25,000. They use this information to estimate the cost of a new, similar project. What type of estimation technique is being used?

A. Bottom-Up Estimating.
B. Analogous Estimating.
C. Parametric Estimating.
D. Three-Point Estimating.

38. What is the primary purpose of a formal change control process for an information security project?

A. To prevent scope creep and ensure the project remains on track, on budget, and achieves its security objectives.
B. To give the project manager absolute authority over all project decisions.
C. To ensure that every project change is implemented without any impact on the budget or timeline.
D. To automatically approve all requested changes to the project scope.

39. In a formal change control process, what is the function of a Request for Change (RFC) document?

A. It is a formal contract with a new vendor.
B. It provides a detailed description of a proposed modification, its justification, and an initial impact estimate.
C. It serves as a final report on a completed project.
D. It is used to track the project's earned value.

40. What is a "contingency reserve" in the context of a project budget?

A. Funds set aside for a specific, known risk that has a high likelihood of occurring.
B. A fund to handle unforeseen and unknown risks.
C. A fund set aside to handle known, but uncertain, risks.
D. An emergency fund for major security incidents.

41. What is the difference between a contingency reserve and a management reserve?

A. Contingency reserve is for known risks, and management reserve is for unknown risks.
B. Contingency reserve is managed by the CISO, while management reserve is managed by the project manager.
C. Contingency reserve is for minor projects, and management reserve is for major projects.
D. There is no difference; the terms are interchangeable.

42. According to the document, which of the following is an example of an "Architecture & Design" resource for a security program?

A. SIEM.
B. GRC Professionals.
C. Threat Modeling Methodologies.
D. Security Engineers.

43. The document defines the "Governance" component of a security program as the foundation that defines what?

A. The technical controls and hardware.
B. The day-to-day operational procedures.
C. Policies, standards, and procedures that guide the program.
D. The metrics for reporting and measurement.

44. In a security project, what does a negative cost variance (CV) typically indicate?

A. The project is behind schedule.
B. The project is ahead of schedule.
C. The project is under budget.
D. The project is over budget.

45. Which of the following is NOT one of the four phases of the security program lifecycle mentioned in the document?

A. Assess & Plan.
B. Operate & Monitor.
C. Design & Implement.
D. Audit & Report.

47. The document describes a shift from a reactive to a proactive approach in security. What does this shift enable the business to do?

A. Fight fires more effectively.
B. Reduce the likelihood and impact of security incidents and pursue new opportunities securely.
C. Reduce the security budget.
D. Eliminate all cybersecurity threats.

48. What is the most critical resource for a security program, according to the ISBK?

A. Technology & Tools.
B. Architecture & Design.
C. People.
D. Budget.

49. When developing a business case for security resources, what should the focus be on?

A. The specific technical needs of the security team.
B. Quantifying risk reduction and ROI.
C. The features of the new technology.
D. The opinions of a single senior leader.

50. What is the role of a GRC (Governance, Risk, and Compliance) professional?

A. To implement and manage security tools.
B. To ensure the program meets regulatory requirements and internal policies.
C. To design the overall security posture.
D. To monitor for threats and respond to incidents.

51. What is a key responsibility of the Security Engineering role?

A. Setting the strategic direction of the program.
B. Designing the security architecture.
C. Implementing, testing, and maintaining security technologies and controls.
D. Managing the security budget.

52. According to the document, what is the primary purpose of a "Shared Knowledge Base" within a security team?

A. To store personal employee data.
B. To centralize project management tasks.
C. To maintain a repository for documentation, policies, and best practices for all teams to access.
D. To track employee performance metrics.

53. What is the "human element" often described as in a security program?

A. The strongest link.
B. The most predictable element.
C. The weakest link.
D. The most expensive resource.

54. The document mentions that a CISO should use clear, non-technical language when engaging with stakeholders. Why is this important?

A. To impress them with technical knowledge.
B. To build alliances by aligning security goals with business objectives.
C. To demonstrate their deep technical expertise.
D. To justify the need for more technical personnel.

55. A security project to deploy a new firewall is experiencing delays due to issues in getting necessary approvals from the network team. What type of variance does this represent?

A. Cost Variance (CV).
B. Scope Variance118.
C. Schedule Variance (SV).
D. Quality Variance.

56. The document states that a Work Breakdown Structure (WBS) is a deliverable-oriented hierarchy. What does this mean?

A. It organizes and defines the total scope of a project by breaking down the work into tangible outputs or deliverables.
B. It lists all the tasks that need to be completed in a linear fashion.
C. It provides a detailed list of all the people required for a project.
D. It focuses on the budget and financial aspects of a project.

57. According to the ISBK, what is the purpose of conducting a "Current State Assessment" in Phase 1 of the program execution plan?

A. To identify new technologies to purchase.
B. To establish a baseline of existing security controls, policies, and procedures for future improvements.
C. To estimate the total cost of the program.
D. To define the program's charter and scope.

58. In the context of the program's staffing plan, which role is responsible for ensuring that security is built-in from the ground up?

A. Security Engineer.
B. Security Analyst.
C. CISO.
D. Security Architect.

59. When managing a security team, what is a key management practice that helps measure team effectiveness and provide feedback?
A. Continuous Training & Development.
B. Performance Monitoring with KPIs.
C. Cross-Functional Projects.
D. Recruitment and Vetting.

60. The document describes the Project Scope Statement. Which of the following is an example of an "out-of-scope" item for an MFA project?

A. User training materials.
B. Implementation of MFA for non-critical systems.
C. A new security policy mandating MFA.
D. A vulnerability assessment report.

61. The Information Security Program Execution Plan outlines four key phases.

Which phase involves the continuous, day-to-day activities of security teams, such as monitoring systems and enforcing policies?

A. Phase 1: Program Foundation.
B. Phase 2: Policy & Control Implementation.
C. Phase 3: Operational Integration.
D. Phase 4: Maintenance & Improvement.

62. What is the purpose of "cross-functional drills" in a team coordination plan?

A. To test the security of physical infrastructure.
B. To simulate real-world scenarios to test response and coordination.
C. To provide individual, specialized training.
D. To develop new security policies.

63. Which of the following is a primary benefit of fostering "psychological safety" within a security team?

A. It eliminates the need for formal reporting procedures.
B. It encourages team members to admit mistakes or report vulnerabilities without fear of blame.
C. It allows team members to work without any supervision.
D. It reduces the need for external audits.

64. The document mentions that a key to retaining top talent is fostering a positive work environment and providing growth opportunities. What is a specific example of providing growth opportunities mentioned in the chapter?

A. Reducing workloads to prevent burnout.
B. Implementing mentorship and coaching programs.
C. Providing higher salaries to all employees.
D. Discouraging participation in industry conferences.

65. The document states that a security budget should be a direct response to what?

A. The latest security trends.
B. The specific risks identified in a thorough risk assessment.
C. The requests of the CISO.
D. The total number of employees.

66. What is a key step in managing and monitoring the security budget, as described in the document?

A. Spending all the allocated money as quickly as possible.
B. Continuously tracking actual vs. planned spending.
C. Ignoring unexpected costs.
D. Avoiding variance analysis.

67. What is the term for a project management tool that breaks down a project's work into smaller, more manageable components in a deliverable-oriented hierarchy?

A. Project Scope Statement.
B. Work Breakdown Structure (WBS).
C. Gantt Chart.
D. Project Charter.

68. What is the key distinction between a work package and a WBS element?

A. A work package is a task, while a WBS element is a deliverable.
B. A WBS element is at the lowest level of the hierarchy, and a work package is at a higher level.
C. A work package is a deliverable, and a WBS element is a task.
D. They are the same thing.

69. What is the most accurate method for estimating project costs according to the ISBK?

A. Analogous Estimating.
B. Bottom-Up Estimating.
C. Top-Down Estimating.
D. Expert Judgment.

70. What is a critical element to include in a Request for Change (RFC) document?

A. A detailed list of all project team members.
B. A justification for the proposed modification and its estimated impact on the project.
C. The project manager's personal opinion of the change.
D. A complete legal analysis of the change.

71. In a security project, who is typically responsible for conducting the impact analysis of a proposed change?

A. The end users.
B. The project sponsor.
C. The project manager and the Change Control Board (CCB).
D. The procurement department.

72. Which of the following is a primary goal of the change control process?

A. To prevent any changes from being made to the project.
B. To ensure that every change is approved by the CISO.
C. To ensure accountability and create a documented audit trail of all project changes.
D. To make the project schedule more flexible.

73. A security manager is working on a new budget. Based on the document, if their primary risk is a data breach from a sophisticated cyberattack, what should they prioritize in the budget?

A. Employee lunch and learns.
B. Advanced threat detection tools and employee training.
C. New office furniture.
D. Upgrading the company website.

74. The document mentions that security should be an "enabler, not a roadblock." What does this mean?

A. Security should be a separate function from the business.
B. The security budget must be aligned with and support the business's strategic objectives.
C. The security team should always approve new initiatives without question.
D. Security should only focus on blocking threats.

75. According to the document, what is the importance of a project's "baseline" in the change control process?

A. It is used to justify additional funding.
B. It is the original scope, budget, and schedule against which all RFCs are

evaluated.
C. It is the final version of the project deliverables.
D. It is the minimum viable product (MVP) of the project.

76. The document refers to the "Plan-Do-Check-Act (PDCA)" model. Which phase involves monitoring the results and verifying the effectiveness of changes?

A. Plan.
B. Do.
C. Check.
D. Act.

77. According to the document, why is a negative schedule variance a significant risk for an infosec project?

A. It means the project is over budget.
B. It could leave a critical system unprotected for longer than planned.
C. It indicates that the project scope has expanded.
D. It suggests that the project team is not working hard enough.

78. A security manager is implementing a program to help new security analysts learn from senior experts. What is this practice called?

A. Cross-training.
B. Mentorship and coaching.
C. Formalized career paths.
D. Performance monitoring.

79. Which of the following is a key responsibility of the IT Operations & Systems Staff in a security program?

A. Strategic leadership.
B. Designing the security framework.
C. Assisting with vulnerability remediation and managing user access.
D. Ensuring legal and regulatory compliance.

80. What does the document describe as the purpose of the "Review & Improve" phase of the security program lifecycle?

A. To design and implement security controls.

B. To assess the organization's current security posture.
C. To regularly review the program's effectiveness against metrics and objectives for continuous improvement.
D. To centralize day-to-day operations and monitoring.

81. The document mentions that a robust incident response plan is critical for what?

A. Preventing all security breaches.
B. Minimizing damage during a breach.
C. Implementing a new security framework.
D. Conducting regular audits.

82. A project manager is breaking down a "Phishing Simulation Project" into smaller tasks like "Select Vendor," "Develop Training Content," and "Report Results." This is an example of what?

A. Variance analysis.
B. Developing a project scope statement.
C. Creating a Work Breakdown Structure (WBS).
D. Gold Plating.

83. A CISO is creating a new budget. They are allocating funds for salaries, benefits, and training. What budget category do these items fall under?

A. Technology & Tools.
B. Personnel.
C. Governance, Risk, and Compliance (GRC).
D. Incident Response.

84. What is a key purpose of a Project Scope Statement?

A. To get legal approval for a project.
B. To provide a shared understanding among all stakeholders about what the project will and will not achieve.
C. To define the security team's responsibilities.
D. To outline the company's entire security program.

85. What is the role of a Compliance Officer in a security program?
A. To manage the IT infrastructure.

B. To implement security controls.
C. To ensure the program meets all regulatory and legal obligations.
D. To design the security architecture.

86. The document states that a security program moves from a reactive to a proactive approach by becoming what?

A. Crisis-driven.
B. Reactive.
C. Strategic.
D. Unstructured.

87. Which of the following is a core component of a security program?

A. Human Resources.
B. Sales & Marketing.
C. Security Architecture & Engineering.
D. Procurement.

88. When developing an information security budget, which step involves working with executive leadership and department heads to understand the organization's priorities?

A. Conducting a Thorough Risk Assessment.
B. Aligning with Business Objectives.
C. Categorizing and Prioritizing Spending.
D. Managing and Monitoring the Budget.

89. A CISO has an annual budget of $500,000 for a new security program. They have set aside $50,000 to cover potential unexpected costs related to known, uncertain risks. What is this $50,000 called?

A. Management Reserve.
B. Contingency Reserve.
C. Gold Plating fund.
D. Scope Creep fund.

90. A security team manager wants to improve communication and coordination. What is a key action they can take, according to the document?

A. Limit meetings to only the CISO and senior staff.

B. Establish a centralized knowledge base for all documentation and policies.
C. Discourage cross-departmental communication.
D. Rely solely on informal communication.

91. What is a key responsibility of the Security Analyst role?

A. Designing a secure network architecture.
B. Implementing security controls.
C. Day-to-day security monitoring, incident triage, and vulnerability management.
D. Providing overall strategic leadership.

92. The document highlights the importance of regular security drills. What is the primary purpose of these drills?

A. To practice for future audits.
B. To simulate real-world scenarios to test response and coordination.
C. To provide individual training.
D. To justify the need for more budget.

93. A security manager is looking to build a resilient security program that can adapt to new threats. According to the document, what should they focus on?

A. A one-time security project.
B. Continuous improvement through regular review and updates based on new threats.
C. Eliminating all vulnerabilities at once.
D. Ignoring minor incidents.

94. What is the "Act" phase of the Plan-Do-Check-Act (PDCA) model described as?

A. Implementing the changes.
B. Monitoring the results.
C. Taking action to standardize successful changes and address new issues188.
D. Planning the changes.

95. The document states that a negative schedule variance can result from a shortage of trained personnel. What is the primary risk associated with this?

A. The project will be over budget.
B. The project will have expanded scope.
C. A critical system could be left unprotected for longer than planned.
D. The project will fail to get vendor buy-in.

96. What is the purpose of the "Impact Analysis and Assessment" phase in a project change control process?

A. To approve or deny the change request.
B. To formally submit the change request.
C. To conduct a thorough analysis of the change's impact on the project's security, scope, timeline, and budget.
D. To implement the approved change.

97. In the context of team development, what is the purpose of cross-training opportunities?

A. To reduce the need for external consultants.
B. To broaden team members' skill sets and provide a holistic view of the security landscape.
C. To prevent staff from leaving the organization.
D. To limit the scope of their work.

98. When developing a project scope statement, what does the "Project Justification and Business Need" section explain?

A. The technical details of the project.
B. The "why" behind the project and how it links to organizational goals.
C. The specific tasks to be performed.
D. The total budget for the project.

99. What is a key purpose of establishing a Change Control Board (CCB) for a project?

A. To ensure that only the project manager can make decisions.
B. To include all project stakeholders in the decision-making process.

C. To implement the changes without review.
D. To prevent any project changes from being considered.

100. The document states that a strong security program is built on several interconnected pillars. What are they?

A. People, Process, and Technology.
B. Hardware, Software, and Services.
C. Governance, Risk Management, Architecture & Engineering, Operations & Incident Response, Awareness & Training, and Measurement & Reporting.
D. Budget, Timeline, and Resources.

101. In the context of a project budget, what is the purpose of a contingency reserve?

A. To cover unforeseen, unknown risks.
B. To cover known, but uncertain, risks.
C. To pay for regular, planned project expenses.
D. To fund gold plating.

102. According to the document, what is the role of a "Project Sponsor"?

A. To manage the day-to-day project tasks.
B. To provide technical guidance to the team.
C. To provide strategic leadership and approval for the project, often the CISO.
D. To implement the project deliverables.

103. A CISO is leading a project to implement new security policies. A key deliverable is a report confirming the successful implementation. This deliverable best aligns with which phase of the security program lifecycle?

A. Assess & Plan.
B. Design & Implement.
C. Operate & Monitor.
D. Review & Improve.

104. What is a key benefit of a structured security program, as described in the document?

A. It moves an organization from a reactive, crisis-driven approach to a proactive,

strategic one.
B. It eliminates all security incidents.
C. It guarantees a 100% compliant posture.
D. It completely removes the need for human oversight.

105. A security team is facing a high turnover rate. What is a key people management strategy to improve retention?

A. Increasing workload.
B. Fostering a positive work environment and providing growth opportunities.
C. Limiting training budgets.
D. Discouraging teamwork.

106. Which of the following is an example of an "Infrastructure & Technology" resource?

A. A Security Architect.
B. Threat Modeling
C. An Endpoint Detection and Response (EDR) system.
D. A security policy.

107. A CISO is defining SMART goals for a new security project. What does the "M" stand for?

A. Maintenance.
B. Measurable.
C. Mitigation.
D. Management.

Answer Key

1. **B.** Program management is a continuous effort that oversees multiple projects to achieve a cohesive and mature security posture, whereas project management is a single initiative with a defined start and end.
   - **Incorrect Options:**
   - A and C are incorrect because they reverse the roles and approaches described in the document.
   - D is incorrect as governance is a component of a program, not a type of management.

2. **B.** This option frames the SIEM in terms of business outcomes (reducing MTTR and preventing financial loss) rather than just technical specifications, which is the key to demonstrating business value and gaining stakeholder buy-in.
   - **Incorrect Options:**
   - A, C, and D are incorrect as they use technical or internal jargon and do not tie the request directly to business value, as recommended in the document.

3. **B.** The document explicitly states that "The core of any security program is a strong risk management framework"
   - **Incorrect Options:**
   - A, C, and D are all key components of a security program but are not identified as the "core" in the document. Governance is the "foundation," while Operations and Awareness are other pillars.

4. **D.** The Measurement & Reporting component is specifically designed to track program effectiveness using KPIs and metrics and to report this to leadership to demonstrate the program's value.
   - **Incorrect Options:**
   - A, B, and C are all important components, but Measurement & Reporting is the one focused on proving the value and maturity of the entire program to leadership.

5. **B.** The document outlines the security program lifecycle in this specific order: Assess & Plan, Design & Implement, Operate & Monitor, and Review & Improve.
   - **Incorrect Options:**
   - A, C, and D all present the phases in an incorrect order, which would disrupt the logical flow of a strategic security program.

6. **B.** The document states that "By implementing a formal security program, an organization moves from a reactive, crisis-driven approach to a proactive, strategic one".
   - **Incorrect Options:**
   - A is incorrect because a formal program involves more than just technology. C is a component of the program, not the overall strategy. D is incorrect because a program is a continuous, not a one-time, effort.

7. **B.** The document's section on "Identifying Resources" is explicitly broken down into three areas: "People," "Infrastructure & Technology," and "Architecture & Design".
   - **Incorrect Options:**
   - A, C, and D are incorrect as they do not match the specific categories mentioned in the document.

8. **D.** The document identifies Governance, Risk, and Compliance (GRC) Professionals as individuals who "ensure the program meets regulatory requirements and internal policies".
   - **Incorrect Options:**
   - A, B, and C have different responsibilities as described in the document, such as implementing controls (Engineer), designing architecture (Architect), and providing strategic leadership (CISO).

9. **C.** The document describes a SIEM as "A platform to centralize and analyze security alerts".
   - **Incorrect Options:**
   - A describes EDR, B describes IAM, and D describes firewalls, all of which are distinct from a SIEM.

10. **B.** The document highlights the human element as the "weakest link" and that security awareness and training is about "educating employees... and understanding their role in protecting the organization's data". This is the most direct and compelling business case for the training.
    - **Incorrect Options:**
    - A, C, and D focus on the product's features or cost, which are secondary to the business value it provides.

11. **C.** The document explicitly states that the key to negotiation and acquisition is "to frame your requests in terms of business value"220.
    - **Incorrect Options:**

- A, B, and D are all part of the process but not identified as the "key" to making a compelling case to leadership.

12. **B.** The document states that a key aspect of Infrastructure Management is "Cost Optimization," which involves continuously monitoring the usage and cost of security tools to ensure you get the most out of your budget.
    - **Incorrect Options:**
    - A, C, and D are important security practices but are not explicitly described as part of infrastructure management in the document.

13. **C.** The document defines Measurement & Reporting as the component that involves "defining key performance indicators (KPIs) and metrics to track the effectiveness of the security program" and providing "visibility into the program's maturity and demonstrates its value". A decrease in incidents is a perfect example of such a metric.
    - **Incorrect Options:**
    - While a decrease in incidents is a result of effective operations (B), the act of measuring and reporting on it falls under the Measurement & Reporting component. Governance and Architecture are not the primary components for this activity.

14. **B.** The document states that a project scope statement "provides a shared understanding among all stakeholders about what the project will achieve, what it won't, and how its success will be measured".
    - **Incorrect Options:**
    - A, C, and D are incorrect as they describe specific parts of a project or are not the primary purpose of the scope statement.

15. **A.** The objective "Implement multi-factor authentication (MFA) for all critical systems, ensuring at least 95% of users are enrolled by the end of Q3" is Specific (MFA implementation), Measurable (95% enrollment), Achievable (assuming feasibility), Relevant (reduces risk), and Time-bound (by the end of Q3), which perfectly aligns with the SMART criteria.
    - **Incorrect Options:**
    - B, C, and D are project management methodologies, not criteria for setting objectives.

16. **C.** The "Scope and Deliverables" section, particularly the "Out-of-Scope" part, explicitly lists what the project will not include, which is essential for preventing

"scope creep".

- **Incorrect Options:**
- A, B, and D are all important parts of the document but do not serve the specific purpose of preventing scope creep by defining what is explicitly excluded.

17. **C.** The document defines "Constraints" as "any limitations that will affect the project's execution," and provides budget, timeline, and resources as examples.
    - **Incorrect Options:**
    - A, B, and D are distinct parts of the scope statement with different purposes.

18. **C.** The document states that an Information Security Program Execution Plan "outlines a strategic plan for the successful execution of an information security program" with the goal to "establish a robust and comprehensive security posture that protects organizational assets and data".
    - **Incorrect Options:**
    - A, B, and D describe individual projects, legal documents, or a specific type of plan, not the overarching program plan.

19. **D.** The document identifies Phase 1 as "Program Foundation (Initial Setup)" and includes "Program Charter & Scope Definition," which involves defining objectives, scope, and governance.
    - **Incorrect Options:**
    - A, B, and C are subsequent phases that build upon the foundation established in Phase 1.

20. **B.** The document states that the Security Engineer's responsibilities include "Implements, tests, and maintains the security technologies and controls," and explicitly links this role to "Activity 5: Technical Control Implementation".
    - **Incorrect Options:**
    - A, C, and D are activities that fall under the responsibilities of other roles, such as the CISO or Security Analyst.
21. **C.** The document places security monitoring and incident response under Phase 3: Operational Integration, which is described as the phase where the program "becomes operational". The Security Analyst's role aligns directly with these day-to-day operations.
    - **Incorrect Options:**
    - A, B, and D are incorrect as they represent different phases of the security program lifecycle.

22. **C.** The CISO's responsibilities are described as "Overall strategic leadership, program governance, risk management oversight, and reporting to executive leadership".
    - **Incorrect Options:**
    - A is the responsibility of a Security Architect, B is the responsibility of a Security Engineer, and D is the responsibility of a Security Analyst.

23. **C.** The document suggests assigning team members to "Cross-Functional Projects" to broaden their skill sets and promote a holistic understanding of the project.
    - **Incorrect Options:**
    - A, B, and D are all counterproductive to fostering a culture of continuous learning and growth.

24. **C.** The document states that defining clear metrics and KPIs provides "objective measures of success" and helps to "demonstrate the value of the security budget".
    - **Incorrect Options:**
    - A is incorrect as the purpose is to justify funding by showing results. B is the opposite of the document's guidance. D is incorrect as KPIs measure success, not limit scope.

25. **B.** The document defines "Psychological Safety" as the shared belief that the team is safe for interpersonal risk-taking, which is crucial for preventing critical errors and encouraging vulnerability reporting without fear of blame.
    - **Incorrect Options:**
    - A is a related concept but not the term used in the document. C and D are practices that contribute to psychological safety but are not the term for the concept itself.

26. **B.** The document advises shifting from "Blame to Learning" and focusing the post-mortem on what can be learned and what processes can be improved, rather than on who is at fault.
    - **Incorrect Options:**
    - A, C, and D are all counterproductive and do not align with the document's guidance on fostering psychological safety and continuous improvement.

27. **B.** The document states that "Prioritizing internal promotions and career

growth is essential for retaining talent and building institutional knowledge" and mentions "Formalized Career Paths" as a key strategy.

- **Incorrect Options:**
- A, C, and D would all likely increase employee turnover.

28. **C.** The document states that a well-planned budget "is directly tied to the organization's strategic goals and risk profile".

- **Incorrect Options:**
- A, B, and D are all factors that might influence a budget but are not the primary, overarching foundation.

29. **C.** The document lists "Conduct a Thorough Risk Assessment" as the first step in developing an information security budget, stating that the budget should be a direct response to these risks.

- **Incorrect Options:**
- A, B, and D are all subsequent steps in the budget development and management process.

30. **C.** The document defines "Variance Analysis" as the process used to investigate why there is a significant difference between budgeted and actual spending.

- **Incorrect Options:**
- A is a management practice, not a specific analysis technique. B is a goal, not a process. D is a review that happens after an event, while variance analysis is a continuous process.

31. **B.** The document defines Cost Variance (CV) as the difference between the earned value (EV) and the actual cost (AC), and states that a "positive CV means the project is under budget for the work completed".

- **Incorrect Options:**
- A is what a negative CV indicates. C and D relate to Schedule Variance, not Cost Variance.

32. **B.** The document explicitly provides the formula for Schedule Variance (SV) as "SV = Earned Value (EV) - Planned Value (PV)".

- **Incorrect Options:**
- A, C, and D are all incorrect formulas for calculating Schedule Variance.

33. **C.** The document explicitly defines "Scope Creep" as a common form of negative

scope variance where "new requirements or features are added without a corresponding adjustment to the budget or schedule," and uses the example of a new mandate to include MFA for a system that was not in the original scope.

- **Incorrect Options:**
- A is incorrect as Gold Plating is adding features that were not requested. B is the process of analyzing the variance, and D is a project management methodology.

34. **B.** The document defines "Gold Plating" as when "team members add extra work or features that were not requested" and uses the example of a security team implementing an advanced logging system with more features than required.

- **Incorrect Options:**
- A is incorrect as Scope Creep is the addition of new requirements. C is a general concept, not this specific action. D is incorrect as it consumes extra time and resources, which is not a characteristic of a successful deliverable.

36. **B.** The document states that the core principle of a WBS is the "100% Rule," which "states that the WBS must include 100% of the work defined by the project scope and capture all internal, external, and interim deliverables".

- **Incorrect Options:**
- A, C, and D are incorrect as they do not align with the definition of the 100% Rule as described in the document.

37. **B.** The document defines "Analogous Estimating" as the method where you "use a similar past project to reference" and gives an example of using a past project's cost as a starting point for a new one.

- **Incorrect Options:**
- A is a different, more accurate method that involves estimating each individual task. C and D are not mentioned in the document.

38. **A.** The document states that the goal of the change control process is to "prevent 'scope creep' and ensuring the project remains on track, on budget, and achieves its security objectives without creating new vulnerabilities".

- **Incorrect Options:**
- B is incorrect as the process is a collaboration, not a dictatorship. C is unrealistic, as changes often impact budget and schedule. D is incorrect as the purpose is to carefully evaluate, not automatically approve.

39. **B.** The document defines a Request for Change (RFC) as a formal document that "provides a detailed description of the proposed modification, its justification..., and an initial estimate of its impact on the project's budget, timeline, and resources".

- **Incorrect Options:**
- A, C, and D are incorrect as they describe different project documents or processes.

40. **C.** The document defines a contingency reserve as a fund set aside "to handle known, but uncertain, risks".

- **Incorrect Options:**
- A is too specific. B is the definition of a management reserve, not a contingency reserve. D is a general concept.

41. **A.** The document explicitly distinguishes between the two, stating that a "Contingency Reserve: This is for known risks" and a "Management Reserve: This is for unknown risks".

- **Incorrect Options:**
- B, C, and D are incorrect as they misrepresent the distinction between the two types of reserves.

42. **C.** The document lists "Threat Modeling" as a resource under the "Architecture & Design" category, which is described as the strategic blueprint for the security program.

- **Incorrect Options:**
- A is an Infrastructure & Technology resource. B and D are People resources.

43. **C.** The document states that Governance "is the foundation, defining the policies, standards, and procedures that guide the program".

- **Incorrect Options:**
- A, B, and D are all parts of a security program but not the specific definition of "Governance" as described in the document.

44. **D.** The document defines a negative Cost Variance (CV) as an indication that "the project is over budget for the work completed".

- **Incorrect Options:**
- A and B relate to Schedule Variance. C is what a positive CV indicates.

45. **D.** The four phases listed in the document are Assess & Plan, Design & Implement, Operate & Monitor, and Review & Improve. Audit & Report is not one of the four phases.

- **Incorrect Options:**
- A, B, and C are all correct phases of the security program lifecycle.

47. **B.** The document states that moving to a proactive approach "not only reduces the likelihood and impact of security incidents but also ensures compliance, builds stakeholder trust, and enables the business to pursue new opportunities securely".

- **Incorrect Options:**
- A is the opposite of the shift described. C and D are not guaranteed by this approach.

48. **C.** The document explicitly states that "People" are the "most critical resource".

- **Incorrect Options:**
- A, B, and D are all important resources, but the document gives special emphasis to "People."

49. **B.** The document states that when developing a business case, the focus should be on quantifying the benefits and framing them in terms of how they will "reduce risk, prevent financial loss, maintain compliance, and protect the brand's reputation".

- **Incorrect Options:**
- A is a narrow, technical focus that the document advises against. C and D are incorrect as they are not the central focus of a business case.

50. **B.** The document states that GRC Professionals "ensure the program meets regulatory requirements and internal policies".

- **Incorrect Options:**
- A, C, and D are the responsibilities of a Security Engineer, Architect, and Analyst, respectively.

51. **C.** The document states that the Security Engineer's responsibilities include "Implements, tests, and maintains the security technologies and controls," and that this role is "essential for Activity 5: Technical Control Implementation".

- **Incorrect Options:**
- A, B, and D are the responsibilities of the CISO, Security Architect, and CISO/Program Manager, respectively.

52. **C.** The document states that a "Shared Knowledge Base" is a "centralized repository for documentation, policies, and best practices so all teams can access

the most current information".

- **Incorrect Options:**
- A, B, and D are not the purpose of a shared knowledge base as described in the document.

53. **C.** The document explicitly states that "The human element is often the weakest link" in a security program.

- **Incorrect Options:**
- A, B, and D are incorrect as they do not align with the statement in the document.

54. **B.** The document states that using clear, non-technical language is key to engaging stakeholders and helping to "align security goals with their business objectives to build alliances".

- **Incorrect Options:**
- A, C, and D are incorrect as they are not the primary purpose of using non-technical language with stakeholders.

55. **C.** The document defines "Schedule Variance (SV)" as an indication of whether a project is ahead of or behind schedule and provides "delays in obtaining necessary approvals" as a cause for a negative SV.

- **Incorrect Options:**
- A and B are different types of variances. D is not a variance type.

56. **A.** The document defines a WBS as a "deliverable-oriented hierarchy that breaks down the project's work into smaller, more manageable components".

- **Incorrect Options:**
- B, C, and D are incorrect as they do not match the document's definition of a WBS.

57. **B.** The document states that a "Current State Assessment" establishes "a baseline for future improvements" by conducting "a thorough review of the existing security controls, policies, and procedures".

- **Incorrect Options:**
- A, C, and D are activities that may occur in other phases, but they are not the purpose of the current state assessment.

58. **D.** The document states that the Security Architect "Designs and plans the security framework for the organization's networks, systems, and applications," and that this role is key to ensuring "that security is built-in from the ground up".

- **Incorrect Options:**

- A, B, and C are other key roles, but their primary responsibility is not to design the initial secure architecture.

59. **B.** The document states that a key management practice is to "Define Clear Metrics and KPIs" and to "track key performance indicators (KPIs) relevant to your project," as these provide "objective measures of success".

- **Incorrect Options:**
- A, C, and D are important for team development, but they are not the primary method for measuring effectiveness and providing feedback.

60. **B.** The document's example of a Project Scope Statement for an MFA project explicitly lists "Implementation of MFA for non-critical systems" as an "Out-of-Scope" item.

- **Incorrect Options:**
- A, C, and D are all listed as "In-Scope" deliverables for the project.

61. **C.** The document describes Phase 3 as "Operational Integration," which is where "the program becomes operational" and where security teams "monitor systems, manage incidents, and enforce policies".

- **Incorrect Options:**
- A, B, and D are other phases with different focuses.

62. **B.** The document states that "Cross-Functional Drills" are used to "simulate real-world scenarios... to test response and coordination".

- **Incorrect Options:**
- A, C, and D are not the purpose of cross-functional drills as described.

63. **B.** The document states that psychological safety is crucial because it creates a "non-punitive culture where team members feel safe to admit mistakes or report vulnerabilities without fear of blame or reprisal".

- **Incorrect Options:**
- A, C, and D are not described as benefits of psychological safety in the document.

64. **B.** The document mentions "Mentorship and Coaching" as a way to provide growth opportunities by pairing "junior team members with senior experts".

- **Incorrect Options:**
- A, C, and D are either not mentioned or are counter-productive to employee retention.

65. **B.** The document states that the security budget is "directly tied to the

organization's strategic goals and risk profile" and should be a "direct response to these risks".

- **Incorrect Options:**
- A, C, and D are all factors, but not the primary driver for the budget.

66. **B.** The document lists "Track Actual vs. Planned Spending" as the first step in managing and monitoring a budget, stating that "Regularly monitor your expenditures".

- **Incorrect Options:**
- A, C, and D are poor budget management practices.

67. **B.** The document defines a "Work Breakdown Structure (WBS)" as a "deliverable-oriented hierarchy that breaks down the project's work into smaller, more manageable components".

- **Incorrect Options:**
- A, C, and D are other project management tools, but they do not match the definition of a WBS.

68. **A.** The document states that WBS Elements are "tangible outputs" or deliverables, while "Work Packages" are at the lowest level and are "the smallest unit of work that can be realistically managed".

- **Incorrect Options:**
- B, C, and D are incorrect as they either misrepresent the relationship or incorrectly define the terms.

69. **B.** The document states that "Bottom-Up Estimating... is the most accurate method" and involves estimating the resources for each task in the WBS.

- **Incorrect Options:**
- A is a faster but less precise method. C and D are not mentioned in the document.

70. **B.** The document states that an RFC "provides a detailed description of the proposed modification, its justification..., and an initial estimate of its impact on the project's budget, timeline, and resources".

- **Incorrect Options:**
- A, C, and D are not the purpose of an RFC.

71. **C.** The document states that "a designated project manager and the project's Change Control Board (CCB) conduct a thorough impact analysis".

- **Incorrect Options:**

- A, B, and D are all stakeholders but are not the primary group responsible for the impact analysis.

72. **C.** The document lists several purposes, including "Ensure accountability" and "Create a clear, documented audit trail of all project changes and their approvals".

- **Incorrect Options:**
- A is incorrect as the purpose is to manage changes, not prevent them. B is incorrect as the CCB, not just the CISO, is responsible for approval. D is incorrect as change control often introduces rigidity, not flexibility.

73. **B.** The document provides this exact scenario, stating that if the primary risk is a data breach from a sophisticated cyberattack, the budget should "prioritize advanced threat detection tools and employee training".

- **Incorrect Options:**
- A, C, and D are not relevant to addressing the specific risk of a cyberattack.

74. **B.** The document states that security should be an enabler and that the budget "must support these objectives" and provides an example of securing a new product launch.

- **Incorrect Options:**
- A and D are incorrect as they would create silos or roadblocks. C is incorrect as security should be a partner with the business, not simply an approver.

75. **B.** The document advises to "Clearly define the project's original scope, budget, and schedule (the baselines)," and that "All RFCs should be evaluated against these baselines to measure their impact".

- **Incorrect Options:**
- A, C, and D are incorrect as they do not match the definition of a project baseline.

76. **C.** The document defines the "Check" phase of the PDCA model as where you "Monitor the results and verify the effectiveness of the changes".

- **Incorrect Options:**
- A, B, and D are all other phases in the cycle.

77. **C.** The document warns that a negative schedule variance "could leave a critical system unprotected for longer than planned".

- **Incorrect Options:**
- A relates to cost variance, B relates to scope variance, and D is not mentioned as a direct risk.

78. **B.** The document describes "Mentorship and Coaching" as a program that "pairs experienced team members with those who are earlier in their careers," which fosters knowledge transfer and provides guidance.

- **Incorrect Options:**
- A, C, and D are other management practices but do not match the specific description.

79. **C.** The document states that the responsibilities of the IT Operations & Systems Staff include "Implementing and maintaining technical security controls, managing user access, and assisting with vulnerability remediation".

- **Incorrect Options:**
- A, B, and D are the responsibilities of a CISO, Security Architect, and Compliance Officer, respectively.

80. **C.** The document states that in the "Review & Improve" phase, "The program's effectiveness is regularly reviewed against its metrics and objectives" and that this "feedback loop is essential for... continuously improving the program's maturity".

- **Incorrect Options:**
- A, B, and D are all other phases of the program lifecycle.

81. **B.** The document states that "A robust incident response plan is critical for minimizing damage during a breach".

- **Incorrect Options:**
- A is unrealistic. C is a separate process. D is part of a separate phase.

82. **C.** The document provides this exact example to illustrate how to "Use a Work Breakdown Structure (WBS)" to break a project down into "smaller, manageable tasks".

- **Incorrect Options:**
- A, B, and D are incorrect as they are different project management processes.

83. **B.** The document lists "Personnel" as a budget category that includes "Salaries, benefits, and training for your security team," as well as contractors and consultants.

- **Incorrect Options:**
- A, C, and D are other budget categories.

84. **B.** The document states that a project scope statement provides a "shared

understanding among all stakeholders about what the project will achieve, what it won't, and how its success will be measured".

- **Incorrect Options:**
- A, C, and D are too broad or too specific to be the primary purpose of the document.

85. **C.** The document lists the Compliance Officer's responsibilities as "Ensuring the program meets all regulatory and legal obligations".

- **Incorrect Options:**
- A, B, and D are the responsibilities of IT Operations, Security Engineer, and Security Architect, respectively.

86. **C.** The document states that a formal security program transforms an organization's approach from reactive to "a proactive, strategic one".

- **Incorrect Options:**
- A, B, and D are not the desired outcome or are the opposite of what a structured program achieves.

87. **C.** The document lists six interconnected pillars or core components of a successful security program, and "Security Architecture & Engineering" is one of them.

- **Incorrect Options:**
- A, B, and D are all related to a program but are not listed as the core pillars.

88. **B.** The document lists "Align with Business Objectives" as the second step in developing a budget and states that it involves working with key stakeholders to understand the organization's priorities.

- **Incorrect Options:**
- A, C, and D are other steps in the process, but they do not involve this specific alignment activity.

89. **B.** The document defines a "Contingency Reserve" as a fund set aside "to handle known, but uncertain, risks". This is exactly what the $50,000 is for in this scenario.

- **Incorrect Options:**
- A is for unknown risks. C and D are not related to project reserves.

90. **B.** The document suggests creating a "Shared Knowledge Base" as a robust communication plan component to ensure all teams can access current information.

- **Incorrect Options:**
- A, C, and D are all practices that would hinder, not help, communication and

coordination.

91. **C.** The document states that a Security Analyst's responsibilities include "Day-to-day security monitoring, incident triage and response, and vulnerability management".

- **Incorrect Options:**
- A, B, and D are the responsibilities of the Security Architect, Security Engineer, and CISO, respectively.

92. **B.** The document states that cross-functional drills "simulate real-world scenarios, such as a phishing campaign or a denial-of-service attack, to test response and coordination".

- **Incorrect Options:**
- A, C, and D are not the primary purpose of these drills.

93. **B.** The document states that the program enters a "continuous cycle of training, auditing, and improvement" in Phase 4 and that this continuous improvement involves "Regularly review and update the security program based on new threats, technologies, and business needs".

- **Incorrect Options:**
- A, C, and D are not aligned with a continuous improvement model.

94. **C.** The document defines the "Act" phase of the PDCA model as taking "action to standardize the successful changes and address any new issues that arose".

- **Incorrect Options:**
- A, B, and D are the "Do," "Check," and "Plan" phases, respectively.

95. **C.** The document states that a negative schedule variance "could leave a critical system unprotected for longer than planned".

- **Incorrect Options:**
- A relates to cost variance, B relates to scope variance, and D is not a risk mentioned in the document.

96. **C.** The document states that a designated team conducts an "Impact Analysis and Assessment" to thoroughly analyze the change's impact on the project's security, scope, timeline, and budget.

- **Incorrect Options:**
- A, B, and D are all other steps in the change control process.

97. **B.** The document states that cross-training opportunities "broaden their skill sets and provide a holistic view of the security landscape".

- **Incorrect Options:**
- A, C, and D are not the purpose of cross-training.

98. **B.** The document states that the "Project Justification and Business Need" section explains the "why" behind the project, clearly stating the problem or opportunity and linking it to organizational goals.

- **Incorrect Options:**
- A, C, and D are other sections or components of a project plan.

99. **B.** The document states that a CCB should include the project manager, a security lead, key stakeholders, and a technical expert "to ensure all perspectives are considered".

- **Incorrect Options:**
- A, C, and D are incorrect as the CCB's purpose is to facilitate controlled, collaborative decision-making, not to limit it.

100. **C.** The document explicitly lists these six pillars as the interconnected components of a successful security program.

- **Incorrect Options:**
- A, B, and D are incorrect as they do not match the list of components in the document.

101. **B.** The document defines a contingency reserve as a fund of money or time "to handle known, but uncertain, risks".

- **Incorrect Options:**
- A is a management reserve. C and D are incorrect as they describe regular or unapproved spending.

102. **C.** The document identifies the "Project Sponsor" as a key stakeholder, typically the CISO, responsible for providing strategic leadership and support for the project. **Incorrect Options:**

- A, B, and D are the responsibilities of the Project Manager or technical team.

103. **B.** A report confirming successful implementation is a tangible deliverable that is created during the "Design & Implement" phase of the program lifecycle.

- **Incorrect Options**:
- A, C, and D are other phases in the cycle and do not typically involve the creation

of final implementation reports.

104. **A.** The document states that a structured security program transforms an organization's approach from "a reactive, crisis-driven approach to a proactive, strategic one".

- **Incorrect Options**:
- B, C, and D are unrealistic claims and are not supported by the document's content.

105. **B.** The document highlights that fostering a positive work environment and providing growth opportunities are essential for retaining top talent.

- **Incorrect Options**:
- A, C, and D are all counter-productive to employee retention.

106. **C.** The document lists Endpoint Detection and Response (EDR) as a technology under the "Infrastructure & Technology" category.

- **Incorrect Options**:
- A is a person, B is an architecture resource, and D is a design resource.

107. **B.** The document defines the "M" in the SMART criteria as "Measurable".

- **Incorrect Options:**
- A, C, and D are incorrect as they are not part of the SMART acronym as defined in the document.

CCISO Explain IT Like I Am 5: Domain 4

4. Information Security Core Competencies

Access control is a security method that regulates who or what can view or use resources in a computing environment. It is a fundamental component of any robust security policy, serving to protect sensitive data and systems from unauthorized access.

Five Different Types of Access Control

The five main types of access control are Mandatory Access Control (MAC), Discretionary Access Control (DAC), Role-Based Access Control (RBAC), Rule-Based Access Control (RBAC), and Attribute-Based Access Control (ABAC).

1. Mandatory Access Control (MAC)

MAC is a very strict model often used in high-security environments, such as military and government organizations.

Key Features:

- **Centralized Control:** A central authority makes all access decisions based on a predefined security policy.
- **Subject/Object Labels:** Every user (subject) and every resource (object) is assigned a sensitivity label. Access is granted only if the subject's label meets or exceeds the object's label.
- **Strict Rules:** Prevents information from flowing from a higher security level to a lower one.

Pros:

- Highly secure and effective at preventing unauthorized data leakage.
- Access decisions are not left to the discretion of individual users, reducing the risk of human error.
- Ideal for environments with extremely sensitive or classified data.

Cons:

- Extremely rigid and complex to administer and manage.

- Difficult to implement and maintain in large, dynamic organizations.
- Can hinder business efficiency due to its strictness.

Example Implementation:

A classified military document system. A user with a "Confidential" clearance can access files marked "Confidential" but is denied access to files marked "Secret" or "Top Secret," regardless of the file's owner. The system itself enforces these rules, and the file's creator cannot grant higher-level access to a user with a lower clearance.

2. Discretionary Access Control (DAC)

DAC is a more flexible model where the owner of a resource can decide who has access to it. It is the most common type of access control used in commercial and general-purpose operating systems.

Key Features:

- **Identity-Based:** Access decisions are based on the identity of the user or a group they belong to.
- **Owner's Discretion:** The creator or owner of a resource can grant or deny access to other users.

Pros:

- Highly flexible and easy to implement in basic environments.
- The owner has full control over their resources.
- Requires less administrative overhead for initial setup.

Cons:

- Can be less secure as it relies on individual users to make good security decisions.
- Can lead to inconsistent security policies and accidental data exposure.
- Difficult to audit and manage access rights across a large organization.

Example Implementation:

A personal computer operating system (e.g., Windows or macOS). You create a folder on your desktop and can individually choose to give "read-only" or "full control" permissions to other user accounts on the computer. Similarly, on cloud storage services like Google Drive, you can share a document and specify who can view, comment on, or edit it.

3. Role-Based Access Control (RBAC)

RBAC is a widely adopted model in modern enterprise environments. Instead of managing permissions for individual users, it groups permissions into roles.

Key Features:

- **Role Assignment:** Users are assigned roles (e.g., "Human Resources," "Finance," "Marketing") based on their job function.
- **Permission Sets:** Each role has a predefined set of permissions that allows users to perform their job.
- **Scalable:** Managing access for roles rather than individual users makes it highly scalable.

Pros:

- Simplifies administration and management of access rights.
- Enforces the principle of least privilege effectively.
- Increases consistency and security across the organization.

Cons:

- Can become complex to manage if there are too many roles or a high turnover of employees.
- Not suitable for every scenario, as some access decisions might require more granular control.
- A user with multiple roles might end up with too many privileges.

Example Implementation:

A company's internal payroll system. A user is assigned the "Payroll Administrator" role. This role automatically gives them permissions to view and edit employee salary information. A user with the "General Employee" role would not have access to this information. If an employee changes departments from Marketing to Finance, their role is simply updated, and their access rights are automatically adjusted.

4. Rule-Based Access Control (RuBAC)

Note: This is different from Role-Based Access Control. Rule-based access control uses a set of rules, or logical conditions, to determine access.

Key Features:

- **Conditional Logic:** Access is granted or denied based on specific, predefined rules.
- **Dynamic:** The rules can consider a variety of factors, such as time of day, location, or the state of a system.
- **Policy-Driven:** The rules are directly derived from the organization's security policy.

Pros:

- Offers a high degree of control and automation.
- Can be very effective for enforcing specific, complex security policies.
- Provides more granular control than DAC and RBAC in certain situations.

Cons:

- Difficult to implement and manage if the rules are not carefully designed.
- Can be complex and time-consuming to set up and update.
- Potential for rule conflicts if not properly managed.

Example Implementation:

A network firewall. A rule might be configured to DENY all incoming traffic from IP addresses located outside of North America. Another rule might be to ALLOW all SSH access, but only if the request originates from within the corporate network between 9 AM and 5 PM on weekdays.

5. Attribute-Based Access Control (ABAC)

ABAC is a dynamic and context-aware model that grants access based on the evaluation of a set of attributes associated with the user, the resource, and the environment.

Key Features:

- **Flexible and Granular:** ABAC is highly flexible and can grant very fine-grained access.
- **Policy-Based:** Access is determined by a policy that uses attributes as variables.
- **Context-Aware:** Considers "who," "what," "where," and "when" to make an access decision.

Pros:

- Extremely flexible and scalable, ideal for complex, large-scale systems.

- Provides the most granular control of any model, allowing for highly specific access policies.
- Reduces the administrative burden of role management as new resources or users are added.

Cons:

- Significantly more complex to design, implement, and manage.
- Requires a robust attribute management system.
- Can be more difficult to audit and troubleshoot access issues due to its dynamic nature.

Example Implementation:

A project management software. An access policy might state: "A user can edit a document if: (user.department == document.owner.department) AND (document.status == 'Draft') AND (user.location == 'Office')." This single policy could apply to thousands of documents without creating specific roles for each team or project.

Factors for Implementing Access Controls

When implementing any access control model, several factors must be considered to ensure effectiveness:

Policies and Procedures:

This is the foundation. You need a clear, well-documented policy that defines security roles, responsibilities, and rules for data access. Policies should cover everything from password requirements to data classification.

Authentication and Authorization:

Authentication: The process of verifying a user's identity. This is achieved through one or more of the following methods, often referred to as "factors."

Something You Know (Knowledge-Based Authentication)

Definition: Relies on a shared secret that only the user is supposed to know.

Key Features: Simple, widely adopted, and easy to implement.

Pros: Cost-effective and familiar to users.

Cons: Susceptible to brute-force attacks, phishing, and password sharing.

Example: A password, PIN, or security question.

Something You Have (Possession-Based Authentication)

Definition: Relies on a physical object or digital token that the user possesses.

Key Features: Provides an additional layer of security beyond a simple password. Can be a physical device or a mobile app.

Pros: More difficult to compromise than knowledge-based methods, as an attacker must steal the physical item.

Cons: The item can be lost, stolen, or damaged. Can be inconvenient for the user.

Example: A key card, security token, or a one-time passcode (OTP) sent to a phone.

Something You Are (Biometric-Based Authentication)

Definition: Relies on a unique biological trait of the user to verify identity.

Key Features: Highly secure and convenient.

Pros: Extremely difficult to forge or steal. Eliminates the need for users to remember passwords.

Cons: Can be expensive to implement. Privacy concerns exist regarding the storage of biometric data.

Example: Fingerprint scanning, facial recognition, or iris scanning.

Multi-Factor Authentication (MFA)

Definition: Requires a user to provide two or more different authentication factors from the categories above.

Key Features: Combines different factors to create a stronger security posture.

Pros: Significantly increases security by making it much harder for attackers to gain access, even if one factor is compromised.

Cons: Adds a step to the login process, which can be seen as less convenient for users.

Example: Logging in with a password (something you know) and then entering a code from a mobile app (something you have).

Single Sign-On (SSO)

Definition: A method that allows a user to authenticate once with a single set of credentials and then access multiple, related, but independent software systems without having to re-enter their password for each one.

Key Features: Centralized authentication point, shared credentials for multiple services.

Pros: Improves user experience and security by reducing "password fatigue" and the need to remember multiple passwords.

Cons: A single compromised account can grant an attacker access to multiple services.

PasswordlessAuthentication

Definition: This modern approach aims to eliminate the need for traditional passwords entirely. Instead, it relies on a combination of other factors like biometrics, push notifications to a trusted device, or "magic links" sent via email.

Key Features: Eliminates passwords, relies on alternative authentication methods.

Pros: More secure than passwords, which are often weak and reused. More convenient for the user.

Cons: Requires a trusted device or email access, which could be a point of failure if lost or compromised.

AdaptiveAuthentication

Definition: Also known as risk-based authentication, this dynamic method assesses a user's risk level based on contextual factors like their location, device, time of day, and behavior.

Key Features: Dynamic, context-aware, risk-based.

Pros: Provides a flexible security layer that adapts to the situation, reducing friction for low- risk logins and increasing security for high-risk ones.

Cons: Can be complex to configure and manage. False positives could inconvenience users with legitimate but unusual login attempts.

Authorization:

The process of granting a user specific permissions to access a resource. Once a user is authenticated, the system determines what they are allowed to do. Authorization is the security process of granting or denying a user access to a specific resource (e.g., a file, a database, an application feature) based on a set of predetermined rules or policies. It determines what an authenticated user is permitted to do.

Authorization vs. Authentication

It's crucial to differentiate these two fundamental security concepts:

- **Authentication:** Answers the question, "Are you who you say you are?" It's the process of verifying a user's identity. Think of it as showing your ID to a bouncer to prove you are old enough to enter a club.
- **Authorization:** Answers the question, "What are you allowed to do here?" It's the process of determining what a user is permitted to access or do once inside. Think of it as the bouncer then giving you a wristband that only lets you into certain areas of the club.

Least Privilege:

This is a core security principle. It dictates that users should be granted the minimum level of access required to perform their job functions and nothing more. This minimizes the potential for accidental or malicious data exposure.

Key Features:

- **Need-to-Know Basis:** Access is granted strictly on a "need-to-know" basis.
- **Default Deny:** The default policy is to deny all access unless it is explicitly granted.
- **Granular Permissions:** Permissions are often fine-grained, allowing for control over specific actions (e.g., read, write, delete) on individual resources.

Pros:

- Reduces the attack surface by limiting the potential for a compromised account to access sensitive data.

- Minimizes the risk of insider threats and data breaches.
- Makes it easier to detect and contain malicious activity.

Cons:

- Can be difficult and time-consuming to implement and manage, especially in large organizations.
- Requires continuous monitoring to ensure that access rights are still appropriate.
- Can lead to "permission creep," where users accumulate unnecessary access rights over time.

Example Implementation:

In a customer relationship management (CRM) system, a sales representative is only given permission to view and edit their own customer accounts. They are denied access to the accounts of other sales reps, as well as to the financial data stored in a separate database.

Separation of Duties:

Critical tasks should be divided among multiple individuals to prevent any single person from having complete control over a process.

Key Features:

- **Task Segmentation:** A single, high-risk process is broken down into multiple sub-tasks.
- **Role-Based Access:** Different roles are assigned to different individuals, each with unique permissions for their sub-task.
- **Reduced Fraud and Error:** Prevents a single individual from being able to perform a fraudulent or erroneous action from start to finish.

Pros:

- Acts as a powerful deterrent against fraud and malicious activity.
- Reduces the risk of human error by requiring multiple people to verify a process.
- Enhances accountability and transparency.

Cons:

- Can increase complexity and slow down business processes.
- Requires careful planning and management to be effective.

- May not be feasible in small organizations with limited staff.

Example Implementation:

In a finance department, the employee who creates a vendor payment request is not the same person who approves the payment. A third person may be responsible for processing the actual transfer of funds.

Auditing and Monitoring:

All access activities must be logged and monitored.

Key Features:

- **Activity Logging:** The system records all access attempts, both successful and unsuccessful.
- **Monitoring and Alerting:** Automated systems monitor logs for suspicious patterns and alert security personnel to potential threats in real time.
- **Forensic Analysis:** Logs provide a trail of evidence that can be used to investigate security incidents and breaches after they occur.

Pros:

- Provides a crucial layer of accountability and deterrence.
- Allows organizations to proactively detect and respond to threats.
- Essential for compliance with regulatory requirements (e.g., HIPAA, SOX).

Cons:

- Can generate a massive amount of data, which can be difficult and expensive to store and analyze.
- Requires dedicated tools and personnel to be effective.
- Can be a privacy concern if not implemented carefully.

Example Implementation:

An organization's security information and event management (SIEM) system collects logs from all servers, firewalls, and applications. The SIEM is configured to trigger an alert if a user attempts to log in from a new country and a corporate VPN is not used. This allows the security team to investigate the suspicious activity in real time.

Designing an Access Control Plan

An access control plan is a strategic document that outlines how an organization will manage and enforce access to its resources.

An access control plan is a formal document that outlines the policies, procedures, and technical mechanisms a company uses to manage and control who can access its resources. It is a critical component of an organization's overall information security strategy.

Purpose

The primary purpose of an access control plan is to:

- Ensure that only authorized users can access sensitive data and systems.
- Prevent data breaches, insider threats, and unauthorized modifications.
- Enforce the principle of least privilege, granting users the minimum access required for their job.
- Maintain a clear record of access decisions for auditing and compliance purposes.

Key Components

A comprehensive access control plan should address both the logical access (to networks, data, and applications) and physical access (to buildings and hardware) to an organization's resources. A typical plan includes the following elements:

1. **Policies and Procedures**

    - **User Roles:** Defines user roles (e.g., "HR Manager," "IT Administrator") and the baseline access rights for each.
    - **Onboarding/Offboarding:** Establishes a process for granting and revoking access for new and departing employees.
    - **Password Policies:** Specifies requirements for password complexity, expiration, and management.
    - **Principle of Least Privilege:** A statement of commitment to this principle, ensuring that access is granted on a need-to-know basis.

2. **Access Control Models**

This section defines the specific model(s) the organization uses to manage permissions. Common models include:

- **Role-Based Access Control (RBAC):** Assigning permissions based on job function. This is the most widely used model.
- **Attribute-Based Access Control (ABAC):** Granting access dynamically based on a set of attributes (e.g., user's location, time of day).
- **Mandatory Access Control (MAC):** A stricter model often used in high-security environments.

3. **Technical Controls**

- **Authentication Mechanisms:** Details the methods used to verify user identity, such as passwords, multi-factor authentication (MFA), or biometrics.
- **Authorization Software:** Lists the specific tools or software used to enforce access policies (e.g., Active Directory, identity and access management (IAM) solutions).
- **Logging and Auditing:** Describes how access events are logged, who is responsible for reviewing them, and the procedures for responding to suspicious activity.

4. **Responsibilities**

- **Owners:** Identifies who is responsible for the overall plan, typically a security officer or IT manager.
- **Administrators:** Specifies which individuals or teams manage user accounts and permissions.
- **Users:** Outlines the responsibilities of all employees, such as protecting their credentials and reporting security incidents.

Example Scenarios

A well-defined plan helps manage access in various scenarios:

- **New Hire:** A new marketing employee is granted access to the marketing department's shared drives and software but is denied access to the HR and finance servers.
- **Job Change:** When an employee moves from marketing to IT, their marketing access is immediately revoked, and they are granted the necessary IT-related permissions.

- **Contractor Access:** A third-party contractor is granted temporary, time-limited access to a specific database for a project. Their permissions expire automatically upon project completion.

Designing an Information Security Access Control Plan: A Step-by-Step Guide

Developing a robust access control plan is a foundational element of any organization's information security strategy. This guide outlines the key steps to create a plan that ensures data is protected while allowing authorized users to perform their jobs efficiently.

Step 1: Define the Scope

The first step is to clearly define what you are protecting. This involves creating a comprehensive inventory of your assets.

- **Identify Critical Assets:** List all information systems, data, and resources that need access control. This can include servers, databases, cloud storage, confidential documents, and intellectual property.
- **Establish Business Requirements:** Understand the business context for each asset. Who needs to access it, and for what purpose? This helps in avoiding overly restrictive policies that hinder productivity.

Step 2: Classify Data

Not all data is created equal. Classifying your data by sensitivity level is a critical prerequisite for establishing appropriate access rules. A common classification scheme includes:

- **Public:** Data available to the general public.
- **Internal:** Data for internal use, but not highly sensitive (e.g., company memos).
- **Confidential:** Data that, if exposed, could cause minor to moderate harm to the organization (e.g., employee information).
- **Restricted/Secret:** Data that, if exposed, would cause severe harm, financial loss, or legal issues (e.g., trade secrets, financial records).

Step 3: Identify User Roles

Instead of granting permissions on an individual basis, which is difficult to manage and prone to error, you should group users into logical roles. These roles should be based on job functions and responsibilities.

- **Create Role Definitions:** Define specific roles such as "Finance Team," "HR Administrator," "IT Support," or "Marketing User."
- **Map Users to Roles:** Assign each user to one or more of these defined roles. This simplifies the management of permissions as users join, leave, or change roles.

Step 4: Establish Access Policies

Now, you can define the rules that govern access. These policies link user roles to the data classifications you established in the previous steps.

- **Principle of Least Privilege:** This is a fundamental concept in security. Users and processes should only be granted the minimum level of access necessary to perform their required functions.
- **Separation of Duties:** For critical functions, require the involvement of more than one person to complete a task. This prevents fraud and errors by ensuring no single person has too much power.

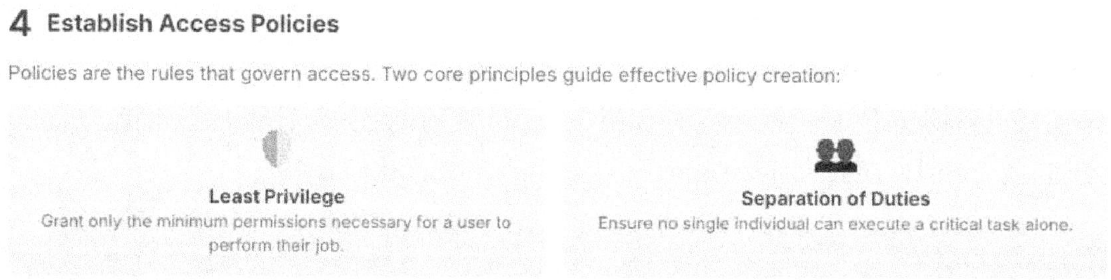

Step 5: Choose an Access Control Model

There are several models to implement your policies. The most common and effective for most organizations is Role-Based Access Control (RBAC).

- **Role-Based Access Control (RBAC):** This model grants or denies access rights based on the user's role within the organization. A user's permissions are tied directly to their job function, making it intuitive and scalable.
- **Other Models:** Other models exist, such as Discretionary Access Control (DAC) where the data owner controls access, and Mandatory Access Control (MAC) which is used in high-security environments. A more advanced option is Attribute-Based Access Control (ABAC), which uses attributes (e.g., user's location, time of day) to make access decisions.

Role-Based Access Control (RBAC) is the industry standard, linking permissions to roles, not individuals.

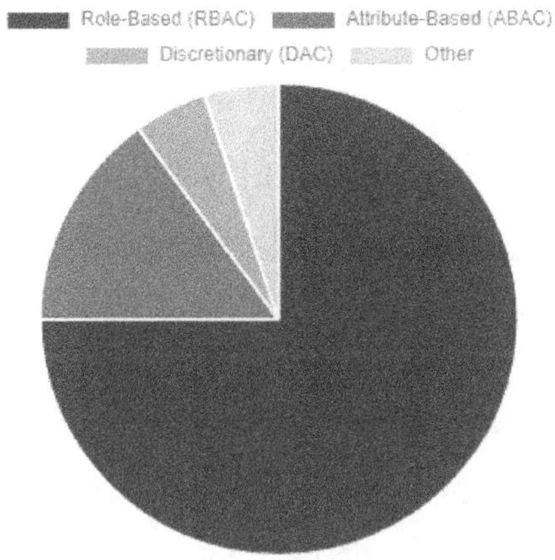

Step 6: Implement the Controls

With your policies and models in place, you can now implement the technical controls to enforce them.

- **Authentication:** Use strong authentication methods like Multi-Factor Authentication (MFA) to verify a user's identity before granting access.
- **Authorization:** Utilize directory services like Microsoft Active Directory or LDAP to manage user roles and permissions centrally. Ensure your systems are configured to enforce the defined access policies.
- **Centralized Management:** Use a centralized system for identity and access management to reduce complexity and improve consistency.

Step 7: Monitor and Audit

A plan is only as good as its execution and maintenance. Ongoing monitoring and auditing are essential to ensure the controls remain effective.

- **Activity Logging:** Log all access attempts, both successful and failed. This provides a trail for security analysis and forensic investigations.
- **Regular Reviews:** Conduct periodic reviews of user access rights. Remove access for employees who have left the company or changed roles.
- **Automated Alerts:** Set up automated alerts for suspicious activity, such as multiple failed login attempts or access to highly sensitive data outside of business hours.

Step 8: Train and Communicate

The human element is often the weakest link in security. Your plan must include an element of user education.

- **User Training:** Train employees on the importance of the access control plan, their responsibilities, and how to protect sensitive information.
- **Policy Communication:** Ensure all employees are aware of and acknowledge the access control policies.

An effective access control plan is a living document that requires regular review and adaptation to the changing needs of the business and the evolving threat landscape. By following these steps, you can create a plan that is both secure and manageable.

The Importance of Warning Banners in Access Control

In the realm of information security, access control is the process of regulating who or what can view or use resources in a computing environment. A crucial, yet often overlooked, component of this process is the use of warning banners. These are the messages displayed to a user before they log in to a system, server, or application.

Warning banners serve a vital function that goes beyond a simple "Welcome" message. They provide a strong legal basis for prosecuting unauthorized access. Without a clear and prominent warning banner, it can be difficult to prove that a user was aware that their access was unauthorized. The banner acts as a form of implied consent; by proceeding past the banner, the user is acknowledging and agreeing to the terms of use. It is the digital equivalent of a "No Trespassing" sign, but with the added weight of an explicit warning about monitoring and the consequences of misuse.

Beyond the legal aspect, warning banners act as a significant deterrent. They explicitly state that the system is private property and that all activity may be monitored. This serves as a psychological barrier, discouraging casual or malicious attempts at unauthorized access by making the potential consequences clear from the outset.

The banners also promote user awareness and accountability. They remind authorized users of their responsibilities, such as proper data handling and security protocols, before they even begin their work. This reinforces a culture of security within an organization. For example, a banner might state that the system contains confidential information and that unauthorized disclosure is prohibited. By clicking "Accept" or "OK," the user has actively acknowledged this responsibility, creating a loggable record that can be used for accountability if a security incident occurs.

In summary, warning banners are not just a formality. They are a fundamental part of a robust access control framework, providing a strong legal foundation, acting as a deterrent, promoting user awareness, and establishing accountability for all system access.

Ensure Users Are Aware Of Their Identity & Access Responsibilities

1. Policy and Acknowledgment

The foundation of any robust access control procedure is a clear and concise Acceptable Use Policy (AUP). This document must explicitly outline the user's responsibilities and the organization's expectations for handling data and using systems. Before a user is granted any system access, they must formally acknowledge that they have read, understood, and agree to abide by this policy.

Key elements to include in the AUP:

- **Data Handling:** Clear guidelines on how to handle different classifications of data (e.g., public, internal, confidential, restricted).
- **Password Management:** Requirements for creating strong passwords, storing them securely, and changing them periodically.
- **System Usage:** Prohibitions on unauthorized software installation, circumventing security controls, and using systems for non-business purposes.
- **Incident Reporting:** A clear procedure for reporting any suspected security incidents, vulnerabilities, or breaches.
- **Enforcement:** A statement outlining the consequences of non-compliance, which may include disciplinary action up to and including termination or legal action.

2. Mandatory Information Security Awareness Training

Access should be contingent upon the successful completion of mandatory information security awareness training. This training should be a dynamic and engaging experience, not just a static document. It should directly cover the contents of the AUP and provide practical examples.

Training topics should include:

- **Phishing and Social Engineering:** How to identify and avoid malicious emails, texts, and phone calls.
- **Secure Browsing and Email Habits:** Best practices for web usage and handling attachments.
- **Clean Desk Policy:** The importance of locking workstations and securing physical documents when away from a desk.
- **Data Privacy and Confidentiality:** Understanding the legal and ethical obligations related to handling sensitive information.

A quiz or knowledge check at the end of the training is highly recommended to ensure the user has retained the critical information. Access is only granted after a passing score is achieved.

3. **The Access Request and Grant Process**

Once the pre-requisites are met, the actual access request and grant process should follow a defined workflow.

- **Request Initiation:** The user's manager or a designated sponsor submits an official request for access, specifying the required systems and level of access (e.g., read-only, write, administrative).
- **Security Review:** An information security officer or team reviews the request to ensure the principle of least privilege is applied. This means granting the minimum level of access required to perform the job function, and no more.
- **Verification:** The security team verifies that the user has completed the mandatory training and signed the AUP.
- **Access Provisioning:** The IT or security team provisions the account and grants access based on the approved request.
- **User Notification:** The user is notified that their access has been granted, often with a reminder to adhere to the AUP.

4. **Ongoing Reinforcement and Audits**

The process doesn't end after access is granted. A continuous approach is essential to maintain a strong security posture.

- **Annual Re-certification:** Require users to re-certify their understanding of the AUP and complete refresher training on an annual or bi-annual basis.

- **Regular Audits:** Conduct regular audits of user access rights to ensure they are still appropriate for their current role. Remove access for users who have changed roles or left the organization promptly.
- **Randomized Drills:** Conduct simulated phishing attacks or other social engineering drills to test user awareness in a controlled environment.

By implementing these procedures, an organization can create a systematic and verifiable process that ensures all users are fully aware of their responsibilities, significantly reducing the risk of a security incident.

Social Engineering, Phishing, and Identity Theft: A Comprehensive Overview

1. Social Engineering: The Psychology of Deception

Social Engineering is the art and science of manipulating individuals into divulging confidential information or performing actions that compromise security. It leverages human psychology, exploiting natural inclinations such as trust, helpfulness, and curiosity. Key concepts include:

Key concepts include:

- **Urgency:** Creating a sense of a time-sensitive situation to pressure victims into making quick, irrational decisions. For example, an email warning that an account will be disabled in 10 minutes unless the user acts immediately.
- **Authority:** Impersonating a person or entity with power or influence, such as a CEO, IT administrator, or law enforcement officer, to make a request seem legitimate and unquestionable.
- **Intimidation/Fear:** Using threats or warnings of negative consequences (e.g., legal action, financial penalties) to coerce compliance.

Real-World Example:

In a high-profile 2020 Twitter breach, attackers used social engineering to gain initial access. They called Twitter employees, claiming to be from the company's IT department, and convinced them to provide their login credentials to a fake internal VPN page. Once inside, the attackers hijacked accounts of prominent figures like Elon

Musk and Barack Obama to promote a cryptocurrency scam (Sanger, 2020).

2. Phishing Attacks: The Digital Lure

Phishing is a fraudulent attempt, typically made through email, text message, or phone call, to steal sensitive information such as usernames, passwords, and credit card details. Attackers disguise themselves as a trustworthy entity in an electronic communication. There are several variations of phishing:

There are several variations of phishing:

- **Spear Phishing:** Highly targeted attacks against specific individuals or companies. The attacker researches the target to make the message appear more personal and legitimate.
- **Whaling:** A form of spear phishing that specifically targets high-ranking executives and other influential individuals within an organization.
- **Smishing & Vishing:** Phishing conducted via SMS text messages (smishing) or voice calls (vishing).
- **Pharming:** A more advanced form of phishing that redirects a user from a legitimate website to a fraudulent one, even if the user types the correct URL.

Real-World Example:

The 2016 cyberattack on the Democratic National Committee (DNC) was initiated by a spear-phishing email. Attackers sent a malicious link disguised as a Google security notification to DNC staff members. When an aide to John Podesta, the campaign chairman, clicked the link, his credentials were stolen, allowing attackers to access thousands of emails (Perlroth & Shane, 2016).

3. Identity Theft: The Ultimate Goal

Identity Theft is the fraudulent acquisition and use of a person's private identifying information, such as their Social Security number, credit card details, or medical information, without their consent. The ultimate goal is typically financial gain, though it can also be used to commit other crimes. Types of identity theft include:

Types of identity theft include:

- **Financial Identity Theft:** The most common form, where a thief opens new credit accounts, makes fraudulent purchases, or takes out loans in the victim's name.

- **Criminal Identity Theft:** Posing as another person when apprehended for a crime to avoid prosecution.
- **Medical Identity Theft:** Using another person's information to obtain medical services or prescription drugs.

Real-World Example:

The Equifax data breach of 2017 was a massive incident that led to the potential exposure of personal information for 147 million people. While not a direct result of social engineering, the stolen data, which included names, birth dates, Social Security numbers, and addresses, became a goldmine for future identity theft. This incident highlights the scale at which personal data can be compromised and used for fraudulent purposes (Equifax, 2017).

4. Best Practices to Counter Social Engineering

To effectively counter these attacks, a multi-layered approach is essential, addressing both technological and human vulnerabilities.

- **Employee Training and Awareness:** Regular, mandatory training sessions and simulated phishing exercises are crucial to help employees recognize and report suspicious activity.
- **Multi-Factor Authentication (MFA):** Implementing MFA on all accounts adds a critical layer of security. Even if an attacker obtains credentials, they cannot access the account without the second factor of authentication.
- **Email and Web Filtering:** Automated systems should be in place to detect and block malicious emails, links, and attachments before they reach employees' inboxes.
- **Incident Response Planning:** A clear, well-rehearsed plan for how to respond to a breach or a successful social engineering attempt can minimize damage and expedite recovery.

5. The Role of Artificial Intelligence in Social Engineering

Artificial intelligence (AI) and generative AI have become powerful tools for attackers, enabling them to create more sophisticated, convincing, and scalable attacks. AI enhances social engineering by automating tasks that were previously time-consuming for humans, such as data gathering, content creation, and real-time communication.

How AI is Incorporated

- **Hyper-Personalized Phishing:** Large Language Models (LLMs) can be used to generate highly realistic and grammatically flawless phishing emails that mimic the writing style of a target's colleague or manager. By analyzing a target's online footprint (social media, public posts), AI can craft messages that are incredibly personalized, referencing specific events, interests, or even a recent purchase to build trust.
- **AI Voice and Deepfakes:** AI can clone a person's voice from just a few seconds of audio, creating synthetic but highly convincing audio. This is used in vishing scams where an attacker impersonates a family member, colleague, or CEO in an urgent phone call. In more advanced cases, deepfake videos can be used in live video calls to impersonate an executive and authorize fraudulent financial transfers.

Real-World Examples

- **The Hong Kong Deepfake Scam (2024):** A finance employee in a multinational company's Hong Kong office was defrauded of $25 million after participating in a video conference call with what appeared to be the company's chief financial officer and other senior staff. The employee was unaware that all the participants were AI-generated deepfakes. The attackers convinced the employee to make multiple transfers to accounts controlled by the fraudsters.
- **The UK Voice Cloning Scam (2019):** Attackers used AI-generated audio to perfectly mimic the voice of the CEO of a German energy firm. They called the CEO of the firm's UK subsidiary and successfully convinced him to urgently transfer $243,000 to a fraudulent Hungarian supplier. The cloned voice was so convincing it even replicated the German CEO's accent and speech patterns.

Mitigation Strategies

- **Verbal Codewords:** Establish a private, verbal codeword with family members or colleagues. If an urgent or suspicious request comes over the phone, the codeword must be used to verify the person's identity. This is particularly effective against voice cloning scams.
- **Question Everything:** Foster a "zero-trust" culture where employees are trained to verify all unusual requests, even if they seem to come from a trusted source. Encourage them to use a separate, known channel (e.g., call the person back on a number from the company directory, not the one provided in the message) to

confirm.

- **AI for Defense:** Just as AI is used for attacks, it can also be used for defense. AI-powered security tools can analyze communication patterns, detect anomalies in email content, and identify AI-generated text or deepfakes more effectively than traditional methods.

Organizational Phishing Attack Response Plan

Phishing is a major threat to any organization. This document outlines a structured, multi-phased plan to proactively prevent, effectively respond to, and recover from phishing attacks. The plan covers actions for the Information Security team, IT, and all employees.

Phase 1: Proactive Prevention (Before an Attack)

The most effective way to handle phishing is to prevent it from ever reaching your users. This phase is about building a strong defense.

Security Awareness Training:

- **Simulated Phishing Drills:** Regularly send fake phishing emails to employees to test their awareness and response.
- **Interactive Training:** Provide clear, concise training on how to identify phishing attempts, including recognizing suspicious sender addresses, urgent language, and malicious links or attachments.
- **Reporting Protocol:** Establish a simple, one-click button or a clear process for employees to report suspicious emails immediately.

Technical Controls:

- **Email Filtering:** Implement robust email security gateways that can scan for and block malicious content, links, and attachments before they reach an employee's inbox.
- **DMARC, DKIM, and SPF:** Configure these protocols to authenticate incoming emails and prevent attackers from spoofing your domain.
- **Multi-Factor Authentication (MFA):** Enforce MFA across all critical systems to prevent attackers from using stolen credentials.
- **Patch Management:** Keep all operating systems and software up to date to patch vulnerabilities that could be exploited.

Phase 2: Detection & Triage (During an Attack)

This phase focuses on identifying a live phishing attempt as soon as it happens.

- **Automated Alerting:** Set up automated alerts for unusual activity, such as a high volume of emails with the same subject line or a sudden increase in failed login attempts from a specific IP address.
- **User Reporting:** Actively monitor the phishing report inbox. Every user report should be treated as a potential live threat.
- **Initial Assessment:** As soon as an alert or report is received, a security analyst must quickly triage it to determine if it is a legitimate attack or a false positive.

Phase 3: Incident Response & Containment (Immediate Action)

If a phishing attack is confirmed, immediate action is required to contain the threat and minimize damage.

- **Email Quarantine:** If the phishing email is still in users' inboxes, use the email security gateway to search for and quarantine all copies.
- **Threat Intelligence:** Analyze the malicious link or attachment to identify the attacker's infrastructure (e.g., Command & Control servers) and indicators of compromise (IOCs).
- **Block Malicious Infrastructure:** Block the identified malicious URLs, IP addresses, and file hashes at the firewall and web proxy levels.
- **User Notification:** Send an internal alert to all employees, warning them of the specific phishing attempt and reminding them not to click on any links or open any attachments.

Phase 4: Eradication & Recovery (After Containment)

This phase focuses on cleaning up any damage from the attack and restoring normal operations.

- **Investigate Compromised Users:** Identify any users who clicked the malicious link or opened the attachment. If credentials were stolen, force a password reset and check for any unauthorized activity.
- **Clean Systems:** Scan any potentially compromised user workstations for malware or

other malicious software. Restore systems from clean backups if necessary.

- **Restore Access:** Once systems are confirmed to be clean and secure, restore access to affected accounts and systems.

Phase 5: Post-Incident Review & Improvement

This final phase is crucial for learning from the incident and enhancing your organization's security posture.

- **Post-Mortem Meeting:** Hold a meeting with all relevant team members to review the incident from start to finish.
- **Analyze Weaknesses:** Identify what went wrong and where the plan could be improved. For example, was a user's training insufficient? Did the email filter fail to catch the attack?
- **Update Plan & Training:** Update the phishing response plan with lessons learned. Create new training modules to address the specific attack vector that was used, ensuring the same incident does not happen again.

Physical Security: A Comprehensive Overview

Physical security is a fundamental component of a complete information security program. It is the practice of protecting physical assets, such as buildings, hardware, and data from physical threats like theft, unauthorized access, and vandalism.

1. Governing Principles: Standards, Procedures, and Laws

Effective physical security is guided by a hierarchy of rules and regulations.

- **Standards:** These are best practices that an organization can choose to adopt. For instance, ISO 27001 and NIST SP 800-53 are widely recognized frameworks that include controls for physical and environmental protection.
- **Procedures:** These are the step-by-step instructions for personnel. Examples include how to handle visitor check-ins or the protocol for managing keys and access cards.
- **Directives & Policies:** These are internal organizational rules. A Physical Security Policy defines an organization's high-level approach to securing its physical assets.
- **Regulations & Laws:** These are external and legally binding. HIPAA mandates

physical safeguards for patient data, while local fire codes and building regulations dictate safety measures for facilities.

2. Asset Value and Impact Analysis

Before you can secure an asset, you must understand its value and the consequences of its loss.

- **Determine Asset Value:** This is not just the purchase price of equipment. It includes the cost of replacing hardware, the time and effort to rebuild infrastructure, and the potential value of any sensitive information stored on or accessed through the asset.
- **Determine Impact if Unavailable:** This process, known as a Business Impact Analysis (BIA), assesses the consequences of a security event. Consider the impact of a data center fire or a flood—this could lead to significant financial losses, service outages, and damage to the organization's reputation.

3. Designing and Managing a Security Plan

A strong physical security plan is not a single measure, but a holistic system of interconnected controls.

- **Layers of Defense (Defense-in-Depth):** The most effective approach uses multiple layers of security. This could start with a perimeter fence, followed by locked gates, security guards, keycard access to buildings and individual rooms, and finally, surveillance cameras monitoring critical areas.
- **Implementation:** This involves deploying all the physical controls identified in the design. Examples include installing access control systems (keycards, biometrics), surveillance cameras (CCTV), and environmental controls (fire suppression, cooling systems).
- **Management & Auditing:** Physical security is an ongoing process. The plan must include a schedule for regular audits to ensure all controls are functioning as intended. Key performance metrics, such as the number of security incidents, alarm response times, and the frequency of access log reviews, are used to measure the plan's effectiveness and identify areas for improvement.

A Step-by-Step Guide to Physical Security

A comprehensive physical security plan is essential for protecting people, assets, and information from a variety of threats. The best plans are not a one-time setup but a continuous cycle of assessment, implementation, and refinement. Here is a step-by-step guide to help you design and manage your plan.

Step 1: Conduct a Comprehensive Risk Assessment

Before you can secure a location, you need to understand what you're protecting and from what. This foundational step involves:

- **Asset Identification:** Create a complete list of everything you need to protect. This includes people, physical property (e.g., buildings, equipment, inventory), and intellectual property (e.g., servers, data centers).
- **Threat Analysis:** Identify potential threats, both internal and external. Threats could include theft, vandalism, terrorism, natural disasters, or unauthorized access.
- **Vulnerability Assessment:** Analyze your current security measures to identify weaknesses. This could be anything from a broken lock to a lack of trained staff.
- **Risk Determination:** Combine your asset, threat, and vulnerability analyses to determine the likelihood and potential impact of each risk. Prioritize risks based on their severity.

Step 2: Define Clear Security Objectives

Based on your risk assessment, establish specific, measurable, achievable, relevant, and time-bound (SMART) security goals. Your objectives should directly address the highest-priority risks. For example, an objective might be "Reduce the risk of unauthorized access to the data center by 50% within six months" or "Ensure all external access points are secured with an alarmed lock system."

Step 3: Develop Security Policies and Procedures

These written rules and guidelines form the backbone of your security program. They dictate how people should behave and how security systems should operate. Key policies and procedures to develop include:

- **Access Control:** Who is authorized to access certain areas, and how is their access verified? (e.g., key cards, biometric scanners).
- **Visitor Management:** How are visitors vetted, registered, and escorted while on the property?
- **Incident Reporting:** What is the protocol for reporting a security breach or suspicious activity?

- **Emergency Procedures:** What are the steps for responding to a fire, medical emergency, or active threat?

Step 4: Implement a Layered Security System (Defense-in-Depth)

The most effective security plans use a layered approach, meaning they don't rely on a single control. This is often called "defense-in-depth." The layers work together to deter, detect, delay, and respond to threats.

- **Deterrence:** Use elements like signage ("Warning: Security Cameras in Use"), bright lighting, and visible security patrols to discourage would-be intruders.
- **Detection:** This layer identifies when a threat is present. Examples include security cameras, motion sensors, alarms, and trained security personnel.
- **Delay:** Physical barriers are used to slow down an intruder, giving the response team more time to arrive. This includes fences, reinforced doors, strong locks, and bollards.
- **Response:** This is the final layer. It involves the actions taken once a threat has been detected and delayed. This could be a security guard's response, an automatic lock-down, or an alert to law enforcement.

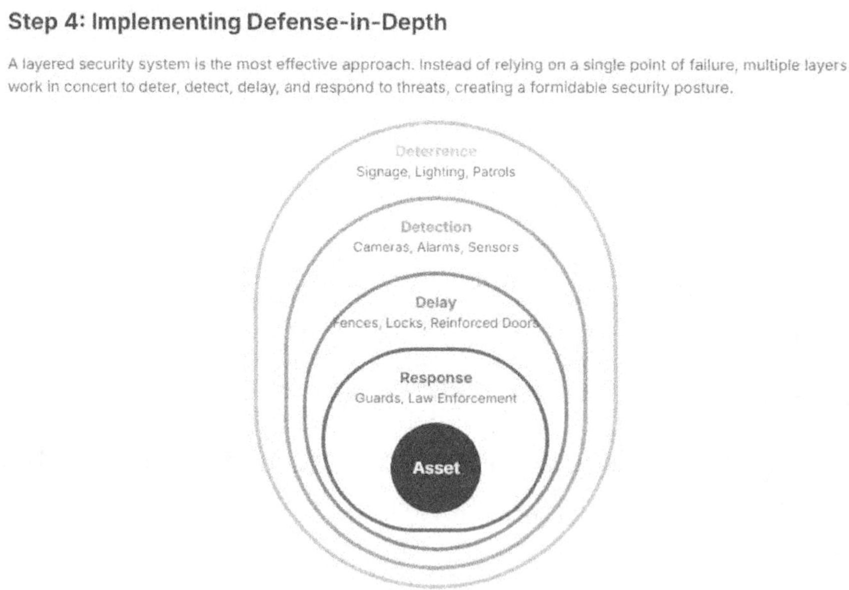

Step 5: Train Personnel

People are often the weakest link in any security chain. A well-designed plan is useless if employees don't know how to follow it. Conduct regular training sessions for all personnel on:

- Security policies and procedures.

- How to identify and report suspicious behavior.
- Using security equipment (e.g., how to properly use a key card).
- Emergency and incident response protocols.

Step 6: Create an Incident Response Plan

A detailed plan for what to do during a security incident is crucial. The plan should outline roles and responsibilities, communication protocols, and steps for:

- **Notification:** Who needs to be informed and in what order?
- **Containment:** How do you stop the threat from escalating?
- **Investigation:** How do you gather information about what happened?
- **Recovery:** How do you restore normal operations and fix the security weakness?

Step 7: Conduct Regular Audits and Reviews

A security plan is not static. Threats evolve, technology changes, and your organization's needs shift. Regularly review and audit your plan to ensure it remains effective. This includes:

- **Penetration Testing:** Hire a third party to test your physical security controls and procedures.
- **Drills and Exercises:** Practice your incident response plan to ensure everyone knows their role.
- **Reviewing and Updating:** Formally review your plan at least annually, or after any significant change (e.g., new building, new technology, new threats).

By following these steps, you can create a comprehensive and adaptable physical security plan that provides a strong defense against a wide range of threats.

Disaster Recovery and Business Continuity Planning

Developing, implementing, and monitoring robust disaster recovery (DR) and business continuity (BC) plans is a fundamental responsibility for an information security professional. These plans are the backbone of an organization's resilience, ensuring that essential operations can withstand and recover from disruptive events, whether they are natural disasters, cyberattacks, or technical failures.

The Core Concepts: BCP vs. DRP

While often used together, Business Continuity Planning (BCP) and Disaster Recovery Planning (DRP) have distinct focuses.

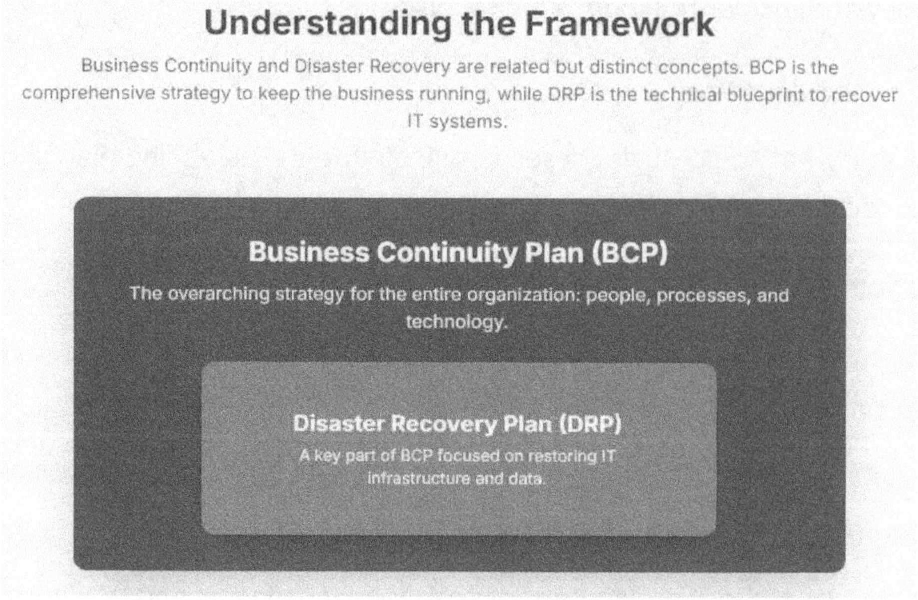

Business Continuity Planning (BCP): This is the overarching strategy. It's about keeping the entire business functioning and operational during and after a crisis. It addresses every aspect of the organization—from people and processes to facilities and technology. From an information security perspective, BCP ensures the continued confidentiality, integrity, and availability of critical information assets and systems that enable business operations. A BCP answers the question: "How do we keep the business running no matter what?"

Disaster Recovery Planning (DRP): This is a critical component of the BCP. The DRP focuses specifically on the recovery of the organization's IT infrastructure and data. It is the technical plan that details how to restore hardware, software, networks, and data after a disruptive event. A DRP answers the question: "How do we get our IT systems back online?"

Think of it this way: the BCP is the full emergency manual for the entire company, while the DRP is a specific chapter in that manual focused on the IT department.

Information Security's Role in BCP

For a BCP to be effective, information security must be an integral part of its development, addressing key questions and concepts for both the security program and the organization.

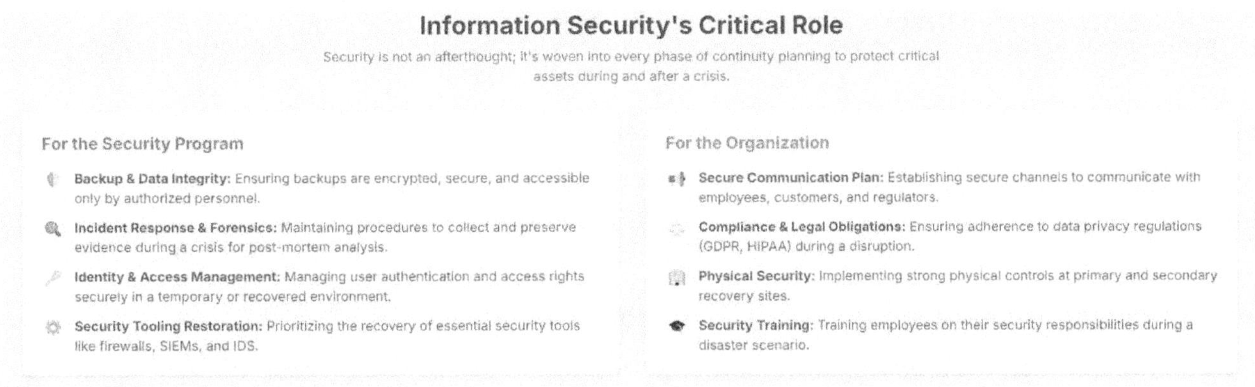

For the Information Security Program and Operations:

- **Backup and Data Integrity:** How are backups of critical data and security configurations protected? Are they encrypted? Who has access to them?
- **Incident Response and Forensics:** What is the process for collecting and preserving evidence during a disruptive event for forensic analysis? How do we perform a post-mortem to identify the root cause?
- **Identity and Access Management:** How will user access rights and identities be managed and authenticated in a temporary or recovered environment? Is there a secure way to handle password resets or new user provisioning?
- **Security Tooling Restoration:** What is the priority for restoring security tools like firewalls, intrusion detection systems (IDS), and security information and event management (SIEM) systems?

For the Organization as a Whole:

- **Communication Plan:** Who is responsible for communicating security-related information to employees, stakeholders, customers, and regulatory bodies during a crisis? How is this communication secured?
- **Compliance and Legal Obligations:** How will the organization maintain compliance with data privacy regulations (e.g., HIPAA, GDPR, CCPA) during and after a disruptive event?
- **Physical Security:** If a recovery site is used, what physical security controls are in place to protect sensitive equipment and data?
- **Security Training:** Are employees trained on their security responsibilities during a disaster? Do they know how to report a security incident from a secondary location?
- **Prioritization:** How are business processes prioritized for recovery based on their

criticality and the sensitivity of the data they handle? This helps determine what must be restored first to minimize security risks.

Key Components of a Plan

A well-structured plan, developed from an information security perspective, should include:

- **Risk Assessment:** Identifying potential threats (e.g., ransomware, power outages, natural disasters) and their potential impact on the organization's assets.
- **Business Impact Analysis (BIA):** This is a critical step in understanding which business processes are most vital. The BIA determines the Recovery Time Objective (RTO), which is the maximum acceptable duration of a business process outage, and the Recovery Point Objective (RPO), which is the maximum amount of data loss a process can tolerate.
- **Strategy and Solutions:** Based on the BIA, you develop strategies to meet your RTOs and RPOs. This includes selecting backup solutions (e.g., cloud, tape), identifying off-site recovery locations, and establishing communication plans.
- **Plan Development:** Writing the plan itself, which should be a clear, step-by-step guide. It should detail who is responsible for what, what systems need to be restored in what order, and how to communicate with stakeholders.

Implementation and Monitoring

Developing the plan is only the first step. To ensure it is effective and aligns with organizational goals, you must:

- **Regular Testing:** Conduct frequent drills and exercises to simulate different disaster scenarios. This helps identify gaps and train personnel. Testing should be a regular part of the IT and security calendar.
- **Continuous Improvement:** After each test or real event, the plan must be reviewed and updated to reflect new technologies, organizational changes, and lessons learned.
- **Alignment with Organizational Goals:** The entire process must be viewed through the lens of business value. The plan's objectives (RTO, RPO) must align with what the business needs to survive. The plans should support, not hinder, the achievement of the organization's mission, ensuring that critical information assets are protected and available when needed most.

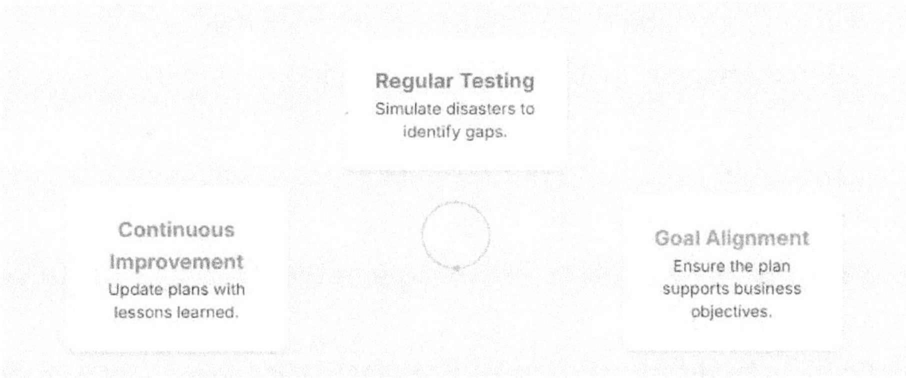

What is a Business Impact Assessment (BIA)?

A Business Impact Assessment (BIA) is a systematic process used to determine and evaluate the potential effects of a disruption to critical business operations. The primary goal is to identify which business functions are most essential and to quantify the operational, financial, and reputational impacts of a service outage or disaster.

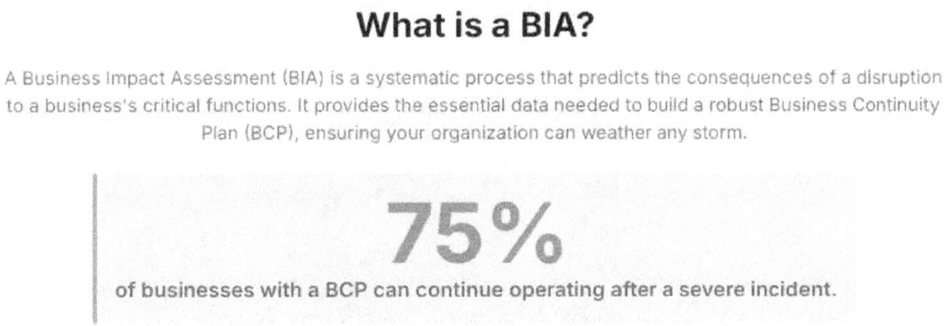

A BIA is not a one-time event; it's an ongoing process that provides the data needed to create a robust Business Continuity Plan (BCP). It helps an organization prioritize recovery efforts and allocate resources effectively to minimize downtime and loss.

Key Components of a BIA

A comprehensive BIA typically focuses on these key areas:

- **Criticality:** Identifying the essential business functions and processes that must continue to operate. This involves understanding which services, products, or operations are vital for the organization's survival.
- **Impact Analysis:** Assessing the consequences of a disruption. This can include:
  - **Financial Impact:** Lost sales, delayed payments, increased expenses (overtime,

outsourcing), regulatory fines, and contractual penalties.

- **Operational Impact:** Inability to produce goods, provide services, or fulfill orders.
- **Reputational Impact:** Loss of customer trust, negative media coverage, and brand damage.
- **Legal & Regulatory Impact:** Failure to meet legal obligations or comply with industry regulations.

- **Recovery Objectives:** Establishing specific targets for restoring operations. The two most critical metrics defined in a BIA are:
  - **Recovery Time Objective (RTO):** The maximum tolerable period of time for a business function to be offline before the resulting impact becomes unacceptable.
  - **Recovery Point Objective (RPO):** The maximum tolerable amount of data that can be lost from a system due to a disruption.

Breakdown of Business Impacts

A disruption can have far-reaching effects. A BIA quantifies these potential impacts to prioritize recovery efforts.

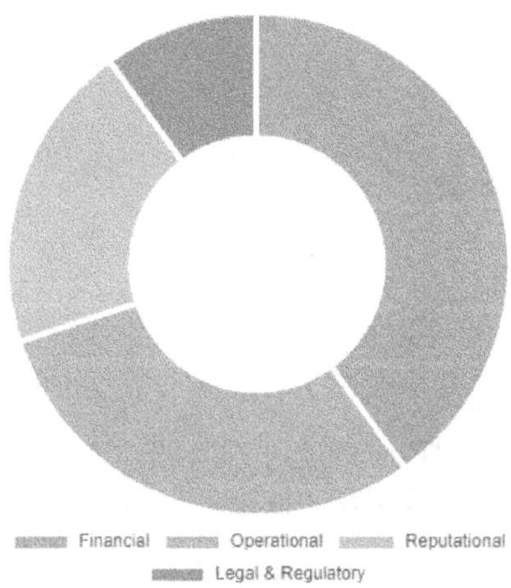

Information Security's Role in the BIA

Information security is a key stakeholder throughout the BIA process. Their expertise is essential for identifying and assessing threats and for developing effective recovery strategies. Their primary responsibilities include:

- **Risk Identification:** Working with business units to identify and document potential threats and vulnerabilities related to information technology and data. This includes everything from cyberattacks and data breaches to hardware failures and software corruption.

- **Dependency Mapping:** Helping to map the critical interdependencies between business functions and the IT systems, data, and applications that support them. This ensures that the BIA accurately reflects the impact of a system outage on business operations.
- **Security Controls Assessment:** Assessing the current security controls in place and their effectiveness in protecting critical data and systems. This analysis can reveal gaps that need to be addressed in the business continuity plan.
- **Recovery Strategy Input:** Providing technical expertise to help define the RTOs and RPOs for IT systems and data. This includes recommending and helping to design technical recovery strategies, such as data backups, redundant systems, and disaster recovery sites, to meet the business's recovery objectives.

The BIA Process: A Step-by-Step Guide

Conducting a BIA involves a structured, collaborative effort across the organization.

Step 1: Planning and Scoping

Define the purpose and scope of the BIA. This includes identifying which departments, business units, or processes will be analyzed. Assemble a cross-functional team with representatives from key areas like IT, finance, operations, and human resources.

Step 2: Data Collection

Gather information on critical business functions. This is typically done through interviews, workshops, and surveys. For each function, ask questions to understand:

- The function's description and purpose.
- Its dependencies (people, technology, facilities, suppliers).
- The financial and operational impacts of a disruption over time.
- The required RTO and RPO.

Step 3: Impact Analysis & Prioritization

Analyze the collected data to quantify the impacts identified in the previous step. Evaluate the interdependencies between functions and systems. Based on the severity of the potential impacts and the required recovery objectives, prioritize each function. This step creates a ranked list of critical processes that will guide the subsequent recovery planning.

Step 4: Report and Review

Compile all findings into a comprehensive BIA report. This document should include an executive summary, the project's scope and methodology, the detailed findings for each business function, and recommendations for recovery strategies. The report should be reviewed and approved by senior management to ensure alignment with organizational goals.

Step 5: Maintenance and Updates

A BIA is a living document. It should be reviewed and updated regularly (at least annually) or whenever a significant change occurs within the business, such as a new product launch, a system upgrade, or a change in regulations. This ensures the data remains accurate and the business continuity plan stays relevant.

Disaster Recovery and Business Continuity Documentation Process

Introduction and Scope

This document outlines a systematic process for designing, creating, and maintaining documentation for Disaster Recovery (DR) and Business Continuity (BC) plans. Its primary purpose is to provide a clear, actionable framework to ensure the organization can continue its critical operations during and after a significant disruption. The scope of this plan covers the identification of critical information assets, the establishment of recovery teams and procedures, and the integration of information security principles to protect the confidentiality, integrity, and availability of data. This documentation is a living blueprint for organizational resilience, designed to be regularly tested and updated.

Roles and Responsibilities

A clear command structure is fundamental to a successful response. This section defines the roles and responsibilities of the crisis management and technical recovery teams.

Crisis Management Team (CMT):

This team is responsible for high-level decision-making, external communications, and managing the overall business impact of the event. They will authorize the activation of the plan and approve resource allocation.

Information Security Incident Response Team (IRT):

This team focuses specifically on security-related incidents. Their responsibilities include forensic analysis, containing security breaches, and monitoring for secondary attacks during the recovery process.

Disaster Recovery Team:

This team is responsible for the technical execution of the recovery plan, including system restoration, data recovery, and hardware procurement.

Business Continuity Team:

This team ensures the continuity of non-technical business functions, such as human resources, finance, and supply chain management.

Phase 1: Foundation and Scoping

The goal of this initial phase is to establish the scope and a security baseline for the entire program.

Step 1: Business Impact Analysis (BIA) & Asset Identification

Purpose:

To identify and document the organization's critical business functions and the information systems and data that support them.

Security Focus:

Document the data classification for each asset (e.g., Public, Internal, Confidential). This will guide recovery priorities. Establish Recovery Time Objectives (RTO) and Recovery Point Objectives (RPO) for each critical system and its data. The RTO is the maximum tolerable downtime, while the RPO is the maximum tolerable data loss. These are the key metrics for success.

Step 2: Threat & Risk Assessment

Purpose:

To document potential threats (both natural and man-made) and the vulnerabilities of identified assets.

Security Focus:

Document the likelihood and impact of security-related threats such as cyberattacks, data breaches, or insider threats. This documentation should highlight the specific security controls that are currently in place and those that need to be implemented or improved as part of the DR/BC plan.

Phase 2: Strategy and Planning

This phase details the specific security strategies and plans to be implemented in a disaster.

Step 1: Incident Response Plan (IRP) Integration

Purpose:

To integrate the organization's IRP into the DR/BC documentation. The IRP is the "first responder's guide," detailing the initial actions to contain and mitigate an event.

Security Focus:

Document the explicit triggers for transitioning from the IRP's containment phase to the DR/BC plan's recovery phase. The IRP should be a referenced document that clearly hands off to the DR/BC plan once the incident is contained and recovery can begin.

Step 2: Activation Procedures

Purpose:

To define the triggers and initial steps for activating the DR/BC plan.

Security Focus:

Clearly document the criteria for declaring a disaster (e.g., loss of a critical data center, a major cyberattack). The initial steps should include secure, pre-determined communication channels to notify the Crisis Management Team and the Information Security Incident Response Team. This ensures a swift and secure response, minimizing confusion and potential for further compromise.

Step 3: Recovery Strategies

Purpose:

To document the chosen technical and procedural methods for restoring critical functions.

Security Focus:

Document security considerations for each strategy. For example, if using a hot site, specify how network security (firewalls, IDS/IPS) will be maintained. For cloud failover, detail the access controls, encryption protocols, and identity management procedures. Include a list of all required certificates, encryption keys, and credentials, stored securely and accessible only to authorized personnel.

Step 4: Communication Plan

Purpose:

To document how information will be shared during an event.

Security Focus:

Define and document secure communication channels for the DR/BC team and key stakeholders. Specify methods to securely notify personnel and external parties (e.g., customers, regulators) about a security incident. The plan must detail what information can be shared and what must remain confidential.

Step 5: Data Backup and Restoration Plan

Purpose:

To document how critical data will be backed up and recovered.

Security Focus:

Document the encryption methods used for data at rest and in transit. Specify the process for verifying the integrity of backups to prevent the restoration of corrupted or compromised data. Clearly outline access controls for backup media and recovery systems.

Phase 3: Implementation and Maintenance

This final phase focuses on putting the plan into practice and ensuring its long-term viability.

Step 1: Procedural Playbooks

Purpose:

To create detailed, step-by-step instructions for all recovery activities.

Security Focus:

Each playbook must include specific security checks and verification steps. For example, a "System Recovery Playbook" should include steps to scan systems for malware, check for unauthorized configuration changes, and ensure all patches are applied before bringing the system back online.

Step 2: Testing and Exercise Reports

Purpose:

To document the testing of the DR/BC plan to prove its viability.

Security Focus:

Each test (from a simple tabletop exercise to a full-scale simulation) must be documented. The report should include the objectives, scenario, participants, results, and lessons learned. This feedback loop is essential for continuous improvement and is a core principle of information security's "plan-do-check-act" cycle.

Step 3: Change Management

Purpose:

To ensure the DR/BC documentation remains current and accurate.

Security Focus:

Implement a formal change management process. Any change to a critical system, its security controls, or its supporting infrastructure must trigger a review and update of the DR/BC documentation to reflect the change and its potential impact on security and recovery.

Appendices and Supporting Documents

This section includes critical, supplementary information that must be kept current.

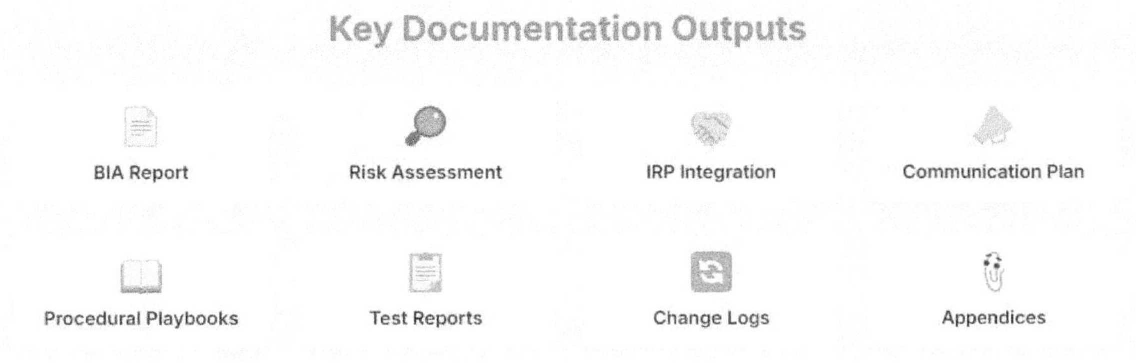

Contact Lists:

A comprehensive list of all personnel, key vendors, and emergency services. This should include multiple forms of contact (phone, email, secure messaging app).

Inventory Lists:

Up-to-date lists of all critical hardware, software, and physical assets required for recovery.

Communication Templates:

Pre-written templates for internal and external messaging to ensure consistent and accurate communication during an event.

Documentation Template Summary

A complete documentation package should include the following sections:

- **Executive Summary:** A high-level overview.
- **Roles and Responsibilities:** A clear command structure for all teams.
- **DR/BC Team Contact List:** Secure and up-to-date contact information.
- **Business Impact Analysis (BIA) Report:** Critical functions, RTOs, RPOs, and data classifications.
- **Risk Assessment Report:** Identified threats, vulnerabilities, and security controls.
- **Incident Response Plan Integration:** The relationship between the IRP and the DR/BC plan.

- **Activation Procedures:** The triggers and initial steps for plan activation.
- **Recovery Strategies:** Detailed plan for each critical system with security considerations.
- **Communication Plan:** Secure communication channels and notification procedures.
- **Procedural Playbooks:** Step-by-step instructions for recovery.
- **Test and Exercise Reports:** A log of all tests, results, and lessons learned.
- **Change Management Log:** A record of all changes to the plan.
- **Appendices and Supporting Documents:** Contact lists, inventory, and communication templates.

Testing and Updating a Continuity of Operations Program

From an information security perspective, a robust Disaster Recovery (DR) and Business Continuity (BC) plan is only as good as its last test. The goal of testing and updating is to ensure that the plan is not a static document, but a living, effective tool that can be used to protect an organization's critical data and systems in the face of a disruption. This process is crucial for identifying weaknesses, validating recovery capabilities, and training personnel.

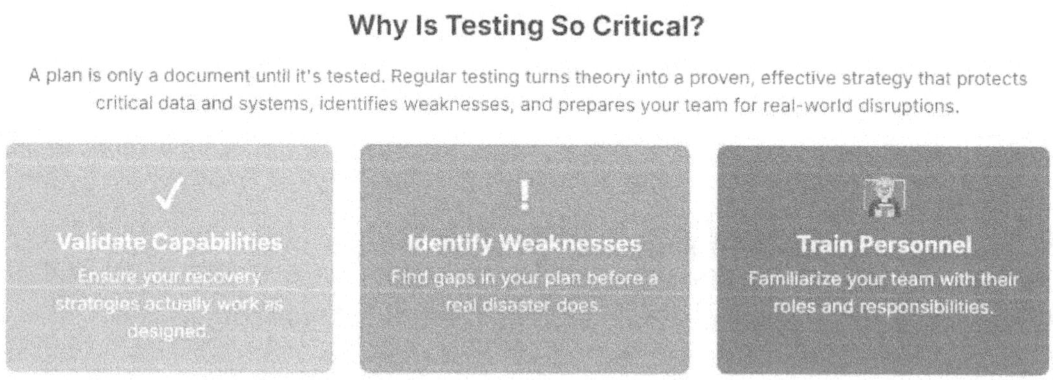

Phase 1: Designing the Test Plan

A well-designed test plan should align with the organization's Recovery Time Objectives (RTO) and Recovery Point Objectives (RPO). The RTO is the maximum acceptable duration of time an application or business process can be down after a disaster, and the RPO is the maximum acceptable amount of data loss. These objectives are determined during the Business Impact Analysis (BIA) and serve as the benchmarks for a successful test.

The test plan should be a formal document that includes:

- **Test Objectives:** What is the specific goal of this test? (e.g., "Verify the successful failover of the core financial server to the hot site within four hours.")
- **Scope:** What systems, applications, and teams will be involved?
- **Test Scenarios:** Realistic, threat-based scenarios are essential from an information security standpoint. These could include a major cyberattack like a ransomware event, a denial-of-service (DoS) attack, or a physical disaster that affects a data center.
- **Success Criteria:** Clearly defined metrics for what constitutes a successful test. This could include meeting RTO/RPO metrics, successful restoration of specific data, or the correct execution of communication protocols.
- **Roles and Responsibilities:** A clear list of who will do what, including an observer or auditor role to document the test.

Phase 2: Executing the Test

Execution should be methodical and documented. There are several types of tests that can be performed, each with a different level of complexity and disruption.

Tabletop Exercise:

This is a discussion-based drill where key personnel walk through the plan step-by-step. It's a low-cost, low-impact way to identify gaps and errors in the plan. From an information security perspective, this is where you discuss how to handle an insider threat, or a data breach while systems are down.

Walkthrough Drill:

In this test, teams physically walk through the steps of the plan without actually disrupting live systems. They may simulate restoring a server or logging into a backup system to verify access controls.

Simulation/Full-Scale Test:

This is the most complex type of test and involves a near-complete shutdown or failover of production systems. This is the ultimate test of the DR plan and allows for real-world verification of RTO and RPO. From an information security perspective, it's crucial to test the effectiveness of data restoration from backups and the integrity of the restored systems. This also verifies that security controls, like firewalls and access lists, are correctly configured in the recovery environment.

Test Types by Complexity

Different tests offer varying levels of assurance and require different levels of investment and potential disruption.

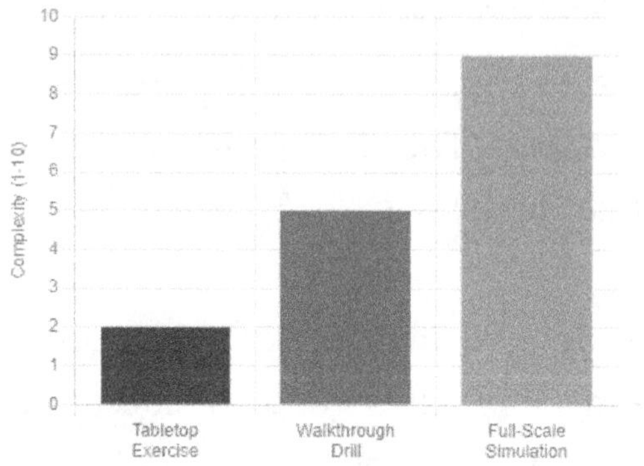

During execution, all actions and their results must be meticulously logged. This includes timestamps for each step, any errors or unexpected outcomes, and the duration of each task.

Phase 3: Post-Test Review and Updating

After the test, a formal post-mortem review, or After-Action Report, must be conducted. This meeting should include all participants and observers. The purpose is to analyze the logged data, discuss what went well, and identify areas for improvement.

Post-Test Action Items

The After-Action Report is the catalyst for improvement. Our latest test cycle generated several key action items to strengthen our resilience.

CATEGORY	ACTION ITEM	STATUS
Plan Update	Update contact list for network team	Completed
Technical Remediation	Increase bandwidth to failover site	In Progress
Personnel Training	Conduct specialized training on data restoration protocol	Scheduled

The After-Action Report should result in a clear, prioritized list of action items, which may include:

- **Updating the Plan:** Correcting errors in contact information, updating system configurations, or revising procedures.
- **Technical Remediation:** Fixing issues with backup systems, network

failover, or server configurations.

- **Personnel Training:** Providing additional training for employees on their roles and responsibilities.

The DR/BC plan must be treated as a living document. Any significant changes to the organization's IT infrastructure, such as adding a new application, changing a network configuration, or migrating to the cloud, should trigger a review and, if necessary, an update of the plan. A new test should be scheduled after any major changes have been implemented to ensure the plan remains effective and relevant.

Information Assurance (IA) in Disaster Recovery & Business Continuity

When building a Continuity of Operations Plan (COOP), integrating Information Assurance (IA) is crucial for ensuring that an organization can recover from a disaster while maintaining the security of its data and systems.

From an information security perspective, this integration is all about maintaining the Confidentiality, Integrity, and Availability (CIA) triad of mission-essential data and systems. A fast recovery is useless if the recovered systems are vulnerable or the data is corrupt.

Key Components of Integration

- **Risk Assessment:** A COOP must be built on a foundation of a comprehensive risk assessment. This goes beyond natural disasters to identify threats like cyberattacks, hardware failures, and human error. Identifying these risks allows for the creation of proactive security measures within the recovery plan.
- **Backup and Recovery:** The plan should detail a robust strategy for backing up and restoring data. To meet IA requirements, this must include secure, encrypted off-site backups and regular testing of the recovery process to ensure data integrity and availability.
- **Alternate Site Operations:** Procedures for moving to an alternate site must include security protocols. This means securely establishing network connectivity, verifying the physical security of the new location, and having a secure method for accessing or transporting sensitive data and systems.
- **Incident Response:** A well-integrated COOP includes a clear and actionable incident response plan for security-related events. This plan outlines the steps for detecting a breach, containing the threat, and recovering securely while minimizing data loss and damage.

Why IA Integration is Essential

Failing to integrate IA into the COOP can have severe consequences, including significant financial loss, legal penalties, and irreparable damage to an organization's reputation.

A COOP without IA might allow operations to resume quickly, but it could also expose the organization to new vulnerabilities. For instance, a system brought online at a secondary location might lack the necessary security controls, making it an easy target for a cyberattack. By weaving IA into the fabric of the COOP, an organization plans not just to survive a disaster, but to do so securely.

An Introduction to Network Security

The move to cloud computing has changed the landscape of network security. While many of the fundamental principles of protecting data and systems remain, new challenges and shared responsibilities have emerged. Understanding network defense in the cloud means recognizing these differences and implementing strategies tailored for a dynamic, distributed environment.

Cloud security refers to the set of policies, controls, and technologies that work together to protect cloud-based systems, data, and infrastructure. Unlike traditional on-premise networks where an organization owns and controls every part of the infrastructure, cloud security operates under a shared responsibility model. This model, which is central to all cloud security discussions, divides the security duties between the cloud provider (like Google Cloud, Amazon Web Services, or Microsoft Azure) and the cloud customer. The provider is generally responsible for securing the cloud itself (the underlying infrastructure, hardware, and facilities), while the customer is responsible for security in the cloud (their data, applications, and network configurations).

On-Premise Network Security

In a traditional on-premise setup, an organization owns and manages the entire IT infrastructure. This approach focuses on building a strong, layered defense around a defined network perimeter. Key characteristics include:

- **Perimeter-Based Defense:** Security is centered on controlling access at the network edge. This often involves physical firewalls, intrusion detection/prevention systems (IDS/IPS), and other hardware-based solutions placed at the boundary between the internal network and the outside world.

- **Hardware and Software Ownership:** The organization is responsible for purchasing, installing, configuring, and maintaining all physical security hardware and software, from network appliances to endpoint protection.
- **Centralized Control:** Security teams have complete, direct control over all components within their network. This can simplify management in some ways but also creates a single point of failure if the perimeter is breached.
- **Scaling Challenges:** Expanding security capacity often requires purchasing and installing new physical hardware, which can be a slow and expensive process.

Perimeter Defense Systems

The concept of perimeter defense relies heavily on systems that create a virtual boundary to control and monitor network access. These include:

Grid Sensors:

In a network context, the term "grid sensor" can refer to a system of interconnected security devices and agents that monitor traffic across a network. These aren't physical tripwires, but rather logical checkpoints that use software to look for suspicious activity. They work in concert with firewalls and IDS/IPS to create a comprehensive view of network activity, acting as distributed "eyes" that report back to a central monitoring system.

Access Control Lists (ACLs):

ACLs are a fundamental part of perimeter defense on network devices like routers and firewalls. An ACL is a sequential list of "permit" or "deny" statements used to filter network traffic. The device processes a packet by checking it against each rule in the list, from top to bottom, until a match is found. Once a match is made, the packet is either allowed or dropped, and no further rules are evaluated. They are used to control which sources can communicate with which destinations on a network and are a simple yet powerful way to enforce a security policy.

Foundational Network Concepts

To understand network security, you first have to understand the basic architecture and components that make up a network. The most important model is the TCP/IP Model, a four-layer framework that defines how data moves across networks and the internet.

Layer	Function	Security Implications
Application	Provides services to user applications (e.g., web browsing, email).	This layer is where application-level security, such as **data encryption (HTTPS)** and **user authentication**, happens. Attacks like phishing and malware target this layer.
Transport	Manages communication between two devices, ensuring data arrives correctly.	Firewalls and IPS can filter traffic based on **port numbers** (e.g., blocking all traffic on a specific port), a function that operates at this layer.
Internet	Routes data packets across networks to their final destination.	Security here involves **packet filtering** based on **IP addresses.** Routers and firewalls analyze and make decisions on traffic at this layer.
Network Access	Manages the physical connection to the network (e.g., Ethernet cables, Wi-Fi).	Physical security and control over which devices can connect to the network are key at this layer.

Key Network Components and Their Security Roles

Physical and virtual devices play a critical role in directing and securing network traffic. Their security capabilities vary widely.

Routers:

Often called the "gatekeepers" of a network, routers connect different networks together (e.g., your home network to the internet). They make intelligent decisions about where to send data packets based on their destination IP address. For security, routers are crucial as they can host firewall services and enforce Access Control Lists (ACLs) to filter traffic moving between networks.

Switches:

These devices connect multiple devices within the same network. Unlike a hub, a switch is intelligent; it learns the MAC address (a unique hardware address) of each connected device and sends data only to the intended recipient. This is a significant security improvement over hubs as it prevents a single device from "eavesdropping" on all network traffic.

Hubs:

A much older and simpler device, a hub connects devices by broadcasting all incoming traffic to all other ports. Any device connected to the hub can see all the traffic passing through it. Because they provide no filtering or intelligence, hubs are considered insecure and are rarely used in modern networks.

Common Network Architectures and Models

Network architecture refers to the overall design of a computer network, including the physical and logical layout of devices, wiring, and software. Network models, like the TCP/ IP and OSI models, are frameworks that provide a structured way to understand how networks operate by dividing communication into distinct layers.

Common Network Architectures

The way a network is structured has a direct impact on its performance, scalability, and security.

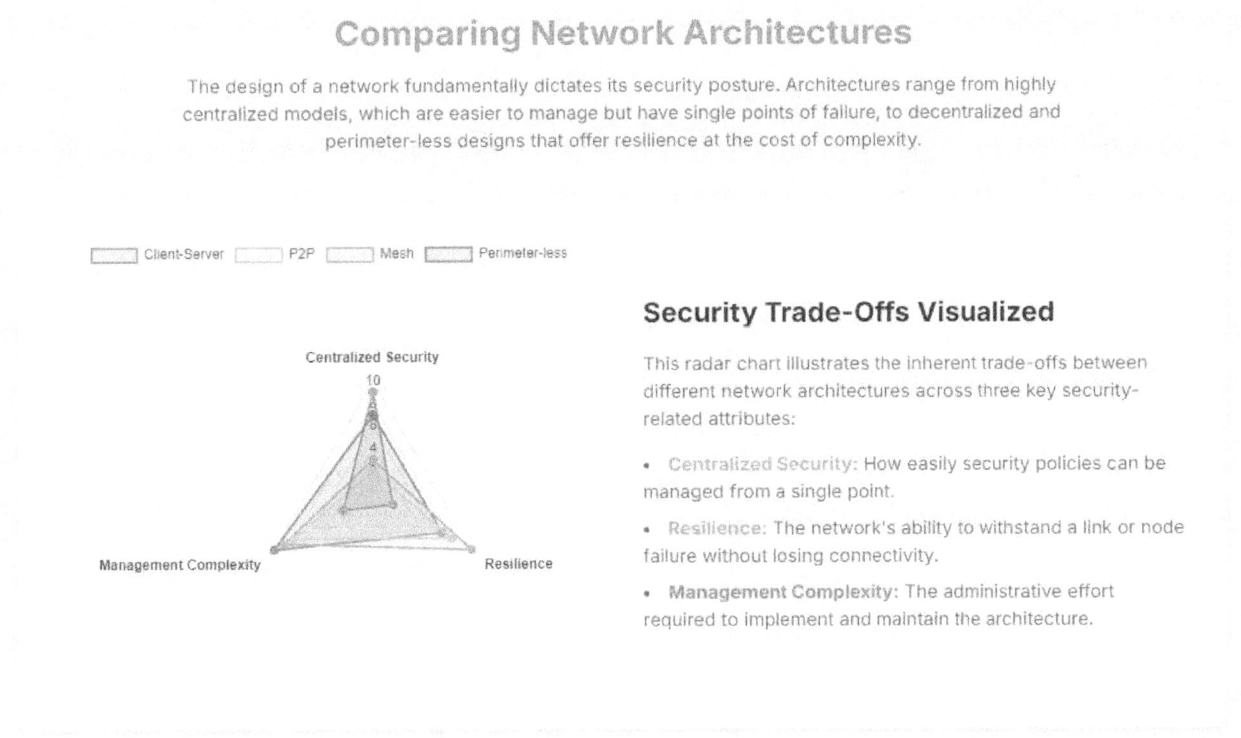

Client-Server:

In this architecture, a central powerful computer, the server, provides resources, data, and services to other computers, the clients. The clients rely on the server to perform most of the work. This is the most common model for modern business networks and the internet.

Security Implications:

Security is centralized and easier to manage because all critical data and services are located on the server. Security controls like firewalls, authentication, and access policies can be enforced at this single point. However, the server is a single point of failure; if it is compromised, the entire network can be affected.

Peer-to-Peer (P2P):

In a P2P architecture, all computers on the network are equal and can act as both clients and servers, sharing resources directly with each other without a central server.

Security Implications:

P2P is often more resilient because there is no single point of failure. However, security is much harder to manage. Since every machine can hold data and services, it's difficult to enforce consistent security policies, perform centralized backups, and monitor for threats across the network.

Hub-and-Spoke:

This architecture has a central hub that connects to multiple remote sites or networks, known as spokes. All traffic between the spokes must pass through the central hub.

Security Implications:

This model centralizes security controls. You can deploy a single, strong firewall and other security appliances at the hub to inspect and control all traffic. This simplifies management and provides consistent security policy enforcement. However, like the client-server model, the hub represents a single point of failure; if it is compromised or goes down, all communication between the spokes is lost.

Mesh:

In a mesh architecture, every device or node is interconnected with every other device. This creates multiple paths for data to travel from one point to another.

Security Implications:

A mesh network is highly resilient and reliable because if one link or node fails, data can simply be rerouted through another path. From a security perspective, this model is complex. It's difficult to enforce a consistent security policy across all the decentralized nodes, and monitoring traffic is challenging because there is no single point of entry or exit. Security needs to be managed at each individual node, which can be a significant administrative burden.

Perimeter-less:

This modern architecture is built on the Zero Trust principle. Instead of securing a perimeter, the focus is on securing every single device, user, and application. It assumes that there is no implicit trust, even for traffic that originates inside the network.

Security Implications:

A perimeter-less model is highly secure by design. It minimizes the attack surface by not relying on a single, vulnerable perimeter. Every access request is authenticated and authorized, and traffic is often encrypted end-to-end. This is the most secure model for distributed, cloud-based environments. However, it is also the most complex to implement and manage, requiring advanced identity management and security orchestration tools.

Bus:

Description: All devices connect to a single communication line (bus), with data transmitted along it.

Characteristics: An early LAN architecture, often using coaxial cable or twisted-pair.

Advantages: Simple, cost-effective for small networks.
Disadvantages: Single point of failure; if the bus breaks, the entire network fails. Limited range and speed.

Security Implications: Highly insecure. All data is visible to every device on the bus, making it easy for an attacker to "eavesdrop" and capture traffic.

Star:

Description: All devices connect to a central hub or switch, which manages data flow.

Characteristics: The most common LAN topology, using Ethernet switches.

Advantages: Easy to install and isolate faults. If one device fails, the rest of the network remains operational. It's easily scalable.

Disadvantages: The central hub or switch is a single point of failure; if it fails, the entire network goes down. It requires more cabling than a bus topology.

Security Implications: More secure than a bus as a switch sends data only to the intended recipient. However, the central switch is a critical point that needs to be secured with firewalls and access controls.

Ring:

Description: Devices are connected in a circular loop, with data passing in one direction.

Characteristics: Historically used in Token Ring networks or FDDI (Fiber Distributed Data Interface).

Advantages: Provides equal access to the network for all devices, leading to efficient data transfer.

Disadvantages: A break in the ring disrupts all communication. It is less flexible to expand or add new devices.

Security Implications: Similar to a bus, data passes through every node in the ring, which can make it vulnerable to interception if not properly secured with encryption.

Tree:

Description: A hierarchical structure with a root node branching out into sub-networks.

Characteristics: Combines bus and star topologies, common in large organizations.

Advantages: Highly scalable and easy to expand.
Disadvantages: The higher-level nodes or root node represent a higher risk of failure, which can segment the network.

Security Implications: Security policies can be enforced at the root node and cascaded down to the branches. However, a failure at the top can impact the entire tree below it.

Hybrid:

Description: Combines two or more architectures (e.g., star-bus) to meet specific needs.

Characteristics: A flexible architecture tailored to complex, large-scale environments.

Advantages: Customizable, balancing the strengths of multiple topologies.

Disadvantages: Complex design and management, and can be more expensive.

Security Implications: Security is a mix of the combined topologies. For example, a star-bus hybrid can be more secure at the star nodes but vulnerable at the bus backbones if not properly segmented and controlled.

Key Threats to Cloud Networks

Cloud environments, like any other network, face a range of security threats. However, certain threats are more prevalent or take on new forms in the cloud:

Misconfiguration:

This is one of the most common causes of cloud breaches. A simple mistake, such as leaving a storage bucket publicly accessible or improperly configuring a firewall rule, can expose sensitive data to the internet.

Unauthorized Access:

If an attacker gains access to an organization's cloud account credentials, they can bypass traditional defenses and gain control of entire environments. This makes strong authentication and access controls critical.

Insecure APIs:

Cloud services are managed through Application Programming Interfaces (APIs). If these APIs are not properly secured, they can be a major attack vector for malicious actors.

Lack of Visibility:

The complex and dynamic nature of the cloud can make it difficult for security teams to have a clear view of all their assets, traffic, and potential vulnerabilities.

Essential Network Defense Systems

Effective network defense requires a combination of robust technologies and sound practices. Many of the tools used in traditional networks have cloud-native equivalents or are used differently.

Cloud Firewalls:

These are digital barriers that filter incoming and outgoing network traffic based on a set of security rules. In the cloud, firewalls are typically managed as a service, allowing you to control traffic to and from virtual machines and other cloud resources without managing the underlying hardware. They are the first line of defense for network security.

Identity and Access Management (IAM):

IAM is arguably the most important security control in the cloud. It's the framework that controls who can access what resources and what actions they can perform. Instead of just controlling physical access, IAM focuses on managing digital identities and permissions for both humans and services.

Zero Trust Architecture:

The Zero Trust model operates on the principle of "never trust, always verify." It assumes that no user or device, whether inside or outside the network, should be automatically trusted. In a cloud environment, where the traditional network perimeter is gone, Zero Trust is a fundamental philosophy. It requires all access to be authenticated and authorized, regardless of location.

Intrusion Detection/Prevention Systems (IDS/IPS):

These systems are critical for monitoring network traffic for suspicious activity and known threats. While often used together, it's important to understand their distinct roles and types.

Expanded Network Defense Systems

Beyond firewalls and IAM, other technologies are essential for securing specific parts of a network's infrastructure, especially in hybrid or on-premise environments.

Demilitarized Zone (DMZ):

Description: A DMZ is a small, isolated network located between a company's internal network and the public internet. Its purpose is to host public-facing services like web servers, email servers, and DNS servers.

Security Implications: By placing public-facing servers in the DMZ, an organization protects its internal network from direct attacks. If a server in the DMZ is compromised, an attacker cannot easily access the more sensitive data and systems on the internal network. The DMZ is typically secured by firewalls on both sides: one to control traffic from the internet, and another to control traffic to the internal network.

Security Principle: The DMZ is a classic example of a "defense-in-depth" strategy, creating a buffer zone to slow down and contain attackers.

Virtual Private Network (VPN):

Description: A VPN creates a secure, encrypted tunnel over a public network (like the internet), allowing remote users to access a private network as if they were physically present.

Security Implications: VPNs ensure the confidentiality and integrity of data transmitted over an untrusted network. All traffic within the tunnel is encrypted, preventing it from being intercepted or read by a third party. They are a critical tool for securing remote access and connecting distributed offices.

Security Principle: VPNs provide strong data in transit protection and are a key component of a secure remote access strategy.

Telecommunication Technologies (PBX and VoIP):

Description:

- **PBX (Private Branch Exchange):** A private telephone network used within a company. It allows a single access number to have multiple extensions and handles internal and external calls.
- **VoIP (Voice over Internet Protocol):** A technology that allows telephone calls to be made over a computer network (like the internet) instead of traditional phone lines.

Security Implications: PBX systems can be vulnerable to unauthorized access, toll fraud, and denial-of-service attacks. Securing them requires strong authentication, regular software updates, and network segmentation. VoIP systems, since they run on the same network as data traffic, are exposed to common IP-based attacks. Securing them requires isolating VoIP traffic on its own VLAN, encrypting call data, and using dedicated firewalls to inspect and filter VoIP-specific protocols like SIP.

Identifying and Mitigating Network Vulnerabilities

Identifying vulnerabilities is the first step in protecting a network. This proactive process involves systematically scanning and testing systems to find weaknesses that an attacker could exploit.

Vulnerability Scanning:

An automated process that uses specialized software to scan systems and networks for known vulnerabilities. The scanner compares the system's configuration against a large database of known weaknesses, such as unpatched software, weak passwords, and misconfigurations.

Penetration Testing:

Unlike a scanner, a penetration test is a manual, goal-oriented process where a security professional (a "pentester") simulates a real-world attack against a network. The pentester uses a combination of automated tools and manual techniques to try to exploit vulnerabilities, gain access, and move laterally through the network.

Transmission Security: SSL and TLS

One of the most critical aspects of network security is protecting data as it moves between systems. SSL (Secure Sockets Layer) and its successor, TLS (Transport Layer Security), are protocols that provide this protection by encrypting data in transit.

What they do:

SSL/TLS create a secure, encrypted connection between a client (like your web browser) and a server. This prevents third parties from eavesdropping on the communication, ensuring that sensitive information like passwords, credit card numbers, and personal data remains private.

How it works:

The process, known as a TLS handshake, involves a series of steps:

- **Hello:** The client and server exchange "hello" messages to agree on a version of TLS and cryptographic algorithms.
- **Certificate Exchange:** The server sends its digital certificate to the client. This certificate contains the server's public key and is signed by a trusted Certificate Authority (CA).
- **Authentication:** The client verifies the server's certificate to ensure it is authentic and not a fake.
- **Key Exchange:** The client and server use the public keys to securely exchange a shared secret key, which will be used for symmetric encryption.
- **Encrypted Data Transfer:** All subsequent communication between the client and server is encrypted using the shared secret key, ensuring a private and secure session.

The Core Principles of Zero Trust

Zero Trust is a fundamental security model that operates on the principle of "never trust, always verify." It is not a single technology but a security philosophy built on three core principles.

Verify Explicitly:

This principle means that every access request must be verified with as much data as possible, rather than assuming trust based on location. This verification process should take into account the user's identity, the device's health, the application being used, and the context of the request. For example, a user attempting to access a sensitive file from a new location or a non-compliant device would be subject to stronger authentication measures, such as multi-factor authentication (MFA).

Use Least Privilege Access:

This principle means that every user, device, and service should be given the minimum amount of access necessary to perform its specific task, and no more. This limits the potential damage from a compromised account. For example, a marketing analyst might have read-only access to a customer database, but not the ability to edit or delete records. This prevents an attacker who compromises the analyst's account from gaining a wider foothold in the network.

Assume Breach:

This principle assumes that an attacker could already be present inside the network. Because of this, security controls are not just focused on preventing external threats but also on containing and minimizing the damage from a breach that has already occurred. This involves microsegmentation of networks (dividing a network into smaller, isolated zones) and continuous monitoring of all traffic, both external and internal.

Secure Access Service Edge (SASE)

As networks evolve from a centralized, on-premise model to a distributed, cloud-based model, security and networking must also change. Secure Access Service Edge (SASE) represents this evolution. SASE is a modern security framework that converges networking capabilities, such as SD-WAN, with network security functions, like Cloud Firewalls and Zero Trust Network Access (ZTNA), into a single, cloud-delivered service.

The core idea of SASE is to provide a comprehensive, flexible, and centralized security policy that can be applied to any user, on any device, anywhere they work. It's a fundamental shift from securing the data center to securing the user.

Core Components of a SASE Architecture

A full SASE platform combines several key technologies into a unified service. These components work together to provide a seamless and secure experience for the end-user while simplifying management for IT teams.

Zero Trust Network Access (ZTNA):

This is a key part of SASE and a direct replacement for traditional VPNs. ZTNA establishes a secure, encrypted connection only to the specific application the user needs to access, rather than to the entire corporate network. This drastically reduces the attack surface.

Cloud Firewall (FWaaS):

A firewall delivered as a service from the cloud. This ensures that every user, whether they are in the office or working from a coffee shop, is protected by the same set of security rules and policies.

Secure Web Gateway (SWG):

An SWG inspects all web traffic, blocking malicious websites, preventing malware downloads, and enforcing company internet usage policies. In a SASE model, this is delivered from the cloud, ensuring consistency for all users.

Cloud Access Security Broker (CASB):

A CASB provides visibility and control over data and user activity in cloud-based applications (like Google Workspace or Microsoft 365). It can enforce security policies, protect against data loss, and identify shadow IT.

Software-Defined Wide Area Network (SD-WAN):

While the other components are for security, SD-WAN is a networking technology that intelligently routes traffic over the best available connection. It ensures users have a reliable, high-performance connection to cloud services and applications, which is essential for a SASE architecture.

Key Benefits of SASE

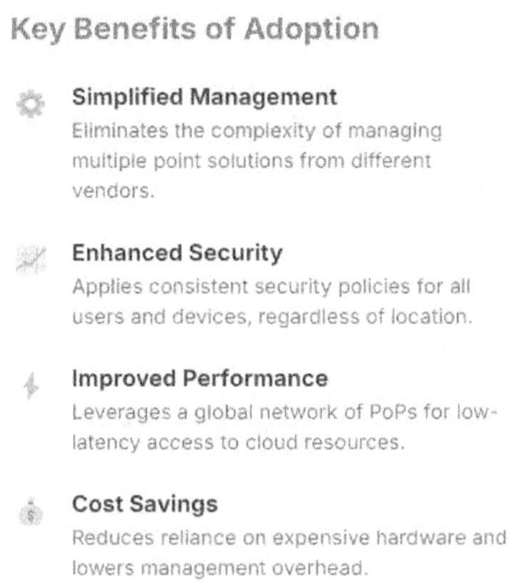

Simplified Management:

By converging networking and security into a single platform, SASE eliminates the complexity of managing multiple point solutions from different vendors.

Enhanced Security:

SASE provides consistent security policies for all users and devices, regardless of their location, reducing the risk of a breach.

Improved Performance:

SASE platforms are often built on a global network of PoPs (Points of Presence), which can provide low-latency access to cloud resources for users around the world.

Cost Savings:

By eliminating the need for expensive hardware and reducing management overhead, SASE can lead to significant cost savings.

Considerations

- Adoption requires careful planning to integrate with existing infrastructure.
- Organizations should assess vendor capabilities and compliance needs.

SASE is increasingly vital as businesses shift to cloud and remote work environments, making it a strategic choice for robust, scalable security.

Network as Code (NaC)

Network as Code (NaC) is a security and network management approach that applies the principles of Infrastructure as Code (IaC) to network devices and configurations. Instead of manually configuring network hardware like routers and firewalls, NaC uses scripts and declarative code to define, deploy, and manage the network. This approach treats the network as a programmable and version-controlled asset, just like application software.

The NaC Workflow: From Code to Configuration

Key Principles of NaC

Automation:

NaC automates repetitive and time-consuming manual tasks, such as configuring new firewalls, updating access control lists, or deploying new network segments. This reduces the risk of human error and speeds up deployment.

Version Control:

NaC leverages version control systems like Git to track every change made to the network configuration. This allows teams to easily review changes, collaborate, and, most importantly, roll back to a previous, stable configuration if an error is introduced.

Declarative Configuration:

In a declarative model, you define the desired state of the network (e.g., "The firewall should allow traffic on port 443 from this IP address"). The NaC tool then automatically takes the necessary steps to achieve that state, regardless of the current configuration.

Testing and Validation:

Just as developers test code before deploying it, NaC enables network teams to test configurations in a virtual environment before applying them to a live network. This helps to catch errors and security vulnerabilities early.

Security Implications of NaC

NaC has a significant positive impact on network security.

Consistency and Policy Enforcement:

NaC ensures that security policies are applied consistently across the entire network. This prevents configuration drift and reduces the risk of misconfigurations that can lead to security vulnerabilities.

Auditability and Compliance:

Every change to the network is documented and version-controlled, creating a clear audit trail that can be used to demonstrate compliance with regulatory requirements.

Faster Response to Threats:

In the event of a security incident, NaC can be used to quickly deploy new security controls or quarantine a compromised network segment by simply updating and deploying a configuration file.

Elimination of Manual Error:

Many security breaches are the result of simple manual errors, such as forgetting to apply a patch or misconfiguring a firewall rule. NaC eliminates these manual steps, leading to a more secure and reliable network.

NaC is an important part of a modern, automated network defense strategy, working alongside concepts like Zero Trust and SASE to create a secure, scalable, and agile network environment.

Software-Defined Networking (SDN)

Software-Defined Networking (SDN) is a network architecture that separates the network's control plane from its data plane. In a traditional network, each device (like a router or a switch) contains its own control logic that determines how to forward traffic. In an SDN environment, a centralized controller takes over this control function, making all the forwarding decisions. The network devices simply execute the instructions they receive from the controller.

Think of it like this: In a traditional network, every train conductor on every train has to decide which tracks to take. In an SDN network, there is a central command center that tells every train exactly where to go. This centralization provides unprecedented control and flexibility.

The Three Planes of SDN

SDN is built on the concept of three distinct "planes" that work together:

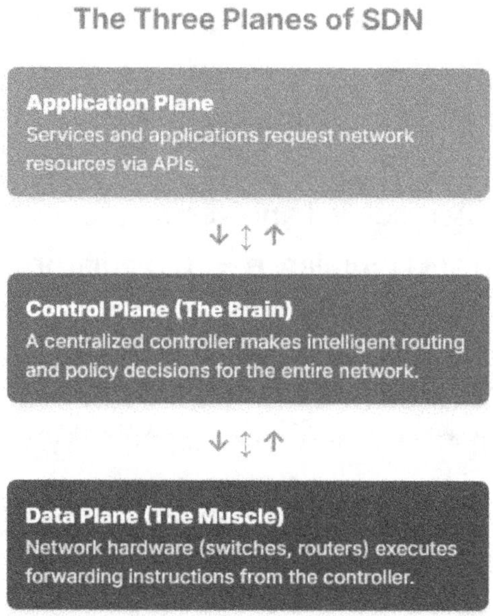

Data Plane (Forwarding Plane):

This is where the actual network traffic moves. It consists of the network devices (routers and switches) that forward data packets based on instructions from the control plane. These devices are often referred to as "dumb" or "stateless" because they no longer make their own routing decisions.

Control Plane:

This is the "brain" of the SDN network. It's a centralized controller that collects information about the entire network topology and uses this information to make intelligent decisions about how traffic should be routed and what security policies should be applied.

Application Plane:

This is where the applications and services that run on top of the SDN network live. Applications can communicate with the control plane through APIs, allowing them to dynamically request network resources and services. This enables powerful automation and integration.

Security Implications of SDN

SDN offers significant security benefits, but it also introduces new risks.

Security Benefits:

- **Centralized Policy Management:** Security policies can be defined and enforced from a single point, ensuring consistency across the entire network. This makes it much easier to manage firewalls, access control lists, and other security controls.
- **Automated Threat Response:** Because the network is programmable, it can be configured to respond to security threats automatically. For example, the SDN controller can be programmed to quarantine a compromised device or redirect malicious traffic to a security appliance in real-time.
- **Enhanced Visibility:** The central controller has a complete view of all network traffic, which provides unparalleled visibility for monitoring and security analytics.

Security Risks:

- **Single Point of Failure:** The central controller is a high-value target for attackers. If the controller is compromised or goes down, it can affect the entire network. This makes the controller's security a top priority.
- **New Attack Vectors:** The APIs that allow applications to communicate with the controller are a new potential attack vector. If these APIs are not properly secured, an attacker could use them to take control of the network.
- **Vulnerability in the Protocol:** The communication protocol between the controller and the network devices (often OpenFlow) must be secured with encryption to prevent an attacker from intercepting and manipulating the control instructions.

Security Implications: A Double-Edged Sword

Benefits ✓

- Centralized policy management ensures consistency.
- Automated threat response quarantines devices in real-time.
- Enhanced visibility across all network traffic.

Risks ✗

- The central controller is a single point of failure.
- Controller APIs introduce new potential attack vectors.
- Control plane communication must be securely encrypted.

SDN is a foundational technology that enables modern network management approaches like NaC and is a key component of SASE architectures.

Management of Accounts and Access Control

Effective network defense relies on strict control over who can access what. This involves a set of administrative procedures and security principles designed to minimize the risk of unauthorized access.

Account Management

Proper account management is the foundation of network access control. It ensures that every user and service has a unique, manageable identity.

Account Lifecycle:

This refers to the process of creating, maintaining, and deleting user accounts. A robust process ensures that accounts are created correctly with the minimum necessary permissions, that they are regularly reviewed, and that they are promptly disabled or deleted when a user's role changes or they leave the organization.

Strong Authentication:

Passwords alone are not enough. Strong authentication methods, such as Multi-Factor Authentication (MFA), require users to provide at least two different pieces of evidence to prove their identity (e.g., a password and a code from their phone).

Privileged Account Management (PAM):

These are accounts with elevated permissions, such as administrator accounts. They are a primary target for attackers. PAM involves a set of tools and practices to secure and monitor these accounts, including limiting their use, requiring special approval to access them, and rotating their credentials automatically.

Network Rights

Network rights, or permissions, define what an authenticated user or device is allowed to do on the network. The guiding principle is Least Privilege.

Principle of Least Privilege:

This is a fundamental security concept that states a user should be granted the minimum necessary permissions to perform their job, and no more. For example, a marketing employee should not have administrative access to the company's financial database. This limits the potential damage if their account is compromised.

Role-Based Access Control (RBAC):

RBAC is a security model that simplifies permission management. Instead of assigning rights to individual users, you assign them to roles (e.g., "HR Manager," "IT Administrator"). When a new employee joins, you simply assign them the appropriate role, and they automatically inherit the correct permissions. This is much more scalable and easier to manage than assigning permissions on a user-by-user basis.

Access to Systems and Equipment

Controlling access to physical and virtual systems and equipment is a key part of network defense.

Physical Security:

This includes securing physical data centers, server rooms, and network closets. Controls such as security cameras, keycard access, and visitor logs prevent unauthorized physical tampering with network hardware.

Logical Access Control:

This refers to the controls that regulate access to systems, applications, and data on the network. Technologies like firewalls, VPNs, and IAM policies are all forms of logical access control.

Remote Access:

Securing remote access is more important than ever. Technologies like VPNs (Virtual Private Networks) create a secure, encrypted tunnel for remote workers to access the corporate network, while Zero Trust architectures ensure that every access attempt is verified, regardless of the user's location.

Support, Monitor, Test& Troubleshoot Network Defense Systems

While deploying security systems is crucial, the ongoing, day-to-day work of managing them is just as important. A robust network defense strategy includes continuous support, monitoring, testing, and troubleshooting.

Monitoring and Support

Continuous monitoring is the practice of actively watching network traffic, system logs, and security alerts to detect and respond to threats in real time.

Log Management and SIEM:

All security devices and systems—including firewalls, IDS/IPS, and servers—must be configured to send their logs to a central location. A Security Information and Event Management (SIEM) system collects, aggregates, and analyzes these logs to identify security events and anomalies. By correlating events from different devices, a SIEM can detect complex attacks that might go unnoticed by a single system.

Performance Monitoring:

Network performance monitoring tools are used to track the health of network hardware (e.g., routers, switches) and software. These tools can identify bottlenecks, hardware failures, or unusual traffic patterns that could be a sign of a security incident or a denial-of-service attack.

Patch Management:

A critical part of support is keeping all software and firmware up to date. Patch management is the process of acquiring, testing, and installing patches to fix security vulnerabilities. Automated tools are often used to ensure that all systems are patched in a timely manner, reducing the window of opportunity for attackers to exploit known vulnerabilities.

Testing

Proactive testing is essential to confirm that security controls are effective and to find vulnerabilities before an attacker does.

Security Audits:

These are systematic reviews of security configurations, access controls, and policies. Audits ensure that systems are configured in a way that aligns with the organization's security standards and regulatory requirements.

Vulnerability Scanning and Penetration Testing:

While previously mentioned as part of identifying vulnerabilities, these are also continuous testing activities. Regular vulnerability scans help to quickly identify new weaknesses introduced by new software or configuration changes, while periodic penetration tests simulate an attack to validate the effectiveness of the entire security posture.

Troubleshooting Issues

When a security or network issue arises, a systematic troubleshooting approach is key to a quick and effective resolution.

Define the Problem:

Clearly identify the symptoms of the issue. Is a specific service unreachable? Is a firewall blocking legitimate traffic? Are users unable to access a VPN?

Gather Information:

Collect data from all relevant sources, including logs from firewalls, servers, IDS/IPS, and network monitoring tools. Look for error messages, unusual traffic patterns, or alerts that occurred around the time of the issue.

Form a Hypothesis:

Based on the information you've gathered, formulate a theory about what is causing the problem. For example, "The new firewall rule is blocking port 443 traffic to the web server."

Test the Hypothesis:

In a controlled environment, test your theory. This might involve temporarily disabling a firewall rule or checking a configuration setting to see if the problem is resolved.

Implement the Solution:

Once the root cause is confirmed, apply the fix. This might be a simple change to a configuration file or a more complex update to a system.

Verify and Document:

Confirm that the fix has resolved the issue and has not introduced any new problems. Document the entire process—the symptoms, the cause, and the solution—to create a knowledge base that can be used to solve similar problems in the future.

Choosing the Right IDS/IPS for Your Organization

Intrusion Detection Systems (IDS) and Intrusion Prevention Systems (IPS) are essential tools for identifying and responding to malicious activity. An IDS is a passive tool that monitors network traffic and logs or alerts on suspicious activity, while an IPS is an active tool that can automatically block or drop malicious traffic.

Organizations can choose from several types of IDS/IPS, often deploying a combination for a layered defense. The appropriate system depends on the organization's network architecture, budget, and security posture.

Network-based IDS/IPS (NIDS/NIPS):

- **Function:** These systems monitor traffic at key points in the network, such as the perimeter or between different network segments. They analyze traffic flows for signatures of known attacks or for anomalous behavior.
- **Best For:** Protecting the overall network infrastructure and detecting attacks targeting multiple systems. NIPS is excellent for blocking common, well-known attacks before they reach a target.

Host-based IDS/IPS (HIDS/HIPS):

- **Function:** HIDS/HIPS are installed directly on individual servers or endpoints. They monitor the system's internal activity, including file integrity changes, system logs, and process execution.
- **Best For:** Detecting attacks that have bypassed the network perimeter or internal threats. They provide deep visibility into a single host's activity and can stop an attack that has already landed.

Cloud-based IDS/IPS:

- **Function:** Offered as a service by cloud providers or third-party vendors, these systems are designed to monitor traffic within the cloud environment. They integrate with the cloud's native logging and traffic flow systems.
- **Best For:** Organizations with cloud-native or hybrid cloud environments. These systems can protect a distributed workload and are often more scalable and dynamic than traditional hardware-based solutions.

A Comparison of Security Approaches

The fundamental difference between these two models is a philosophical shift from securing a **physical perimeter** to securing **virtual identities and configurations.**

Feature	On-Premise Security	Cloud Security
Core Philosophy	**Perimeter-based defense.** Trust is assumed once inside the network.	**Zero Trust.** No user, device, or application is trusted by default, regardless of location.
Responsibility	**Solely the organization's.** The organization is responsible for all hardware, software, and data security.	**Shared responsibility model.** The cloud provider secures the infrastructure, while the customer secures their data, applications, and configurations.
Primary Control	**Network Firewalls.** The main focus is on keeping external threats out of the internal network.	**Identity and Access Management (IAM).** The main focus is on controlling who (or what) can access specific resources, no matter where they are located.
Scalability	**Manual and time-consuming.** Requires procuring and installing new hardware.	**Automated and dynamic.** Security tools scale as resources are provisioned.

An Examination of Wireless Security

The proliferation of wireless networks has fundamentally reshaped how we connect and share information. From personal home networks to large corporate infrastructures, wireless technology offers unparalleled convenience. However, this accessibility also introduces significant security risks. Wireless security, therefore, is the practice of safeguarding these networks and the data they transmit from unauthorized access and malicious attacks. Understanding the importance of this security, the different protocols that exist, and the key practices for maintaining a secure network is crucial in today's digital world.

The importance of robust wireless security cannot be overstated. Unlike wired connections, which require a physical tap into the network, wireless signals are broadcast through the air. This makes them vulnerable to interception by anyone within range. Without proper security, a malicious actor could eavesdrop on data transmissions, steal sensitive information like passwords and financial details, or even gain unauthorized access to a connected network. Such breaches can lead to serious consequences, including identity theft, financial loss, and damage to a company's reputation. Thus, securing wireless networks is not just a technical formality, but a fundamental necessity for protecting privacy and data integrity.

Wireless Vulnerabilities and Attacks

Wireless networks are susceptible to several key vulnerabilities that can be exploited by attackers. A vulnerability is a weakness in a system that can be exploited, while an attack is the deliberate action taken to exploit it.

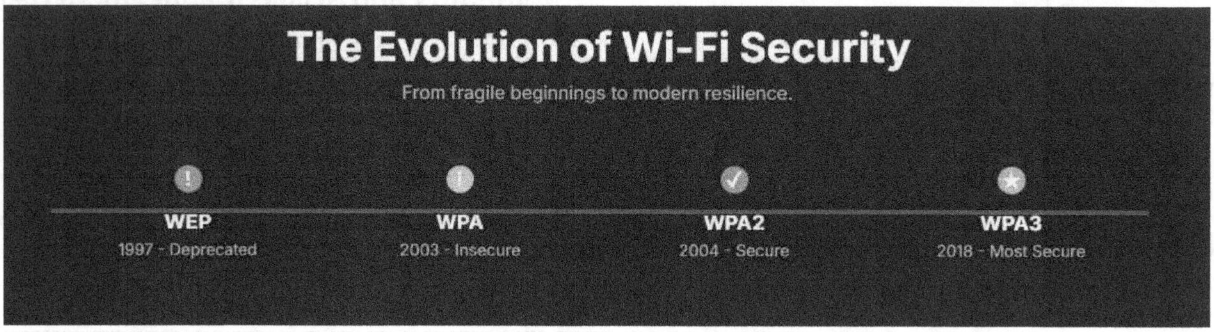

Configuration and Setup Vulnerabilities

Default Settings:

Many wireless devices (e.g., routers, access points) come with default SSIDs, passwords, or admin credentials that are easily guessable or widely known (e.g., "admin/admin"). Failure to change these increases the risk of unauthorized access.

Description: The vulnerability stems from the use of pre-set, non-unique credentials that are either public knowledge or easily guessed.

Target: The network's administrative interface and overall security.

Impact: Full unauthorized access to the router's settings, allowing an attacker to change configurations, monitor traffic, or launch other attacks.

Mitigation: Always change default administrative credentials immediately after setup. Use a strong, unique password for the Wi-Fi network itself.

Weak Encryption:

Using outdated protocols like WEP (Wired Equivalent Privacy) or WPA (Wi-Fi Protected Access) instead of WPA3 makes networks susceptible to decryption attacks.

Description: The network's encryption is too weak to effectively protect data, allowing it to be easily cracked or bypassed.

Target: The encrypted data transmitted over the network.

Impact: Data interception and exposure of confidential information.

Mitigation: Configure your router to use the latest and most secure protocol available, which is WPA3. If WPA3 is not an option, use WPA2 with AES encryption.

Misconfigured Access Points:

Incorrectly configured settings, such as disabling encryption or enabling overly permissive access, can expose the network.

Description: Human error in the configuration process creates a security gap.

Target: The network's security posture.

Impact: Unauthorized network access, data exposure, and potential for further attacks.

Mitigation: Ensure encryption is always enabled. Only enable services you absolutely need, and configure access controls properly.

Eavesdropping and Data Interception

Packet Sniffing:

Attackers intercept unencrypted or weakly encrypted wireless traffic using tools like Wireshark or Kismet to capture sensitive data (e.g., passwords, emails).

Description: An attacker " listens" to the wireless traffic by capturing data packets transmitted over the air.

Target: The data being transmitted between devices and the access point.

Impact: Exposure of confidential information, including login credentials and personal data.

Mitigation: Use end-to-end encryption for all traffic. The use of HTTPS is critical for websites, and a VPN (Virtual Private Network) can encrypt all your internet activity, especially on public networks.

Man-in-the-Middle (MITM) Attacks:

Attackers position themselves between the victim's device and the access point to intercept or manipulate data. This is often accomplished through techniques like creating a Rogue

Access Point or an Evil Twin Attack:

Description: The attacker secretly relays and potentially alters communications between two parties who believe they are communicating directly with each other.

Target: The communication channel between a user's device and the internet.

Impact: Theft of credentials, session hijacking, or injection of malicious content.

Mitigation: Be cautious of suspicious network names on public Wi-Fi. Check for SSL/TLS certificates (the padlock icon in your browser) and, most importantly, use a VPN.

Session Hijacking:

Attackers steal session cookies or tokens from a user's active session to impersonate them and gain unauthorized access to services.

Description: An attacker intercepts a valid session token and uses it to take over a user's authenticated session without needing a password.
Target: The user's active session with a website or service.

Impact: Unauthorized access to accounts and services, leading to data theft or fraud.

Mitigation: Ensure that all sensitive websites and services use HTTPS. Log out of accounts when you are finished, especially on a public computer or network.

Authentication and Access Control Vulnerabilities

Weak Passwords:

Simple or easily guessable Wi-Fi passwords can be cracked using brute-force or dictionary attacks.

Description: An attacker uses automated tools to try thousands or millions of password combinations until they find the correct one.

Target: The Wi-Fi network's password.

Impact: Unauthorized network access.

Mitigation: Use a strong, complex password that is at least 12 characters long and includes a mix of uppercase letters, lowercase letters, numbers, and symbols.

MAC Spoofing:

Attackers can forge the MAC address of a legitimate device to bypass MAC filtering and gain network access.

Description: An attacker changes their device's MAC address to match that of a whitelisted device on the network.

Target: A network's MAC address filter.

Impact: Unauthorized network access.

Mitigation: Avoid relying on MAC filtering as a primary security measure. Instead, focus on using strong encryption protocols (WPA3/WPA2) and a robust password.

Phishing via Fake Hotspots:

Attackers set up malicious public Wi-Fi hotspots to lure users into entering sensitive information on fake login pages.

Description: An attacker creates a fake Wi-Fi network to redirect users to a fraudulent login page that mimics a legitimate one.

Target: The user's trust and their login credentials.

Impact: Credential theft or malware infection.

Mitigation: Never enter personal or financial information on a website while connected to an unsecured public Wi-Fi network. Use a VPN or your mobile data instead.

Firmware Exploitation:

Attackers exploit outdated or vulnerable firmware in routers or access points to gain control, extract credentials, or install malicious code.

Description: An attacker takes advantage of unpatched software bugs in the router's operating system.

Target: The router's firmware and control panel.

Impact: Full device compromise, persistent network access, and the ability to monitor or manipulate all traffic.

Mitigation: Regularly check for and install firmware updates from your router manufacturer's website. Consider enabling automatic updates if available.

Protocol and Implementation Vulnerabilities

WEP Vulnerabilities:

WEP's weak encryption can be cracked in minutes using tools like Aircrack-ng due to flaws in its key management and initialization vectors.

Description: An attacker captures a sufficient number of data packets and uses known flaws in the WEP algorithm to quickly determine the encryption key.

Target: The WEP encryption key.

Impact: Complete compromise of the network and all data transmitted on it.

Mitigation: Do not use WEP under any circumstances. Upgrade your router and network settings to use WPA2 or, preferably, WPA3.

WPA/WPA2 Flaws:

Vulnerabilities like KRACK (Key Reinstallation Attack) in WPA2 allow attackers to decrypt data or inject malicious packets, though patches have mitigated this.

Description: An attacker forces the reinstallation of an already-in-use key, which can be manipulated to decrypt data packets.

Target: The WPA2 handshake and encryption key.

Impact: Data interception or manipulation (mitigated by patches in most modern devices).

Mitigation: Keep all of your operating systems and wireless device drivers up to date to ensure that patches for known vulnerabilities are installed.

WPS (Wi-Fi Protected Setup) Weaknesses:

WPS PINs can be brute-forced, granting attackers access to the network without needing the Wi-Fi password.

Description: The eight-digit PIN is flawed, with a much smaller number of combinations to guess than intended. An attacker can quickly brute-force the PIN to gain access.

Target: The WPS PIN.

Impact: Unauthorized network access.

Mitigation: Disable WPS on your router. It is a convenience feature that presents a significant security risk.

Denial-of-Service (DoS) Attacks

Jamming:

Attackers use signal jammers to disrupt wireless communications, rendering the network unusable.

Description: An attacker transmits radio signals on the same frequency as the Wi-Fi network, overwhelming the legitimate signal.

Target: The wireless network's radio signal.

Impact: Prevents legitimate devices from connecting or staying connected to the network. **Mitigation:** This attack is difficult to prevent, as it is a physical layer problem. You can try to change the Wi-Fi channel to a less congested one, but the best defense is to secure the physical location of your access points.

Deauthentication Attacks:

Attackers send deauthentication packets to disconnect devices from the network, causing service disruptions. This can also be a preliminary step to capturing WPA handshakes for cracking.

Description: An attacker spoofs the identity of a client or access point and sends a deauthentication command to force a device to disconnect.

Target: A specific device or all devices connected to the network.

Impact: Denial of service (DoS) or capturing WPA handshakes for cracking.

Mitigation: The primary mitigation is to keep router firmware and device drivers updated, as newer versions often have better defenses against these attacks.

Flooding:

Overloading the network with fake requests or traffic to overwhelm the access point and degrade performance.

Description: An attacker sends a high volume of traffic to an access point to consume its resources and prevent it from handling legitimate requests.

Target: The access point's processing power and bandwidth.

Impact: Network downtime or severely degraded performance.

Mitigation: Modern routers have built-in security features to detect and prevent flooding attacks. Ensure these features are enabled.

Physical and Environmental Vulnerabilities

Signal Leakage:

Wireless signals extending beyond the intended area (e.g., outside a building) allow attackers to connect or eavesdrop from a distance.

Description: The physical range of the wireless signal extends beyond the intended secure area.

Target: The network's signal itself.

Impact: Unauthorized connection attempts and data interception from outside the physical premises.

Mitigation: Place your router in a central location within your home or office. If your router has adjustable power settings, you can lower the signal strength to reduce its range.

Device Theft:

Physical access to wireless devices like routers can allow attackers to reset them, extract credentials, or install malicious firmware.

Description: An attacker gains physical control of the network device.

Target: The router or access point.

Impact: Complete network compromise, as the attacker can reset the device to default settings, bypass security, or install malicious software.

Mitigation: Secure your router and other network devices in a locked cabinet or a physically secure location.

Wireless Security Protocols and Best Practices

Over time, several protocols have been developed to address the vulnerabilities of wireless networks, each offering a different level of protection. The earliest, Wired Equivalent Privacy (WEP), was quickly proven to be weak and easily exploited. It was succeeded by Wi- Fi Protected Access (WPA), which introduced stronger encryption and dynamic keys. A significant improvement came with WPA2, which adopted the more secure Advanced Encryption Standard (AES) and has long been the industry standard for most Wi-Fi networks. The latest and most secure protocol is WPA3, which offers enhanced security features, including individualized data encryption for each user on a public network, making it even more resilient against attacks. While WPA2 is still considered a viable option, WPA3 is the preferred choice for new devices and networks.

An Introduction to Malicious Code Threats

Malicious code, often referred to as malware (a blend of "malicious" and "software"), is a broad term for any software designed to cause harm, disrupt systems, or gain unauthorized access to computer systems, networks, or data. Below is a concise overview of these threats, their key characteristics, and how they operate.

What's the Difference?

While they are all designed to cause harm, their primary distinction lies in how they spread and operate.

1. Viruses

Definition: A type of malicious code that attaches itself to legitimate programs or files, spreading when the infected file is executed.

Behavior: A virus cannot spread on its own and requires a human action to activate. Once active, it can replicate and spread to other files, often corrupting or deleting data, slowing down systems, or stealing information.

Examples: File infectors (infect executable files) and Boot sector viruses (target system boot processes).

Spread: Via infected email attachments, downloads, or removable media.

Example Impact: The ILOVEYOU virus (2000) spread via email, overwriting files and causing billions in damages.

2. Trojans

Definition: Malware that disguises itself as legitimate software, tricking users into installing it.

Behavior: A Trojan does not self-replicate but creates backdoors for attackers. It is often used for data theft, remote control, or delivering other types of malware.

Examples: Banking Trojans (e.g., Emotet) steal financial credentials, while Remote

Access Trojans (RATs) allow attackers to control devices.

Spread: Via phishing emails, fake software updates, or malicious downloads.

Example Impact: The Zeus Trojan (2007) targeted banking credentials, leading to millions in financial losses.

3. Worms

Behavior: Unlike a virus, a worm does not need to attach itself to a host file. It can spread independently across networks by exploiting software vulnerabilities, making it very effective at infecting multiple machines quickly.

Key Types of Malware

Malware is an umbrella term for a wide range of malicious software. Here are some of the most common types.

Ransomware:

This is a particularly destructive type of malware that locks or encrypts a user's files and systems, making them inaccessible. The attacker then demands a ransom payment, usually in cryptocurrency, in exchange for a decryption key. Modern ransomware often uses a "double extortion" tactic, where attackers not only encrypt data but also steal it and threaten to leak it publicly if the ransom is not paid.

Spyware:

This malware is designed to secretly monitor a user's activity and collect information without their knowledge or consent. It can capture sensitive data such as keystrokes (via a keylogger), browsing history, login credentials, and personal information. This stolen data is then sent to a third party, often for financial gain.

Adware:

While often more of a nuisance than a direct threat, adware is a type of software that automatically displays unwanted advertisements, such as pop-ups or banner ads. It often comes bundled with free software and can slow down your system and redirect your browser to malicious websites. Some forms of adware can also track your browsing habits and sell your information to advertisers.

Rootkits:

A rootkit is a stealthy and sophisticated set of tools designed to hide its presence on a compromised system. By gaining "root" or privileged access to the operating system's core functions, it can conceal malicious processes, files, and network connections from standard security software. This makes it extremely difficult to detect and remove, allowing an attacker to maintain persistent, undetected control over a device.

Botnets:

A botnet is a network of compromised devices (called "bots" or "zombies") that are controlled remotely by a single attacker, known as a "bot-herder." These networks are created by infecting devices with bot-malware, and they are typically used to carry out large-scale, coordinated attacks. The most common use of a botnet is to launch a Distributed Denial of Service (DDoS) attack, which overwhelms a target website or server with a flood of traffic, causing it to crash or become unavailable.

Fileless Malware:

Unlike traditional malware that relies on executable files, fileless malware operates entirely within a computer's memory. It uses legitimate, built-in system tools (like PowerShell or WMI) to run malicious code, leaving no traces on the hard drive. This "living off the land" approach allows it to bypass traditional antivirus software that scans for malicious files, making it a particularly evasive and dangerous threat.

How Threats Get On My Computer

Malicious code threats use a variety of delivery mechanisms to infect a system.

Phishing:

This is a form of social engineering where attackers send deceptive emails, text messages, or instant messages that appear to be from a trustworthy source. The goal is to trick the user into clicking on a malicious link, downloading an infected attachment, or revealing sensitive information. The messages often create a sense of urgency, fear, or curiosity to bypass the user's critical thinking.

Drive-by Downloads:

This refers to the unintentional download of malicious software onto your computer or mobile device. This can happen simply by visiting a compromised or malicious website. The site exploits vulnerabilities in your web browser, operating system, or plugins to automatically download and install the malware without your knowledge or consent. It often works in the background and can be hard to detect.

Exploits:

An exploit is a piece of malicious code or data that takes advantage of a security flaw or vulnerability in a software application or operating system. These vulnerabilities can exist in web browsers, plug-ins (like Adobe Flash or Java), or even the operating system itself. An exploit delivers a malicious payload by targeting and bypassing the system's security controls. For example, a zero-day exploit targets a vulnerability that is unknown to the software developer, making it a highly effective and dangerous attack vector.

Infected Media:

Malware can be spread through physical media like USB drives, CDs, or external hard drives. If an infected drive is plugged into a computer, the malware can either automatically transfer and run (if the system has an enabled autorun feature) or spread when the user manually opens an infected file on the drive. Sharing infected external devices is a common way this type of malware spreads.

Prevention and Mitigation

Fortunately, there are several steps you can take to protect your devices and data.

Antivirus/Antimalware Software:

These tools are your first line of defense. They work by scanning files and memory for patterns that match known malware signatures and by using behavioral analysis to detect suspicious activity from unknown threats. For maximum protection, enable real-time scanning, set up periodic full-system scans, and make sure the software is configured to automatically download the latest malware definitions.

Keep Your Software Updated:

Regularly updating your operating system, web browser, and other applications is one of the most critical steps you can take. These updates often contain "patches" that fix newly discovered security vulnerabilities that cybercriminals could otherwise exploit to install malware. You should also enable automatic updates whenever possible to ensure you're protected against the latest threats.

Be Skeptical of Suspicious Emails:

Phishing is a primary attack vector. Always be wary of emails from unknown senders or messages with unexpected attachments or links. Instead of clicking, hover over links to see the true destination URL, and manually navigate to websites you know and trust. Never open an attachment or download a file unless you are absolutely certain of its source.

Use Strong Passwords and Multi-Factor Authentication (MFA):

This is one of the most effective ways to protect your accounts. MFA requires a second form of verification beyond just a password, such as a code sent to your phone or a biometric scan like a fingerprint. Even if an attacker steals your password, they can't access your account without that second factor, making credential theft much less useful to them.

Back Up Your Data:

Regularly back up your important files to an external hard drive or a cloud service. This is your best defense against destructive malware like ransomware. If a ransomware attack encrypts your files, you can wipe your system and restore your data from your clean backup without paying the ransom.

Use a Firewall:

Think of a firewall as a digital gatekeeper. It is a security system that monitors and filters incoming and outgoing network traffic based on a set of security rules. A firewall blocks unauthorized access attempts and prevents malicious data packets from entering your network or computer. Both hardware firewalls (often built into your home router) and software firewalls (installed on your device) are essential for a multi-layered defense.

Practice Zero Trust:

The principle of Zero Trust means "never trust, always verify." Instead of assuming that users and devices inside your network are safe, this model requires strict identity verification and authorization for every single access request. It operates on the assumption that a breach is always possible and uses a least-privilege approach, only granting users the minimum access required for their task. This limits the damage an attacker can do if they manage to get into the system.

Current Trends and Real-World Examples

The world of malicious code is constantly evolving. Staying informed about current trends is key to protection.

AI-Driven Malware:

Attackers are using generative AI to create more sophisticated and adaptive threats.

Recent discoveries include PromptLock, a new ransomware strain that uses an AI language model to dynamically generate malicious scripts, making it unpredictable and harder to detect with traditional signatures. This technology lowers the barrier to entry, allowing less skilled cybercriminals to create complex, multi-stage attacks.

Deepfake Phishing & Social Engineering:

AI-generated deepfakes—fake audio, video, and images—are now a primary tool for social engineering. Attackers use voice cloning to impersonate CEOs, colleagues, or family members to manipulate victims into transferring funds or revealing sensitive information. A recent example is the $25 million deepfake video call scam that fooled a finance worker into sending money to a fraudulent account after the attacker impersonated multiple people in a single video conference.

Ransomware-as-a-Service (RaaS):

Cybercriminals can now easily purchase or rent ransomware kits on dark web markets to launch attacks without needing advanced technical skills.

Supply Chain Attacks:

Targeting software vendors to infect thousands of users downstream (e.g., the SolarWinds attack).

IoT Vulnerabilities:

Increasing attacks on smart devices due to their weak security.

A recent example is the CrowdStrike Incident (2024).

A software failure caused widespread outages, and malicious actors exploited the chaos by distributing fake recovery tools laced with malware, highlighting the need for vigilance even during non-malicious system events.

Secure Coding and Web Application Security

Secure coding is the practice of writing code in a way that protects an application from security vulnerabilities. It involves anticipating and mitigating potential threats throughout the software development lifecycle. By adopting these principles, developers can significantly reduce the risk of data breaches, system compromise, and other security incidents.

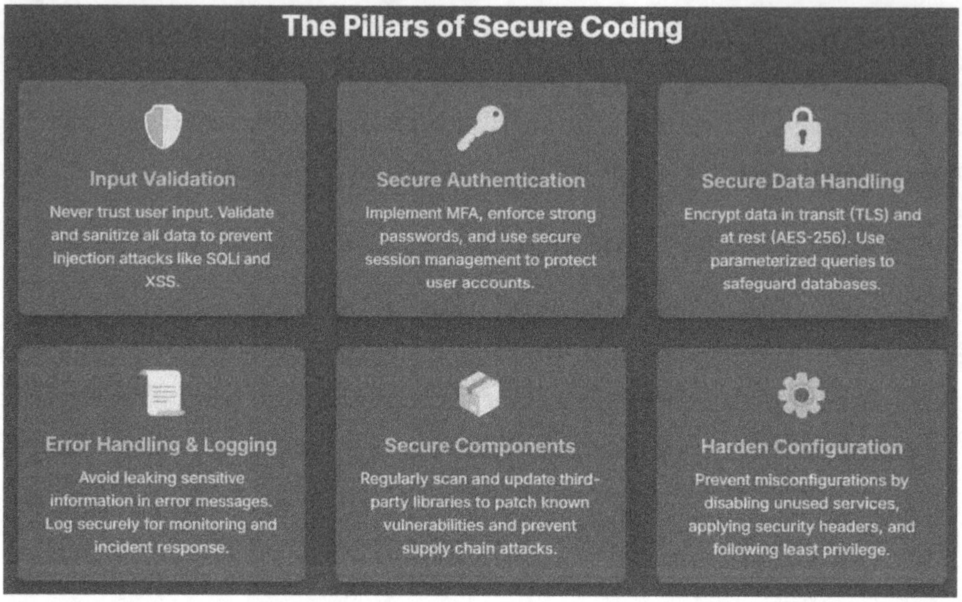

1. Secure Coding Best Practices

Secure coding minimizes vulnerabilities in software, reducing the risk of exploitation by malware, Trojans, or viruses. These practices align with OWASP Top 10 (2021) and NIST guidelines.

1.1 Input Validation and Sanitization

Why: Prevents injection attacks (e.g., SQL injection, XSS) that deliver malware or steal data (OWASP A03:2021). How:

- Validate all inputs (client and server-side) for type, length, format, and range.
- Use allowlists (e.g., regex for expected formats) over blocklists.
- Sanitize inputs to remove malicious code (e.g., strip HTML tags for XSS).

Tools: OWASP ESAPI, libraries like sanitize-html (JavaScript), bleach (Python).

Example:

```
from bleach import clean user_input =
"malicious_code()"
sanitized = clean(user_input, tags=['p', 'b'], attributes={'a': ['href']})
```

1.2 Secure Authentication and Session Management

Why: Prevents broken authentication (OWASP A01:2021), enabling Trojans to hijack sessions. How:

- Enforce strong passwords (e.g., 12+ characters, mixed types).
- Use secure session cookies (HttpOnly, Secure, SameSite=Strict).

- Implement multi-factor authentication (MFA).
- Hash passwords with bcrypt or Argon2; never store plaintext.

Tools: OAuth 2.0, OpenID Connect, jsonwebtoken (Node.js).

Example:

```
// Express.js secure session cookie app.use(session({ secret: process.env.SESSION_SECRET,
cookie: { secure: true, httpOnly: true, sameSite: 'strict' }
}));
```

1.3 Secure Data Handling

Why: Prevents data exposure (OWASP A02:2021) exploited by spyware or ransomware. How:

- Encrypt sensitive data in transit (TLS 1.3) and at rest (AES-256).
- Avoid logging sensitive data (e.g., passwords, API keys).
- Use parameterized queries for databases to prevent SQL injection.

Tools: Let's Encrypt for TLS, crypto module (Node.js), pylibcrypto (Python).

Example:

```
-- Parameterized query in PostgreSQL
SELECT * FROM users WHERE username = $1 AND password = $2;
```

1.4 Error Handling and Logging

Why: Prevents information leakage (OWASP A09:2021) that aids attackers in crafting Trojans. How:

- Avoid exposing stack traces or system details in errors.
- Log errors securely without sensitive data.
- Use structured logging for monitoring.

Tools: Winston (Node.js), Log4j (Java), ELK Stack for analysis.

Example:

```
// Node.js error handling app.use((err, req, res, next)
=> {
logger.error('Error occurred', { error: err.message }); res.status(500).send('Internal Server Error');
});
```

1.5 Secure Software Components

Why: Prevents exploitation of vulnerable dependencies (OWASP A06:2021). How:

- Use tools to scan for outdated or vulnerable libraries.
- Regularly update dependencies and apply patches.
- Avoid unverified third-party code.

Tools: Dependabot, Snyk, OWASP Dependency-Check.

Example:

```
<h1>Check dependencies in Node.js</h1> npm install -g  npm-audit
npm audit
```

1.6 Secure Coding in Development Lifecycle

Why: Embeds security in design, coding, and testing to prevent malware entry points. How:

- Conduct threat modeling in design (STRIDE methodology).
- Use static/dynamic analysis tools (SAST/DAST) in CI/CD pipelines.
- Perform code reviews with security checklists.

Tools: SonarQube (SAST), OWASP ZAP (DAST), GitHub CodeQL.

Example:

```
<h1>GitHub Actions for SAST</h1> name:
CodeQL
on: [push] jobs:  analyze:
runs-on: ubuntu-latest steps:
- uses: github/codeql-action/analyze@v2
```

2. Securing Web Applications

Web applications are prime targets for malware delivery (e.g., via XSS, CSRF). These practices focus on hardening web apps.

2.1 Implement Content Security Policy (CSP)

Why: Mitigates XSS by restricting script sources, blocking malicious code. How:

- Define strict CSP headers to allow only trusted domains.

- Use nonces or hashes for inline scripts.

Example:

```
<meta http-equiv="Content-Security-Policy" content="default-src 'self'; script-src 'self'  trusted.com; style-src 'self' trusted.com;">
```

2.2 Protect Against Cross-Site Request Forgery (CSRF)

Why: Prevents unauthorized actions by authenticated users. How:

- Use CSRF tokens in forms and AJAX requests.
- Validate tokens server-side.

Tools: CSRFGuard (Java), csurf middleware (Express.js).

Example:

```
const csurf = require('csurf'); app.use(csurf());
app.post('/form', (req, res) => {
if (req.csrfToken()) { /* Process form */ }
});
```

2.3 Secure API Endpoints

Why: APIs are entry points for Trojans exploiting SSRF (OWASP A10:2021). How:

- Use rate limiting and input validation.
- Authenticate API requests with JWT or API keys.
- Avoid exposing unnecessary endpoints.

Tools: Postman for testing, express-rate-limit.

Example:

```
const rateLimit = require('express-rate-limit'); app.use(rateLimit({ windowMs: 15 * 60 *  1000, max: 100 }));
```

2.4 Harden Server Configuration

Why: Prevents server misconfiguration (OWASP A05:2021) exploited by worms or ransomware. How:

- Disable unnecessary services and ports.
- Use secure headers (e.g., X-Frame-Options, HSTS).
- Regularly scan for misconfigurations.

Tools: Mozilla Observatory, helmet (Express.js).

Example:

```
const helmet = require('helmet'); app.use(helmet({
hsts: { maxAge: 31536000, includeSubDomains: true }, xFrameOptions: { action: 'deny' }
}));
```

2.5 Regular Testing and Patching

Why: Identifies vulnerabilities before exploitation. How:

- Conduct penetration testing and vulnerability scans.
- Apply patches promptly (within 30 days).
- Test for OWASP Top 10 vulnerabilities.

Tools: Burp Suite, Nessus, OWASP ZAP.

3. Training for Teams

Security Teams:

- **Advanced SSDLC training:** OWASP Secure Coding Practices, ISC2 CSSLP.
- **Hands-on labs:** Use TryHackMe or Hack The Box for XSS/CSRF scenarios.
- **Frequency:** Quarterly, with certifications every 2 years.

Non-Security Teams (Developers, Others):

- Basics of OWASP Top 10 and secure coding (e.g., input validation).
- Use gamified platforms like Secure Code Warrior or Immersive Labs.
- **Frequency:** Bi-annual refreshers, 1-2 hours per session.

4. Implementation Tips

Tools Budget:

$500-$2000/year for SAST/DAST tools; free options like OWASP ZAP are available.

Timeline:

Integrate practices in 3-6 months; start with input validation and CSP.

Metrics:

Reduce vulnerabilities by 30% in scans; achieve 95% patch compliance.

Resources:

OWASP Cheat Sheets, NIST SP 800-53, Microsoft Learn SSDLC modules.

Integrating Secure Coding into the Software Development Life Software development Life Cycle (SDLC)

Software assurance programs are designed to integrate security practices and principles throughout every phase of the SDLC. This shifts security from a reactive, last-minute check to a proactive, continuous process.

1. Requirements and Design Phase

- **Threat Modeling:** Identify potential threats and vulnerabilities early in the design process. This helps in understanding the attack surface of the application and prioritizing security efforts.
- **Secure Design Principles:** Incorporate security-by-design concepts, such as the principle of least privilege, defense in depth, and separation of duties.
- **Defining Security Requirements:** Explicitly state security requirements alongside functional requirements to ensure they are considered from the start.

2. Implementation and Coding Phase

This is where the general secure coding best practices outlined above are applied. Developers write code with security in mind, including:

- Securely handling all inputs and outputs.

- Using secure APIs and libraries.
- Writing well-commented and clean code to make security reviews easier.
- Conducting peer code reviews focused on security flaws.

3. Testing and Verification Phase

- **Static Application Security Testing (SAST):** Use automated tools to analyze the source code for security vulnerabilities without executing the application.
- **Dynamic Application Security Testing (DAST):** Test the running application from the outside to identify vulnerabilities like cross-site scripting and SQL injection.
- **Penetration Testing:** Ethical hackers attempt to find and exploit vulnerabilities to evaluate the application's overall security posture.
- **Vulnerability Scanning:** Regularly scan for known vulnerabilities in all dependencies and components.

4. Deployment and Operations Phase

- **Secure Configuration:** Ensure the production environment is configured securely, with unnecessary services and ports disabled.
- **Continuous Monitoring:** Use logging, monitoring, and intrusion detection systems to watch for suspicious activity.
- **Patch Management:** Implement a process to promptly apply security patches to the application and its underlyin g infrastructure.
- **Incident Response Plan:** Have a clear plan in place for how to respond to a security breach, including steps for containment, eradication, and recovery.

Understanding System Engineering Practices

System engineering is an interdisciplinary approach that focuses on the design, integration, and management of complex systems over their life cycles. It's a key practice for ensuring that a system is not only functional but also secure, reliable, and maintainable.

1. Requirements Management

- This practice involves defining, documenting, and managing the requirements of a system throughout its life cycle. From a security perspective, this means ensuring that security requirements are clear, testable, and prioritized alongside functional requirements.

2. Architectural Design

- System architecture is the conceptual model that defines the structure, behavior, and more views of a system. Secure architectural design involves making decisions that minimize the attack surface, enforce the principle of least privilege, and incorporate security controls at every layer.

3. System Integration

- This is the process of bringing together the component subsystems into one complete system. Integration can introduce new vulnerabilities, so it's critical to perform security testing at each integration point and to ensure secure communication between components.

4. Verification and Validation (V&V)

- V&V practices ensure that a system meets its specified requirements (verification) and serves its intended purpose (validation). From a security standpoint, this includes testing to confirm that all defined security requirements are met and that the system is resilient against anticipated threats.

5. Risk Management

- Risk management involves identifying, assessing, and mitigating risks to a system. This practice is foundational to security and includes activities like threat modeling, vulnerability assessments, and the development of a formal security risk register.

6. Configuration Management

- Configuration management is the process of managing changes to a system's configuration. This practice is vital for maintaining a secure baseline. It ensures that changes are tracked, approved, and that secure configurations are consistently deployed across all environments.

Software Vulnerability Analysis Techniques and Tools

Understanding how to find and analyze vulnerabilities is as crucial as knowing how to write secure code. These techniques use specialized tools to automate the process of discovering security flaws.

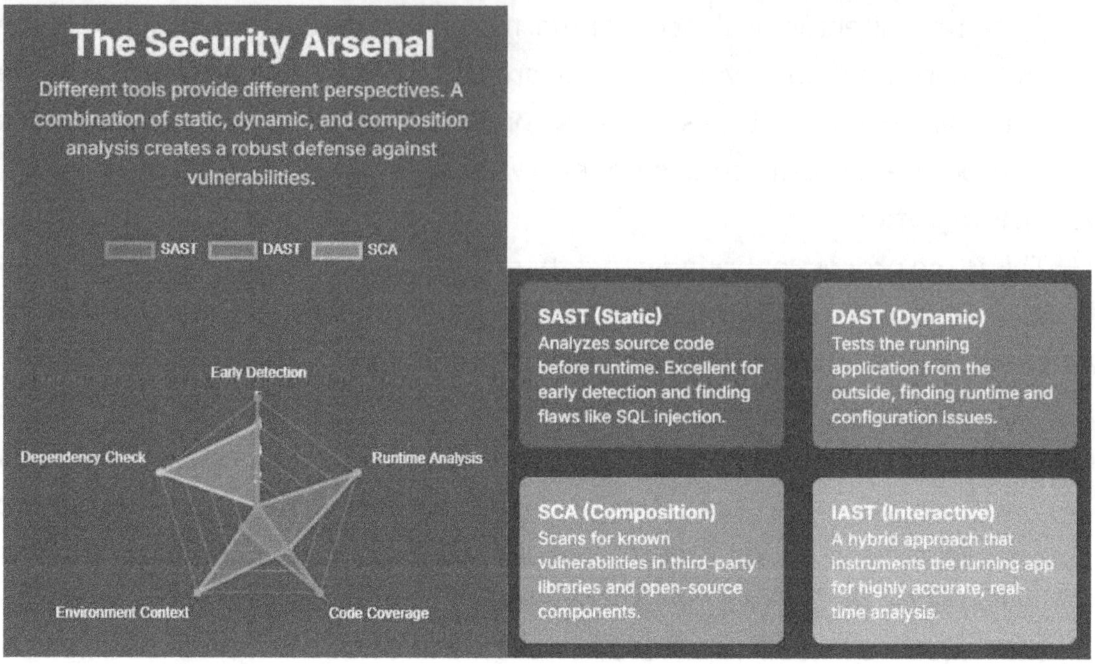

1. Static Code Analysis (SAST)

- Static analysis is the process of examining an application's source code without running it. SAST tools scan the code for patterns that indicate known security vulnerabilities. This technique is highly effective for finding issues early in the development process, often before the code is even compiled. Key benefits include:
- **Early Detection:** Finds vulnerabilities in the development phase, making them cheaper and easier to fix.
- **Comprehensive Coverage:** Can analyze the entire codebase, including parts that may not be executed during dynamic testing.
- **Specific Location:** Pinpoints the exact line of code where a vulnerability exists, helping developers quickly remediate the issue.

2. Dynamic Code Analysis (DAST)

- Dynamic analysis involves testing a running application to find security vulnerabilities. DAST tools simulate attacks and monitor the application's responses to identify weaknesses. This technique is particularly useful for detecting runtime vulnerabilities, such as configuration errors, weak authentication, and session management flaws.
- **Real-world Context:** Tests the application in its operational environment, including its interactions with databases, web servers, and other services.
- **Black-Box Testing:** Can be performed without access to the source code, making it suitable for testing third-party applications.

- **Discovering Misconfigurations:** Effective at finding vulnerabilities that result from incorrect server or application configurations.

3. Software Composition Analysis (SCA)

- SCA is a technique used to identify open-source components, their licenses, and any known vulnerabilities within them. With most modern applications relying heavily on open-source libraries, SCA is a critical part of a security program. SCA tools automatically scan an application's dependencies and compare them against public vulnerability databases.
- **Dependency Mapping:** Creates a complete inventory of all open-source and third- party components used by the application.
- **Vulnerability Monitoring:** Continuously monitors for new vulnerabilities announced for the components in use.
- **License Compliance:** Helps ensure that the use of open-source components adheres to their licensing terms.

4. Interactive Application Security Testing (IAST)

- IAST is a hybrid approach that combines elements of both SAST and DAST. It works by instrumenting the application from within the running environment, allowing it to perform detailed analysis of code and data flow in real-time. This provides more accurate results with fewer false positives, as it can trace the path of data from an input to an output.

Secure IT System Installation and Operation

This practice focuses on ensuring that IT systems are installed and operated in a controlled, secure manner, particularly within a test configuration. The primary goal is to prevent any changes to the program's code or any compromise of the security measures put in place during development.

- **Isolated Test Environments:** Utilize dedicated and isolated testing environments that are a near-perfect replica of the production system. This ensures that tests are conducted under realistic conditions without the risk of affecting the live system.
- **Read-Only Access:** Configure test accounts and automated tools with read-only access to the program code. This prevents accidental or malicious alterations to the source code during the testing phase.

- **Non-Production Data:** Use sanitized or dummy data in test environments. Never use real, sensitive production data to avoid the risk of a data breach during testing.
- **Configuration as Code:** Manage environment configurations using scripts or templates (e.g., Terraform, Ansible). This ensures consistency across development, testing, and production environments and reduces the risk of manual configuration errors that could introduce security flaws.
- **Immutable Infrastructure:** Use an immutable infrastructure model where servers and components are never updated in place. Instead, a new, fully configured instance is deployed to replace the old one. This guarantees that every environment is built from a secure, approved image.
- **Audit and Monitoring:** Implement robust logging and monitoring for all activities within the test environment. This provides a clear audit trail to detect any unauthorized access, configuration changes, or attempts to bypass security controls.

What is Operating System (OS) Hardening?

Operating system (OS) hardening is a security process that involves configuring a system to reduce its attack surface and minimize potential vulnerabilities. In simple terms, it's about "locking down" an OS by removing or disabling unnecessary components, services, and features that could be exploited by an attacker.

Unlike simply installing antivirus software or a firewall, hardening is a proactive measure that changes the fundamental configuration of the system itself. This makes the OS more resilient to a wide range of cyberattacks, from malware and phishing to sophisticated exploits.

The core principle behind hardening is the "Principle of Least Functionality," which states that a system should only have the bare minimum functionality required to perform its purpose. Every additional service, port, or user account adds a potential entry point for a malicious actor.

What is OS Hardening?

OS hardening is the process of securing a system by reducing its attack surface. This involves removing unnecessary software, disabling non-essential services, and configuring security settings to their most secure state. It's a foundational step in protecting against cyberattacks.

The core idea is the "Principle of Least Functionality": a system should only have the features and access necessary to perform its intended function, and nothing more.

Reduce Your Attack Surface

80%

Proper hardening can eliminate up to 80% of potential entry points for attackers by removing default and unused components.

Common OS Vulnerabilities and Attacks

Before a system can be secured, it's essential to understand the types of vulnerabilities and attacks that an OS can face.

Common Vulnerabilities

- **Software and Configuration Bugs:** Flaws in code or misconfigured settings that can be exploited. These are often the easiest to fix through proper patch management and configuration.
- **Unpatched Software:** Known weaknesses in software that have not been addressed with the latest security updates.
- **Default Settings:** Leaving default usernames, passwords, or open ports can create easy entry points for attackers.
- **Weak User Authentication:** Using simple passwords, shared accounts, or not enforcing multi-factor authentication.
- **Unnecessary Services:** Running services or applications that are not critical for the system's function, increasing the attack surface.

Common Attacks

- **Malware:** Malicious software (e.g., viruses, ransomware, spyware) designed to disrupt or gain unauthorized access to a system.
- **Denial of Service (DoS):** An attack that overwhelms a system's resources, making it unavailable to legitimate users.
- **Unauthorized Access:** Gaining control of a system or data without proper permissions, often through exploited vulnerabilities or stolen credentials.

- **Privilege Escalation:** An attacker who has gained basic access to a system seeks to gain higher-level permissions (e.g., from a standard user to an administrator).
- **Man-in-the-Middle (MitM):** An attack where an attacker secretly intercepts and relays messages between two parties who believe they are communicating directly.

Developing a Hardening Plan

Creating a comprehensive hardening plan is a critical step to ensure that security measures are applied consistently and effectively.

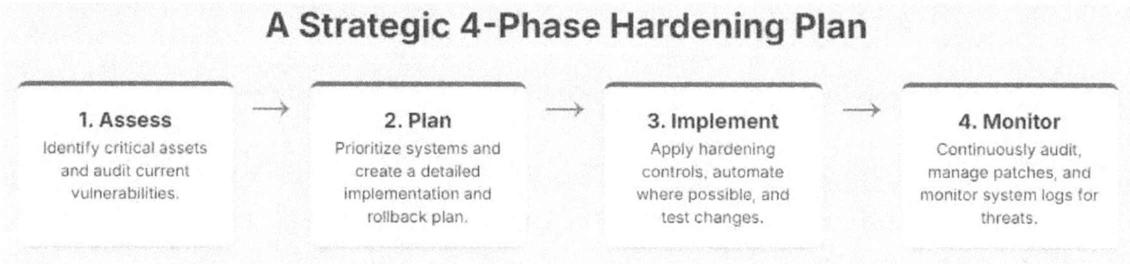

Phase 1: Assessment and Discovery

- **Identify Critical Assets:** Determine which systems are most critical to your organization. These should be prioritized for hardening.
- **Conduct a Baseline Audit:** Perform a security audit of your current systems to identify existing vulnerabilities and misconfigurations.
- **Define Security Requirements:** Based on the audit and business needs, establish a clear set of security requirements and policies.

Phase 2: Planning and Strategy

- **Prioritize Systems:** Based on the assessment, create a prioritized list of systems to be hardened, starting with the most critical and vulnerable.
- **Create a Rollback Plan:** Before making any changes, have a plan to revert to the previous state in case of unexpected issues.
- **Define Roles and Responsibilities:** Clearly assign who is responsible for each step of the hardening process.

Phase 3: Implementation and Remediation

- **Apply Hardening Controls:** Systematically apply the security controls and best practices outlined in this guide.
- **Use Automation:** Wherever possible, use configuration management tools to automate the hardening process, ensuring consistency and efficiency.

- **Test After Changes:** After applying each set of changes, test the system to ensure that its functionality has not been negatively impacted.

Phase 4: Monitoring and Maintenance

- **Establish Continuous Auditing:** Regularly audit the hardened systems to detect any configuration drift or new vulnerabilities.
- **Implement Patch Management:** Follow a regular schedule for identifying, testing, and deploying patches.
- **Monitor Logs and Alerts:** Continuously monitor system logs for signs of suspicious activity and respond to security alerts promptly.

Key OS Hardening Practices

Hardening is not a one-time task but an ongoing process that should be integrated into a system's lifecycle. Below is a concise overview of key practices for hardening an operating system, applicable to common systems like Windows, Linux, or macOS.

Windows	Linux	macOS
• Use Group Policy to enforce security settings.	• Use SELinux or AppArmor for access control.	• Enable Gatekeeper to restrict apps.
• Apply Microsoft Security Baselines.	• Harden SSH: disable root login, use keys.	• Configure privacy settings to limit data access.
• Restrict PowerShell access for non-admins.	• Regularly check for outdated packages.	• Use the built-in `pf` firewall.

1. Minimize Attack Surface

- **Remove Unnecessary Software**: Uninstall unused applications and disable unnecessary services or daemons to reduce potential entry points.
- **Disable Unused Features**: Turn off features like remote desktop, file sharing, or unused protocols (e.g., SMBv1) unless required.

2. Patch Management Process

Patch management is the process of identifying, acquiring, testing, and deploying patches to address software vulnerabilities. A well-defined process is crucial for maintaining a secure and stable environment.

- **Regular Patching**: Keep the OS and all software up to date with the latest security patches to address known vulnerabilities.
- **Enable Automatic Updates**: Configure the system to automatically download and

install updates where feasible.

- **Assessment**: Continuously identify new security patches and updates from software vendors. This can be done through vendor websites, mailing lists, or automated tools.
- **Testing**: Before deploying patches to a production environment, test them in a non- production or staging environment to ensure they don't cause new problems or disrupt critical services.
- **Deployment**: Deploy patches systematically, starting with non-critical systems and gradually moving to more critical ones. Use automated tools to streamline this process across many systems.
- **Verification**: After deployment, verify that the patches have been applied successfully and the systems are functioning as expected.

3. Configure User Accounts and Permissions

- **Least Privilege Principle**: Use non-administrative accounts for daily tasks. Restrict root or administrator access to essential tasks.
- **Strong Password Policies**: Enforce complex passwords, multi-factor authentication (MFA), and regular password rotation.
- **Disable Guest Accounts**: Remove or disable default guest accounts to prevent unauthorized access.

4. Secure File System and Permissions

- **Restrict File Permissions**: Limit access to sensitive files and directories (e.g., /etc, C:\Windows) to authorized users only.
- **Use Encryption**: Enable full-disk encryption (e.g., BitLocker for Windows, FileVault for macOS, LUKS for Linux) to protect data at rest.

5. Network Security

- **Firewall Configuration:** Enable and configure a firewall to block unauthorized inbound and outbound traffic. Allow only necessary ports and services.
- **Disable Unused Network Services**: Turn off services like Telnet, FTP, or unnecessary ports (e.g., 445 for SMB).
- **Use Secure Protocols**: Prefer SSH over Telnet, HTTPS over HTTP, and enforce TLS for network communications.

6. Configuration Management for Information System Security

Configuration management is the process of maintaining a consistent and known state of your systems. It ensures that security policies and hardening measures are consistently applied and not inadvertently reverted.

- **Automate Security Policies**: Use configuration management tools like Ansible, Puppet, or Chef to define security configurations as code. This allows you to automatically enforce security settings across your entire infrastructure.
- **Baseline Configuration**: Establish a secure baseline configuration for all system types. Any deviations from this baseline should be flagged and remediated.
- **Drift Detection**: Regularly audit systems to detect "configuration drift," where a system's configuration has changed from the secure baseline.

7. Understanding and Monitoring System Logs

System logs are a critical source of information for security monitoring and incident response. They record events, user activities, and system processes.

- **Enable Auditing**: Configure system logs to track user activity, system events, and potential security incidents.
- **What to Look For**: Monitor logs for key security events, such as:
    - Failed login attempts (potential brute-force attacks)
    - Changes to user accounts or permissions
    - Service restarts or shutdowns
    - Firewall block messages and unauthorized network traffic
    - Execution of suspicious scripts or programs
- **Centralized Logging**: Use tools like Syslog or Windows Event Forwarding to aggregate logs from multiple systems into a central location. This makes analysis easier and protects logs from being tampered with on a compromised system.
- **Monitor for Anomalies**: Regularly review logs for suspicious activity using tools like Splunk or ELK Stack.

8. Antivirus and Endpoint Protection

- **Install Antivirus Software**: Use reputable antivirus or endpoint detection and response (EDR) tools to detect and mitigate malware.
- **Regular Scans**: Schedule periodic scans to identify and remove threats.

9. Backup and Recovery

- **Regular Backups**: Maintain secure, encrypted backups of critical data and system configurations.
- **Test Restores**: Periodically verify that backups can be restored to ensure data integrity.

10. Physical Security

- **Secure Location**: Store servers in a locked room or data center with limited physical access.

- **Access Control**: Use strong access control measures, such as key cards, biometric scanners, or security personnel to control entry.
- **Environmental Controls**: Protect systems from environmental risks like fire, water damage, and extreme temperatures. Use fire suppression systems and maintain proper cooling and power redundancy.

11. Security Policies and Compliance

- **Follow Standards**: Adhere to frameworks like CIS Benchmarks, NIST 800-53, or DISA STIGs for OS-specific hardening guidelines.
- **Regular Audits**: Conduct security assessments to identify and address misconfigurations or vulnerabilities.

OS-Specific Considerations

Windows:

- Use Group Policy to enforce security settings (e.g., password policies, account lockout).
- Disable PowerShell for non-admin users if not needed.
- Apply Microsoft Security Baselines for standardized configurations.

Linux:

- Use tools like SELinux or AppArmor for mandatory access control.
- Harden SSH by disabling root login and using key-based authentication.
- Regularly check for outdated packages with apt, yum, or dnf.

macOS:

- Enable Gatekeeper to restrict unverified apps.
- Configure privacy settings to limit app access to sensitive data.
- Use pf firewall for network traffic control.

Tools for OS Hardening

- **CIS-CAT**: Assesses compliance with CIS Benchmarks.
- **Lynis**: Open-source auditing tool for Linux/Unix systems.
- **Microsoft Defender**: Built-in security for Windows.
- **OpenSCAP**: Security compliance for Linux systems.

Best Practices

- **Document Configurations:** Maintain records of all hardening steps for consistency and audits.

- **Test Changes**: Apply changes in a test environment before deploying to production to avoid disruptions.
- **Stay Informed**: Monitor CVE databases and vendor advisories for emerging threats.

An Overview of Encryption Technologies

Encryption technologies are methods and tools used to secure data by transforming it into an unreadable format, accessible only to those with the correct key or credentials. They're critical for protecting sensitive information in transit and at rest, ensuring confidentiality, integrity, and authenticity. Below is an overview of key encryption technologies, concepts, and their applications, tailored to provide a clear and concise understanding.

The Core of Digital Trust

Encryption is the bedrock of online privacy, transforming readable data into a secure, scrambled format. Let's explore the fundamental concepts that make this possible.

98%

of all internet traffic is now encrypted

Core Encryption Concepts

- **Symmetric Encryption**: Uses a single key for both encryption and decryption. Fast and efficient for large data volumes but requires secure key sharing.
    - Examples: AES (Advanced Encryption Standard), DES (Data Standard, now outdated).
- **Asymmetric Encryption**: Uses a pair of keys (public and private). The public key encrypts, and the private key decrypts. Slower but secure for key exchange and authentication.
    - Examples: RSA, ECC (Elliptic Curve Cryptography).
- **Hashing**: Converts data into a fixed-length string (hash) to verify integrity, not reversible. Not encryption but often used alongside it.
    - Examples: SHA-256, MD5 (less secure).
- **Key Exchange Protocols:** Enable secure sharing of encryption keys over insecure channels.
    - Examples: Diffie-Hellman, ECDH (Elliptic Curve Diffie-Hellman).

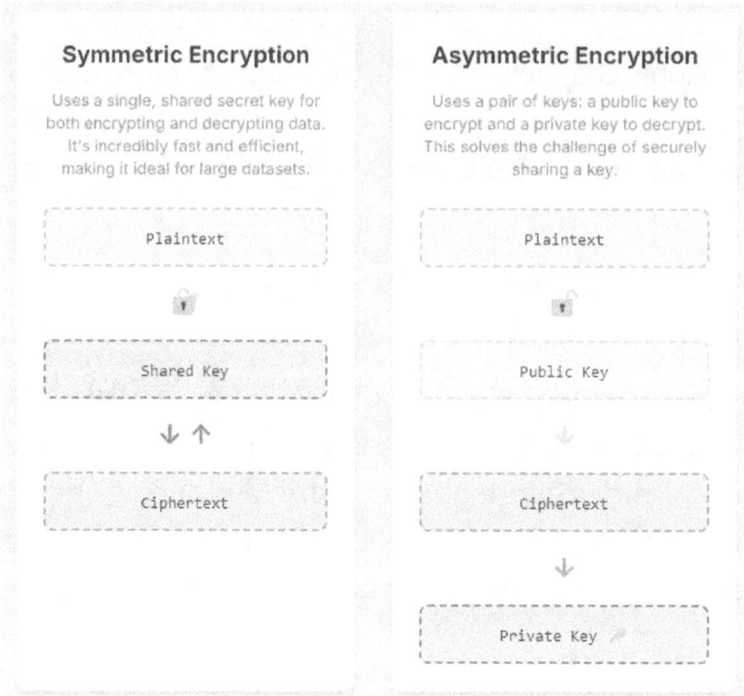

Components of a Cryptosystem

A cryptosystem is a complete set of algorithms and practices that provide secure communication. It is made up of several key components that work together to transform data from a readable form to a secure one and back again.

- **Plaintext**: The original, unencrypted message or data that is human-readable. This is the information you want to protect.
- **Ciphertext**: The encrypted, scrambled, or unreadable data that is the output of the encryption process. It is the protected version of the plaintext.
- **Algorithm (or Cipher)**: The mathematical procedure or set of rules used for both the encryption and decryption processes. This defines how the plaintext is transformed into ciphertext and vice-versa.
- **Key**: A piece of secret information—typically a string of bits—that is used with the algorithm to perform the encryption and decryption. The key is what makes the encryption process unique and secure. Without the correct key, it is computationally infeasible to decrypt the ciphertext.
- **Encryption**: The process of using the algorithm and key to convert plaintext into ciphertext. This is the act of securing the data.
- **Decryption**: The reverse process of using the algorithm and key to convert ciphertext back into plaintext. This is the act of restoring the original, readable data.

Major Encryption Technologies

AES (Advanced Encryption Standard):

- Widely used symmetric encryption algorithm.
- Key sizes: 128, 192, or 256 bits (AES-256 is most secure).
- Applications: Disk encryption (BitLocker), VPNs, secure communications (TLS/SSL).
- Strength: Highly secure, fast, and adopted by NIST as a standard.

RSA (Rivest-Shamir-Adleman):

- Asymmetric algorithm based on prime number factorization.
- Key sizes: Typically 2048 or 4096 bits.
- Applications: Secure key exchange, digital signatures, SSL/TLS certificates.
- Limitation: Slower than symmetric encryption, used for small data like keys.

ECC (Elliptic Curve Cryptography):

- Asymmetric encryption using elliptic curve mathematics.
- Smaller key sizes (e.g., 256-bit ECC ≈ 3072-bit RSA) for equivalent security).
- Applications: Mobile devices, blockchain (e.g., Bitcoin wallets), TLS.
- Advantage: Efficient for resource-constrained environments.

RSA vs. ECC: A Comparison

The choice between RSA and ECC depends on the specific application and its security requirements. While both are powerful asymmetric algorithms, they differ significantly in their underlying mathematics, performance, and key sizes.

RSA vs. ECC: The Asymmetric Showdown

Elliptic Curve Cryptography (ECC) provides the same level of security as RSA but with significantly smaller key sizes, making it faster and more efficient for modern devices.

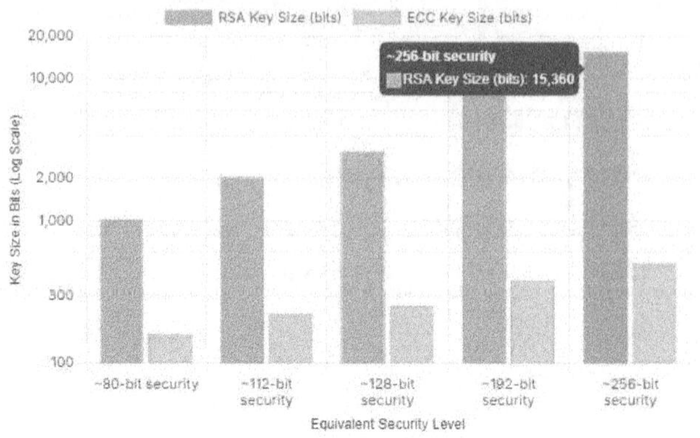

Feature	RSA (Rivest-Shamir-Adleman)	ECC (Elliptic Curve Cryptography)
Mathematical Foundation	Based on the difficulty of factoring large integers.	Based on the difficulty of solving the elliptic curve discrete logarithm problem.
Key Size	Requires much larger key sizes for equivalent security. e.g., 2048-bit key for standard security.	Requires significantly smaller key sizes for equivalent security. e.g., 256-bit key for standard security.
Performance	Slower for key generation, signing, and encryption. Becomes computationally expensive as key size increases.	Faster for key generation and signing. More efficient for both encryption and decryption.
Resource Usage	Higher CPU and memory consumption. Not ideal for low-power or IoT devices.	Lower CPU and memory consumption. Well-suited for mobile, embedded systems, and IoT devices.
Security	Considered secure against classical attacks. Vulnerable to quantum attacks via Shor's algorithm.	Considered secure against classical attacks. Also vulnerable to quantum attacks via Shor's algorithm.

Common Use Cases	Digital certificates (SSL/TLS), secure email (PGP/GPG), general data encryption.	Mobile communications, cryptocurrencies (Bitcoin, Ethereum), secure messaging, and IoT.
Adoption	A long-standing, well-understood, and widely adopted standard.	Increasing in adoption due to its efficiency and smaller key sizes.

Major Encryption Technologies (Continued)

TLS/SSL (Transport Layer Security/Secure Sockets Layer):

- Protocols combining symmetric and asymmetric encryption to secure internet communications.
- Applications: HTTPS websites, email, VPNs.
- Process: Asymmetric encryption (e.g., RSA/ECC) for key exchange, then symmetric encryption (e.g., AES) for data transfer.

PGP (Pretty Good Privacy) and GPG (GNU Privacy Guard):

- Combines symmetric and asymmetric encryption for secure file and email encryption.
- Applications: Email encryption, file signing, secure data sharing.
- Example: Encrypts email with recipient's public key, decryptable only with their private key.

Post-Quantum Cryptography (PQC)

PQC refers to cryptographic algorithms designed to be secure against attacks from both classical and quantum computers. This field is a critical response to the threat posed by quantum computers, which with algorithms like Shor's, could break widely used asymmetric cryptography (RSA, ECC). The "harvest now, decrypt later" threat is a major driver for PQC, where adversaries steal encrypted data today, knowing they can decrypt it in the future once a sufficiently powerful quantum computer exists.

- **NIST Standardization**: The National Institute of Standards and Technology (NIST) has been leading a global effort to standardize new PQC algorithms. In 2024, they announced the first set of algorithms to be standardized:
    - **CRYSTALS-Kyber (now ML-KEM)**: A key-establishment algorithm based on lattice-based cryptography, intended as the primary standard for general encryption. It offers a secure and efficient way for two parties to agree on a shared secret key.
    - **CRYSTALS-Dilithium (now ML-DSA)**: A digital signature algorithm also based on lattices, designated as the primary standard for protecting digital signatures.
    - **SPHINCS+ (now SLH-DSA)**: A hash-based digital signature algorithm that serves as a secondary standard. It is stateless and does not require a trusted setup, making it a robust backup in case lattice-based methods are later found to be vulnerable.

- **Underlying Mathematical Problems**: Unlike RSA and ECC which rely on number theory problems that quantum computers can solve, PQC algorithms are based on different, "hard" mathematical problems that are believed to be resistant to quantum attacks. The NIST-selected algorithms primarily rely on **lattice-based cryptography**, which involves high-dimensional grids and problems that are computationally difficult to solve, even for a quantum computer.
- **Implementation and Migration**: The transition to PQC is a massive, multi-year undertaking. Governments and organizations are now developing roadmaps to migrate their systems, with many implementing a **hybrid approach** that combines both classical and PQC algorithms. This provides a defense-in-depth strategy, ensuring that systems remain secure even if one of the algorithms is compromised.

Homomorphic Encryption (HE):

Allows computations on encrypted data without first decrypting it. The result of a homomorphic operation is a new ciphertext, which, when decrypted, is the same as the result of the same operation on the original plaintext.

Types of HE:

- **Partially Homomorphic Encryption (PHE)**: Supports a single type of mathematical operation (e.g., addition or multiplication) an unlimited number of times. RSA is a type of multiplicative PHE.
- **Somewhat Homomorphic Encryption (SHE)**: Supports a limited number of both addition and multiplication operations.
- **Fully Homomorphic Encryption (FHE)**: The most advanced type, allowing for an unlimited number of both addition and multiplication operations. This enables any arbitrary computation on encrypted data, often referred to as cryptography's "holy grail."
- **Applications**: Secure cloud computing (data can be processed by a third-party cloud provider without them ever seeing the plaintext), secure data analysis in healthcare or finance, and private machine learning.
- **Limitation**: Still very computationally intensive and slower than traditional encryption, requiring significant resources.

Zero-Knowledge Proofs (ZKP):

A method for a "prover" to demonstrate to a "verifier" that a statement is true without revealing any information other than the validity of the statement itself. A classic example is proving you know the secret to a cave without revealing the secret.

Key Properties:

- **Completeness**: If the statement is true, an honest prover can always convince the verifier.
- **Soundness**: If the statement is false, a dishonest prover cannot convince the verifier.
- **Zero-Knowledge**: If the statement is true, the verifier learns nothing except that the statement is true.

Common Types:

- **zk-SNARKs** (Zero-Knowledge Succinct Non-Interactive Argument of Knowledge): Generate very small, easily verifiable proofs. They require a "trusted setup" to generate a public parameter string, which can be a point of security concern if not handled properly.

- **zk-STARKs** (Zero-Knowledge Scalable Transparent Argument of Knowledge): Do not require a trusted setup, making them "transparent" and more scalable for large computations. They are also considered quantum-resistant but typically produce larger proofs than zk-SNARKs.
- **Applications**: Blockchain (e.g., Zcash for private transactions, scalable Layer 2 solutions), secure authentication (proving age or identity without revealing personal details), and verifiable computation where a user can prove they ran a computation correctly without revealing the inputs.

The Role of AI in Cryptography

The relationship between artificial intelligence and cryptography is a complex and evolving one, with AI serving as both a new threat and a powerful tool for enhancing security.

AI as a Threat to Cryptography

AI can be used by malicious actors to scale and automate attacks in ways that were previously impossible, creating new risks for cryptographic systems.

- **Accelerated Cryptanalysis**: AI and machine learning algorithms can analyze vast amounts of data to find patterns and vulnerabilities in cryptographic algorithms or their implementations. While they are not yet capable of breaking well-designed, modern ciphers like AES, they can exploit weaker or custom ciphers and accelerate existing attack methods.
- **Side-Channel Attacks**: AI models can be trained on "side-channel data" such as power consumption, electromagnetic emissions, or timing variations from a device to deduce the cryptographic key being used. This form of attack bypasses the mathematical strength of the encryption and targets the physical implementation.
- **Sophisticated Social Engineering**: AI, particularly Large Language Models, can generate highly convincing phishing emails, deepfakes, and other forms of social engineering content that are difficult for humans to detect. These attacks aim to trick individuals into revealing plaintext data or cryptographic keys, rendering the encryption useless.
- **Implementation Flaws**: The primary threat from AI is not that it will break the math behind encryption, but that it will find and exploit flaws in how we implement and use it. AI is excellent at pattern recognition and can discover subtle weaknesses in code,

metadata, and user behavior.

AI as an Enhancement for Cryptography

AI is also being used as a critical tool to build stronger and more resilient cryptographic systems, helping defenders stay ahead of attackers.

- **Adaptive and Automated Encryption**: AI can enable systems to adapt their security in real-time. For example, a system could use machine learning to detect suspicious network activity and automatically increase the encryption strength or rotate keys more frequently to counter a potential attack.
- **Enhanced Key Generation**: Traditional key generation relies on pseudorandom number generators. AI can be used to analyze large datasets to find more complex, irregular, and truly random patterns, creating more robust and unpredictable keys that are much harder to guess or brute-force.
- **Predictive Threat Detection**: AI-powered security systems can analyze real-time network traffic and logs to predict and detect security breaches before they occur. This allows organizations to proactively strengthen their defenses, moving from a reactive to an anticipatory security posture.
- **Development of Post-Quantum Cryptography (PQC)**: AI is being used as a research tool to help design and evaluate new PQC algorithms. By analyzing complex mathematical structures, AI can help cryptographers identify potential weaknesses or efficiencies in quantum-resistant algorithms, accelerating the development of a secure post-quantum future.

Applications of Encryption Technologies

- **Data Protection**: Encrypting sensitive data (e.g., credit card info, health records) in databases or storage.
- **Secure Communication**: HTTPS, VPNs, and encrypted messaging (e.g., Signal, WhatsApp using Signal Protocol).
- **Authentication**: Digital signatures and certificates to verify identity (e.g., in blockchain, SSL certificates).
- **Cloud Security**: Encrypting data before uploading to cloud services.
- **IoT Security**: Protecting data on resource-constrained devices using lightweight encryption like ECC.

Emerging Trends and Challenges

- **Quantum Threat**: Quantum computers, using algorithms like Shor's, could efficiently factor the large prime numbers that secure asymmetric encryption like RSA and ECC. This poses a "harvest now, decrypt later" threat, where encrypted data is stolen today to be decrypted in the future. PQC, such as lattice-based cryptography, is being developed to counter this, and the NIST Post-Quantum Cryptography Standardization project is a major global effort to establish new, quantum-resistant algorithms.
- **Regulatory Compliance**: Laws like GDPR (General Data Protection Regulation) and CCPA (California Consumer Privacy Act) mandate the use of "reasonable" and "appropriate" security measures for personal data, with encryption often being a core requirement. Other regulations like HIPAA for health data and PCI DSS for payment cards also require specific encryption standards. Non-compliance can result in significant fines and legal action.
- **Performance vs. Security**: There is a constant trade-off between strong encryption (larger key sizes, more complex algorithms) and performance (speed, CPU usage, battery life). For resource-constrained devices like those in the Internet of Things (IoT), this is a critical challenge. Developers must balance the need for robust security with the practical limitations of the hardware, often leading to the use of more efficient, yet still secure, algorithms like ECC.
- **Key Management**: Securely generating, storing, distributing, and revoking cryptographic keys is one of the most significant challenges in maintaining a secure system. If a key is compromised, all data it protects is at risk. This is why robust key management systems (KMS) and hardware security modules (HSMs) are essential for protecting the keys themselves from theft or misuse.

Notable Implementations

- **Signal Protocol**: The Signal Protocol is a non-federated cryptographic protocol that provides end-to-end encryption for voice, video, and instant messaging conversations. It uses a combination of cryptographic primitives, including the **Extended Diffie-Hellman (X3DH) key agreement protocol** to establish a shared secret, and the **Double Ratchet Algorithm** for ongoing perfect forward secrecy and future secrecy. It also employs algorithms like AES-256 for symmetric encryption and Curve25519 for elliptic curve cryptography.

- **Tor Network**: The Tor network is an open-source software project that enables anonymous communication. It directs Internet traffic through a free, worldwide, volunteer overlay network, consisting of more than seven thousand relays, to conceal a user's location and usage from network surveillance. Tor uses layered encryption, often referred to as **onion routing**. The user's data is encrypted multiple times with the public keys of each relay in the circuit. This ensures that each relay only knows the identity of the previous and next relay, making it extremely difficult to trace the traffic back to its source.
- **Blockchain**: Blockchain is a distributed digital ledger that relies heavily on cryptography to ensure security and integrity. The technology uses **Elliptic Curve Cryptography (ECC)** for generating the public and private key pairs that secure user wallets. A private key is used to digitally sign a transaction, which can be verified by anyone using the corresponding public key. Furthermore, blockchains use **cryptographic hash functions**, such as **SHA-256**, to link blocks together and to create a tamper-proof record of transactions. The Proof-of-Work consensus mechanism, used by Bitcoin, also relies on solving a cryptographic puzzle that involves repeated hashing.

Algorithm and Technology Recommendations

When building a secure system, a layered and modern approach is best. Here are some general recommendations for algorithm and technology choices:

For Data at Rest (e.g., database, file storage): Use a strong, symmetric encryption algorithm.

- **Recommendation: AES-256-GCM**. AES-256 provides the highest level of security for the AES standard, and GCM (Galois/Counter Mode) adds authenticated encryption, which protects both confidentiality and integrity of the data.

For Data in Transit (e.g., web traffic, API calls): Use a secure, standardized protocol that combines asymmetric and symmetric encryption.

- **Recommendation: TLS 1.3.** This is the latest version of the Transport Layer Security protocol. It uses ephemeral Diffie-Hellman key exchange for perfect forward secrecy and a modern symmetric cipher like AES-256-GCM. Using TLS 1.3 is an industry best practice for all web traffic (HTTPS).

For Digital Signatures and Authentication: Use a modern, efficient asymmetric algorithm.

- **Recommendation**: **ECC (specifically, Ed25519).** Ed25519 is a specific elliptic curve digital signature algorithm that is known for its high speed, small key sizes, and strong security. It is an excellent modern alternative to RSA for digital signatures.

For Key Exchange: Use a key exchange protocol that provides perfect forward secrecy.

- **Recommendation**: **ECDH (Elliptic Curve Diffie-Hellman).** ECDH is a core component of modern TLS and other secure protocols. It allows two parties to agree on a shared secret key over an insecure channel, ensuring that if a long-term key is compromised, past communications remain secure.

For Post-Quantum Readiness: Plan for a smooth transition to quantum-resistant cryptography.

- **Recommendation**: **Hybrid approach**. While PQC algorithms are not yet widely adopted, it is best practice to begin planning for a hybrid approach. This involves

  using both a classical algorithm (like ECC or RSA) and a new, quantum-resistant one (like ML-KEM or ML-DSA) in parallel. This provides a robust defense and ensures security against both classical and future quantum threats.

For Hashing: Use a modern, collision-resistant hash function.

- **Recommendation**: **SHA-256 or SHA-384**. These algorithms are part of the SHA-2 family and are currently considered secure for a wide range of applications, including data integrity checks and password storage. Avoid older algorithms like MD5 or SHA-1, which have known vulnerabilities.

Vulnerability Assessment and Penetration Testing (VAPT)

Vulnerability Assessment and Penetration Testing (VAPT) are critical cybersecurity practices to identify and mitigate security weaknesses in systems, networks, or applications. Below, I'll explain each, their differences, and key considerations, aiming for clarity and conciseness while addressing the topic comprehensively.

What is VAPT?

Vulnerability Assessment and Penetration Testing (VAPT) are two distinct but complementary security disciplines. A Vulnerability Assessment provides a broad, automated scan to find potential weaknesses, while a Penetration Test simulates a real-world attack to see if those weaknesses can actually be exploited. Together, they offer a holistic view of an organization's security posture.

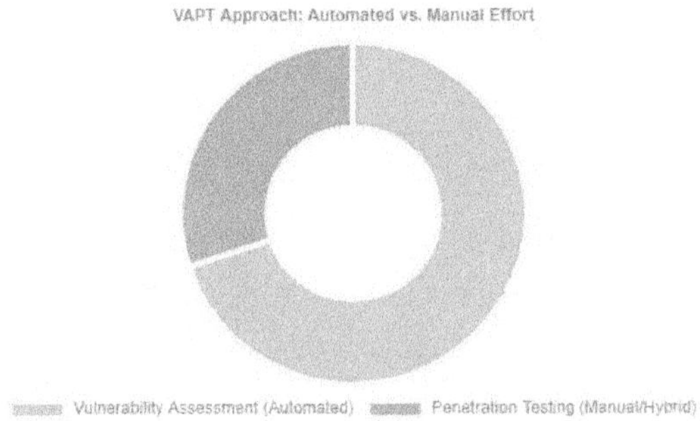

Vulnerability Assessment

A **Vulnerability Assessment** is a systematic process to identify, classify, and prioritize security vulnerabilities in a system. It's typically automated, using tools to scan for known weaknesses, misconfigurations, or outdated software.

- **Purpose**: Discover potential security gaps before they can be exploited.
- **Process**:
    - **Discovery**: Scan systems, networks, or applications to identify assets (e.g., servers, endpoints, software).
    - **Vulnerability Scanning**: Use tools like Nessus, Qualys, or OpenVAS to detect known vulnerabilities (e.g., unpatched software, weak passwords).
    - **Analysis**: Categorize vulnerabilities by severity (e.g., critical, high, medium, low) based on CVSS scores or exploitability.
    - **Reporting**: Provide a detailed report with vulnerabilities, their impact, and remediation recommendations.
- **Tools**: Nessus, Qualys, Burp Suite Scanner, Nmap, OWASP ZAP.
- **Frequency**: Regular scans (e.g., quarterly, after major changes) to maintain security posture.

- **Output**: A list of vulnerabilities with details like CVE IDs, affected systems, and suggested fixes.

Penetration Testing

A **Penetration Test** (pen test) simulates real-world cyberattacks to exploit vulnerabilities and assess the system's resilience. It's typically manual or semi-automated, conducted by ethical hackers mimicking attacker techniques.

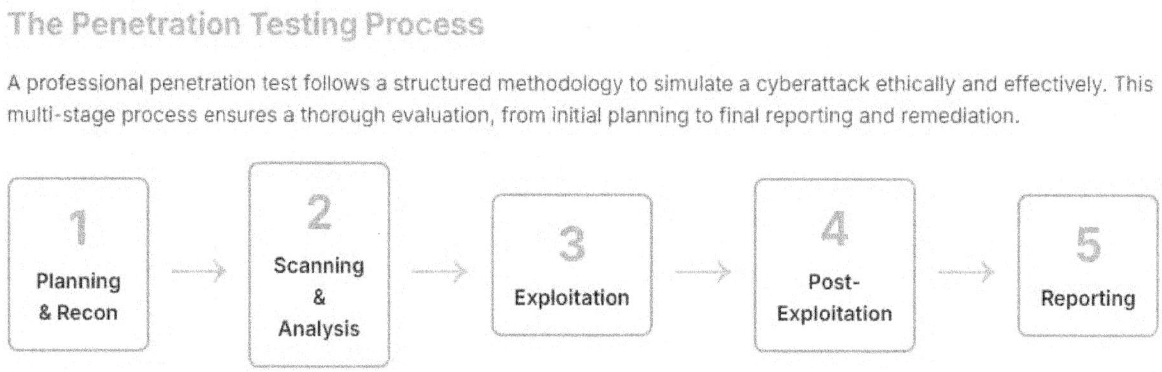

- **Purpose**: Test the exploitability of vulnerabilities and evaluate defenses under realistic attack scenarios.
- **Process**:
    - **Planning**: Define scope, goals, and rules of engagement (e.g., systems to test, allowed techniques).
    - **Reconnaissance**: Gather information about the target (e.g., OSINT, network mapping).
    - **Exploitation**: Attempt to exploit vulnerabilities to gain unauthorized access, escalate privileges, or extract data.
    - **Post-Exploitation**: Assess the impact (e.g., data exfiltration, persistence) and test detection capabilities.
    - Reporting: Document findings, exploited vulnerabilities, attack paths, and remediation steps.
- Types:
    - **Black Box**: No prior knowledge of the system (external attacker perspective).
    - **White Box**: Full knowledge of system architecture (insider perspective).
    - **Gray Box**: Partial knowledge (hybrid approach).

- **Tools**: Metasploit, Burp Suite, Kali Linux, Nmap, Wireshark, custom scripts.
- **Frequency**: Conducted periodically (e.g., annually) or after a system change.

- **Output**: A detailed report with exploited vulnerabilities, attack success, and mitigation strategies.

Key Differences

Aspect	Vulnerability Assessment	Penetration Testing
Objective	Identify and prioritize vulnerabilities	Exploit vulnerabilities to test defenses
Approach	Mostly automated	Manual or semi-automated
Depth	Broad, surface-level scanning	In-depth, targeted exploitation
Skill Level	Moderate (tool-driven)	High (requires expertise)
Time	Faster (hours to days)	Slower (days to weeks)
Cost	Lower	Higher due to expertise and effort
Outcome	List of potential vulnerabilities	Proof of exploitation and impact

Combined Approach (VAPT)

VAPT combines both practices for a comprehensive security evaluation:

- **Vulnerability Assessment** identifies weaknesses.
- **Penetration Testing** validates which vulnerabilities are exploitable and their real- world impact.
- **Benefits**:
    - Holistic view of security posture.
    - Prioritizes remediation based on exploitability.
    - Reduces false positives from automated scans.
- **Use Case**: Required for compliance (e.g., PCI DSS, ISO 27001) or to secure critical systems.

Best Practices

- **Define Scope**: Clearly outline systems, applications, or networks to be tested to avoid unintended disruptions.
- **Engage Experts**: For pen testing, hire certified professionals (e.g., CEH, OSCP, CISSP).
- **Use Reputable Tools**: Combine open-source (e.g., OpenVAS) and commercial tools for accuracy.

- **Remediate Promptly**: Prioritize high-severity vulnerabilities and verify fixes through retesting.
- **Regular Testing**: Schedule assessments and pen tests to address new vulnerabilities and evolving threats.
- **Compliance**: Align with standards like NIST, GDPR, or industry-specific requirements.
- **Documentation**: Maintain detailed reports for audits and future reference.

Challenges

- **False Positives**: Vulnerability scans may flag non-issues, requiring manual validation.
- **Scope Creep**: Pen testing can disrupt operations if not carefully scoped.
- **Resource Intensive**: Pen testing requires skilled professionals and time.
- **Evolving Threats**: New vulnerabilities emerge constantly, requiring continuous monitoring.

The Gap Between VAPT and Real-World Attacks

While VAPT is a powerful and necessary security measure, it's crucial to understand that it does not provide a complete defense against all real-world attacks. A significant gap exists between the controlled, time-bound nature of a VAPT and the persistent, adaptive nature of an attacker's campaign.

Key Factors Creating the Gap

- **Scope and Time Limitations**: A VAPT is a snapshot in time. It is conducted over a defined period (e.g., a few weeks) and focuses on a specific, agreed-upon scope (e.g., one application, a few IP addresses). A real attacker, by contrast, has unlimited time and is not bound by any scope. They can conduct long-term reconnaissance and pivot to any target in the organization, including targets explicitly out-of-scope for the test.
- **Motivation and Creativity**: Ethical hackers are bound by a contract and an ethical framework. Their goal is to find vulnerabilities and demonstrate them. A real-world attacker is driven by financial gain, espionage, or other malicious intent. They will

use every possible vector, including those that are not part of the standard VAPT process, such as social engineering, physical access, and insider threats.

- **Evolving Threat Landscape**: The security landscape is a dynamic environment. New vulnerabilities, especially "zero-day" exploits, are discovered constantly. A VAPT report is only accurate for the moment it was completed. A new vulnerability could emerge the very next day and be exploited by an attacker, rendering the report's findings outdated.
- **The Human Factor**: VAPT focuses on technical weaknesses. Real-world attacks frequently exploit human vulnerabilities through phishing, social engineering, and manipulating employees into revealing credentials or sensitive information. These "human hacks" are often outside the scope of a technical penetration test but are a primary attack vector for threat actors.

Impacts of the Security Gap

- Failing to account for the gap can have severe consequences for an organization:
- **Undetected Breaches**: A clean VAPT report can create a false sense of security. If the organization does not implement continuous monitoring and threat intelligence, it may be vulnerable to attacks that exploit weaknesses outside the VAPT's scope, leading to a breach that goes undetected for months.
- **Financial and Reputational Damage**: A successful real-world attack can result in significant financial losses from data theft, regulatory fines, and business interruption. It also causes severe reputational damage, eroding customer trust and stakeholder confidence.
- **Compliance Failures**: While VAPT can help achieve compliance, the real-world consequences of an attack can lead to compliance failures and legal action if the organization's security posture is found to be inadequate.

Recent Trends (as of August 2025)

- **Cloud Security**: Increased focus on assessing cloud environments (AWS, Azure, GCP) for misconfigurations.
- **Zero-Day Threats**: Growing emphasis on identifying unknown vulnerabilities through advanced pen testing.
- **Automation**: AI-driven tools are enhancing vulnerability scanning speed and accuracy.

- **Ransomware Simulation**: Pen tests now include ransomware attack simulations to test backup and recovery processes.
- **Compliance Mandates**: Stricter regulations (e.g., DORA, NYDFS) drive demand for regular VAPT.

How to Get Started

For Organizations:

- Hire a reputable VAPT provider or build an in-house team.
- Start with a vulnerability assessment to identify low-hanging fruit.
- Follow with targeted pen testing for critical systems.
- Check provider credentials (e.g., CREST, Offensive Security).

For Individuals:

- Learn tools like Nmap, Burp Suite, or Metasploit via platforms like TryHackMe or Hack The Box.
- Pursue certifications (e.g., CEH, OSCP, CompTIA PenTest+).
- Stay updated on vulnerabilities via CVE databases or X posts from cybersecurity experts.

Implementing a Penetration Testing Program

To ensure organizational security, a penetration testing program must be formally designed, developed, and implemented as a continuous cycle.

Pre-Engagement Procedures

These steps ensure the test is conducted legally, ethically, and effectively.

- **Define Objectives and Scope**: A formal agreement must specify what the test is intended to achieve (e.g., meet compliance, find all vulnerabilities, achieve compliance). The scope defines the systems, applications, and network ranges that are authorized for testing.

- **Rules of Engagement (RoE)**: The RoE document is a critical component of the agreement. It outlines the hours of operation for the test, permitted attack types, and communication protocols. It also defines what is explicitly forbidden (e.g., denial-of- service attacks, social engineering, physical access attempts).
- **Establish Communication Channels**: Define the primary points of contact for both the testing team and the client organization. A communication plan should specify how critical findings will be reported and what to do in case of an incident or an unintended disruption.
- **Legal Authorization**: Ensure all necessary legal documents are signed, including a master service agreement (MSA), a non-disclosure agreement (NDA), and the formal RoE document.

Post-Engagement Procedures

The work doesn't end when the test is over. These procedures are crucial for translating findings into actionable security improvements.

- **Post-Test Debriefing**: A meeting between the testing team and the client to discuss the findings, demonstrate exploited vulnerabilities, and answer questions.
- **Reporting**: The final report is the primary deliverable of a penetration test. It should include the following sections:
- **Executive Summary**: A high-level overview of the test's findings for a non-technical audience.
- **Technical Findings**: Detailed descriptions of each vulnerability, including proof-of- concept, and a clear explanation of how it was exploited.
- **Risk Rating**: A rating for each vulnerability based on its severity and the likelihood of exploitation.
- **Remediation Recommendations**: Specific, actionable steps to fix each vulnerability. This may include code changes, configuration updates, or the application of patches.

Vulnerability Management and Remediation

Effective vulnerability management is a continuous process that ensures findings from the penetration test lead to a more secure environment.

- **Develop a Remediation Plan**: Based on the test report, create a prioritized plan for fixing vulnerabilities. High-risk issues should be addressed first, and owners should be assigned for each task.

- **Implement Corrections**: The IT and development teams implement the necessary changes to correct the vulnerabilities identified in the report.
- **Retesting and Verification**: After the fixes are in place, the testing team or an internal security team should retest the system to verify that the vulnerabilities have been successfully closed and that no new issues were introduced.
- **Integrate a Vulnerability Management System (VMS)**: A VMS is a software solution that automates the lifecycle of vulnerability management. It can:
    - **Track and Prioritize Findings**: Centralize all vulnerabilities (from scans, pen tests, etc.) and prioritize them based on risk scores.
    - **Assign and Manage Tasks**: Automatically assign remediation tasks to the appropriate teams and track their progress.
    - **Generate Reports and Metrics**: Provide real-time dashboards and reports to monitor the organization's security posture and demonstrate compliance.
    - **Continuous Scanning**: Continuously scan the environment to identify new vulnerabilities as they emerge.

Common Vulnerabilities in Information Systems

Vulnerabilities are weaknesses that can be exploited by an attacker to compromise a system. Here are some of the most common types found in information systems:

- **Injection Flaws**: These occur when an attacker sends untrusted data to an application that is then executed as a command or query. Common examples include SQL Injection (SQLi), Cross-Site Scripting (XSS), and Command Injection.
- **Broken Authentication and Session Management**: Flaws in the way applications handle user authentication and session tokens can allow attackers to compromise passwords, keys, or session tokens, and impersonate other users. This includes weak password policies, lack of multi-factor authentication (MFA), and insecure session IDs.
- **Sensitive Data Exposure**: Many applications fail to properly protect sensitive data, such as financial information, personal health information, or credentials. This can happen due to a lack of encryption in transit or at rest, or through improper handling of sensitive data in logs or error messages.

- **Security Misconfigurations**: These are often the easiest vulnerabilities to find and exploit. They include insecure default configurations, open storage buckets, unnecessary enabled features, and misconfigured permissions on cloud services.
- **Vulnerable and Outdated Components**: Using components, libraries, or frameworks with known vulnerabilities can expose an entire system to risk. This includes using old versions of software that have not been patched.
- **Broken Access Control**: This occurs when an attacker can act as a user with higher privileges or access data they are not authorized to see. For example, a standard user could gain access to an administrative page by simply changing the URL.

Legal Issues in Penetration Testing

Penetration testing is a simulated cyberattack, and without proper legal authorization, it can be considered a crime. Ethical hackers and organizations must be aware of and adhere to the following legal principles:

- **Written Authorization and Scope**: The most crucial legal requirement is a signed contract or a "Rules of Engagement" document. This provides explicit, written permission from the system owner to conduct the test. It must clearly define the scope, including which IP addresses, applications, and systems are in-scope and out-of-scope, as well as the types of attacks that are permitted.
- **Data Protection and Privacy Laws**: Penetration tests can involve accessing or handling sensitive data. Testers must comply with relevant data protection laws, such as the General Data Protection Regulation (GDPR) in the European Union or the California Consumer Privacy Act (CCPA) in the US. This requires protecting personal data, avoiding unnecessary access, and ensuring any data collected is anonymized or handled securely.
- **Computer Fraud and Abuse Act (CFAA)**: In the United States, the CFAA criminalizes unauthorized access to a computer. Without a clear, written contract, a penetration test could be viewed as a violation of this act, leading to severe penalties, even if the intent was to improve security. Similar laws exist in other countries, such as the Computer Misuse Act in the UK.
- **Liability and Confidentiality**: The contract should also clearly define liability for any accidental damage or business disruption caused during the test. Additionally, a Non-Disclosure Agreement (NDA) is essential to ensure that all findings and sensitive information are kept confidential and are not disclosed to unauthorized parties.

The Impact of AI on VAPT Activities

Artificial intelligence is rapidly transforming the cybersecurity landscape, influencing both the techniques used by attackers and the methods used to defend against them. Here's how AI is impacting the activities covered in this document:

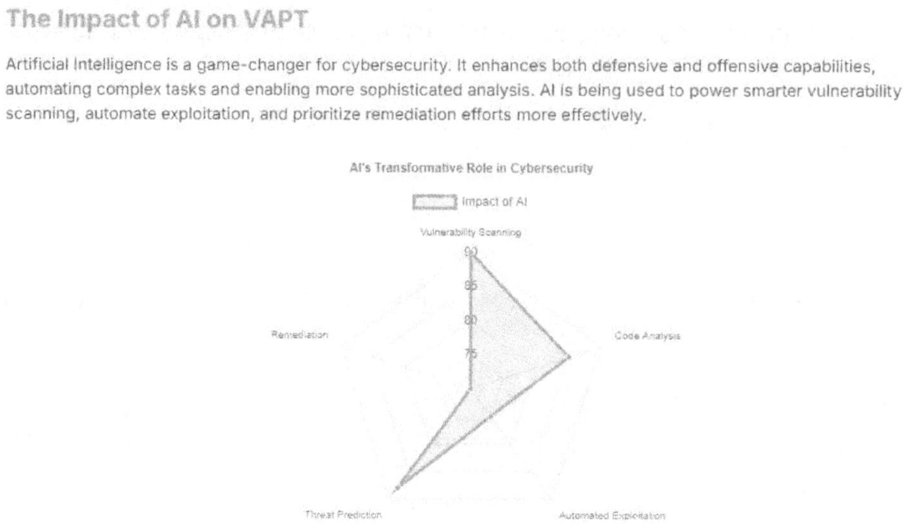

AI in Vulnerability Identification

- **Enhanced Vulnerability Scanning**: Traditional vulnerability scanners rely on a database of known signatures. AI-powered scanners can go beyond this by analyzing code and system behavior to identify new or "zero-day" vulnerabilities that haven't been documented yet. They can learn from past data to predict where new weaknesses might appear.
- **Code Analysis**: AI can be trained to analyze large codebases for security flaws much faster and more accurately than a human. It can spot subtle patterns that might indicate a vulnerability, such as a potential injection point or a weak cryptographic implementation.
- **Predictive Analytics**: AI models can analyze threat intelligence data, past incidents, and known vulnerabilities to predict which systems are most likely to be targeted and what types of attacks are most probable. This allows organizations to prioritize their VAPT efforts more effectively.

AI in Penetration Testing

- **Automated Exploitation**: AI can automate parts of the reconnaissance and exploitation phases of a penetration test. It can identify a vulnerability, develop a custom exploit, and execute it against the target system without human intervention.
- **Adaptive Attack Paths**: AI-driven pen testing tools can dynamically change their attack strategy based on the system's response. For example, if one attack vector fails, the AI can automatically switch to another, mimicking the adaptability of a human attacker.
- **Red Team Automation**: For organizations with internal security teams, AI can be a powerful tool for automating repetitive tasks. This frees up the human "red team" to focus on more complex and creative attack scenarios.

AI in Vulnerability Management and Remediation

- **Automated Patch Management**: AI can analyze a system's dependencies and vulnerabilities to recommend and even automatically apply patches in a way that minimizes disruption. It can predict potential conflicts before a patch is deployed.
- **Prioritization**: With the massive number of vulnerabilities discovered daily, prioritization is key. AI-powered VMS can use machine learning to score vulnerabilities not just on their CVSS score, but also on their real-world exploitability, the value of the asset they're on, and the current threat landscape. This allows for a more risk-based approach to remediation.
- **Root Cause Analysis**: AI can analyze logs and security data from a penetration test to help identify the underlying root cause of a vulnerability, rather than just treating the symptom. This can lead to more effective, long-term security improvements.

While AI offers significant advantages, it's also a double-edged sword. Malicious actors are also using AI to automate attacks, create more sophisticated phishing campaigns, and find new vulnerabilities. This makes the partnership between human security experts and AI- powered tools more critical than ever.

Threat Management: A Comprehensive Overview

Threat management is a comprehensive process used to identify, assess, prioritize, and respond to potential cyber threats to protect an organization's data, systems, and networks. It involves proactive strategies to prevent cyberattacks, detect threats in real-time, and respond effectively to minimize damage and ensure business continuity. Below is an overview of key strategies and best practices for effective threat management, based on current industry standards and insights.

Key Components of Threat Management

Many organizations adopt the **NIST Cybersecurity Framework (NIST CF)**, which outlines five core functions for effective threat management: Identify, Protect, Detect, Respond, and Recover. These functions provide a structured approach to managing cyber risks.

NIST Cybersecurity Framework Diagram

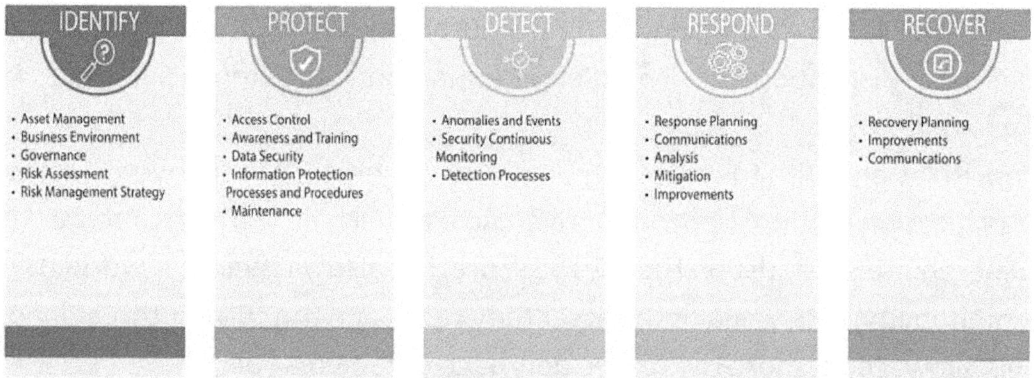

Identify:

- **Purpose**: Understand the organization's assets, vulnerabilities, and potential threats.
- **Actions**:
    - Conduct asset inventories to map critical systems, data, and resources.
    - Perform risk assessments to prioritize vulnerabilities and threats.
    - Use threat intelligence feeds to stay informed about emerging risks, such as malware, phishing, or advanced persistent threats (APTs).
- **Example**: Identify unpatched software or misconfigured systems that could be exploited by attackers.

Protect:

- **Purpose**: Implement safeguards to prevent or minimize the impact of threats.
- **Actions**:
    - Deploy firewalls, intrusion detection/prevention systems (IDS/IPS), encryption, and access controls.
    - Conduct regular employee training to reduce human errors, such as clicking phishing links.
    - Implement patch management to address known vulnerabilities.
- **Example**: Use multi-factor authentication (MFA) to secure access to sensitive systems.

Detect:

- **Purpose**: Continuously monitor systems to identify threats early.
- **Actions**:
    - Use Security Information and Event Management (SIEM) systems, behavioral analytics, and AI/ML-powered tools to detect anomalies.
    - Monitor network traffic, endpoints, and logs for signs of compromise.
    - Leverage real-time alerts and threat intelligence to identify zero-day attacks or insider threats.
- **Example**: Detect unusual login attempts from unfamiliar locations using User and Entity Behavior Analytics (UEBA).

Respond:

- **Purpose**: Contain and mitigate threats to limit damage.
- **Actions**:
    - Develop and test an incident response plan to ensure quick action during a breach.
    - Use automation to streamline containment and eradication processes.
    - Communicate effectively with stakeholders to manage the incident.
- **Example**: Isolate an infected endpoint to prevent malware from spreading across the network.

Recover:

- **Purpose**: Restore systems and data to normal operations and improve defenses.
- **Actions**:
    - Restore data from backups and verify system integrity.
    - Conduct post-incident analysis to identify root causes and improve processes.
    - Update security policies and train staff to prevent recurrence.

- **Example**: Rebuild a compromised server and apply lessons learned to strengthen security controls.

Key Strategies for Threat Management

Proactive Threat Hunting:

- Actively search for threats using threat intelligence, analytics, and automated platforms.
- Focus on identifying unknown or emerging threats, such as mutating malware or insider risks, before they cause harm.

Unified Threat Management (UTM):

- Combine multiple security tools (e.g., firewalls, malware protection, URL filtering) into a single platform for streamlined management.
- UTM solutions simplify operations and improve visibility across the threat landscape.

Vulnerability Management:

- Regularly scan for and patch vulnerabilities in software, hardware, and configurations.
- Prioritize remediation based on risk scoring and exploitability.

Leverage AI and Automation:

- Use AI-powered tools for faster threat detection and response, such as anomaly detection or automated patch management.
- Automation reduces manual workloads, allowing security teams to focus on strategic tasks.

Employee Training and Awareness:

- Educate staff on recognizing phishing, maintaining password hygiene, and reporting suspicious activity.
- Foster a security-aware culture to reduce unintentional threats caused by human error.

Incident Response Planning:

- Develop and regularly test a comprehensive incident response plan.
- Include clear procedures for containment, eradication, and recovery to minimize downtime.

Third-Party Risk Management:

- Assess the cybersecurity posture of vendors and partners to mitigate supply chain risks.
- Enforce contractual security obligations to ensure compliance.

Common Challenges in Threat Management

This chart highlights the most common hurdles organizations face in managing cyber threats. Information fragmentation and the rapid evolution of threats are often the most significant challenges.

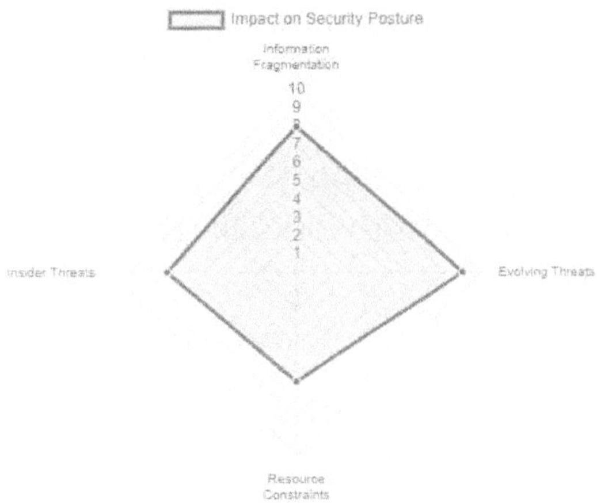

- **Information Fragmentation**: Disparate tools and data sources can create blind spots, reducing visibility into the threat landscape.
- **Evolving Threats**: Attackers use advanced techniques like AI-powered malware or zero-day exploits, requiring adaptive defenses.
- **Resource Constraints**: Limited budgets and skilled personnel can hinder effective threat management.
- **Insider Threats**: Both intentional (e.g., malicious employees) and unintentional (e.g., negligent actions) threats require tailored mitigation strategies.

Best Practices

- **Adopt Industry Frameworks**: Use NIST, ISO 27001, or other standards to guide your threat management strategy.
- **Continuous Monitoring**: Implement real-time monitoring to detect and respond to

threats quickly.

- **Prioritize Risks**: Focus resources on high-impact, high-probability threats using risk-based scoring.
- **Integrate Tools and Teams**: Foster collaboration between IT, security, HR, and compliance teams to align efforts and share insights.
- **Stay Informed**: Subscribe to threat intelligence feeds and stay updated on emerging threats to adapt strategies.

Benefits of Effective Threat Management

- **Reduced Risk**: Proactive measures minimize the likelihood and impact of cyberattacks.
- **Cost Savings**: Early detection and response can save millions in breach remediation costs.
- **Business Continuity**: Robust strategies ensure minimal disruption to operations.
- **Compliance:** Aligning with frameworks like NIST helps meet regulatory requirements.
- **Reputation Protection**: Strong security builds trust with customers and stakeholders.

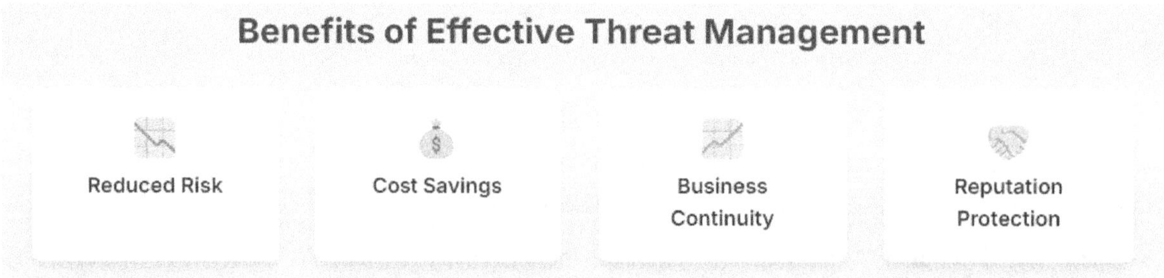

Example Tools and Technologies

- **SIEM Systems**: Splunk, IBM QRadar, or ArcSight for centralized log management and threat detection.
- **Threat Intelligence Platforms**: Recorded Future, ThreatConnect, or Cyble for real-time threat insights.
- **Endpoint Protection**: CrowdStrike, SentinelOne, or Palo Alto Networks for malware and intrusion prevention.
- **Automation Tools**: SOAR (Security Orchestration, Automation, and Response) platforms like Splunk SOAR to streamline incident response.

Critical Perspective

While frameworks like NIST provide structured guidance, over-reliance on standardized approaches can lead to complacency or a one-size-fits-all mentality. Organizations must tailor strategies to their unique environments, as generic solutions may not address specific risks, such as those in operational technology (OT) or IoT environments. Additionally, the rapid evolution of threats, such as AI-driven attacks, requires constant adaptation beyond traditional tools like signature-based detection, which struggles against unknown threats. Finally, the human element—whether through insider threats or burnout among security staff—remains a critical vulnerability that technology alone cannot solve.

For organizations seeking to implement or improve threat management, start by assessing your current security posture, aligning with a framework like NIST, and investing in both technology and employee training.

Incident Response and Computer Forensics

Incident response and computer forensics are two distinct but deeply interconnected fields within cybersecurity. While incident response focuses on the immediate, tactical handling of a cyberattack to minimize damage, computer forensics is a meticulous, investigative discipline that seeks to uncover the truth and gather evidence after the fact.

What is Incident Response?

Incident response (IR) is the proactive and reactive process an organization follows to prepare for, detect, contain, and recover from a cybersecurity incident. The primary goal is to limit the impact of a breach, reduce recovery time, and restore business operations as quickly as possible. An effective IR plan is crucial for managing the chaos of a live attack.

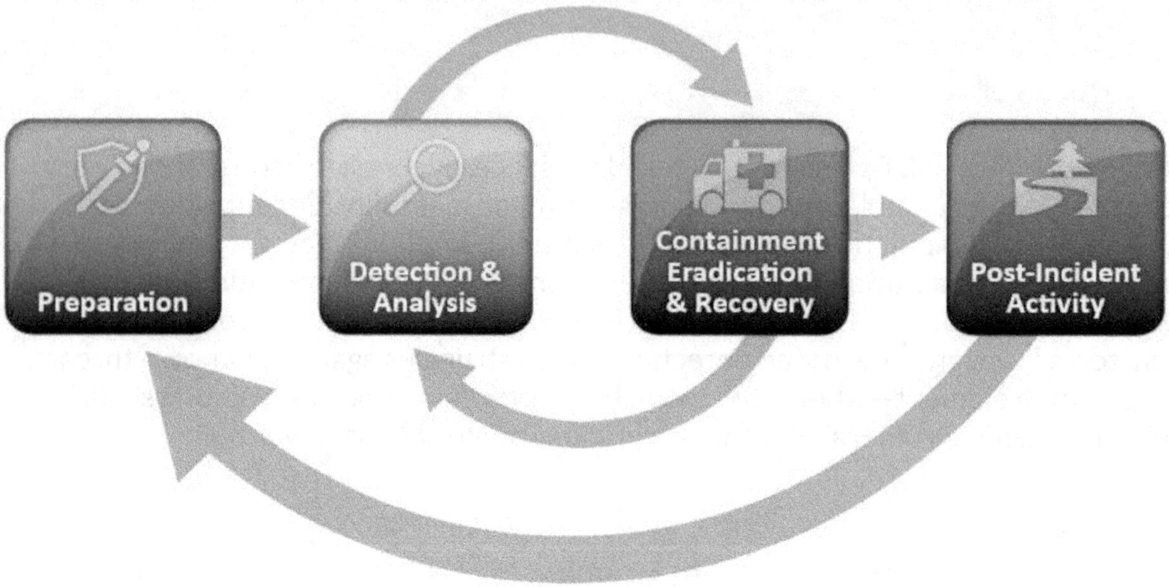

The incident response lifecycle is typically broken down into a series of phases:

- **1. Preparation:** This phase happens before an incident. It involves creating a formal IR plan, building a Computer Security Incident Response Team (CSIRT), acquiring necessary tools, defining roles and responsibilities, and conducting regular training and drills.
- **2. Identification:** The team actively monitors for signs of an incident, such as alerts from security systems, unusual network traffic, or user reports. Once a potential incident is detected, it is analyzed to confirm if a breach has occurred and to determine its scope and nature.
- **3. Containment:** This is a crucial phase where the team takes immediate action to prevent the threat from spreading. This might involve isolating affected systems, disconnecting them from the network, or blocking malicious traffic. The goal is to "stop the bleeding."
- **4. Eradication & Recovery:** After the threat is contained, the team works to remove the malicious elements from the environment. This includes deleting malware, patching vulnerabilities, and restoring systems to a clean, secure state from trusted backups.
- **5. Post-Incident Activity (Lessons Learned):** Once the incident is resolved and operations are back to normal, a post-mortem analysis is conducted. The team reviews what happened, what worked well in the response, and what could be improved. This feedback loop is essential for strengthening future security defenses and updating the IR plan.

Key Operational Procedures

This section details critical steps for designing and executing effective incident response and forensics.

1. Designing Incident Response Procedures

A successful incident response is a planned event, not a chaotic reaction. It relies on a well- defined process that the team has practiced repeatedly.

- **Playbooks:** These are step-by-step guides for handling specific types of incidents (e.g., a malware infection, a phishing attack, a data breach). They detail the exact actions to take, the tools to use, and the personnel to involve.
- **Tabletop Exercises:** These are simulated, discussion-based walkthroughs of an incident scenario. They test the IR plan without an actual attack, allowing the team to identify gaps, refine communication protocols, and clarify roles and responsibilities in a low-stress environment.
- **Red Team/Blue Team Drills:** A red team simulates an attack on the organization, while a blue team defends against it. This is a hands-on exercise that provides a real- world test of the IR plan, the team's skills, and the effectiveness of security controls.

2. Guidelines for Legal Action

Not all security incidents require legal action, but it's vital to have a process to determine if a violation of law has occurred. This requires close collaboration with legal counsel.

- **Indicators of a Legal Violation:**
    - The incident involves the theft or exposure of sensitive data, such as personally identifiable information (PII) or protected health information (PHI).
    - There is evidence of financial fraud or unauthorized transactions.
    - The attack is linked to organized crime or state-sponsored actors.
    - The incident violates specific regulatory frameworks like GDPR or HIPAA.
- **Legal Reporting:** The IR team must have clear guidelines on when to contact the legal department, who to inform, and what information to provide. All evidence must be preserved according to a strict chain of custody to ensure it is admissible in potential legal proceedings.

3. Volatile vs. Persistent System Information

During a forensic investigation, it is critical to understand the difference between volatile and persistent data and to collect them in the correct order.

- **Volatile Data:** This is temporary information that is lost when a system is powered down. It is often the most valuable evidence in a live investigation. Examples include:

  - System memory (RAM)
  - Running processes and open files
  - Network connections and active user sessions
  - Contents of the clipboard

- **Persistent Data:** This is information that is stored on a device and remains after a system is turned off. It provides a historical record of events. Examples include:
  - Hard drives and solid-state drives
  - Registry files
  - Log files
  - File metadata and timestamps
  - Backups
- Proper forensic procedure dictates that volatile data is collected first, as it is the most at risk of being lost, followed by persistent data.

What is Computer Forensics?

Computer forensics (also known as digital forensics) is a specialized branch of forensic science that involves the systematic collection, preservation, analysis, and presentation of digital evidence for legal or investigative purposes. Its goal is to reconstruct events, identify the root cause of an incident, and pinpoint the perpetrators while maintaining a strict chain of custody for all evidence.

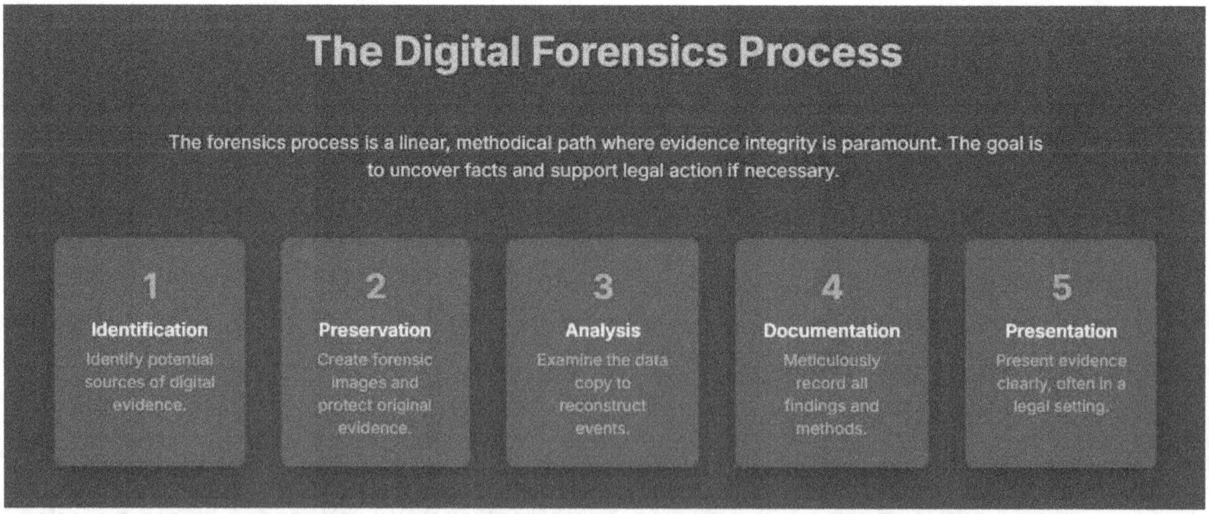

The digital forensics process is meticulous and follows a structured methodology to ensure evidence is legally admissible:

- **1. Identification:** This initial phase involves identifying all potential sources of digital evidence, such as computers, servers, mobile devices, and cloud storage.

- **2. Preservation:** The most critical step. Investigators use specialized tools to create an exact, bit-for-bit copy (a "forensic image") of the original data. The original evidence is then secured to ensure it remains unaltered, which is essential for maintaining its integrity in court.
- **3. Analysis:** The forensic investigator examines the acquired data copy to recover and interpret relevant information. This can involve recovering deleted files, analyzing network logs, and investigating system artifacts to piece together a timeline of events.
- **4. Documentation & Reporting:** All findings, methods, and evidence are meticulously documented. A comprehensive report is prepared to summarize the investigation's conclusions, detailing how the evidence was found and analyzed.
- **5. Presentation:** In a legal context, the investigator may be required to present their findings and testify as an expert witness in court.

The Relationship between Incident Response & Computer Forensics

Incident response and computer forensics are often performed by the same team and are considered a single practice known as **Digital Forensics and Incident Response (DFIR)**. Incident response is the immediate, broad-level action taken to mitigate a threat, while computer forensics is the deep-dive, post-incident investigation.

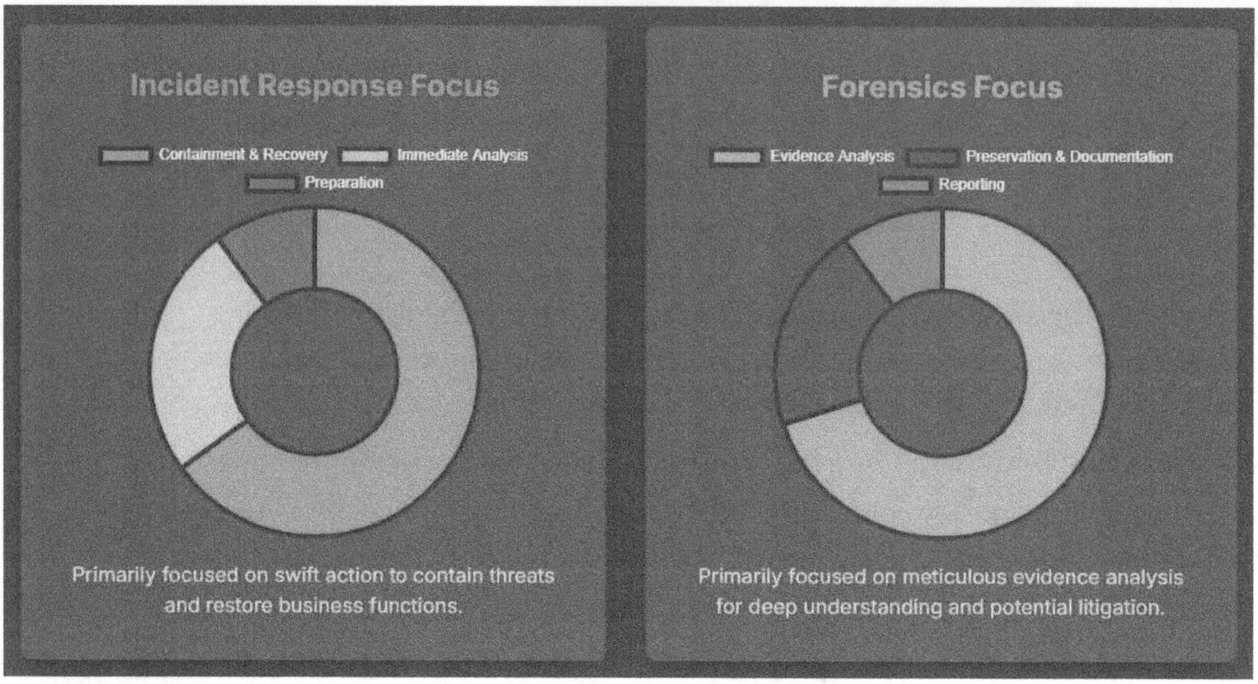

Here is a summary of their key differences

Aspect	Incident Response	Computer Forensics
Primary Goal	To minimize damage and restore operations quickly.	To preserve evidence and investigate to determine what happened.
Timing	During and immediately after an incident.	After containment, or as a dedicated post-incident investigation.
Scope	Broader; addresses the entire business impact.	Narrower; focuses on the technical investigation of digital evidence.
Legality	May involve preserving some evidence, but legal admissibility is not the primary concern.	Strict adherence to legal standards and chain of custody is paramount.
Skills	Requires quick thinking, network security knowledge, and systems administration skills.	Requires highly specialized knowledge of forensic tools, file systems, and legal procedures.

Establishing and Managing a Digital Forensics Program

A robust cybersecurity posture requires a formalized digital forensics program. This section outlines the key components of establishing and managing such a program.

- **1. Setting up a Forensic Lab and Program** A digital forensics program requires a dedicated environment for investigations. A forensic lab is a controlled physical or logical space designed to prevent contamination of evidence. Key components of a forensic lab include:
    - **Secure Storage:** Physically secure lockers or safes to store original digital evidence (e.g., hard drives, mobile devices).
    - **Forensic Workstations:** High-performance computers with specialized hardware and software. These workstations often have write-blockers to prevent accidental changes to original evidence.
    - **Software Suites:** Licensed forensic software (e.g., EnCase, FTK) for data imaging, analysis, and reporting.

- **2. Developing and Managing an Organizational Program** A successful program requires more than just tools. It needs a strategic framework and clear policies.
    - **Program Policies:** Formal documents that define the scope, authority, and procedures for all forensic investigations. These policies ensure consistency and legal defensibility.
    - **Standard Operating Procedures (SOPs):** Detailed, step-by-step instructions for every task, from evidence collection to analysis. SOPs are crucial for maintaining the chain of custody.
    - **Training and Certification:** The program must invest in continuous training and professional certification for its team members to stay current with evolving technology and threats.
- **3. Establishing and Managing Forensic Investigation Teams** A skilled and well- structured team is the backbone of the program.
    - **Team Roles:** A team may include a lead investigator, forensic analysts, malware reverse engineers, and legal or compliance liaisons. Each role has a specific responsibility in the investigative process.
    - **Clear Authority:** The team must have the authority and mandate from management to perform its duties, including seizing equipment and

accessing sensitive data, in accordance with established policies.

- **4. E-Discovery Principles and Practices** E-Discovery (Electronic Discovery) is the process of identifying, collecting, and producing electronically stored information (ESI) in response to a request for production in a lawsuit or investigation. Digital forensics is a key part of this process.
  - **Legal Hold:** The moment an investigation is initiated, a legal hold must be placed on all relevant ESI to prevent its deletion or alteration.
  - **Targeted Collection:** E-Discovery is often a targeted collection of specific data, whereas a forensic investigation may involve a complete, bit-for-bit copy of an entire drive.

- **5. Designing an Investigative Process** The investigative process is a series of methodical steps to handle evidence.
  - **Evidence Collection:** The initial stage, where the team secures and documents all potential sources of evidence, both volatile and persistent. This includes photographing the scene and documenting the state of the systems.
  - **Imaging & Data Acquisition:** The process of creating a forensically sound copy of the original data. This is typically done using a hardware write-blocker to ensure the original media is not modified. The resulting copy is an exact, bit-for-bit duplicate.
  - **Analysis:** The most time-consuming stage. Analysts use specialized tools to examine the acquired data, looking for artifacts of an attack. This may include recovering deleted files, analyzing log files, and carving for specific keywords.

- **6. Best Practices for Evidence Handling** Proper handling of digital evidence is non- negotiable for maintaining its integrity.
  - **Chain of Custody:** A document that records every person who has handled the evidence, the date and time of the transfer, and the reason for the transfer. It is a legal record that proves the evidence has not been tampered with.
  - **Media Storage:** Store original evidence in a secure, climate-controlled environment. The forensic images and analysis results should be stored on a separate, dedicated network drive.
  - **Cryptographic Hashing:** Create a cryptographic hash (e.g., SHA256) of the original media before and after imaging. If the hashes match, it proves the

integrity of the acquired data.

- **7. Understanding Digital Media and File Systems** Forensic professionals must have a deep understanding of how data is stored on various media devices and organized by different file systems.
  - **Digital Media:** This includes traditional hard disk drives (HDDs), solid-state drives (SSDs), USB drives, and removable media. Each has its own characteristics that affect the forensic acquisition process.
  - **File Systems:** The method used to store and organize files on a disk. Common examples include NTFS (Windows), ext4 (Linux), and HFS+ (macOS). Understanding the nuances of each file system is critical for finding and recovering data.

Advanced Forensic Concepts and Tools

This section outlines the use of specialized tools and the methods employed by attackers to evade detection.

Forensic Investigation Tools

Forensic professionals rely on a diverse set of tools to perform their investigations. These tools are designed to work on copies of data to ensure the integrity of the original evidence.

- **Imaging and Acquisition Tools:** These tools are used to create bit-for-bit copies of digital media. Hardware write-blockers prevent any changes to the original source.
  - **Examples:** AccessData's FTK Imager, Magnet AXIOM, and open-source tools like the dd command in Linux.
- **Analysis Tools:** These are comprehensive software suites that allow investigators to examine and interpret the data from a forensic image. They can recover deleted files, search for keywords, analyze a timeline of events, and identify artifacts of malicious activity.
  - **Examples:** EnCase, Magnet AXIOM, and open-source options like Autopsy and The Sleuth Kit (TSK).
- **Network Forensics Tools:** Used to capture and analyze network traffic (e.g., pcap files) to reconstruct network-related events.
  - **Examples:** Wireshark, NetworkMiner.

Anti-Forensic Techniques

Anti-forensic techniques are methods used by an adversary to impede a forensic investigation. Understanding these techniques is critical for investigators to counter them.

- **Data Wiping and Sanitization:** The complete destruction of data on a drive using specialized tools.
- **Steganography:** Hiding data within a seemingly harmless file, such as an image or audio file.
- **Encryption:** Using strong encryption on files or entire disk volumes to make data unreadable without the correct key.
- **Timestomp:** Manipulating the timestamps of files (e.g., creation, modification, and access times) to mislead investigators and obscure the true timeline of events.
- **Rootkits:** Malware that gains deep-level access to a system to hide its presence and malicious activity from forensic tools.

Forensic professionals must use specialized tools and techniques, like memory analysis and live system acquisition, to bypass these anti-forensic measures and uncover hidden evidence.

CCISO Domain 4: Questions

1. A CISO is designing an access control policy for a highly sensitive government system that handles classified data. The primary objective is to prevent information from being downgraded and to ensure that a user's access is strictly determined by their security clearance, regardless of who owns the file. Which access control model is the most appropriate for this scenario?

   A) Discretionary Access Control (DAC)
   B) Role-Based Access Control (RBAC)
   C) Mandatory Access Control (MAC)
   D) Attribute-Based Access Control (ABAC)

2. A large, decentralized organization is struggling to manage a complex web of user permissions, leading to "permission creep" where employees accumulate excessive rights over time. The CISO wants to implement a new access control model that simplifies administration by linking permissions to job functions rather than individual users. Which model should the CISO recommend?

   A) Mandatory Access Control (MAC)
   B) Role-Based Access Control (RBAC)
   C) Discretionary Access Control (DAC)
   D) Rule-Based Access Control (RBAC)

3. An organization is deploying a new project management system. The CISO wants to create an access policy that states, "A user can edit a document if they are in the same department as the document owner, and the document's status is 'Draft'." Which access control model is best suited to implement this dynamic, context-aware policy?

   A) Mandatory Access Control (MAC)
   B) Rule-Based Access Control (RBAC)
   C) Role-Based Access Control (RBAC)
   D) Attribute-Based Access Control (ABAC)

4. A security analyst receives an alert from the SIEM system indicating a user is attempting to log in from an unusual geographical location outside of their normal business hours. The system automatically prompts the user for a second form of verification, such as a one-time code from a mobile app. This is an example of which type of authentication?

   A) Single Sign-On (SSO)
   B) Multi-Factor Authentication (MFA)
   C) Adaptive Authentication

D) Passwordless Authentication

5. A CISO is reviewing the company's Acceptable Use Policy (AUP). Which of the following elements is considered a critical component of a comprehensive AUP designed to ensure user accountability?

   A) A list of approved software for business use.
   B) Guidelines for creating a strong password and handling sensitive data.
   C) A detailed list of all system administrators.
   D) A schedule for mandatory annual employee vacations.

6. An organization requires employees to log in to the network using their password and then to enter a one-time passcode generated by a mobile app. This is an example of which security concept?

   A) Single Sign-On (SSO)
   B) Separation of Duties
   C) Multi-Factor Authentication (MFA)
   D) Role-Based Access Control (RBAC)

7. A security team is investigating a potential insider threat. They discover that an employee with no administrative rights was able to access and exfiltrate sensitive customer data from a database. This finding suggests a failure to enforce which core security principle?

   A) Separation of Duties
   B) Principle of Least Privilege
   C) Single Sign-On (SSO)
   D) Discretionary Access Control (DAC)

8. An organization's security policy requires that all vendor payment requests must be created by one employee and then approved by a different employee before the funds are transferred by a third. This is a practical application of which security principle?

   A) Principle of Least Privilege
   B) Mandatory Access Control (MAC)
   C) Separation of Duties
   D) Zero Trust

9. A security analyst is conducting a post-incident review of a recent data breach. During the investigation, they find that an attacker exploited a vulnerability in the company's public-facing web server that had been known for over two years but was never patched. This highlights a failure in which key security process?

   A) Threat modeling
   B) Social engineering
   C) Patch management

D) Digital forensics

10. A threat actor sends a malicious email to a finance department employee. The email, which appears to be from the CEO, urgently requests an immediate wire transfer to a new vendor. The
employee, under pressure, initiates the transfer without confirming the request through another channel. This attack is an example of which technique?

A) Phishing
B) Session Hijacking
C) Drive-by Download
D) Zero-day exploit

11. An attacker gains access to a corporate network by using a fake Wi-Fi network that spoofs the name of a legitimate one at a local coffee shop. The attacker then intercepts the traffic of unsuspecting users. This type of attack is known as:

A) DNS Poisoning
B) Man-in-the-Middle (MITM) attack
C) DoS (Denial-of-Service) attack
D) Cross-Site Scripting (XSS)

12. A CISO is reviewing the logs of a Security Information and Event Management (SIEM) system. They notice a large number of failed login attempts from a single IP address located in a foreign country, followed by a successful login using stolen credentials. This indicates a successful execution of which type of attack?

A) Drive-by Download
B) Session Hijacking
C) Brute-force attack
D) Spear phishing

13. A CISO is implementing a new security measure to combat phishing attacks. They are considering a policy that requires employees to formally acknowledge an Acceptable Use Policy (AUP) and pass a mandatory security awareness training quiz before being granted system access. This measure is primarily designed to address which of the following?

A) Technical vulnerabilities
B) Human element risks
C) Network misconfigurations
D) Physical security threats

14. A user reports that their files have been encrypted and a ransom note is on their desktop,

demanding payment in Bitcoin to restore access. Which type of malicious software is responsible for this?

A) Trojan
B) Worm
C) Spyware
D) Ransomware

15. An organization's finance team needs to access a secure application only during specific business hours (9 AM - 5 PM) and only from a company-issued device connected to the corporate network. Which access control model is best suited to enforce these time and location-based rules?

A) Role-Based Access Control (RBAC)
B) Mandatory Access Control (MAC)
C) Discretionary Access Control (DAC)
D) Rule-Based Access Control (RBAC)

16. Which of the following is an example of "Something You Have" authentication?

A) A password
B) A fingerprint scan
C) A security token generating a one-time passcode
D) The answer to a security question

17. In the context of secure coding, which of the following is the primary purpose of input validation and sanitization?

A) To prevent Denial-of-Service (DoS) attacks
B) To encrypt data in transit
C) To prevent injection attacks like SQL injection and XSS
D) To ensure multi-factor authentication is used

18. A CISO is drafting a business continuity plan. Which of the following roles is responsible for high-level decision-making and managing the overall business impact of a significant disruption?

A) Information Security Incident Response Team (IRT)
B) Crisis Management Team (CMT)
C) Disaster Recovery Team
D) Business Continuity Team

19. A security team is performing a post-incident review. They are using log data to determine the sequence of events and identify the source of a breach. This activity is a key part of

which phase of the incident response lifecycle?

A) Containment
B) Eradication
C) Identification
D) Post-Incident Review & Improvement

20. What is the primary function of a Security Information and Event Management (SIEM) system as described in the document?

A) To automatically quarantine all incoming emails.
B) To collect logs from various systems and monitor them for suspicious activity.
C) To prevent users from installing unauthorized software.
D) To perform automated penetration tests on the network.

21. A security professional is tasked with preparing for a digital forensics investigation. Which tool or practice is specifically designed to prevent accidental changes to original evidence on a hard drive?

A) A forensic workstation with a write-blocker
B) A SIEM system
C) A Vulnerability Assessment scanner
D) A password hash cracking tool

22. A software company is implementing secure coding practices. Which of the following best describes the purpose of hashing passwords with an algorithm like bcrypt instead of storing them in plaintext?

A) To make the password easier for users to remember.
B) To prevent an attacker from using stolen passwords on other systems if the database is breached.
C) To speed up the login process for users.
D) To ensure the password can be recovered by an administrator if a user forgets it.

23. What is the primary difference between a Vulnerability Assessment and a Penetration Test?

A) A Vulnerability Assessment uses automated tools, while a Penetration Test is always a manual process.
B) A Vulnerability Assessment identifies potential weaknesses, while a Penetration Test actively attempts to exploit those weaknesses to assess the impact.
C) A Vulnerability Assessment is only performed on external systems, while a Penetration Test is only performed on internal systems.
D) A Vulnerability Assessment is a proactive measure, while a Penetration Test is only

performed after a breach has occurred.

24. A CISO is concerned about the risk of a supply chain attack. Which recent real-world event is a prime example of this type of attack, as mentioned in the document?

   A) The CrowdStrike incident (2024)
   B) The Twitter breach (2020)
   C) The SolarWinds attack
   D) The $25 million deepfake scam

25. A security team discovers a new type of malware that uses an AI language model to dynamically generate malicious scripts. What trend does this new threat exemplify?

   A) Ransomware-as-a-Service (RaaS)
   B) AI-driven malware
   C) IoT vulnerabilities
   D) Deepfake social engineering

26. An organization's new CISO wants to ensure that all employees are aware that their activity on company systems is monitored and that unauthorized use is prohibited, both for legal and deterrent reasons. Which of the following is the most effective and legally sound method to accomplish this?

   A) Sending out a company-wide email.
   B) Posting a sign on the main entrance to the office.
   C) Implementing a prominent warning banner that users must acknowledge before logging in.
   D) Including a statement in the employee handbook.

27. What is the primary purpose of a Business Impact Analysis (BIA) as it relates to information security?

   A) To perform a full penetration test on all critical systems.
   B) To identify and document critical business functions and the IT systems that support them.
   C) To train employees on how to identify phishing emails.
   D) To manage privileged accounts and their access rights.

28. The concept of Homomorphic Encryption (HE) is described as a futuristic approach that allows computations to be performed on data while it is in what state?

   A) In transit
   B) Encrypted
   C) In a database

D) In plaintext

29. A CISO is reviewing their organization's disaster recovery plan. What is the primary difference between a Recovery Time Objective (RTO) and a Recovery Point Objective (RPO)?

A) RTO is the time to restore business operations, while RPO is the maximum acceptable data loss.
B) RTO is the maximum data loss, while RPO is the time to restore business operations.
C) RTO is the cost of downtime, while RPO is the cost of recovery.
D) RTO and RPO are different terms for the same concept.

30. A user reports that their computer is behaving strangely, and a forensic investigator suspects an anti-forensic technique is being used. Which of the following is a technique that an attacker might use to hide their presence and malicious activity from forensic tools?

A) Timestomp
B) Patch management
C) Input validation
D) Least privilege

31. An attacker gains access to a web server and injects a malicious script into a comment field that, when viewed by other users, steals their session cookies. Which secure coding practice was most likely not followed, allowing this Cross-Site Scripting (XSS) attack?

A) Secure Authentication
B) Input Validation and Sanitization
C) Error Handling
D) Proper Logging

32. What is the main purpose of an Acceptable Use Policy (AUP) in an organization?

A) To define the hardware specifications for all company computers.
B) To outline the legal consequences of non-compliance.
C) To explicitly outline a user's responsibilities and the organization's expectations for system usage and data handling.
D) To provide a list of all company-approved websites.

33. Which of the following best describes the purpose of a Forensic Workstation in a digital forensics lab?

A) A computer used for everyday administrative tasks.
B) A server that stores all network logs.
C) A high-performance computer with write-blockers to prevent changes to original evidence.

D) A machine for running automated vulnerability scans.

34. The concept of Zero Trust is a modern security model that operates on which core assumption?

A) All internal network traffic is trustworthy.
B) A breach is always possible, and every access request must be verified.
C) External threats are the only ones that need to be considered.
D) All devices within the corporate network are inherently secure.

35. The document describes a recent scam where a finance worker was tricked into transferring $25 million after an attacker used fake audio and video to impersonate multiple people on a video call. This is a real-world example of:

A) A denial-of-service attack
B) A phishing attack
C) A deepfake social engineering scam
D) A SQL injection attack

36. Which of the following is a key feature of Mandatory Access Control (MAC)?

A) The owner of a resource can grant or deny access to others.
B) Access is determined by a central authority using sensitivity labels.
C) Users are grouped into roles based on their job function.
D) Access is granted based on the user's location and time of day.

37. Discretionary Access Control (DAC) is the most common model used in:
A) Military and government organizations
B) Highly secure data centers
C) Commercial and general-purpose operating systems
D) Large-scale cloud services

38. The principle of Least Privilege is best described as:

A) Granting users full administrative rights by default.
B) Giving users only the minimum access required to perform their job functions.
C) Restricting all users to read-only access.
D) Allowing users to grant access to others at their discretion.

39. What is the primary purpose of an Authentication process?

A) To determine what a user is allowed to do.
B) To grant a user specific permissions to a resource.

C) To verify a user's identity.
D) To prevent unauthorized network traffic.

40. What is the main characteristic that distinguishes Authorization from Authentication?

A) Authentication verifies identity, while Authorization determines what a user can do.
B) Authentication determines what a user can do, while Authorization verifies identity.
C) They are two different terms for the same process.
D) Authentication is used for physical access, while Authorization is used for logical access.

41. A Separation of Duties policy is designed to:

A) Allow a single employee to handle all aspects of a critical task.
B) Divide critical tasks among multiple individuals to prevent fraud and errors.
C) Grant an employee all the permissions they need for their job.
D) Simplify the process of managing user permissions.

42. What is the main drawback of Discretionary Access Control (DAC)?

A) It is too rigid and complex to administer.
B) It can lead to inconsistent security policies and accidental data exposure.
C) It is not scalable for large organizations.
D) It is only suitable for high-security environments.

43. Which access control model is considered the "most flexible and granular" because it grants access based on a set of attributes associated with the user, the resource, and the environment?

A) Role-Based Access Control (RBAC)
B) Mandatory Access Control (MAC)
C) Attribute-Based Access Control (ABAC)
D) Rule-Based Access Control (RBAC)

44. In a digital forensics investigation, what is the primary purpose of a write-blocker?

A) To prevent an investigator from deleting evidence.
B) To prevent accidental changes to the original evidence on a hard drive.
C) To write data onto an encrypted hard drive.
D) To speed up the process of data acquisition.

45. A CISO is establishing a data classification scheme. Which of the following data classifications, if exposed, would cause the most severe harm, financial loss, or legal issues?

A) Public
B) Internal

C) Confidential
D) Restricted/Secret

46. What is the main benefit of a centralized management system for identity and access management?

A) It makes it easier for attackers to compromise a single point.
B) It increases complexity and administrative overhead.
C) It reduces complexity and improves consistency.
D) It allows individual users to manage their own permissions.

47. What is the primary purpose of an Incident Response Plan (IRP)?

A) To define the long-term recovery strategy after a disaster.
B) To document potential threats to the organization.
C) To serve as a "first responder's guide" detailing initial actions to contain and mitigate an event.
D) To provide a list of all company assets.

48. According to the document, which of the following is an example of an anti-forensic technique?

A) Using an antivirus program
B) Implementing Multi-Factor Authentication (MFA)
C) Timestomp, which manipulates file timestamps
D) Performing a vulnerability assessment

49. What is the main goal of the Containment phase in the incident response lifecycle?

A) To identify the source of the attack.
B) To prevent the threat from spreading further.
C) To recover systems from backups.
D) To conduct a post-mortem review of the incident.

50. The practice of writing code in a way that anticipates and mitigates potential security vulnerabilities is known as:

A) Digital Forensics
B) Secure Coding
C) Penetration Testing
D) Risk Management

51. An attacker intercepts a user's session token and uses it to take over their authenticated session without needing a password. This type of attack is known as:

A) Session Hijacking
B) Phishing
C) Drive-by Download
D) SQL Injection

52. The document mentions a type of malware that can be unintentionally downloaded by simply visiting a compromised website, as the site exploits vulnerabilities in the web browser. What is this called?

A) Infected Media
B) A Rootkit
C) A Drive-by Download
D) Ransomware

53. Which of the following is NOT a phase of the incident response lifecycle as described in the document?

A) Preparation
B) Identification
C) Eradication
D) Notification

54. What is the primary role of an Information Security Incident Response Team (IRT) in a disaster recovery scenario?

A) To manage high-level decision-making.
B) To ensure the continuity of non-technical business functions.
C) To focus on security-related incidents, including forensic analysis and containing breaches.
D) To handle external communications with the public and media.

55. According to the document, what is the primary purpose of a warning banner before a user logs in to a system?

A) To provide a friendly welcome message.
B) To serve as a strong legal basis for prosecuting unauthorized access.
C) To advertise the company's security policies.
D) To inform users about system maintenance schedules.

56. The document outlines a phishing attack response plan. In the Proactive Prevention phase, what is the purpose of conducting simulated phishing drills?

A) To identify system vulnerabilities.
B) To punish employees who fail to identify phishing emails.

C) To test employees' awareness and response to phishing attempts.
D) To automatically block all suspicious emails.

57. In the context of the phishing attack response plan, what is the purpose of the Eradication & Recovery phase?

A) To identify the attacker's command and control servers.
B) To contain the threat and prevent it from spreading.
C) To clean up any damage from the attack and restore normal operations.
D) To conduct a post-mortem review of the incident.

58. What is the key difference between Rule-Based Access Control (RBAC) and Role-Based Access Control (RBAC)?

A) Role-Based uses conditional logic, while Rule-Based uses roles.
B) Role-Based uses roles, while Rule-Based uses a set of logical conditions.
C) They are the same model with different names.
D) Rule-Based is for high-security environments, while Role-Based is for commercial environments.

59. What is a key component of a Phishing Attack Response Plan that falls under the Proactive Prevention phase?

A) Incident analysis
B) Threat intelligence gathering
C) Enforcement of Multi-Factor Authentication (MFA)
D) Forensic investigation

60. Which of the following best describes the Threat & Risk Assessment step in designing a Disaster Recovery/Business Continuity (DR/BC) plan?

A) It involves defining the purpose and scope of the plan.
B) It documents potential threats and the vulnerabilities of identified assets.
C) It focuses on the technical execution of the recovery plan.
D) It is an optional step that is not critical for the plan's success.

61. What is the primary responsibility of the Crisis Management Team (CMT) in a disaster or business disruption?

A) To handle the technical execution of system recovery.
B) To manage non-technical business functions.
C) To provide high-level decision-making and manage the overall business impact.
D) To perform forensic analysis of a security breach.

62. The document discusses a trend where cybercriminals can easily purchase or rent ransomware kits on dark web markets to launch attacks without needing advanced technical skills. This is known as:

A) Ransomware-as-a-Service (RaaS)
B) Deepfake Social Engineering
C) Supply Chain Attacks
D) AI-Driven Malware

63. The use of a VPN is recommended to mitigate the risk of which type of network attack?

A) SQL Injection
B) On-path attacks (formerly known as man-in-the-middle attacks)
C) Denial-of-Service (DoS)
D) Cross-Site Scripting (XSS)

64. What is a key feature of Passwordless Authentication?

A) It relies solely on a user's password.
B) It aims to eliminate traditional passwords entirely, using alternative methods like biometrics.
C) It requires a user to enter their password twice.
D) It is a type of Single Sign-On (SSO) system.

65. What is the primary purpose of a Post-Mortem Meeting after a security incident?

A) To assign blame to the individuals responsible.
B) To announce the successful recovery to the public.
C) To review the incident from start to finish and identify weaknesses in the response plan.
D) To create new user accounts and permissions.

66. Which of the following is a key reason for implementing an Auditing and Monitoring process for access activities?

A) To give all users the same level of access.
B) To eliminate the need for an access control plan.
C) To provide a trail of evidence for forensic analysis and compliance.
D) To make the login process faster for all users.

67. The document states that a key feature of Mandatory Access Control (MAC) is the use of sensitivity labels. What is the purpose of these labels?

A) To identify the file owner.

B) To determine the file's size and creation date.
C) To assign a security clearance to both users and resources.
D) To indicate the file's format (e.g., .docx, .pdf).

68. What is a significant risk associated with Single Sign-On (SSO)?

A) A single compromised account can grant an attacker access to multiple services.
B) Users have to remember multiple passwords.
C) It is less convenient for users.
D) It requires a separate account for each service.

69. What is the primary purpose of the Preparation phase of the incident response lifecycle?

A) To contain an active threat.
B) To identify the source of the incident.
C) To create the formal IR plan, build a team, and conduct training before an incident occurs.
D) To remove the threat from the affected systems.

70. The document describes a scenario where an employee's access to marketing materials is immediately revoked when they change departments and are instead granted access to finance- related resources. This is an example of an effective process for managing which of the following?

A) Onboarding/Offboarding
B) Data classification
C) Password policies
D) Authentication mechanisms

71. In a digital forensics investigation, what is the primary purpose of data sanitization or wiping?

A) To prevent data from being read.
B) To completely destroy data on a drivc to makc it unrecoverable.
C) To hide data within a seemingly harmless file.
D) To manipulate the timestamps of files.

72. What is the main drawback of Attribute-Based Access Control (ABAC)?

A) It is less granular than other models.
B) It is significantly more complex to design, implement, and manage.
C) It is not scalable for large organizations.
D) It relies on the discretion of individual users.

73. The document emphasizes the importance of a Centralized Authentication Point for which

of the following concepts?

A) Discretionary Access Control (DAC)
B) Separation of Duties
C) Single Sign-On (SSO)
D) Mandatory Access Control (MAC)

74. A security analyst is conducting a code review and finds that a web application is not properly stripping HTML tags from user-submitted comments. This could lead to what type of attack?

A) SQL Injection
B) Cross-Site Scripting (XSS)
C) Buffer Overflow
D) Brute-force attack

75. According to the document, what is the primary benefit of enforcing Multi-Factor Authentication (MFA) across critical systems?

A) It reduces the number of passwords a user has to remember.
B) It makes it significantly harder for attackers to gain access even if one factor is compromised.
C) It makes the login process faster and more convenient.
D) It eliminates the need for any other security controls.

76. The document mentions Vulnerable and Outdated Components as a common web application security risk. What is the best way to mitigate this risk?

A) Disabling unused network services.
B) Ensuring that all libraries and frameworks are kept up to date.
C) Implementing a new password policy.
D) Using a firewall to block all incoming traffic.

77. What is the primary function of a firewall as a security control?

A) To hide data within a seemingly harmless file.
B) To scan files for patterns that match known malware signatures.
C) To monitor and filter incoming and outgoing network traffic.
D) To encrypt data on a hard drive.

78. The document describes a core security principle that dictates that a user should only be granted the minimum level of access required to perform their job, and that the default policy should be to deny all access unless it is explicitly granted. This is known as:

A) Single Sign-On (SSO)

B) Separation of Duties
C) Least Privilege
D) Discretionary Access Control (DAC)

79. What is a significant drawback of Mandatory Access Control (MAC)?
A) It relies on the data owner to make access decisions.
B) It can lead to "permission creep."
C) It is highly rigid and complex to administer.
D) It is not suitable for high-security environments.

80. A finance worker receives an email that looks legitimate, with a link that appears to go to a corporate portal but actually directs them to a fraudulent website. This is an example of what kind of attack?

A) Vishing
B) Smishing
C) Phishing
D) Hoaxing

81. According to the document, a key component of a Disaster Recovery (DR) and Business Continuity (BC) plan is the integration of the Incident Response Plan (IRP). What is the role of the IRP in this context?

A) The IRP replaces the DR/BC plan.
B) The IRP acts as the "first responder's guide," detailing the initial actions to contain and mitigate an event.
C) The IRP is used for long-term recovery after a disaster.
D) The IRP is an optional component.

82. The document lists several types of anti-forensic techniques. Which technique involves hiding data within a seemingly harmless file, such as an image or audio file?

A) Timestomp
B) Steganography
C) Data Wiping
D) Encryption

83. What is the main purpose of a Business Impact Analysis (BIA)?

A) To determine the cost of implementing a new security system.
B) To identify and document the organization's critical business functions.
C) To conduct a technical vulnerability assessment.
D) To define the roles and responsibilities of the IT team.

84. What is a key step in a Phishing Attack Response Plan's Detection & Triage phase?

A) Investigating compromised user accounts.
B) Blocking the malicious infrastructure.
C) Immediately notifying all users of the attack.
D) Triaging alerts and user reports to determine if an attack is legitimate.

85. In secure coding, what is the purpose of using a secure session cookie with the HttpOnly and Secure attributes?

A) To allow JavaScript to access the cookie.
B) To prevent the cookie from being transmitted over an unencrypted connection.
C) To make the cookie accessible to all websites.
D) To prevent Cross-Site Request Forgery (CSRF) attacks.

86. What is the main purpose of a Threat & Risk Assessment in the context of a DR/BC plan?

A) To define the scope of the plan.
B) To document the data classification for each asset.
C) To document potential threats and the vulnerabilities of identified assets.
D) To establish the roles and responsibilities of the recovery teams.

87. Which of the following best describes the principle of Default Deny?

A) The default policy is to allow all access unless it is explicitly denied.
B) The default policy is to deny all access unless it is explicitly granted.
C) All user requests are automatically denied.
D) All user requests are automatically granted.

88. What is the primary purpose of Regular Reviews of user access rights?

A) To ensure that users are maintaining their passwords.
B) To ensure that access rights are still appropriate for a user's current role and to remove unnecessary privileges.
C) To test the user's knowledge of the Acceptable Use Policy.
D) To identify any unauthorized software installed on the network.

89. A CISO wants to implement a new authentication method that is both highly secure and convenient for users, as it eliminates the need to remember passwords. Which method should they consider?

A) Knowledge-Based Authentication
B) Biometric-Based Authentication
C) Single-Factor Authentication

D) Password-Based Authentication

90. The document states that the Incident Response Plan (IRP) is a referenced document that hands off to the Disaster Recovery (DR)/Business Continuity (BC) plan once a specific action is completed. What is that action?

A) When the attack is eradicated.
B) When the incident is identified.
C) Once the incident is contained.
D) When the recovery phase begins.

91. Which of the following is a common drawback of implementing the Principle of Least Privilege?

A) It increases the attack surface.
B) It can be difficult and time-consuming to manage, especially in large organizations.
C) It leads to inconsistent security policies.
D) It does not minimize the risk of insider threats.

92. A security analyst is analyzing a hard drive and finds a file with a creation timestamp that has been manipulated to appear older than it is. This is an example of which anti-forensic technique?

A) Steganography
B) Encryption
C) Data Wiping
D) Timestomp

93. The document highlights the importance of user education in an access control plan. What is a key component of this education?

A) Creating a detailed log of user activity.
B) Defining user roles and permissions.
C) Conducting regular training on phishing and social engineering.
D) Implementing a firewall.

94. What is the primary function of a Software Suite in a digital forensics program?

A) To prevent physical access to the forensic lab.
B) To image a hard drive and then analyze the data for evidence.
C) To provide a secure internet connection.
D) To manage user accounts and permissions.

95. A CISO is reviewing the risks of a system outage. They are concerned about the

maximum tolerable amount of data loss. What is the term for this metric?

A) Recovery Time Objective (RTO)
B) Recovery Point Objective (RPO)
C) Mean Time to Recovery (MTTR)
D) Service Level Agreement (SLA)

96. Which of the following best describes the Single Sign-On (SSO) authentication method?

A) It requires a user to enter their credentials for every application they use.
B) It uses multiple factors for authentication.
C) It allows a user to authenticate once and access multiple related systems without re-entering their password.
D) It relies solely on biometrics for authentication.

97. An organization is planning for a disaster. The Disaster Recovery Team has a specific responsibility. What is it?

A) To manage external communications.
B) To handle the technical execution of the recovery plan, including system restoration.
C) To manage the company's finances.
D) To handle high-level decision-making.

98. A security audit reveals that a production database is running on an outdated version of a software with known vulnerabilities. This is an example of which of the following?

A) Cross-Site Scripting (XSS)
B) SQL Injection
C) Vulnerable and Outdated Components
D) Security Misconfiguration

99. A CISO wants to ensure that all employee activity on the network is logged for potential forensic analysis. This falls under which component of a comprehensive access control plan?

A) Onboarding/Offboarding procedures
B) Access Control Models
C) Policies and Procedures
D) Technical Controls (Logging and Auditing)

100. The document describes a recent cyberattack in which a software failure caused widespread outages, and malicious actors exploited the chaos by distributing fake recovery tools laced with malware. This is an example of an attack vector related to:

A) Supply Chain Attacks
B) Social Engineering
C) Denial-of-Service
D) Business Impact Analysis

Answer Key

1. **C) Mandatory Access Control (MAC)**

- **Explanation:** MAC is a very strict model used in high-security environments like the military. Access is based on sensitivity labels, ensuring that a user's access is strictly determined by their security clearance and preventing information from flowing to a lower security level. The file's owner cannot grant access that would violate the system's policy.
- **Why others are wrong:** DAC relies on the owner's discretion, which is not the objective. RBAC is based on roles and job functions, which may not be strict enough for classified data. ABAC uses attributes but is more dynamic and complex, while MAC is specifically designed for the strict hierarchical control required.

2. **B) Role-Based Access Control (RBAC)**

- **Explanation:** RBAC is a widely adopted model in modern enterprises because it simplifies administration by grouping permissions into roles based on job function. This approach makes it highly scalable and effectively enforces the principle of least privilege, reducing "permission creep".
- **Why others are wrong:** MAC is too rigid and complex to manage in a large, dynamic organization. DAC is flexible but relies on individual users, which can lead to inconsistent security policies and is difficult to manage across a large organization. Rule-Based Access Control uses conditional logic and is also a different model from RBAC.

3. **D) Attribute-Based Access Control (ABAC)**

- **Explanation:** ABAC is a dynamic and context-aware model that grants access based on a set of attributes associated with the user, resource, and environment. The example provided in the document directly aligns with this scenario: "A user can edit a document if: (user.department == document.owner.department) AND (document.status == 'Draft') AND (user.location == 'Office')".
- **Why others are wrong:** MAC is based on fixed sensitivity labels, not dynamic attributes. Rule-Based Access Control uses predefined rules, but ABAC is specifically designed for this level of granular, context-aware policy. RBAC is based on predefined roles and would not

be able to dynamically adjust permissions based on a document's status.

4. **C) Adaptive Authentication**

- **Explanation:** Adaptive authentication is also known as risk-based authentication and assesses a user's risk level based on contextual factors like location and behavior[18]. It provides a flexible security layer that adds a step for high-risk logins, like this one, while reducing friction for low-risk ones.
- **Why others are wrong:** SSO allows a single login to access multiple systems. MFA requires multiple factors regardless of risk, while adaptive authentication only requests it in high-risk scenarios. Passwordless authentication eliminates passwords entirely.

5. **B) Guidelines for creating a strong password and handling sensitive data.**

- **Explanation:** An Acceptable Use Policy (AUP) is a foundation for access control that outlines user responsibilities[23]. Key elements include data handling guidelines and password management requirements[24].
- **Why others are wrong:** While the other options may be part of a company's policies, they are not core, critical components of the AUP as described in the document.

6. **C) Multi-Factor Authentication (MFA)**

- **Explanation:** MFA requires a user to provide two or more different authentication factors. A password is "something you know," and a one-time passcode from a mobile app is "something you have". Combining them is the core principle of MFA.
- **Why others are wrong:** SSO is about authenticating once for multiple services. Separation of Duties divides tasks among multiple people. RBAC assigns permissions based on roles.

7. **B) Principle of Least Privilege**

- **Explanation:** The Principle of Least Privilege dictates that users should be granted the minimum level of access required to perform their job functions and nothing more. A failure to adhere to this principle would allow a user to have unnecessary access, leading to the type of data exfiltration described.
- **Why others are wrong:** Separation of Duties is about dividing critical tasks. SSO is about single authentication for multiple services. DAC is a specific access control model, and while related, the core principle being violated is Least Privilege.

8. **C) Separation of Duties**

- **Explanation:** Separation of Duties requires critical tasks to be divided among multiple individuals to prevent any single person from having complete control over a process. The example of a finance department's payment process is directly used in the document to illustrate this principle.
- **Why others are wrong:** Least Privilege is about limiting access to the minimum needed. MAC is a strict access control model. Zero Trust is a broader security model.

9. C) Patch management

- **Explanation:** Patch management is the process of identifying, acquiring, testing, and deploying patches to address software vulnerabilities. The document states that updates often contain "patches" that fix newly discovered vulnerabilities that cybercriminals could otherwise exploit41. The failure to apply a patch for a known vulnerability is a direct failure in this process.
- **Why others are wrong:** Threat modeling is a proactive process for identifying threats before implementation. Social engineering is a type of attack. Digital forensics is the investigation of a security incident after it has occurred.

10. A) Phishing

- **Explanation:** Phishing is a type of social engineering attack that uses emails or other electronic communications to trick a user into performing an action like transferring funds. The attacker impersonates an authority figure (the CEO) to pressure the victim into acting quickly.
- **Why others are wrong:** Session Hijacking involves taking over an authenticated session. A Drive-by Download is the unintentional download of malware from a website. A Zero-day exploit is a specific type of vulnerability that is unknown to the software vendor.

11. B) Man-in-the-Middle (MITM) attack

- **Explanation:** An MITM attack involves an attacker secretly relaying and altering the communication between two parties who believe they are communicating directly with each other. The example of a fake Wi-Fi network that intercepts traffic is a classic example of this attack.
- **Why others are wrong:** DNS poisoning is a different network attack that modifies domain name records. A DoS attack aims to make a system unavailable. XSS is an injection attack that targets web applications.

12. C) Brute-force attack

- **Explanation:** A brute-force attack is an attempt to gain access by systematically trying every possible password combination until the correct one is found. The scenario of a large number of failed login attempts from a single IP is a classic indicator of this type of attack.
- **Why others are wrong:** A Drive-by Download is unintentional malware installation. Session Hijacking steals a session token. Spear phishing is a targeted phishing attack.

13. B) Human element risks

- **Explanation:** The document explicitly states that the human element is often the weakest link in security and that a plan must include an element of user education59. The AUP and mandatory training are designed to make users aware of their responsibilities and reduce risks like phishing.

- **Why others are wrong:** While these measures can have an indirect effect on other areas, their primary purpose as described is to address the risk posed by user behavior.

14. **D) Ransomware**

- **Explanation:** Ransomware is a type of malicious software that encrypts a victim's files and demands a ransom payment to restore access. This is the exact scenario described.
- **Why others are wrong:** Trojans are malware that appears legitimate. Worms are self-replicating malware. Spyware is designed to steal information.

15. **D) Rule-Based Access Control (RBAC)**

- **Explanation:** Rule-Based Access Control uses a set of rules and logical conditions to determine access. The document gives an example of a network firewall rule that uses time of day and location to grant access, which directly aligns with this scenario.
- **Why others are wrong:** RBAC uses job roles. MAC is based on sensitivity labels. DAC is based on owner discretion.

16. **C) A security token generating a one-time passcode**

- **Explanation:** "Something You Have" authentication relies on a physical object or digital token that the user possesses. A security token or a one-time passcode sent to a phone are given as examples.
- **Why others are wrong:** A password is "something you know". A fingerprint scan is "something you are". A security question is "something you know".

17. **C) To prevent injection attacks like SQL injection and XSS**

- **Explanation:** The document explicitly states that input validation and sanitization prevents injection attacks like SQL injection and XSS. These attacks are a common way to deliver malware or steal data.
- **Why others are wrong:** While these practices contribute to overall security, their primary purpose is to prevent injection attacks. Encryption is a separate control.

18. **B) Crisis Management Team (CMT)**

- **Explanation:** The document defines the Crisis Management Team (CMT) as the team responsible for "high-level decision-making, external communications, and managing the overall business impact of the event".
- **Why others are wrong:** The IRT focuses on security-related incidents, the Disaster Recovery Team handles the technical execution of the recovery, and the Business Continuity Team handles non- technical functions.

19. **D) Post-Incident Review & Improvement**

- **Explanation:** The post-incident review phase focuses on "learning from the incident". A key component is holding a post-mortem meeting to review the incident from start to finish and analyze weaknesses.
- **Why others are wrong:** Containment is about stopping the spread. Eradication is about cleaning up the damage. Identification is about detecting a potential incident.

20. **B) To collect logs from various systems and monitor them for suspicious activity.**

- **Explanation:** The document describes a SIEM system as one that "collects logs from all servers, firewalls, and applications" and is configured to "monitor logs for suspicious patterns and alert security personnel".
- **Why others are wrong:** While a SIEM may be part of a broader security strategy, its primary purpose is log management and monitoring. The other options are functions of different security tools (e.g., email gateways, vulnerability scanners).

21. **A) A forensic workstation with a write-blocker**

- **Explanation:** The document explicitly states that a forensic workstation should have a "write-blocker to prevent accidental changes to original evidence".
- **Why others are wrong:** A SIEM system monitors logs. A Vulnerability Assessment scanner identifies weaknesses. A password cracking tool is used to break password hashes.

22. **B) To prevent an attacker from using stolen passwords on other systems if the database is breached.**

- **Explanation:** The document states that password hashing with algorithms like bcrypt prevents broken authentication. Hashing makes the password unreadable, so even if an attacker steals the database, they cannot use the passwords on other systems because the plaintext password is not stored.
- **Why others are wrong:** Hashing makes the password unreadable and does not make it easier for users to remember. It can slow down the login process slightly, but the security benefit outweighs this. Hashing is a one-way function and does not allow for recovery of the original password.

23. **B) A Vulnerability Assessment identifies potential weaknesses, while a Penetration Test actively attempts to exploit those weaknesses to assess the impact.**

- **Explanation:** The document states that a Vulnerability Assessment is a "passive approach" to identify and categorize weaknesses, while a Penetration Test is an "active approach" that simulates an attack to exploit those vulnerabilities and assess the impact.
- **Why others are wrong:** The document clearly differentiates between the two, noting that a pen test is an active attempt to exploit vulnerabilities. They can be performed both internally and externally. Both are proactive measures, not post-breach activities.

24. **C) The SolarWinds attack**

- **Explanation:** The document directly mentions the SolarWinds attack as an example of a supply chain attack, where attackers "target software vendors to infect thousands of users downstream".
- **Why others are wrong:** The CrowdStrike incident was a software failure. The Twitter breach was due to social engineering. The deepfake scam was a form of social engineering.

25. **B) AI-driven malware**

- **Explanation:** The document describes AI-driven malware as a trend where attackers use generative AI to create more sophisticated and adaptive threats. It specifically mentions a ransomware strain, PromptLock, that uses a language model to dynamically generate malicious scripts.
- **Why others are wrong:** RaaS is about selling ransomware kits. IoT vulnerabilities are a separate trend. Deepfake social engineering is a different use of AI for attacks.

26. **C) Implementing a prominent warning banner that users must acknowledge before logging in.**

- **Explanation:** The document states that warning banners provide a "strong legal basis for prosecuting unauthorized access" and act as a "significant deterrent" by explicitly stating that the system is private and monitored. A user's acknowledgment of the banner creates a loggable record.
- **Why others are wrong:** The other methods are less effective. A company-wide email can be missed, a sign at the entrance is for physical access, and an employee handbook may not be reviewed by all employees. A warning banner requires active acknowledgment.

27. **B) To identify and document critical business functions and the IT systems that support them.**

- **Explanation:** The document defines a Business Impact Analysis (BIA) as the process to "identify and document the organization's critical business functions and the information systems and data that support them"108. This is a foundational step for business continuity and disaster recovery planning.
- **Why others are wrong:** A BIA is not a technical assessment or training program. Its purpose is to understand the business-side impact, not to manage privileged accounts.

28. **B) Encrypted**

- **Explanation:** The document defines Homomorphic Encryption (HE) as a method that "allows computations on encrypted data without first decrypting it".
- **Why others are wrong:** The other options describe the state of data in other contexts, but HE is specifically about performing computations on encrypted data.

29. **A) RTO is the time to restore business operations, while RPO is the maximum acceptable data loss.**

- **Explanation:** The document explicitly defines the two metrics: "The RTO is the maximum tolerable downtime, while the RPO is the maximum tolerable data loss".
- **Why others are wrong:** The definitions are reversed in option B. Options C and D are incorrect as the two metrics are distinct and have different purposes.

30. **A) Timestomp**

- **Explanation:** The document lists several anti-forensic techniques, defining "Timestomp" as "manipulating the timestamps of files...to mislead investigators and obscure the true timeline of events".
- **Why others are wrong:** The other options are security processes or principles, not anti-forensic techniques.

31. **B) Input Validation and Sanitization**

- **Explanation:** The document states that input validation and sanitization are practices that prevent injection attacks like XSS by sanitizing inputs to remove malicious code, such as stripping HTML tags.
- **Why others are wrong:** While the other options are part of secure coding, the specific issue of a malicious script being injected into a comment field is prevented by input validation and sanitization.

32. **C) To explicitly outline a user's responsibilities and the organization's expectations for system usage and data handling.**

- **Explanation:** The document defines the Acceptable Use Policy (AUP) as the document that "must explicitly outline the user's responsibilities and the organization's expectations for handling data and using systems".
- **Why others are wrong:** The AUP is not about hardware specifications, and while it may mention consequences, its main purpose is to outline responsibilities and expectations. It is also not a list of approved websites.

33. **C) A high-performance computer with write-blockers to prevent changes to original evidence.**

- **Explanation:** The document defines a forensic workstation as a "high-performance computer with specialized hardware and software" that often has "write-blockers to prevent accidental changes to original evidence".
- **Why others are wrong:** The other options describe different types of systems or tools, not a forensic workstation.

34. **B) A breach is always possible, and every access request must be verified.**

- **Explanation:** The document defines the principle of Zero Trust as "never trust, always verify". It operates on the assumption that a breach is always possible and requires strict identity verification and authorization for every single access request.
- **Why others are wrong:** The other options describe outdated or incorrect assumptions that Zero Trust is designed to replace.

35. **C) A deepfake social engineering scam**

- **Explanation:** The document describes a real-world example of a "deepfake video call scam" where an attacker impersonated multiple people to trick a finance worker into transferring funds. This falls under the category of deepfake social engineering.
- **Why others are wrong:** A denial-of-service attack is a different type of network attack. Phishing is a broader category and this is a specific, modern example using deepfake technology. SQL injection is an attack on a database.

36. **B) Access is determined by a central authority using sensitivity labels.**

- **Explanation:** The document states that a key feature of MAC is "Centralized Control" where a central authority makes all access decisions based on a predefined security policy. It also notes that every user and resource is assigned a "sensitivity label".
- **Why others are wrong:** Option A describes DAC. Option C describes RBAC. Option D describes ABAC.

37. **C) Commercial and general-purpose operating systems**

- **Explanation:** The document states that DAC "is the most common type of access control used in commercial and general-purpose operating systems".
- **Why others are wrong:** MAC is used in high-security environments. The other options are not mentioned as the primary use case for DAC.

38. **B) Giving users only the minimum access required to perform their job functions.**

- **Explanation:** The document defines the Principle of Least Privilege as a core concept that dictates "users should be granted the minimum level of access required to perform their job functions and nothing more".
- **Why others are wrong:** The other options describe incorrect or dangerous practices that violate this principle.

39. **C) To verify a user's identity.**

- **Explanation:** The document defines authentication as the process of "verifying a user's identity" and answers the question, "Are you who you say you are?"
- **Why others are wrong:** Authorization is the process that determines what a user is allowed to do. The other options are not the primary purpose of authentication.

40. **A) Authentication verifies identity, while Authorization determines what a user can**

do.

- **Explanation:** The document clearly differentiates the two concepts: Authentication answers, "Are you who you say you are?", while Authorization answers, "What are you allowed to do here?".
- **Why others are wrong:** The other options incorrectly describe or confuse the two distinct concepts.

41. **B) Divide critical tasks among multiple individuals to prevent fraud and errors.**
- **Explanation:** The document defines Separation of Duties as a policy where "critical tasks should be divided among multiple individuals to prevent any single person from having complete control over a process". This prevents a single person from performing a fraudulent or erroneous action from start to finish.
- **Why others are wrong:** Options A and C describe practices that violate this principle. Option D is a benefit of RBAC, not Separation of Duties.

42. **B) It can lead to inconsistent security policies and accidental data exposure.**
- **Explanation:** The document lists the cons of DAC, stating that it "relies on individual users to make good security decisions" which "can lead to inconsistent security policies and accidental data exposure".
- **Why others are wrong:** Option A describes MAC's drawback. Option C is a drawback of DAC's manageability in large organizations139, not its core function. Option D is a purpose for MAC, not DAC.

43. **C) Attribute-Based Access Control (ABAC)**
- **Explanation:** The document describes ABAC as the most advanced and dynamic model, providing the "most granular control of any model" because it grants access based on a set of attributes.
- **Why others are wrong:** RBAC is based on roles. MAC is based on labels. Rule-based access control uses logical conditions but ABAC's strength is its granularity based on a variety of attributes.

44. **B) To prevent accidental changes to the original evidence on a hard drive.**
- **Explanation:** The document states that forensic workstations have "write-blockers to prevent accidental changes to original evidence".
- **Why others are wrong:** The other options describe different functions and are not the purpose of a write-blocker.

45. **D) Restricted/Secret**
- **Explanation:** The document defines the Restricted/Secret data classification as data that, "if exposed, would cause severe harm, financial loss, or legal issues".
- **Why others are wrong:** The other classifications (Public, Internal, Confidential) are defined as causing progressively less harm if exposed.

46. C) It reduces complexity and improves consistency.

- **Explanation:** The document states that centralized management for identity and access management is a key implementation control that helps to "reduce complexity and improve consistency".

- **Why others are wrong:** The other options are either incorrect or describe a disadvantage. A centralized system can be a single point of failure if not properly secured.

47. **C) To serve as a "first responder's guide" detailing initial actions to contain and mitigate an event.**

- **Explanation:** The document explicitly defines the IRP as the "first responder's guide," which details the "initial actions to contain and mitigate an event".
- **Why others are wrong:** The other options are not the primary purpose of an IRP, but rather components of a broader DR/BC plan.

48. **C) Timestomp, which manipulates file timestamps**

- **Explanation:** The document defines "Timestomp" as an anti-forensic technique that involves "manipulating the timestamps of files (e.g., creation, modification, and access times) to mislead investigators".
- **Why others are wrong:** Antivirus, MFA, and vulnerability assessments are security practices, not anti- forensic techniques.

49. **B) To prevent the threat from spreading further.**

- **Explanation:** The document defines containment as the "crucial phase where the team takes immediate action to prevent the threat from spreading". The goal is to "stop the bleeding".
- **Why others are wrong:** The other options describe different phases of the incident response lifecycle.

50. **B) Secure Coding**

- **Explanation:** The document defines Secure Coding as the practice of "writing code in a way that protects an application from security vulnerabilities".
- **Why others are wrong:** The other options are separate security disciplines.

51. **A) Session Hijacking**

- **Explanation:** The document defines Session Hijacking as an attack where "attackers steal session cookies or tokens from a user's active session to impersonate them".
- **Why others are wrong:** The other options are different types of attacks. Phishing uses deception, Drive-by Downloads are unintentional downloads, and SQL Injection targets databases.

52. **C) A Drive-by Download**

- **Explanation:** The document defines a Drive-by Download as the "unintentional download of malicious software onto your computer or mobile device" that can happen "simply by visiting a compromised or malicious website".

- **Why others are wrong:** Infected Media uses physical devices158. A Rootkit hides its presence. Ransomware encrypts files.

53. D) Notification

- **Explanation:** The document lists the phases of the incident response lifecycle as: Preparation, Identification, Containment, Eradication, Recovery, and Post-Incident Review. Notification is an action within these phases, not a phase itself.
- **Why others are wrong:** Preparation, Identification, and Eradication are all explicitly listed as phases in the document.

54. **C) To focus on security-related incidents, including forensic analysis and containing breaches.**

- **Explanation:** The document defines the IRT's responsibilities as focusing on "security-related incidents" and specifically mentions "forensic analysis, containing security breaches, and monitoring for secondary attacks".
- **Why others are wrong:** The other options describe the responsibilities of different teams (CMT, Business Continuity Team, etc.).

55. **B) To serve as a strong legal basis for prosecuting unauthorized access.**

- **Explanation:** The document states that warning banners are a "crucial...component" that provides a "strong legal basis for prosecuting unauthorized access".
- **Why others are wrong:** While the banner may promote awareness, its primary purpose as described in the document is to establish a legal foundation and act as a deterrent.

56. **C) To test employees' awareness and response to phishing attempts.**

- **Explanation:** Under the "Proactive Prevention" phase, the document lists "Simulated Phishing Drills" with the purpose of regularly sending fake emails to "test their awareness and response".
- **Why others are wrong:** The other options are either incorrect or describe the purpose of different tools or activities. Drills are for testing and training, not for punishment or automatic blocking.

57. **C) To clean up any damage from the attack and restore normal operations.**

- **Explanation:** The document states that the Eradication & Recovery phase "focuses on cleaning up any damage from the attack and restoring normal operations".
- **Why others are wrong:** The other options describe actions in different phases of the response plan.

58. **B) Role-Based uses roles, while Rule-Based uses a set of logical conditions.**

- **Explanation:** The document explicitly notes that Rule-Based Access Control is "different from Role- Based Access Control". It defines RBAC as grouping permissions into roles and Rule-Based as using a "set of rules, or logical conditions".
- **Why others are wrong:** The other options either confuse the two models or incorrectly describe their function.

59. C) Enforcement of Multi-Factor Authentication (MFA)

- **Explanation:** Under the "Proactive Prevention" phase of the phishing response plan, the document lists "Technical Controls," and one of them is to "Enforce Multi-Factor Authentication (MFA)".

- **Why others are wrong:** Incident analysis, threat intelligence, and forensic investigation are actions that occur during or after an attack, not in the proactive prevention phase.

60. **B) It documents potential threats and the vulnerabilities of identified assets.**

- **Explanation:** The document states that the purpose of the Threat & Risk Assessment is to "document potential threats (both natural and man-made) and the vulnerabilities of identified assets".
- **Why others are wrong:** Defining the scope is Step 1 of the process. Technical execution is the responsibility of the Disaster Recovery team. It is a critical step, not an optional one.

61. **C) To provide high-level decision-making and manage the overall business impact.**

- **Explanation:** The document defines the Crisis Management Team (CMT) as responsible for "high- level decision-making, external communications, and managing the overall business impact of the event".
- **Why others are wrong:** The other options describe the responsibilities of the Disaster Recovery, Business Continuity, and IRT teams.

62. **A) Ransomware-as-a-Service (RaaS)**

- **Explanation:** The document defines RaaS as a trend where "Cybercriminals can now easily purchase or rent ransomware kits on dark web markets to launch attacks without needing advanced technical skills".
- **Why others are wrong:** The other options are different types of attacks or trends.

63. **B) On-path attacks (formerly known as man-in-the-middle attacks)**

- **Explanation:** The document states that a VPN is a key mitigation for on-path attacks, as it encrypts the user's traffic and prevents an attacker from intercepting it.
- **Why others are wrong:** The other attacks are not primarily mitigated by a VPN. SQL injection targets databases, DoS attacks flood a system with traffic, and XSS is an injection attack on a web application.

64. **B) It aims to eliminate traditional passwords entirely, using alternative methods like biometrics.**

- **Explanation:** The document defines Passwordless Authentication as a modern approach that "aims to eliminate the need for traditional passwords entirely" and instead relies on a combination of other factors like biometrics.
- **Why others are wrong:** The other options describe traditional password-based authentication or MFA.

65. **C) To review the incident from start to finish and identify weaknesses in the response plan.**

- **Explanation:** The document states that a Post-Mortem Meeting is held to "review the incident from start to finish" and to "Analyze Weaknesses" in the plan.
- **Why others are wrong:** The other options are not the primary purpose of a post-mortem review. The goal is to learn from the incident, not to assign blame.

66. **C) To provide a trail of evidence for forensic analysis and compliance.**

- **Explanation:** The document states that auditing and monitoring "provide a trail of evidence that can be used to investigate security incidents and breaches after they occur" and are "essential for compliance with regulatory requirements".
- **Why others are wrong:** The other options are incorrect. Auditing and monitoring do not give all users the same access or eliminate the need for a plan.

67. **C) To assign a security clearance to both users and resources.**

- **Explanation:** The document states that in a MAC model, "Every user (subject) and every resource (object) is assigned a sensitivity label" and that "Access is granted only if the subject's label meets or exceeds the object's label".
- **Why others are wrong:** The other options are incorrect as the purpose of sensitivity labels is to enforce the access policy.

68. **A) A single compromised account can grant an attacker access to multiple services.**

- **Explanation:** The document lists the cons of SSO, stating that "A single compromised account can grant an attacker access to multiple services".
- **Why others are wrong:** SSO actually improves user experience by reducing "password fatigue" and the need for multiple passwords.

69. **C) To create the formal IR plan, build a team, and conduct training before an incident occurs.**

- **Explanation:** The document states that the Preparation phase "happens before an incident" and involves "creating a formal IR plan, building a Computer Security Incident Response Team (CSIRT), acquiring necessary tools, defining roles and responsibilities, and conducting regular training and drills".
- **Why others are wrong:** The other options describe actions in different phases of the incident response lifecycle.

70. **A) Onboarding/Offboarding**

- **Explanation:** The document lists "Onboarding/Offboarding" as a key component of an access control plan that "Establishes a process for granting and revoking access for new and departing employees". The scenario of an employee changing departments is an example of an effective offboarding/onboarding process.
- **Why others are wrong:** While related, the scenario specifically describes the process of granting and revoking access, which is the purpose of an onboarding/offboarding procedure.

71. **B) To completely destroy data on a drive to make it unrecoverable.**

- **Explanation:** The document defines "Data Wiping and Sanitization" as "The complete destruction of data on a drive using specialized tools".

- **Why others are wrong:** The other options describe different anti-forensic techniques like encryption and steganography.

72. **B) It is significantly more complex to design, implement, and manage.**
- **Explanation:** The document lists the cons of ABAC, stating that it is "Significantly more complex to design, implement, and manage" and "Requires a robust attribute management system".
- **Why others are wrong:** The other options are incorrect. ABAC is the most granular and scalable model.

73. **C) Single Sign-On (SSO)**
- **Explanation:** The document states that a key feature of SSO is a "Centralized authentication point" that uses "shared credentials for multiple services".
- **Why others are wrong:** The other options are different security principles or access control models.

74. **B) Cross-Site Scripting (XSS)**
- **Explanation:** The document states that one of the purposes of input validation and sanitization is to "sanitize inputs to remove malicious code (e.g., strip HTML tags for XSS)". This attack occurs when an attacker injects a malicious script that is not properly sanitized.
- **Why others are wrong:** The other attacks are different types of web application vulnerabilities.

75. **B) It makes it significantly harder for attackers to gain access even if one factor is compromised.**
- **Explanation:** The document states that MFA "Significantly increases security by making it much harder for attackers to gain access, even if one factor is compromised".
- **Why others are wrong:** MFA can be seen as less convenient. It is a strong control but does not eliminate the need for others.

76. **B) Ensuring that all libraries and frameworks are kept up to date.**
- **Explanation:** The document lists "Vulnerable and Outdated Components" as a risk and states that using components with known vulnerabilities can expose the entire system. The solution is to keep all software and components updated with security patches.
- **Why others are wrong:** The other options are different security controls.

77. **C) To monitor and filter incoming and outgoing network traffic.**
- **Explanation:** The document defines a firewall as a "security system that monitors and filters incoming and outgoing network traffic based on a set of security rules".
- **Why others are wrong:** The other options describe the functions of different security

tools (e.g., steganography, antivirus, encryption).

78. **C) Least Privilege**

- **Explanation:** The document defines the Principle of Least Privilege, stating that it dictates that a user should only be granted the minimum level of access and that the "Default Deny" policy is to deny all access unless it is explicitly granted.
- **Why others are wrong:** The other options are different security principles or models.

79. **C) It is highly rigid and complex to administer.**

- **Explanation:** The document lists the cons of MAC, stating that it is "Extremely rigid and complex to administer and manage".
- **Why others are wrong:** Option A describes DAC. Option B describes a drawback of DAC and RBAC if not managed correctly. Option D is incorrect, as MAC is ideal for high-security environments.

80. **C) Phishing**

- **Explanation:** The document defines phishing as the use of a "deceptive message designed to trick a person into revealing sensitive information or taking a malicious action". The scenario of a fake link in a legitimate-looking email is a classic phishing attack.
- **Why others are wrong:** Vishing and smishing are phishing attacks over voice and SMS, respectively. Hoaxing is a broader term for a deceptive message, but phishing is the specific type of attack described.

81. **B) The IRP acts as the "first responder's guide," detailing the initial actions to contain and mitigate an event.**

- **Explanation:** The ISBK explicitly states that the IRP is the "first responder's guide," which details "the initial actions to contain and mitigate an event". It is integrated into the DR/BC documentation to provide a seamless transition from incident response to recovery.
- **Why others are wrong:** The other options incorrectly describe the relationship between the IRP and the DR/BC plan.

82. **B) Steganography**

- **Explanation:** The document defines Steganography as "Hiding data within a seemingly harmless file, such as an image or audio file".
- **Why others are wrong:** The other options are different anti-forensic techniques. Timestomp manipulates timestamps, Data Wiping destroys data, and Encryption makes data unreadable.

83. **B) To identify and document the organization's critical business functions.**

- **Explanation:** The document defines a BIA as a process to "identify and document the organization's critical business functions and the information systems and data that

support them".
- **Why others are wrong:** The other options describe different security processes.

84. **D) Triaging alerts and user reports to determine if an attack is legitimate.**
- **Explanation:** The document states that in the Detection & Triage phase, "a security analyst must quickly triage it to determine if it is a legitimate attack or a false positive".
- **Why others are wrong:** The other options describe actions in different phases of the plan.

85. **B) To prevent the cookie from being transmitted over an unencrypted connection.**
- **Explanation:** The document notes that secure session cookies should use the Secure attribute, which "ensures the browser will only send the cookie over an encrypted connection (HTTPS)". The HttpOnlyattribute prevents client-side scripts from accessing the cookie.
- **Why others are wrong:** The other options are either incorrect or describe a different attribute.

86. **C) To document potential threats and the vulnerabilities of identified assets.**
- **Explanation:** The document states that the purpose of the Threat & Risk Assessment is to "document potential threats...and the vulnerabilities of identified assets" to guide the DR/BC plan.
- **Why others are wrong:** The other options describe different steps in the planning process.

87. **B) The default policy is to deny all access unless it is explicitly granted.**
- **Explanation:** The document defines this as a key feature of the Principle of Least Privilege. This is a fundamental concept in security.
- **Why others are wrong:** The other options are incorrect and describe insecure practices.

88. **B) To ensure that access rights are still appropriate for a user's current role and to remove unnecessary privileges.**
- **Explanation:** The document states that organizations should "Conduct regular audits of user access rights to ensure they are still appropriate for their current role" and "Remove access for employees who have left the company or changed roles promptly". This helps to prevent "permission creep".
- **Why others are wrong:** While a security audit might uncover other issues, the primary purpose of this review is to manage permissions.

89. **B) Biometric-Based Authentication**
- **Explanation:** The document describes Biometric-Based Authentication as a method that is "Highly secure and convenient" and "Eliminates the need for users to remember passwords" because it relies on a unique biological trait.
- **Why others are wrong:** The other options are either less secure (Knowledge-Based)

or do not eliminate the need for a password.

90. C) Once the incident is contained.

- **Explanation:** The document states that the IRP is a referenced document that "clearly hands off to the DR/BC plan once the incident is contained and recovery can begin".
- **Why others are wrong:** The other options describe actions that happen either before containment or during the recovery phase.

91. B) It can be difficult and time-consuming to manage, especially in large organizations.

- **Explanation:** The document lists the cons of the Principle of Least Privilege, stating that it "Can be difficult and time-consuming to implement and manage, especially in large organizations".
- **Why others are wrong:** Least Privilege *reduces* the attack surface and minimizes insider threats. Inconsistent policies are a drawback of DAC, not Least Privilege.

92. D) Timestomp

- **Explanation:** The document defines "Timestomp" as the anti-forensic technique of "Manipulating the timestamps of files (e.g., creation, modification, and access times) to mislead investigators".
- **Why others are wrong:** The other options are different anti-forensic techniques.

93. C) Conducting regular training on phishing and social engineering.

- **Explanation:** The document states that the human element is often the weakest link and that an access control plan must include user education. It specifically recommends training topics that include "Phishing and Social Engineering: How to identify and avoid malicious emails, texts, and phone calls".
- **Why others are wrong:** The other options are technical controls or administrative procedures, not part of user education.

94. B) To image a hard drive and then analyze the data for evidence.

- **Explanation:** The document defines forensic software suites as tools that "allow investigators to examine and interpret the data from a forensic image" and can "recover deleted files, search for keywords, analyze a timeline of events, and identify artifacts of malicious activity".
- **Why others are wrong:** The other options describe functions of different tools or security controls.

95. B) Recovery Point Objective (RPO)

- **Explanation:** The document defines the RPO as the "maximum tolerable data loss".
- **Why others are wrong:** RTO is the maximum tolerable downtime. MTTR and SLA are not

defined in the same context in the document.

96. **C) It allows a user to authenticate once and access multiple related systems without re- entering their password.**

- **Explanation:** The document defines SSO as a method that "allows a user to authenticate once with a single set of credentials and then access multiple, related, but independent software systems without having to re-enter their password for each one".
- **Why others are wrong:** The other options are incorrect descriptions of SSO.

97. **B) To handle the technical execution of the recovery plan, including system restoration.**

- **Explanation:** The document states that the Disaster Recovery Team is responsible for the "technical execution of the recovery plan, including system restoration, data recovery, and hardware procurement".
- **Why others are wrong:** The other options are the responsibilities of other teams.

98. **C) Vulnerable and Outdated Components**

- **Explanation:** The document lists "Vulnerable and Outdated Components" as a common web application security risk, stating that using components with known vulnerabilities can expose an entire system to risk.
- **Why others are wrong:** The other options describe different types of attacks or misconfigurations.

99. **D) Technical Controls (Logging and Auditing)**

- **Explanation:** The document states that a comprehensive access control plan includes "Technical Controls," and one of the key elements under this section is "Logging and Auditing," which describes how access events are logged and reviewed.
- **Why others are wrong:** The other options are different components of an access control plan, but not the one that specifically covers the logging of user activity.

100. **A) Supply Chain Attacks**

Explanation: The document mentions the CrowdStrike Incident (2024) as a recent example of attackers exploiting a software failure and distributing fake recovery tools, which highlights the risk of supply chain attacks.

Why others are wrong: While social engineering was used in the incident, the core attack vector related to the chaos and distribution of fake tools falls under the broader category of a supply chain attack. Denial-of-service and business impact analysis are different concepts.

CCISO Explain IT like I Am 5: Domain 5

DOMAIN 5: Strategic Planning, Finance, Procurement, and Third-Party Management

Integrating Business Functions with Information Security Management

Effective information security is no longer a siloed technical function. It is a fundamental business imperative that must be deeply integrated with core organizational processes to protect valuable assets, ensure business continuity, and maintain stakeholder trust. In the context of information security management programs, Strategic Planning, Finance, Procurement, and Third-Party Management form a critical domain, particularly as outlined in the Certified Chief Information Security Officer (CCISO) certification from EC-Council. This domain, known as Domain 5, emphasizes aligning security initiatives with organizational goals, managing resources effectively, and handling external partnerships to mitigate risks. This section outlines how these four critical business functions are essential to building a robust and resilient security posture, equipping security leaders to integrate them into a cohesive information security management system (ISMS).

Strategic Planning and Information Security

Strategic planning in information security involves designing and maintaining an enterprise information security architecture (EISA) that aligns business processes, IT systems, networks, personnel, and projects with the organization's overall security strategy. This integration ensures that security initiatives directly support the business's mission, vision, and objectives.

Key areas of integration include:

- **Risk-Based Prioritization:** Strategic planning begins with a comprehensive risk assessment. Security teams must identify and prioritize risks based on their potential impact to business operations, not just technical vulnerabilities. This process helps allocate resources to protect the most critical assets. Key activities include conducting external analyses (e.g., market trends and industry environments) and internal analyses (e.g., risk management and organizational capabilities) to ensure the security program supports business objectives.

- **Defining Risk Appetite:** Senior leadership, in collaboration with security and business leaders, must define the organization's risk appetite—the level of risk it is willing to accept to achieve its goals. This provides a clear directive for the security team, guiding decisions on what risks to accept, mitigate, transfer, or avoid.
- **Security Roadmap Development:** The security strategy should be a long-term roadmap that aligns with business objectives over a 3- to 5-year horizon. This includes engaging key stakeholders to clarify organizational goals and define a visionary strategic plan with clear targets. It also involves establishing key performance indicators (KPIs) for ongoing measurement of effectiveness. This forward-looking process helps prevent misalignment between security efforts and business needs, fostering a proactive security posture.

Enterprise Information Security Architecture (EISA) Guide

This guide provides a comprehensive overview of the process for designing, developing, and maintaining an Enterprise Information Security Architecture (EISA). The goal of EISA is to align an organization's business processes, technology, people, and projects with a cohesive security strategy, creating a resilient and secure operational environment.

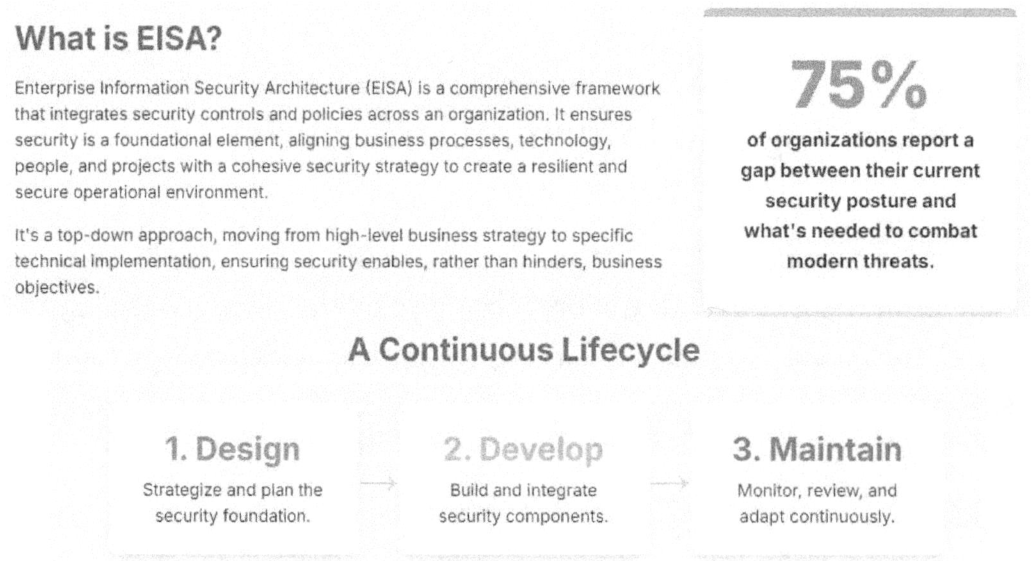

Phase 1: Design

The design phase is foundational, focusing on understanding the organization's strategic goals and translating them into clear security requirements. It is a top-down approach, focusing on business alignment before diving into technical details.

Key Steps in Design

➢ **Strategic Alignment & Scoping:**
Assess the current state, understand business objectives, and define the scope of the EISA.

➢ **Define Principles & Requirements:**
Establish core principles like "least privilege" and categorize critical assets.

➢ **Create Target Architecture:**
Envision the future state, define security domains, and select appropriate frameworks like SABSA or TOGAF.

Defining Security Domains

A balanced EISA provides coverage across multiple security domains. The radar chart below shows a sample assessment of focus areas in a target architecture.

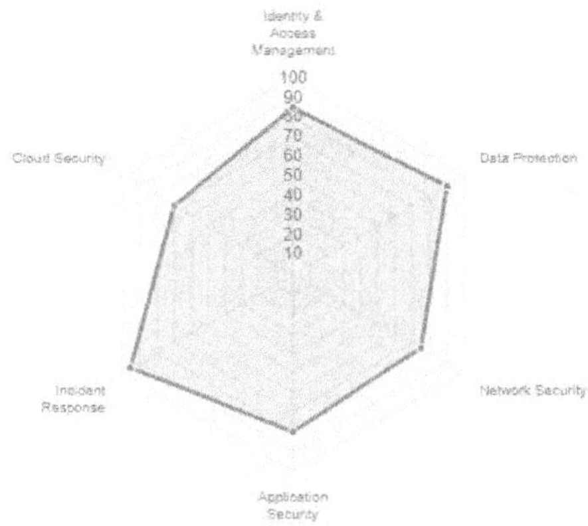

Step 1: Strategic Alignment and Scoping

- **Assess the Current State and Business Strategy:** Begin by understanding the organization's mission, business objectives, and risk appetite. Conduct a thorough risk assessment to identify gaps, vulnerabilities, and compliance issues in existing security postures. Security must be an enabler of business, not a roadblock.
- **Identify Stakeholders:** Engage with key personnel from business units, IT, legal, HR, and executive leadership to gather their perspectives and requirements.
- **Define Scope:** Clearly define what the EISA will cover, including specific business units, geographic locations, technologies, and regulatory requirements.

Step 2: Define Security Principles and Requirements

- **Establish Principles:** Establish high-level principles, such as "defense in depth" or "least privilege," tailored to the organization's risk appetite.
- **Categorize Assets:** Classify data, systems, and networks based on their sensitivity (e.g., critical vs. non-critical).
- **Integrate People and Processes:** Incorporate people factors, like training needs and role-based access, and operational elements, like incident response protocols.

Step 3: Create Logical and Target State Architecture (To-Be)

- **Develop the Security Vision:** Based on business needs and risk analysis, create a clear, high-level vision for the future state of the organization's security posture.
- **Define Security Domains:** Design a conceptual model that outlines security domains, such as identity and access management, network security, data protection, and application security.

- **Leverage Frameworks:** Use established frameworks like SABSA (Sherwood Applied Business Security Architecture) for business-driven security attributes, COBIT for governance, and TOGAF for integration with broader enterprise architecture.
- **Select Technologies and Controls:** Choose the technologies, frameworks, and processes to achieve the target state. These must be scalable and aligned with the organization's IT roadmap.

Phase 2: Develop

The development phase involves creating a detailed roadmap and integrating the EISA into daily operations and project lifecycles.

Prioritizing Security Initiatives

The EISA roadmap prioritizes projects based on risk and business impact. High-priority items address the most critical vulnerabilities first.

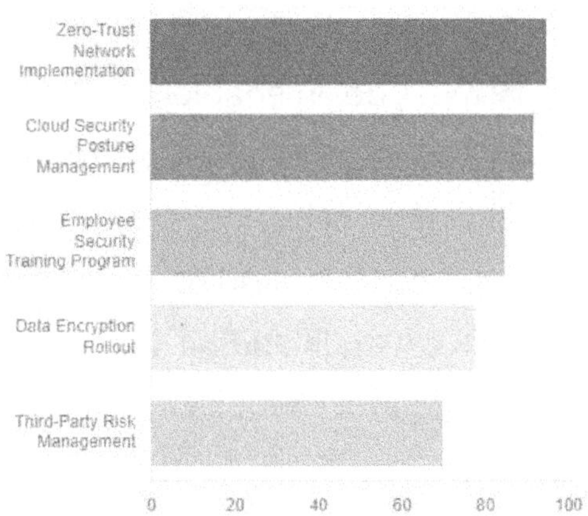

Key Steps in Development

- **Create EISA Roadmap:** Prioritize initiatives and develop a multi-year plan with secured funding.
- **Build Physical Architecture:** Implement technologies like firewalls, SASE, and endpoint protection. Develop policies and standards.
- **Integrate & Validate:** Embed security into business processes, train staff, and conduct penetration testing to verify effectiveness.

Step 1: Create an EISA Roadmap

- **Prioritize Initiatives:** Based on risk, business impact, and resource availability, prioritize security initiatives from the target state.
- **Develop a Phased Plan:** Create a multi-year roadmap that outlines the sequence of projects and initiatives needed to achieve the target state.
- **Secure Funding and Resources:** Work with leadership to secure the necessary budget and personnel for implementation.

Step 2: Build Physical and Component Architecture

- **Select and Configure Technologies:** Implement firewalls, intrusion detection systems (IDS), endpoint protection for hardware, and secure access service edge (SASE) for networks.

- **Develop Policies and Standards:** Create guidelines for software development (e.g., secure coding), hardware procurement, and network configurations (e.g., zero-trust models).
- **Align with Projects:** Embed security reviews into agile or waterfall methodologies to ensure security is "baked in" from the start.

Step 3: Integrate with Business Elements

- **Align Business Processes:** Embed security controls into workflows, such as automated approvals for data access.
- **Address People and Operations:** Roll out training programs, define roles (e.g., security champions), and establish monitoring for operational anomalies.
- **Ensure Network Alignment:** Design segmented LAN/WAN with encryption and access controls to support remote work and cloud integrations.

Step 4: Test and Validate

- **Perform Testing:** Conduct penetration testing, vulnerability scans, and simulations to verify alignment.
- **Use Metrics:** Use metrics like Mean Time to Detect (MTTD) and compliance rates to measure effectiveness.
- **Iterate:** Refine the architecture based on feedback from cross-functional teams.

Phase 3: Maintain

Security is not a one-time project; it's a continuous process. The maintenance phase ensures the EISA remains effective and adaptable.

Prioritizing Security Initiatives

The EISA roadmap prioritizes projects based on risk and business impact. High-priority items address the most critical vulnerabilities first.

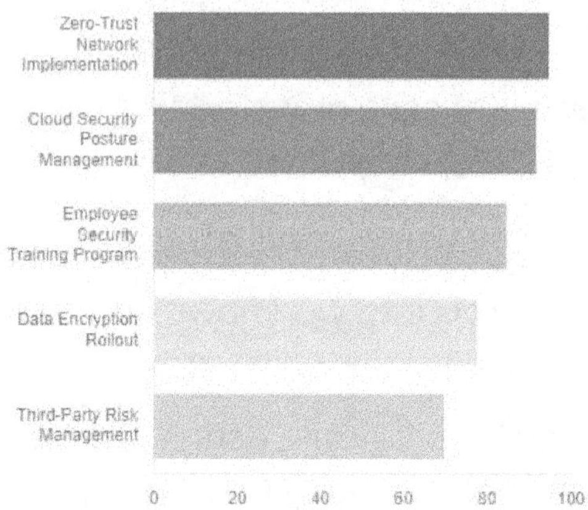

Key Steps in Development

- **Create EISA Roadmap:** Prioritize initiatives and develop a multi-year plan with secured funding.
- **Build Physical Architecture:** Implement technologies like firewalls, SASE, and endpoint protection. Develop policies and standards.
- **Integrate & Validate:** Embed security into business processes, train staff, and conduct penetration testing to verify effectiveness.

Step 1: Continuous Monitoring and Management

- **Implement Monitoring Tools:** Use security information and event management (SIEM) systems and other monitoring tools to continuously collect and analyze security data. Implement Security Operations Centers (SOCs) for real-time monitoring.
- **Manage Security Controls:** Regularly review and update configurations for security controls to ensure they are operating effectively.

Step 2: Audit and Review

- **Conduct Regular Audits:** Perform internal and external audits to verify compliance with security policies and standards.
- **Review Architecture Periodically:** The EISA should be reviewed at least annually, or after significant business changes, to ensure it remains aligned with the organization's evolving needs.

Step 3: Incident Response and Threat Management

- **Develop an Incident Response Plan:** Create a clear, well-documented plan for how to respond to and recover from security incidents.
- **Threat Intelligence:** Continuously monitor the threat landscape and update the EISA to defend against new and emerging threats.

Benefits and Best Practices

A well-aligned EISA reduces risks, improves efficiency, and supports innovation. Best practices include:

- **Holistic Integration:** Treat security as part of the enterprise architecture, not a silo.
- **Collaboration:** Involve IT, business units, and external experts.
- **Scalability:** Design for growth, such as hybrid cloud environments.
- **Compliance Focus:** Align with standards like NIST, ISO 27001, or GDPR.

By following this framework, organizations can create a robust EISA that not only protects assets but also enables strategic goals.

Enterprise Information Security Architecture (EISA) Frameworks

An Enterprise Information Security Architecture (EISA) is a structured approach for designing, implementing, and managing an organization's security strategy. It is a subset of enterprise architecture that focuses specifically on securing the organization's digital assets, including data, networks, and systems. The primary purpose of an EISA is to ensure that security initiatives are strategically aligned with the overall business objectives and are not just a collection of siloed, ad-hoc solutions.

What is an EISA?

An Enterprise Information Security Architecture (EISA) is a structured approach for designing, implementing, and managing an organization's security strategy. It's the blueprint that ensures all security initiatives are strategically aligned with business objectives, moving beyond a collection of separate, siloed solutions to create a cohesive defense.

Key Components of an EISA Framework

A robust EISA framework typically involves several layers, which help to translate high-level business goals into specific technical security controls. These layers include:

- **Business Context Layer:** This is the highest and most abstract layer. It defines the organization's business goals, risk tolerance, and the value of its information assets. The EISA must be defined by and support these business needs.
- **Conceptual Layer:** This layer provides a high-level, "big picture" view of the security architecture. It outlines the core security principles, the overall security vision, and the major security domains (e.g., network security, data security, application security).
- **Logical Layer:** Here, the conceptual principles are translated into a logical design. It defines how security will be implemented across various systems and

processes, including defining security controls, policies, and procedures. This layer is often where the "what" and "how" of security are determined.

- **Implementation Layer:** This is the practical, hands-on layer. It details the specific technologies, tools, and processes required to implement the logical design. This includes the selection of firewalls, encryption software, access control systems, and incident response plans.

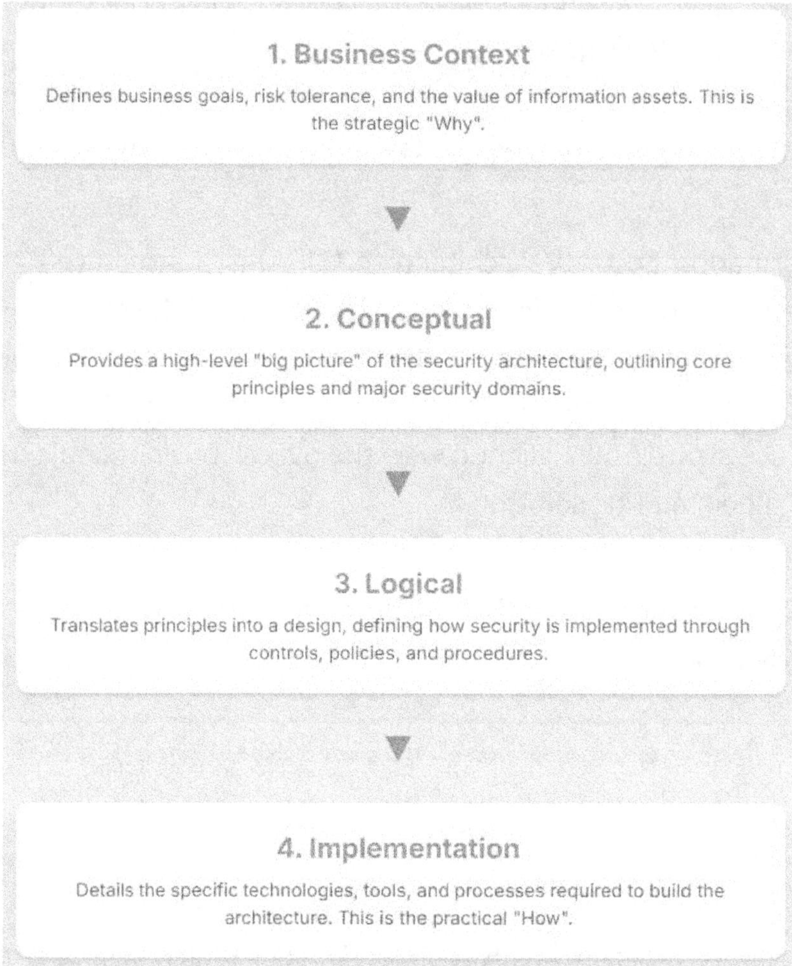

Benefits of an EISA

Adopting an EISA framework provides numerous benefits for an organization:

- **Strategic Alignment:** It ensures that security investments and efforts directly support business objectives, rather than being seen as a separate cost center.

- **Proactive Security:** By identifying and mitigating security vulnerabilities at the architectural level, EISA helps organizations move from a reactive to a proactive security posture.
- **Risk Management:** The framework provides a systematic way to identify, assess, and manage risks across the entire enterprise.
- **Compliance:** A well-documented EISA can assist in meeting regulatory requirements and industry standards, which is crucial for sectors like finance and healthcare.

Key EISA Frameworks

Yes, several established frameworks can guide the design, development, and maintenance of an Enterprise Information Security Architecture (EISA). These frameworks provide structured methodologies to align security with business objectives, integrate with IT systems, and address risks across processes, people, and technology. Below is a concise overview of key frameworks relevant to EISA:

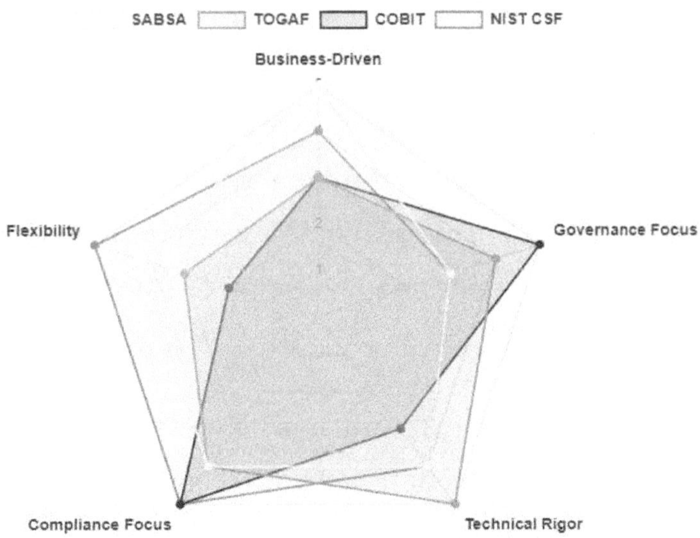

SABSA (Sherwood Applied Business Security Architecture)

Overview: A business-driven, risk-based framework that aligns security with organizational goals. It uses a layered approach (conceptual, logical, physical, and component) to create a holistic security architecture.

- **Relevance to EISA:** SABSA is ideal for aligning business processes, IT systems, networks, and people with the organization's security strategy. It emphasizes attributes like confidentiality, integrity, and availability tailored to business needs.

- **Key Features:**
    - Business attribute profiling to map security requirements to business outcomes.
    - A top-down approach starting with business context, ensuring alignment with strategy.
    - Scalable and adaptable for enterprises of all sizes.
- **Use Case:** Best for organizations needing a comprehensive, business-focused security architecture that integrates with enterprise architecture frameworks like TOGAF.

TOGAF (The Open Group Architecture Framework) with Security Extensions

Overview: While primarily an enterprise architecture framework, TOGAF includes security architecture components that can be adapted for EISA. It provides a structured process (Architecture Development Method, ADM) to integrate security into IT, networks, and business processes.

- **Relevance to EISA:** TOGAF's security extensions ensure alignment of hardware, software, and operations with the organization's security strategy, focusing on governance and risk management.
- **Key Features:**
    - Integrates security into enterprise-wide architecture.
    - Supports governance through the Architecture Board and compliance checks.
    - Provides templates for security requirements and risk assessments.
- **Use Case:** Suitable for organizations already using TOGAF for enterprise architecture, seeking to embed security holistically.

COBIT (Control Objectives for Information and Related Technologies)

Overview: A governance and management framework focused on IT processes, including security. COBIT aligns IT and security with business goals through defined controls and metrics.

- **Relevance to EISA:** COBIT helps structure security processes for operations, projects, and IT assets, ensuring compliance and risk management align with business strategy.
- **Key Features:**
    - Focuses on governance, risk, and compliance (GRC).
    - Provides a maturity model to assess and improve security processes.

- Aligns with standards like ISO 27001 and NIST.

- **Use Case:** Ideal for organizations prioritizing governance and measurable security outcomes across people, processes, and technology.

NIST Cybersecurity Framework (CSF)

Overview: A risk-based framework developed by the National Institute of Standards and Technology, focusing on five core functions: Identify, Protect, Detect, Respond, and Recover.

- **Relevance to EISA:** NIST CSF provides a flexible structure to secure IT systems, networks, and operations while aligning with business objectives and regulatory requirements.
- **Key Features:**
    - Customizable profiles to align security with business priorities.
    - Focuses on risk management and continuous improvement.
    - Widely adopted for compliance with standards like GDPR and HIPAA.
- **Use Case:** Best for organizations needing a straightforward, compliance-driven framework that integrates with existing IT and network architectures.

ISO/IEC 27001 (Information Security Management System)

Overview: An international standard for establishing, implementing, maintaining, and improving an information security management system (ISMS).

- **Relevance to EISA:** ISO 27001 provides a systematic approach to securing IT assets, networks, and processes, with a focus on risk management and alignment with business goals.
- **Key Features:**
    - Defines controls for hardware, software, networks, and people (e.g., access management, training).
    - Supports certification, ensuring compliance with global standards.
    - Integrates with enterprise-wide risk management.
- **Use Case:** Suitable for organizations seeking a globally recognized standard to structure their EISA, especially for compliance-driven industries.

Zachman Framework (Security-Focused Adaptation)

- **Overview:** A structured matrix for enterprise architecture that can be adapted for security by mapping security controls across perspectives (e.g., planner, designer) and aspects (e.g., data, function, network).
- **Relevance to EISA:** Helps organize security components across business processes, IT systems, and operations, ensuring comprehensive coverage.
- **Key Features:**
    - Provides a taxonomy for aligning security with enterprise components.
    - Supports detailed mapping of people, processes, and technology.
    - Less prescriptive, allowing customization.
- **Use Case:** Useful for complex organizations needing a flexible, high-level framework to integrate security with enterprise architecture.

Comparison and Selection

- **SABSA:** Best for business-driven, strategic alignment with comprehensive security integration.
- **TOGAF:** Ideal for organizations with existing enterprise architecture practices.
- **COBIT:** Strong for governance and compliance-focused EISA.
- **NIST CSF:** Flexible and practical for risk-based, compliance-driven security.
- **ISO 27001:** Preferred for organizations needing certified, standardized security processes.
- **Zachman:** Good for highly customized, taxonomy-driven approaches.

Best Practices for Applying Frameworks

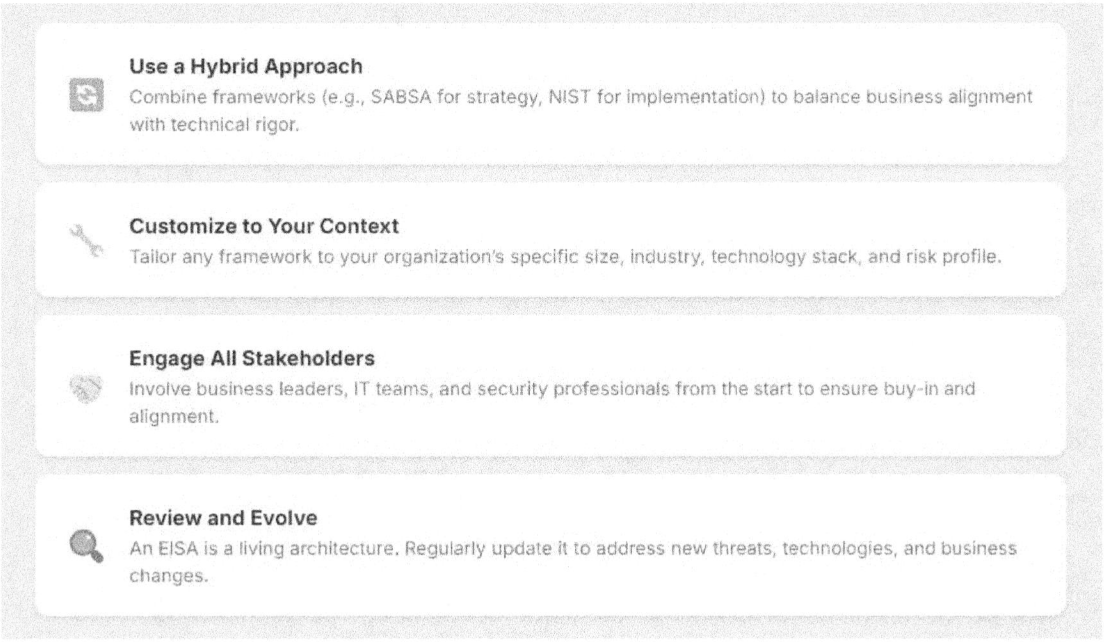

- **Hybrid Approach:** Many organizations combine frameworks (e.g., SABSA for strategy, NIST for implementation) to balance business alignment and technical rigor.
- **Customization:** Tailor frameworks to the organization's size, industry, and risk profile.
- **Stakeholder Engagement:** Involve business leaders, IT teams, and security professionals to ensure alignment with strategy, operations, and projects.
- **Continuous Review:** Regularly update the framework to address new threats, technologies, and business changes.

Ultimately, an EISA framework is a critical tool for organizations seeking to create a cohesive, effective, and business-aligned information security program.

ISMS Strategic Planning Document

This document provides a strategic framework for the development and management of an Information Security Management System (ISMS). It is a template designed to be customized with specific organizational data to ensure the information security program is effectively aligned with business objectives.

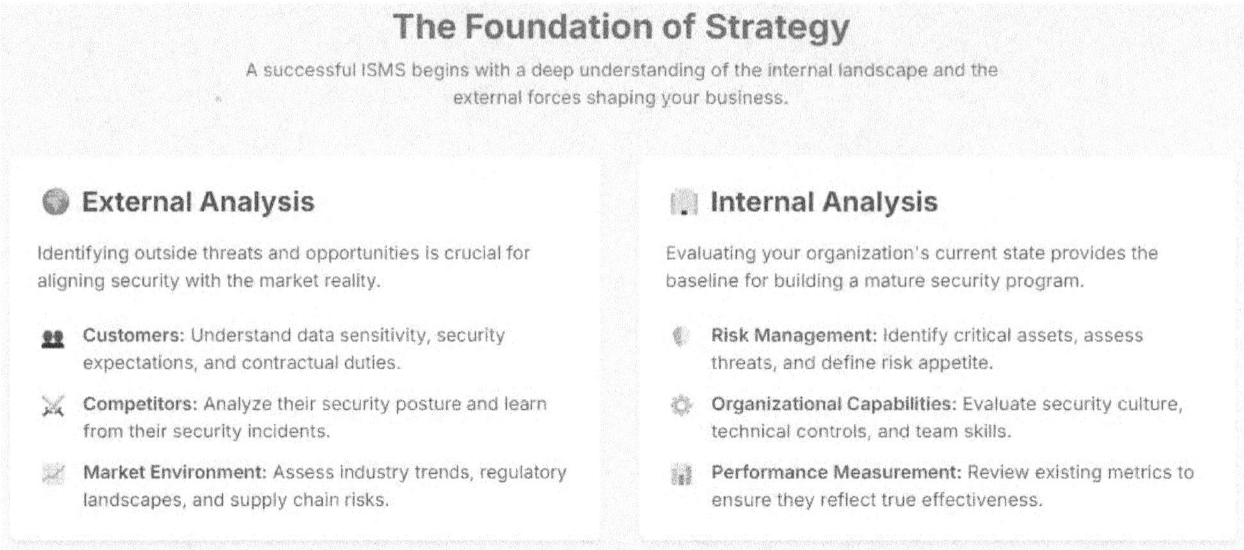

1. External Analysis

Understanding the external environment is crucial for identifying information security requirements and potential threats. This section outlines the key areas for analysis.

a. Customers

- **Customer Data:** What type of sensitive data do we handle for our customers (e.g., PII, financial information, intellectual property)?
- **Security Expectations:** What are our customers' expectations regarding the security and privacy of their data? Do they require specific certifications (e.g., ISO 27001, SOC 2)?
- **Contractual Obligations:** What are the contractual requirements for information security and data protection?

b. Competitors

- **Security Posture:** How do our competitors manage their information security? Are they leveraging security as a competitive advantage?
- **Breach History:** Have any competitors experienced a data breach or security incident? What were the impacts, and what lessons can we learn?
- **Market Perception:** How is information security perceived within our industry? Is a strong security posture a differentiator?

c. Markets and Industry Environment

- **Industry Trends:** What are the major trends in our industry (e.g., cloud adoption, IoT, remote work) that impact information security?
- **Regulatory Landscape:** What laws and regulations apply to our business and data handling (e.g., GDPR, CCPA, HIPAA, local government regulations)?

- **Supply Chain:** Who are our key suppliers and third-party vendors? What are their security requirements, and how do we assess their risk?

2. Internal Analysis

A thorough internal analysis provides a baseline for the current security posture and identifies areas for improvement.

a. Risk Management

- **Asset Identification:** What are our critical information assets (e.g., data, systems, intellectual property)?
- **Threat and Vulnerability Assessment:** What are the most significant threats to our assets, and what are their existing vulnerabilities?
- **Risk Appetite:** What is the organization's tolerance for information security risk?
- **Incident History:** What security incidents or near-misses have we experienced in the past?

b. Organizational Capabilities

- **Information Security Culture:** How is information security perceived throughout the organization? Is it a priority?
- **Technical Controls:** What security tools and technologies are currently in place (e.g., firewalls, EDR, SIEM)? Are they effective?
- **Human Resources:** Do we have the necessary staff and skills to manage information security effectively? What training and awareness programs are in place?
- **Policy and Procedures:** Are our information security policies, standards, and procedures documented, communicated, and regularly reviewed?

c. Performance Measurement

- **Existing Metrics:** What metrics are we currently using to measure security performance (e.g., number of incidents, time to resolution)?
- **Effectiveness:** Do these metrics provide a true picture of our security program's effectiveness? Are they tied to business outcomes?
- **Reporting:** How is security performance reported to leadership and other stakeholders?

Alignment with Organizational Objectives

The goal of this strategic plan is to ensure the ISMS directly supports and enables business success. This requires aligning security controls with key business objectives.

a. Identify Business Objectives

Example Objectives:

- Increase market share by 15% in the next two years.
- Launch a new product line in Q3.
- Enter the European market.
- Improve operational efficiency by 10%.

b. Define a Visionary Strategic Plan

The information security program should not be seen as just a reactive measure, but a forward-looking, visionary, and innovative business function. Its strategic plan should have clear goals, objectives, and targets that directly support the operational needs of the organization.

c. Map Security Objectives to Business Objectives

For each business objective, define one or more corresponding information security objectives.

BUSINESS OBJECTIVE	ALIGNED INFORMATION SECURITY OBJECTIVE
INCREASE MARKET SHARE BY 15%	Objective: Enhance customer trust by achieving ISO 27001 certification.
LAUNCH A NEW PRODUCT LINE IN Q3	Objective: Implement "security by design" principles and conduct a full penetration test before launch.
ENTER THE EUROPEAN MARKET	Objective: Ensure full compliance with GDPR through data residency and privacy controls.
IMPROVE OPERATIONAL EFFICIENCY	Objective: Automate security patch management to reduce manual effort and system downtime.

Information Security Program Strategic Roadmap

An information security program strategic roadmap is a high-level, visual representation that outlines how security initiatives and objectives will be achieved over a defined timeframe, typically 1–3 years. Its primary purpose is to translate the strategic plan into actionable, phased initiatives that are easily understood by both technical teams and business stakeholders.

a. **Key Components**

- **Phased Approach:** The roadmap breaks down the plan into distinct phases or quarters.
- **Key Initiatives:** Each phase contains major projects or initiatives (e.g., "Implement Multi- Factor Authentication," "Achieve ISO 27001 Certification").
- **Dependencies:** It shows how initiatives are linked and which projects must be completed before others can begin.
- **Resource Allocation:** It provides a high-level view of the resources (budget, personnel) required for each phase.
- **Milestones:** It includes specific, measurable milestones to track progress.

b. **Examples and Use Cases**

Ongoing Governance

This section outlines the continuous processes and resources required to execute and maintain the ISMS strategic plan effectively.

- **Identify Stakeholders:** This includes senior leadership (C-suite), IT department heads, legal and compliance teams, human resources, and business unit leaders. Each group provides a unique perspective on the organization's needs and challenges.
- **Conduct Interviews & Workshops:** Use these sessions to ask targeted questions about business goals, current security pain points, and future growth plans. This ensures the

security strategy is a business enabler, not a roadblock.

a. Stakeholder Engagement

Identify and consult with key stakeholders (e.g., executive leadership, department heads, legal counsel, HR, and technical teams) to ensure a shared understanding of the organization's business objectives and the role of the information security program in achieving them. A clear communication plan is essential for building a strong security culture and securing buy-in.

b. Continuous Performance Measurement

Define key performance indicators (KPIs) and measure their effectiveness on a continuous basis. This moves beyond basic metrics to assess the true impact and value of security initiatives.

Example KPIs:

- **Strategic:** Percentage of critical business objectives supported by a security initiative.
- **Operational:** Mean Time to Detect (MTTD) and Mean Time to Respond (MTTR) for incidents.
- **Cultural:** Phishing simulation click-through rates and completion rates for security awareness training.

c. Resource Assessment and Adjustment

Regularly assess and adjust security resources (budget, technology, and personnel) to ensure they are sufficient and aligned with the organization's strategic objectives. This includes a forward-looking analysis of future needs based on business growth and market changes. A strategic plan is only as good as the resources supporting it. Regularly assess your security resources to ensure they are aligned with the plan's objectives.

- **Budget Alignment:** Ensure the security budget adequately funds the planned initiatives, technology, and personnel. Advocate for increased investment by demonstrating the value and risk reduction provided by the security program.
- **Technology & Tools:** Evaluate whether existing security technologies are sufficient or if new investments are needed to achieve the plan's goals. This may involve exploring new tools for automation, threat intelligence, or cloud security.
- **Talent & Skills:** Assess the current team's skills and identify any gaps. This

may require hiring new specialists, upskilling current staff through training, or leveraging external managed security services.

d. Monitoring and Accountability

Establish a robust process to monitor all activities, track progress against the strategic roadmap, and ensure accountability. Regular progress reports to leadership are essential to demonstrate the value of the information security program and maintain support for ongoing initiatives.

This framework is designed to move your ISMS from a purely technical function to a strategic business enabler.

The strategic plan is a living document that requires continuous monitoring and adaptation to remain effective.

- **Accountability:** Assign ownership for each strategic initiative to a specific individual or team. This ensures clear accountability for progress and results.
- **Regular Review:** Conduct quarterly or bi-annual reviews of the strategic plan with stakeholders to discuss progress, challenges, and new risks.
- **Adaptation:** Be prepared to adjust the plan in response to changes in the threat landscape, new business initiatives, or shifts in organizational priorities.

Finance and Information Security

Financial management within information security focuses on budgeting, resource allocation, and cost oversight to support security operations. Integrating finance and security ensures that security spending is justified, transparent, and linked to tangible business outcomes.

Core elements include:

- **Budgeting and Resource Allocation:** The security budget must be developed collaboratively with finance. This involves analyzing, forecasting, and developing the operational budget for the security department, and acquiring and managing resources needed for implementing and maintaining the information security plan. Funds are allocated to projects and units, while monitoring costs and alignment with the strategic plan.
- **Return on Security Investment (ROSI):** Demonstrating the value of security can be

challenging, as its primary purpose is to prevent negative events. Security leaders must frame investments in business terms, calculating ROSI by comparing the cost of a security control against the financial losses it helps prevent. Effective financial practices ensure that security investments deliver value, such as through cost-benefit analyses during procurement and understanding concepts like Total Cost of Ownership (TCO).

- **Metrics and Reporting:** Regular reporting to finance and executive teams should use business-oriented metrics. This includes reporting on financial metrics to stakeholders and balancing the security investment portfolio based on the EISA and enterprise priorities.

Information Security Operational Budget Analysis and Forecast

This document outlines a comprehensive framework for analyzing, forecasting, and developing the operational budget for a security department within a financial institution. The core objective is to ensure that security investments are strategically aligned with business objectives, regulatory requirements, and the organization's risk appetite.

Anatomy of a Security Budget

A modern security budget is a balanced portfolio of investments across personnel, technology, and services. Understanding this breakdown is the first step toward strategic allocation.

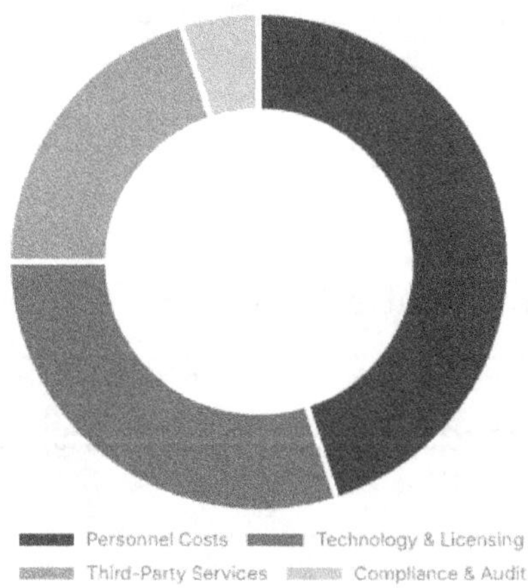

1. Current State Analysis: Budget Breakdown

An effective budget starts with a clear understanding of current and past expenditures. The operational budget for a security department can be broken down into the following key categories:

- **Personnel Costs ($):**

- **Salaries and Benefits:** The largest component, covering security analysts, engineers, incident responders, and management.
- **Training and Certifications:** Continuous professional development is critical to keep the team's skills current with evolving threats.
- **Contractors/Consultants:** Costs for specialized temporary staff or consulting services for specific projects.

- **Technology and Licensing ($):**
    - **Security Software:** Licensing for core tools such as Security Information and Event Management (SIEM), antivirus/endpoint detection and response (EDR), data loss prevention (DLP), and vulnerability scanners.
    - **Cloud Security:** Costs associated with security controls and services within cloud environments (e.g., Cloud Access Security Broker - CASB, identity and access management
    - IAM).
    - **Hardware:** Costs for security appliances like firewalls, intrusion detection/prevention systems (IDS/IPS), and dedicated servers.
- **Third-Party Services:**
    - **Managed Security Services (MSSP):** Retainer fees for outsourced security operations centers (SOC) or managed detection and response (MDR).
    - **Penetration Testing & Red Teaming:** Costs for regular security assessments and simulated attacks to test defenses.
    - **Incident Response Retainers:** A critical line item for rapid access to specialized expertise in the event of a major breach.
- **Compliance and Audit:**
    - **Audit Fees:** Costs for external audits required by regulations like PCI DSS, SOX, or GDPR.
    - **Compliance Tools:** Software or services to monitor and report on compliance status.

2. Forecasting Future Needs

Forecasting the next fiscal year's budget requires a forward-looking view of the threat landscape and business priorities. The following factors must be considered:

- **Evolving Threat Landscape:** The financial sector is a prime target for sophisticated attacks, including ransomware, phishing, and state-sponsored attacks. The budget must account for new tools and technologies to counter these emerging threats.

- **Regulatory Changes:** New or updated regulations (e.g., changes to SEC or FINRA rules, international data privacy laws) can mandate new security controls, training, and reporting, all of which require budget allocation.
- **Business Growth and Digital Transformation:** As the company launches new products (e.g., mobile banking apps), expands into new markets, or adopts new technologies (e.g., AI, blockchain), the security budget must grow to protect these new assets.
- **Technology Refresh Cycles:** Plan for the replacement of aging hardware and software to ensure security effectiveness and vendor support.

Budget Development and Justification

The budget development process should be risk-based and collaborative.

Step-by-Step Budget Development:

- **Review Current Spend:** Analyze the past 12-24 months of expenditures to identify trends, cost-savings opportunities, and areas of over/under-investment.
- **Conduct a Risk Assessment:** Partner with business leaders to identify and prioritize key assets and potential threats. The budget should directly fund controls that mitigate the highest-priority risks.
- **Map Needs to Investments:** For each identified need (e.g., better cloud security), propose a specific investment (e.g., a new cloud security posture management tool) and its associated cost.
- **Build a Tiered Budget:** Create a baseline budget (must-have items for core operations and compliance) and one or two tiered proposals for "strategic investments" that are critical for future growth or risk reduction.

- **Develop Justification:** Each budget item should have a clear business case. Justification should be framed in terms of risk reduction, return on investment (ROI), compliance with regulations, and support for key business initiatives.

Resource Acquisition and Management

Once the budget is approved, the focus shifts to acquiring and managing the necessary resources.

Personnel Acquisition:

- **Recruitment and Onboarding:** Work with Human Resources to develop a clear talent acquisition strategy for open roles. This includes defining job descriptions, conducting technical interviews, and providing structured onboarding to ensure new team members are productive quickly.
- **Skill Augmentation:** In cases where specialized skills are needed for a short period, engage third-party consultants or contractors. This can be more cost-effective than hiring a full-time employee for a temporary project.

Technology Procurement:

- **Vendor Selection:** The budget proposal should be followed by a formal vendor selection process. This involves issuing a Request for Proposal (RFP) to potential vendors, evaluating their offerings against a set of technical and financial criteria, and conducting proof-of-concept tests.
- **Contract Negotiation:** Work with the legal and procurement departments to negotiate contracts that include clear Service Level Agreements (SLAs), data security clauses, and termination rights. This is particularly crucial for third-party services.

Operational Management:

- **Asset Management:** Implement a robust system to track all security hardware and software licenses. This ensures that the organization is not overpaying for unused licenses and that all security tools are properly configured and maintained.
- **Performance Monitoring:** For all new tools and services, establish clear metrics for success and regularly review performance. For example, monitor a new EDR solution's ability to detect and block threats to validate its effectiveness and justify its ongoing cost.

Financial Management and Performance Metrics

To prove the value and ensure the effective use of the security budget, a department must engage in diligent financial management and robust reporting.

Key Financial Metrics for Stakeholders

Effective communication with stakeholders requires translating security operations into financial terms. Reporting these metrics demonstrates fiscal responsibility and program effectiveness.

- Project Budget Adherence
- ROI on Major Purchases
- Cost-Per-Incident Reduction
- Strategic Plan Alignment

- **Project Cost Oversight:** The security department must actively monitor and oversee the costs of all security projects to ensure they stay within budget and on schedule. This includes tracking labor, software, and hardware costs and reporting on any variances.
- **Return on Investment (ROI):** It is critical to measure and report the ROI of key security and IT infrastructure purchases. This can be qualitative (e.g., reduced risk of a breach) or quantitative (e.g., a new tool reducing manual effort by X hours, or preventing a breach that would have cost $Y).
- **Strategic Alignment:** All financial decisions and expenditures must be directly aligned with the organization's strategic plan and risk management objectives. The budget serves as a financial representation of the security strategy.
- **Financial Metrics Reporting:** The security team is responsible for identifying and reporting key financial metrics to stakeholders, including project budget adherence, ROI on major investments, and the cost-per-incident. This demonstrates fiscal responsibility and provides a clear business case for security spending.

These financial metrics, combined with operational KPIs, provide a comprehensive view of the security program's health and effectiveness:

- **Mean Time to Detect (MTTD):** How quickly threats are identified.
- **Mean Time to Respond (MTTR):** How long it takes to contain and remediate an incident.
- **Vulnerability Remediation Rate:** The speed at which known vulnerabilities are patched.

- **Number of Phishing Clicks:** A measure of security awareness program effectiveness.
- **Incident Cost Reduction:** Demonstrating how proactive security investments reduce the financial impact of breaches.

Procurement and Information Security

The procurement process is a critical checkpoint for managing supply chain risk. By embedding security early in the vendor selection and acquisition lifecycle, organizations can avoid introducing new vulnerabilities through third-party products and services.

Key areas of integration include:

- **Security Requirements:** Security teams must provide clear, non-negotiable security requirements for all new purchases. These should be incorporated into Requests for Proposals (RFPs) and contracts, covering areas such as data encryption, access controls, vulnerability management, and incident response capabilities. This process begins with performing a Business Impact Analysis (BIA) to determine the procurement's importance.
- **Vendor Due Diligence:** Before any purchase is made, a thorough security assessment of the vendor is necessary. This due diligence collaborates with stakeholders (e.g., legal, IT security, privacy teams, and suppliers) to include risk-based security requirements in contracts and Service Level Agreements (SLAs).
- **Contractual Clauses:** The final contract with a vendor must include specific security clauses that define responsibilities, liability, and breach notification requirements. Key concepts such as Statement of Objectives (SOO) and Statement of Work (SOW) are used to design vendor selection processes and contract administration policies.

Balancing the IT Security Investment Portfolio

Balancing an IT security investment portfolio is the process of strategically allocating resources across various security initiatives to achieve the greatest possible risk reduction and business enablement. This goes beyond simply buying the latest tools; it involves a holistic approach that aligns with the organization's overall mission and risk appetite.

- **Assessing Enterprise Security Priorities:** Before any investment is made, a clear understanding of enterprise security priorities is essential. These priorities should stem directly from the organization's business goals, such as maintaining customer trust, protecting intellectual property, ensuring regulatory compliance (e.g., GDPR, HIPAA), or enabling new business ventures. The security portfolio should be weighted to protect the assets and processes most critical to these goals. For instance, a financial institution would prioritize investments in fraud detection and data encryption, while a manufacturing company might focus on securing its operational technology (OT) systems. These priorities are typically derived from risk assessments and are often ranked using tools like risk heat maps.

- **EISA Considerations (Enterprise Information Security Architecture):** EISA provides a strategic blueprint for the organization's security posture. It ensures that security investments are not made in a silo but are part of a cohesive, long-term plan. EISA emphasizes aligning security with business objectives through layers like policy, standards, and technical controls. Key EISA considerations for investment balancing include:
    - **Defense-in-Depth:** Investing in multiple layers of security controls (e.g., firewalls, intrusion detection systems, endpoint protection) to create a robust defense. A balanced portfolio should diversify investments across preventive (e.g., firewalls), detective (e.g., SIEM systems), and corrective (e.g., incident response tools) measures.
    - **Integration and Interoperability:** Prioritizing tools that integrate seamlessly with existing infrastructure to avoid complexity and "shelfware" (unused software).
    - **Scalability:** Choosing solutions that can grow with the business, supporting new technologies and expanding operations without requiring a complete security overhaul.

- **Portfolio Management Techniques:**
    - **Risk-Based Allocation:** Allocate budgets proportional to risk levels (e.g., 40% to high- risk areas like cyber threats, 30% to compliance).
    - **ROI Evaluation:** Calculate the Return on Security Investment (ROSI) to justify expenditures. A more granular formula for this is:
    - ROSI=Mitigation Cost(Risk Exposure−Mitigation Cost)
    - **Diversification:** Avoid over-reliance on one vendor or technology to mitigate vendor lock-in risks.
    - **Regular Reviews:** Conduct annual portfolio reviews to rebalance based on emerging threats, such as AI-driven attacks or supply chain vulnerabilities.

The goal is to move from a reactive, tool-centric approach to a proactive, risk-based strategy. This involves continuous monitoring and adjusting the portfolio as threats evolve and business priorities shift.

The Acquisition Life Cycle and Business Impact Analysis (BIA)

The acquisition of an information system is a critical process, and integrating security from the very beginning is far more cost-effective than trying to add it later. The acquisition life cycle provides a structured framework for this process, with the Business Impact Analysis (BIA) serving as a foundational step. The cycle typically follows established frameworks like NIST SP 800-64 or ISO 27001.

Phases of the Acquisition Life Cycle:

1. **Planning:** Initial needs assessment and strategic planning.
2. **Requirements Definition:** Detailing the functional and security requirements for the system, specifying security controls (e.g., encryption standards, audit logs).
3. **Procurement:** The formal process of soliciting, evaluating, and selecting a vendor.
4. **Implementation:** The deployment and integration of the system.
5. **Operations & Maintenance:** Ongoing use, support, and updates.
6. **Disposal:** Securely retiring the system at the end of its life.

- **Importance of Procurement via Business Impact Analysis:** A Business Impact Analysis (BIA) is a systematic process to determine the potential effects of a disruption to an organization's critical business functions and processes. By performing a BIA, the organization can:
    - **Identify Critical Assets:** Determine which information systems and data are essential for survival and operations.
    - **Assess Impact of Disruption:** Quantify the financial and operational impact of a security incident, including lost revenue, regulatory fines, and reputational damage.
    - **Prioritize Security Controls:** Use the BIA findings to prioritize procurement efforts. For example, if the BIA reveals that a customer database is a critical asset, it justifies a higher investment in a robust database security solution. This ensures that procurement decisions are based on business needs rather than technical preference.

Procurement Strategies and Cost-Benefit Analysis (CBA)

Once the needs are identified via the BIA, the organization must choose the right procurement strategy and perform a rigorous analysis to ensure a sound investment.

Basic Procurement Concepts

- **Statement of Objectives (SOO):**
  - **Definition:** A document that outlines the high-level objectives and desired outcomes of a procurement project without specifying how the work should be performed. It provides contractors with flexibility to propose solutions that meet the stated goals.
  - **Purpose:** Guides suppliers in developing their proposals by focusing on the "what" and "why" rather than the "how." It encourages innovation and allows contractors to propose cost-effective, creative approaches.
  - **Key Elements:** Clear, concise objectives tied to the organization's mission or needs; Performance outcomes or deliverables expected; Evaluation criteria for assessing proposals.
  - **Example in IT Security:** An SOO for procuring a cybersecurity solution might state the objective of achieving 99.9% uptime for a network security system, reducing threat detection time to under 5 minutes, and ensuring compliance with specific regulations (e.g., GDPR or NIST 800-53).

- **Statement of Work (SOW):**
  - **Definition:** A detailed document that specifies the tasks, deliverables, timelines, and standards that a contractor must follow to fulfill the contract. It focuses on the "how" of the work.
  - **Purpose:** Provides clear instructions to ensure the contractor delivers the required products or services according to the organization's expectations.
  - **Key Elements:** Detailed description of tasks and deliverables; Performance standards and quality requirements; Timelines, milestones, and deadlines; Roles and responsibilities of both parties.
  - **Example in IT Security:** An SOW for an IT security service might include tasks like conducting penetration testing, delivering a report within 10 days, adhering to OWASP standards, and providing ongoing monitoring for 12 months.

- **Total Cost of Ownership (TCO):**

- **Definition:** A financial estimate that considers all costs associated with acquiring, operating, and maintaining a product or service over its entire lifecycle, not just the initial purchase price.
- **Purpose:** Helps organizations make informed procurement decisions by evaluating long- term costs, including indirect and hidden expenses.
- **Key Elements:** Initial acquisition costs (e.g., purchase price, licensing fees); Operating costs (e.g., maintenance, training, energy usage); End-of-life costs (e.g., decommissioning, disposal, or replacement).
- **Example in IT Security:** For a firewall system, TCO would include the hardware/ software purchase price, annual maintenance fees, staff training, energy costs for running the system, and eventual replacement or upgrade costs over a 5- year period.

Collaborating with Stakeholders in IT Security Procurement

Effective procurement of IT security products and services requires collaboration with a diverse group of stakeholders to ensure alignment with organizational needs, compliance requirements, and technical specifications. Key stakeholders and their roles include:

- **Internal Client:** Defines business needs and desired outcomes.
- **Lawyers:** Ensure contracts comply with legal and regulatory requirements.
- **IT Security Professionals:** Provide technical expertise on security requirements and integration.
- **Privacy Professionals:** Ensure compliance with data privacy regulations.
- **Security Engineers:** Provide insights into technical implementation and operational feasibility.
- **Suppliers:** Provide the products or services and propose solutions.
- **Other Stakeholders:** The Finance Team and Procurement Team ensure the project aligns with budgets and organizational policies.

Incorporating Risk-Based Security Requirements

It is critical to embed security requirements directly into procurement documents from the outset. This includes:

- **Acquisition Plans and Cost Estimates:** Include a risk assessment and factor in costs for security features.

- **Statements of Work (SOW) and Contracts:** Define specific security tasks and include clauses for compliance with security standards.
- **Evaluation Factors for Award:** Prioritize vendors with strong security certifications and proven track records.
- **Service Level Agreements (SLAs):**Define security-related performance metrics and penalties for violations.

Procurement Strategies

- **Request for Information (RFI):** An initial, exploratory document used to gather general information from a broad range of potential vendors.
  - **Pros:** Low effort and risk; excellent for initial market research.
  - **Cons:** Not a formal commitment; responses can be general.
  - **When to Use:** When you're in the early stages of a project and need to understand what solutions are available in the market.

- **Request for Proposal (RFP):** A more detailed and formal process, an RFP is issued to solicit specific, customized solutions from a pre-screened group of vendors.
  - **Pros:** Provides detailed, comparable proposals; good for complex projects.
  - **Cons:** High effort for both the organization and the vendors; can be lengthy.
  - **When to Use:** For complex, high-value projects where you know your specific requirements but want to see different vendor approaches.

- **Competitive Bidding:** This strategy is designed to achieve the best possible value for a product or service by inviting multiple, qualified vendors to submit bids.
  - **Pros:** Ensures transparency and fairness; often leads to a lower price.
  - **Cons:** Can be time-consuming and labor-intensive.
  - **When to Use:** For well-defined products or services where the primary goal is to get the best price.

- **Sole-Source:** Buying from a single vendor, often used for proprietary technology or a trusted existing partner.
  - **Pros:** Fastest procurement method; simplifies the process.
  - **Cons:** No price competition; potential for vendor lock-in.
  - **When to Use:** When a specific vendor has unique, proprietary technology, or when

time is of the essence.

The Importance of Cost-Benefit Analysis (CBA)

A CBA is a crucial step in evaluating potential security investments. It provides a quantitative method for comparing the projected costs of a project against its expected benefits.

Steps to Perform a CBA during Procurement:

- **Identify and Quantify Costs:** Include both direct and indirect costs over the entire lifecycle.
- **Identify and Quantify Benefits:** Include tangible benefits (e.g., reduced losses from a breach) and intangible benefits (e.g., enhanced reputation).
- **Compare Costs and Benefits:** Calculate the Return on Security Investment (ROSI) to justify the expenditure.

Vendor Selection and Management Policy

This policy outlines a structured approach to selecting and managing vendors for IT security products and services. It emphasizes risk-based decision-making, stakeholder involvement, and ongoing oversight to ensure alignment with organizational security objectives.

Vendor Selection Process

The selection process follows a multi-stage framework to identify, evaluate, and onboard vendors. It incorporates best practices such as clear requirements definition, competitive bidding, and rigorous due diligence.

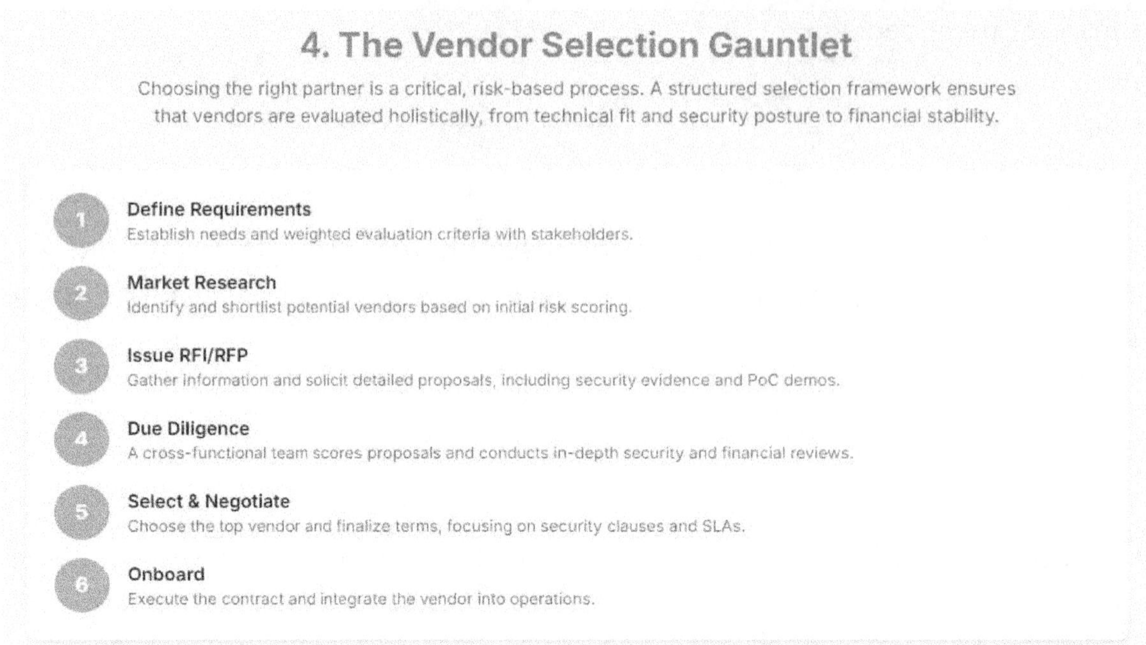

- **Define Requirements and Criteria:** Establish clear needs based on the SOO or SOW and develop weighted evaluation criteria that prioritize risk-based factors, such as cybersecurity certifications.
- **Market Research and Vendor Identification:** Identify potential vendors using industry reports and databases. Shortlist vendors based on preliminary filters and use vendor risk scoring to assess initial risks.
- **Request for Information/Proposal (RFI/RFP):** Issue an RFI to gather preliminary information, followed by an RFP for detailed proposals. Require vendors to submit evidence of security practices and include requirements for proof-of-concept (PoC) demonstrations.
- **Evaluation and Due Diligence:** Form a cross-functional evaluation team to score proposals using a standardized rubric. Perform in-depth due diligence, including security questionnaires, site visits, and financial reviews.
- **Selection and Negotiation:** Select the top vendor(s) and negotiate terms, focusing on security clauses, SLAs, and exit strategies.
- **Onboarding:** Execute the contract and integrate the vendor into operations.

Vendor Management Policy

This policy governs ongoing relationships to ensure performance, compliance, and risk mitigation.

- **Performance Monitoring:** Conduct quarterly reviews against SLAs and security metrics.
- **Risk Management:** Implement continuous monitoring and reassess risks annually or after incidents.
- **Compliance and Auditing:** Require vendors to provide annual audit reports and enforce penalties for non-compliance.
- **Termination and Off-boarding:** Define criteria for contract termination and procedures for data repatriation.

Contract Administration Policies

These policies provide guidelines for managing contracts post-award, focusing on the evaluation, acceptance, and security assessments of IT security products and services. They align with federal standards like the Federal Acquisition Regulation (FAR) and emphasize proactive oversight.

Evaluation and Acceptance of Delivered IT Security Products and Services

- **Inspection Procedures:** Upon delivery, conduct inspections to verify compliance with SOW specifications, including functional testing and performance benchmarks.
- **Acceptance Process:** Use a staged acceptance process, with provisional acceptance after initial tests and final acceptance after a trial period. Document non-conformities and tie payments to milestones.
- **Change Management:** Establish protocols for contract modifications, requiring a security impact assessment for any changes.

Security Evaluation of IT and Software Being Procured

- **Pre-Delivery Security Assessments:** During procurement, mandate vendor-submitted security artifacts (e.g., vulnerability scans).
- **Post-Delivery Security Reviews:** Upon receipt, perform security audits to confirm no backdoors or weaknesses.
- **Ongoing Evaluations:** Require periodic security reassessments and immediate reviews after vendor-reported incidents.

Measures and Reporting Standards

To track the effectiveness of IT security procurements, it is essential to establish key performance indicators (KPIs) and reporting frameworks aligned with security policies. These focus on risk reduction, efficiency, and compliance, enabling data-driven improvements.

Core Vendor & Procurement Metrics

A comprehensive measurement program tracks metrics across risk, performance, and financial dimensions to provide a holistic view of procurement health.

Vendor Risk Score
Target: < 20/100 (Low Risk). Measures the average risk rating from continuous assessments.

Compliance Adherence Rate
Target: 100%. Ensures vendors comply with standards like NIST and GDPR.

Incident Response Time
Target: < 4 hours. Aligns with incident management policies for timely vendor action.

TCO Savings
Target: > 10%. Promotes cost-effective procurement by tracking savings against estimates.

Key Measures (KPIs)

Use the following table to outline core KPIs, targets, and alignment with objectives:

KPI	DESCRIPTION	TARGET	ALIGNMENT WITH IT SECURITY POLICIES	MEASUREMENT FREQUENCY
VENDOR RISK SCORE	Average risk rating from assessments (e.g., based on breach history, compliance).	< 20/100 (low risk)	Ensures vendors meet risk thresholds per policy.	Quarterly
ON-TIME DELIVERY RATE	Percentage of deliverables met on schedule.	> 95%	Supports operational continuity and SLA adherence.	Per contract milestone

COMPLIANCE ADHERENCE RATE	Percentage of vendors compliant with standards (e.g., NIST, GDPR).	100%	Directly ties to security policy enforcement.	Annual
MEAN TIME TO DETECT (MTTD) VULNERABILITIES	Average time to identify issues in procured products/ services.	< 24 hours	Measures effectiveness of security evaluations.	Monthly

Reporting Standards

- **Framework:** Use dashboards for real-time visibility; generate monthly reports for management and quarterly for executives.
- **Content:** Include KPI trends, variance analysis, and recommendations.
- **Distribution:** Share via secure channels; escalate red flags immediately.

Practical Example: Procuring a Cloud Security Solution

This example combines concepts from the entire ISBK, demonstrating a comprehensive approach.

- **SOO:** The objective is to secure cloud-based applications with 99.9% availability, GDPR compliance, and real-time threat detection.
- **SOW:** The tasks include deploying a cloud access security broker (CASB), conducting monthly vulnerability scans, and providing 24/7 monitoring with a 2-hour incident response time.
- **TCO:** Includes initial licensing costs ($50,000), annual maintenance ($10,000/year), training ($5,000), and potential breach recovery costs ($20,000 over 5 years).

Stakeholder Collaboration:

- **Internal Client:** Confirms the need for a CASB to secure SaaS applications.
- **Lawyers:** Add GDPR compliance clauses to the contract.
- **IT Security Professionals:** Validate CASB compatibility with existing SIEM tools.
- **Privacy Professionals:** Ensure data residency requirements are met.
- **Security Engineers:** Conduct a proof-of-concept (PoC) to test CASB performance.

- **Suppliers:** Provide demos and respond to the RFP with detailed proposals.

Risk-Based Requirements:

- **Acquisition Plan:** Require GDPR-compliant data encryption.
- **Cost Estimate:** Budget for ongoing compliance audits.
- **SOW:** Mandate weekly patch updates and annual penetration testing.
- **Contract:** Include penalties for non-compliance with GDPR.
- **SLA:** Guarantee 99.9% uptime and a 2-hour incident response time.
- **Evaluation Factors:** Prioritize vendors with SOC 2 certification and proven cloud security expertise.

- **Vendor Selection and Management:** The company uses a standardized rubric to evaluate vendors. After selecting a vendor, it tracks the incident response time as a key KPI.
- **Contract Administration:** Upon delivery, the company performs vulnerability scans to verify the software's security. It also establishes protocols for any future changes to the contract to ensure security is not compromised.
- **Measures and Reporting:** The company reports quarterly on the vendor's compliance rate and the number of security incidents attributable to the new software. If these metrics fall below the target, a formal vendor review is triggered.

Requirements for Statements of Work (SOWs) & Procurement Documents

The following requirements should be included in procurement documents and statements of work to ensure that vendors and contractors adhere to a strong security posture. These elements protect sensitive data, maintain system integrity, and ensure compliance with regulatory standards.

The Unseen Risk

Embedding security requirements into Statements of Work (SOWs) from day one is not just a best practice; it's a critical defense against systemic vulnerabilities. It transforms security from an afterthought into a foundational pillar of every project.

60%

of data breaches are attributed to vulnerabilities in third-party vendor systems.

Key Considerations for Including IA Requirements

When drafting SOWs or procurement documents, the following principles are essential to ensure the security requirements are effective and enforceable:

- **Tailor to the Acquisition:** Base requirements on the system's security categorization (e.g., low, moderate, or high impact per FIPS 199), risk assessments, and the nature of the work (e.g., cloud services, software development, or hardware procurement).
- **Reference Applicable Standards:** Cite relevant policies, laws, and guidelines to establish baselines.
- **Define Responsibilities:** Specify roles for the contractor, system owner, and government oversight (e.g., Contracting Officer's Representative or Authorizing Official).
- **Incorporate Deliverables:** Require security documentation, plans, reports, and testing results with timelines.
- **Ensure Flowdown:** Mandate that requirements apply to subcontractors if they handle sensitive data.
- **Address Lifecycle:** Cover planning, development, testing, operation, maintenance, and disposal.
- **Compliance Verification:** Include self-attestation, audits, or third-party assessments.

Foundational Security Principles (CIA Triad)

All services and systems provided by the contractor must be designed, implemented, and managed in a way that upholds the three core principles of information security:

- **Confidentiality:** Protection of data from unauthorized disclosure. The SOW should require the contractor to implement controls that prevent unauthorized access to sensitive information.
- **Integrity:** Ensuring the accuracy and completeness of data. This includes protecting against unauthorized modification, deletion, or creation of data.
- **Availability:** Ensuring that authorized users have timely and reliable access to information and systems. The contractor must provide a clear plan for system uptime and disaster recovery.

Compliance and Governance

The contractor must comply with all relevant information security policies, laws, and regulations.

- **Standards Adherence:** Specify adherence to a recognized security framework, such as FISMA, the Computer Security Act of 1987, E-Government Act, OMB A-130, FIPS 200 (Minimum Security Requirements), and NIST SP 800-53 (Security Controls). Adherence to other standards like ISO 27001 or CMMC (Cybersecurity Maturity Model Certification) should also be specified as applicable.
- **Reporting:** The contractor must provide a summary of their security controls and an attestation of compliance upon request.
- **Audits and Assessments:** The client reserves the right to perform or request third-party security audits, vulnerability assessments, and penetration tests on the contractor's systems.

Personnel Security

The contractor is responsible for ensuring that all personnel with access to the client's information or systems are trustworthy and properly vetted.

- **Background Checks:** Require background investigations commensurate with the level of access.
- **Security Training:** Personnel must complete security and awareness training, including annual refreshers, covering topics like data handling, phishing, and incident reporting.

- **Roles and Responsibilities:** The SOW should define clear roles, responsibilities, and access levels for contractor personnel.

Non-Disclosure Agreements (NDAs)

NDAs are a fundamental security and legal requirement to protect sensitive information. The SOW must mandate that the contractor and its subcontractors sign legally binding NDAs.

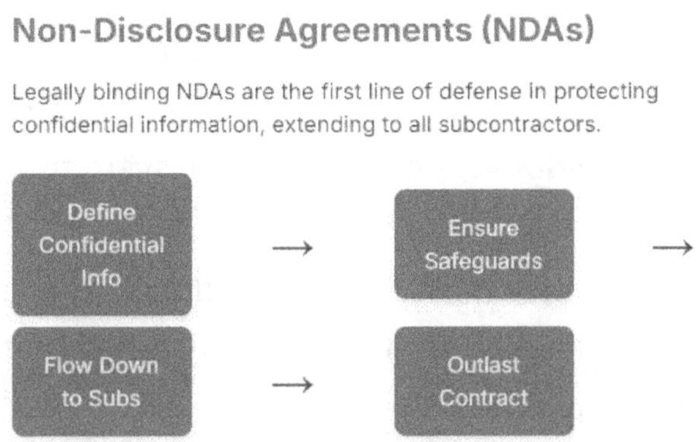

- **Scope:** The NDA must clearly define what constitutes "Confidential Information," including but not limited to proprietary data, intellectual property, trade secrets, personal information, and any information marked as confidential by the client.
- **Contractor Obligations:** The agreement must require the contractor to use confidential information only for the specified purpose of the contract and to implement adequate physical, technical, and administrative safeguards to prevent its unauthorized disclosure.
- **Subcontractor Flowdown:** The NDA must explicitly require the contractor to ensure all subcontractors with access to confidential information are also bound by a similar, enforceable non-disclosure agreement.
- **Duration:** The confidentiality obligations must survive the termination or expiration of the contract for a specified period, or indefinitely for certain types of information.

Deliverables and Documentation

The contractor must provide a set of security-related documents and artifacts throughout the contract lifecycle to demonstrate compliance and the effectiveness of security controls.

Key Documentation Deliverables

Formal documentation provides a clear record of a system's security posture, risks, and incident history, ensuring transparency and accountability.

- **System Security Plan (SSP):** Details the implementation of security controls.
- **Risk Assessments:** Formal analysis of threats and vulnerabilities.
- **Security Assessment Reports (SARs):** Documents findings from audits and tests.
- **Incident Reports:** Formal records of security breaches and responses.

- **System Security Plan (SSP):** An SSP is a formal document that details the security controls and requirements for a system. The contractor is responsible for developing, maintaining, and submitting an SSP for all systems and applications under their control.
- **Risk Assessments:** The contractor must perform and submit formal risk assessments at specified intervals (e.g., annually or after a significant change) to identify, analyze, and mitigate threats and vulnerabilities.
- **Security Assessment Reports (SARs):** Following security testing or an audit, the contractor must provide an SAR that documents the findings, identified weaknesses, and a plan for remediation.
- **Incident Reports:** All security incidents and breaches must be documented in a formal report that includes a timeline of events, impact analysis, and corrective actions taken.

Supply Chain Risk Management

The contractor must implement and maintain security controls to manage risks throughout the supply chain.

Licensed by Google

This is crucial to prevent the introduction of malware, counterfeit products, or other vulnerabilities into the systems and services delivered.

- **Subcontractor and Supplier Vetting:** The contractor must vet all suppliers and subcontractors to ensure they meet the security requirements of the contract.
- **Component Authenticity:** The contractor is responsible for verifying the authenticity and integrity of all hardware and software components. This may include using trusted sources and cryptographic integrity checks.
- **Reporting:** The contractor must promptly notify the client of any confirmed or suspected supply chain security incidents.
- **Flowdown of Requirements:** The contractor must ensure that all security requirements, including those related to the supply chain, are contractually flowed down to all subcontractors.

1. System and Data Security

These requirements focus on the technical and procedural controls for protecting information throughout its lifecycle.

- **Access Control:** The contractor must implement the principle of least privilege, ensuring that personnel only have access to the data and systems necessary to perform their duties.

- **Encryption:** All sensitive data must be encrypted both in transit (e.g., using TLS/SSL) and at rest (e.g., using AES-256).
- **Data Handling:** The SOW should detail procedures for how data is collected, stored, processed, and transmitted. It must also include requirements for proper media sanitization upon disposal.
- **Configuration Management:** The contractor must use secure baselines for all hardware and software components to prevent vulnerabilities.

2. Physical and Environmental Security

The contractor's facilities must be protected to prevent unauthorized physical access to systems and data.

- **Access Control:** Require physical access controls such as keycard systems, biometric scanners, or security guards at data centers and critical areas.
- **Monitoring:** The use of video surveillance and access logs to monitor physical activity should be specified.

3. Incident Response and Reporting

A clear and well-defined process for handling security incidents is crucial.

- **Notification:** The SOW must specify a mandatory timeline for notifying the client of any security incident, breach, or compromise. This is typically within 24 hours of discovery.
- **Incident Handling:** The contractor must have a documented incident response plan and provide a point of contact for all security-related communications.
- **Forensics:** The contractor must preserve all relevant evidence and cooperate fully with any subsequent investigation.

4. Continuous Monitoring and Auditing

Security is an ongoing process, not a one-time event.

- **Vulnerability Scanning:** The contractor must perform regular vulnerability scans and promptly remediate any discovered weaknesses.
- **Security Logs:** Require the collection and retention of security logs for a specified

period (e.g., 90 days or more) to support forensic analysis.

5. Plan of Action and Milestones (POA&M)

The contractor must establish a formal process for addressing and remediating security weaknesses.

- **Remediation Plan:** The contractor must develop and maintain a POA&M for any identified security deficiency. The plan must include a detailed description of the weakness, the corrective actions, required resources, and a timeline with specific milestones for completion.
- **Client Approval:** The POA&M must be submitted to the client for review and approval prior to implementation.
- **Status Reporting:** The contractor must provide regular status reports on the progress of all open POA&Ms.

6. Contract Termination and Data Return/Destruction

The SOW must include clear procedures for handling data at the conclusion of the contract.

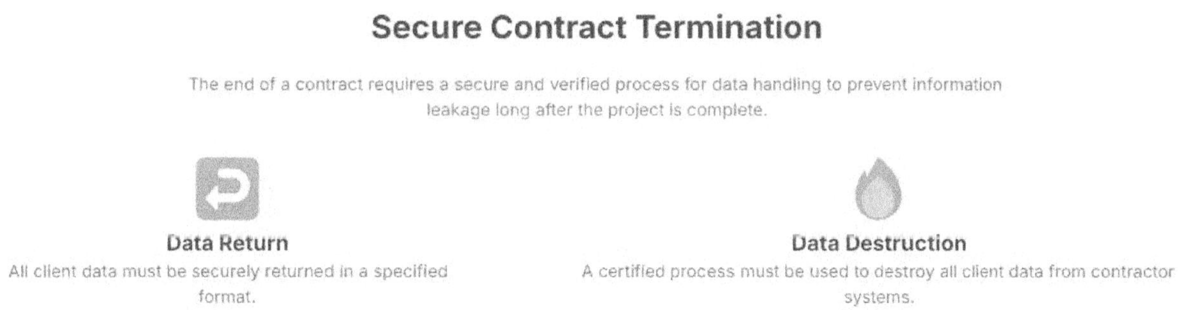

- **Data Return:** The contractor must securely return all client data in a specified format.
- **Data Destruction:** A process for the certified destruction of all client data stored on the contractor's systems must be defined and validated.

Third-Party Management and Information Security

Third-party management addresses risks from external vendors, suppliers, and partners, which is increasingly critical in interconnected digital ecosystems. A robust Third-Party Risk Management (TPRM) program is essential for protecting the supply chain.

Key areas of integration include:

- **Risk Tiering:** Not all vendors pose the same level of risk. A TPRM program should categorize vendors into tiers to prioritize assessment and monitoring efforts. This includes designing selection processes, management policies, metrics, and ongoing compliance assessments for third parties.
- **Continuous Monitoring:** A TPRM program is not a one-time activity. It requires ongoing monitoring of vendor security postures. This involves incorporating risk-based security, privacy, and compliance requirements into procurement documents and managing assessments to ensure continuous compliance.
- **Incident Response Coordination:** In the event of a breach involving a third party, a pre- defined incident response plan is crucial. TPRM programs identify, assess, and mitigate risks such as data breaches or supply chain disruptions, often involving tools for vendor evaluations and incident response planning. In 2025, TPRM has evolved to include advanced strategies for cyber threat protection in procurement outsourcing.

The Importance of Third-Party Security

In today's interconnected business environment, organizations rarely operate in isolation. They rely on a vast ecosystem of third-party vendors, suppliers, and partners to provide essential services, from cloud hosting and software to data analytics and managed services. While these relationships are vital for innovation and efficiency, they also introduce significant security risks. A vulnerability or a security lapse at a third-party vendor can directly impact an organization's own data and operations, leading to data breaches, financial loss, reputational damage, and regulatory penalties.

A report from 2024 found that more than one-third of all data breaches originated from third-party compromises, highlighting this as a major threat vector. Therefore, a robust Third-Party Risk Management (TPRM) program is not just a best practice; it is a fundamental requirement for a strong cybersecurity posture.

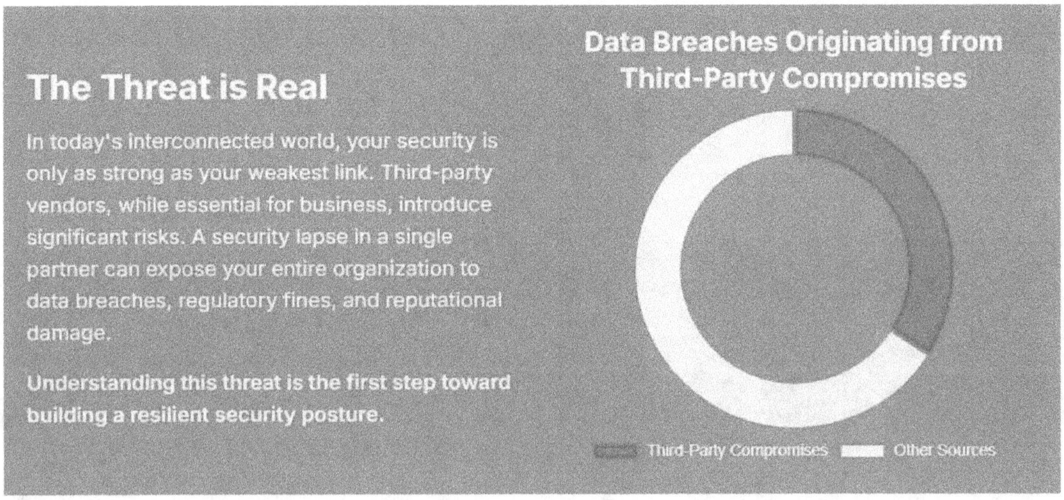

Key Risks Introduced by Third Parties

Working with external partners can expose an organization to various risks, including:

- **Data Breaches:** This is the most common and devastating risk. If a third-party vendor with access to your sensitive data (e.g., customer PII, financial information, or intellectual property) suffers a breach, your organization is directly impacted.
- **Compliance and Regulatory Fines:** Many regulations, such as GDPR, HIPAA, and CCPA, hold the primary organization accountable for the security practices of its third-party providers. A vendor's non-compliance can lead to massive fines and legal action for your company.
- **Operational Disruptions:** A security incident or service outage at a critical third party can disrupt your business continuity and ability to serve customers.
- **Reputational Damage:** A public security incident involving a third party can erode customer trust and harm your brand, even if the breach did not originate within your own systems.
- **Fourth-Party Risk:** The risk chain doesn't stop at your immediate vendors. Many third parties rely on their own vendors (known as "fourth parties"), creating a complex supply chain that can be difficult to monitor and secure.

The Third-Party Risk Management Lifecycle

An effective TPRM program should be a continuous, cyclical process, not a one-time assessment. The lifecycle can be broken down into several key phases:

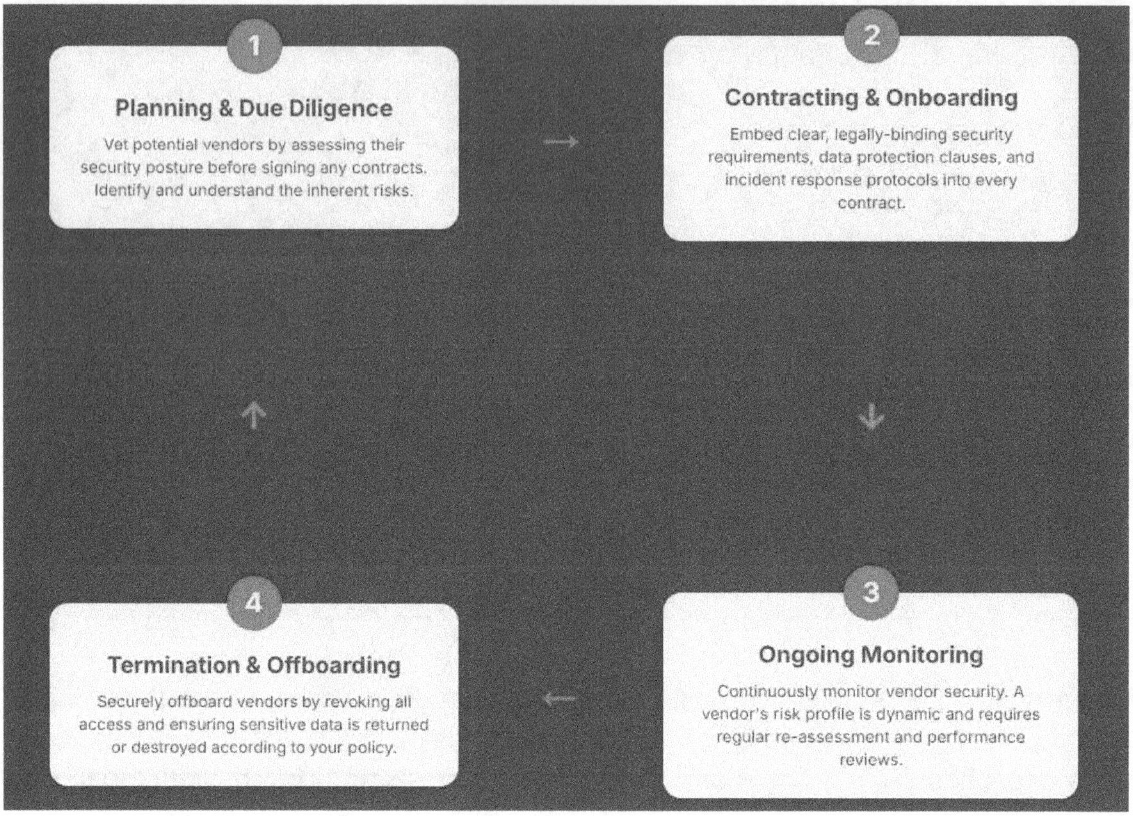

- **Planning and Due Diligence:** This initial phase involves identifying the need for a new third party, defining the scope of their access, and thoroughly vetting potential vendors. Key activities include:
  - Creating a comprehensive inventory of all third parties.
  - Categorizing vendors based on the criticality of their service and the level of data access they will have.
  - Conducting a security assessment of prospective vendors, often through security questionnaires, audits, and analysis of their security posture.

- **Contracting and Onboarding:** Once a vendor is selected, the contract must include clear security requirements. This is where security is baked into the legal agreement. Key provisions include:
  - Data protection and privacy clauses.
  - Defined security controls and standards (e.g., ISO 27001 or SOC 2 compliance).
  - Incident response and notification protocols.
  - Audit and access rights for your organization.
  - Liability and indemnification clauses.

- **Ongoing Monitoring:** Third-party risk is dynamic. A vendor's security posture can change over time due to new vulnerabilities, mergers, or changes in staff. Continuous monitoring is essential to detect and respond to these changes. Methods include:
    - Regular security ratings and automated monitoring of the vendor's attack surface.
    - Periodic re-assessments and security audits.
    - Regular communication and performance reviews.

- **Termination and Off-boarding:** When a relationship ends, a secure off-boarding process is crucial to ensure the vendor no longer has access to your data or systems. This phase involves:
    - Revoking all logical and physical access.
    - Ensuring all sensitive data has been securely returned or destroyed.
    - Confirming that all contractual obligations related to data retention and security have been met.

Designing the Third-Party Selection Process

A well-defined selection process ensures that security is a core factor from the very beginning of a new relationship.

Defining a High-Risk Vendor

A "high-risk vendor" is a third party that, if compromised or mismanaged, could cause significant financial, operational, or reputational damage to your organization. This classification is not about the size of the vendor, but rather the level of risk they introduce based on several key factors:

- **Access to Sensitive Data:** The most critical factor. This includes vendors who handle your customer's Personally Identifiable Information (PII), Protected Health

Information (PHI), financial data, or your organization's intellectual property.

- **Criticality of the Service:** A vendor providing a service that is essential for your business's core operations. For example, a cloud provider hosting your primary applications or a managed security service provider. A disruption to their service would directly impact your ability to function.
- **System Connectivity:** Vendors that have direct, privileged access to your internal network, systems, or databases.
- **Regulatory and Compliance Impact:** A vendor whose failure to meet security or privacy standards could put you in violation of regulations like GDPR, HIPAA, or CCPA.

Steps before Engaging a Vendor

- **Initial Triage and Scoping:** Before engaging with a vendor, determine the business criticality and the type of data they will access. This initial classification will dictate the level of security scrutiny required. A low-risk vendor (e.g., a janitorial service) requires less due diligence than a high-risk vendor that will handle customer data.

- **Risk-Based Questionnaires:** Develop a tiered set of questionnaires. A basic questionnaire can be used for all vendors, while more detailed, in-depth assessments are reserved for high-risk vendors. These should cover key areas like:
  - Information security policies and governance.
  - Data handling and encryption practices.
  - Physical security controls.
  - Incident response and business continuity plans.
  - Compliance with relevant regulations and industry standards.

- **Due Diligence and Evidence Review:** Don't rely solely on self-attested information. Request supporting documentation such as SOC 2 reports, ISO 27001 certificates, penetration test results, and audit findings to validate the vendor's security claims.

- **Vendor Security Scoring:** Create a scoring system to evaluate and compare vendors objectively. This helps in making an informed decision and can be used to justify vendor selection to stakeholders.

Developing Management Policies, Metrics, and Processes

A robust TPRM program requires clear policies and measurable goals.

- **Third-Party Management Policy:** Create a formal policy that outlines your organization's commitment to managing third-party risk. This policy should define:
  - The scope and roles of the TPRM program.
  - Responsibility and accountability for vendor relationships.
  - The complete TPRM lifecycle, from selection to termination.
  - Criteria for risk classification.

- **Establish Metrics (Key Performance Indicators):** Track and report on metrics to demonstrate the program's effectiveness. Examples include:
  - Number of high-risk vendors assessed.
  - Average time to complete a vendor security review.
  - Number of open security issues identified with third parties.
  - Percentage of critical vendors with up-to-date security assessments.

- **Standardized Processes:** Create repeatable, automated processes for all stages of the lifecycle. This ensures consistency and reduces manual effort. These processes should include workflows for:
  - Requesting and tracking new vendor reviews.
  - Notifying stakeholders of new risks.
  - Managing remediation plans for identified issues.

Designing and Managing the Third-Party Assessment Process

The assessment process is the heart of TPRM. It's how you identify and mitigate risks.

Due Diligence vs. Due Care

Within the context of cybersecurity and risk management, "due diligence" and "due care" are two distinct but related concepts. Both are legal and ethical standards for responsible behavior, but they apply at different stages of the vendor lifecycle.

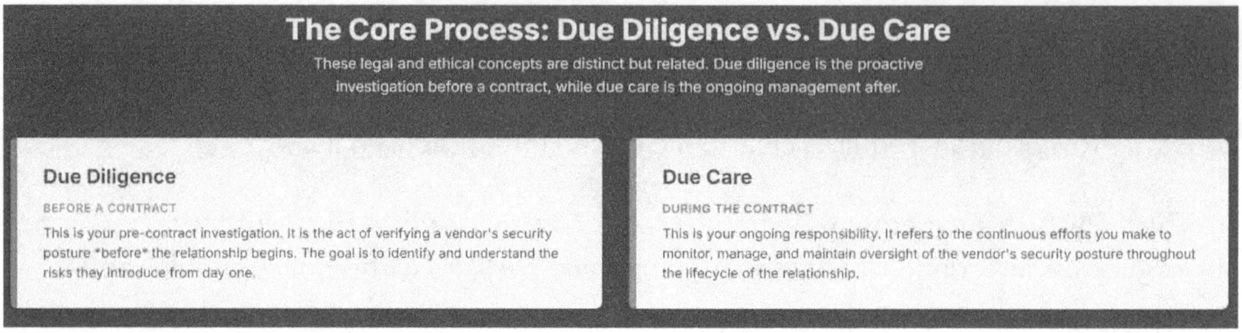

- **Due Diligence:** This is a proactive and pre-contract investigation. It is the act of investigating and verifying the security posture, controls, and practices of a potential third-party vendor before you enter into a contract with them. The purpose of due diligence is to identify and understand the inherent risks a vendor might introduce to your organization. This is a one-time effort per vendor at the start of the relationship.

- **Due Care:** This is an ongoing and continuous responsibility. It refers to the reasonable efforts an organization must make to protect its assets and data from foreseeable risks. In the context of third-party risk management, due care means actively monitoring, managing, and maintaining oversight of a vendor's security posture throughout the entire lifecycle of the relationship. It's about ensuring a vendor continues to meet the security standards you set.

ASPECT	DUE DILIGENCE	DUE CARE
TIMING	Pre-contractual, one-time action.	Post-contractual, continuous responsibility.
NATURE	An investigation or assessment.	An ongoing management and monitoring process.
GOAL	To understand and identify inherent risks.	To mitigate and manage identified risks over time.
ACTIVITY	Security questionnaires, audits, evidence review.	Continuous monitoring, periodic re-assessments, remediation tracking.

- **Initial Assessment:** This is the first comprehensive review of a vendor's security posture. It's typically done during the due diligence phase and involves the questionnaires and evidence review mentioned earlier. The goal is to identify inherent risk before a contract is signed.

- **Ongoing Compliance Management:** After a vendor is onboarded, the risk management continues. This is not a "set it and forget it" process.
    - **Continuous Monitoring:** Use automated tools to monitor the vendor's external security posture. These tools can alert you to new vulnerabilities, changes in security ratings, or public security incidents.
    - **Periodic Re-assessments:** High-risk vendors should be re-assessed annually. This helps verify that they are maintaining their security controls and are still in compliance with your requirements.
    - **Remediation and Follow-up:** If an assessment or monitoring tool identifies a security issue, work with the vendor to create a remediation plan. Track these issues to closure and ensure the vendor takes appropriate action.
- **Performance and Compliance Audits:** For your most critical vendors, consider conducting your own on-site or virtual audits to verify their security controls.

Third-Party Incident Response Management

A proactive and well-defined incident response plan for third parties is crucial for minimizing the impact of a security event. While you cannot control a vendor's environment, you can control the response process and ensure timely communication and action.

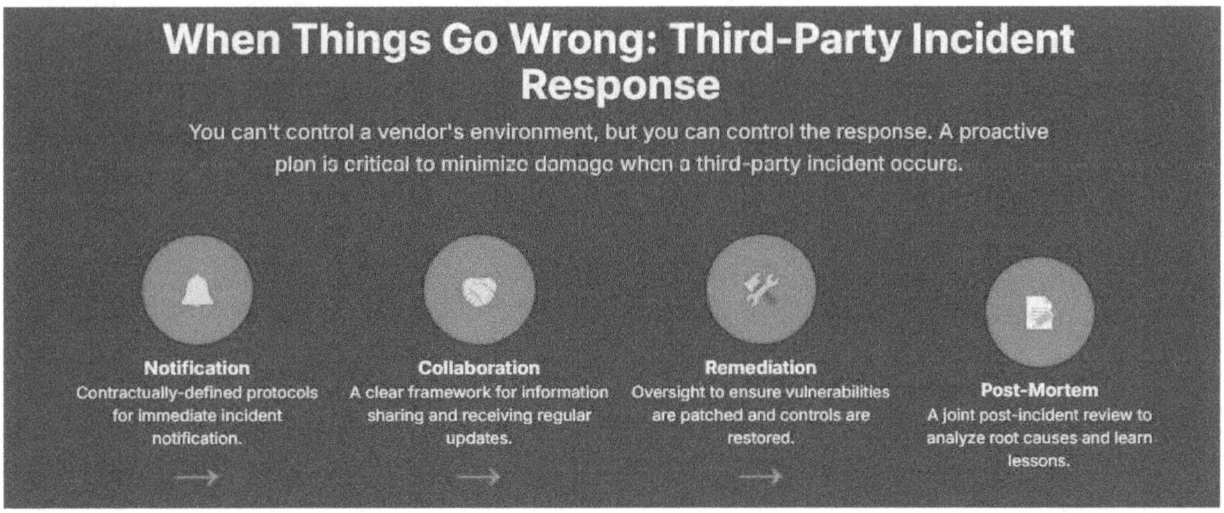

Key Components of a Third-Party Incident Response Plan:

- **Defined Notification Protocols:** Your contracts must include a clear, unambiguous requirement for vendors to notify you of a security incident. This should specify:
  - **Timeframe:** The maximum number of hours from discovery to notification (e.g., "within 24 hours of discovery").
  - **Method:** The secure communication channels to use (e.g., a dedicated phone number, secure email address, or a pre-defined portal).
  - **Content:** The minimum information to be included in the initial notification (e.g., nature of the incident, estimated scope, and initial impact).

- **Information Sharing and Collaboration:** Once an incident is reported, establish a clear framework for information sharing. You need a dedicated point of contact at the vendor to receive regular, detailed updates on the investigation, remediation efforts, and any affected data. Your own legal and PR teams need this information to manage your company's response and meet regulatory requirements.

- **Remediation and Recovery Oversight:** Your organization has a vested interest in the vendor's recovery. The plan should outline your right to review and approve the vendor's remediation plan. You should have a process to track progress and ensure that all identified vulnerabilities are fully patched and controls are restored.

- **Post-Incident Review:** After the incident is resolved, a joint post-mortem should be conducted with the vendor. The purpose of this review is to analyze what happened, identify root causes, and discuss lessons learned. This information is vital for strengthening your contract requirements and improving your own TPRM program in the future.

Measures and Reporting for Secure Procurement

To ensure procurement is consistently aligned with IT security policies, it's essential to establish clear measures and a formal reporting process. This allows you to track progress, identify gaps, and communicate the value of the security program to leadership.

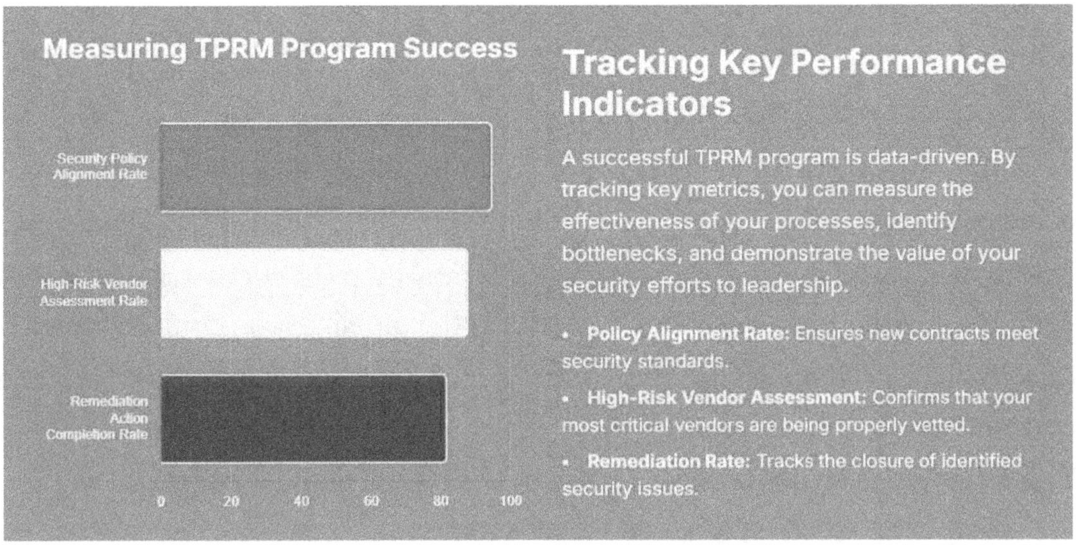

Key Measures and Metrics:

- **Security Policy Alignment Rate:** The percentage of all new procurement contracts that include the mandatory IT security clauses and requirements. This metric directly measures policy enforcement at the point of entry.
- **Time-to-Security-Approval:** The average time it takes for a new third-party request to receive security approval. A high value may indicate bottlenecks in the review process.
- **Risk Categorization Accuracy:** The percentage of vendors correctly classified according to their risk level (e.g., low, medium, high) during the initial triage phase.
- **Remediation Action Completion Rate:** The percentage of identified security issues with vendors that have been fully remediated and closed within the agreed-upon timeframe.
- **Critical Vendor Compliance Status:** A continuous score or rating for your most critical vendors, based on the results of ongoing monitoring and periodic re-assessments.
- **Third-Party Security Incidents:** The number of security incidents that originated from a third party and their impact (e.g., data loss, service disruption). This is a lagging indicator of the program's effectiveness.

Reporting Standards and Procedures

- **Reporting Cadence:** Reports should be generated and distributed on a regular schedule (e.g., monthly, quarterly, or annually).
- **Audience-Specific Content:** Tailor reports to the audience. Leadership and stakeholders require high-level summaries of key risks and the program's overall health. Security teams

need detailed, actionable data on specific vendor issues.

Key Components of a Report:

- **Executive Summary:** A concise overview of the program's status, highlighting major achievements and top risks.
- **Dashboard View:** A visual representation of key metrics, such as the number of vendors by risk tier, new vendor requests in the pipeline, and compliance scores.
- **Risk Register:** A detailed list of all open security issues, their severity, and their current remediation status.
- **Trend Analysis:** An analysis of metrics over time to identify trends, show improvement, or highlight new areas of concern.

Integrating Security into Procurement Documents

Security should be embedded into every step of the procurement process, not just treated as a final check. By including specific security requirements in procurement documents, you create a legally binding framework that holds vendors accountable for their security posture.

How They Work Together: A One-to-Many Relationship

The most effective structure is a single, robust MSA that governs multiple SOWs. This streamlines the process of starting new projects. The foundational legal terms are already agreed upon, so you only need to define the new project's specific scope, timeline, and deliverables in a new SOW.

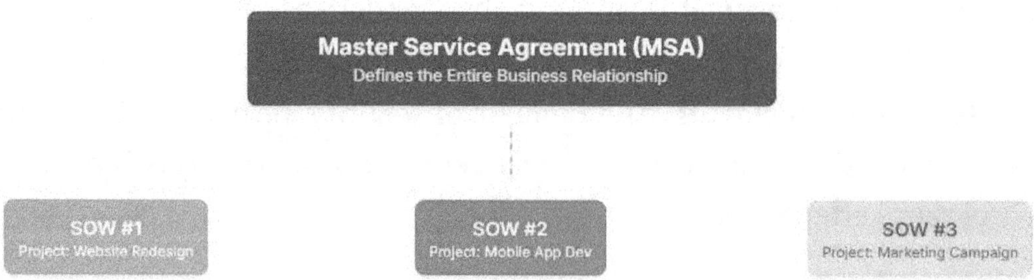

A Deeper Dive into Key Procurement Documents: SOW vs. MSA

- **SOW (Statement of Work):** A formal document that outlines the specific project-based work to be performed by a vendor. It defines the scope, deliverables, timeline, milestones, and specific tasks for a single project or a defined period. The SOW is tactical and details the "what" of a specific engagement.

- **MSA (Master Service Agreement):** A contract that establishes the general terms and conditions for a long-term business relationship between two parties. It covers broad, overarching legal and business terms that apply to all future projects, without defining the specifics of any one project. The MSA is strategic and governs the "how" of the entire relationship.

Key Differences and Use Cases:

ASPECT	STATEMENT OF WORK (SOW)	MASTER SERVICE AGREEMENT (MSA)
PURPOSE	Defines a specific project's deliverables and scope.	Establishes general legal and business terms for a long-term partnership.
SCOPE	Tactical and project-specific.	Strategic and relationship-wide.
DURATION	Limited to the lifespan of a single project.	Long-term and evergreen, unless terminated.
CONTENT FOCUS	Deliverables, tasks, timeline, resources.	Liability, jurisdiction, confidentiality, indemnification, data protection clauses.
SECURITY USE CASE	Specifies project-specific security controls (e.g., "All data for this project must be encrypted with AES-256").	Contains foundational, non-negotiable security and compliance requirements for the entire relationship (e.g., "Vendor agrees to comply with all relevant data privacy regulations like GDPR").

Security Requirements in SOW and MSA

Statements of Work (SOW) and Master Service Agreements (MSA):

- **Data Handling and Privacy:** Explicitly define the types of data the vendor will handle and the specific security controls required. This includes outlining data residency requirements and mandating the use of encryption for data both at rest and in transit. A Data Processing Agreement (DPA) should be included for compliance with regulations like GDPR and CCPA, detailing the roles and responsibilities of the data controller and processor.
- **Security Incident Response:** Mandate a specific, measurable incident response plan. Require the vendor to notify your organization within a defined timeframe (e.g.,24 hours) of a suspected or confirmed security breach. The SOW should define the format and content of these notifications and what remediation actions are expected.
- **Audit and Assessment Rights:** Secure the right for your organization to conduct security audits, penetration tests, or vulnerability assessments of the vendor's environment. The MSA should outline the general right to audit, while the SOW can detail the specifics for a particular engagement.
- **Secure Development Lifecycle (SDLC):** If the vendor is developing software, require them to follow a secure SDLC, including regular vulnerability scanning and penetration testing.

- *Contracts:*
  - **Liability and Indemnification:** Ensure that the contract clearly outlines the vendor's liability in the event of a security incident caused by their negligence or breach of contract.
- *Evaluation Factors for Award:*
  - **Security Posture:** Make security posture a formal, weighted criterion in the vendor selection process. This incentivizes vendors to maintain a strong security program.
  - **Third-Party Certifications:** Require proof of relevant certifications (e.g., SOC 2, ISO 27001) as part of the evaluation.

- *Service Level Agreements (SLAs):*
  - **Availability:** Define security-related uptime and availability requirements to prevent service disruption from security events.

- **Response Time:** Set specific, measurable timelines for the vendor to respond to and remediate security vulnerabilities or issues discovered during monitoring.
- **Remediation:** Specify the timeframe within which high-severity vulnerabilities must be patched or mitigated.

By implementing these measures and reporting standards, an organization can effectively demonstrate the value of its third-party security program and ensure that all new procurements are aligned with established IT security policies.

Summary of Key Components

COMPONENT	KEY FOCUS AREAS	BENEFITS TO ISMS
STRATEGIC PLANNING	Alignment with business objectives, KPI measurement	Ensures proactive, visionary security integration
FINANCE	Budgeting, ROI analysis, resource allocation	Optimizes costs and supports sustainable security investments
PROCUREMENT	Vendor selection, contract security requirements	Minimizes risks in acquiring security tools and services
THIRD-PARTY MANAGEMENT	Risk assessments, compliance monitoring	Protects against external threats and enhances supply chain security

By integrating these elements, information security management programs can achieve holistic governance, as seen in frameworks like CCISO, which prepare leaders to navigate complex organizational landscapes.

Multiple-Choice Questions

Scenario-Based Questions (1-35)

1. A CISO is leading an initiative to secure a new product launch in the European market. The strategic plan requires ensuring full compliance with GDPR. According to the provided document, which of the following actions is the most aligned with the "Implement 'security by design' principles" objective for this project?

A. Conducting an internal audit of existing systems to verify their compliance with ISO 27001.
B. Automating security patch management for the new product to reduce manual effort.
C. Integrating threat modeling and a secure architecture review during the initial design phase.
D. Enhancing customer trust by achieving a SOC 2 certification for the company.

2. A CISO is tasked with developing a security strategy for a financial institution that has a low-risk appetite. The strategy must guide decisions on what risks to accept, mitigate, transfer, or avoid. Which of the following is the most critical first step for the CISO to take in collaboration with senior leadership?

A. Develop a multi-year roadmap for security technology implementation.
B. Conduct an external market analysis to identify emerging threats.
C. Define the organization's risk appetite and risk tolerance.
D. Secure funding and resources for an enterprise-wide security architecture.

3. A CISO is reviewing the IT security budget for the upcoming fiscal year. A new government regulation requires specific data protection measures for all citizen data. The CISO needs to justify a significant budget increase to the board. Which of the following is the most effective approach for the CISO to justify the new expenditure?

A. Demonstrate the return on security investment (ROSI) by calculating the potential financial impact of a breach without the new controls1.
B. Present a detailed breakdown of all IT security expenditures over the past two years to show historical trends
C. Highlight the need for new tools and technologies to counter evolving threats
D. Explain that the new regulation is a form of regulatory change, which mandates new security controls.

4. An organization is preparing to acquire a new cloud-based customer relationship management (CRM) system. As the CISO, you are responsible for ensuring security is integrated early in the process. According to The ISBK, which of the following is the most critical step to take during the Procurement phase to mitigate supply chain risk?

A. Perform a cost-benefit analysis (CBA) to compare the projected costs and benefits of the CRM system.
B. Define specific security requirements that must be incorporated into the Request for Proposal (RFP) and contract.
C. Use a Statement of Objectives (SOO) to outline the desired outcomes of the procurement project.
D. Conduct a thorough risk assessment of the vendor after the contract is signed and the system is deployed.

5. A company's CISO is implementing a new third-party risk management (TPRM) program. The CISO needs to classify vendors based on the risk they introduce. A new vendor, a managed security service provider (MSSP), will have direct, privileged access to the internal network. How should the CISO classify this vendor, and what level of scrutiny is required?

A. Low-risk vendor, requiring a basic security questionnaire.
B. Medium-risk vendor, requiring a detailed security questionnaire and a financial review.
C. High-risk vendor, requiring an in-depth due diligence process, including SOC 2 reports and penetration test results.
D. No-risk vendor, as they are a security service provider and assumed to be secure.

6. A CISO is tasked with improving the organization's security posture by moving from a reactive to a proactive model. The CISO's strategic plan involves implementing new security controls. Which of the following is the most critical action to ensure these investments are part of a cohesive, long-term plan?

A. Invest solely in preventive controls like firewalls and IDS.
B. Prioritize tools that integrate seamlessly with existing infrastructure.
C. Use a risk-based allocation method for the budget.
D. Align the security investment portfolio with an Enterprise Information Security Architecture (EISA).

7. A CISO is presenting a security budget proposal to the executive board. One of the key arguments is the need to improve vulnerability remediation rates. Which of the following is the most relevant financial metric the CISO can use to demonstrate the business case for this investment?

A. Mean Time to Detect (MTTD).
B. Incident Cost Reduction.
C. Number of Phishing Clicks.
D. Mean Time to Respond (MTTR).

8. An organization is launching a new public-facing mobile application. The CISO wants to embed security into the development lifecycle. Which of the following security program roadmap phasing examples would be most appropriate for this project?

A. Phase 1: Deploy Endpoint Detection and Response (EDR); Phase 2: Develop incident response playbooks.
B. Phase 1: Conduct a compliance gap analysis; Phase 2: Implement controls, document policies.
C. Phase 1: Threat modeling and secure architecture review; Phase 2: Integrate SAST/DAST tools

into the CI/CD pipeline6.

D. Phase 1: Implement continuous monitoring tools; Phase 2: Conduct regular audits.

9. A CISO is evaluating a new vendor that will handle the company's intellectual property. Before signing a contract, the CISO's team performs an extensive review of the vendor's security policies, and requests their SOC 2 report. Which of the following concepts does this activity best represent?

A. Due Care.
B. Due Diligence.
C. Risk Acceptance.
D. Third-Party Management.

10. An organization's ISMS strategic plan identifies a business objective to "Increase market share by 15%." As the CISO, your task is to define a corresponding security objective. Which of the following objectives is the most direct and effective alignment with this business goal, according to The ISBK?

A. Implement a new SIEM to improve threat detection.
B. Enhance customer trust by achieving a global security certification, such as ISO 27001.
C. Automate security patch management to reduce system downtime.
D. Conduct a thorough risk assessment of internal systems.

11. A large enterprise is already using TOGAF for its broader enterprise architecture. The new CISO wants to establish a comprehensive and integrated security architecture. According to The ISBK, which of the following is the most logical EISA framework to adopt?

A. SABSA, due to its business-driven, risk-based approach.
B. COBIT, because it focuses on governance and compliance.
C. TOGAF with its security extensions, as it ensures alignment with the existing enterprise-wide architecture.
D. NIST CSF, for its flexible and practical risk-based functions.

12. A CISO is leading a multi-year project to migrate the company's on-premises infrastructure to a hybrid cloud environment. A key challenge is ensuring the security architecture can scale with the business. What best practice, mentioned in The ISBK, should the CISO prioritize during the design of this new architecture?

A. Limiting the number of security tools to reduce complexity.
B. Designing a zero-trust network model.
C. Prioritizing solutions that support new technologies and expanding operations.
D. Focusing on a single, comprehensive framework like ISO 27001.

13. A CISO is creating a security program roadmap. A critical dependency is that a new threat intelligence platform must be operational before the security operations center (SOC) can be fully implemented. This dependency should be included in which component of the roadmap?

A. Milestones.

B. Key Initiatives.
C. Phased Approach.
D. Dependencies.

14. A CISO wants to move the organization's security posture from a reactive, "firefighting" mode to a proactive one. Which of the following benefits of adopting an Enterprise Information Security Architecture (EISA) is most relevant to this goal?

A. Simplified Compliance.
B. Holistic Risk Management.
C. Strategic Alignment.
D. Proactive Security.

15. A CISO is conducting an internal analysis to inform the new ISMS strategic plan. The CISO wants to identify the most significant threats to the organization's assets. Which of the following activities is most directly related to this goal?

A. Reviewing existing security metrics.
B. Evaluating the security culture.
C. Assessing threats and vulnerabilities.
D. Identifying critical information assets.

16. A CISO's team discovers a critical zero-day vulnerability in a third-party software component used by a key business application. According to The ISBK, what is the most appropriate action that falls under the concept of Due Care?

A. Revoking the vendor's logical access to the company's network.
B. Requesting the vendor's most recent SOC 2 report.
C. Working with the vendor to create and track a remediation plan to closure.
D. Conducting a one-time security assessment of the vendor's security posture.

17. A CISO is using a risk heat map to rank security priorities. The map shows that the highest risk is a data breach of customer PII. Which of the following is the most appropriate action for the CISO based on this finding?

A. Prioritize investments in fraud detection and data encryption.
B. Prioritize securing the organization's operational technology (OT) systems.
C. Prioritize investments in a robust database security solution.
D. Re-evaluate the organization's risk appetite with senior leadership.

18. The procurement team has requested a cost-benefit analysis (CBA) for a new security information and event management (SIEM) system. The CISO needs to quantify the intangible benefits of the investment. Which of the following is an example of an intangible benefit?

A. Reduced losses from a breach.

B. Enhanced company reputation.
C. Reduced manual effort.
D. Reduced system downtime.

19. A CISO wants to create a security architecture that is business-driven and adaptable, starting from the highest-level business context. Which EISA framework is best suited for this top-down approach, as highlighted in The ISBK?

A. COBIT.
B. NIST CSF.
C. SABSA.
D. TOGAF.

20. A CISO is in the "Develop" phase of building an Enterprise Information Security Architecture (EISA). The CISO's team is now selecting and configuring specific technologies. Which of the following is a primary goal of this activity?

A. Aligning security reviews with agile or waterfall methodologies.
B. Developing a multi-year roadmap.
C. Building the physical and component architecture, including firewalls and endpoint protection.
D. Securing funding and resources.

21. A CISO is leading the security strategy for a new e-commerce platform. The CISO is concerned about the security of third-party payment gateways and shipping partners. This type of risk is known as:

A. Direct risk.
B. Internal risk.
C. Fourth-party risk.
D. Procurement risk.

22. A CISO is working with the legal department to finalize a contract with a new cloud service provider. The CISO wants to ensure that specific security performance metrics and penalties are defined in the agreement. Which contractual element should the CISO focus on for this purpose?

A. Statement of Work (SOW).
B. Statement of Objectives (SOO).
C. Service Level Agreements (SLAs).
D. Request for Proposal (RFP).

23. A company is considering a new SaaS solution for its HR department. The CISO's team is responsible for vendor due diligence. The vendor claims to be SOC 2 certified. What is the most important action for the CISO's team to take, according to The ISBK?

A. Rely on the vendor's self-attested information.

B. Request and review the SOC 2 report and other supporting documentation.
C. Ask for a list of the vendor's other clients.
D. Conduct a site visit to the vendor's office.

24. A CISO is implementing a security program that aligns with an Enterprise Information Security Architecture (EISA). The CISO has defined the high-level security principles and vision. The next step, according to The ISBK, is to translate these principles into a logical design that defines how security will be implemented through controls and policies. Which EISA layer does this describe?

A. Conceptual Layer.
B. Business Context Layer.
C. Implementation Layer.
D. Logical Layer.

25. A company has recently experienced a significant data breach due to a misconfiguration in a third-party cloud service. The CISO is now tasked with rebuilding customer trust. According to The ISBK, what is the most significant consequence of a third-party security incident that the CISO must address?
A. Increased operational costs.
B. Financial losses due to a direct breach.
C. Reputational damage that erodes customer trust.
D. A violation of internal policies.

26. A CISO is leading an organization-wide initiative to achieve a new security certification. The CISO needs to identify and engage with key personnel to gather their perspectives and requirements. According to The ISBK, which of the following groups should the CISO engage with to ensure a comprehensive security strategy?

A. Only IT and legal teams.
B. Only business unit leaders and executive leadership.
C. All personnel from business units, IT, legal, HR, and executive leadership.
D. Only external consultants and vendors.

27. A CISO needs to select a vendor for a new endpoint protection solution. The CISO knows the specific security requirements but wants to see different vendor approaches before making a final decision. Which procurement strategy is most suitable for this scenario?

A. Sole-Source.
B. Competitive Bidding.
C. Request for Information (RFI).
D. Request for Proposal (RFP).

28. An organization is adopting a hybrid approach to its EISA, combining different frameworks. The CISO has chosen SABSA for the strategic, business-driven aspects. Which framework would be the most effective complement for the technical implementation phase, according to The ISBK?

A. COBIT, for its focus on governance and GRC.
B. NIST CSF, for its practical, risk-based functions.
C. TOGAF, for its broader enterprise architecture focus.
D. ISO 27001, for its certification focus.

29. A CISO's team has completed a thorough risk assessment and identified that the organization's customer database is its most critical asset. According to The ISBK, how should this finding influence the procurement of new security solutions?

A. It justifies a higher investment in a robust database security solution.
B. It requires a detailed Cost-Benefit Analysis (CBA).
C. It proves the need for a formal Statement of Work (SOW).
D. It mandates the use of a Request for Proposal (RFP) for the procurement.

30. The CISO of a manufacturing company is developing a security roadmap. The company is heavily reliant on its operational technology (OT) systems for production. According to The ISBK, which of the following security investments should the CISO prioritize?

A. Fraud detection and data encryption for financial transactions.
B. Security investments focused on securing the OT systems.
C. Endpoint detection and response (EDR) for corporate laptops.
D. A new SIEM system for general log analysis.

31. A CISO is leading a security program that has been operating in a reactive, "fix-it" mode. The CISO needs to demonstrate the value of a proactive, strategic approach to the board. Which of the following is the most direct benefit of a well-aligned EISA that the CISO can present to justify this shift?

A. It ensures security investments directly support and enable business objectives.
B. It provides a systematic way to identify and manage risks across the enterprise.
C. It streamlines adherence to regulatory and industry standards.
D. It moves the organization from a reactive to a proactive security posture.

32. A CISO is negotiating a contract with a new third-party vendor. The CISO wants to ensure that in the event of a security incident originating from the vendor, the vendor is held financially accountable. Which contractual clause is most critical for the CISO to include?

A. Incident response and notification protocols.
B. Audit and access rights for your organization.
C. Data protection and privacy clauses.
D. Liability and indemnification clauses.

33. A CISO is leading a project to secure remote work capabilities for all employees. The CISO's team is now in the "Develop" phase of the EISA lifecycle. Which of the following activities is most relevant to this project during this phase?

A. Defining the organization's risk appetite.
B. Creating a high-level vision for the future state of the security posture.
C. Designing a segmented LAN/WAN with encryption and access controls.
D. Conducting an annual review of the EISA.

34. A CISO is asked to present a detailed project plan for a new data encryption rollout. The plan must specify the tasks, deliverables, and timelines. Which of the following procurement concepts is most relevant for this purpose?

A. Total Cost of Ownership (TCO).
B. Statement of Objectives (SOO).
C. Cost-Benefit Analysis (CBA).
D. Statement of Work (SOW).

35. An organization's CISO is implementing a formal third-party management policy. According to The ISBK, what is the most critical first step in the TPRM lifecycle to identify the full scope of risk?

A. Negotiating contractual security clauses.
B. Continuous monitoring of vendor security posture.
C. Creating a comprehensive inventory of all third parties and categorizing them based on criticality.
D. Revoking all logical and physical access for a terminated vendor.

Knowledge-Based Questions (36-100)

36. Which of the following is a primary purpose of a security roadmap?

A. To provide a high-level overview of the current security posture.
B. To translate the strategic plan into actionable, phased initiatives.
C. To define the organization's risk appetite.
D. To detail the specific technologies and tools required for implementation.

37. The highest and most abstract layer of a robust EISA framework is the:

A. Implementation Layer.
B. Logical Layer.
C. Conceptual Layer.
D. Business Context Layer.

38. What is the primary purpose of a Business Impact Analysis (BIA) in the context of IT security procurement?

A. To identify and quantify the Total Cost of Ownership (TCO) of a new system.
B. To determine the potential effects of a disruption to an organization's critical business functions.
C. To compare the projected costs and benefits of a security investment.
D. To guide suppliers in developing their proposals for a project.

39. According to The ISBK, what is the term for a high-level, visual representation that outlines how security initiatives and objectives will be achieved over a defined timeframe, typically 1-3 years?

A. Enterprise Information Security Architecture (EISA).
B. Information Security Management System (ISMS).
C. Information Security Program Strategic Roadmap.
D. Business Impact Analysis (BIA).

40. Which of the following frameworks is described as being a governance and management framework focused on IT processes, including security, and aligning IT with business goals through defined controls and metrics?

A. TOGAF.
B. NIST Cybersecurity Framework (CSF).
C. COBIT.
D. SABSA.

41. Which of the following is an example of a detective control, as mentioned in The ISBK's discussion on Defense-in-Depth?

A. Endpoint protection.
B. Firewalls.
C. SIEM systems.
D. Data encryption.

42. What is the term for a financial estimate that considers all costs associated with acquiring, operating, and maintaining a product or service over its entire lifecycle?

A. Return on Security Investment (ROSI).
B. Total Cost of Ownership (TCO).
C. Cost-Benefit Analysis (CBA).
D. Return on Investment (ROI).

43. What is the primary purpose of a Request for Proposal (RFP)?

A. To gather general information from a broad range of potential vendors.
B. To solicit specific, customized solutions from a pre-screened group of vendors
C. To achieve the best possible value for a well-defined product.
D. To buy from a single vendor for proprietary technology.

44. What is the term for the level of risk an organization is willing to accept to achieve its goals?

A. Risk assessment.
B. Risk appetite
C. Risk transfer.
D. Risk mitigation.

45. Which EISA layer is where the "what" and "how" of security are determined by translating conceptual principles into a logical design?

A. Business Context Layer.
B. Logical Layer
C. Conceptual Layer.
D. Implementation Layer.

46. According to The ISBK, which of the following is not a phase in the EISA lifecycle?

A. Design.
B. Develop.
C. Maintain.
D. Implement.

47. The concept of "Defense in Depth" involves investing in multiple layers of security controls. Which of the following best describes this approach?

A. Prioritizing investments in a single, robust security solution.
B. Relying on a single vendor for all security technologies.
C. Diversifying investments across preventive, detective, and corrective measures
D. Focusing on a single security domain, such as network security.

48. What is a key feature of the COBIT framework, as noted in The ISBK?

A. It is a business-driven, risk-based framework.
B. It provides a maturity model to assess and improve security processes
C. It is an enterprise architecture framework.
D. It focuses on five core functions: Identify, Protect, Detect, Respond, and Recover.

49. A CISO must define the organization's risk appetite with senior leadership. This provides the security team with a clear directive to guide decisions on which of the following?

A. Which technologies to purchase.
B. How to allocate the budget.
C. What risks to accept, mitigate, transfer, or avoid
D. Which security frameworks to adopt.

50. A security strategic plan should be a long-term roadmap that aligns with business objectives over what timeframe, as mentioned in The ISBK?

A. 1-2 years.
B. 3-5 years
C. 5-10 years.
D. 6-12 months.

51. The procurement concept known as an SOO (Statement of Objectives) focuses on defining the:

A. "How" of the work.
B. Specific tasks, deliverables, and timelines.
C. "What" and "why" of the project
D. Total cost over the lifecycle.

52. What is the term for the act of investigating and verifying the security posture of a potential vendor before entering into a contract?

A. Due Care.
B. Due Diligence
C. Vendor Management.
D. Risk Mitigation.

53. Which of the following is considered a proactive, continuous responsibility that involves actively monitoring and managing a vendor's security posture after the contract is signed?

A. Due Diligence.
B. Due Care
C. Initial Assessment.
D. Vendor Selection.

54. What is the purpose of conducting a security assessment of prospective vendors during the Third-Party Risk Management (TPRM) lifecycle?

A. To terminate the vendor relationship.
B. To create a comprehensive inventory of all third parties.
C. To vet potential vendors before a contract is signed
D. To monitor a vendor's security posture over time.

55. The ISBK states that an EISA must be reviewed at least annually, or after significant business changes, during which phase of its lifecycle?

A. Design.
B. Develop.
C. Maintain.

D. Implement.

56. Which of the following is a key component of an Information Security Program Strategic Roadmap?

A. A detailed breakdown of all financial expenditures.
B. A list of all hardware and software to be purchased.
C. A high-level visual representation of phased initiatives
D. A set of specific, technical security controls.

57. According to The ISBK, which EISA framework is best suited for organizations that need a globally recognized standard to structure their security and seek certification?

A. ISO/IEC 27001.
B. NIST Cybersecurity Framework (CSF).
C. COBIT.
D. SABSA.

58. The "Implementation Layer" of an EISA framework is described as the practical, hands-on layer that details the specific technologies and tools required. This layer is also referred to as the:

A. Strategic "Why".
B. Conceptual "Big Picture".
C. Logical "What and How".
D. Practical "How"

59. Which of the following is a key feature of the NIST Cybersecurity Framework (CSF)?

A. It provides a maturity model to assess processes.
B. It is a business-driven, risk-based framework.
C. It focuses on five core functions: Identify, Protect, Detect, Respond, and Recover.
D. It includes security extensions for enterprise architecture.

60. What is the purpose of conducting an external analysis as part of an ISMS strategic plan?
A. To evaluate the organization's current security culture.
B. To identify outside threats and opportunities.
C. To assess the effectiveness of existing security tools.
D. To define the organization's risk tolerance.

61. Which of the following is a key element of the "Develop" phase in the EISA lifecycle?

A. Conducting a comprehensive risk assessment.
B. Defining security principles like "least privilege".
C. Creating a detailed EISA roadmap with a phased plan
D. Implementing a SIEM for continuous monitoring.

62. What is the primary purpose of an Enterprise Information Security Architecture (EISA)?

A. To create a collection of siloed, ad-hoc security solutions.
B. To ensure security initiatives are strategically aligned with overall business objectives
C. To define the specific technologies and tools to be used.
D. To detail a vendor's security posture before a contract.

63. Which of the following is a metric used to measure the effectiveness of a security program, as described in The ISBK?

A. Total Cost of Ownership (TCO).
B. Return on Security Investment (ROSI).
C. Mean Time to Detect (MTTD).
D. Statement of Work (SOW).

64. Which of the following frameworks is described as an enterprise architecture framework that includes security components and provides a structured process (Architecture Development Method, ADM) to integrate security?

A. COBIT.
B. SABSA.
C. NIST CSF.
D. TOGAF.

65. What is the term for a document that specifies the high-level objectives and desired outcomes of a procurement project without detailing how the work should be performed?

A. Request for Proposal (RFP).
B. Statement of Work (SOW).
C. Statement of Objectives (SOO)
D. Service Level Agreement (SLA).

66. Which of the following is a key component of the "Design" phase of an EISA?

A. Conducting penetration testing.
B. Creating a multi-year roadmap.
C. Defining security domains and principles
D. Implementing SIEM systems.

67. What is the primary focus of the Zachman Framework (Security-Focused Adaptation)?

A. Providing a systematic way to identify, assess, and manage risks.
B. Aligning security with business objectives.
C. Providing a taxonomy for aligning security with enterprise components

D. Defining controls for hardware, software, and networks.

68. What is the goal of balancing an IT security investment portfolio?

A. To purchase the latest security tools.
B. To reduce the number of security vendors.
C. To achieve the greatest possible risk reduction and business enablement
D. To focus solely on compliance-driven investments.

69. What is the primary reason for a company to conduct an internal analysis as part of its ISMS strategic planning?

A. To identify new market trends and industry regulations.
B. To understand customer security expectations.
C. To provide a baseline for the current security posture
D. To assess the security posture of competitors.

70. According to The ISBK, which of the following is a key benefit of a well-documented EISA?
A. It eliminates the need for third-party risk management.
B. It assists in meeting regulatory requirements and industry standards
C. It ensures the organization moves from a proactive to a reactive posture.
D. It simplifies the process of acquiring new technology.

71. What is the purpose of the "Onboarding" phase in the vendor selection process?

A. To perform in-depth due diligence.
B. To negotiate contractual terms.
C. To execute the contract and integrate the vendor into operations
D. To identify potential vendors through market research.

72. Which of the following is a common security principle mentioned in The ISBK?

A. Cost-Benefit Analysis.
B. Total Cost of Ownership.
C. Least Privilege
D. Return on Security Investment.

73. The EISA framework provides a blueprint for the organization's security posture. What is the main benefit of this blueprint when balancing security investments?

A. It ensures investments are part of a cohesive, long-term plan
B. It provides a detailed breakdown of all expenditures.
C. It prioritizes the purchase of new tools.
D. It focuses on a single layer of security control.

74. What does the term "shelfware" refer to, in the context of security investments?

A. Unused or ineffective software
B. Software purchased for a specific project.
C. Proprietary software from a single vendor.
D. Security software that is highly integrated.

75. Which of the following is a characteristic of a "high-risk vendor," as defined in The ISBK?

A. A vendor with a small team and limited resources.
B. A vendor that handles the organization's customer PII or intellectual property
C. A vendor that provides a non-essential service, such as janitorial work.
D. A vendor that only has direct access to the public-facing website.

76. What is the primary purpose of a security strategic plan, as described in The ISBK?

A. To define the organization's technical security controls.
B. To outline the specific budget for the security department.
C. To ensure security initiatives directly support the business's mission, vision, and objectives
D. To document past security incidents.

77. When conducting a Cost-Benefit Analysis (CBA) for a security investment, what is a tangible benefit that can be quantified?

A. Enhanced brand reputation.
B. Improved customer trust.
C. Reduced losses from a breach
D. Increased operational efficiency.

78. What is the term for a continuous, cyclical process for managing supply chain risk from a new third party?

A. Vendor Selection Process.
B. Acquisition Life Cycle.
C. Third-Party Risk Management Lifecycle
D. Procurement Strategy.

79. In the "Maintain" phase of the EISA lifecycle, what is the purpose of continuously monitoring the threat landscape?

A. To perform internal and external audits.
B. To verify compliance with policies.
C. To update the EISA to defend against new and emerging threats
D. To create a well-documented incident response plan.

80. Which of the following is a key feature of SABSA?
A. It provides a maturity model to assess and improve security processes.
B. It is a business-driven, risk-based framework that aligns security with organizational goals
C. It focuses on five core functions: Identify, Protect, Detect, Respond, and Recover.
D. It is primarily an enterprise architecture framework.

81. What is the primary purpose of a Request for Information (RFI)?

A. To solicit a formal proposal from a vendor.
B. To gather general information from a broad range of potential vendors for market research.
C. To negotiate specific contract terms and conditions.
D. To compare the costs of different solutions.

82. Which of the following best describes the "Internal Analysis" section of an ISMS strategic planning document?

A. It identifies outside threats and opportunities.
B. It provides a baseline for the current security posture
C. It focuses on regulatory changes and market trends.
D. It outlines contractual obligations with customers.

83. The purpose of an EISA's "Conceptual Layer" is to provide a:

A. Detailed view of specific technologies.
B. High-level "big picture" view of the security architecture
C. Breakdown of all financial costs.
D. Detailed description of the tasks and deliverables.

84. According to The ISBK, what is the primary purpose of a security program strategic roadmap?

A. To create a list of all security incidents.
B. To translate the strategic plan into actionable, phased initiatives
C. To define the organization's risk tolerance.
D. To document a detailed threat assessment.

85. What is the term for the process of strategically allocating resources across various security initiatives to achieve the greatest possible risk reduction?

A. Cost-Benefit Analysis (CBA).
B. Risk-Based Prioritization.
C. Balancing an IT Security Investment Portfolio
D. Total Cost of Ownership (TCO).

86. According to The ISBK, which of the following is a key benefit of adopting an EISA framework?

A. It simplifies business processes.
B. It guarantees a 100% secure environment.
C. It provides a systematic way to identify, assess, and manage risks
D. It eliminates the need for ongoing monitoring.

87. A procurement strategy that involves buying from a single vendor, often used for proprietary technology, is known as:

A. Competitive Bidding.
B. Request for Proposal (RFP).
C. Sole-Source
D. Request for Information (RFI).

88. Which of the following is a key activity in the "Planning and Due Diligence" phase of the TPRM lifecycle?

A. Continuous monitoring of a vendor's attack surface.
B. Revoking a vendor's logical and physical access.
C. Conducting a security assessment of prospective vendors
D. Conducting periodic re-assessments of existing vendors.

89. What is the purpose of the "Internal Analysis" component of an ISMS strategic plan?

A. To understand customer security expectations.
B. To evaluate the organization's current state and identify areas for improvement
C. To learn from competitors' security incidents.
D. To assess industry trends and regulatory landscapes.

90. Which of the following is a key feature of ISO/IEC 27001?

A. It provides a maturity model to assess processes.
B. It focuses on governance, risk, and compliance (GRC).
C. It supports certification, ensuring compliance with global standards
D. It is a business-driven, risk-based framework.

91. What is the key difference between a Statement of Objectives (SOO) and a Statement of Work (SOW)?

A. SOO focuses on the "what" and "why," while SOW details the "how"
B. SOO is a formal contract, while SOW is a preliminary document.
C. SOO is for hardware procurement, while SOW is for software.
D. SOO is used for competitive bidding, while SOW is for sole-source.

92. Which EISA layer is focused on defining the organization's business goals, risk tolerance, and the value of its information assets?

A. Conceptual Layer.
B. Logical Layer.
C. Implementation Layer.
D. Business Context Layer

93. According to the ISBK, an Information Security Program Strategic Roadmap should typically cover what timeframe?

A. 1-3 years
B. 3-5 years.
C. 5-10 years.
D. 6-12 months.

94. What is the primary goal of the "Design" phase of the EISA lifecycle?

A. To build and integrate security components.
B. To monitor and review the architecture continuously.
C. To understand the organization's strategic goals and translate them into security requirements
D. To conduct a vulnerability assessment.

95. What is the purpose of conducting a "continuous review" of the security framework?

A. To ensure a "set it and forget it" approach.
B. To address new threats, technologies, and business changes
C. To reduce the need for stakeholder engagement.
D. To focus solely on a single framework.

96. What is the term for a high-level, "big picture" view of the security architecture that outlines core security principles?

A. Business Context Layer.
B. Conceptual Layer
C. Logical Layer.
D. Implementation Layer.

97. The ISBK defines a "high-risk vendor" based on several key factors. Which of the following is considered the most critical factor?

A. The size of the vendor.
B. Access to sensitive data
C. The number of employees.
D. The vendor's financial stability.

98. Which of the following is a key step in the "Develop" phase of the EISA lifecycle?

A. Conducting an external analysis.
B. Defining the scope of the EISA.
C. Building the physical and component architecture
D. Defining the organization's risk appetite.

99. What is a key purpose of the EISA's "Implementation Layer"?

A. To create a logical design.
B. To outline security principles.
C. To detail the specific technologies, tools, and processes required to build the architecture
D. To define business goals and risk tolerance.

100. What is the main reason for a CISO to involve a diverse group of stakeholders, including lawyers and HR, in the IT security procurement process?

A. To accelerate the vendor selection process.
B. To ensure alignment with legal, compliance, and human resources needs
C. To reduce the need for vendor due diligence.
D. To identify new market trends.

Answer Key

1. C. Integrating threat modeling and a secure architecture review during the initial design phase is a direct application of the "security by design" principle. The ISBK's example roadmap for a new product launch explicitly lists "Threat modeling and secure architecture review" in the first phase.

- **A** is incorrect because an internal audit is a measure of an existing system, not an action during the design of a new one.
- **B** is incorrect because automated patch management is an operational efficiency objective, not a security by design principle for a product launch.
- **D** is incorrect as achieving SOC 2 is a broader objective to enhance customer trust, not a specific action for secure product design.

2. C. The ISBK states that defining the organization's risk appetite is a key area of strategic planning. This provides a clear directive for the security team, guiding decisions on what risks to accept, mitigate, transfer, or avoid. Without this, a CISO cannot effectively develop a strategy.

- **A** and **B** are part of the strategic planning process but are subsequent steps that build upon a defined risk appetite.
- **D** is a result of the strategic planning process, not a prerequisite.

3. A. The most effective way to justify a security expenditure to the board is to present it in financial terms. The ISBK highlights the use of metrics like "Incident Cost Reduction" and the formula for Return on Security Investment (ROSI) to justify expenditures. This approach directly ties the investment to a potential financial loss.

- **B, C, and D** are all valid points, but they do not provide the direct financial justification (the "business case") that is most persuasive to a board of directors, as described in The ISBK.

4. B. The ISBK emphasizes that security teams must "provide clear, non-negotiable security requirements" that should be "incorporated into Requests for Proposals (RFPs) and contracts". This is presented as a primary method for embedding security early in the procurement process to mitigate supply chain risk.

- **A** is a crucial step but is part of the broader financial analysis, not the specific action to embed security requirements in the contract.
- **C** is a high-level document and does not specify the detailed security requirements needed for risk mitigation.
- **D** is incorrect because due diligence must be performed *before* a purchase is made.

5. C. The ISBK defines a "high-risk vendor" as one that could cause significant damage if compromised. Key factors include "criticality of the service" and "system connectivity". An MSSP with privileged network access meets these criteria. The ISBK further states that for high-risk vendors, an in-depth due diligence process, including evidence review of SOC 2 reports and penetration test results, is required.

- **A** and **B** are incorrect because a vendor with direct, privileged network access is explicitly defined as high- risk, not low or medium.
- **D** is incorrect as no vendor is "no-risk"; all third parties introduce some level of risk.

6. D. The ISBK states that EISA provides a strategic blueprint that ensures security investments are not made in a silo but are part of a "cohesive, long-term plan". This aligns with moving from a reactive to a proactive strategy.

- **A** is incorrect because a balanced portfolio should diversify across preventive, detective, and corrective measures.

- **B** is a good practice, but it is a consideration within the EISA framework, not the overarching strategic action.
- **C** is a technique for managing the portfolio, but it relies on a clear understanding of priorities, which is provided by EISA.

7. B. The ISBK lists "Incident Cost Reduction" as a financial metric that demonstrates how proactive security investments reduce the financial impact of breaches. Improving vulnerability remediation rates is a proactive measure that directly contributes to this.

- **A, C, and D** are operational metrics (KPIs) and while important, they are not direct financial metrics that demonstrate a business case for a budget increase.

8. C. The ISBK provides a specific example roadmap phasing for "Securing a New Product Launch," which includes "Threat modeling and secure architecture review" and "Integrate SAST/DAST tools into the CI/CD pipeline". This aligns with a proactive, "security by design" approach.

- **A** is a roadmap for maturing security operations.
- **B** is a roadmap for compliance and certification.
- **D** is part of the EISA maintenance phase.

9. B. The ISBK explicitly defines "Due Diligence" as a "proactive and pre-contract investigation" that involves "investigating and verifying the security posture, controls, and practices of a potential third-party vendor before you enter into a contract"[92]. The actions described—reviewing policies and a SOC 2 report

before a contract—are textbook examples of this.

- **A** (Due Care) is the ongoing, continuous responsibility after the contract is signed.

- **C** (Risk Acceptance) is a decision made after due diligence, not the act of due diligence itself.
- **D** (Third-Party Management) is the overall program, not the specific pre-contractual activity.

10. B. The ISBK provides a table that directly maps the business objective "Increase market share by 15%" to the aligned security objective "Enhance customer trust by achieving ISO 27001 certification".

This is because a globally recognized security certification can be leveraged as a competitive advantage to build customer trust.

- **A, C, and D** are all valid security objectives, but they do not directly align with the business goal of increasing market share as specified in The ISBK's example.

11. C. The ISBK states that TOGAF is an enterprise architecture framework that includes security extensions. It recommends TOGAF for organizations "already using TOGAF for enterprise architecture, seeking to embed security holistically".

- **A, B, and D** are all valid frameworks, but they are not presented as the most logical choice when an organization is already committed to a different enterprise architecture framework.

12. C. The ISBK lists "Scalability" as a best practice for a well-aligned EISA, specifically stating that a CISO should prioritize "solutions that can grow with the business, supporting new technologies and expanding operations without requiring a complete security overhaul".

- **A** is incorrect; a balanced approach requires investing in multiple layers of controls.
- **B** and **D** are specific strategies, but they are not the overarching principle of designing for future growth.

13. D. The ISBK's description of a security roadmap's "Key Components" explicitly lists "Dependencies" as showing "how initiatives are linked and which projects must be completed before others can begin".

- **A, B, and C** are other components of a roadmap, but "Dependencies" is the most specific and correct answer for this scenario.

14. D. The ISBK lists "Proactive Security" as a key benefit of EISA, stating that it helps organizations "move from a reactive 'firefighting' mode to a proactive posture of mitigating risks at the design level".

- **A, B, and C** are also benefits, but they do not directly describe the shift from a reactive to a proactive security posture.

15. C. The "Internal Analysis" section of The ISBK lists "Threat and Vulnerability Assessment" as a key activity for "Risk Management" and defines it as "What are the most significant threats to our assets, and what are their existing vulnerabilities?".

- **A, B, and D** are also part of the internal analysis, but they are not directly related to identifying threats.

16. C. The ISBK defines "Due Care" as an "ongoing and continuous responsibility" to "actively monitor, manage, and maintain oversight of a vendor's security posture". The example activity for due care is "Remediation and Follow-up". Working with a vendor to fix a discovered vulnerability falls under this category.

- **A** and **D** are actions that might be part of the TPRM lifecycle, but they do not specifically represent the concept of ongoing "due care."
- **B** is an activity that falls under Due Diligence, the pre-contractual investigation[103103103].

17. C. The ISBK states that the CISO's priorities should stem from the organization's business goals, and that "These priorities are typically derived from risk assessments and are often ranked using tools like risk heat maps". The example given is that if a BIA reveals a "customer database is a critical asset, it justifies a higher investment in a robust database security solution".

- **A** is incorrect because the example given for fraud detection and data encryption is for a financial institution, which may not be the case here.
- **B** is incorrect as this is for a manufacturing company.
- **D** is incorrect; the risk appetite is defined before the risk assessment.

18. B. The ISBK provides a list of tangible and intangible benefits to consider in a CBA. "Reduced losses from a breach" is a tangible, quantifiable benefit. "Enhanced reputation" is listed as an example of an intangible benefit.

- **A, C, and D** are examples of tangible benefits, such as reduced costs or improved efficiency.

19. C. The ISBK explicitly describes SABSA as a "business-driven, risk-based framework" that uses a "top-down approach starting with business context". This perfectly matches the CISO's goal.

- **A, B, and D** are other valid frameworks but are not described as having this specific top-down, business- driven approach.

20. C. The ISBK states that a key step in the "Develop" phase is to "Build Physical and Component Architecture" by implementing "firewalls, intrusion detection systems (IDS), endpoint protection for hardware, and secure access service edge (SASE) for networks".

- **A** is a separate step ("Align with Projects") within the same phase.
- **B** is a step within the "Develop" phase, but it's about creating the plan, not implementing the technologies.
- **D** is a step to secure resources for implementation, not the implementation itself.

21. C. The ISBK mentions that the risk chain does not stop at immediate vendors and that "Many third parties rely on their own vendors (known as 'fourth parties'), creating a complex supply chain that can be difficult to monitor and secure". A payment gateway or shipping partner is a third party, but their reliance on their own vendors (e.g., cloud providers) introduces fourth-party risk.

- **A** and **B** are not defined in The ISBK.
- **D** is a general category, not the specific type of risk from a vendor's supply chain.

22. C. The ISBK states that Service Level Agreements (SLAs) are where "security-related performance metrics and penalties for violations" are defined.

- **A** is a detailed document on tasks and deliverables.
- **B** is a high-level objectives document.
- **D** is a request for a proposal, not a final contract element.

23. B. The ISBK states, "Don't rely solely on self-attested information" and advises that during due diligence, a CISO should "Request supporting documentation such as SOC 2 reports, ISO 27001 certificates, penetration test results, and audit findings to validate the vendor's security claims".

- **A** is explicitly stated as something to avoid.
- **C** and **D** are not mentioned as the primary actions for this specific scenario.

24. D. The ISBK defines the "Logical Layer" as the layer where "conceptual principles are translated into a logical design," which "defines how security will be implemented across various systems and processes, including defining security controls, policies, and procedures".

- **A** and **B** are higher-level layers, while **C** is the hands-on layer.

25. C. The ISBK explicitly mentions "Reputational Damage" as a consequence of a third-party security incident, stating that it "can erode customer trust and harm your brand, even if the breach did not originate within your own systems".

- **A, B, and D** are also consequences, but the loss of customer trust and brand damage is highlighted as a significant reputational impact.

26. C. The ISBK emphasizes stakeholder engagement as a key component of strategic planning and governance. It lists "Engage with key personnel from business units, IT, legal, HR, and executive leadership" as a step in the design phase of EISA.

- **A, B, and D** are incomplete and do not reflect the comprehensive, cross-functional approach recommended.

27. D. The ISBK defines an RFP as a process for complex, high-value projects where the organization knows its specific requirements but wants to see different vendor approaches. This matches the CISO's needs.

- **A** is for a single, proprietary vendor.
- **B** is for well-defined products where the primary goal is the best price.
- **C** is for initial market research, not for soliciting proposals.

28. B. The ISBK suggests a "Hybrid Approach" as a best practice, with the example of combining "SABSA for strategy" with "NIST for implementation" to "balance business alignment with technical rigor".

- **A, C, and D** are other frameworks, but NIST is specifically mentioned as a complement to SABSA for implementation.

29. A. The ISBK states that a BIA (which identifies critical assets) can be used to "Prioritize Security Controls" and that if a BIA reveals a "customer database is a critical asset, it justifies a higher investment in a robust database security solution".

- **B** and **C** are separate procurement concepts.
- **D** is not necessarily mandated.

30. B. The ISBK states that a manufacturing company "might focus on securing its operational technology (OT) systems" when balancing its security investment portfolio, as these systems are critical to production.

- **A** is the example given for a financial institution.
- **C** and **D** are general security investments, not specific to the unique needs of a manufacturing company.

31. D. The ISBK's section on EISA benefits explicitly lists "Proactive Security" and states that it helps an organization "move from a reactive 'firefighting' mode to a proactive security posture". This is the most direct benefit that justifies the shift the CISO wants to make.

- **A, B, and C** are other benefits, but they are outcomes of a well-designed EISA, not the core concept of moving from reactive to proactive.

32. D. The ISBK states that "liability and indemnification clauses" are key provisions that must be included in a contract with a vendor to define responsibilities. This clause is crucial for assigning financial accountability.

- **A, B, and C** are also important clauses, but they do not specifically address financial liability in the way that an indemnification clause does.

33. C. The "Develop" phase includes building the physical and component architecture, which involves "designing segmented LAN/WAN with encryption and access controls to support remote work and cloud integrations". This is the most direct action related to securing remote work capabilities.

- **A, B, and D** are actions from the "Design" or "Maintain" phases.

34. D. The ISBK defines a "Statement of Work (SOW)" as a "detailed document that specifies the tasks, deliverables, timelines, and standards that a contractor must follow to fulfill the contract". This is exactly what the CISO needs for the project plan.

- **A** is a financial estimate.
- **B** is a high-level objectives document.
- **C** is a financial analysis.

35. C. The ISBK's section on the "Third-Party Risk Management Lifecycle" lists "Planning and Due Diligence" as the initial phase and a key activity is "Creating a comprehensive inventory of all third parties" and "Categorizing vendors based on the criticality of their service". This is the foundational step to define the scope of risk.

- **A, B, and D** are all later steps in the lifecycle.

36. B. The ISBK states that the primary purpose of a security program strategic roadmap is to "translate the strategic plan into actionable, phased initiatives".

- **A, C, and D** are all parts of the strategic planning process but are not the primary purpose of the roadmap itself.

37. D. The "Key Components of an EISA Framework" section lists the "Business Context Layer" as the "highest and most abstract layer".

38. B. The ISBK explicitly defines a BIA as a "systematic process to determine the potential effects of a disruption to an organization's critical business functions and processes".

39. C. The ISBK defines the "Information Security Program Strategic Roadmap" as a "high-level, visual representation that outlines how security initiatives and objectives will be achieved over a defined timeframe, typically 1–3 years".

40. C. The "Key EISA Frameworks" section provides an overview of COBIT, stating it is a "governance and management framework focused on IT processes, including security".

41. C. The ISBK, when discussing defense-in-depth, lists SIEM systems as an example of a "detective" measure.

- **A, B, and D** are listed as preventive measures.

42. B. The ISBK defines "Total Cost of Ownership (TCO)" as a "financial estimate that considers all costs associated with acquiring, operating, and maintaining a product or service over its entire lifecycle".

43. B. The ISBK defines a Request for Proposal (RFP) as a document issued to "solicit specific, customized solutions from a pre-screened group of vendors"

44. B. The ISBK defines "risk appetite" as the "level of risk it is willing to accept to achieve its goals"[136].

45. B. The "Logical Layer" is described as where "conceptual principles are translated into a logical design" and where the "what" and "how" of security are determined.

46. D. The EISA lifecycle phases described are Design, Develop, and Maintain. "Implement" is not a lifecycle phase, but rather a layer within the framework and a step within the Develop phase.

47. C. The ISBK states that a balanced portfolio should "diversify investments across preventive (e.g., firewalls), detective (e.g., SIEM systems), and corrective (e.g., incident response tools) measures".

48. B. The ISBK lists a key feature of COBIT as providing a "maturity model to assess and improve security processes".

49. C. The ISBK explicitly states that defining the risk appetite guides the security team's decisions on "what risks to accept, mitigate, transfer, or avoid".

50. B. The ISBK states that a security strategy should be a "long-term roadmap that aligns with business objectives over a 3- to 5-year horizon".

51. C. The ISBK states that an SOO "guides suppliers in developing their proposals by focusing on the 'what' and 'why' rather than the 'how'".

52. B. The ISBK defines "Due Diligence" as a "proactive and pre-contract investigation".

53. B. The ISBK defines "Due Care" as an "ongoing and continuous responsibility" that involves "actively monitoring, managing, and maintaining oversight of a vendor's security posture throughout the entire lifecycle of the relationship".

54. C. The ISBK states that a key activity in the "Planning and Due Diligence" phase is "Conducting a security assessment of prospective vendors".

55. C. The ISBK states that during the "Maintain" phase, the EISA should be reviewed at least annually.

56. C. The ISBK defines the roadmap as a "high-level, visual representation" of phased initiatives.

57. A. The ISBK's description of ISO/IEC 27001 states it is suitable for organizations that need a "globally recognized standard" and "Supports certification".

58. D. The ISBK defines the "Implementation Layer" as the "practical, hands-on layer" that is the "practical 'How'" of the framework.

59. C. The ISBK states that NIST CSF is a risk-based framework that focuses on five core functions: "Identify, Protect, Detect, Respond, and Recover".

60. B. The ISBK states that "Understanding the external environment is crucial for identifying information security requirements and potential threats" and that "external analysis" is for "Identifying outside threats and opportunities".

61. C. The ISBK lists "Create an EISA Roadmap" and "Develop a Phased Plan" as a key step in the "Develop" phase.

62. B. The ISBK states that the primary purpose of an EISA is to "ensure that security initiatives are strategically aligned with the overall business objectives".

63. C. The ISBK lists Mean Time to Detect (MTTD) as a metric used to measure a security program's effectiveness.

64. D. The ISBK states that TOGAF is an "enterprise architecture framework" that includes security components and provides a "structured process (Architecture Development Method, ADM) to integrate security".

65. C. The ISBK defines a Statement of Objectives (SOO) as a document that "outlines the high-level objectives and desired outcomes of a procurement project without specifying how the work should be performed".

66. C. The "Design" phase includes a step to "Define Security Principles and Requirements," which involves establishing high-level principles.

67. C. The ISBK states that a security-focused adaptation of the Zachman Framework "Provides a taxonomy for aligning security with enterprise components".

68. C. The ISBK defines balancing an IT security investment portfolio as "strategically allocating resources... to achieve the greatest possible risk reduction and business enablement".

69. C. The ISBK states that a "thorough internal analysis provides a baseline for the current security posture and identifies areas for improvement".

70. B. The ISBK lists "Compliance" as a benefit of EISA, stating that it "can assist in meeting regulatory requirements and industry standards".

71. C. The "Vendor Selection Process" section states that "Onboarding" involves executing the contract and "integrat[ing] the vendor into operations".

72. C. The ISBK lists "least privilege" as a high-level security principle to establish during the EISA design phase.

73. A. The ISBK highlights that EISA provides a strategic blueprint that ensures security investments are not made in a silo but are part of a "cohesive, long-term plan".

74. A. The ISBK mentions that prioritizing tools that integrate seamlessly can help "avoid complexity and 'shelfware' (unused software)".

75. B. The ISBK lists "Access to Sensitive Data" as the "most critical factor" for defining a high-risk vendor.

76. C. The ISBK states that the strategic planning process ensures "security initiatives directly support the business's mission, vision, and objectives".

77. C. The ISBK lists "reduced losses from a breach" as a tangible, quantifiable benefit of a security investment.

78. C. The ISBK defines the "Third-Party Risk Management Lifecycle" as a "continuous, cyclical process".

79. C. The ISBK states that during the "Incident Response and Threat Management" step of the "Maintain" phase, a CISO should "Continuously monitor the threat landscape and update the EISA to defend against new and emerging threats".

80. B. The ISBK's overview of SABSA states it is a "business-driven, risk-based framework that aligns security with organizational goals".

81. B. The ISBK defines an RFI as "an initial, exploratory document used to gather general information from a broad range of potential vendors".

82. B. The ISBK states that "A thorough internal analysis provides a baseline for the current security posture and identifies areas for improvement".

83. B. The ISBK defines the "Conceptual Layer" as providing a "high-level, 'big picture' view of the security architecture".

84. B. The ISBK states that the primary purpose of the roadmap is to "translate the strategic plan into actionable, phased initiatives".

85. C. The ISBK defines "Balancing an IT security investment portfolio" as the process of "strategically allocating resources across various security initiatives to achieve the greatest possible risk reduction and business enablement".

86. C. The ISBK lists "Holistic Risk Management" as a benefit of EISA, which provides a "systematic way to identify, assess, and manage security risks across the entire enterprise".

87. C. The ISBK defines "Sole-Source" as buying from a "single vendor, often used for proprietary technology or a trusted existing partner".

88. C. The ISBK lists "Conducting a security assessment of prospective vendors" as a key activity in the "Planning and Due Diligence" phase.

89. B. The ISBK states that a thorough "Internal Analysis" provides a baseline for the current security posture and identifies areas for improvement.

90. C. The ISBK states a key feature of ISO/IEC 27001 is that it "Supports certification, ensuring compliance with global standards".

91. A. The ISBK explicitly states that an SOO focuses on the "what" and "why," while an SOW details the "how" of the work.

92. D. The ISBK defines the "Business Context Layer" as the layer that "defines the organization's business goals, risk tolerance, and the value of its information assets".

93. A. The ISBK states that the strategic roadmap typically outlines initiatives over a "defined timeframe, typically 1–3 years".

94. C. The ISBK states that the "Design phase is foundational, focusing on understanding the organization's strategic goals and translating them into clear security requirements".

95. B. The ISBK states that "Review and Evolve" is a best practice for applying frameworks and that organizations should "Regularly update it to address new threats, technologies, and business changes".

96. B. The ISBK defines the "Conceptual Layer" as the one that provides a "high-level, 'big picture' view of the security architecture".

97. B. The ISBK states that the "most critical factor" for defining a high-risk vendor is their "Access to Sensitive Data".

98. C. The ISBK lists "Build Physical and Component Architecture" as a key step in the "Develop" phase.

99. C. The ISBK states that the "Implementation Layer" details "the specific technologies, tools, and processes required to implement the logical design".

100. B. The ISBK states that effective procurement requires collaboration with a "diverse group of stakeholders" to "ensure alignment with organizational needs, compliance requirements, and technical specifications". Lawyers and HR are included to ensure legal and human resources needs are met.

References

American Institute of Certified Public Accountants. (2020). *SOC 2® - SOC for Service Organizations: Trust Services Criteria.* https://www.aicpa.org/interestareas/frc/assuranceadvisoryservices/socforserviceorganizations.html

Cheung, E. (2024, February 4). Finance worker pays out $25 million after video call with deepfake 'chief financial officer.' *CNN.* https://www.cnn.com/2024/02/04/asia/deepfake-cfo-scam-hong-kong- intl-hnk/index.html

Committee of Sponsoring Organizations of the Treadway Commission. (2013). *Internal control— Integrated framework.* https://www.coso.org/Documents/990025P-Executive-Summary-final- may20.pdf

EC-Council. (2020). C|CISO candidate handbook v4. https://cert.eccouncil.org/images/doc/CCISO- Handbook-v4.pdf

EC-Council. (2021). CCISO blueprint v2. https://cert.eccouncil.org/images/doc/CCISO-New- Blueprint-v2.pdf

EC-Council. (n.d.). *Certified Chief Information Security Officer (CCISO).* Retrieved September 1, 2025, from https://www.eccouncil.org/programs/certified-chief-information-security-officer-cciso/

EC-Council. (n.d.). *CCISO program overview.* Retrieved September 1, 2025, from https://www.eccouncil.org/certified-chief-information-security-officer-cciso-program/

Equifax. (2017, September 7). *Equifax announces cybersecurity incident involving consumer information*
[Press release]. https://investor.equifax.com/news-and-events/news/2017/09-07-2017-213000628

European Union. (2016). *Regulation (EU) 2016/679 of the European Parliament and of the Council of 27 April 2016 on the protection of natural persons with regard to the processing of personal data and on the free movement of such data (General Data Protection Regulation).* Official Journal of the European Union, L119, 1–88. Retrieved September 1, 2025, from https://eur-lex.europa.eu/legal-content/EN/TXT/? uri=CELEX%3A32016R0679

FAIR Institute. (n.d.). *Factor Analysis of Information Risk (FAIR).* Retrieved September 1, 2025, from https://www.fairinstitute.org/

Institute for Security and Technology. (n.d.). *Cybersecurity considerations for regulatory reform.* Retrieved September 1, 2025, from https://securityandtechnology.org/

International Organization for Standardization. (2018). *ISO 31000:2018 Risk management – Guidelines.* https://www.iso.org/standard/65694.html

International Organization for Standardization. (2022). *ISO/IEC 27001:2022 Information security, cybersecurity and privacy protection – Information security management systems – Requirements.* https://www.iso.org/standard/27001

International Organization for Standardization. (2013). *ISO/IEC 27001:2013: Information technology — Security techniques — Information security management systems — Requirements.* https://www.iso.org/standard/54534.html

ISACA. (2019). *COBIT 2019 framework: Introduction and methodology.* https://www.isaca.org/resources/cobit

ISO 31000 for Complementary Risk Management International Organization for Standardization. (2018). *ISO 31000:2018 Risk management – Guidelines.* https://www.iso.org/standard/65694.html

National Institute of Standards and Technology. (n.d.). *Cybersecurity Framework (CSF) 2.0.* Retrieved September 1, 2025, from https://www.nist.gov/cyberframework

National Institute of Standards and Technology. (n.d.). *Risk Management Framework (RMF) overview.* Retrieved September 1, 2025, from https://csrc.nist.gov/projects/risk-management/about-rmf

National Institute of Standards and Technology. (2012). *Guide for conducting risk assessments (NIST SP 800-30 Rev. 1).* U.S. Department of Commerce. https://doi.org/10.6028/NIST.SP.800-30r1

National Institute of Standards and Technology. (2020). *Security and privacy controls for information systems and organizations (NIST SP 800-53 Rev. 5).* U.S. Department of Commerce. https://doi.org/10.6028/NIST.SP.800-53r5

New York State Department of Financial Services. (2020, October 14). *Report on investigation of Twitter's July 15, 2020 cybersecurity incident and the implications for election security.* https://www.dfs.ny.gov/Twitter_Report

Official COSO ERM Framework (2017) Committee of Sponsoring Organizations of the Treadway Commission. (2017). *Enterprise risk management—Integrating with strategy and performance.* https://www.coso.org/Documents/2017-COSO-ERM-Integrating-with-Strategy-and-Performance- Executive-Summary.pdf

PCI Security Standards Council. (n.d.). *Payment Card Industry Data Security Standard (PCI DSS).* Retrieved September 1, 2025, from https://www.pcisecuritystandards.org/

Perlroth, N., Sanger, D. E., & Shane, S. (2016, December 20). How we identified the D.N.C. hack's 'patient zero.' *The New York Times.* https://www.nytimes.com/2016/12/20/insider/how-we- identified-the-dnc-hacks-patient-zero.html

SecurityScorecard. (2025, March 28). *Global third party breach report.* https://securityscorecard.com/resource/global-third-party-breach-report/

Sherwood, J., Clark, A., & Lynas, D. (2005). *Enterprise security architecture: A business-driven approach.* CMP Books.

Stupp, C. (2019, August 30). Fraudsters used AI to mimic CEO's voice in unusual cybercrime case. *The Wall Street Journal.* https://www.wsj.com/articles/fraudsters-use-ai-to-mimic-ceos-voice-in-unusual-cybercrime-case-11567157402

The Open Group. (2018). *The TOGAF® standard, version 9.2.* https://pubs.opengroup.org/architecture/togaf9-doc/arch/

U.S. Department of Health and Human Services. (n.d.). *Summary of the HIPAA Security Rule.* Retrieved September 1, 2025, from https://www.hhs.gov/hipaa/for-professionals/security/laws-regulations/ index.html

Zachman, J. A. (1987). A framework for information systems architecture. *IBM Systems Journal, 26*(3), 276–292. https://doi.org/10.1147/sj.263.0276

www.ingramcontent.com/pod-product-compliance
Lightning Source LLC
LaVergne TN
LVHW082011200926
848481LV00010B/2839
* 9 7 9 8 2 3 2 6 3 2 5 7 1 *